Introduction to Legal Studies

Dr. Frances E. Chapman
Ph.D., LL.M., J.D., B.A. (Hons.)
St. Jerome's University, University of Waterloo

NELSON EDUCATION

NELSON EDUCATION

Introduction to Legal Studies
by Dr. Frances E. Chapman

Vice President, Editorial Higher Education:
Anne Williams

Executive Editor:
Lenore Taylor-Atkins

Marketing Manager:
Terry Fedorkiw

Developmental Editor:
Suzanne Simpson Millar

Photo Researcher/Permissions Coordinator:
Julie Pratt

Senior Content Production Manager:
Imoinda Romain

Production Service:
MPS Limited

Copy Editor:
Valerie Adams

Proofreader:
MPS Limited

Indexer:
MPS Limited

Manufacturing Manager:
Joanne McNeil

Design Director:
Ken Phipps

Managing Designer:
Franca Amore

Interior Design:
Sharon Lucas Creative

Cover Design:
James Genge, Strong Finish

Cover Image:
© OGphoto

Chapter Opener Image:
© Brandon Bourdages/Dreamstime.com

Feature Box Icons:
Gavel: © Arrow/Dreamstime.com; ice cream cone: © iStockphoto.com/appleuzr

Compositor:
MPS Limited

Printer:
Edwards Brothers Malloy

Printed and bound in the United States of America
1 2 3 4 15 14 13 12

For more information contact Nelson Education Ltd., 1120 Birchmount Road, Toronto, Ontario, M1K 5G4. Or you can visit our Internet site at http://www.nelson.com

Library and Archives Canada Cataloguing in Publication

Chapman, Frances E. (Frances Elizabeth), 1975-

Introduction to legal studies/ Frances E. Chapman.

Includes bibliographical references and index.
ISBN-13: 978-0-17-650338-3

1. Law—Canada—Textbooks. 2. Sociological jurisprudence—Canada—Textbooks. I. Title.

KE444.C53 2013 349.71 C2012-906925-6
KF385.C53 2013

ISBN-13: 978-0-17-650338-3
ISBN-10: 0-17-650338-2

Dedication

My legal curiosity is boundless, but unfortunately, sometimes realities get in the way. I dedicate this book to what I have learned:

1. *Sometimes you win cases that you didn't think you were going to win, sometimes you unexpectedly lose, and sometimes the other lawyers at the firm tell you not to come back unless you win.*
2. *Sometimes you get through a day in court and don't wet your pants (which is a victory).*
3. *Sometimes sump-pumps don't vibrate as much as you want them to.*
4. *I've had (and have) the best mentors.*
5. *I have the best students in the world: past, present, and future.*

Brief Contents

Contents

CHAPTER 6: FAMILY LAW 144

CHAPTER 10: THE *CHARTER*, CRIMINAL PROCEDURE, AND EVIDENCE 254

CHAPTER 11: CRIMINAL LAW DEFENCES 279

Preface

When I started teaching undergraduate courses in legal studies full-time in 2007, it soon became apparent to me that there were so many things about the law that I wish I had known before I went to law school. If only I had known the basics of civil litigation, torts, contracts, and criminal law, life would have been perfect. OK, maybe not perfect, but life would have been a little easier. When I started to research how students learn the law, I was really surprised that there is very little written on the topic. The scholarship on the processes of teaching and learning has been concentrated within a variety of disciplines, but it has been infrequently applied to legal studies. It was then that I realized the purpose of this text: to present legal information to first-year undergraduate students in the case law based method employed at Canadian law schools.

When students begin their education in law, they do not have much time to think about *how* they are learning the law. However, in a history that goes back centuries, law school students are exposed to case law to create an understanding of the law beyond a recital of Latin terms. What many students learn in law school is at a much deeper level of understanding of the law at the graduate level, but I know for myself, having the context behind the law made a huge difference in the retention and understanding of complex legal language and concepts. Giving undergraduate students the opportunity to engage with legal cases allows for a deeper level of learning as it provides them with opportunities to engage with real examples.

Legal cases are the shorthand used by lawyers, and teaching first-year undergrad legal studies students with this method creates great results. I have seen the informal proof that the case-based method can transform many students into extremely critical and thoughtful learners. Giving actual legal cases to undergraduate not only provides them with a context within which new material is embedded and thus more easily retained but it also gives more tools to the learner and a framework that makes the information more personally relevant to interpret and understand.

TOPIC COVERAGE

In this text, students will also be exposed to the fundamentals of the Canadian legal system in several areas of the law, including ethics and professional responsibility, civil litigation, tort law, contract law, administrative law, family law, constitutional law, criminal law, criminal procedure, evidence, the *Charter of Rights and Freedoms*, criminal defences, criminal sentencing, and alternative dispute resolution. I know that many of my lawyer friends will read this text and immediately email me to say, "but what about ...," "but you left out ...," "but you simplified ..." in the context of their favourite legal principles in their areas of practice. I am very aware that I could have written tomes on every concept in the book, but I wanted to restrict the material to that first goal: "what I wish I had known." So, this is what I wish I had known when I started law school at the University of Western Ontario in 1999.

The key to this text has always been my students. It is for this reason that every word of this textbook has been student read and student vetted. I have had a group of students who have poured themselves into the text to tell me what they love and—just as important—what they hate. Every bit of this book was read and commented on by my students, and this text is really for them.

PEDAGOGY

The text consists of many elements to help the students learn by focusing on material that is interesting to first year undergraduate students in addition to:

- **Learning Objectives:** Each chapter begins with Learning Objectives to help students understand what issues will be raised in the chapter. These Learning Objectives are then revisited and summarized at the end of the chapter.
- **Case boxes** are used throughout the text to illustrate concepts and have the students connect with the legal principles.
- **Food for Thought** and other boxes are used in this text to help provide additional and interesting examples for students to challenge their assumptions about the law.
- **Self-Evaluation Questions** at the end of each chapter act as a study tool to guide students on important elements of the chapter.

ABOUT THE AUTHOR

Frances E Chapman was born and raised in rural Southwestern Ontario and worked in her family's business from a young age. In 1994, she moved to Waterloo, Ontario, to complete her undergraduate degree at the University of Waterloo in Sociology, with an option in Legal Studies and Criminology in 1998. Frances then moved to London, Ontario, where she graduated from law school at the University of Western Ontario with her JD degree in 2002.

After completing her articles at Cohen Highley LLP in London, Frances gained a broad range of experience in family law, criminal law, personal injury and tort law, administrative law, contract law, and civil and commercial litigation. She was re-hired by the firm as an associate lawyer in the department of the senior litigation partner, and was called to the bar in July 2003. Frances practised for almost two years working with real property disputes, mortgage actions, wrongful dismissal, and class actions.

Frances returned to school in September 2005 to pursue her passion for criminal law. She focused specifically on criminal law defences including automatism, duress, and necessity, and completed her Master of Laws degree at the University of Western Ontario while teaching part-time at Fanshawe College. She then moved to Toronto to complete her PhD in law at Osgoode Hall Law School at York University while working as a Teaching Assistant at both York University and Ryerson University. Frances finished her PhD in 2009 while teaching full-time at St. Jerome's University at the University of Waterloo since 2007. Her areas of interest are in criminal law, focusing on defences including brainwashing, mental disorder, and she focuses particularly on violence against women and domestic violence.

Frances currently teaches Legal Studies as an assistant professor in the Department of Sociology and Legal Studies at St. Jerome's in the same program that she graduated from in 1998. Frances received the "Professor of the Term Award" from the University of Waterloo Arts Student Union for Fall 2008. In her spare time, Frances is an avid pug dog enthusiast.

ACKNOWLEDGEMENTS

A textbook like this does not get written without a huge support system. I have been very lucky to have some wonderful students touch this book that I have put so much of myself into. It is student vetted, student developed, and let me assure you—they had opinions that they were not shy to express.

I would love to thank, in particular, my following students and colleagues:

- Melody Jahanzadeh, my beloved articling student (and former University of Waterloo student) who volunteered so much of her time and energy and who will almost be a (wonderful) lawyer by the time this book is published.
- Mehrnaz Jahanzadeh, my second beloved Jahanzadeh, who took up where her sister left off and did such a wonderful job. Thank you for being my details expert (and I love you more than your sister. She told me to say that).

- Cydney Wood-Lyons, who put so much care into this text. Thank you for all of your big-picture ideas.
- Rachele Broome, who spent her co-op term helping with this textbook.
- Nora Sleeth, who was one of my first research assistants on this project (and who will also be a lawyer soon after this book is published).
- Shelley Chornaby, who wrote a fantastic essay about polygamy that I ended up adding in a shortened form to this text. She was so committed to this project, and it came through in her great research.
- Jessica Whitehead, who did some wonderful research on the long-gun registry for me.
- Mark Poland and Chris Cowie for their wonderful contributions and expertise.
- A big thank you to St. Jerome's University for their support with this project.

Thank you to the following reviewers who took the time to make so many wonderful suggestions about the content of this text:

Amanda Burgess	University of Windsor
James Butler	St. Lawrence College
Leo de Jourdan	Canadore College
Elizabeth Strutt-MacLeod	St. Clair College of Applied Arts and Technology
Deirdre Way	Loyalist College

Thank you to my Nelson team and especially Suzanne Simpson Millar, Julie Pratt, Lenore Taylor-Atkins, Anne Williams, Terry Fedorkiw, Amanda Henry, Imoinda Romain, and Manoj Kumar for all of their constant encouragement over the years. Thank you for trusting me with this huge project.

Thank you to my law family: JJ, Lucy, Lianne, JP, Kenny, Mark, and Brad. I have learned so much from all of you.

Another big thank you to my "academic family"—Toni, Tracy, and Steven (and their spouses Andrzej, Thom, and Leslie). I could not do it without you all. Thank you to my mentor Sally Gunz for all of your support, and also to my lawyer's group at UW including Lowell, Neil, and Darren.

I was also privileged to have a great support system at home. This book is dedicated to my beloved Bryan for listening to my woes about drafts and publishing (thank you so much for all of your love and support), and to my Mom and Dad, Ashley, Lesya, Olivia, Nicola, Terry, Christina, Andrea, Steve, Dave, Emeley, Ivy, and my beloved pugs, Gillian and Simon, who saw me through this project. A final thank you to my sister-in-law Tracy who gave me the confidence to pursue this project—it would not have been possible without you.

Introduction

> *"Who are you? Who are you to dictate who should be part of the litigation system. Who are you to decide why parties decide to litigate? Who. Are. You?"*[1]

Learning Outcomes

After completing this chapter, you should be able to:

1. Define "law."
2. List the defining characteristics of natural law, legal positivism, and legal realism.
3. Identify one of the most common charges in seventeenth-century Europe.
4. Analyze the father of the "atavistic" theory. What were the characteristics of the "atavistic man"?

I was once severely chastised by a law school professor for asking a novice question about why one particular party decided to sue another party in court. In front of the entire class, the professor pointed a finger at me and asked, "Who are you? Who are you to dictate who should be part of the litigation system. Who are you to decide why parties decide to litigate?" Although I felt like crawling under my desk at the time, I have come to realize that this is actually a pretty wise response (but I will never tell him that). The parties get to decide how they choose to use the justice system, what issues they have, and what specific topics they want a judge to decide. No one else has the right to dictate what litigants do; this is the beauty of our system. So, if cases throughout this text seem not to make sense for the moment, try to think about the wider reasons behind their decisions to litigate, proceed, or end their case. As students of the law, we must analyze the case that come before the court, and not the hypothetical case we wish it to be.

This textbook draws heavily from a "case-based" philosophy of law. This means that the student analyzes actual cases that have been decided by judges and adjudicators of various types. This is something that is often not done until a student is at law school after an

1. Law professor to frightened student, 1999.

undergraduate degree. I believe that there is much for the undergraduate student to gain by looking at the law under this lens, and I hope it expands the rote learning behind stale legal concepts.

As you read this text, it is a perfectly valid decision for you to say that the judge simply got it wrong. We have all been taught that questioning the law is not allowed; yet in this textbook questions are the key to learning. It would be impossible to learn every case on a particular topic, so it is important to look at some representative cases that allow students to see the extremes and sometimes the lesser-known aspects of a legal principle. The study of law is learning how to think—not the miniscule details of cases that happened many years ago. However, tracking the history of a topic is essential to understanding how a law was formed, and what it might look like in the future.

One of the worst comments that I have ever received on a professor evaluation form was from a student who said, "Great course, but I don't know what the answers were." The bottom line in law is that there is almost never one *correct* answer. Simply looking for a rule book for what is right and what is wrong is an ineffective study of the law. As professor and author SM Waddams has noted, the law is better conceptualized as a "continuing process of attempting to solve the problems of a changing society, [rather] than as a set of rules."[2] Those students who look for black-and-white answers concerning the law will quickly realize that there is often no such thing.

As will be seen in this text, the outcome may be very specific to a certain case, the parties involved, the admissible evidence, the proof before the court, and of course to that judge and jury. Being able to predict what will be the result in any case is often impossible, and clients spend a great deal of money to test their case in court and hope for a positive outcome in what are called **test cases**. The issue in the case has often never been explored before, and a ruling needs to be made for future cases. Although the system strives to be predictable and even-handed, this cannot always be the situation. Modern realities (technology, unique facts) occur daily, and the law must struggle to keep up with this constant change.

The study of law at the undergraduate level is a very particular beast. Some think that the law should only be purely talked about in the abstract, and others argue that there is no way to divorce law from the practical realities of the system (the documents that need to be filed, rules of procedure, etc.). This text attempts to do both. We can talk about the theoretical underpinnings of the system and what it should strive to accomplish, but it is also important to look at actual decisions that have been handed down from the courts so we know how the law developed, where it currently stands, and how it will progress in the future. Call it an academic discipline or a practical administrative program, but it is important for students to get the full picture of the law. As SM Waddams has said the "study of law, however, can never divorce itself from a living working system," and I add that the living system cannot be divorced from the theory.[3]

However, it is difficult to define what "law" is. The fact is that the word *law* can apply to many different things. It can refer to a system that governs human activities through threat of punishment in an organized society by the government. It can refer to the documents behind the law; the legislation (federal and provincial), including proclamations, regulations or orders, the Constitution, judicial decisions, and legal principles that form the law. Law can refer to the subspecialty of a type of practice, for example, personal injury law. It can also refer to the whole structure behind the process—including the judges and courthouses, as well as the legal profession.

Law is usually imposed by an external body in order to control conflict so that individual needs are met, but so that the good of society is preserved. A very important aspect of the law is that it has to be enforced. The system must decide what sanctions will be applied to individuals who do not follow the law. The enforcement mechanism is the state, which is comprised of the

2. SM Waddams, *Introduction to the Study of Law,* 7th ed. (Toronto: Carswell 2010) at 4. Reprinted by permission of Carswell, a division of Thomson Reuters Canada Ltd.

3. *Ibid* at 3.

courts, police, government, and Crown attorneys who draw these boundaries. The law and legal institutions play an increasingly important role in regulating our day-to-day behaviour.

The law is a complex system of control which permeates almost all of our social interactions. Laws govern tuition fees, taxation, landlord and tenant matters, marriage and divorce, child support and custody, vehicle regulations, business contracts, wills and estates, and property ownership, among other matters. It is difficult to think of anything in life that is not directly or indirectly influenced or governed by law. However, are there situations in which the law extends too far? For example, should you be limited as to what you can name your child? See the Food for Thought box for one answer to that question.

FOOD FOR THOUGHT...

In Ontario, the Office of the Registrar General registers names through birth certificates and name changes. Should any particular name be rejected? This issue has recently become an issue in New Zealand, with a nine-year-old girl who is the subject of a custody fight between her parents. Since New Zealanders may only change their own names if they are 18 years of age or married, this young girl was made a ward of the state by a judge so that she could change her name, which was legally "Talula Does the Hula from Hawaii." The girl was so embarrassed of this moniker that she kept her name from friends and told them that her name was "K."

tomas del amo/Shutterstock

What's in a name?

The judge in the custody case found that her name "makes a fool of the child and sets her up with a social disability and handicap" and that her parents had exercised "very poor judgment" in selecting this name. K was made a ward of the state in order to change her name, but the girl's new name was kept confidential to protect her identity.

During this case, the court listed other names that had been rejected by New Zealand registration officials, including "Violence," "Midnight," "Chardonnay" "Number 16 Bus Shelter," "Fish and Chips," "Yeah Detroit," "Stallion," "Twisty Poi," "Keenan Got Lucy" and (my personal favourite) "Sex Fruit."[4] An official with the New Zealand Office of Births, Deaths, and Marriages said that he tries to talk to parents to convince them of the embarrassment that the child may encounter with an unusual name.[5]

In the United States, even adults have been prevented from changing their own names. Those names rejected include "1069," which was denied by the North Dakota Supreme Court in 1976 and the Minnesota Supreme Court in 1979, because a name cannot be a number; also denied were "III" pronounced "three," again denied by the California Court of Appeal in 1984 because a symbol cannot be a name; "Santa Claus" was denied by the Ohio courts in 2000 because Santa is a "treasure that society passes on from generation to generation" but allowed by the Utah Supreme Court in 2001 because although it may be "unwise," the petitioner was allowed to select his own name. Conversely, the name "They" was allowed by a Missouri court, and the name "Bean!" (to be pronounced with a raise in pitch and volume) was allowed by the California Court of Appeal in 2006.[6] However, a 2010 case before the Pennsylvania court denied a request of a man to change his name to "Boomer the Dog."[7]

---

4. Bonnie Malkin, "'Talula Does the Hula from Hawaii' Not a Girl's Name, New Zealand Court Rules," Telegraph.co.uk, online: <http://www.telegraph.co.uk/news/newstopics/howaboutthat/2452593/Talula-Does-The-Hula-From-Hawaii-not-a-girls-name-New-Zealand-court-rules.html>.
5. CBC News, "Talula Does the Hula from Hawaii, 9, Gets Court-Ordered Name Change," online: <http://www.cbc.ca/news/world/story/2008/07/24/talula-nz-name.html>.
6. Eugene Volokh, "Talula Does the Hula from Hawaii and Other Names So Weird That Judges Forbade Them," *Slate*, online: <http://www.slate.com/id/2196204/pagenum/all/#p2>.
7. Tim McNulty, "Boomer the Dog to Remain Gary Guy Mathews: Judge Denies Green Tree Man's Petition to Change His Name," post-gazette.com, online: <http://www.post-gazette.com/pg/10224/1079431-455.stm>.

TYPES OF LAW IN CANADA

This textbook is a tale of two main types of law: the **civil law** and the **criminal law**. Although the criminal law is much more familiar to many, civil law is practised by many more lawyers in Canada today. A 2004 study by the Law Society of Upper Canada, "Diversity and Change: The Contemporary Legal Profession in Ontario," looked at the gender differences in areas of practice, and found that criminal law is only one rather small area of law practised by both men and women in Canada (see Figure 1.1). Only 10 percent of women and 10 percent of men practise in the area of criminal law. The other 90 percent for both sexes is made up of various civil law areas of practice.[8]

Many Canadians believe that we are far less likely to sue someone in Canada than people are in the United States. Fasken Martineau, one of the world's leading international business law and litigation law firms, conducted a survey of businesses and found that, contrary to the view that Canada is not litigious, over "40 percent of respondents have had at least one legal dispute commenced against their company in the last year ... and an average of 8.3 disputes per year."[9]

Disputes can arise between individuals, between individuals and companies, between an individual and the community, between an individual and the government, and even within different levels of government (municipal, provincial, and federal). Disputes between

Figure 1.1 Fields of Law by Gender

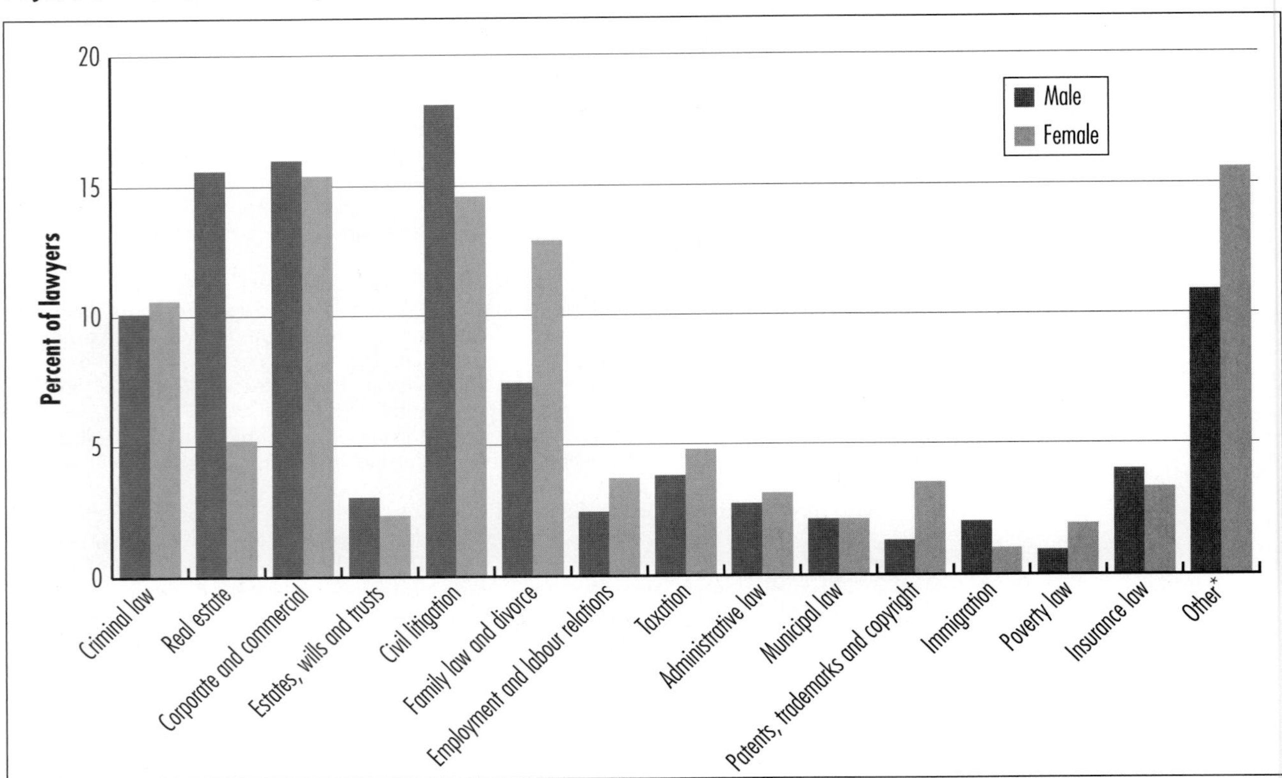

* Other includes Aboriginal Rights, Adjudication/Mediation, Constitutional Law, Debtors' and Creditors' Rights, Human Rights and *Charter*, Landlord and Tenant, and Legal Policy Work.

Source: Figure 3.5 titled *Fields of Law by Gender* found at page 34 of the document titled *Diversity And Change: The Contemporary Legal Profession in Ontario*, A Report to The Law Society of Upper Canada, September 2004 prepared by FM Kay, C Masuch, and P Curry.

8. Law Society of Upper Canada, "Diversity and Change: The Contemporary Legal Profession in Ontario," online: <http://rc.lsuc.on.ca/pdf/equity/diversityChange.pdf>.
9. Fasken Martineau, "2008 Litigation Trends in Canada," online: <http://www.fasken.com/files/FileControl/04da904b-f84e-4d9f-b2f4-0a8efcbb47e3/7483b893-e478-44a4-8fed-f49aa917d8cf/Presentation/File/LTS_English_WEB.pdf>.

Figure 1.2 The Legal Systems of the World

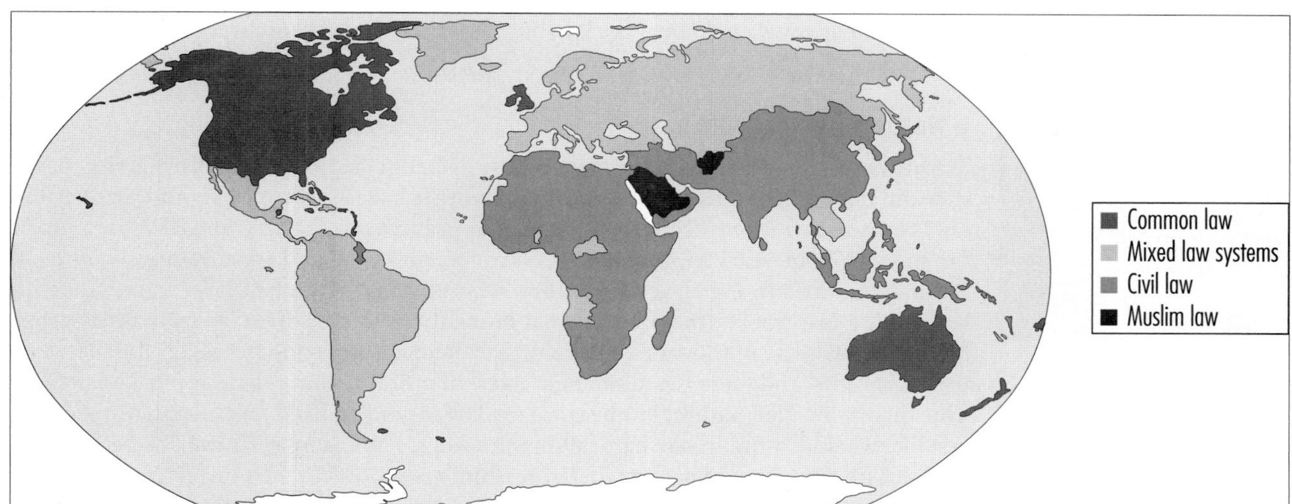

Most of the world uses civil law, with the exception of the majority of North America, New Zealand and Australia, which use common law.

Source: ChartsBin statistics collector team 2010, Legal Systems of the World, ChartsBin.com, <http://chartsbin.com/view/aq2>.

individuals are called **private law**, or **civil law**, and include matters such as tort law, contract law, and civil litigation. Conflict between the individual and the state is called **public law**, and concerns areas of law such as **criminal law**, administrative law, constitutional law, and international law. The study of law is generally a dissection of statutes drafted by the government, and case law that is decided by judges.

Just to make things complicated, the term "civil law" has another meaning. In addition to its meaning as law in relation to matters between individuals, **civil law** also means a system of law based on the Roman tradition. Most of Western Europe adopted the Roman system of law, which eventually came be known as the Civil Code system. Other countries, such as Scotland, are also based on a civil law tradition, in addition to the state of Louisiana in the United States, and in Canada the province of Quebec. Although largely not used in the majority of North America, civil law is the most widespread legal system in the world (see Figure 1.2).

There are also similar meanings to the term **common law**. Common law can mean the system of law based on judicial decisions. All of Canada, other than Quebec, uses a common law system, as do some other countries, including the United States (except Louisiana), England, New Zealand, and Australia. However, the term "common law" can also mean the system of case-based law that is in contrast to statute law. When talking about case law, many refer to this as the common law. For the purposes of this text, common law will almost always refer to the system of case law unless otherwise specified. Table 1.1 summarizes these differences.

Table 1.1 Various Meanings of "Common Law" and "Civil Law"

	Common Law	**Civil Law**
Legal System	Legal system practised in many countries in the world, including most of Canada and the United States	Roman tradition that is the most practised system of law in the world, including Quebec and Louisiana
Type of Law	—	The topics of law in Canada, which includes torts, contracts, corporate law, etc.
Source of the Law	Referring to the British tradition of law based on cases establishing precedent as distinguished from statute law	—

Socrates

Hulton Archive/Getty Images

Different Views of the Law

There are many ways to look at the law, but there are certain theoretical positions that one may take.

1. Natural Law Approach

Traditionally, people obeyed the law because of habit, custom, or the fear of violence if they did not conform. However, over time theorists have asked: Why should we obey the law? **Natural law** is one of the most ancient approaches to the law, which has developed for thousands of years through Plato, Socrates, Aristotle, and most famously with St. Thomas Aquinas in the eleventh century, who said that an unjust law "seems to be no law at all."[10] Natural law theorists say that **morality** cannot be divorced from the law; but rather they are one in the same. They say that there is a clear and necessary link between these concepts, and there is a fundamental test of morality that can be applied to any law. This theory is called natural law because the law should be fixed and has a natural order, just like what is found in our natural surroundings. For example, Christians believe that God ordered the ways of nature; therefore, humans should do the same. Humans should live in line with what was in nature, and a law could only be if it was consistent with this natural function. Thus, there were God-given moral values that must be assumed in the law.

Natural law theorists say that it is possible to understand true morality, and the law should therefore reflect these principles. They would say that if a law does not conform to morality, then it is not a valid law, and if a law is not valid, you do not need to obey. This is based on the Latin term ***lex iniusta non est lex***, or "an unjust law is not a law." This means that moral validity is necessary to have a law, and to follow an unjust law would be to disobey God's plan and to act immorally. Thus, if a plaintiff comes before the court to enforce a Nazi law that he should be able to confiscate all of the possessions of a Jewish defendant, should the judge be able to assert that this law is immoral and refuse to enforce that provision? Natural law theorists would say this law was immoral and not a law and the judge would not have to enforce that man-made provision.

Many are very critical of this way of thinking. How does one determine what is moral? There is no experiment where morality can be described in scientific terms. There is also a danger that one can twist this theory to suit the purposes of a particular situation. In addition, what morality should be used? In a country such as Canada, which diverse and often-divergent religious or secular principles should be used? Some say that natural law is virtually dead in Canada, as it is just too "difficult to discern a moral soul with such a product of conflict and compromise."[11] However, it is important to note that different concepts like the freedom of religion, conscience, and association are based on natural law ideals and are still found today within the *Canadian Charter of Rights and Freedoms*. However, the tradition that is now more dominant in our current Canadian system is one of legal positivism.

2. Legal Positivism

Legal positivism is the predominant approach in our courts today. It is a concept that came from the historic British concept of **parliamentary supremacy** or the thought that only Parliament can make laws and that no individual should be able to be above those laws. Unlike natural law proponents, legal positivists say that law should be divorced from morality. Positivism uses science to explain law, and they observe what can be empirically proven through logic. This theory derives from scientific positivism, where all knowledge can be observed and measured and does not consist of things like morality and religion.

10. Thomas Aquinas, *Summa Theological*, translated by Fathers of the English Dominican Province, 1952, at ques 95, art 2, ques 96, art 4.

11. Neil Boyd, *Canadian Law: An Introduction*, 5th ed (Toronto: Nelson, 2007) at 10.

Positivists say that there can be a mechanical analysis of the law and it can be viewed with logic to determine how the law works. These theorists say one cannot possibly identify only what is moral and determine the law, and the scope of the law, on that basis.

These proponents say that the process behind law is more important than the individual laws themselves. Thus, there should be liberty and democratic institutions that do not allow the abuse of power, but again it is the process that is important. The task of those in the legal system is to interpret the law set down by the lawmakers and not to make their own moral decisions. Our lawmakers are elected and express the will of the people, so this concept of the law should be supreme. Is this the case in Canada? See the next Food for Thought box.

Positivists say that language is the key. One must use language that clearly expresses what the lawmakers wanted it to say, and nothing else matters. If people do not agree with a law then they should work to re-draft legislation, not just ignore what they consider an immoral law. This system is guided by the Latin phrase ***nulla poena sine lege,*** or "there is no penalty without a valid law." Positivists adhere to what is known as **black-letter law** or what is written and established is what should be applied.

Thus, one can determine if there is a law by looking at the situation empirically and deciding whether it came from the sovereign or our lawmakers. This is why the police or the Crown attorney can agree to release an accused person if they are ordered to do so by a judge. They might have to do this even though they believe the individual is guilty of the crime, but they respect that the system will work as designed, and they are not in a position to overrule this decision.[12]

However, in this perspective it is important to recognize that the law is human-made. People sat down and drafted a law for a particular purpose (or perhaps for a purpose that they never considered.) So, the question remains, if the law is completely human-made, why do we follow the law? Legal philosopher HLA Hart said that we have a "habit of obedience" in that we learn the right and wrong things to do during our childhood. We are all taught that it is wrong to steal that chocolate bar from the store, and it is right to pay for anything

FOOD FOR THOUGHT...

A current example of legal positivism can be observed through the "long-gun registry" in Canada. In the 1990s, the *Firearms Act, SC 1995, c 3,* was adopted to keep guns from those who could be a danger to the Canadian public. For the first time, rifle and shotgun owners were required to register their firearms. This expanded registry kept information on every owner, their licence, registration certificate, and all authorizations or rejections and disobedience of these new restrictions, which could result in up to a 14-year jail sentence. Firearm owners were given five years after the creation of the law to obtain a firearm licence and seven years to register the firearms.

The program had only succeeded in enrolling 75 percent of Canadian gun owners by January 1, 2003 (the seven-year deadline for firearm registration), leaving approximately 1.9 million firearms unaccounted for. The updated registry was first estimated to be an initial investment of $2 million and that it would cost no more than $85 million over five years; however, the cost ballooned to over $2 billion at the expense of Canadian taxpayers. On October 25, 2011, *Bill C-19: An Act to Amend the Criminal Code and the Firearms Act* was submitted by Vic Toews, Canada's Minister of Public Safety. *Bill C-19* aims to remove the requirement to register firearms that are neither prohibited nor restricted, and the bill received Royal Assent in 2012. Positivists would say that this is the way to change the law. The government had certain aims with the first piece of legislation, but it was unsuccessful and not supported by the Canadian public, so new legislation was introduced to attempt to respond to this problem. In this process, few are asking whether gun ownership is moral, but just what serves the public. The policy goals of the government and public may change, and the law should react to this need accordingly. The public has spoken.

12. Jeffrie G Murphy and Jules L Coleman, *Philosophy of Law: An Introduction to Jurisprudence* (Boulder, CO: Westview, 1990).

we pick up as we are shopping. Some think that the law is simply an extension of what we learned as children as a form of social control. Institutions like school and work have enforced these concepts, and most of us conform to what we believe is the right or "legal" thing to do.

Many criticize positivism for not taking some morality into account. Others say that the language we use is ambiguous, and the system has its flaws, so blind obedience to what the state tells us is very dangerous.

3. Judicial (Legal) Realism

A third theory, developed in the United States early in the twentieth century, said that it is the judges that are the most important element in a case. **Judicial realism** was a reaction to the failure of many to predict what was going to happen in a particular case. Realists decided that something more than the law must be occurring, and that one must be aware of the economics, social context, and political situation in which the case arises. This was a rejection of natural law and positivism, and belief that a "correct" solution would emerge if the law is applied.

FOOD FOR THOUGHT...

Shai Danziger, Jonathan Levav, and Liora Avnaim-Pesso from the Ben-Gurion University of the Negev and Columbia Business School wrote an article entitled "Extraneous Factors in Judicial Decisions," which looked at 1112 rulings by judges in Israel who were granting or denying parole to prisoners. This study had some interesting results (see Figure 1.3). At the beginning of the session 65 percent of prisoners were granted parole, but by the end of the morning session almost no prisoners were granted release. After a meal break, the release rate went back up to 65 percent, and fell again throughout the rest of the day.[13]

Figure 1.3 Judges' Rulings at Specific Time of Day

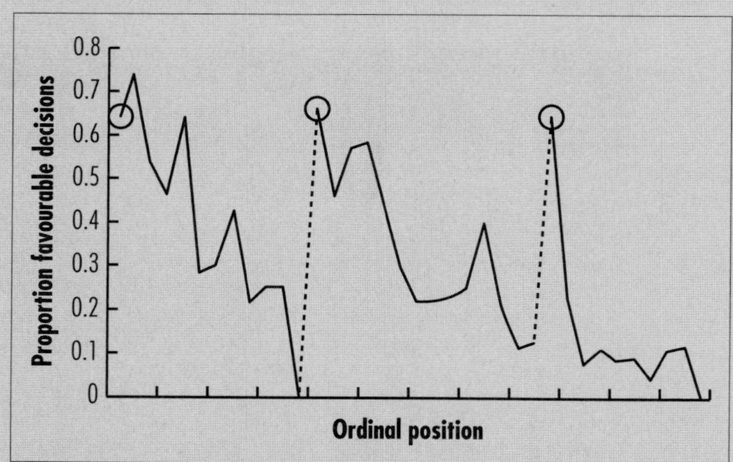

This graph shows the rulings in favour of prisoners by the time they appeared in the sessions. Circles indicate the first decision in each of the three decision sessions; tick marks on the horizontal axis denote every third case, and dotted lines denote food breaks.

Source: From Shai Danzigera, Jonathan Levavb, and Liora Avnaim-Pesso," Extraneous factors in judicial decisions," *Proceedings of the National Academy of Sciences of the USA*, vol. 108, no. 17, (26 April 2011) 6889-6892

Should a favourable ruling depend on whether a judge's blood sugar is low?

13. *The Lawyers Weekly*, "A Rested, Full Judge Equals a Lenient Judge?" online: <http://www.lawyersweekly-digital.com/lawyersweekly/3101?pg=25#pg25>.

Realists argue that the law is not neutral like the legal positivists say, but rather it depends on who the parties are, their life experience, and their values in relation to the case. The law cannot be analyzed mechanically because, whether or not they are consciously aware, the parties in the case inject their beliefs. This perspective has led these theorists to conclude that the law is what a particular judge deems it to be. This theory is sometimes referred to as the "right side of the bed" theory (did that judge wake up on the right side of the bed that morning?). These theorists say that the psychosocial makeup of the judges lets us understand how they interpret and apply the law, and that it is not surprising that judges protect the property and rights of the rich, given their own privileged class position.

Critics of judicial realism say that it is naïve to base a theory on a "what the judge had for breakfast" school of jurisprudence. Many say that there is far too much of an emphasis on the judge and not the case, and the theory assumes that judges cannot be objective and fair. Again, others say that morality should again be involved, and say that there is a real lack of a vision within this theory. Although this theory seems absurd to some, a scientific perspective may confirm this theory, as seen in the Food for Thought box on the previous page.

Although these three methods have emerged as dominant perspectives, be aware that there are many other theories which have been developed. These include the Marxist theory of law, which looks at the law through the political and economic theories of Karl Marx; the critical legal perspective, which was developed among academics to look at the law with a great deal of skepticism; and an anarchist perspective, which is suspicious of all state control within the law. There are also various feminist theories of law, which explore law from many perspectives. Theorist Susan B Boyd sums up the importance feminist theory in law saying that it is

> important because women continue to encounter barriers in gaining access to justice for reasons related to gender, in addition to other factors such as poverty. For example, despite the many law reforms in relation to sexual assault and evidence law, female complainants continue to encounter significant barriers in the criminal law system. Feminism also has much to contribute to complex questions ... because feminism itself has been challenged and complicated over the years by engagement with diversities of race, class, culture, religion, and sexuality.[14]

Of course, most people do not look at the law solely within artificial categories, but rather these approaches are used to look at the law in a very specific way with a particular complainant, and any individual may wish to adopt different elements of different theories. Consider the issue of "vehicles" in the park, discussed in the following box.

HLA HART—NO VEHICLES IN THE PARK

One of the best-known examples of looking at these different legal perspectives is known as the "No Vehicles in the Park" example, by HLA Hart, which said that "a legal rule forbids you to take a vehicle into the public park. Plainly this forbids an automobile, but what about bicycles, roller skates, toy automobiles? What about airplanes? Are these, as we say, to be called 'vehicles' for the purpose of the rule or not?"[15]

How would this situation be interpreted by natural lawyers, positivists, and legal realists?

What about a stroller? Wheelchair?

Is a law ever not a law?

What if no one believes in the law?

HLA Hart

Steve Pyke/Premium Archive/Getty Images

14. Susan B Boyd, "Spaces and Challenges: Feminism in Legal Academia" (2011) 44 *UBC Law Review*, 205 at para 3.

15. HLA Hart, "Positivism and the Separation of Law and Morals," (1958) 71 *Harvard Law Review* 593 at 607.

PRELIMINARY CASE EXAMPLES

Looking at the law in the abstract is not always the best method. As discussed, cases can be dealt with either by the civil law (tort, contract system) or the criminal law system. So at this point in the text, consider the three following real court cases, which will be examined through a civil and criminal law perspective:

1. A mother goes into the bathroom of her home, inserts a pellet gun into her vagina, and fires a pellet into her uterus. She is in the late stages of pregnancy, and two days later she gives birth to a child. After initially claiming she did not know her baby had an injury, the child develops a serious infection, and the results of a brain scan surprises doctors when it reveals a metal pellet lodged in the baby's brain. The doctors successfully remove the pellet and save the baby's life.

Should the mother be charged in the criminal justice system with attempted murder? Should her child be able to sue her civilly for the injuries he sustained?

2. A pregnant woman is an accident when the car she is driving collides with another vehicle. The crash results in prenatal injuries to her fetus, which is born by Caesarean section later that day. The child has permanent mental and physical injuries.

Can the child sue his mother for her negligent driving and for the injuries he suffered before he was born? Can she be charged criminally for the injuries to her child?

3. A doctor prescribes an acne medicine called Accutane to the plaintiff. This medication is very damaging to a fetus. The plaintiff's husband had a vasectomy four-and-a-half years before, but the operation failed, and a child is conceived while the plaintiff is taking the medicine.

Can the child sue the doctor for "wrongful life," saying that he or she should never have been born? Can the child sue the parents? Can the parents be charged criminally for failing to provide the necessaries of life?

These cases will be further considered at the end of the chapter. See if your opinion changes after reading the rest of this chapter on the introduction to legal studies.

INTRODUCTION TO CIVIL LAW

Law is something that many people think is ancient and staid. Many presume that legal tomes have been handed down through the ages, and that everything we know about law has already been decided. Hopefully, throughout the course of this textbook, you will see that these stereotypes are untrue. What is true is that law is a universal part of our society that attempts to limit and minimize the conflict based on our individual interests. People will have possessions and property, and others will want to claim those belongings.

It is a very common trait of students to ask, "What is going to happen in this particular case?" The unfulfilling answer to that question much of the time is that no one knows until the courts decide that case or a similar case. The law continues to evolve, as it is continuously looking at issues in different ways, and the law may be expanded or limited depending on the case before the courts. There may be strong arguments on both sides of the issue, and it is up to the courts to decide the future direction of the issue. Lord Denning, a very famous British judge, said in the case of *Packer v Packer,* [1953] 2 All ER 127 (CA), that "if we never do anything which has not been done before, we shall never get anywhere. The law will stand still while the rest of the world goes on; and that will be bad for both." Thus, it is important to look at the law as a **living tree** that evolves and expands as time goes on. This term was originally used in *Edwards v Canada (Attorney General),* [1930] AC 124, where Lord Sankey stated that the Constitution "planted in Canada a living tree capable of growth and expansion within its natural limits ... the approach must be capable of growth to meet the future." The overall approach to the Canadian system of law can be looked at in the same way.

kosam/Shutterstock

Constitution as a "living tree"

It is also important to note that the law is not always concerned with what we would call "justice." As will be seen in this text, many times an individual may be successful in a legal case because of a technical detail, such as the way that the evidence was collected, or the filing of certain documents. Only looking for an artificial concept such as "justice" (whatever that might mean) will be unsatisfying to the student of law. Our legal system is not one that is wholly trying to achieve this elusive goal; that is not something that the legal system will necessarily achieve because it is not always possible. Many people will ultimately be unsuccessful in the realm of civil law, as parties often compromise at a solution that makes both parties unfulfilled. We might even think that some people who "deserved" to be heard will not be. What we can do is to adhere to certain fundamental principles of our system, and keep striving to make improvements as we realize them.

The law attempts to make the best decisions possible, given the available evidence and parties involved. Yet, it is a maxim of the law that "hard cases make bad law"; in some cases, the judge tries to push the boundaries or ignore principles of law to help sympathetic parties. Trying to find justice for a wronged individual may result in a legal principle that is not applicable to the wider community. We may strive to get a just result for one person, but judges must always keep an eye on what this decision might mean to future cases. Judges must weigh what is good for the community and what is good for the individual, what principles will create stability for the future rather than just the wishes of one individual, and whether the predictability of the law in a certain case will be changed for all other similar cases in the future. A distinguished Canadian educator once said that the "law is a part of Western society's dream of a life governed by reason."[16] However, as you will see in this text, you might not always agree that reason was used. Chapters 2–7 will further explore the civil law in Canada, and in particular law, ethics, and professional responsibility; civil litigation; contract law; tort law; family law; and administrative law.

16. John Willis, as cited in SM Waddams, *Introduction to the Study of Law*, 7th ed (Toronto: Carswell 2010) at 5. Reprinted by permission of Carswell, a division of Thomson Reuters Canada Ltd.

Quebec functions within the civil law system.

Kurt De Bruyn/Shutterwork.

A NOTE ON QUEBEC LAW

Like many countries around the world, Quebec's system of law is based on Roman law. Although the rest of Canada is governed by a system of common law, Quebec operates with a system through a Civil Code, and is also called **civil law**. Although some federal statutes, such as the *Criminal Code of Canada*, are in operation within Quebec, the whole system of commercial obligations, property law, and most family law may not be the same as it is in the rest of Canada. Often lawyers who practise in the common law system know very little about the system of law in Quebec.

Those using the civil law system do not rely on case law the same way that we do in a common law system. The primary source of law is the legislation that the judge needs to interpret, so the judge does not need to find another case to support their decision, finding a principle in the Code is enough. Sometimes cases are used when a situation is not addressed in their Code and they need to find a case to form an analogy. Civil law countries might also use doctrine or written work by scholars on the meaning of the provisions in the Code (as is also done in the common law system to a certain extent). However, it is important to remember that Quebec also uses the common law system with regard to criminal law matters. The civil and common law systems both work together within their system.

INTRODUCTION TO CONSTITUTIONAL LAW

In the space between civil law and criminal law, is the area of law the law called constitutional law. This type of law includes elements of the civil law, but also reaches over to the criminal law. Chapter 8 on constitutional law will discuss the applicability of constitutional law to both of the areas of our system. Some have said that the rules found in the Canadian Constitution are the most fundamental laws of our system because they govern how the state can act at its most basic level. A constitution is a body of law that establishes the framework for a government, which frames the supreme law of the country. Constitutional law is the system of written (and unwritten) principles that defines what power we give to our government while still protecting individuals and certain groups.

Chapter 8 will discuss Canada's constitutional law from a civil law perspective, and its ties to the criminal law system will be discussed in Chapter 10. This constitutional framework for our laws will provide the link between these two very different, but related parts of our law.

INTRODUCTION TO CRIMINAL LAW

"Nobody cares about criminal law except theorists and habitual criminals."

—Sir Henry Maine

As discussed, there are many differences between the two distinct areas of law. **Tort** is a private wrong, while crime is a public matter, and the purpose of the criminal law is to protect society from dangerous conduct. A case involving assault and battery can be both a civil and a criminal matter, but the results are very different. A civil matter will involve procedural matters, including the filing of a statement of claim and defence (usually by trained lawyers), where the victim has control of the matter and will usually seek damages in the form of money, and the case is proven on a balance of probabilities.

In a criminal court, the case is heard by a provincially or federally appointed judge, with or without a jury, and the case is brought in the name of the state (e.g., *Regina v Chapman* or *R v Chapman*). The Crown attorney employed by the state will prepare the case (largely without the input of the victim), and the accused will plead "guilty" or "not guilty." The victim will have very little control over the matter, and the injured person often gets no personal benefit, as the convicted will either face incarceration by the state (after being found guilty beyond a reasonable doubt) or he or she must pay a fine, which also goes to the state and not the victim (although there are some provisions for reparation, as will be seen in Chapter 12 on sentencing). The injured party in criminal law is deemed to be the state—not only the person physically or psychologically impacted by the crime.

The differences between the two systems are reflected by the different terms used. In a civil trial there is a *plaintiff* and a *defendant*, while in a criminal proceeding there is a *victim* and an *accused*. In a civil matter, the defendant is found liable and collects damages after the judgment, while the accused in a criminal trial is found guilty and will be convicted and punished. The maxim that it is "better to let nine guilty persons go free than convict one innocent person" is a cornerstone of the criminal system. If the wrong judgment is given on a civil trial, only a few individuals will be impacted; however, in a criminal trial, the fundamental basis of our system is brought into question for all if an innocent person is found guilty.

The differences between civil and criminal law in this context is the legal consequences that follow the act and whether a person chooses to pursue a criminal and/or civil remedy. Arguably, criminal law is the most intrusive form of public law, and theorists have attempted to understand the criminal law for centuries. Winston Churchill said in 1910 that the "mood and temper of the public with regard to the treatment of crime and criminals is one of the most unfailing tests of the civilization of any country."[17] However, dealing with those we label "criminal" and attempting to understand why these individuals decide not to conform like the rest of us has occupied theorists of all sorts.

Historically, we have not always treated the criminal among us well. In the fourteenth century in England, it was a crime to be a **vagabond**—this was any person who was unemployed and "idle." Vagabonds had their ears burned with a hot iron so that they could be identified, and more and more of the homeless and poor were branded this way. However, society was unable to explain *why* some would be vagrants and criminals, so people turned to familiar explanations, including the supernatural.

Supernatural Theories of Crime

No one explanation of deviance explains all crimes or all criminals, but the earliest attempts to explain deviance and the problems of crime looked for causes in the supernatural world. Before sociological, psychological, and criminological theories were created, individuals relied on the supernatural.

Particularly prior to the eighteenth century, supernatural causes were used to explain such occurrences as crop failures, diseases, and other disasters. Using a demonic perspective, crime, mental disorder, birth defects, and even minor vices such as drinking could be blamed on the supernatural. Burning a "witch" at the stake was often believed to be a good thing, as the state was driving out the devil from the person and saving the victim's soul. Two solutions to evil (and therefore crime) included exorcism, which was meant to cleanse or rid the person of the demon, or punishment and death used to destroy the devil by killing or torturing the individual.

By the late sixteenth century, hundreds and thousands of individuals were being killed because they were found to be witches. Author and legal historian Colin Wilson summarizes these murders saying that:

> in Toulouse, forty witches were burned in 1557, and in 1582, eighteen witches were burned in Avignon; between 1581 and 1591, nine hundred witches were sentenced in Lorraine, and in 1609, four hundred witches were burned in four months. In Germany, it was the same story: in 1572, five witches burnt in Treves; between 1587

17. Mark MacGuigan, Report to Parliament, by the Sub-Committee on the Penitentiary System in Canada (Ottawa: Government of Canada, 1977) at 1.

> and 1594, more than three hundred people were tried for witchcraft; then, in the early seventeenth century, there were literally thousands of burnings. One "witch-finder," Franz Buirmann, burned half the population of one village of three hundred inhabitants between 1631 and 1636; in Bamberg, sixteen hundred people were burned; in Würzburg, seven hundred and fifty-seven—these included children whose ages ranged from three to fifteen.[18]

It is estimated that witch hunts from 1400 to 1700 killed hundreds of thousands of innocent people in Europe.

There were also witch hunts in the American colonies leading to deaths, most famously, of victims in the township of Salem in 1692. The clergyman in the village, Samuel Parris, was convinced that a maid from the Barbados was teaching children to practise voodoo. Several young girls, aged 9 to 12, said that they were having convulsions and that spirits were "pinching" them. The maid, Tituba, was beaten, she confessed to being a witch, and she named several older women as witches, who were then arrested and tortured. The whole village became convinced that witches were among them. Approximately 20 persons (and at least one dog) were tried and executed, and approximately 142 persons were named by the girls. The girls initially accused mainly low-status women in the community, but it was only when they began accusing prominent members of society that the witch hunt ended and the authorities put an end to the trials. Sociologists say that these executions served a number of purposes: they provided a form of entertainment for the population; they made people fearful and obedient to authorities; and they reinforced the power of the church.

Witchcraft was one of the most common crimes in Europe in the seventeenth century. Crime was constructed in relation to religion, and any crime was an offence against God. The law was very commonly used to punish those thought to be consumed by evil influences. Author Rick Linden notes that common charges against witches were having a "pact with the Devil; journeys through the air over vast distances mounted on broomsticks; unlawful assembly at sabbats; worship of the Devil; kissing the Devil under the tail; copulation with incubi, male devils equipped with ice-cold penises; copulation with succubi, female devils ... killing the neighbour's cow; causing hailstorms; ruining the crops; stealing and eating babies."[19]

Witch trials in Salem, Massachusetts, in 1692

18. Colin Wilson, *A Criminal History of Mankind* (London: Mercury, 2005) at 357.
19. Rick Linden, *Criminology: A Canadian Perspective*, 7th ed (Toronto: Nelson, 2012) at 263.

The victims of these witch hunts give us some hint as to why they occurred. Many academics have looked at this phenomenon from a feminist legal perspective, as it has been estimated that 85 percent of those executed as witches were women.[20] In particular, those who were targeted were likely to be poor, unmarried, and women whose sexuality was questioned because they were promiscuous, adulterous, lesbians, or prostitutes. Accused individuals who were of low social or economic status or who were not well connected to the Church were particularly vulnerable to accusations.

The witch hunts contributed to social order and deterred people from challenging those in positions of power and authority. This was a form of **moral panic** based on no empirical evidence. This type of panic spreads through rumour, gossip, innuendo, and superstition. It is accepted uncritically and passed on from person to person. Those who start, promote, and fuel the panic do so for their own motives and self-interest.

FOOD FOR THOUGHT...

Do we still have moral panics today?
How is the media involved today?
What groups of people are vilified today?

Torture was often used to extract confessions from suspected witches because conviction under the Roman code of **canon** law used in most European courts required two eyewitnesses or a confession. It was often difficult to get eyewitnesses to this type of activity, so getting a confession from the "witch" was essential. Torture was also used to get the witch to name other witches, who were subsequently arrested, tortured, convicted, and killed. Accused witches who were was cooperative might be strangled before they were burned to death. Torture at this time included pulling the prisoner's fingernails off with pincers; inserting needles under fingernails; using a rack to painfully stretch the body; leg screws, which broke the shin-bone into pieces; a "witch chair," which was a seat of spikes heated from below; and crushing of the body by weights, often stones, like those used in Salem. See the box entitled "How to Find a Witch" for further discussion on identifying witches.

HOW TO FIND A WITCH

In the Middle Ages in Europe, authorities believed that God would indicate who was innocent and who was guilty. The first way was by "trial by battle," where the victim of a crime (or a family member) would physically fight the offender or the offender's family. The winner of the battle would be the innocent party.

There was also trial by ordeal (also called "trial by water"), where the accused person would be subjected to painful or difficult tests. Suspected witches were often tied up and thrown into a body of water. If the accused sank to the bottom of the water, she was innocent (but often was dead); if she floated, she was determined to be a "witch" and was executed, and justice was seen to be done because people believed God's will was being followed. Some would also be forced to "run a gauntlet" (or to endure attack from all sides) or would be forced to walk on fire. These trials were replaced by something called **compurgation**, where approximately 11 people would gather to swear that the accused was innocent. This was done on the principle that this number of people would not lie under oath and face God's wrath.

20. Rick Linden, *Criminology: A Canadian Perspective*, 6th ed (Toronto: Nelson, 2009) at 222.

As deviance became harder to explain with reference to the supernatural, individuals sought another way to understand the crimes of others.

ISSUE DISCUSSION

Does witchcraft have a place today? Look at s 365 of the *Criminal Code* and discuss in terms of the discussion on supernatural theories of crime.

Biological Theories of Crime

When reliance on the supernatural failed to provide a workable system of criminal law, the criminal law turned toward the biological and psychological to target those in need of punishment by the system. Stemming from supernatural theories that those with mental or physical disabilities are somehow criminal, Italian physician Giambattista della Porta (1535–1615) founded the school of **physiognomy,** which is the study of facial features in relation to the behaviour of humans. Next, Johann Kaspar Spurzheim (1776–1832) and Franz Joseph Gall (1758–1828) developed the science of **phrenology**, or the study of the contours of the skull to determine human interaction. All of this work led to the study of human behaviour by other theorists, including Cesare Lombroso.

Lombroso's Theory of Atavism

Cesare Lombroso (1835–1909), an Italian anthropologist and doctor, developed the first scientific theories of criminology with his concept of the "born criminal" and adopted a positivist theory. Although his research was fundamentally flawed, Lombroso was one of the first theorists to use this "scientific" method. Lombroso began his research when he worked in the Italian army as a prison physician and took an interest in the association between body type, appearance, and behaviour, and he systematically measured and observed some 3000 soldiers. He later studied inmates and the bodies of dead criminals in Italian prisons and soon began to report finding distinct physical differences between criminals and the so-called normal men.

Lombroso claimed that criminals could be identified by sight and by various **atavistic** characteristics. Those who were criminal had a huge lower jaw, strong canine teeth, ears that were found in savages or apes, an abnormal nose, insensitivity to pain, extreme sight, prominent lips, and "ape-like" arms, and were thus criminals who were a "throwback" to some primitive man. Lombroso found that these individuals had a "love of orgies, and the irresistible craving for evil for its own sake, the desire not only to extinguish life in the victim, but to mutilate the corpse, tear its flesh, and drink its blood."[21]

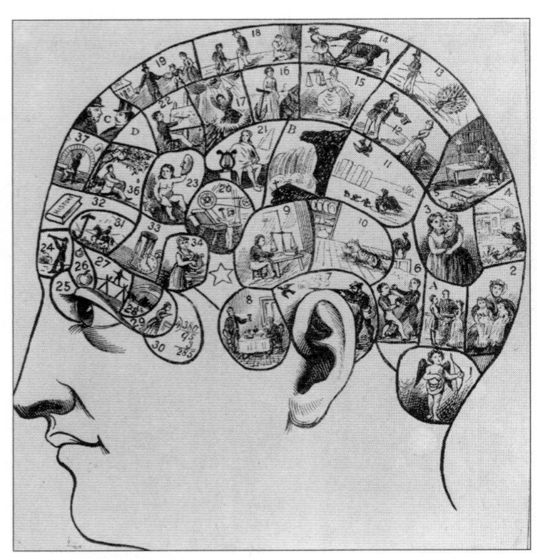
Hulton Archive/Getty Images

A phrenology chart mapping the brain.

Lombroso developed the science of phrenology, which involves measuring the size and shape of the skull, and concluded that there were significant and measurable differences in the skulls of criminals. He concluded that the criminal was less evolutionary evolved, thus explaining criminals' propensity to commit crime. For instance, criminals had not developed moral capacity and were thus unable to feel guilt or remorse and could not help themselves because their biology made them predisposed to crime.

This view of the atavistic offender was not well received by many, in part because it ran counter to prevailing philosophical views that people exercised free will. Social control of criminals from this perspective suggests that the criminal justice system should simply be a method of incapacitation of these dangerous criminals who cannot control themselves because they were born with this problem. Thus, they should be subject only to lengthy imprisonment or death. Treatment or rehabilitation was

21. Marvin E Wolfgang, "Cesare Lombroso," in Hermann Mannheim, ed, *Pioneers in Criminology* (Montclair, NJ: Patterson Smith, 1972).

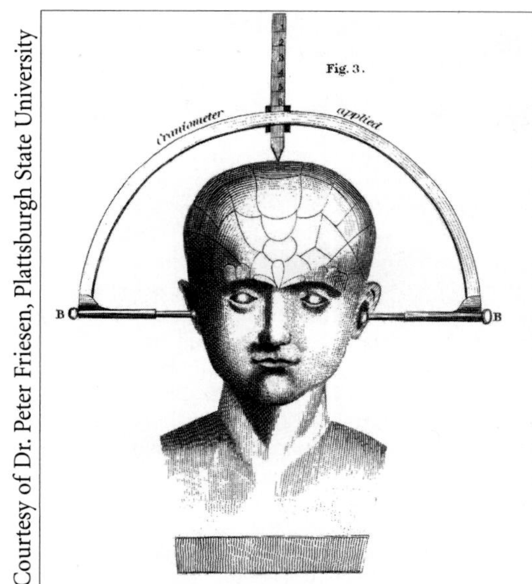

Courtesy of Dr. Peter Friesen, Plattsburgh State University

In craniometry, a craniometer was used to measure the size of the skull, which in turn was thought to correspond to intellectual capacity and personality traits.

not feasible since the problem was genetic and incurable. Lombroso even went as far as testifying as an "expert witness" in murder trials. In one case, the court was trying to determine which stepson had murdered a woman, and Lombroso testified that one of them was the perfect born criminal. He described this man as having "huge jaws, swollen sinuses, extremely pronounced cheekbones, a thin upper lip, huge incisors ... a large head capacity ... and left-handedness."[22] To Lombroso, this was a clear example of an atavistic criminal and the man was convicted.

LOMBROSO AND THE FEMALE OFFENDER It was clear to Lombroso that women were less prone to crime than men. According to Lombroso's theory, it could be argued that women were more evolutionary advanced than men and thus committed less crime. This was not consistent with Lombroso's patriarchal beliefs in the inferiority of women, so Lombroso had to adjust his theory to explain this discrepancy. Lombroso said that women had "many traits in common with children" but that a woman could be "transformed into a born criminal more terrible than any man.... The criminal woman is consequently a monster. Her normal sister is kept in the paths of virtue by many causes, such as maternity, piety, weakness, and when these counter influences fail, and a woman commits a crime, we may conclude that her wickedness must have been enormous before it could triumph over so many obstacles."[23] Thus, for a woman to be criminal she was worse than any man because she had to overcome her natural childlike weaknesses.

Lombroso argued that criminal women must be born with masculine qualities (like intelligence and activeness) conducive to criminal activity. He argued that when not restrained by religious sentiments, maternal feelings, and stupidity, this terrible criminal emerges. Lombroso felt that prostitutes were representative of atavistic women. He conducted autopsies of prostitutes and claimed to find that they were more masculine and had darker skin, a virile cranium, and excess body hair. Many question whether this was a researcher looking for characteristics that support his theory, and many also question the overall validity of his research.

DISCREDITING LOMBROSO Many academics had concerns about Lombroso's theory and research, but a number of studies done in Europe failed to replicate his findings. Charles Goring (1870–1919), a doctor and medical officer in the British prison system, collected data on over 3000 English convicts. When he compared his measurements with control samples of students and military men, he found no correlation between body and head measurements and criminality. Goring concluded that Lombroso's atavistic monster did not exist.

Lombroso's research was very sloppy by today's standards. His groups were chosen unscientifically, and he assumed that those in prison were all criminals and all those outside were not criminals. He did not make careful measurements, did not select or use control groups properly, suppressed data that did not fit his theory, and perhaps even fabricated some of his data. Many have looked for the meaning behind these findings. One theory is that the traits described by Lombroso were largely correlated with Sicilians who were, at the time, stereotyped as more criminal than the rest of Italian society. Goring and others discredited Lombroso's research and theory but not before it had been widely accepted throughout the world. His theories also played a major role in giving rise to the eugenics movement.

Are We Just Making It Up?

So many theories have tried to explain human criminality. The **eugenics** movement believed that they could cure the ills of society by "better breeding," a theory much accepted in Nazi Germany. **Craniometry** made use of skull measurements to determine criminal propensity. The point of this introduction has shown that we do not necessarily have it all figured out

22. Cesare Lombroso, *Criminal Man*, translation and introduction by Mary Gibson, Nicole Hahn Rafter (North Carolina: Duke University Press, 2006).
23. Cesar Lombroso and William Ferrero, *The Female Offender* (New York: Appleton, 1895) at 151–152.

FOOD FOR THOUGHT...

In 1928, the *Sexual Sterilization Act*, SA 1928, c 37, was passed in Alberta and created a "Eugenics Board" to see to the sterilization of those who were discharged from a mental institution. The Eugenics Board was tasked with determining whether patients were in danger of reproducing and transmitting their disease or "evil" to their children.[24] Patients deemed at risk of having children were forcibly sterilized. The person being sterilized was not permitted to refuse the procedure, and the decision was based only on the "best interests" of the individual. This movement was headed by the United Farm Women of Alberta (UFWA), but was also supported by the medical and legal professions, as well as many politicians, who some have noted were mainly from the "white, Anglo-Saxon, Protestant population of Alberta, who had a firm belief in their natural superiority over other races and classes."[25] The province of Alberta approved 4725 cases, and 2822 sterilizations were performed.[26] By 1945, Saskatchewan debated whether to adopt this legislation based on a report by Dr. CM Hincks of the Canadian National Committee for Mental Hygiene, which found that there was a real need for "sterilization in connection with physically attractive moron girls prior to discharge from residential school [for mental defectives.]"[27]

These provisions were ultimately repealed in the 1970s because the eugenics theories on which it was based were questioned, and on the basis that the legislation violated human rights.

Should we fear that eugenics may occur again today in Canada?
What do we currently think is socially unacceptable?
Who do we think is unacceptable?
How could Canadians allow this to happen less than a century ago?

when it comes to crime. Sociologists, psychologists, and criminologists have spent centuries trying to figure out why people commit crime. The truth is that we may be little closer today than we were with supernatural theories. See above Food for Thought box and the history of sterilization of women in Canada for a sad example of the results of these biological theories.

The job of the law student and lawyer is not to determine why an individual may have committed a crime, but to focus on what to do with that person when he or she enters the legal system. The truth with many topics is that we may be learning as we go. We once thought the earth was flat (and apparently some people still think it is), but we eventually altered that theory. We thought that the earth was the centre of the universe, but we eventually altered that approach. Much is left to be desired about science, and the same can be said about the law. No one theory works with every individual, and we are changing our legal theories all of the time, and one will fall into favour over another as we develop. As students of the law, we are looking at most things *ex post facto*, or "after the fact." Instead of an absolute focus on why crime occurs, the law student recognizes the need to take the available evidence and deal with people accused of crime in the legal system as best as we can.

CASE STUDIES

An interesting way to examine the similarities and differences in the civil law and criminal law systems and reactions to the offender or the person bringing a lawsuit is to look at various cases that deal with the same issues in various ways. Compare and contrast the cases in the following box that were briefly introduced earlier in the text.

24. As cited in Naomi Nind, "Solving an 'Appalling' Problem: Social Reformers and the Campaign for the Alberta *Sexual Sterilization Act*, 1928" (2000) 38 *Alberta Law Review* 536 at 537.

25. Naomi Nind, "Solving an 'Appalling' Problem: Social Reformers and the Campaign for the Alberta *Sexual Sterilization Act*, 1928" (2000) 38 *Alberta Law Review* 536 at 544.

26. As cited in Laura Fraser, "Sterilization: Choice, Right, or Requirement? A Comment on the Best Interests Test in *Re Eve*" (1998) 7 *Dalhousie Journal of Legal Studies* 163 at 167.

27. *Time Magazine*, "Canada: Saskatchewan: Sterilization Cry" (1945).

1. *R v DRUMMOND*, [1996] OJ NO. 4597 (ONT CJ)

This case is the only one of the three examples which was dealt with in the criminal law system. In a very controversial case from 1996, 28-year-old Brenda Drummond went into the bathroom of her home, inserted a pellet gun into her vagina, and fired a pellet into her uterus. Mrs. Drummond was pregnant at the time of the shooting and had her other children playing in the house. Two days later, Mrs. Drummond gave birth to an almost-full-term six-pound child that she named Johnathan Drummond. After Mrs. Drummond initially claimed she did not know her baby had an injury, Johnathan developed a serious infection. The results of a brain scan surprised doctors when it revealed a metal pellet lodged in the baby's brain. Ninety hours after Johnathan was born, doctors removed the pellet surgically and saved his life.

Mrs. Drummond alleged that she did not know that she was pregnant when she shot herself with the gun. Although there was evidence that Mrs. Drummond was a good mother with no criminal history, she was charged with the attempted murder of her child under s 223(2) of the *Criminal Code.* Section 223 provides that

> a child becomes a human being within the meaning of this Act when it has completely proceeded, in a living state, from the body of its mother, whether or not (*a*) it has breathed; (*b*) it has an independent circulation; or (*c*) the navel string is severed. (2) A person commits homicide when he causes injury to a child before or during its birth as a result of which the child dies after becoming a human being.

This section provides that homicide is committed if a child dies *after* birth from injuries inflicted by that person *before* birth. Lawyers for Mrs. Drummond said that Johnathan had no legal status when he was inside the womb, and since he did not die from his injuries, s 223(2) did not apply. The Crown lawyers said that this law made no sense, but the judge refused to alter the law as written by Parliament. The judge said that "no matter how desirable it may be, I cannot construe section 223 in a manner that removes the words at the end of 223(2): 'As a result of which the child dies after becoming a human being.'" At the time of the injury, Johnathan was not a human being, and he did not die after birth. Although the judge said that Mrs. Drummond's actions could be seen as immoral, it was not illegal and Mrs. Drummond could not be found guilty of the crime of attempted homicide. The Crown chose not to appeal if Mrs. Drummond agreed to plead guilty to another charge of failing to provide the necessaries of life and received 30 months probation.

Was this a just use of the criminal law system?
Did Mrs. Drummond "get off" on a technicality?
Should Mrs. Drummond be found guilty of a crime?
Would the civil law system have found differently?

2. *DOBSON (LITIGATION GUARDIAN OF) v DOBSON*, [1999] SCJ NO 41 (SCC)

In *Dobson,* which was dealt with in the civil law, the Supreme Court examined the case of the defendant who was 27 weeks pregnant when the car she was driving collided with another vehicle. The crash resulted in prenatal injuries to her fetus, later named Ryan, who was born by Caesarean section later that day. The child had permanent mental and physical injuries. The child's grandfather brought an action against the child's mother alleging her negligent driving. The court had to determine whether Ryan had the capacity to bring a tort action against his mother for her negligence before he was born.

First, the court had to determine if there was a legal duty owed by a pregnant woman towards her child who is "born alive." The court debated whether limitations should be placed on a woman who is pregnant. Should she drive? Leave the home? The court found that the public policy concerns raised are so great that a legal duty cannot, and should not, be imposed on a pregnant woman toward her fetus, and subsequent child. The court should not impose restrictions on a pregnant woman, such as her right to drive, and they should be hesitant to impose any additional burdens on pregnant women. Trying to artificially impose the standard of a "reasonable pregnant woman" has many implications for lifestyle choices, and undermines the rights of women. The court concluded that if any imposition on women is going to be made, it must be made by the legislature.

Do you agree with this decision?
Should a mother's "lifestyle choices" be examined by the court—including tobacco use, drug use, recreational activities, her diet, and stress at work?
Compare this case to cases termed "wrongful birth."

3. *PAXTON* ET AL *v RAMJI*, [2008] 92 OR (3D) 401 (ONT CA)

The parties in *Paxton* decided to sue civilly. There have been several cases trying to determine whether a fetus injured during pregnancy could recover damages after the child was born alive. There has been a spike in these reproductive cases in the last few decades, and the issue of liability to the unborn has been progressing. It was established in law that a child born alive could sue for prenatal injuries even though no tort is committed while the child was still a fetus. Thus, if the child is not born alive, there is no action, but once he or she is born alive the child is a person and may sue for any injuries suffered.

Liability has been imposed for negligent pharmaceutical companies for the drugs given to mothers during pregnancy, and for doctors who have prescribed harmful medications or injured the child during birth. The issue in these cases is based on a health-care professional's duty to inform patients about treatment, or avoiding or terminating pregnancy. Cases have come to the court from parents who were not informed of their genetic risk to have children with a particular disease, cases where mothers were not warned of the effects of post-conception illnesses (like chickenpox) that the mother might have, and cases where there was a failure to test for abnormalities or failure to read certain tests correctly.

Because of the overwhelming cost of a disabled child, many parents have sought to find the defendant doctor negligent because a reasonable person in the circumstances would have prevented or terminated the pregnancy. The court has found damages for special expenses for the child and for loss of income of the caregivers of the child, in addition to emotional suffering. However, the *Paxton* case imposed some limitations on this type of tort litigation.

In *Paxton*, the defendant doctor prescribed an acne medicine called Accutane to the plaintiff. Accutane is a drug that can cause fetal malformation. The plaintiff's husband had a vasectomy four-and-a-half years earlier, but the operation failed and a child was conceived. The trial judge found that this was not a case of "wrongful life," which has not been recognized in Canadian law, but a matter of whether there was a duty and standard of care from the doctor to a child that was not conceived. The trial judge found that the doctor did owe a duty of care not to prescribe the medication without taking all reasonable steps to ensure that the mother would not become pregnant.

The court of appeal disagreed and said that there is not even a duty of care from the doctor to the unborn child. The court found that there is no jurisprudence in Canada on whether a doctor can be in a relationship with a future child who was not conceived or born at the time of the prescription. A doctor cannot have a duty of care to any future child of the doctor's female patient. There would be a conflict of interest between what was best for the female patient and any potential child. The doctor cannot advise or take instructions from that non-existent child, and cannot be in a position of a duty of care to the child.

The court reaffirmed that until a child is born alive, the doctor must act in the best interest of the female patient.

There has been some speculation that a tort of "wrongful life" might be successful in the future. The argument would be that the plaintiff child argues that if the defendant parent had been warned, the child would not have been born with the mental and physical disabilities present. The plaintiff's claim would be that he or she should not have been born. There are many policy considerations for this type of claim, although some cases have been successful in a few American states. It is difficult to measure damages on something that is theoretical and did not happen. Some say that this devalues the life of many disabled individuals and devalues the sanctity of life because they are arguing that they would be better off dead.

Was this the right decision?
Could someone sue another party on the grounds that he or she should not have been alive? Is this a total contradiction that the law should not have to deal with?
What is the difference between the criminal case and the civil law cases?

CONCLUSION

Throughout the text you will find the following things: the law is full of uncertainty; the law is full of rapid change; no one can say for sure what the law is until the courts decide; and "hard cases make bad law." The law may seem not to make sense, it might seem contradictory, but as Waddams says, "it would be very hard upon the profession, if the law was so certain, that everybody knew it."[28] The law is supposed to be difficult, and if we had it all figured out, we would not need to study it so carefully. Our system is a very complex one, but it is also quite flexible. I hope that you will have opinions on many issues, and you will ask yourself how the Canadian justice system should respond. It is important to remember that as Canadian citizens we are presumed to know the law "except Her Majesty's judges, who have a Court of Appeal set over them to correct their errors."[29] So although we are presumed to know our rights, and presumed to stay out of matters that do not concern us (as so eloquently stated by my law school professor), it is important to get a full picture of the Canadian justice system and to question how to improve the function in the future. The law is all about questions—asking the right ones, and refraining from judging others who use the system in their own particular way.

LEARNING OUTCOMES SUMMARIZED

1. Define "law."

The law can refer to the system of justice through the state's threat of punishment under a particular governmental structure. It can refer to the legislation and written documents behind the court system (including regulations, proclamations, the Constitution, and case law). It can refer to the fields of law, such as contract law or criminal law. It can also refer to the structure of the system, including all of the players in the courtroom.

2. List the defining characteristics of natural law, legal positivism, and legal realism.

Natural law:

- Morality cannot be divorced from law, but they have to be understood together.
- There is a link between law and morality, and an unjust law must not be followed.
- The answers can be found in the natural world with a fixed order.

28. SM Waddams, *Introduction to the Study of Law*, 7th ed (Toronto: Carswell 2010) at 4. Reprinted by permission of Carswell, a division of Thomson Reuters Canada Ltd.

29. *Ibid* at 4.

Legal positivism:

- Law is divorced from morality, and all can be explained through science, measurement and logic.
- One must look at the law mechanically to determine the answers.
- Morality does not provide the solutions to legal problems.

Legal realists:

- Context is important to law including economic, social, and political factors.
- The parties are important—their life experiences, how they approach the law, and how they interpret the law.
- Judges and their personal opinions are very important, as they apply the law.

3. Identify one of the most common charges in seventeenth-century Europe.

One of the most common charges was being a "witch." Those who were charged (mostly women) were marginal members of the society, were unconnected to religious faiths, and were economically disadvantaged. Particular targets were women who were unmarried, who were viewed as promiscuous, or who were homosexual.

4. Analyze the father of the "atavistic" theory? What were the characteristics of the "atavistic man"?

Cesare Lombroso was the father of the atavistic theory, and he believed that he could identify criminals by sight by their atavistic characteristics. Those who were criminal had distinct facial features—features found in, what he called, savages or apes. They were insensitive to pain and had "ape-like" arms. They were identified as criminals who were a "throwback" to some primitive man. Lombroso attributed many criminal attributes to those he found to be unfeeling animals.

SELF-EVALUATION QUESTIONS

1. Should laws be prospective or retroactive? Why?
2. What does the phrase "hard cases made bad law" mean?
3. What system of law is the law in Quebec based on?
4. Discuss the differences between private and public law.
5. How could the Canadian legal system be compared to a living tree?
6. In the *Dobson (Litigation Guardian of) v Dobson* case, did the Supreme Court find that it should use a "reasonable person" test? Was it a modified form of this test? Discuss.

CHAPTER

2

Legal Professionals, Rules of Professional Conduct, and Legal Ethics

"The first thing we do, let's kill all the lawyers."
—William Shakespeare, King Henry *VI, Act IV, Scene II*

Learning Outcomes

After completing this chapter, you should be able to:

1. Identify the exceptions to lawyer-and-client confidentiality.
2. List the punishments that a lawyer can face if reprimanded by the law society.
3. Discuss the limitations of a criminal defence lawyer who has an unequivocal confession from a client.
4. Assess the lawyer's options when a client insists on perjuring him- or herself on the witness stand.
5. Evaluate how a lawyer–client relationship can come to an end.

THE ROLE OF THE PARTIES IN THE CANADIAN JUSTICE SYSTEM

The Legal Profession

The legal profession is regulated in several ways. Lawyers are self-regulated; that is, the control of lawyers is by lawyers. However, legal professionals can be sued in the civil law system for incompetence, breach of their duties, or criminal prosecutions for things such as fraud. Lawyers are also regulated by informal means, such as through mentors at law firms, and by the market for legal services.

Lawyers have a monopoly on legal services in Canada, so many think that it is a natural fit for lawyers to discipline other lawyers if they act inappropriately, because of their specialized knowledge of the profession. Legislation prevents non-lawyers from practising law or acting as **barristers** and **solicitors** (in Canada the profession is now "fused," so lawyers are both **barristers and solicitors**).

Law Society of Upper Canada–Benchers
http://www.lsuc.on.ca/WorkArea/DownloadAsset.aspx?id=2147483894

The Law Society

In Canada, the law societies control who can become a lawyer, what admission requirements are necessary, what education is needed, and who can be removed from the profession. The governing body of the law society is called "convocation." It is composed of people called **benchers,** many of whom are elected by lawyers. In Ontario, benchers are tasked with the governance of the law society and the regulation of the province's lawyers and paralegals for a four-year term. Benchers spend an average of 31 days a year attending to law society matters, including sitting on hearing panels, attending monthly committee and convocation meetings, and attending calls to the bar. Benchers are remunerated for some of their services at a rate of $500 per day and $300 per half-day, but benchers must attend 26 times for law society activities before being eligible for remuneration. Benchers may also be reimbursed for expenses.

Some are critical of the relatively modest remuneration for benchers because lawyers from large law firms are more able to participate in the law society than sole practitioners, who would not be able to take this time away from clients. All provincial bar associations belong to the Canadian Bar Association (CBA), which informs all provincial bar associations and law societies. The law society of each province finally approves that a lawyer can act in a particular jurisdiction.

There are 14 law societies in Canada—one for each of the provinces and territories, and Quebec has two societies (one that governs **notaries**, and one that governs lawyers.) Each law society is created by a statute of each province or territory, and these organizations are usually called a "Law Society," though it is called the "Barristers' Society" in Nova Scotia. Each law society has a board of directors known as benchers or "Members of Council," who meet regularly to discuss admission to the society, professional standards, insurance, and discipline of its lawyers. The society can be small (with a support staff of just one person in the Yukon) or have more than 300 staff members, as at the Law Society of Upper Canada (LSUC) in Ontario.

The Federation of Law Societies of Canada (FLSC) governs these 14 law societies and oversees Canada's approximately 95000 lawyers and Quebec's 3500 notaries. Through the National Committee on Accreditation (NCA), the FLSC assesses and certifies those who receive their law degrees internationally and wish to apply for membership in a Canadian law society (except in Quebec). The FLSC also operates the website CanLII, which provides publicly accessible and free online access to legislation and case law.

The Federation of Law Societies of Canada
http://www.flsc.ca/en/about/about.asp
CanLII
http://www.canlii.org/en/index.php
Federation Model Code of Professional Conduct
http://www.flsc.ca/en/federation-model-code-of-professional-conduct//

In 2004, the FLSC created a Model Code of Professional Conduct (MCPC), which was sent to the provinces in 2009. Provincial law societies, such as the LSUC, have recently been investigating having one code of conduct across Canada. For example, the LSUC had a report dated May 24, 2012 by the Professional Regulation Committee that called for input on amendments proposed to the Ontario Rules of Professional Conduct by August 2012 with a next report in early 2013. It is anticipated that the code will be implemented by provinces after feedback is received, and it is expected to be adopted by all provinces in the next few years. Because of this, the exact wording of the sections discussed in this chapter may change slightly in the coming years.

Some critics of the legal system in Canada say that the profession is quick to suppress any unauthorized practice of law under the guise of protecting the public, but is actually protecting lawyers' monopoly on their jobs. However, the unauthorized practice of law can be harmful to the public as seen in *The Law Society of Upper Canada v Boldt* (see the following case box).

THE LAW SOCIETY OF UPPER CANADA v BOLDT, [2006] OJ NO 1142 (ONT SCJ)

Ms. Boldt was never a member of the Law Society of Upper Canada (LSUC) in Ontario, and had never been licensed to practise in Ontario. However, Ms. Boldt was carrying on business as a lawyer through her operation of a "full-service" paralegal business.

Ms. Boldt was previously prosecuted by the LSUC in 1995 and 1998 for the unauthorized practice of law contrary to s 50 of the Law Society Act RSO 1990, c L-8. The previous actions were dealt with by agreement between the accused and the law society. Ms. Boldt pleaded guilty to one count of unlawfully acting or practising as a barrister and solicitor, and she admitted that she had offered services in wills, divorces, and incorporations, and she had represented clients in the Ontario Court of Justice, including the preparation of documents, and she provided advice in wills and separation agreements. She was fined $100 and took an undertaking not to practise law in breach of s 50. However, Ms. Boldt violated this agreement in 1999, and the court ordered Ms. Boldt to stop practising law.

In 2003, Ms. Boldt again came before the court because she had prepared legal documents in the context of a divorce. Her clients believed they had signed a final and binding separation agreement when in fact they had not. The LSUC offers lawyers professional liability insurance if anything goes wrong in the course of work with a lawyer and their clients. However, Ms. Boldt did not have this insurance as she was not a lawyer, and the public was unprotected against services that the LSUC found were below standard. The court found that she dispensed legal advice without being a lawyer, and that she had violated the injunction that said that she should not practise law. Ms. Boldt was held in **contempt of court**.

At sentencing, the court found that Ms. Boldt "showed deliberate and willful contempt of the court's order," and she profited from her unauthorized practice of the law. The LSUC sought a period of imprisonment of Ms. Boldt for four months. Counsel for Ms. Boldt said that a fine of $5000 would be appropriate without a jail sentence. The court sentenced Ms. Boldt to four months of house arrest, a prohibition from carrying on paralegal matters for four months, the publication of the sentence, and a payment for the legal fees of the LSUC in the amount of $35 000.

Do you think this is a very severe sentence for the unauthorized practice of law? In a development (see *Maureen Olivia Boldt v Law Society of Upper Canada*, 2011 ONLSHP 0018), Ms. Boldt later applied for Class P1 paralegal licence under the new paralegal regime. The court found that Ms. Boldt "did not act with high ethical standards in her dealings with her former clients or the Courts. The Candidate, persistently and repetitively, conducted herself in such a manner that she posed a risk to the public and the administration of justice ... the Candidate did not and does not appreciate the difference between right and wrong. She has no moral compass. The administration of justice must be protected from someone such as she who thinks nothing of making unfounded allegations against members of the judiciary and others. The Candidate has demonstrated an unwillingness to be governed by the Society, and is thus ungovernable." Her application for a paralegal licence was denied. Do you agree with this decision that Ms. Boldt cannot practise as a paralegal?

THE ROLE OF LAWYERS

Lawyers are professionals who are educated and trained in the practice of law. The law is highly technical and lawyers are trained in its complex rules and regulations, and most individuals involved in the justice system need lawyers in order to navigate through the courts as an intermediary between their clients and the legal system. Lawyers take a personal complaint and turn it into a legal cause that is **actionable** in law.

Although many lawyers practise law in various areas, there are numerous types of law that one can specialize in. These include corporate law, taxation law, municipal law, bankruptcy, administrative law, real estate, estate and wills, family law, labour and employment law, commercial litigation, intellectual property law (including patents and copyright), criminal law from either the perspective of the defence or Crown

A lawyer's robes

© Julie Pratt

(which may include constitutional issues), immigration, landlord and tenant law, Aboriginal law, sports law, entertainment law, and personal injury litigation, among other specialties. More recently, areas like environmental law and poverty law have emerged.

How a lawyer practises can also be diversified. Every level of government requires lawyers to assist in their day-to-day functions, and may hire their own team to represent their interests. Large corporations may employ a department of lawyers to work within the company to deal with any issues that arise in the course of business. These lawyers are commonly called **in-house counsel**. Lawyers can practise law within large law firms, law firms with only one lawyer (**sole practitioners**), or anywhere in between. Many politicians are also lawyers and use their knowledge on the legislative front.

Lawyers may also teach at law schools, at universities at the undergraduate level, at colleges, or in high schools. These lawyers are academics who seek to change or modify the law through the dissection and discussion of legal issues. Many lawyers take their skills to corporations where they do not directly use their legal training, but use their knowledge for business purposes. No matter what the end result, according to theorist SM Waddams, a "good legal education is worth having for its intellectual discipline, its inherent interest, and for the understanding it gives of legal institutions."[1]

Lawyers also maintain some ceremonial aspects in Canada, and still wear ceremonial robes that consist of the robe itself, a waistcoat, and special court shirts with stiff wing collar and white tabs. The requirements for court attire are specific and lawyers are required to wear black shoes; black or dark grey socks or black, dark grey, or natural hose; and black, dark grey, or dark grey striped trousers or skirt.

What Is the Public Perception of Lawyers?

Waddams has succinctly summarized the (rather pessimistic) opinion of lawyers in our society:

> The legal profession has never enjoyed great popularity. This is no doubt because the lawyer is rarely the supplier of anything pleasant. Legal services never seem to produce a tangible benefit. In civil litigation the loser generally regards his lawyer's fee as the addition of insult to injury. The winner always regards herself as the recipient of simple justice, and resents having to pay a fee for what is, after all, rightfully her own. The successful criminal lawyer may enjoy some reputation in Kingston Penitentiary, but to the public at large he seems to be a threat to public security who is apt to set free dangerous criminals on what everyone knows are mere technicalities. The drawer of wills, the conveyor of real property, the administrator of estates all seem to belong to a parasitic breed who make unnecessarily complex the simple affairs of life in order to benefit themselves and the fellow members of their professions. The only clients who really appreciate the legal services they receive are hard-headed business persons who know the value of good advice about corporate organization, income tax, or labour relations. No wonder corporate practice is so popular.[2]

The public seems to have a love-hate relationship with lawyers. As a group, lawyers tend to be the butt of much criticism—and, of course, lawyer jokes—but these advocates are also championed by those who have benefited from their services. The negative image seems to revolve around what is perceived to be the unethical conduct of lawyers. The practice of law places lawyers in ethical dilemmas on an everyday basis. In addition, lawyers are often tainted by the people they represent, who are sometimes accused of serious liability or brutal crimes.

As such, the public perception of lawyers is not as positive as many would like. A Leger poll in 2004 measured the most admired professions (see Figure 2.1). Only 44 percent of Canadians admired lawyers in 2004, which was a drop from 54 percent in 2002. In contrast, 75 percent of Canadians admired judges in 2004, down from 80 percent in 2002. Firefighters, on the other hand, had a 97 percent admiration rate and nurses had a rate of 95 percent.

1. SM Waddams, *Introduction to the Study of Law*, 7th ed (Toronto: Carswell 2010) at 118–119. Reprinted by permission of Carswell, a division of Thomson Reuters Canada Ltd.
2. *Ibid* at 117.

Figure 2.1 Public Perception of Professions in Canada 2004 Compared to 2002

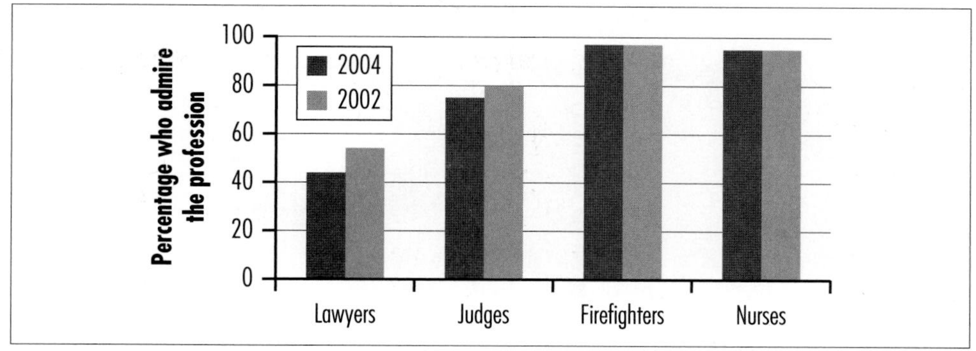

Source: Philip Slayton, *Lawyers Gone Bad: Money, Sex and Madness in Canada's Legal Profession.* (London: Penguin, 2007).

Figure 2.2 Complaints Made to the Law Society of Upper Canada, 2010 and 2011

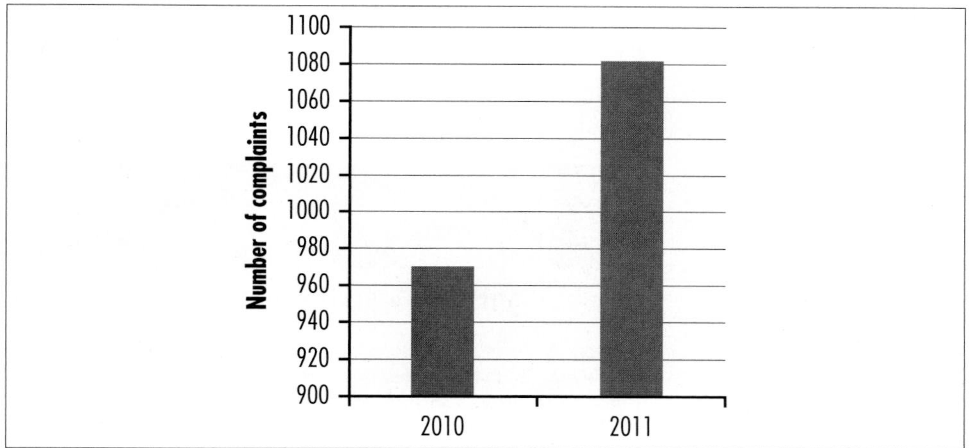

Source: Thomas Claridge, "Complaints Against Ontario Lawyers Jump Nine Per Cent" (4 March 2011) *The Lawyers Weekly.*

There are approximately 14000 complaints per year to Canadian law societies.[3] In Ontario, for the first three months of 2011, there was a 9 percent increase in complaints to the LSUC on Ontario's 40000 lawyers. There were a total of 1082 complaints against lawyers, compared with 971 complaints for the same period of 2010 (see Figure 2.2).[4]

However, a 2009 poll from the United Kingdom (see Figure 2.3) found that only 3 percent of the those surveyed trusted journalists, 2 percent trusted bankers, and 1 percent trusted real estate agents and politicians, but 24 percent trusted lawyers.[5] Similarly, an American Bar Association survey of 300 households found that 76 percent of those polled were satisfied (58 percent) or somewhat satisfied (18 percent) with a lawyer they had retained.[6] Where does the general negative image of lawyers come from in Canada? Could the media be to blame? See the following Food for Thought box.

3. Philip Slayton, *Lawyers Gone Bad: Money, Sex and Madness in Canada's Legal Profession.* (London: Penguin, 2007).
4. Thomas Claridge, "Complaints Against Ontario Lawyers Jump Nine Per Cent" (4 March 2011) *The Lawyers Weekly.*
5. Frances Gibb, "Actually, the Public Do Trust Lawyers ..." (31 March 2009), timesonline.co.uk, online: <http://business.timesonline.co.uk/tol/business/law/article6010141.ece>.
6. Michael Rappaport, "Nobody Likes a Lawyer Until they Need One" (2008) *Lawyers Weekly.*

Figure 2.3 Trust in Professionals—The United Kingdom

Percentage who trust

Journalists	Bankers	Real estate agents	Politicians	Lawyers

Source: Frances Gibb, "Actually, the Public Do Trust Lawyers . . ." (31 March 2009). Times Online timesonline.co.uk

FOOD FOR THOUGHT...

DOES OUR PERCEPTION OF LAWYERS COME FROM THE MOVIES?

Michael Asimow wrote an article in 2000 called "Bad Lawyers in the Movies." In this article, he follows the image portrayed in movies from the 1970s through the 1990s, and concludes that there are many negative views of lawyers portrayed in film. Asimow says,

> Seen any lawyer films recently? Chances are, most of the lawyers in those films were bad. They were unpleasant or unhappy human beings you wouldn't want as friends. And they were bad professionals you wouldn't admire or want as your lawyer. In the majority of films involving law, lawyers and the legal system since the 1970's, the lawyer characters and their law firms were pretty bad. This generalization holds whether the film fits the standard lawyer/courtroom genre, whether it involves legal issues, whether the film is a comedy (black or otherwise) or a drama, or whether it falls into other genres such as romances, mystery stories, or thrillers that just happen to have lawyer roles.[7]

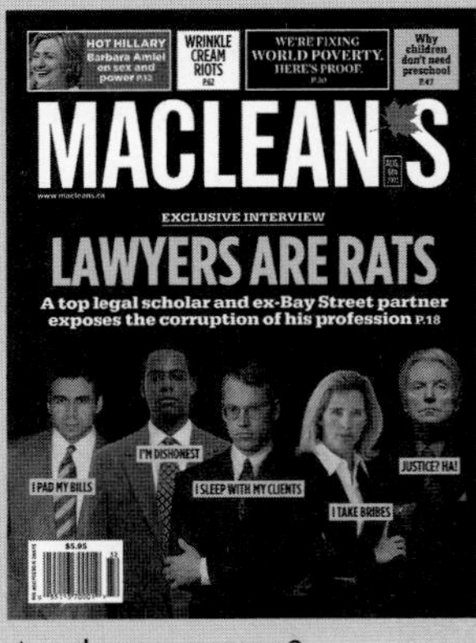

Are lawyers rats?

Asimow looked at movies such as *The Firm*, *Liar Liar*, and *The Devil's Advocate*, and showed that there has been a drop in the public's perception of lawyers in terms of ethics, prestige, and character starting in the 1970s and 1980s and continuing forward to 2000.

What do you think about the portrayal of lawyers in the media?

In August 2007, the cover of *Maclean's* magazine had photos of lawyers, and under the heading "Lawyers are Rats," the pictures had captions such as "I'm dishonest," "I sleep with my clients," "I take bribes," and "Justice? Ha!" Are these labels justified?

7. Michael Asimow, "Bad Lawyers In the Movies" (2000) *Nova Law Review* vol. 24, p. 533.

Lawyers and Demographics

The demographics of the legal profession are changing faster than the public perception is shifting. According to the CBA, there are increasing numbers of females being accepted to law schools and practising law. The 2001 Canadian census reveals that more females than males are being called to the bar, and females comprise more of the lawyers under the age of 30 (see Figure 2.4). However, among older lawyers, the ratio is almost nine males to every female. In Ontario, the 2006 census showed that although women were just 5 percent of lawyers in 1971, they are now nearly 60 percent of young lawyers, and 38 percent of all lawyers in Ontario (see Figure 2.4).[8]

The 1996 census showed that 94 percent of lawyers were white (a figure that remained fairly stable through 2001, at 93 percent), and that three quarters of non-white lawyers were South Asian, black or Chinese in origin.[9] There are still very few Aboriginal lawyers and the number has only increased from 0.6 percent to 1 percent of lawyers in Ontario between 2001 and 2006. In Ontario, 11.5 percent of lawyers are members of a visible minority, but 20 percent of lawyers aged 25–34 are members of a visible minority. It is an alarming reality that women and visible minorities are still earning less money than white male lawyers. Female lawyers aged 45 to 49 earn 16 percent less than their male colleagues. It is estimated that "racialized" (i.e., non-white) lawyers aged 40 to 44 earn $40 000 less than white men of the same age earn per year.[10]

Many law societies are investigating why increasing numbers of women are entering the profession but are also leaving the field at a high rate. The "Final Report—Retention of Women in Private Practice Working Group" by the Law Society of Upper Canada finds that women are leaving because the legal profession has not recognized the needs of women.[11] The report examines how women's realities include childbirth and family responsibilities and how this affects their professional lives and contributes to the huge loss to the legal profession which is failing to retain this group of talented lawyers. This will be an area that will continue to be investigated across Canada.

Figure 2.4 Age Cohorts of Lawyers in Canada, 2001

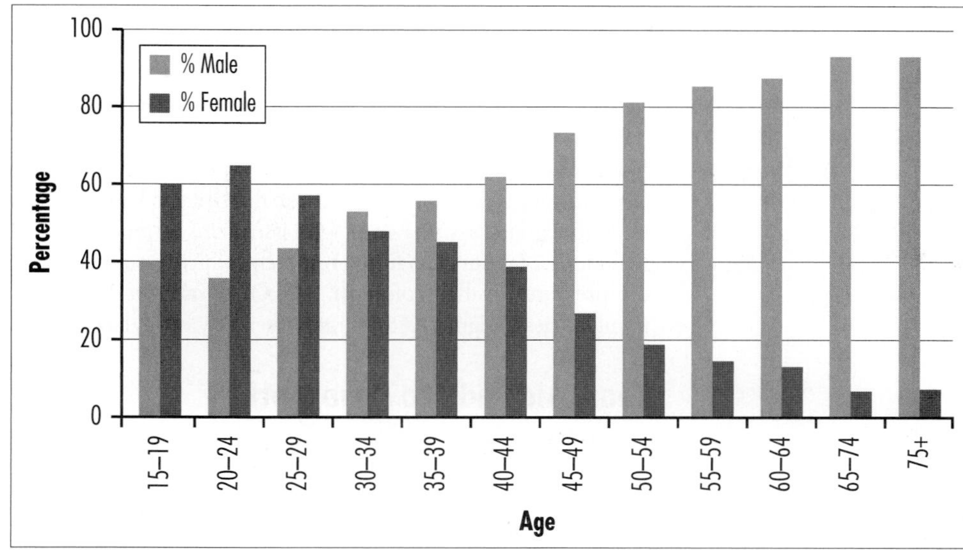

Source: From David Brusegard, *The Implications of Demographic Change in the Legal Profession*, (The Canadian Bar Association, February 3, 2004). Reprinted with permission of the Canadian Bar Association. <http://www.cba.org/cba/futures/pdf/demographics_feb04.pdf> at 3

8. David Brusegard, "The Implications of Demographic Change in the Legal Profession (The Canadian Bar Association, February 3, 2004), online: <http://www.cba.org/cba/futures/pdf/demographics_feb04.pdf at 3>.
9. Law Society of Upper Canada, online: <http://www.lsuc.on.ca/media/convapril10_ornstein.pdf> at i.
10. *Ibid* at ii.
11. Law Society of Upper Canada, "Final Report—Retention of Women in Private Practice Working Group," May 22, 2008).

Figure 2.5 Ontario Lawyers Assistance Plan: New Lawyer Cases 2010

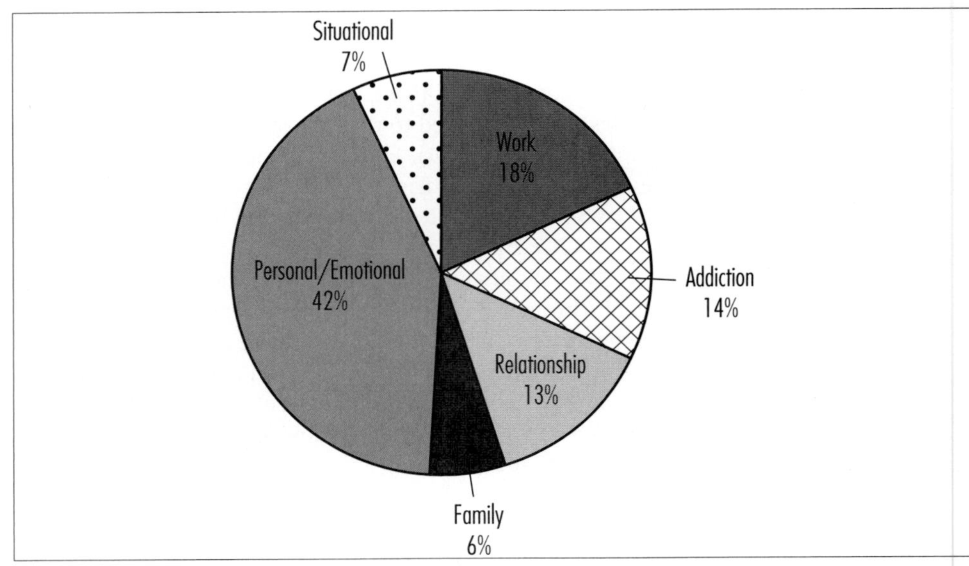

Source: Ontario Lawyers' Assistance Program Annual Report 2010, retrieved from: <http://www.olap.ca/ANNUAL%20REPORT%202010_V2.pdf>. Reproduced by permission of OLAP.

The CBA has also frequently reported that lawyers are at a high risk for developing depression and committing suicide. The CBA notes that of 28 occupations studied by Johns Hopkins, lawyers were the most likely of all of the professions studied to be depressed. A study from Washington state found that although 5–10 percent of the population suffers from depression, the rate is closer to 19 percent among lawyers. The CBA cites Robert Bircher of the Lawyers Assistance Program of British Columbia, who points out that the factors that lead to depression in lawyers are "long hours, the adversarial nature of law, the focus on billable hours, increased competition for clients, the dehumanization of the practice, focusing on the business aspects of law rather than people combined with a culture of materialism, perfectionism, and workaholism."[12]

The CBA also cites an Ontario study of lawyers facing discipline, which found that nearly 50 percent of these lawyers admitted to having issues with drugs, alcohol, or psychiatric health.[13] Since drug and alcohol abuse are such big problems within the legal profession, provinces like Ontario have formed associations like the Ontario Lawyers Assistance Plan (OLAP), which seeks to confidentially assist lawyers with issues of substance abuse and mental disorders. The OLAP includes a 24-hour help line for lawyers, which is staffed by volunteer lawyers who understand the pressures of the profession. The OLAP also helps lawyers having trouble with work and family issues.[14] Figure 2.5 illustrates the many issues faced by lawyers seeking assistance in 2010.

Legal Aid and *Pro Bono* Work

Despite the negative image of lawyers that the Canadian public may have, there are many lawyers who do dedicated and sometimes reduced-fee work on behalf of their clients. In Canada, we have a program of **legal aid**. The legal aid system exists to allow those who could not financially afford a lawyer to nonetheless be represented. A substantive review of the legal aid system in Canada was done in 2001 by the Canadian Centre for Justice Statistics through Statistics Canada. The report explained that legal aid was only available for young offenders and adults who were charged with a serious federal offences. Less serious offences

12. Owen Kelly, "Lawyers and Depression: Three Case Studies" (Canadian Bar Association), online: <http://www.cba.org/cba/practicelink/bwl/depression.aspx>.
13. Canadian Bar Association, "Addiction and Psychiatric Impairment of Lawyers and Judges: A Search for Meaningful Data" (Legal Profession Assistance Conference).
14. Ontario Lawyers Assistance Plan, "Annual Report: 2010," online: <http://www.olap.ca/ANNUAL%20REPORT%202010_V2.pdf>

do not qualify for coverage unless there is a danger that the accused person will go to prison or lose his or her livelihood.[15]

Unless the accused individual has an extremely limited income, he or she will not covered. For example, today in Manitoba a family of two would be eligible if their income is less than $18 000 per year, and a family of four would be eligible if their income was less than $27 000 per year. Legal aid lawyers in Manitoba are paid a maximum of $80 per hour, and often matters are capped with the maximum that a lawyer can receive from legal aid, which is called a "block fee." Today in Ontario, legal aid has deemed that a lawyer making a guilty plea on behalf of a client will only receive $650, no matter how complicated the matter may be. Normally, many lawyers can earn $200–$300 or more per *hour* with a private **retainer.** However, many lawyers accepting legal aid work far beyond the time and money given to them through the government, and will end up working for free in order to do a good job for the accused.[16]

Recently in Ontario, prominent defence lawyer Clayton Ruby wrote a scathing review of legal aid in Ontario, saying that the Attorney General and the chair of Legal Aid Ontario (LAO) should be "ashamed." He noted that although the money given to police and Crown attorneys increases every day, defence lawyers cannot do their work because of underfunding by LAO. He noted that legal aid will only be granted to someone earning less than $12 500 a year, even though the poverty line is $19 000 per year, meaning that "most poor people never get near legal aid."[17]

Ruby noted that lawyers in Ontario are receiving one-sixth to one-third of what other lawyers are paid, and that they "donate dozens or hundreds of free hours to do a case with integrity."[18] He alleges that having a block fee system where lawyers are given a flat rate for certain tasks will result in "dump truck" lawyers who plead guilty for all clients regardless of the need for an investigation into whether the client really is properly pleading guilty. Many times the only way that the system functions is through lawyers donating their time. Ruby quotes José Saramago who said that "charity is what is left when there is neither kindness nor justice."[19]

Lawyers may also help those who cannot afford legal representation through a practice called ***pro bono*** work. Most of the FLSC's Rules of Conduct mandate that lawyers should work for those unable to access justice because of financial reasons. The MCPC Commentary to s 3.01(1) states that

> it is in keeping with the best traditions of the legal profession to provide services *pro bono* and to reduce or waive a fee when there is hardship or poverty or the client or prospective client would otherwise be deprived of adequate legal advice or representation. The Law Society encourages lawyers to provide public interest legal services and to support organizations that provide services to persons of limited means.*

The rationale is that since lawyers have the monopoly on the business of law, they also have a responsibility to provide public service. Lawyers give generously of their time and expertise to those in need, but this is something that is not readily acknowledged by the general public. Perhaps it should be the sacrifices of lawyers, who often work for free giving up significant income, that should be recognized, rather than the unflattering image that is often portrayed. It is also important to note that lawyers still have the duty of competency and must adhere to the rules of conduct for lawyers regardless of the funding source.

Legal aid for civil law matters is only available from "community legal clinics," which are non-profit legal centres run by independent boards of directors from the community. Clinics give access to lawyers, paralegals, and other staff to provide information, legal advice, and representation on civil law matters. These clinics may receive funding from

---

* Federation of Law Societies of Canada, *Model Code of Professional Conduct* (2011), p. 76.

15. Canadian Centre for Justice Statistics through Statistics Canada, "Legal Aid in Canada: Description of Operations," <http://publications.gc.ca/Collection-R/Statcan/85-217-XIB/0000185-217-XIB.pdf>.

16. Legal Aid in Canada, Statistics Canada, online <http://dsp-psd.tpsgc.gc.ca/Collection-R/Statcan/85-217-XIB/0000185-217-XIB.pdf>.

17. Clayton Ruby, "The Shame of Legal Aid Ontario," *The Lawyers Weekly* (February 2011), online: <http://www.lawyersweekly.ca/index.php?section=article&articleid=1355>.

18. Clayton Ruby, "The Shame of Legal Aid Ontario," *The Lawyers Weekly*, online <http://www.lawyersweekly.ca/index.php?section=article&articleid=1355>.

19. *Ibid.*

legal aid, and in Ontario these clinics receive most of their funding from LAO, which supports over 70 legal clinics across the province, including 17 specialty clinics. The areas of assistance may include workplace safety issues, employment insurance matters, disability payments, Canada Pension Plan issues, wills and estates, and appeals of the Landlord and Tenant Board.[20] Legal aid is very limited to these clinics and matters, and although fees are not usually charged, clients may be asked to cover court filing fees and medical expenses if they have the means to do so. Other provinces have similar walk-in clinics, many law schools have free clinics, and individuals can represent themselves in many matters. However, many areas of civil law are not covered. Legal aid is practically inaccessible for most Canadians and only available for criminal law matters where the accused person's freedom is at stake. For example, in Saskatchewan, legal aid does not cover the following:

- actions on municipal bylaws
- *Business Corporation Act*
- change of name
- Employment Insurance appeals
- foreclosure
- immigration matters
- income tax returns
- matrimonial property issues
- refugee matters
- selling property
- small claims actions
- welfare appeals
- wills and estates
- Workers Compensation applications
- wrongful dismissal disputes[21]

RULES OF PROFESSIONAL CONDUCT

Each province has its own rules and regulations for lawyers practising in their jurisdiction. However, there are also general rules that have been established by the CBA. The CBA, which acts as an advocate for the legal profession, represents approximately 37000 lawyers, judges, law educators, and law students across Canada, and more than 60 percent of all practising lawyers in Canada belong to the CBA.[22] The CBA is an advocate to improve the law, the administration of justice, access to justice, and the skill and the ethical standards of the profession. It also deals with issues that cross provincial boundaries.

The CBA adopted its first Code of Professional Conduct (CBA Code) in 1920. Before this time, lawyer conduct was compliant with standards that were understood in the profession: "informed by the ethics and etiquette of a gentleman."[23] However, there came a time when this knowledge had to be formalized. Some of the provinces and territories adopted the CBA Code (P.E.I., for example) with particular modifications for the needs of the jurisdiction. Others simply refer to the CBA Code when they are amending their rules of professional conduct. The CBA Code serves the purpose of being a common code of conduct for all Canadian lawyers. The last edition was modified in 2009, and it is now in a fully searchable form available on the Internet. However, the CBA Code is advisory only, and each province has the ability make specific rules for its members. The courts are also not bound by the rules of conduct, but the courts often take notice of these codes as representing the standard in a particular issue. However, as discussed, it seems that the MCPC from the FLSC is going to be the model for all provinces in the future.

20. Legal Aid Ontario, online: <http://www.legalaid.on.ca/en/getting/type_civil-clinics.asp>.

21. Legal Aid Saskatchewan, online <http://69.27.116.234/legal_help/nature_of_problem/other.php>. Reproduced by permission of Legal Aid Saskatchewan.

22. Canadian Bar Association, online: <http://www.cba.org/CBA/about/main/>.

23. Alice Woolley et al, *Lawyers' Ethics and Professional Regulation* (Markham, ON: LexisNexis, 2008) at 63.

The Canadian Bar Association
http://www.cba.org/

Regardless of the source of a professional code, there have been critics of any written code of conduct for lawyers. Some argue that ethical considerations have to be taken on a case-by-case basis, and behaviour cannot be governed by a set of detailed and specific rules. Critics say that rules take away from rational and focused discussion on the particular details of a unique situation. Others say there is a key problem with self-regulation and that allowing lawyers to govern themselves is eliminating the need for public input, and that lawyers cannot be trusted to put the client's interest above their own. Others question whether lawyers routinely refer to these codes of conduct, or whether they serve just a symbolic function.

For each of the provinces and territories, in the CBA Code, and in the MCPC, there is additional commentary that helps to resolve additional issues that may confront lawyers in practice. There are several common elements of the rules of professional conduct of the CBA, the provinces, and the MCPC. The most important sections of these will be discussed below with reference to the rules of various provinces and the MCPC.[24]

Relationship to the Administration of Justice

Lawyers have a duty to the administration of justice in general, and the MCPC provides at s 1.01 that the lawyer's "conduct should reflect favourably on the legal profession, inspire the confidence, respect and trust of clients and of the community, and avoid even the appearance of impropriety."* To this end, many of the provinces' codes, and the MCPC s 1.01, provide that a "lawyer has a duty to carry on the practice of law and discharge all responsibilities to clients, tribunals, the public and other members of the profession honourably and with integrity."† If a lawyer does not maintain the standard of integrity, there are disciplinary actions that can be taken. This includes lawyers' conduct in their public and/or *private* life that would reflect on our system of justice.

Ontario is specific in its rules about what standards a lawyer must adhere to. It says in rule 1 that:†

> (a) a lawyer has a duty to carry on the practice of law and discharge all responsibilities to clients, tribunals, the public, and other legal practitioners honourably and with integrity,
> (b) a lawyer has special responsibilities by virtue of the privileges afforded the legal profession and the important role it plays in a free and democratic society and in the administration of justice, including a special responsibility to recognize the diversity of the Ontario community, to protect the dignity of individuals, and to respect human rights laws in force in Ontario,
> (c) a lawyer has a duty to uphold the standards and reputation of the legal profession and to assist in the advancement of its goals, organizations, and institutions,
> (d) the rules are intended to express to the profession and to the public the high ethical ideals of the legal profession,
> (e) the rules are intended to specify the bases on which lawyers may be disciplined, and
> (f) rules of professional conduct cannot address every situation, and a lawyer should observe the rules in the spirit as well as in the letter.

---

* Federation of Law Societies of Canada, *Model Code of Professional Conduct* (2011), p. 14.

† Rule 1.03 Interpretation, Standards of the Legal Profession, of the *Rules of Professional Conduct [Amended - June 2009]*, in effect since November 1, 2000 and with respect of the commentary included with rule 1.03 [New -- June 2001], located on the Law Society's website at http://www.lsuc.on.ca/WorkArea/DownloadAsset.aspx?id=10284. © Copyright 2000-2009, The Law Society of Upper Canada. All Rights Reserved. Reprinted with permission of The Law Society of Upper Canada.

24. **FLSC MCPC, online:** <http://www.flsc.ca/_documents/ModelCode-June2012.pdf>; **CBA, online:** <http://www.cba.org/CBA/activities/pdf/codeofconduct.pdf>; **Alberta, Law Society of Alberta Code of Professional Conduct, online:** <http://www.lawsociety.ab.ca/lawyers/regulations/code.aspx>; **British Columbia, Professional Conduct Handbook Law Society of British Columbia, online:** <http://www.lawsociety.bc.ca/page.cfm?cid=383&t=Professional-Conduct-Manual>; **Manitoba, Code of Professional Conduct Law Society of Manitoba, online:** <http://www.lawsociety.mb.ca/lawyer-regulation/code-of-professional-conduct/english-version>; **New Brunswick, Code of Professional Conduct Law Society of New Brunswick, online:** <http://www.lawsociety-barreau.nb.ca/assets/documents/CODEOFPROFESSIONALCONDUCT_February_2009.pdf>; **Newfoundland, Code of Professional Conduct, online** <http://www.lawsociety.nf.ca/code/code.asp>; **the Northwest Territories uses the CBA's code of professional conduct but also has Legal Profession Act, online:** <http://www.justice.gov.nt.ca/Legislation/..%5CPDF%5CACTS%5CLegal%20Profession.pdf>; **Nova Scotia, Legal Ethics Handbook Nova Scotia Barristers' Society, online:** <http://www.nsbs.org/legalethics/toc.htm>; **Nunavut, Rules of the Law Society of Nunavut, online:** <http://lawsociety.nu.ca/act_and_rules/2009%2005%2002%20_%20Con_Rules.pdf>; **Ontario, Law Society of Upper Canada, online:** <http://www.lsuc.on.ca/WorkArea/DownloadAsset.aspx?id=10272>; **P.E.I., Law Society of P.E.I., Code of Professional Conduct, online** <http://www.lspei.pe.ca/ethics_and_code.php>; **Quebec, *Barreau du Québec*, online:** <http://www.barreau.qc.ca/?Langue=en>; **Saskatchewan, Law Society of Saskatchewan, Code of Professional Conduct, online:** <http://www.lawsociety.sk.ca/newlook/Publications/Code2003/CodeCompleteNov03.pdf>; **Yukon, Law Society of Yukon, Code of Professional Conduct, online:** <http://www.lawsocietyyukon.com/pdf/codeofconduct10.pdf>.

Thus, a lawyer must give candid advice to clients without overstating the merits of the case. Lawyers must disclose all the costs of a particular action to their clients. In this profession integrity is important, so that when lawyers give promises, they must live up to their word.

Of particular importance is subsection (f) that the "spirit" of the rules should be observed, as well as the "letter." This means that even though a technicality could be found to exist that would allow a lawyer to circumvent a rule, the lawyer should observe the broader meaning of what was to be prevented by the rule. Even if the specific violation is not listed, one should read the rules beyond the literal language.

Relationship to Other Lawyers and the Court

The rules in most provinces are also specific about the duties owed by the lawyer to others within the system. In Manitoba, rule 4.01(5) provides that "a lawyer must be courteous, civil, and act in good faith to the tribunal and all persons with whom the lawyer has dealings in the course of litigation." This means that lawyers must be honest and open, and must address other lawyers and judges with respect at all times. In court, other lawyers are referred to with the terms "my friend," or "Ms. Smith" and judges as "Your Honour."

This rule also provides that rights cannot be protected if the courtroom procedures are not respected. This is true for administrative tribunals, arbitrators, mediators, and others who resolve disputes, regardless of formality. In civil matters, a lawyer must also avoid frivolous tactics, and the Alberta code is very succinct in Chapter 1, rule 6, which states that if "a client's position or claim is clearly without merit, the lawyer must decline to act." Such actions are a waste of court resources, and may simply be used to hope that the other party runs out of money before fully launching a defence. A lawyer must not bring actions solely to delay or harass the other party, as such behaviour would bring the administration of justice into disrepute.

Lawyers' Responsibility to Clients

Competence

The Rules of Professional Conduct across Canada refer to the competent service that is due to the client. Generally, lawyers must maintain an acceptable degree of professional knowledge in their area of specialization. Secondly, they must adequately prepare and communicate effectively with their clients. It is always a duty of lawyers to admit if they are not competent in the representation of their clients in a particular matter, and to offer the best service to clients and promote confidence in the justice system. It has been established in the case law that Canadians have a constitutional right to competent counsel.[25] Courts that are evaluating whether a client had competent legal representation will look at whether the conduct fell within the range of a competent lawyer. This standard does not mean that a lawyer has to be perfect in all circumstances.

In Ontario, rule 2.01 provides that competent lawyers must have "skills, attributes, and values" needed to represent a client in the substance and procedure of the law, including investigation, implementation of these skills through legal research, analysis, application, writing and drafting, negotiation, alternative dispute resolution, advocacy, problem-solving, and communication. All of these duties must be completed in a diligent, timely, and cost-effective manner with a sufficient intellectual capacity, complying with the rules and spirit of the Rules of Professional Conduct, while recognizing one's limitations, managing the practice of the law through professional development, and adapting to changing standards. If there is a complaint that a lawyer has not fulfilled these duties, the law society can conduct a review of the lawyer's practice.

The rules also provide specific guidelines for competency in the court. For example, rule 4.01(1) of the Ontario rules provide that "when acting as an advocate, a lawyer shall represent the client resolutely and honourably within the limits of the law while treating the tribunal with candour, fairness, courtesy, and respect." Some disagree with the commentary to this section, which states that the "lawyer has a duty to the client to raise fearlessly every issue, advance every argument, and ask every question, however distasteful, which the

25. Michel Proulx and David Layton, *Ethics and Canadian Criminal Law* (Toronto: Irwin Law, 2001) at 143.

lawyer thinks will help the client's case and to endeavour to obtain for the client the benefit of every remedy and defence authorized by law." Some advocates say that this duty is too broad and that a lawyer cannot be made to advance arguments that are not morally reasonable, but others argue that this is a duty of every competent lawyer.

Confidentiality

Confidentiality between solicitor and client is one of the oldest types of privileges, with roots in the sixteenth century, and the promise of a lawyer "as a gentleman to keep his client's secret."[26] The courts have consistently found that the privilege with solicitors and their clients is of the highest confidentialities, even more than the medical/psychiatric confidentialities and religious or marital privileges. Confidentiality has been described as the key to the professional relationship between a lawyer and client. Section 2.03(1) of the MCPC provides that:

> A lawyer at all times must hold in strict confidence all information concerning the business and affairs of a client acquired in the course of the professional relationship and must not divulge any such information unless:
> (a) expressly or impliedly authorized by the client;
> (b) required by law or a court to do so;
> (c) required to deliver the information to the Law Society, or
> (d) otherwise permitted by this rule.*

A similar section is found in section 2.03(1) in Ontario, and many other provinces have an almost identical provisions. The rationality behind this confidentiality is that clients should be able to have full and unreserved communication with their lawyer. Lawyers may not be able to advise their clients and prepare their cases if they do not have a full appreciation of the facts of the case and the needs of the clients, while insuring that their legal rights are preserved. Clients may be asked to talk about some extremely personal information, which might expose them to serious liability, and it is only with confidence that the material will not be exposed that a person can talk honestly about such issues.

This duty is provided to every client, and continues even after the lawyer has ceased acting for that particular client. The duty is broad and can include all conversations, identity of the client, and day-to-day information. A lawyer may not disclose this information to anyone, and this duty is given to all clients even if there is only a brief relationship between the parties (e.g., one consultation where the lawyer is not retained.)

This confidentiality also extends to what lawyers call "shop talk." A lawyer should never engage in gossip, even with friends or family, which could disclose confidential information. This duty becomes complex when lawyers talk to other lawyers within or outside of their law **firm**. Strictly interpreted, lawyers should not talk about their clients to anyone outside of their firm, and should not reveal the identity of their clients to anyone else. However, lawyers often talk about legal strategy with other lawyers in order to provide the best possible representation to their clients. Lawyers need to confirm that other lawyers will understand the need for confidentiality on any discussions of strategy.

The law society can deter and punish those lawyers who breach confidentiality. A breach of confidence can lead to disciplinary hearings for the lawyer, a civil law suit where the lawyer is formally sued for disclosing information, and/or a formal complaint to the law society that the client had ineffective counsel. With modern-day realities of the practice of law, lawyers must be careful not to talk on cell phones in a public location while discussing client information, must not have documents or boxes that have the client's name in a public setting, and should safeguard computers and other electronic devices in public. Lawyers must tell their clients of this duty and what exceptions exist to this rule.

If information is inadvertently disclosed by one of the counsel on a case, the other lawyer may have a duty not to use that information if it was an honest mistake. Several provinces specifically address this situation. For example in British Columbia, the rules provide in s 15 that:

---

* Federation of Law Societies of Canada, *Model Code of Professional Conduct* (2011), p. 30.

26. Shane G Parker, "Solicitor/Client Privilege" in Joel E Pink and David C Perrier, *From Crime to Punishment,* 6th ed (Toronto: Thomson Carswell, 2007) at 499.

> A lawyer who has access to or comes into possession of a document which the lawyer has reasonable grounds to believe belongs to or is intended for an opposing party and was not intended for the lawyer to see, shall:
> (a) return the document, unread and uncopied, to the party to whom it belongs, or
> (b) if the lawyer reads part or all of the document before realizing that it was not intended for him or her, cease reading the document and promptly return it, uncopied, to the party to whom it belongs, advising that party:
> (i) of the extent to which the lawyer is aware of the contents, and
> (ii) what use the lawyer intends to make of the contents of the document.

In Ontario, rule 6.03 specifically addresses mistakes and says that a "lawyer shall avoid **sharp practice** and shall not take advantage of or act without fair warning upon slips, irregularities, or mistakes on the part of other legal practitioners not going to the merits or involving the sacrifice of a client's rights." A lawyer is under a duty not to use mistakes to their advantage because this trickery could result in a bad precedent that would be followed in the future. Thus, this is another limit on the duty of loyalty to a client, but the rules are particular on the allowable actions of one lawyer in relation to another.

This duty can be particularly onerous on the criminal lawyer. There seems to be no duty of a lawyer to reveal the location of a fugitive client, but the lawyer must not aid the client's effort to escape capture. A lawyer also cannot use the confidential information from a client for his or her own interest. The civil law case of *Szarfer v Chodos* (see the following case box) is an interesting example of this principle.

SZARFER v CHODOS, [1986] OJ NO 256 (ONT HCJ)

Mr. Chodos was Mr. Szarfer's lawyer acting in a personal injury case. In getting information about injuries that Mr. Szarfer suffered in an accident, Mr. Chodos learned that there were difficulties in Mr. Szarfer's marriage. In particular, Mr. Szarfer was suffering from erectile dysfunction. The lawyer also knew Mrs. Szarfer because she had previously worked for him as a legal secretary. On the basis of the information that there was sexual dysfunction in the marriage, Mr. Chodos started a sexual affair with Mrs. Szarfer.

The court found that this was confidential information that Mr. Chodos had learned in his role as lawyer. Confidential information must not be used by the lawyer for his own benefit. The onus is on the lawyer to prove that he did not use confidential information for his own benefit, but Mr. Chodos could not do this. Trust between the lawyer and client was destroyed, and Mr. Chodos used the vulnerability of Mrs. Szarfer and her husband to his benefit. The court found that this was a breach of the confidentiality between lawyer and client, and the lawyer was ordered to pay almost $44 000 to Mr. Szarfer. This decision was affirmed on appeal to the Ontario Court of Appeal.

Do you believe that this judgment was justified given that it was two consenting adults who entered into a consensual relationship?

EXCEPTIONS TO CONFIDENTIALITY There are some exceptions to this duty of confidentiality. Lawyers may be forced to reveal elements of what their client has told them when they are required to do so by law or by a court order. In most jurisdictions, the lawyer must only reveal what is absolutely required and nothing more. However, legislation in some provinces provide that a lawyer must report sexual and physical abuse in particular circumstances, and a lawyer might be required to disclose if a crime is about to be committed. In addition, clients may give express permission to their counsel to divulge this information to others. One of the most important exceptions is where a lawyer believes that a "future harm" may occur. The issue of future harm is outlined in the following case box, which looks at *Smith v Jones.*

SMITH v JONES, [1999] SCJ NO 15 (SCC)

In this case, where the names were changed to protect the identity of the parties, the court stressed that confidentiality is important to the administration of justice, but is subject to some exceptions. Mr. Jones was charged with an aggravated sexual assault on a prostitute. Mr. Jones went to a psychiatrist, Dr. Smith, for an assessment for his case. Mr. Jones described in vivid detail his plan for a future crime. He was going to choose a small-statured prostitute who could be overpowered, he was going to sexually assault and kidnap her, and dispose of her body in a wooded area in British Columbia. He told the psychiatrist that the first victim would be a trial-run, and then he would seek out other victims.

Dr. Smith called Mr. Jones's lawyer and informed him that Mr. Jones was a dangerous person who would commit further offences if he did not receive treatment. Mr. Jones pleaded guilty to the aggravated sexual assault he was charged with, but the lawyer decided not to tell the judge about the concerns of Dr. Smith. Dr. Smith made an application to the court to disclose this information even though the doctor and the lawyer had a duty of confidentiality.

The Supreme Court ruled that although confidentiality is important, the risk to the public is also important. Confidentiality is not absolute in doctor patient or lawyer client relationships. Three factors were found to be important in determining if the confidentiality could be breached:

1. Was there a clear risk to an identifiable person or group of persons?
2. Was there a risk of serious bodily harm or death?
3. Is the danger imminent?

The court found that all of these elements were met in the case at hand, and Dr. Smith was allowed to disclose what he was told by Mr. Jones. However, the court said that this disclosure should be as limited as possible to disclose only what was necessary to disclose that there was a risk of serious harm to an identifiable group of prostitutes located in the Downtown Eastside of Vancouver. Only these parts of the report were made available to police. It was believed that this same approach should be followed with lawyers.

Do you think that lawyers and doctors should be able to breach confidentiality?

What about the requirement that they should just reveal as little information as possible? Is that a fair rule?

After *Smith v Jones,* the rules of professional conduct now speak to this kind of exception to confidentiality. For example, in Ontario the Law Society of Upper Canada in s 2.03(3) provides that:

> (3) Where a lawyer believes upon reasonable grounds that there is an imminent risk to an identifiable person or group of death or serious bodily harm, including serious psychological harm that substantially interferes with health or well-being, the lawyer may disclose, pursuant to judicial order where practicable, confidential information where it is necessary to do so in order to prevent the death or harm, but shall not disclose more information than is required.*

The Rules of Professional Conduct for Alberta also provides in Chapter 7, s 8(b), as in most provinces, that "a lawyer must disclose confidential information when required to do so by law." Thus, if a court orders a lawyer to disclose information, he or she must do so.

The communication may also be disclosed if the statement itself is a crime (uttering a threat, for example), but it may also be disclosed when it was made to facilitate a crime. For example, if a client asks his or her lawyer where the best place to bury a dead body would be, this is advice to facilitate a crime, so that communication may not be confidential. However, even if the facts are part of public knowledge, most provinces provide that a lawyer must still protect the client.

* Subrule 2.03(3) Justified or Permitted Disclosure, of the *Rules of Professional Conduct,* in effect since November 1, 2000 and with respect to the commentary following subrule 2.03(3) only, [*Amended - March 2004*], located on the Law Society's website at <http://www.lsuc.on.ca/media/rpc_2.pdf.>

DEBUNKING THE MYTH

Many confuse the confidentiality rules with what is called **solicitor–client privilege,** which is an evidence rule. Solicitor–client privilege simply means that material that is prepared between the lawyer and client may be inadmissible in court.

Conversely, the court has also found that a lawyer is able to defend him- or herself from an allegation of lawyer misconduct. Material is no longer confidential when the client raises the issue of wrongdoing. This rule only makes sense because otherwise, a client could say that the lawyer was incompetent, and the court would have to take the client's word if the lawyer was not able to point to evidence to disprove that allegation.

Does a Lawyer Have to Represent Every Client?

There are many issues for lawyers when accepting clients. Lawyers must be careful that taking a particular client will not breach a code of conduct, or that the lawyer would be placed in a position where loyalty to a client would be compromised. The lawyer client relationship is one of the highest trust positions in law, and the lawyer's loyalty to the client must not be questioned. This duty comes out of what is referred to as a **fiduciary relationship**. It is clear that lawyers have some discretion in choosing clients, but how far that discretion goes is sometimes unclear.

There are some clear areas where a lawyer may refuse to be retained by a client:

1. *Conflict of interest.* If there is a reason that the lawyer should not take on a particular client, the lawyer must not do so. For example, in the *Newfoundland Rules of Professional Conduct*, Chapter V states:

   1. A conflicting interest is one that would be likely to affect adversely the lawyer's judgement or advice on behalf of, or loyalty to a client or prospective client.
   2. The reason for the Rule is self-evident. The client or the client's affairs may be seriously prejudiced unless the lawyer's judgement and freedom of action on the client's behalf are as free as possible from compromising influences.
   3. Conflicting interests include, but are not limited to the duties and loyalties of the lawyer or a partner or professional associate of the lawyer to any other client, whether involved in the particular transaction or not, including the obligation to communicate information.

The commentary of the rules for many provinces also provides that this conflict may be over financial interests. *Ontario Rules of Professional Conduct*, s 2.04(1) commentary notes that "where a lawyer is acting for a friend or family member, the lawyer may have a conflict of interest because the personal relationship may interfere with the lawyer's duty to provide objective, disinterested professional advice to the client." Thus, lawyers might have a relationship issue that would prevent them from taking on a particular client.

2. *Potential to be a witness.* If there is a possibility that a lawyer might be a witness in a case where he or she is representing a client, most jurisdictions prevent that lawyer from being counsel in that case.
3. *Client already has a lawyer.* It often arises that a client wants to switch lawyers, but until that retainer has been terminated, another lawyer cannot take on that case.
4. *Illegality.* If the client asks the lawyer to do something illegal, the lawyer is prohibited from taking on that case. If the lawyer has already been retained and then gets a request to breach the rules of conduct, the lawyer cannot carry out those instructions. Making these types of requests might result in the complete breakdown in the relationship between the parties, and the only option may be to withdraw from representing that client.

When a lawyer does reject a client, there is a duty to provide reasonable assistance, without charge, to find another lawyer who would be a competent advocate in the particular case. The MCPC also reminds lawyers, in s 2.04(3), that "a lawyer must not represent opposing parties in a dispute,"* and the commentary clarifies that

* Federation of Law Societies of Canada, *Model Code of Professional Conduct* (2011), p. 40.

> a lawyer representing a client who is a party in a dispute with another party or parties must competently and diligently develop and argue the position of the client. In a dispute, the parties' immediate legal interests are clearly adverse. If the lawyer were permitted to act for opposing parties in such circumstances even with consent, the lawyer's advice, judgment and loyalty to one client would be materially and adversely affected by the same duties to the other client or clients. In short, the lawyer would find it impossible to act without offending these rules.*

However, there are provisions that allow for this type of representation if the parties have **independent legal advice**, but they must end the relationship if there is a conflicting interest. Thus, both parties will have to be fully informed of the potential conflicts in this relationship, and the parties may be asked to get the opinion of a third-party lawyer. Then, even after all of this preparation, there may still be a conflict. Many lawyers will simply decline to act concurrently for both parties in any circumstance to avoid this complication.

Making Services Available

Although there are many situations where a lawyer is prohibited from taking on a particular client, there is also a duty to make legal services available to the public. The MCPC provides at s 3.01(1) that "a lawyer must make legal services available to the public efficiently and conveniently and, subject to rule 3.01(2), may offer legal services to a prospective client by any means."† Although these responsibilities are quite vague, this has been interpreted to mean that lawyers must seek to ensure that access to the law is made available to as many people as possible, especially the poor and disadvantaged. Others say that lawyers have a positive duty to reform and improve the legal system, including a duty to the public.

Most of the codes of professional conduct also forbid discrimination on the basis of those grounds prohibited in human rights legislation. Thus, a lawyer cannot typically refuse a client based on race, language, national or ethnic origin, colour, religion, age, sex, sexual orientation, marital status, family status, or disability. A lawyer also cannot justify inferior services on these grounds.[27]

Advertising

Many advocates say that advertising is an important part of making services available to clients, and informing them of their services. However, advertising was not permitted in the legal profession until the 1980s, when the rules were relaxed for "tasteful" advertising. Critics say that advertising lowers the public image of lawyers, but others say that advertising is critical to provide access to justice for all. The MCPC s 3.03(1) provides that "an advertisement may also include a description of the lawyer's or law firm's proficiency or experience in an area of law. In all cases, the representations made must be accurate (that is, demonstrably true) and must not be misleading."‡

Most provinces provide what specifically is allowed to be advertised by a lawyer. For example, the Code of Professional Conduct Law § Society of New Brunswick Chapter 16, which deals with advertising and marketing, provides that:

> 3. In engaging in any advertising the lawyer shall not mislead or arouse unattainable hopes or expectations of others; shall not affect adversely the quality of legal services offered by, *e.g.*, a reduction of legal fees from those usually charged in the geographic area; and **shall not advertise in an undignified manner, in bad taste or be otherwise offensive as to be prejudicial to the interests of the public, the legal profession or the administration of justice or the institutions associated** therewith.
> 4. The lawyer contravenes the rule in this chapter if in advertising or in marketing the professional legal services offered the lawyer
>   (*a*) states or causes or permits to have stated anything any part of which is inaccurate, is misleading or is likely to mislead, is derogatory, is not in good taste or that constitutes self-aggrandizement, or

* Federation of Law Societies of Canada, *Model Code of Professional Conduct* (2011), p. 40.

† Federation of Law Societies of Canada, *Model Code of Professional Conduct* (2011), p. 76.

‡ Federation of Law Societies of Canada, *Model Code of Professional Conduct* (2011), p. 79.

§ Law Society of New Brunswick *Code of Professional Conduct* (2009) pp. 73-74. Online at <http://www.lawsociety-barreau.nb.ca/assets/documents/CODEOFPROFESSIONALCONDUCT_February_2009.pdf>. Reproduced by permission of the Law Society of New Brunswick.

27. Michel Proulx and David Layton, *Ethics and Canadian Criminal Law* (Toronto: Irwin Law, 2001) at 84.

(*b*) misrepresents the competence or the experience of the lawyer or of a partner or of an associate of the lawyer, or
(*c*) implies that the lawyer is able to obtain results not achievable by other lawyers or that the lawyer is in a position of influence, or
(*d*) approaches a person known or thought likely to be the client of another with the objective of replacing that other as the lawyer of the person, or
(*e*) directs advertising or marketing efforts toward a specific person or a specific group of persons where the person or the group of persons has apparently suffered injury or loss of any kind within the recent past, or
(*f*) compares the quality of the professional legal services of the lawyer, the time within which results can be obtained or the cost of those services with that of other lawyers, or
(*g*) violates any of the regulations, rules or rulings of the Society with respect to the advertising or the marketing of professional legal services.

How does a lawyer adhere to these very specific rules on advertising? See the above Food for Thought box.

FOOD FOR THOUGHT...

In this difficult economy, lawyers need clients to be attracted to the services of their firm, but there are real limits to how they are able to do this. Read through and discuss the selections from print advertisements (or their derivatives) below.

1. Burchell, Smith, Jost, Willis, and Burchell: "We know Everything. We can do Anything. We stop at Nothing."[28]
2. Richardson's Law Office: "Accidents happen ... But don't let your choice of lawyers be one of them."[29]
3. Foster Townsend Graham: "Damn Fine Litigators."[30]
4. Harris Beach: "Lawyers You'll Swear By. Not at."[31]
5. Jackson Lewis: "All We Do Is Work."[32]
6. Corri Fetman & Associates: On a billboard in Chicago, this firm put a picture of the "six-pack abs of a headless male torso and tanned female cleavage heaving forth from a black lace bra" with the tagline, "Life's Short. Get a Divorce."[33]
7. Syracuse, NY, attorney James Alexander ran a TV spot for his firm showing lawyers offering counsel to space aliens who had crashed their UFO. He also did one with lawyers towering like giants over Syracuse.[34]
8. "I may be a bastard. But I'm your bastard."[35]

ETHICS IN THE CIVIL LAW

There are many ethical issues that may arise in the practice of the civil law. As Alice Woolley and her colleagues have noted, these issues may arise with a "business lawyer negotiating a deal on behalf of a corporate client ... as a labour lawyer negotiating the terms of a new collective bargaining agreement; as a native rights lawyer working with government representatives on a land claim settlement; as a public interest lawyer holding a press conference to raise support for a client's opposition to the creation of a local nuclear waste facility."[36] A civil law lawyer may have ethical issues arise before the litigation, beginning with the initial

28. Online: <http://www.novalawyer.com/>, as cited in Alice Woolley et al, *Lawyers' Ethics and Professional Regulation* (Markham, ON: LexisNexis, 2008) at 132.
29. *Ibid* at 132.
30. Online: < http://www.ftgalaw.com/>.
31. Harris Beach, online: <http://www.harrisbeach.com/about>.
32. Jackson Lewis, online: <http://www.jacksonlewis.com/home.php>.
33. Corri Fetman & Associates, online: <http://www.cfalawfirm.com/press.html>.
34. Alice Woolley et al, *Lawyers' Ethics and Professional Regulation* (Markham, ON: LexisNexis, 2008) at 132 133. See also Nathan Koppel, "Objection! Funny Legal Ads Draw Censure," *Wall Street Journal*, online: <http://online.wsj.com/article/SB120234229733949051.html>.
35. Derived from a previous ad no longer available.
36. Alice Woolley et al, *Lawyers' Ethics and Professional Regulation* (Markham, ON: LexisNexis, 2008) at 203.

consultation with the client, confidentiality, and the drafting of documentation. This is in addition to the host of ethical issues that may arise at trial.

Although there are numerous ways in which a civil law lawyer can be faced with ethical issues, one important way a lawyer may be challenged is within a corporate setting with in-house counsel. If a lawyer works within a company in the legal department, and he or she knows that the company is going to do something that would hurt the public, does that lawyer have an obligation to the public, or to the company he or she works for? If lawyers must be committed advocates for their clients, can they fulfill this role at the expense of the world at large? Do they owe a duty to the individuals who might be harmed by their company's actions or omissions? It is difficult in this situation to even identify who the "client" is. A lawyer may think that the senior executive who gives the lawyer instructions is the client, or the company as a whole is giving directions, and it might be the individuals in the company to which the lawyer feels bound.

The MCPC Code also provides for these situations. The commentary to s 2.02(8) states that:

> A lawyer acting for an organization who learns that the organization has acted, is acting, or intends to act in a wrongful manner, may advise the chief executive officer and must advise the chief legal officer of the misconduct. If the wrongful conduct is not abandoned or stopped, the lawyer must report the matter "up the ladder" of responsibility within the organization until the matter is dealt with appropriately. If the organization, despite the lawyer's advice, continues with the wrongful conduct, the lawyer must withdraw from acting in the particular matter in accordance with Rule 2.07. In some but not all cases, withdrawal means resigning from his or her position or relationship with the organization and not simply withdrawing from acting in the particular matter.*

Thus, the lawyer may need to withdraw from the matter completely in order to adhere to the rules. What if you know that lives are at stake? See the You Decide box.

YOU DECIDE

Ms. Casey is in-house counsel for a car company. The engineers in the company have alerted her that there is a flaw in the car, and if it is hit from the side the doors will likely cause the passengers very severe injuries. The company does a financial cost-benefit analysis and finds that it will be costly to recall the cars to replace the defective equipment. Ms. Casey is asked to prepare a legal opinion on the ability of injured passengers to sue the company, and the amount of damages that may result. Ms. Casey's opinion is that it will financially cost less for the company to leave the design flaw, even though many people will undoubtedly be hurt or killed.

Does Ms. Casey have an obligation to the public?

Does she have an obligation to the company?

What if only one person or very few people would likely be harmed?

Is this decision more difficult for a lawyer who is in-house counsel opposed to those who work within a firm structure?

In short, legal ethics deal with the concept that if there is a conflict between a lawyer's duties and a particular case, how does the lawyer decide what to do? There are many rules that a lawyer must uphold when acting as an advocate for a client in the courtroom. For example, rule 4.01 in the Ontario Rules of Professional Conduct says the lawyer must be on guard in the following situations. Lawyers must not:

> (a) abuse the process of the tribunal by instituting or prosecuting proceedings which, although legal in themselves, are clearly motivated by malice on the part of the client and are brought solely for the purpose of injuring the other party,
> (b) knowingly assist or permit the client to do anything that the lawyer considers to be dishonest or dishonourable,
> (d) endeavour or allow anyone else to endeavour, directly or indirectly, to influence the decision or action of a tribunal or any of its officials in any case or matter by any means other than open persuasion as an advocate;

* Federation of Law Societies of Canada, *Model Code of Professional Conduct* (2011), p. 28.

(e) knowingly attempt to deceive a tribunal or influence the course of justice by offering false evidence, misstating facts or law, presenting or relying upon a false or deceptive affidavit, suppressing what ought to be disclosed, or otherwise assisting in any fraud, crime, or illegal conduct,
(f) knowingly misstate the contents of a document, the testimony of a witness, the substance of an argument, or the provisions of a statute or like authority,
(g) knowingly assert as true a fact when its truth cannot reasonably be supported by the evidence or as a matter of which notice may be taken by the tribunal,
(h) deliberately refrain from informing the tribunal of any binding authority that the lawyer considers to be directly on point and that has not been mentioned by an opponent,
(i) dissuade a witness from giving evidence or advise a witness to be absent,
(j) knowingly permit a witness or party to be presented in a false or misleading way or to impersonate another,
(k) needlessly abuse, hector, or harass a witness,
(l) when representing a complainant or potential complainant, attempt to gain a benefit for the complainant by threatening the laying of a criminal charge or by offering to seek or to procure the withdrawal of a criminal charge, and
(m) needlessly inconvenience a witness.*

ETHICS IN THE CRIMINAL LAW

In addition to the Rules of Professional Conduct and the obligations of all lawyers, the criminal justice system presents unique challenges. There have been many ethical issues that arise within that system, and it is important to remember the duties particular to the criminal lawyer. The answer is often that there is no easy answer. When defending an accused, it is the defence lawyer's duty to protect the client from conviction, except where a judge and/or jury in a properly formed court, with jurisdiction, by legal and properly collected evidence, convicts the accused. The provinces state that a defence lawyer is able to use any defence, including what many in the public call "technicalities" or loopholes in the system.

Although the lawyer owes a duty to the client, there are also duties to the court, society, other lawyers, and to him- or herself. These duties are often in conflict with one another, and this is when the study of legal ethics becomes important. Legal ethics are regularly in conflict with what society would see as morality. For example, a lawyer might have to keep the details of an alleged crime confidential when many in society would say there was an automatic duty to report these crimes.

Ethical Issues for the Crown

From the Perspective of the Crown Attorney: Mark T Poland, Assistant Crown Attorney, Waterloo Region Crown Attorney's Office

Ethical issues present themselves to prosecutors all the time. In fact, exercising good judgment, and resolving these issues in a manner that is fair and in the public interest is a significant part of the work of a Crown attorney. Ethical issues arise primarily as a function of the role of the prosecutor, which requires a Crown attorney to act fairly and dispassionately, in a way calculated to render the most complete justice. This quasi-judicial role can conflict with a prosecutor's co-existing function to engage in the adversarial system of justice by acting as a strong advocate for a trial interest.

The hardest calls to make are those that surround two major issues—when to withdraw charges and what evidence to place before the court. The decision to potentially withdraw charges has to be revisited throughout the progress of a case. In general, a prosecutor is obligated to withdraw a case from consideration by the court at the point that he or she determines that the case lacks "a reasonable prospect of conviction." The precise limits of this test are often practically difficult to ascertain, but they require the prosecutor to make an unvarnished assessment of the strength of the case while keeping perspective on what

* Subrule 4.01(2) The Lawyer as Advocate. Advocacy, of the *Rules of Professional Conduct*, in effect since November 1, 2000, located on the Law Society's website at http://www.lsuc.on.ca/media/rpc_4.pdf.

types of evidence will and should properly be put before the court. The test for "reasonable prospect of conviction" is certainly higher than the test that the police must meet in order to lay charges, which is one of "reasonable grounds to believe" that an offence has been committed. Accordingly, there will be cases where the police were completely correct to lay charges because the evidence meets the "reasonable grounds to believe" test (i.e., a standard similar to "reasonably probable"), yet does not reach the level of presenting a "reasonable prospect of conviction" (i.e., a standard closer to "proof beyond a reasonable doubt").

More rarely, cases are also withdrawn because, notwithstanding the existence of a reasonable prospect of conviction, they are nonetheless considered to be "not in the public interest" to proceed upon. An example of this latter circumstance might occur in a case where an accused person is seriously ill and unable to meaningfully participate in his or her trial. These decisions to withdraw charges are hard to make in many cases. On a human level, they become even more difficult where the case involves serious harm or death by an accused person towards another. You can imagine the difficulty of explaining to someone who has lost a loved one in a homicide case, that the case will be withdrawn against the accused, who will "walk free" from the court without sanction. This is particularly difficult where the police have properly assessed that they have reasonable grounds to believe that this accused actually caused the death of the loved one, but the evidence in the case simply cannot properly support a conviction.

Sometimes Crown attorneys are also faced with hard decisions about what evidence to call. Recent judicial inquiries into wrongful convictions have outlined the dangers of relying upon less-than-perfect eyewitness identification evidence. Similarly, from time to time, information comes forward indicating that an accused person has confessed to a crime, but the information is presented by a person of unsavoury character like a so-called "jailhouse informants." This circumstance arises where an inmate claims to have come into possession of information about a crime as a result of conversations with the accused while incarcerated together. Other times, the Crown can find themselves in possession of information that may be helpful to a case, but which has the potential to endanger the safety of a person close to the accused who has acted as a "confidential informant." There are many judgment calls about evidence-related issues such as these, but they often result in the same outcome: a key potential piece of evidence is not placed before the court, with the inevitable result that the case become less viable, or even impossible to prove.

There are really two requirements in dealing with ethical issues as a Crown prosecutor: The first is to identify the problem as an ethical issue. The second is trying to figure out a plan to deal with it. Sometimes crafting a solution to an ethical dilemma requires convening a meeting of experienced prosecutors, and discussing the issue in detail. For some ethical issues, regularly constituted advisory panels exist. One example of this is the in-custody informant committee of the Ontario Ministry of the Attorney General. This is a mandatory screening mechanism designed to carefully assess all in-custody informant evidence before it is placed before a court. In the ordinary course, though, the resolution of most ethical issues requires the prosecutor to look no further than his or her own moral compass, and to remember the words of the Supreme Court of Canada in *R v Boucher* (1954), 110 CCC 263 (SCC):

> It cannot be overemphasized that the purpose of a criminal prosecution is not to obtain a conviction; it is to lay before a jury what the Crown considers to be credible evidence relevant to what is alleged to be a crime.... The role of prosecutor excludes any notion of winning or losing; his function is a matter of public duty than which in civil life there can be none charged with greater personal responsibility.

How Can You Defend That Guilty Person?

> *"A lawyer has no business with the justice or injustice of the cause which he undertakes, unless his client asks his opinion, and then he is bound to give it honestly. The justice or injustice of the cause is to be decided by the judge."*
>
> —*Samuel Johnson (1709–1784),* Tour to the Hebrides, *15 August 1773*

Every criminal defence lawyer has been asked, "how can you defend *that* person (or monster, or deviant, or killer, or psychopath)?" Many in the public see the role of the defence lawyer as using technicalities to allow guilty clients to go free. Michael Proulx and David Layton sum these feelings up perfectly saying that if "one can accept that the justice system is a necessary and good institution, and that the lawyer must undertake special duties to ensure that the system operates properly, then such duties, to the extent that they may superficially clash with common or non-legal morality, are arguably justified."[37] If we accept that the system works, then we have to have individuals who can put aside their personal thoughts and represent a client to the best of their abilities. As will be discussed in Chapter 10, charges must be proved against the defendant, and therefore it is often essential that the individual has legal representation. Even an accused who confesses guilt needs protection to navigate the very complex legal system.

However, there are certain limitations when a client confesses guilt to his or her lawyer, and it is one of the most trying issues in the ethics of advocacy. What the lawyer thinks, however, is irrelevant to the job to be done. The *personal* opinion of the criminal defence lawyer about the guilt or innocence of the client is irrelevant to the issue, and must *not* be expressed to the court. The Australian case of *Tuckiar v R* examines this duty (see the following case box).

TUCKIAR v R [1934], 52 CLR 335 (HC AUSTRALIA)

In this Australian High Court case, the accused confessed to his lawyer that he had committed the crime, but the client pleaded not guilty and went forward to trial. However, during a meeting with the judge, the lawyer recounted the confession of the accused in front of the judge and the prosecution. Going even further, the lawyer revealed the story in court following the jury's guilty verdict at the end of the trial. This case was appealed to the high court.

The appeal court was very judgmental about the actions of the lawyer. The court found that "whether he be in fact guilty or not, a prisoner is, in point of law, entitled to acquittal from any charge which the evidence fails to establish that he committed, and it is not incumbent on his counsel by abandoning his defence to deprive him of the benefit of such rational arguments as fairly arise on the proofs submitted." This has become one of the most cited statements of why a defendant deserves a full defence, and it is not the place of the lawyer to substitute his or her opinion for that of a judge and jury, including the right to appeal a decision. A criminal lawyer must keep these statements confidential even after the end of the trial.

Should a lawyer be able to express his or her personal opinions by the end of the trial (especially if the lawyer believes the client is guilty)?

Some of the assertions by clients may turn out to be true, however unreliable they may seem at the time. The same assertion is also true for the Crown; they must not express their personal opinion as to guilt. French lawyer Daniel Soulez-Larivière wrote in his text on ethics (translated) that:

> To each their role. To judges to judge, to lawyers to defend. A lawyer who wants to judge his own client is mistaken as to his profession, mixes up respective functions and weakens his own function to the detriment of the entire judicial system.[38]

In the Quebec Court of Appeal case of *R v Delisle* (1999), 133 CCC (3d) 541 (Que CA), the accused insisted that he was not the man who committed a serious assault. The lawyer discounted what his client said based on his theory of the case, and did not investigate a man named "Carl" that the accused said committed the crime. The accused was convicted, and

37. Michel Proulx and David Layton, Ethics and Canadian Criminal Law (Toronto: Irwin Law, 2001), at 86.

38. *Ibid* at 38.

Carl was not called to the witness stand. After the trial, Carl contacted the lawyer and said that he was, in fact, responsible for the assault. The Court of Appeal stated that the lawyer had set himself up as judge, and was found to be incompetent counsel.

Limitations if a Client Confesses

Those lawyers with a certain knowledge of the client's guilt are limited in what defence can be used, as counsel cannot mislead the court. This is the reason that some criminal lawyers will say that they do not necessarily want to know the full truth of what happened. For example, a lawyer who knows that the accused has confessed cannot call a false alibi to the stand to lie to the court. The commentary to s 4.01(1) of the MCPC provides that there are limited actions a lawyer can take. If the accused makes an unequivocal confession to a crime a lawyer may only

> take objection to the jurisdiction of the court, the form of the indictment or the admissibility or sufficiency of the evidence, but must not suggest that some other person committed the offence or call any evidence that, by reason of the admissions, the lawyer believes to be false. Nor may the lawyer set up an affirmative case inconsistent with such admissions, for example, by calling evidence in support of an alibi intended to show that the accused could not have done or, in fact, has not done the act. Such admissions will also impose a limit on the extent to which the lawyer may attack the evidence for the prosecution. The lawyer is entitled to test the evidence given by each individual witness for the prosecution and argue that the evidence taken as a whole is insufficient to amount to proof that the accused is guilty of the offence charged, but the lawyer should go no further than that.*

However, there is a significant grey area in what lawyers may do to defend their clients. Can a lawyer question a witness about the witness's character? Can a lawyer question the witness about witness's vision, and whether the witness clearly viewed the crime? Can a defence lawyer raise a defence even if he or she believes that the client is guilty?

It seems from case law that a defence lawyer does not have absolute rein to challenge a witness whom the lawyer knows to be truthful. According to s 4.01(2)(m) and (o) of the MCPC, the defence lawyer may not "needlessly abuse, hector or harass a witness"† or "needlessly inconvenience a witness."‡ It is proper to expose any holes in the witness's testimony that points to guilt (including the witness's character), but degrading a witness for spite is not permissible. A witness must always be treated with dignity, but the defence has the ability to test the evidence presented in court (see the following case box, which looks at *R v Li*).

R v LI, [1993] BCJ NO 2312 (BC CA) (LEAVE TO THE SCC REFUSED)

Mr. Li was charged with robbing a jewellery store, and he told his lawyer that he was, in fact, involved. Two store clerks identified the accused from a photograph, but neither clerk was sure about the identification and there were some discrepancies based on characteristics of the accused. The clerks had given inaccurate information about his fluency in English and his hairstyle.

At trial Mr. Li did not testify, but the defence lawyer called two witnesses to say what his hairstyle was at the time of the robbery, and his ability to speak English. This evidence was used in order to undermine the clerks' identification. Despite this evidence, the accused was convicted. Mr. Li appealed, saying that his lawyer was under a conflict of interest because he knew Mr. Li was involved. The Court of Appeal said that the lawyer was correct in not calling Mr. Li to testify, given that he knew that Mr. Li had committed the crime.

However, the court commented on the appropriateness of calling witnesses to counteract the evidence of the clerks. The court found that the lawyer was under a duty to test the proof of the case, and it was proper to call witnesses to give evidence about the physical appearance of Mr. Li and his English skills. These elements may have raised a reasonable

* Federation of Law Societies of Canada, *Model Code of Professional Conduct* (2011), p. 81.

† Federation of Law Societies of Canada, *Model Code of Professional Conduct* (2011), p. 83-84.

‡ Federation of Law Societies of Canada, *Model Code of Professional Conduct* (2011), p. 83-84.

doubt about the identification of the accused. The court found that the lawyer did not breach any ethical rule, as he did not put the accused on the stand to lie, and he did not advance any defence inconsistent with the facts as he knew them. A lawyer may point out witness vulnerabilities even if the lawyer knows that the witness's evidence is likely accurate.

Critics have said that this situation might come close to presenting a defence that the lawyer absolutely knows to be false (which a lawyer cannot do). Do you think that this evidence crossed the line?

Client Perjury

Another issue facing lawyers is the difficult situation where a client gives false testimony on the witness stand, or what is known as **perjury**. Every accused has the constitutional right to testify on his or her own behalf, but the MCPC s 4.01(2) provides that a lawyer must not "knowingly attempt to deceive a tribunal or influence the course of justice by offering false evidence, misstating facts or law, presenting or relying upon a false or deceptive affidavit, suppressing what ought to be disclosed or otherwise assisting in any fraud, crime or illegal conduct."* Ethics codes in both British Columbia (Chapter 8) and Alberta (Chapter 10, rule 14) have extensive rules on the topic.

It seems that if a lawyer knows that a client is planning to perjure him- or herself, the lawyer must counsel the client with the consequences of these actions. Perjury is a crime and the accused could jeopardize the current case and the sentence he or she may receive. The lawyer cannot be faulted for putting this fact to his or her client in certain terms, such as in *Nix v Whiteside* (see the following case box).

NIX v WHITESIDE, 475 US 157 [1986] (UNITED STATES SUPREME COURT)

Mr. Whiteside was charged with stabbing a drug dealer to death. He told his lawyer that he killed the drug dealer because he thought the dealer was going to shoot him with a gun. Mr. Whiteside had not seen the gun, but he had based this fear on the drug dealer's reputation, and his movements immediately before the stabbing.

However, Mr. Whiteside decided to change his story at trial. He told his lawyer that his self-defence claim would not be successful unless he testified that he saw something "metallic" in the victim's hand. Mr. Whiteside believed that unless he testified that he saw something in drug dealer's hand, he would not be acquitted through self-defence. The lawyer tried to convince his client that he could not present false evidence, and that it was not believable that he saw something metallic when no gun was found on the deceased. The lawyer said that he would withdraw from the case if Mr. Whiteside insisted on lying, he would tell the court that this testimony was a lie, and he would discredit his client on the stand.

Mr. Whiteside agreed not to lie on the witness stand, and the jury convicted him. Mr. Whiteside appealed saying that the lawyer giving him this severe warning had denied him the right of effective counsel. The Court of Appeal said that the lawyer had done the right thing by threatening to withdraw and telling the court of the perjury (although this was not done). The court found that Mr. Whiteside should not be able to appeal to punish a lawyer who had convinced him not to lie.

Many have criticized this decision that a lawyer should not say that he or she would tell the court that the client was committing perjury. Do you agree?

In Canada, courts have found that, if a client tells you that he or she are going to commit perjury, the lawyer may withdraw from the case, refuse to call the client to the

* Federation of Law Societies of Canada, *Model Code of Professional Conduct* (2011), p. 83-84.

stand, disclose the perjury to the court or another third party, refuse to use this testimony in a summary of the case, or question the accused in a passive way in order not to elicit this incorrect statement. However, these options must be balanced between the client's right to testify, withdrawing in a way that will not put the client into a prejudicial situation, and ideally the court should not know that the lawyer is withdrawing for perjury. Not informing the court of these issues can be an extremely difficult thing to do.

If the perjury has happened suddenly on the stand, there are several options open to the lawyer, but the situation must be handled delicately. If possible, the lawyer should ask for a recess to speak with the client, without alerting the Crown, judge, or jury that something is wrong. This may only be accomplished in the next break in the proceedings. A lawyer may also switch to questioning on an uncontroversial area of testimony. If the client will not be dissuaded from continuing to commit perjury, then the lawyer can withdraw, disclose the matter to the court or Crown (this seems to be a last resort), or continue with the questioning as if nothing is wrong and not refer to that testimony in the **closing argument**.

The Client Who Maintains Innocence and Pleads Guilty

A particularly difficult situation for a lawyer arises where a client maintains his or her innocence but still wishes to plead guilty. The plea bargaining process will be discussed in later chapters, but it is sufficient to recognize that the Crown and defence lawyer may enter into discussions to have the accused plead guilty to a charge in return for a lesser sentence or withdrawal of some charges. It seems that a lawyer may enter into negotiations with the Crown even though the accused is denying guilt, but this should only occur if the client instructs his or her lawyer to do so.

Clients may wish to plead guilty because they have committed the crime, or because they have a defence but believe that it is possible that the defence will fail for one of many reasons at trial. There may also be other reasons—for example, because the accused wishes to protect another party, or to avoid publicity or stress, or because the cost of a trial might be more than the client is willing to take on. A plea may be a quick resolution to an embarrassing situation, or the client may lack the confidence to fight a criminal charge. However, under Canadian law, a judge may not accept a guilty plea if the accused does not admit guilt in court. As will be discussed in later chapters, a judge may question the accused to ensure that the individual is assuming the guilt of the charge. If a judge is not satisfied that this is true, the judge must not accept the guilty plea.

Incriminating Physical Evidence

Incriminating physical evidence involves the classic situation when a lawyer comes into contact with incriminating physical evidence such as the "smoking gun" or "bloody shirt" scenario. A criminal lawyer faces difficult issues when a client brings a piece of evidence and asks for assistance in dealing with the item. The lawyer owes a duty of confidentiality to the client, and this would be a perfect opportunity to help the client in his or her case. However, the lawyer also has an obligation to the administration of justice so that the lawyer are not permitted to destroy such evidence. How lawyers should dispose of this evidence has been the source of much debate.

A lawyer cannot suppress evidence, according to the rules, but in the criminal law there is no disclosure obligation on the defence lawyer to give all material to the Crown. The only exceptions to this rule are where the defence should disclose in reasonable time (1) an alibi, so that it can be investigated; (2) a psychiatric defence should be disclosed so that the Crown can have its own mental-health expert examine the accused; and (3) all other experts should be disclosed 30 days before trial, pursuant to the *Criminal Code*.[39] The Crown may be given an adjournment to prepare for this evidence, but it is still admissible

39. Alice Woolley et al, *Lawyers' Ethics and Professional Regulation* (Markham, ON: LexisNexis, 2008) at 382.

evidence, and it may be protected by the law of privilege. However, a case against a lawyer withholding the smoking gun might come down to the intent of the lawyer taking that evidence. Consider *R v Murray* in the following case box.

R v MURRAY, [2000] 144 CCC (3D) 289 (ONT SCJ)

Mr. Murray was retained by Paul Bernardo in February 1993 to represent him in a series of Scarborough Ontario sexual assaults, and was later retained to defend him in connection with the Leslie Mahaffy and Kristen French murders and some other related offences.

Mr. Murray was later charged with suppressing video evidence that showed his client sexually torturing the two girls, which was proof that Bernardo had committed the crimes with which he was charged. Although Bernardo's house was searched for 71 days by the police, this evidence was not found. On instructions from his client, Mr. Murray went to Mr. Bernardo's home and took the tapes from a pot light in the ceiling in a surreptitious way that prevented the Crown from knowing about the existence of the videos. The lawyer kept the tapes for 17 months without telling the Crown. Mr. Murray then passed on the case to another lawyer, John Rosen. Mr. Bernardo released Mr. Murray from his retainer, but in that letter he directed Mr. Murray not to give the tapes to the new lawyer. This seemed like an ethical issue to Mr. Murray, and he went to the Law Society of Upper Canada for advice.

The Law Society told Mr. Murray to turn over the tapes to a judge who could rule on what to do with the evidence. The judge ruled that the tapes should be given to the new lawyer, Mr. Rosen. Mr. Rosen watched the tapes and used them as a tool for bargaining.

However, Mr. Murray was charged with attempt to obstruct justice by concealment of the videotapes. Those prosecuting the lawyer said that taking the tapes was an obstruction because:

1. the tapes were put in a place that could not be obtained by the police in obstruction of their investigation;
2. the Crown could not put on a full prosecution given that the tapes were an integral piece of evidence and made them negotiate with Bernardo and his wife Karla Homolka when this would not have been done otherwise;
3. the tapes influenced the way Mr. Rosen defended Mr. Bernardo; and
4. keeping the tapes deprived the jury of admissible evidence.

The court found that the concealment of these tapes could affect all aspects of the criminal justice system, but Mr. Murray was acquitted because he lacked the mental element of consciously concealing the evidence. It was not clear that Mr. Murray intended to permanently retain the evidence in order to obstruct justice. With Mr. Murray's duty to confidentiality and his lack of intent, he could not be convicted. The court found that it was a defence strategy to retain the tapes until trial.

Why do many people think that Mr. Murray should have been found guilty? Was this a good decision that strictly enforced the law?

However, after *R v Murray*, there is little doubt that a lawyer must not knowingly conceal evidence to impair the functioning of the justice system, even by temporarily removing evidence. The MCPC provides little guidance on the responsibilities when it comes to evidence other than the lawyer must not "*knowingly* attempt to deceive a tribunal or influence the course of justice by offering false evidence, misstating facts or law, presenting or relying upon a false or deceptive affidavit, suppressing what *ought* to be disclosed or otherwise assisting in any fraud, crime or illegal conduct" Yet, this is still vague and does not present a resolution to the lawyer on what "ought to be disclosed."

Instead of seeking a disciplinary hearing of Mr. Murray after the case, the Law Society of Upper Canada struck a special committee to prepare a new rule to deal with these situations, but this project was never completed. No consensus about the rule could be reached by the committee nor convocation, so no rule resulted. In the end, Mr. Murray was acquitted of obstruction of justice, did not face discipline from the law society, and the rule was not created.

Alberta does have a provision, under Chapter 10, Rule 20, Commentary 20, about the concealment of property. The rules say that it applies to

> criminal matters due to the danger of obstruction of justice if evidence in a criminal matter is withheld. While a lawyer has no obligation to disclose the mere existence of such evidence, it would be unethical to accept possession of it and then conceal or destroy it. The lawyer must therefore advise someone wishing to deliver potential evidence that, if possession is accepted by the lawyer, it is necessary to turn the evidence over to appropriate authorities (unless it consists of communications or documents that are privileged). When surrendering criminal evidence, however, a lawyer must protect confidentiality attaching to the circumstances in which the material was acquired, which may require that the lawyer act anonymously or through a third party.

However, some critics have noted that although Alberta should be commended for attempting to provide lawyers with guidance on this issue, the rule is too broad, and Ontario and the CBA have refused to follow Alberta's lead.

Most agree, even in the absence of clear rules, that lawyers should refrain from taking possession of illegal evidence, and they should deliver that evidence immediately to the police in a way that does not disclose the identity of a client. Lawyers should also not interfere in any way with the evidence that they receive, including destroying that evidence, altering it, or changing it in any way.

Termination of the Client–Lawyer Relationship in Civil and Criminal Law

As discussed earlier, a lawyer may withdraw from the lawyer–client relationship if this decision will not unduly prejudice the client. This is usually in situations where the client has acted in a dishonourable way, or there is a serious loss of confidence between the parties. When the lawyer withdraws, he or she must give back all documentation and property to the client or the new lawyer, disclose all relevant information, account for all outstanding fees, and cooperate with the subsequent legal counsel. The best interests of the client should always be the first consideration, which includes competent and continuing representation without undue delay or cost. To withdraw from a case there must be a good reason with appropriate notice to the client. If there is a breakdown in the relationship, the client will not want a lawyer who is not committed to the case, and the lawyer would not want to keep a client who does not trust the lawyer's authority.

In Ontario, the Law Society of Upper Canada has specific rules when it comes to terminating a lawyer–client relationship. Rule 2.09 provides that a lawyer must have a good reason to withdraw, there has been a serious loss of confidence between the lawyer and client, and there is enough time so that the client can find another lawyer with adequate preparation time before trial. There are also some circumstances where a lawyer must withdraw:

- if the lawyer is fired by the client;
- if the lawyer is asked to do something that is contrary to the lawyer's duty to the court;
- if the client has had "dishonourable conduct" in the proceedings or if the client has proceeded with legal matters simply to "harass or maliciously injure another";
- if the lawyer believes there has been dishonesty or fraud; or
- if the lawyer is not competent in that particular legal matter.

However, the client has the right to discharge a lawyer at any time. There must be confidence and trust between the client and lawyer, and if that confidence is gone, the relationship should end. A client can terminate the retainer with a lawyer even if the trial has already started, if the client will suffer prejudice, or if the client has no reason for firing the lawyer, and whether or not there is any notice. A client cannot be forced to retain or continue working with a particular lawyer.

Discipline

Lawyers are punished under legislation by the respective law society. For example, in Saskatchewan, the *Legal Profession Act*, 1990, c L-10.1, 2(1)(c), provides that a lawyer must not engage in **conduct unbecoming** a lawyer, which is defined as "an act or conduct inimical to the best interests of the public or the members of the society; or, which tends to harm the standing of the legal profession." This may include engaging in fraud, mishandling trust monies, or a breach of the rules of conduct. Conduct unbecoming is one of the most frequent findings of the law societies. The lawyer can go before a hearing panel to determine if he or she has violated this provision and the lawyer can face the following penalties:

1. A **revocation** of the lawyer's licence;
2. An order requiring the lawyer to surrender his or her licence;
3. An order suspending the lawyer's licence,
   I. for a definite period,
   II. until terms and conditions are satisfied, or
   III. both a definite term and when conditions are met.
4. A fine of not more than $10 000, payable to the Law Society;
5. An order that the lawyer obtain or continue treatment or counselling, including testing and treatment for addiction to or excessive use of alcohol or drugs, or participate in other programs to improve his or her health;
6. An order that the lawyer participate in specified programs of legal education or professional training;
7. An order restricting the areas of law that the lawyer can practice in;
8. An order restricting legal services;
9. An order that the lawyer co-operate in a review of the lawyer's business;
10. An order requiring the lawyer to refund to a client all or a portion of the fees paid;
11. An order that the lawyer be reprimanded; or
12 Any other order that the Hearing Panel considers appropriate.

Disbarment

In addition to determining if someone should be admitted to the bar, law societies also govern misconduct by lawyers (including misconduct outside of the practice of law). It is relatively rare for the Bar Association to **disbar** lawyers. A survey of the lists of lawyers under discipline on the Law Society of Upper Canada shows that fewer than ten lawyers a year are disbarred in Ontario (see http://www.lsuc.on.ca/with.aspx?id=690). However, when lawyers are disbarred, it may be for serious reasons (see the following case box).

ADAMS v LAW SOCIETY OF ALBERTA, [2000] AJ NO. 1031 (APPEAL FROM THE LAW SOCIETY OF ALBERTA HEARING)

Mr. Adams appealed the decision of the Law Society of Alberta for disbarring him from the practice of law. Mr. Adams pleaded guilty to sexual exploitation with a 16-year-old prostitute girlfriend of his client. Criminally, Mr. Adams received a 15-month conditional sentence. The law society panel found that he had breached his duty to the client, brought the profession into disrepute and was deserving of punishment. Mr. Adams agreed that he deserved punishment, but that disbarment was unreasonable.

The panel found that the misconduct was within the context of his legal practice, and was a significant beach of the client's trust. The panel found that the breach of trust in a sexual relationship was even more serious than taking money from clients because "money can be restored but honour cannot." The Alberta appeal court found that the hearing panel had considered the relevant factors, and disbarment was an appropriate finding. Mr. Adams was disbarred.

Do you think this punishment was too severe, given that this was a consensual relationship, and the 16-year-old was not a client?
Why do you think that Mr. Adams was disbarred, but Mr. Chodos (see the case box on page 36) was just ordered to pay damages? Do you think that age was a factor?

Most disciplinary proceedings focus on "professional misconduct" and lead to sanctions much less severe than disbarment.

PARALEGALS

The Canadian Association of Paralegals defines a **paralegal** as

> an individual qualified through education, training or work experience, who is employed or whose services have been retained by a legal professional, law firm, governmental agency, private or public corporation or other entity in a capacity or function which involves the performance, under the supervision of a legal professional, of substantive legal work, which may include administrative or managerial duties, requiring sufficient knowledge of legal concepts.[40]

Paralegals are non-lawyers who provide access to justice to members of the Canadian public who may not be able to afford a lawyer. Often paralegal services are performed under the supervision of a lawyer, and there can be specific types of paralegals that specialize in the transfer of property, landlord and tenant matters, and certain types of litigation (e.g., small claims court). Paralegals are distinct from law clerks and legal assistants, who have specific college education programs, and clerks and assistants usually do not appear on matters in court or before tribunals.

Although Ontario has sought to strictly regulate paralegals, other provinces have not yet followed suit, but British Columbia and Alberta have paralegal associations, and Quebec is currently forming its own association. There are also other provincial associations at work in Saskatchewan, Manitoba, and the Maritimes, but they are still in the planning stages. Outside of Ontario, paralegals are still independent and are simply not permitted to practise in certain areas of law. Throughout Canada, paralegals prepare legal documents, maintain records, and perform administrative and clerical functions, but in some provinces they may also assist in personal injury litigation and family law, interview witnesses, appear at administrative tribunals, and file documents for land conveyances. Most provinces require some post-secondary education or experience, usually at the college level, and may require a placement within a law firm or other legal body.

Although other provinces have not formally regulated paralegals, Ontario has taken the lead in this capacity. In 2006, a legislation was introduced called the *Access to Justice Act,* SO 2006, c 21, which brought paralegals (who were previously independent) under the regulation of the Law Society of Upper Canada. To protect the public, these paralegals would now have to be regulated, educated, insured, and licensed in order to practise in Ontario, and the Law Society of Upper Canada began regulating paralegals on May 1, 2007. A *Paralegal Rules of Conduct* was also developed for paralegals to outline their professional and ethical obligations (much like the Rules of Conduct for lawyers). Those paralegals already in practice had to apply for this new licence. The first licences were issued in early 2008 and totalled over 2000 in the first year. After June 30, 2010, all paralegals must graduate from an accredited paralegal program at colleges in Ontario.

Paralegals must also write a paralegal licensing examination to qualify to act as a paralegal in Ontario. The exam, which is three-and-a-half hours in length, contains approximately 130 multiple-choice questions, and is offered three times a year. Paralegals are also

40. Canadian Association of Paralegals, online: <http://www.caplegal.ca/home.php?p=charter&l=&m=1#Scene_1>.

The Law Society of Upper Canada Paralegal Accreditation **http://rc.lsuc.on.ca/jsp/paralegal/accreditation.jsp**

required to submit a statement of "Good Character," as lawyers are required to do, pursuant to By-Law 4 and the *Law Society Act*, RSO 1990, c L-8. For a discussion of the areas of law paralegals are permitted to appear on, see the following box.

IN WHAT AREAS MAY A PARALEGAL PRACTISE IN ONTARIO?

As of May 1, 2007, paralegals are not permitted to appear in Family Court, and they may not draft wills or handle real estate transactions or estates. The Law Society of Upper Canada's By-Law 4 permits paralegals to practise in Small Claims Court; in the Ontario Court of Justice under the *Provincial Offences Act* (e.g., *Highway Traffic Act* matters); before provincial boards and agencies; in summary conviction offences where the maximum penalty does not exceed six months' imprisonment; and in administrative tribunals, including the Financial Services Commission of Ontario. Paralegals may give legal advice about a proceeding, draft or assist in drafting the documents for a proceeding, and negotiate on the behalf of a client who is entering into a proceeding.

JUDGES

> *"It is for the advocates, each in his turn, to examine the witnesses, and not for the judge to take it on himself lest by so doing he appeared to favour one side or the other.... The judge's part in all this is to hearken to the evidence, only himself asking questions of witnesses when it is necessary to clear up any point that has been overlooked or left obscure; to see that the advocates behave themselves seemly and keep to the rules laid down by the law; to exclude irrelevancies and discourage repetition; to make sure by wise intervention that he follows the points that the advocates are making and can assess their worth; and at the end to make up his mind where the truth lies. If he goes beyond this, he drops the matter of a judge and assumes the role of an advocate; and the change does not become him well."*
>
> —*Lord Denning, R v Perrigo (1972), 10 CCC (2d) 336 (Ont Dist Ct)*

The judiciary is the third arm of the government, which is separate from the legislative and the executive. Its role is to uphold the Constitution and administer the law in a fair and impartial way according to the law. Judges are the highest authority inside the courtroom. The judge has the discretion to question a witness to clarify a position or to question counsel and, in the Canadian adversarial system, the judge does not take an interventionist role so as not to appear to favour one side over the other. A judge must maintain **impartiality** at all times. It is the role of the judge to decide all questions of law that might come before the court in substance or in procedure, and judges may be called on to make significant rulings including whether evidence should be excluded, whether a witness is properly called, and what evidence should be presented to the jury.

In a jury trial, the judge does not determine the finding of "guilty" or "not guilty." This is a task left to the jury. However, the judge does get to rule on the interpretation of the law, to decide what principles are given to the jury to **deliberate** upon, and sentencing.

Until 1971, there was no formal training for any judges in Canada, but by 1974 the Canadian Institute for the Administration of Justice ran seminars for judges, including the week-long seminar for new judges. In 1987, the National Judicial Institute was established in Ottawa to provide more voluntary judicial education.[41] The judge occupies a highly symbolic role and the courtroom is designed to reinforce the judge's status. The judge sits at the front of the courtroom in a position that allows him or her to oversee and

41. Ian Greene, *The Courts* (Vancouver: UBC Press, 2006) at 12.

control the proceedings. The judge's chair is higher than anyone else's and is separated by a barrier. The judge has a court clerk to assist him or her with the organization of documents and exhibits.

In addition, the judge has a private chamber, uses a separate entrance to the court after everyone else has already entered (and the judge's entrance is formally announced), and everyone in the courtroom is required to rise when told to do so. The judge is addressed as "Your Honour" ("Your Worship" for a Justice of the Peace) and the judge alone has the power to interpret the rules of law that govern the proceedings. Judges may also charge anyone who shows disrespect with **contempt of court**. This includes making disparaging comments, criticizing a ruling, or engaging in any act that is calculated to embarrass, hinder, or obstruct a court in the administration of justice, or that is calculated to lessen its authority or its dignity.

The judiciary in Canada has independence, job security, and financial security. The base salary for federal judges is approximately $260 000, and the average is similar for the Ontario Court of Justice and Superior Court of Justice judges.[42] Depending on the province, this information may be publically available. In turn, judges are expected to know the law and act in a fair and impartial manner towards everyone in the courtroom including the lawyers, jurors, witnesses, and the accused. Judges represent law and order and their behaviour and words are often the measure of the fairness within our justice system. Judges' independence allows them to make decisions that are unpopular or that may be contrary to the interests of the government, without worrying that they will lose their job. Judges are only bound by the laws of Parliament and what the legislature has enacted.

The highest level of authority is the Supreme Court of Canada. The appointment of judges is governed by the *Supreme Court Act* RSC 1985, c S-26. The Prime Minister may have assistance from the Minister of Justice and, since February 2006, nominees face three hours of questions from an all-party committee of the House of Commons. However, the final decision of appointment or a withdrawal of a nominee rests with the Prime Minister. Justice Minister Irwin Cotler said in testimony to the House of Commons Justice Committee in 2004 that certain characteristics are looked for in identifying a candidate for the Supreme Court. These criteria include professional capacity such as knowledge of the law, personal characteristics like integrity and patience, and diversity. A judge's judicial history may also be examined, which includes judicial decisions the judge has made in the past.[43]

Usually, the judges selected for this highest court are already judges from various provinces and have at least ten years of standing at the bar in their province. The judges hold office until they are 75 years of age "during good behaviour," unless they decide to retire earlier. The Supreme Court traditionally has nine judges—three must be from Quebec (per the *Supreme Court Act*), usually three are from Ontario (by convention), two are from the West, and one is from the Maritimes. When one judge retires, he or she is replaced by a judge from the same geographic region.

The court also has an individual that sits at the highest rank and is called the "Chief Justice." The Chief Justice is selected by the Prime Minister in consultation with the federal cabinet. The Chief Justice decides which of the judges hears motions and cases. In addition, if the Governor General dies or is incapacitated, the Chief Justice is the Administrator of Canada and has the powers of the Governor General. Decisions of the Supreme Court are often made by panels of seven of the nine judges, but as many as nine and as few as five judges can hear a particular case. The Chief Justice makes the decision on who will hear each case depending on the judicial resources available.

Provincial superior court justices, federal court justices and justices of the Supreme Court of Canada are usually addressed as "Mr. Justice Smith" or "Madam Justice Smith," and in court they are traditionally addressed as "My Lady" or "My Lord," but this is becoming rare, especially at the lower levels. In written documents, they are referred to as "Smith J." (or "Smith J.A." in the court of appeal; provincial chief justices are "Smith C.J.O," "Smith C.J.A.," etc., where the last letter refers to the province; and "Smith C.J.C."

42. Ontario Minister of Finance, online: <http://www.fin.gov.on.ca/en/publications/salarydisclosure/2010/judiciary10.html>.

43. Ian Greene, *The Courts* (Vancouver: UBC Press, 2006), at 24.

The current judges of the Supreme Court of Canada. **Back Row:** The Honourable Mr. Justice Michael J. Moldaver, the Honourable Mr. Justice Marshall Rothstein, the Honourable Mr. Justice Thomas A. Cromwell, and the Honourable Madam Justice Andromache Karakatsanis. **Front Row:** The Honourable Mr. Justice Morris J. Fish, the Honourable Mr. Justice Louis LeBel, the Right Honourable Beverley McLachlin, P.C. Chief Justice of Canada, the Honourable Madam Justice Marie Deschamps, and the Honourable Madam Justice Rosalie Silberman Abella.

for the Chief Justice of the Supreme Court of Canada). Judges are formally addressed outside of the court as "The Honourable Mr. (or Madam) Justice A. Smith." It is common to refer to the judge as "Justice Smith" in informal conversation.

Who Is Eligible to Be Appointed a Judge?

To be eligible for an appointment, judicial applicants must be in good standing with their law society (not disbarred or suspended) in one of the Canadian provinces or territories. Superior court judges are appointed by the Canadian government, and the inferior court judges are appointed by the provincial government. This process is much different from the system in the United States, where judges are elected, and the process to appoint a Supreme Court judge is an extremely rigorous process.

Ontario, Saskatchewan, Quebec, New Brunswick, Newfoundland and Labrador, and the Yukon are among the provinces and territories that require judicial candidates to have at least ten years experience as a lawyer before they become a judge. The Northwest Territories requires at least seven years, and Alberta, British Columbia, Manitoba, Nova Scotia, and Prince Edward Island require at least five years' experience. Some provinces, including Saskatchewan, Manitoba, and Quebec, as well as the Yukon, also provide that one may be appointed with "pertinent legal experience" (perhaps in other adjudicative roles) if the individual practised for less than the number of years required. This appropriate legal or judicial experience may qualify one for appointment.[44] Table 2.1 summarizes these requirements.

44. Provincial Court Act, RSA 2000, c P-31; Provincial Court Act, RSBC 1996, c 379; Provincial Court Act, CCSM c C275; Provincial Court Act, RSNB 1973, c P-21; Provincial Court Act, RSNS 1989, c 238; Provincial Court Act, 1991 SNL 1991, c 15; Territorial Court Act, RSNWT, 1988, c T-2; The Nunavut Judicial System Implementation Act, SNWT 1998, c 34; Courts of Justice Act, RSO 1990, c C.43; Provincial Court Act, RSPEI 1988, c P-25; Courts of Justice Act, RSQ, c T-16; The Provincial Court Act, SS 1998, c P-30.11; Territorial Court Act, RSY 2002, c 217.

Table 2.1 Requirements for a Judicial Position

Province/Territory	Years as Lawyer	Pertinent Legal Experience
Ontario, Saskatchewan, Quebec, New Brunswick, Newfoundland, and the Yukon	10 years required	Saskatchewan, Yukon, Quebec—accepted
Northwest Territories	7 years required	
Alberta, B.C., Manitoba, Nova Scotia, and Prince Edward Island	5 years required	Manitoba—accepted

Investigation

Judges can be investigated if it is alleged that they have done something wrong. A Judicial Council is an organization that investigates judges. It is self-regulated just as lawyers are, in that judges investigate judges. The first Judicial Council was formed in Ontario in 1968, and almost all other provinces by the mid-1980s, and a Federal Judicial Council was formed in 1971. Judges can be investigated for complaints by the Canadian Judicial Council (CJC) and can be reprimanded and even removed from the bench for serious breaches of conduct.

The CJC investigates allegations of unethical behaviour, incapacity because of permanent disability, and incompetence. The CJC makes recommendations to Parliament or the provincial government about whether a judge should be removed from the bench or disciplined. Investigating judicial misconduct is the most serious task of the CJC, and it has investigated judges for "apparent bias (for example, sexist or racist comments during the trial, or taking a political stand off the bench), inappropriate conduct (especially towards court staff), and conflicts of interest."[45] Complaints may also be made about criticizing other judges, delay in decisions, and the treatment of the individuals who appear before their court. Can a judge be removed from office? Can a judge plagiarize? See the boxes below.

Tibor Kolley/The Globe and Mail/The Canadian Press

Justice Paul Cosgrove

CAN A JUDGE BE REMOVED FROM THE BENCH?

Although it is very rare for a justice to be removed by the CJC, there is an example in the Ontario Superior Court with Justice Paul Cosgrove. Justice Cosgrove was a former federal cabinet minister who spent 40 years in public service, but was investigated for his actions in a 1998 murder trial, where he was alleged to have abused his powers. The Court of Appeal in the case found that Justice Cosgrove made serious legal errors, and mistakenly found that there was misconduct perpetrated by the Crown counsel and police officers. The appeal court later found that these allegations against the Crown and the police were "unwarranted and unsubstantiated."

The inquiry committee recommended that Justice Cosgrove be removed from the bench, saying that that he did not realize the impact he made on the murder victim's family, and seriously affected the reputation of senior government

continued

45. Lori Hausegger, Matthew Hennigar, and Troy Riddell *Canadian Courts: Law, Politics and Process* (Don Mills, ON: Oxford, 2009) at 185.

officials, including the Crown and police. Justice Cosgrove made a full apology to the CJC, saying that "I deeply and acutely regret the fact that my actions may have done damage to this office."[46]

The CJC did not accept the apology and filed a report with the federal Justice Minister to remove Justice Cosgrove from the bench in April 2009. This removal must be approved by a vote by the Senate and House of Commons. However, instead of waiting for this resolution, Justice Cosgrove resigned in order to avoid being the first federally appointed judge since Confederation to be removed from the bench. Cosgrove was only the second to have been recommended for removal.

Do you think that a judge should be held to a higher standard than lawyers?

CAN JUDGES PLAGIARIZE?

In the personal injury case of *Cojocaru (Guardian Ad Litem) v British Columbia Women's Hospital and Health Centre,* [2011] BCJ No 680 (BC CA), a split court ordered a new trial because Justice Joel Groves was alleged to have plagiarized his decision. When the court examined his reasons for his decision, they found that 321 of the 368 paragraphs of the trial decisions were copied "almost word-for-word" from the closing submissions of the plaintiff, and the judge did not acknowledge that he took this work from the plaintiff's documents. The court found that there was little evidence that the judge even considered the defendant's argument.

The Court of Appeal found that neither the parties "nor the public can be satisfied that justice has been done ... [and by recognizing the decision] this Court would risk undermining the confidence of the public in the administration of justice." The court concluded that the judge overlooked evidence, made errors in his analysis, and did not consider the defence argument. Thus, since the court of appeal could not say that the trial judge dealt with the issues at trial, the court would not be able to review a decision that was not reasoned, and on this ground a new trial was ordered. The court of appeal was reluctant to order a new trial, recognizing the difficulty of the parties in going through the process again, but found that this was the only resolution to this difficult matter.[47]

Is this fair to the parties that they have to go through the expense, time and pain of another trial because of the wrongdoing of a judge?

LEARNING OUTCOMES SUMMARIZED

1. Identify the exceptions to lawyer and client confidentiality.

Lawyers may only breach confidentiality when required to do so by law, court order, or by permission of the client, and only as much as necessary. Lawyers may be required to disclose abuse, or if a crime is about to be committed. In Ontario, the Law Society of Upper Canada in s 2.03(3) has provided that if a lawyer believes there is an imminent risk of death or serious bodily (or psychological) harm to an identifiable person or group, the lawyer may disclose confidential information to prevent that death or harm, but no more information must be disclosed than is necessary. A lawyer may also have to disclose if the communication is a threat, or to facilitate a crime, or if there is a genuine risk of wrongful conviction, or if the lawyer needs to defend him or herself from an allegation of lawyer misconduct.

2. List the punishments that a lawyer can face if reprimanded by the law society.

1. Revocation of licence.
2. An order to surrender his or her licence.
3. An order suspending the lawyer's licence, for a specific term, until conditions are met or both.
4. A fine of not more than $10 000, payable to the Law Society.

46. Thomas Claridge, "Justice Cosgrove Pleads for His Job: Judge Delivered a Second Apology to the Full Council of Chief Justices in Toronto" (20 March 2009), The *Lawyers Weekly*.

47. Gary Oakes, "Trial Decision Overturned for Plagiarism" (29 April 2011), *The Lawyers Weekly,* 2.

5. An order that the lawyer obtain or continue treatment or counselling.
6. An order that the lawyer participate in legal education or professional training.
7. An order restricting the areas of law that the lawyer can practice in.
8. An order restricting legal services.
9. A review of the lawyer's business.
10. An order requiring the lawyer to refund fees paid.
11. An order that the lawyer be reprimanded.
12. Any other order that the Hearing Panel considers appropriate.

3. Discuss the limitations of a criminal defence lawyer who has an unequivocal confession from their client.

If the accused makes an unequivocal confession to a crime a lawyer may object to the jurisdiction of the court, object to the form of the charges, object to the sufficiency or admissibility of the evidence, or test the evidence of each witness to make sure that the evidence is proof that the accused is guilty of the charge. However, the lawyer must *not* suggest that another person committed the offence, and the lawyer must *not* call evidence that he or she believes to be false.

4. Assess the lawyer's options when a client insists on perjuring him- or herself on the witness stand.

If a client is going to commit perjury, appropriate options are withdrawing from the case, refusing to call the client to the stand, disclosing the perjury to the court or another third party, refusing to use this testimony in a summary of the case, or questioning the accused in a passive way to avoid eliciting this incorrect statement. However, these options must be balanced, as the client has the right to testify and make his or her case.

If the perjury happens suddenly on the stand, the lawyer may ask for a recess to speak with the client without alerting the Crown, judge, or jury (perhaps waiting until the next break); switch to questioning on a uncontroversial area of testimony; withdraw from the case; disclose the matter to the court or Crown (as a last resort); avoid referring to that testimony in the closing argument.

5. Evaluate how a lawyer–client relationship can come to an end.

A lawyer may withdraw from the lawyer client relationship if withdrawing will not unduly prejudice the client. This is usually occurs in situations where the client has acted in a dishonourable way, or there is a serious loss of confidence between the parties. The lawyer must give back all documentation and property to the client or the new lawyer, disclose all relevant information, account for all outstanding fees, and cooperate with the subsequent legal counsel. The client deserves competent and continuing representation without undue delay or cost. To withdraw from a case must be for a good reason with appropriate notice to the client.

In most provinces, a lawyer must show that there has been a serious loss of confidence between the lawyer and client, and there must be enough time so that the client can find another lawyer and have enough time to prepare before trial. There are also some circumstances where a lawyer must withdraw: (1) if the lawyer is fired by the client; (2) if the lawyer is asked to do something that is contrary to the lawyer's duty to the court; (3) if the client had "dishonourable conduct" in the proceedings; (4) if the lawyer believes there has been dishonesty or fraud; or (5) or if the lawyer is not competent.

The client also has the right to discharge a lawyer at any time. There must be confidence and trust between the client and lawyer, and if that confidence is gone, the relationship should end even if the trial has already begun.

SELF-EVALUATION QUESTIONS

1. What is the importance of the rule that a lawyer has a duty to "raise fearlessly every issue"?
2. What is "legal aid" and "*pro bono*" work for lawyers?
3. The legal profession is a "self-regulating" profession. What does this mean?
4. List some historical ceremonial features that remain in Canadian courts.

CHAPTER 3

Civil Litigation

Learning Outcomes

After completing this chapter, you should be able to:

1. Understand what parliamentary supremacy is.
2. Discuss what is meant by the court's assertion that you must come with "clean hands."
3. Describe what is meant by the phrase "distinguishing the case."
4. List the main perspectives of statutory interpretation.
5. Identify the purpose of a pre-trial conference.

INTRODUCTION

The civil law governs the interactions between individuals, but can it also include governments and other institutions. This breadth of practice includes all non-criminal cases that come under contract law (Chapter 4), tort law (Chapter 5), family law (Chapter 6), administrative law (Chapter 7), constitutional law (Chapter 8), property disputes, corporate law, environmental law, mediation (Chapter 12), commercial law, estate law, and sports law, as well as immigration and refugee claims. It can also encompass matters as diverse as the inquiry into the tainted blood scandal. The civil law is governed by statutes and/or the common law.

As discussed in Chapter 1, Canadian law is divided into provincial and federal laws, but also into the common law system used by the federal, provincial (except in Quebec), and territorial courts. The civil law system is used in Quebec. The common law system is the predominant system of case law used in Canada, and lawyers also refer to case law as common law to distinguish it from statutory law. In this chapter, the term "civil law" will refer exclusively to torts, contracts, and so forth, and *not* to the system of law practised in Quebec.

LEGAL THEORY

The concept of the **rule of law** comes from the Greek philosopher Aristotle (384–322 B.C.), who distinguished between a government of laws, and a government of men. The Canadian system is a government of laws, as no one "man" is above the law—including monarchs and the government—and there should be no exercise of arbitrary power. This concept tries to ensure equal justice for all under the law, the right to a fair hearing, and all of the rights set out in the *Charter of Rights and Freedoms.* There was also a point in the evolution of the law that it was no longer possible to say, as it once was, that all law came from religion, or was based on morality (see the discussion in Chapter 1 on natural law).

The basis of our system is something called **parliamentary supremacy**. Historically, in England in 1649, Charles I tried to dismiss parliament and rule on his own. Many believed that an elected group of men were the supreme lawmakers (Parliament) and that they should be the one body that is making the laws, not a king or monarch. This concept became fundamental to the common law system of law. The court's role was just to interpret and enforce laws that Parliament created. If a court decision resulted in an injustice, it was contingent on Parliament to fix the problem. Judges were there simply to enforce that principle, and they had to apply the law as it is in the books—even if it was distasteful. The result, however, could be inconsistency in law, and it was difficult to predict the outcome in some cases. There was some question whether this was the best approach, and whether statutory law and case law should work together. Today, statutes and case law do function in tandem to allow a judge to come to the best possible result. It is still incumbent on Parliament to revise any laws that may lead to an injustice, but judges also sometimes fulfill that role.

HIERARCHY OF THE COURTS

Not all courts are created equal. The courts that we will be looking at in this text are in the middle column of Figure 3.1, which illustrates the main court system in Canada and the hierarchy of the courts. Table 3.1 lists the names of trial courts by province. There are **courts of first instance,** which are trial courts such as the Superior Court of Justice for Ontario, where all the evidence is raised, disputed, and decided. All cases above small claims court go to the province's Supreme or Superior Court or the Court of Queen's Bench (depending on the province). Lawyers may prepare for years to go to these trial courts on civil law issues like personal injury, breach of contract, property issues, and so forth.

Figure 3.1 Hierarchy of the Courts in Canada

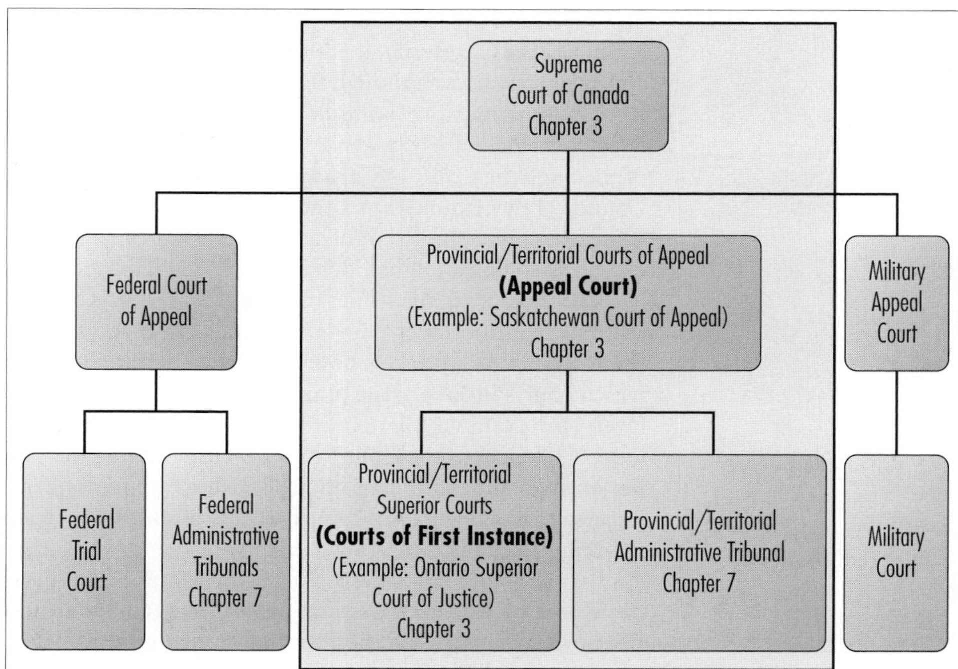

Table 3.1 Names of the Trial Court by Province

Province or Territory	Name of the Trial Court
Alberta	Court of Queen's Bench
British Columbia	Supreme Court
Manitoba	Court of Queen's Bench
New Brunswick	Court of Queen's Bench
Newfoundland and Labrador	Supreme Court
Nova Scotia	Supreme Court
Ontario	Superior Court of Justice
Prince Edward Island	Supreme Court
Quebec	Supreme Court
Saskatchewan	Court of Queen's Bench
Northwest Territories	Supreme Court
Nunavut	Court of Justice
Yukon	Supreme Court

Appellate courts are higher courts which can review the decisions of lower courts if there was a mistake of law. For example, these courts include the Court of Appeal for each of the provinces and territories and the Supreme Court of Canada. These courts do not examine evidence but simply examine written briefs on the law, and hear the submissions of lawyers on the issues. The Court of Appeal usually has a panel of three or more judges. A split between the judges is not uncommon, and both the **majority** and the **minority** may write a decision explaining their thought processes. There may also be a **concurring** decision.

There is also a federal court system, which hears matters such as immigration law, patent law, copyright law, and tax law. The federal court has a trial level, the Federal Court of Appeal, and then appeals go to the Supreme Court. There are also federal administrative tribunals (see Chapter 7). It is also important to note that there are military trial courts and courts of appeal, even though they are not addressed in this text.

The Supreme Court is the ultimate court in Canada and it hears appeals from the common law system, the civil law system in Quebec, and the Federal Court of Appeal. Before the founding of the Supreme Court of Canada, appeal cases went to the Judicial Committee of the Privy Council (Privy Council) in London, England (this ended in 1949). The Supreme Court is sometimes called the "court of last resort." Figures 3.2 and 3.3 outline the geographical origin of appeals to the Supreme Court in Canada, and the area of law that they concern.

There is a distinct hierarchy of courts in Canada. Generally speaking, higher courts can **bind** lower courts that are within the same geographical jurisdiction, and the lower are bound to follow the higher. Figure 3.4 shows the hierarchy and outlines which courts influence the other courts in the country. Decisions by courts on the same level—for example, the Ontario Superior Court of Justice and Saskatchewan Court of Queen's Bench, or the Court of Appeal for Ontario and Court of Appeal for Alberta—are **persuasive**, meaning that their decisions should be respected, but it not binding. However, case law from a higher level is binding. For example, a case in the Nova Scotia Supreme Court is bound by a case from the Nova Scotia Court of Appeal. Case law of another geographic location but on the same level is persuasive. For example, a case at the Court of Appeal for Saskatchewan is persuasive for the Court of Appeal for New Brunswick. A case from the Supreme Court is binding on every geographic region, every province or territory, and every level of court.

Figure 3.2 Appeals Heard, 2010: Origin

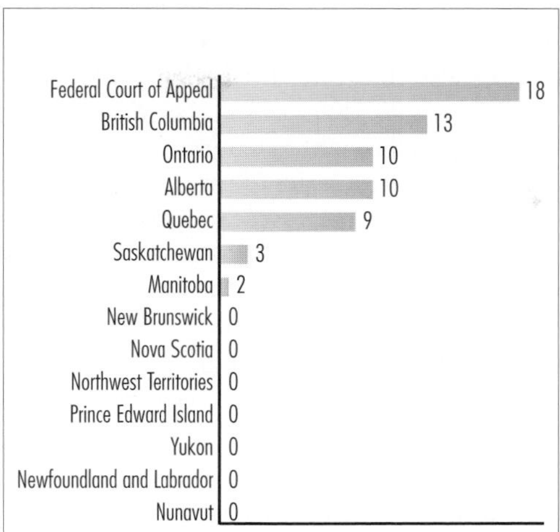

Figure 3.3 Appeals Heard, 2010: Type

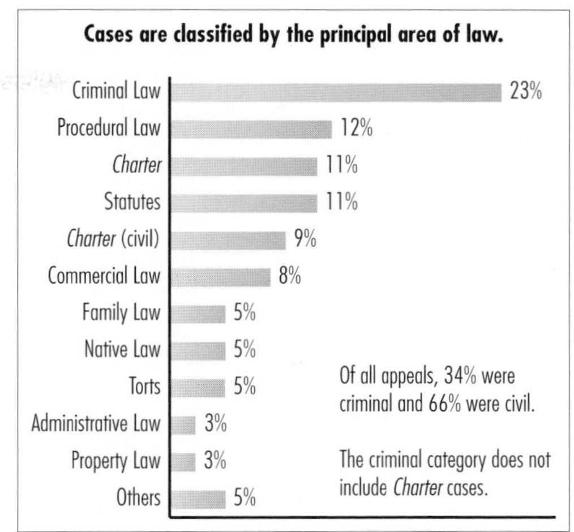

Sources: *Supreme Court of Canada. Statistics 2000–2010 Bulletin of Proceedings: Special Edition*, p. 6. Reproduced with the permission of the Supreme Court of Canada, 2012.

Canadian courts are not bound by cases in the United Kingdom, but it can be persuasive if England or other Commonwealth countries have made a finding on a specific area of law, particularly if there is no case yet in Canada. Some cases in particular areas of law in the United States are persuasive, but it is difficult to summarize the U.S. law because the law changes significantly from state to state. The applicability of a case may be limited

Figure 3.4 Binding Courts in Canada

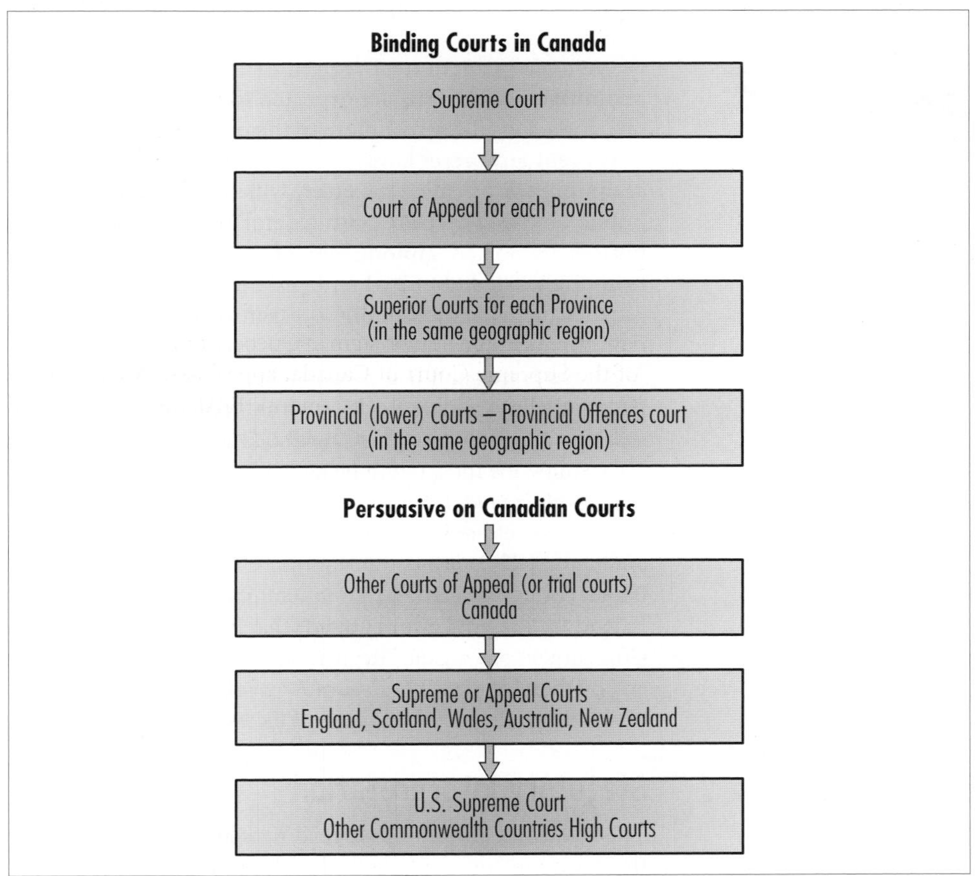

to one state/circuit court in only one or two states. However, over time, Canada is relying more on U.S. cases and less on British cases. The Supreme Court often refers to cases from the British House of Lords, the High Court of Australia, and the Supreme Court of the United States. Figure 3.4 also illustrates the international courts which may be influential on Canadian law.

Judges may also give special weight to Court of Appeal (or Supreme Court) cases where the decision is unanimous, where a series of cases all discuss the same principle, older cases that may begin a new precedent in law; cases decided by prominent judges, or decisions where the judges gave extensive reasons. If the case has a **dissenting** decision, if the judges disagreed on the reasons for the decision, if the case is old or in a quickly changing area of law, or if it is a decision where the court wrongly did not consider a particular statute or case, lesser weight will be given to that decision.

STATUTE LAW

There are three levels of government in Canada—the federal, provincial, and municipal. The Canadian House of Commons and the legislative assemblies of the provinces and territories draft legislation. It is not only Parliament that makes laws, but powers are also delegated to other authorities to make regulations to fulfill the goals of their governing legislation. The legislation may allow the Governor-General, the Lieutenant-Governor, a cabinet minister, board, commission, or tribunal to make laws called **regulations**.

These regulations can be quickly and easily enacted to meet the changing needs of that area of law. However, each level of government must be careful not to go beyond its authority to make law. This is called being ***ultra vires***, the Latin term that means "beyond the power of the body," or acting beyond the given jurisdiction. If law is deemed *ultra vires,* then it is invalid. The goal of those drafting legislation and regulations is to clearly set out in plain language what is expected, so a judge can easily apply that language to a case.

Federal (*Canada Gazette*): **http://www.gazette.gc.ca/**

A major function of legislation is that laws must be published or what is called **promulgated**. Citizens are expected to know what the laws are, as ignorance of the law is no excuse for failing to adhere to the principles. In order to make laws available to all, and to prevent any secret laws, there are formal ways that legislation is made available. There are publications called **gazettes,** which print and make all the new laws available to the public online. There are both federal and provincial/territorial gazettes in which official notices are posted, announcements of government regulations are made, and proclamations are posted about when legislation will be in force. After a law is published in the gazette, the Canadian public is assumed to be aware of the contents, whether they have read them or not.

Statutes are published in volumes each year called the *Statutes of Canada* (SC), or for the different provinces and territories, such as the *Statutes of Saskatchewan* (SS), and are followed by the year they are published. There are also times where there are compilations of federal and provincial statutes, the most recent being 1985. Therefore, you will see a compilation called the *Revised Statutes of Canada, 1985* (RSC 1985). There are also compilations made of provincial statutes that you will see referred to as the *Revised Statutes* of the province. For example, the *Revised Statutes of Ontario* (RSO) is a compilation of Ontario law. Statutes can have a long name and a short name. For example, the *Access to Information Act* RSC, 1985, c A-1 is actually titled "An Act to Extend the Present Laws of Canada that Provide Access to Information under the Control of the Government of Canada." Regulations are named in the same way and are referred to, as statutes are, by their last revision. *Revised Regulations of Ontario* can be cited as (RRO 1990). Figure 3.5 breaks down the individual parts of the New Brunswick *Age of Majority Act,* RSNB 1973, c A-4.

Statutory Interpretation

The law is not simply about reading legislation but about interpreting its meaning. While the common law can only deal with problems as cases arise, and only then at an extremely

Figure 3.5 Analyzing a Statute

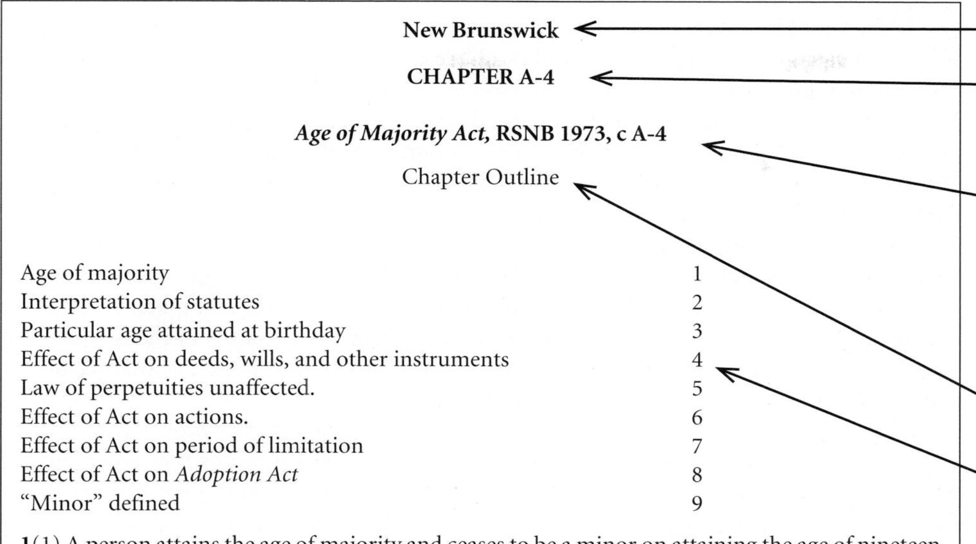

New Brunswick

CHAPTER A-4

***Age of Majority Act,* RSNB 1973, c A-4**

Chapter Outline

Age of majority	1
Interpretation of statutes	2
Particular age attained at birthday	3
Effect of Act on deeds, wills, and other instruments	4
Law of perpetuities unaffected.	5
Effect of Act on actions.	6
Effect of Act on period of limitation	7
Effect of Act on *Adoption Act*	8
"Minor" defined	9

1(1) A person attains the age of majority and ceases to be a minor on attaining the age of nineteen years.

1(2) A person who has attained the age of nineteen years but has not attained the age of twenty-one years, attains the age of majority and ceases to be a minor on the coming into force of this Act.

1(3) Subject to the provisions of this Act, this section applies with respect to every law that is within the legislative competence of the Legislature and in force in the Province on or after the day this Act comes into force.

1972, c 5, s 1.

2(1) When used in

(a) an Act of the Legislature, or any regulation, order or by-law made under an Act of the Legislature, enacted or made before or after the coming into force of this Act,

(b) an Act of Parliament or a provision thereof, that, by an Act of the Legislature, enacted before or after the day this Act comes into force, is made to apply in respect of any Act, matter or thing that is within the legislative competence of the Legislature,

(c) a deed, will or any other instrument whatsoever made on or after August 1, 1972, and

(d) an order or direction of a court made before or after the coming into force of this Act, the words "child," except where used only to indicate a child-parent relationship, "infant," "infancy," "minor," "minority," and similar words shall be construed as referring to a person who has not attained the age of majority, and the words "adult," "full age" and similar words shall be construed as referring to a person who has attained the age of majority.

2(2) Subsection (1) does not apply where it is expressed or implied in the enactment, regulation, order, by-law, direction or instrument that a meaning was intended by the use of a word that is inconsistent with the construction required to be placed on the word by that subsection.

2(3) A reference to any age between the ages of nineteen years and twenty-one years inclusive in

(a) an Act of the Legislature or any regulation, order or by-law made under an Act of the Legislature, or

(b) an order or direction of a court, enacted or made before August 1, 1972, shall be deemed to be a reference to the age of nineteen years.

1972, c 5, s 2.

3 A person attains a particular age expressed in years at the commencement of that anniversary of the date of his birth.

1972, c 5, s 3.

...

Province,where applicable

Chapter number so that the legislation can be found in paper form, catalogued under the chapter number.

Long title of the legislation; RSNB means that it is a "Revised Statute of New Brunswick." So, the legislation was revised in 1973, and again, it is to be found in Chapter A-4 in paper form.

Index of the sections in the legislation

What follows is the body of the legislation, which is numbered by sections and subsections.

Application of the statute to those between the ages of 19 to 21 who are now the age of majority

The statute, and this particular section, was first legislated with the Statutes of New Brunswick in 1972, Chapter 5.

May be a definition of some of the key terms for the legislation

Source: <http://www2.gnb.ca/content/gnb/en/departments/attorney_general/acts_regulations.html>

slow pace, legislation can actually anticipate future disputes. Legislation is much better equipped to accommodate rapid social change.

There should be several goals of all legislation. Laws must be general enough to apply to the population required; they should be clear so there are no contradictory provisions; there should not be a conflict of laws at the municipal, provincial, federal levels and perhaps the international level; laws should not make demands that are not possible to comply with; and they should stand the test of time. It is also important that there is a mechanism to enforce these laws or the legislation is fruitless. To this aim, judges have long sought some structure to the way that they interpret statutes.

Judges play an important role by interpreting what legislation says. Although it is a goal to have legislation that is completely clear in all situations, if legislation is ambiguous in some way, there are several rules to guide judges in how to interpret that material. The first avenue of information is the beginning of the legislation itself. Statutes usually start with a definitions section that states how language is going to be interpreted in that particular statute, which may give judges direction in interpretation.

Judges may also use federal interpretation statutes like the *Interpretation Act,* RSC 1985, c I-21 (each province has its own interpretation statutes, like Ontario's *Interpretation Act,* RSO 1990, c I11), which provide guidance across all jurisdictions if it is not otherwise specified in the legislation. Judges may also look to the legislative documents that lay out the discussion that occurred in parliamentary debates about a new piece of legislation. The transcripts of these debates are published in a record called **Hansard**, and it may be used to assist a judge in interpretation. However, sometimes not even these aids may be fully satisfying to a judge attempting to understand the application of a statute. At this point, a judge may turn to some general rules regarding statutory interpretation.

Traditional Rules of Statutory Interpretation

1. Literal Rule (Plain or Ordinary Meaning Rule)

Under this rule, if the words in the legislation are clear and unambiguous, they must be given their ordinary meaning, and grammatical and normal punctuation rules apply. However, under this rule, the statute alone is the only thing that is to be considered, and no other context is permitted. If this is the case, a judge must apply the law as written, even if it results in an undesirable outcome. Under this rule, there is recognition that Parliament is given the task of legislating, and a judge cannot usurp that function even if the legislation is ambiguous (subject of course to the *Charter of Rights and Freedoms*, which will be discussed in later chapters). Judges must apply the ordinary meaning unless there is a valid reason to do otherwise. If the words are plain, no further inquiry is required. How far should the ordinary meaning of language be pushed? See the Food for Thought box.

FOOD FOR THOUGHT...

In the English case of *R v Harris* in 1836, Ms. Harris was charged with the stabbing, wounding, or cutting of another with a *weapon*. In fact, Ms. Harris bit off the nose of her victim and a police officer's finger. Under the definition of the statute she was charged under, "teeth" were not defined as a weapon. The defence argued that there was no weapon involved, and therefore no crime. Ms. Harris was acquitted.

This was a literal reading of the statute; there was no weapon, and therefore she could not be convicted, even though her acquittal was an undesirable result (for the prosecution). If Parliament had wanted to include someone's teeth in the definition of weapon, it would have done so.

Is this the right result?

Are you persuaded by the literal rule of statutory interpretation?

2. The Absurdity Rule (or the Golden Rule)

This perspective adds to the literal rule in that the normal meaning of the legislation should be used unless this reading would result in an absurdity. Thus, if good results come from the legislation, it is assumed to be part of the purpose of the act. However, if there are absurd or unacceptable results, a judge can assume that this was not the intention of the legislation. A judge is allowed to move from the literal meaning only as much as necessary to remove the conflict. This is a commonsense solution, but it does require a judge to believe there is an absurd result. What may be absurd to one judge may not be absurd to another. The case of *Skoke-Graham v R* (see the following case box) examines an absurdity.

SKOKE-GRAHAM v R, [1988] 1 SCR 513 (SCC)

A reading of legislation that would lead to an absurd result that is contrary to the public interest may be deemed unworkable. The court in *Skoke-Graham* had to determine if church members who deliberately violated church protocol by kneeling to receive communion actually committed a criminal act because s 172 (3) of the *Criminal Code* says it is an offence to: "willfully ... [do] anything that disturbs the order or solemnity of a religious meeting." Several members of the church were charged by the police.

When the court looked at the ordinary meaning of "anything that disturbs," it had to reject that ordinary meaning because it would have absurd consequences. If it said "anything" that disturbs would mean kneeling improperly, then all kinds of "trivial" matters "which would lead to such annoyance, anxiety or emotional upset would be caught by the provision: a man might be convicted under the section for failing to take his hat off in a church, or failing to keep it on in a synagogue." The Supreme Court found that this was clearly an absurd result to convict someone of a crime for not properly kneeling, or something as trivial as wearing (or not wearing) a hat; therefore, the absurd result should be avoided.

Do you think that it was (or should be) a criminal act to wilfully disrupt a religious ceremony in this way?

3. The "Mischief" or Purposive Analysis Rule

Through this technique, the court can seek the legislative purpose of the legislation. To do this, the court can look to the language of the act (perhaps in the **preamble** to the statute) or the Hansard or legislative committee reports. This rule is called the "mischief rule" because it looks to what the legislators were trying to cure to see how the act should be interpreted. The court can look to the reason for the legislation, and what it was trying to prevent.

Judges may also examine how the words in question were used in prior cases, and they may also ask what problem the common law failed to address and examine the need for the particular legislation and what it sought to prevent. The actual words of the legislation have relatively little importance in this perspective. However, many have criticized this rule because it assumes that there is no doubt about the purpose and intention of the legislation. In reality, that element may also be in doubt. This issue is being debated in New York City (see the Food for Thought box).

4. The Contextual Analysis Rule

The court may look not just at the section of the legislation in question, but the act as a whole, other legislation, and perhaps the social conditions surrounding the formation of the legislation. The judge must realize that the legislators had a goal and plan for the legislation, and that their words were selected purposively.

FOOD FOR THOUGHT...

Kyle Peterson, a unicyclist in New York City, filed a US$3 million lawsuit, saying that a ticket should not have been issued to him because the city ordinance he was charged under prevents any "two-or-three-wheeled device" on sidewalks. The cyclist argues that he had a one-wheeled device, which is not covered by the legislation. The city has sought to dismiss the suit because the unicyclist violated the intent of the legislation, which was to prevent pedestrians from being injured by fast-moving cyclists.[1] The city says that the difference between a bicycle and a unicycle is "negligible," and both should be prevented from harming pedestrians.[2]

Should the court look at the intent of the legislation, or was it very specific by saying that it was two or three-wheeled devices that the legislation was targeting?

Are fast-moving wheeled vehicles the "mischief" that the legislation was designed to avoid?

Mikael Damkier/Shutterstock

Is a unicycle allowed where bicycles are not?

5. The Plausible Meaning Rule

The court can depart from the ordinary meaning of a statute only if there is a more plausible meaning to the words. However, courts will be limited in determining what is plausible only with the language that is in the text. Judges will normally not be able to add or delete words or change the intent. The courts do have the ability to change drafting errors in legislation if they are confident about the intent of the drafters.

6. The Modern Rule of Interpretation

Finally, there is what has come to be known as the modern rule of interpretation. This rule takes on many of the characteristics of the other rules in one approach. The entire act is to be read grammatically and in an ordinary meaning, and the context of the legislation and the intent of Parliament are all to be taken into account. This includes the literal rule in that the plain meaning is to be examined, the mischief rule in that the purpose of the law is to be ascertained, the absurdity rule in the inclusion of context, and the possibility of drawing on the wider contextual analysis and the plausible meaning rules. It is still rather unclear which perspective should have priority, but there is room for all of these approaches.

It is important to remember that there is no hard-and-fast rule about which method of statutory interpretation is called for in the situation. These rules are not binding and constraining on judges, but rather are simply tools to be used in situations where the legislation is not as clear as it should be.

1. Natalie Fraser, "Unicyclist Fights Two-Wheel Rule" (10 June 2011) *Lawyers Weekly*, online: <http://www.lawyersweekly-digital.com/lawyersweekly/3106#pg15>.
2. Associated Press, "NYC to Fight Unicyclist Kyle Peterson's Lawsuit" (18 March 2011), CBS, online: <http://newyork.cbslocal.com/2011/03/18/nyc-to-fight-unicyclists-lawsuit>.

Case Law

> Some suppose that the lawyer's job is to learn as many long words as possible, preferably in Latin and Law French, so as to make himself incomprehensible. Presumably, the harder he is to understand the better he must be as a lawyer. Nothing could be further from the truth. The good lawyer expresses herself with clarity, simplicity and brevity.[3]

There is a real move in law to use more straightforward and simple language. The "wheretofore," "heretofore," and flowery language is largely a thing of the past. Judges attempt to have well-written decisions so that they can be followed in the future. However, case law needs to be distinguished from court transcripts. A transcript is a word-for-word account of what happened at trial, including all of the testimony of witnesses, questions by the judge, and so on. A written decision is much shorter and only discusses the judge's (or the panel of judges) conclusion and the rationale for reaching that conclusion. A judgment is what must be relied upon in the future. As discussed in Chapter 1, the common law system is built on previous cases, which are referred to as **case law**. But how does a judge come to the right decision in a case?

Oliver Wendell Holmes put the role of judges into a realistic perspective in *Southern Pacific Company v Jensen*, 244 US 205, 222 (1917), when he said that the "common law is not a brooding omnipresence in the sky." There is no magic to knowing what the "correct" decision is in any particular case. You cannot pluck the decision from some otherworldy place and fix all legal problems. Historically, some thought that the law would become more certain as judges filled in the holes between every case that could occur; this, of course, is just not practical. Cases are largely fact-specific, and the principles that they decide upon can be individual. However, each decided case forms a **precedent** to be followed in the future.

Stare Decisis, *Ratio Decidendi*, and *Obiter Dicta*

When a future judge is hearing a similar case to one that has already been decided, that judge may be bound to apply the same reasoning that was used in that earlier case. Later cases may also be used to explain or expand on the reasons from the first case in order to address the **case at hand**. The legal system relies on this reporting of decisions so precedent can be established.

This general reliance on decided cases is called ***stare decisis***, or to "stand by decided matters." This Latin term provides that courts are bound to follow precedent and to adhere to decided cases that have similar facts. This principle of our system allows stability, consistency, and predictability in matters that come before the court. This comes from the historic reasoning that a judge is not making new law when he or she decides a case, but discovering legal principles that had always existed. Once cases are treated alike, those in our society can make decisions about their own rights and obligations. This precedent is binding on all future judges providing for fairness and respect for the law. This expectation has become a fundamental part of our justice system.

However, there are ways that a judge can decide not to follow a precedent, and this is called **distinguishing the case**. A judge may find key differences in law, procedures, or in the facts of the case, suggesting that it should not be followed. Distinguishing a case is very much an art (again there is no right or wrong reason), but it can give flexibility to the system to circumvent a particular case if it is felt that it should not be binding. Finding a way around earlier cases can become a battle of the precedents, as each side might present 10 cases about why a certain principle applies, while the other side has 11 cases that show that another principle is really the one that should be followed. The court must look at the level of court in the precedent cases (being mindful of the hierarchy of the courts), and determine how persuasive the argument is about whether the principle applies or does not.

The value of a precedent case is not just who won or lost, but the reasons the judge decided the case in a particular way. This reason is formally called the ***ratio decidendi*** (*ratio*

3. SM Waddams, *Introduction to the Study of Law*, 7th ed (Toronto: Carswell 2010) at 37. Reprinted by permission of Carswell, a division of Thomson Reuters Canada Ltd.

WHAT IS AN EXAMPLE OF A *RATIO*?

The *ratio* of a case could be something short, as in the old English case of *Harmony Shipping Co SA v Davis,* [1979] 3 All ER 177 (CA), per Lord Denning, MR, that there is "no property in a witness." This means that you do not own a witness in a trial; therefore, either side can interview and call them to the witness stand. The *ratio* could also be something relying on a historic principle applied to a particular case, such as in *Montana Mustard Seed Co v Gates* [1963] SJ No 37 (Sask Ct QB): "it is interesting to observe that although many cases support the principle that an *agreement to agree* is not a contract, it is not the law that mere difficulty in establishing what is a reasonable price renders void what is otherwise a contract." The *ratio* of an "agreement to agree is not a contract" is applied to the next case with this particular issue.

for short), a Latin term that means "root of the decision." A student of law may read a case that is 50 pages long, but the root of the decision is one paragraph, or one sentence, or one phrase. A case usually summarizes the facts, sets out what reasoning the judge or judges used, and concludes with a decision. Only the *ratio* is binding on future courts; all of the other material in the case is just background. Other courts and lawyers may interpret what forms the *ratio*, and may interpret it in different ways. However, if a higher court overrules that *ratio,* that principle and case is no longer valid, as the other court may find that *ratio* was decided in error. For an example of a *ratio*, see the What is an example of a *ratio*? box.

However, in some cases at the appeal level, judges sit in panels of several judges. In these cases, different judges may come to the same conclusion, but for completely different reasons. In this case there might not be a single *ratio* for the case on which a precedent is built. Depending on the cases that come later, one judge's *ratio* may be more relevant than the other. The reputation of a judge may make one *ratio* carry more weight than the other, or there might not be a clear *ratio* at all. Finding the *ratio* is not a precise matter; judges will often not label their *ratio* with neon blinking lights. Finding the *ratio* is a subjective skill, and it will be improved only with practice.

However, as noted earlier, not everything that a judge says in a decision can be binding on future decisions. Although the *ratio* of a case is binding to cases in the future, everything else a judge says is called ***obiter dicta***, which is a Latin term that means "words in passing" (*dicta* for short, but many people shorten it to *obiter*). All of the other discussions in the case are not binding on future courts. Yet, for that next case that comes along, the *obiter* could be persuasive to future judges. Some Supreme Court *obiter* has been found to be binding on lower courts if it is relevant. In the case of *R v Sellars,*[1980] 1 SCR 527 (SCC), the Supreme Court found that *obiter* from the majority decision of the Supreme Court could be binding on lower courts, but only in rare situations.

It can be concluded that a decision by a judge really has two functions: (1) to decide that particular case and solve the dispute, and (2) to establish a legal principle for the future. As S M Waddams notes, "every decision is at once an application of the law and a contribution to the fabric of the law itself."[4]

It is important to note that the courts do sometimes make mistakes. However, decided cases cannot simply be reopened if there is an allegation that the wrong decision was made. The Latin term ***res judicata***, or "a matter adjudicated," is the goal of our system. We want individuals to have finality from the legal system. Once their matter has been heard and dealt with, that is the end. It is a difficult reality in our system that a litigant may lose a case but then another similar case goes to the Supreme Court the next day that says that the **authority** the first case was based on was wrong. That first party is still bound by that wrong decision; the first case is bound by that old case and cannot be re-opened on that ground.

There are many advantages to following precedent. The parties are given predictability and practicality, and the courts can deal with matters through incremental changes. However, there are several disadvantages to a case-based system, including rigidity. There is

4. SM Waddams, *Introduction to the Study of Law*, 7th ed (Toronto: Carswell 2010) at 86. Reprinted by permission of Carswell, a division of Thomson Reuters Canada Ltd.

also a danger in making illogical distinctions between cases, and the lawyers and judges may lose touch with the intention of the legislation. The Supreme Court does have the power to reverse its past decisions, but many say this is getting far too close to a legislative role. It is difficult for a judge to simply create a new legal principle; thus, the system is rather inflexible and slow to change. This leaves the responsibility to Parliament to be the source of new law through the members we have elected to represent our needs as citizens.

Law Reports

Quicklaw
http://www.lexisnexis.ca/en/quicklaw
Westlaw Canada
http://canada.westlaw.com/signon/default.wl?vr=2.0&fn=_top&rs=WLCA12.01&bhcp=1

Although historically lawyers and clerks went to court to write down what a judge said from the bench, we now have all sorts of ways to see what a judge decided in a case. There are now many electronic sources to search exactly what a judgment said, including services like LexisNexis Quicklaw, and Westlaw. These services are often available through university library systems.

A case report should be a discussion of what the judge was thinking as he or she came to a decision. Sometimes reports use headings that you can easily follow, but sometimes (sadly) the reasoning can be almost incomprehensible. These decisions written down by judges are published in books called "case reporters" or just "reporters." Not all decisions are published; only those that have a significant impact on future cases will be published in this way. Reporters can have different focuses. The *Supreme Court Reports* (SCR) publishes important cases from the Supreme Court of Canada; the *Dominion Law Reports* (DLR) publishes all sorts of cases of interest from the Supreme Court, courts of appeal, and some lower courts. Other reporters publish material from a particular province, like the *Ontario Reports* (OR); particular areas, such as the *Western Weekly Reports* (WWR); or in particular subject areas, such as the *Canadian Criminal Cases* (CCC), which only publishes cases in criminal law.

The editors of these journals decide what cases to publish, and then they write a **headnote**. A headnote is helpful because it is a summary of the facts, the issues, and the decision in the case. However, it is extremely important to remember that the judge in the case did *not* write this material—this is only what the editor of the particular reporter thought was relevant. This information can be misleading or simply incorrect. One must always verify that what is in the headnote is actually reflected in the case. However, this material is under copyright, and must be cited appropriately like the rest of the case. A student may believe that the *ratio* is properly stated in the headnote, but one must check the case to ensure that the *ratio* is properly reported, or found at all in the headnote.

CanIII
http://www.canlii.org

Every case **citation** tells you important information and exactly where you can find a case. In a citation such as *R v McCraw,* [1991] 3 SCR 72 (SCC), you know many things about this case. First, it is a criminal case because it begins with "*R*" for Regina or Rex (the Queen or King), so the state is one of the parties. Next, it was decided in 1991, and you can find this case in the third volume of the 1991 book of the SCR's, or the *Supreme Court Reports.* You could go to a law library, find the *Supreme Court Reports*, pull out the third volume of 1991, and turn to page 72, and you will find that exact case.

Most cases are reported online, including the free service of CanLII, which provides the full text of cases for free in a searchable form. Note that there are similar sites for other countries.

iQoncept/Shutterstock

Search for the relevant facts within a case.

Format of a Written Case

There are many elements to a written case. Figure 3.6 is a line-by-line breakdown of how to read a case.

The Case Brief

A fundamental way to read cases and remember the important information is to create a case brief. The purpose of a student case brief is to summarize a case in order to identify the parties, issues, and the legal reasoning used. Briefing a case breaks it down to the component parts and analyzes them in order to understand the case. In practice, this helps you understand the cases that are important precedents for those that follow, and how that might apply to future cases.

Figure 3.6 Reading a Case

Stergios v Kim

Between
Shaun James Stergios, Applicant, and Eun Ju Kim, Respondent

[2010] OJ No. 3299
2010 ONSC 4195
Court File No. 20169-04
Ontario Superior Court of Justice

CF Graham J.

Heard: October 23, 2008; January 12–15, 20, 22, and July 2–3, 2009
Judgment: July 28, 2010

(355 paras)

Family law – Maintenance and support – spousal support – considerations – agreement – enrichment and corresponding impoverishment – economic disadvantage of marriage Quantum – Duration of Marriage – Payor's annual income – order – time-limited – Amount award – Periodic monthly award – motion by Kim, the respondent, for spousal support allowed.

Motion by Kim, the respondent, for an order for spousal support. Kim was born and raised in South Korea. Stergios was born and raised in Canada. The parties married in South Korea in 2000 and separated in 2004. There were no children of the marriage. Kim postponed her acceptance into a joint Med/PhD programme as a result of Stergios' unexpected proposal of marriage and his promise that he would support Kim while she finished her studies in Canada.

HELD: Motion allowed. As a result of her reliance on the promises made by Stergios, Kim suffered significant economic disadvantages while Stergios enjoyed significant economic advantages from the marriage. Kim also suffered economic disadvantages and hardship as a result of the marriage's breakdown. Furthermore, Kim required assistance from Stergios in order to achieve economic self-sufficiency.

Statutes, Regulations and Rules Cited: *Divorce Act*, RSC 1985, c 3 (2nd Supp), s 15.2, 15.2(4), s 15.2(5), s 15.2(6) *Immigratio*n Act, RSC 1985, c I-2, Spousal Support Advisory Guidelines.

Counsel: Andrea Di Batista, for the Applicant; Kevin S Dunsmuir for the Respondent.

REASONS FOR JUDGMENT

CF Graham J

Introduction

1 Ms. Kim was born and raised in South Korea. All of her family live there. Mr. Stergios was born and raised in Canada.

2 Mr. Stergios and Ms. Kim were married in South Korea in 2000. He was 28 and she was 27. They separated in 2004. They have no children.

3 Ms. Kim seeks an order for spousal support, commencing on the date of separation to allow her to pursue further education, a career, and a life in Canada.

4 Mr. Stergios submits that Ms. Kim is not entitled to spousal support and that she should return to South Korea where she can pursue further education, a career, and a life.

5 Mr. Stergois submits that the monies he paid to Ms. Kim from January 1, 2006 until May of 2007 pursuant to a without prejudice temporary consent order for spousal support should be returned.

Style of Cause
Parties
Citation
Court File Number
Court
Judge
Trial
Decision
Length of Decision
Keywords
Headnote
Judgment
Authorities
Lawyers
Decision
Judge
Reasons

The case name is always written in italics separated by a "v," which is the short form of the Latin word "versus," meaning "against." However, when reading a case name out loud, it will be "Stergios AND Kim."

The parties in a civil action are referred to as the Plaintiff, which is often indicated with the Greek symbol π, and the Defendant, which is represented with the symbol Δ. In a civil law case, the Plaintiff's name comes first, and the Defendant's name comes last. If there are many parties, the first party will be named, but the rest of the parties will be noted with the abbreviation "et al" which is the Latin phrase for "and others." The parties here are the "Applicant" and "Respondent" because this is an appeal of a motion.

Break down the citation—2010 is the year that the judgment came out, OJ is Ontario Journal at page 3299. This next citation is called a "neutral citation," which does not refer to a specific reporter but to a neutral location where this case can be looked up online.

This is the number used to find the case in the court system at the court house where the trial was held.

The court can be in a short form, and this will be seen after citations. For example, this court will be Ont SCJ in short form. Other common courts are the Supreme Court of Canada, or SCC.

Court of Appeal and Supreme Court of Canada cases will have multiple judges listed. There may be a majority decision, minority, and a concurring reason.

A trial may occur over several dates, and the judgment may not come out for several months after those hearing dates. If this is a Court of Appeal or Supreme Court of Canada decision it will say the history of the case: "On Appeal from the Court of Appeal for British Columbia" etc.

The date of judgment is the most important date.

You will refer to citations in the case by paragraph number so the reader can pinpoint your reference.

Keywords provide a summary of the issues in the case. This is a family law case about spousal support. These keywords will provide searchable terms electronically.

This is a brief summary of the case. Do not simply rely on the headnote as it could give you incorrect information.

This is the headnote of the decision in the case; Kim was to receive spousal support because of her disadvantages as part of her marriage. In an upper level court there might be summaries of the majority decision, minority decision(s) and concurring decisions.

This is the legislation that the court relied on, including the *Divorce Act*. The judge may also list academic articles that they might have referred to, or previous cases.

The names of the lawyers and who they represent. Depending on which party appeals, the parties are referred to as the Applicant—the person who appeals—and the Respondent who responds to the appeal.

Look through the entire decision to see what part of the text is the majority decision, and what might be a minority decision. A separate decision will be a judge's name (Per Fish J.) and then the text of their opinion. Only the majority decision is important for the outcome of that particular case, but the minority might be used in the future.

Source: *Stergios v Kim*, 2010 ONSC 4195 (CanLII), <http://canlii.ca/t/2bx88> retrieved on 2012-03-09.

Tips to Briefing a Case

It is important to know the court structure and where this case fits within the hierarchy. A good way to do this is to make a chronology of the case. Is this the court of first instance? Appeal court? The Supreme Court of Canada? What was the decision at the lower courts? Then make a list of the parties. Identify the plaintiff/defendant, appellant/respondent, and so forth. Are there multiple decisions? Which judges wrote the majority, minority, or concurring decisions? Is there something important in a minority opinion?

Next, read the case more than once. Sort out the facts and determine if the parties are disputing not only the law but the facts as well. Determine the relevant *essential* facts. If the fact that one of the parties had a mental disorder is not relevant to the ultimate decision of the court, it should not be mentioned in the brief. What are the legal issues? If you can find the conclusion to the issue, you might find the *ratio*. What is the reasoning used? Did the judge focus in on one specific element, or did the judge decide on several different issues? Are there *obiter dicta* worth mentioning? Is there something important in there that might relate to future cases? Are there flaws or gaps in the reasoning? Are there things that the judges have missed?

THE ROLE OF LEGISLATION AND CASE LAW IN A JUDICIAL DECISION—SUMMARY

It is important to remember that there is a partnership between case law and legislation. If a statute is introduced that does not follow previous case law, the statute overrules the old case law. However, case law regularly interprets legislation, giving meaning and correcting any mistakes. At sometimes case law can change the applicability of statute law and continue to evolve with the times, but there is always the option of legislators to introduce new statutes if the courts are taking the law in a direction that they do not intend.

So, judges are tasked with weighing evidence, following procedural rules, and pointing to the law they are following. Notably, judges must consider these questions:

1. *Is there a statute that applies?* If yes, apply it with the plain meaning, and then add other statutory interpretation tools (absurdity rule, etc.) if need be.
2. *Is there a case that addresses this situation?* If yes, apply that case. However, can those cases be distinguished from the case at hand? Are the facts materially different from the case at hand? What will be the impact of establishing this principle as precedent?

CIVIL LITIGATION AND THE TRIAL PROCESS

> *"Procedural regulations are the door, and the only door, to make real what is laid down by substantive law."*[5]

Introduction

It is important for any student of legal studies to have a preliminary understanding of the procedural elements of a civil law matter. The rules of civil procedure can be important not only in the province where you practise, but also when you are dealing with a matter that might involve a defendant in Manitoba, and a plaintiff in Saskatchewan. The rules of each particular province can be important. In addition, it is important that a student know that there are limitations on the time periods in which you can sue another person. If you are outside of the time limitations, you may lose your right to sue another party forever. A study of Ontarians who used civil legal services found a variety of matters where individuals may seek the help of a lawyer (see Table 3.2).

5. Karl Llewellyn, *The Bramble Bush* (New York: Oceana, 1960) at 17.

Table 3.2 Types of Legal Problems in Ontario, June 2009

	Total Sample %	Had Legal Problem %
Family relationship problems	12	30
Wills and powers of attorney problems	5	13
Housing or land problems	4	10
Real estate transactions	4	9
Employment problems	4	9
Criminal problems	3	9
Personal injury problems	3	7
Money or debt problems	2	5
Legal action problems	1	3
Neighbourhood problems/property damage	1	3
Traffic/speeding offences/violations/tickets	1	3
Disability-related issues	1	2
Consumer problems	1	2
Immigration problems	1	2
Small or personal business issues	1	2
Discrimination/harassment problems	1	2
Welfare or social assistance problems	1	1
Hospital treatment or release problems	*	1
Treatment by police	–	–
Other	3	8
None	62	1
Don't know/not applicable	*	*

* less than 1 percent

Source: The survey results titled *Types of Legal Problems – June 2009*, found at page 21 of the document titled *Listening to Ontarians, the 2010 Report of the Ontario Civil Legal Needs Project*, located on the Law Society's website at <http://www.lsuc.on.ca/media/may3110_oclnreport_final.pdf.> © Copyright 2010 Joint: The Law Society of Upper Canada, Legal Aid Ontario & Pro Bono Law Ontario. All Rights Reserved. Reproduced with permission of the copyright holders.

When a potential client comes to a lawyer, a good lawyer will not automatically start a civil action, but will explore the problem with the client. Civil actions are time-consuming, emotionally draining, and financially costly. Lawyers will usually first explore the possibility of settling out of court with the other party. They may send a letter on behalf of the client to see if the other side would be willing to negotiate. This could lead to what is called an **out of court settlement**. The parties may agree to divide the **damages**—drop some of the elements and negotiate with others. As will be discussed, about 90–99 percent of cases (depending on the type of civil law) end in **default judgment**, **settlement**, **abandonment**, or **diversion** to alternative dispute resolution (ADR; which will be examined in Chapter 12), without ever getting to trial.[6]

6. Lori Hausegger, Matthew Hennigar, and Troy Riddell, *Canadian Courts: Law, Politics and Process* (Don Mills, ON: Oxford, 2009) at 334.

However, if this settlement is unsuccessful, the lawyer must also determine if the client has a **cause of action**. This means that a person must have an established right to use the civil law court system, and the lawyer can guide the client into the part of the system the client should proceed in (e.g., if the amount of money sought is less than $25 000, litigants in Ontario must proceed in the small claims system, which is described later in this chapter).

The lawyer will usually give an opinion to the client on the likelihood of success in court. The lawyer will review with the client whether he or she believes that the client's version of the facts will be accepted, how much the client might expect to recover, and how much the client may be liable to pay in costs. Also, a client must be made to understand that even if he or she wins the case against the other party, that party may try to hide assets to prevent the client from collecting the money that is owed.

In addition, the civil law system is set up to screen out cases and to discourage them from going forward by helping or forcing plaintiffs and defendants to settle. Some provinces, such as Ontario, have instituted a **mandatory mediation** process before the case can proceed to determine whether or not there is a possibility of settling the dispute rather than taking the case to trial.

Once an individual decides to proceed with the formal process of **litigation**, he or she is regulated by a complex series of rules about how to act within the system. Although each province is a little different, the Ontario system will be the focus of this section of the text.[7] In Ontario, lawyers are governed by the *Courts of Justice Act,* RSO 1990, Chapter c 43, and the regulations under the *Rules of Civil Procedure* (RCP) RRO 1990, Regulation 194. The process of litigation is governed and regulated by procedural law that outlines the various steps that each side must take before moving to the next stage of the process.

Most small claims courts have their own rules, as do family law courts, and courts of appeal. In Ontario, these rules are all within the *Courts of Justice Act*. Most civil cases require the services of a lawyer who has familiarity with the legal procedures and knows how to fill in the required paperwork and make the appropriate **motions** and requests.

Before starting an action, a lawyer also has to ensure that the parties have **standing,** which is an important part of the process. Generally, if you are hit by a car, you are directly related to the injury, and you may personally sue in court. If there was a car accident down the street where you were headed, but you did not see the accident, you cannot go to the court and sue that driver of the car. To have standing to sue in civil law, you must have a particular kind of relationship to the facts of the case. This may include a spouse, child, or parent of the person who has been injured or wronged. You may also have standing if you were a witness or have some other personal stake in the action. A person may also have third-party standing in order to protect the rights of others (like a child or injured person) who may not be able to represent themselves.

There are four main stages in litigation: (1) pleadings, (2) pre-trial, (3) trial, and (4) post-trial.

Pleadings

The first step in an action is filing the **pleadings** with the court. This step is often called filing the **originating process**, and simply refers to the beginning of the paperwork. In Ontario, an action is started by filing a **notice of action** (some provinces have a writ of summons) that informs the defendant that an action has been started. With this document, you are telling the other side that you are going to sue them in court, and it provides a brief summary with enough detail so that the defendant knows what is being alleged against him or her. This puts the other party on notice that there will only be a certain period of time to defend him- or herself from this action.

7. *Alberta Rules of Court,* Alta Reg 390/1968, *British Columbia and Yukon, Rules of Court,* BC Reg 221/90; *Manitoba, Court of Queen's Bench Rules,* Man Reg 553/88; *New Brunswick, Rules of Court,* NB Reg 82–73; *Newfoundland and Labrador, Rules of the Supreme Court,* SNL 1986, c 42, Sch DR; *Northwest Territories and Nunavut, Rules of the Supreme Court,* NWT Reg 010-96; *Nova Scotia, Judicature Act,* RSNS 1989, c 240; *Civil Procedure Rules,* R 20.03, 20.04 and 20.05; *Prince Edward Island, Supreme Court Act,* RSPEI 1988, c S-10, *Rules of Civil Procedure; Saskatchewan, Queen's Bench Act,* RSS 1978, c Q-1, *Queen's Bench Rules, R 214; Quebec, Code of Civil Procedure,* RSQ c C-25.

The notice is filed by the plaintiff and is taken to a court to register (this starts the action), where a fee is paid and the **seal** of the court is affixed to make it an official court document. This is called **issuing** the document. The person who filed the documents keeps the original document, and a copy goes to the court file.

The plaintiff must **serve** the notice of action on the defendant in person (or to the corporation office) or by mail. There are precise rules of service to make sure that all the parties have received all the documents, and one must be able to prove that the other party was given all material. There are special ways the plaintiff has to serve the defendant so to be sure that the defendant has received it, and many documents must be served through **personal service,** where the document is given directly to the person being served, or an agent, director, or officer of a corporation if a business is being served.

Lawyers may retain "process servers," whose job it is to go find the individual and hand him or her the documents. If a party's lawyer is known, documents can be left with the lawyer, or, in some cases, the documents may be sent to the last known address, or to that person's place of residence. Whatever way the documents are sent, the person sending them out must file an **affidavit of service** with the court house. This affidavit must state the person's name and information, the day and time when the materials were sent, and this document is sworn to be true. The defendant is given a specified time period to respond to the action or the plaintiff can go to court to seek a **default judgment**.

Now that the defendant has been put on notice, under s 14.01 (3) of the RCP, the plaintiff must make a **statement of claim** that outlines his or her allegations and damages, which must be filed within 30 days of issuing the notice of action. This is an official notice of all of the details of the action, and the defendant must respond to this statement of claim. The statement of claim is *not* an argument about the facts of the case, but instead it is a broad statement of the alleged harm caused by the defendant, and includes the dollar amounts being demanded as damages. It has an introduction that states the parties that are involved, the material facts, and the place of the trial proposed by the plaintiff (see the box entitled "What Does a Statement of Claim Look Like?").

The defendant has options on how to respond to the statement of claim. The defendant may either pay the amount in the statement of claim, do nothing (which may have severe consequences), or defend the action. If the defendant wishes to dispute the claim, the defendant prepares a **statement of defence** and files it with the court registry, and this time a copy is served on the plaintiff. The defendant must respond to each of the plaintiff's allegations. In the statement of defence, the defendant can either

WHAT DOES A STATEMENT OF CLAIM LOOK LIKE?

After the standard formatting at the beginning and ending of a statement of claim, most statements look similar. The statement of claim must state the full name of the parties, their addresses, and the names of their lawyers (if known). Each of the paragraphs is numbered for easy reference. The following fictitious statement of claim is based on the following facts.

A client comes to your firm, where you are a successful up-and-coming junior lawyer. Her name is Serena Van der Woodsen, and she wants to sue the defendant, a personal investigator named Chuck Bass, for a home invasion. Serena says that Chuck damaged her property when he broke into her house, and she wants to sue Chuck in civil law for damages in the form of money for the loss of her property. She tells you that she called the police when this happened, and the police identified Chuck as the party responsible for being in Serena's house. You inform Serena that she may start an action against Chuck in the civil law system. You draft a statement of claim for Serena. A statement of claim begins with what damages are requested. See Figure 3.7.

Figure 3.7 Statement of Claim

FORM 14A
Courts of Justice Act
STATEMENT OF CLAIM (GENERAL)

(*Court seal*)

STATEMENT OF CLAIM

TO THE DEFENDANT

A LEGAL PROCEEDING HAS BEEN COMMENCED AGAINST YOU by the plaintiff. The claim made against you is set out in the following pages.

IF YOU WISH TO DEFEND THIS PROCEEDING, you or an Ontario lawyer acting for you must prepare a statement of defence in Form 18A prescribed by the Rules of Civil Procedure, serve it on the plaintiff's lawyer or, where the plaintiff does not have a lawyer, serve it on the plaintiff, and file it, with proof of service in this court office, WITHIN TWENTY DAYS after this statement of claim is served on you, if you are served in Ontario.

If you are served in another province or territory of Canada or in the United States of America, the period for serving and filing your statement of defence is forty days. If you are served outside Canada and the United States of America, the period is sixty days.

Instead of serving and filing a statement of defence, you may serve and file a notice of intent to defend in Form 18B prescribed by the Rules of Civil Procedure. This will entitle you to ten more days within which to serve and file your statement of defence.

IF YOU FAIL TO DEFEND THIS PROCEEDING, JUDGMENT MAY BE GIVEN AGAINST YOU IN YOUR ABSENCE AND WITHOUT FURTHER NOTICE TO YOU. IF YOU WISH TO DEFEND THIS PROCEEDING BUT ARE UNABLE TO PAY LEGAL FEES, LEGAL AID MAY BE AVAILABLE TO YOU BY CONTACTING A LOCAL LEGAL AID OFFICE.

(*Where the claim made is for money only, include the following:*)

IF YOU PAY THE PLAINTIFF'S CLAIM, and $__________ for costs, within the time for serving and filing your statement of defence you may move to have this proceeding dismissed by the court. If you believe the amount claimed for costs is excessive, you may pay the plaintiff's claim and $400 for costs and have the costs assessed by the court.

Date ____________________

Issued by ____________________
Local registrar
Address of
court office ____________________
____

TO (*Name and address of each defendant*)

CLAIM

1. The Plaintiff, Serena Van der Woodsen ("Van der Woodsen") claims damages from the Defendant, Chuck Bass ("Bass") as follows:
   (a) General damages in the amount of $50 000.00;
   (b) Special Damages in the amount of $9500.00;
   (c) Exemplary and punitive damages in the amount of $50 000.00;
   (d) Pre- and post-judgment interest; and
   (e) The costs of this action on a substantial indemnity basis.

(*continued*)

Figure 3.7 Statement of Claim (*continued*)

2. At all material times, the Plaintiff was a homeowner residing in the property municipally known as 190 Blackacre Avenue, Waterloo, Ontario Canada.
3. At all material times, the Defendant was a resident of Kitchener Ontario Canada and was unknown to the Plaintiff.
4. On or about July 13, 2011, at approximately 11:45 a.m., the Defendant entered the home of the Plaintiff while she was at the home. His unauthorized entry constituted break-and-enter, contrary to section 348 of the *Criminal Code of Canada.* The Defendant had no colour of right to enter the home, nor to handle any of the furnishings found in the home. Despite this, the Defendant damaged a vase. The details of how the vase was damaged are best known to the Defendant. The replacement cost of the vase, which was a Louis XIV antique, was $7500.
5. As a consequence of the Defendant's trespass, the Plaintiff suffered severe emotional trauma, treatment of which required psychotherapy and other counselling services. Some of these treatments are not covered by the Plaintiff's provincial health insurance, and was paid by the Plaintiff personally. The cost of these out-of-pocket expenses totalled $2000.
6. The Plaintiff Van der Woodsen further claims general damages for pain and suffering in the amount of $50 000.
7. The unlawful actions of the Defendant were so egregious as to be "reprehensible and malicious." Accordingly, the Plaintiff is seeking an award of $50 000 in exemplary and punitive damages.
8. Should a trial of this action be necessary, the Plaintiffs ask that it take place in Kitchener, Ontario, Canada.

(*Date of issue*) (*Name, address and telephone number of lawyer or plaintiff*)

RCP-E xxA (July 1, 20xx)

admit that the allegation(s) are true (usually the obvious truths in the statement); deny the allegations, which puts the facts in issue that must be proven at trial; state that the defendant lacks the knowledge on a particular allegation, which again the plaintiff will have to prove; or the defendant can give his or her own version of the facts, but not arguments. If there was a defence to the statement of claim on page 75–76, what would it look like? See Figure 3.8.

Often, the defendant will make a **counterclaim** against the plaintiff, saying that there is actually a claim against the plaintiff (e.g., Chuck could sue for the injuries he suffered when Serena threw the vase at him). The plaintiff will now have to respond to this counterclaim. This document can be defended by the plaintiff. The defendant may also bring what is called a **third-party claim,** saying that there are additional parties who should be added to the suit. In cases where there are two or more defendants, the defendants can claim against each other in what is called a **crossclaim.** Each of these claims needs its own pleadings, which need to be filed, issued, and served on the other parties.

If the defendant does not respond, the plaintiff can ask the court for a default judgment, saying that if the defendant did not bother to respond and the plaintiff's entire claim must be true. Therefore, the plaintiff wins the action, receives the amount of money requested, and gets any related costs. Lawyers are typically involved in these proceedings and may request further information from either party. Lawyers may also engage in pretrial motions to dismiss the proceedings or ask for a change of venue. At one time, the pleadings had to be perfect or they would be dismissed, but today judges have the power to amend pleadings if it is fair to the parties.

Figure 3.8 What Does a Statement of Defence Look Like?

FORM 18A

Courts of Justice Act

STATEMENT OF DEFENCE

(*General heading*)

STATEMENT OF DEFENCE

1. The Defendant admits the allegations contained in paragraphs 3, 4 (to the extent that he was present on the property in question on the day in question, and to the extent that he saw the vase).
2. The Defendant denies the allegations contained in paragraphs 1, 4 (to the extent that he knowingly committed a break-and-enter, that he had no colour of right to enter the home, that he damaged her vase) of the statement of claim and puts the Plaintiff to the strict proof thereof.
3. The Defendant has no knowledge of the allegations listed in paragraphs 2, 4 (to the value of the vase set), 5 (to the extent of the Plaintiff's injuries, if any), 6 and 7.
4. At all material times, the Defendant was employed as a private investigator, and was licensed in that field. The Defendant pleads and relies on the *Private Security and Investigative Services Act,* SO 2005, c 34.
5. In July 2011, the Defendant was retained to seize a missing vase that had been stolen from the Royal Ontario Museum ("the ROM") in Toronto, Ontario.
6. After completing a thorough investigation, the Defendant arrived at the conclusion that the vase in question was the property of the ROM, and the Plaintiff had no colour or right to the property, but the vase was in the care of the Plaintiff at her home.
7. Relying on the statutory and common law authority, the Defendant took steps to lawfully repossess the vase by entering the Plaintiff's residence to reclaim the property.
8. On or about July 13, 2011, the Defendant entered the Plaintiff's home and found the Plaintiff there. The Defendant identified himself as a private investigator working for the ROM, and announced that she was in possession of the stolen property, and that by right of statute he was repossessing the vase.
9. Rather than accede to the Defendant's lawful request, the Plaintiff became violent and attempted to injure the Defendant. Fearing for his safety, the Defendant fled, despite which the Plaintiff continued to follow him and threw the vase at the Defendant. This act of the Plaintiff resulted in the harm to the vase in question.
10. The Defendant states that the Plaintiff's losses and/or injuries (which are not admitted but expressly denied) are exaggerated and excessive. Additionally, or in the alternative, they were preventable by the Plaintiff, and/or the Plaintiff could have taken steps to mitigate her losses or injuries.
11. The Defendant states that his actions were lawful in his role as private investigator, and by statute.
12. The Defendant asks that the Plaintiff's claim be dismissed with costs.

(*Date*) (*Name, address and telephone number of defendant's solicitor or defendant*)

TO (*Name and address of plaintiff's solicitor or plaintiff*)

RCP-E xxA (November 1, 20xx)

It is important to remember that the vast majority of actions that are in the pleadings stage never go to trial. Hausegger and her colleagues have noted that in a study in Ontario since 1978, only 1 to 9 percent of the actions started actually go to trial each year.[8] It is a main goal of the civil system to allow for resolution of cases before they get to trial. This can happen because the parties negotiate a settlement because the action is allowed to lapse due to inaction, or because something goes wrong at some stage in the process.

8. Lori Hausegger, Matthew Hennigar, and Troy Riddell, *Canadian Courts: Law, Politics and Process.* (Don Mills, ON: Oxford, 2009) at 323.

Discovery

One objective in the early stages of civil litigation is to uncover as much information as possible before the case comes to trial. This means that the factual and legal issues must be identified and both sides need to be fully informed and prepared in advance of the trial. Each side delivers to the other an **affidavit of documents**, and each side can request to view any or all of these documents that the other side has in its possession. This includes all documents, whether they are helpful or harmful.

Examination for discovery is usually the term used for the process that allows the parties to gather information before trial but after all pleadings have been submitted. The party may be required to go to a place where the party's answers can be recorded at a specific time and place. The process involves testimony under **oath** or **affirmation** of both parties by the lawyers for the plaintiff and the defendant. All evidence and allegations are disclosed to the other side before the trial begins and to ensure that there are no surprises in court. These proceedings are transcribed by a court reporter and become part of the evidence at trial. Having this process of question and answer outside of trial allows for the reduction of court time, money spent, and sometimes allows for settlement when the parties see all of the evidence that may be for or against them.

The questions asked of the parties at discovery are detailed and specific, and may refer to specific documents. These documents must be made available to the other party. Lawyers can object to certain lines of questioning of their clients if they are not relevant to the issue. Generally, lawyers allow each other broad leeway in the questioning of their clients. A lawyer can give an **undertaking** about additional documents or recollections of the client. If a lawyer is unsure whether the client will be able to produce additional documents, the lawyer may tell the other side that the lawyer will take it under **advisement** in order to investigate the matter with the client or others. Originals of documents can be viewed by one lawyer in the office of the other, and physical objects can be inspected. Photographs, X-rays, and medical material may be made available at this time, and a party can be made to submit to medical examinations to determine injuries.

If an answer that a party gives at trial is different from the answer that that party gave at the discovery, the transcript of that answer will be read to the court show that the party may be untrustworthy because that person has given different answers at different times.

Pre-Trial Procedures and Conferences

If discovery is complete and the parties still cannot settle the matter, the plaintiff or the defendant can **set down the matter for trial** by filing a **trial record** with the court. Parties are also subject to a **pre-trial conference,** which is the last step before trial. The lawyers and often the plaintiff and the defendant informally (although sometimes it may be more formal) meet with a judge, who does not actually hear the trial, to explain why a settlement cannot be reached. This often occurs in the judge's **chambers**. Judges will question the merits of the case, point out weaknesses, and may pressure both sides to come to an agreement. If no settlement is reached, officials at the court house will put the case on the list to go to trial. There may be a significant wait to get to trial when a judge and courtroom are available.

Pre-trial conferences are a tool used to discourage people from proceeding with the court case and encourage settlement, but it may be dependent on the judge that is hearing the material at the pre-trial. Some judges are proactive in encouraging settlement, and other judges are not motivated to bring the parties together in resolving the issues. However, the parties may take these pre-trials seriously because a judge is telling them that their case may not have any chance of success. Jurisdictions like Toronto, Ottawa, and Windsor are increasingly requiring **mediation** for some disputes, and this might be a continuing trend in the future.

The Trial

The lawyers for the parties start the trial with an **opening statement,** where the case is summarized. The civil trial is similar to criminal trials, with both the plaintiff and defendant testifying under oath and being **examined in chief** and **cross-examined** on the **witness stand.** Civil cases are largely heard by a judge without a jury. According to the RCP, there are strict rules of evidence to be followed in the course of a civil law trial. All of the testimony is recorded by a court reporter, or by electronic recording methods. Both sides will have an opportunity to make a **closing statement** about their version of the facts.

At the end of the trial, the judge and/or jury comes to a **verdict**. The judge makes a determination based on the **balance of probabilities** and usually sums up his or her argument in writing and releases the judgment a few days, weeks, or months later, which is called a reserved judgment. The offending party is found **liable** or not legally responsible (not guilty or not guilty as in a criminal trial). It is important to realize that in one case, the accused in a criminal trial could be found not guilty, but could be found liable on the same facts in a civil matter (O.J. Simpson is an American example of this situation. Mr. Simpson was acquitted of all criminal charges proven on a standard of beyond a reasonable doubt related to the murder of his ex-wife and her friend, but he was later found civilly responsible to the families for their deaths. See Chapter 9 for more details on the criminal standard.) The plaintiff has the **burden** of proving that the judge and/or jury should accept the plaintiff's version of what happened.

There is some question about the actual time of a case from beginning to end, but most wait times before trial are approximately two years, although a small percentage are still not resolved after five years.[9]

Civil Juries

Although much is written on the criminal law jury system, very little is said about civil juries. Section 108 (1) of the Ontario *Courts of Justice Act* provides that in "an action in the Superior Court of Justice that is not in the Small Claims Court, a party may require that the issues of fact be tried or the damages assessed, or both, by a jury, unless otherwise provided." This right to have a civil matter heard by a jury dates to back before Confederation. In Ontario, juries were mandatory in civil actions, but many believed they were being abused, because sheriffs had control over the juror rolls and could stack the jury in favour of one of the parties. After reforms in 1868, civil actions were to be heard only by a judge unless one of the parties requested a jury.[10]

Today in Ontario, juries are selected according to the *Juries Act* RSO 1990, c C.43. According to s 2, everyone is eligible to sit on a civil jury in the Superior Court of Justice in the county where they reside if the individual:

(a) resides in Ontario;
(b) is a Canadian citizen; and
(c) is at least 18 years old in the year prior to being selected.

Civil law juries are composed of six to eight members (unlike the 12 members in a criminal trial) and a decision can be made with a majority of the civil jury. Each province has different rules, but in British Columbia, s 22 of the *Jury Act,* RSBC 2006, c 242, provides that

> (1) If a jury does not reach a unanimous verdict within 3 hours from the time it retired to consider its verdict, the judge of the court may receive the verdict of 75% of those jurors.
> (2) A verdict under subsection (1) is as binding in all respects and has the same effect as if it had been the unanimous verdict of the full jury.

9. Lori Hausegger, Matthew Hennigar, and Troy Riddell *Canadian Courts: Law, Politics, and Process* (Don Mills, ON: Oxford, 2009), at 336.

10. WA Bogart, "'Guardian of Civil Rights ... Medieval Relic': The Civil Jury in Canada," 62 *Law and Contemporary Problems* 305.

Some individuals are ineligible to serve as jurors. In Ontario under s 3 and s 4 of the *Juries Act* RSO 1990, c C.43, certain groups are not permitted to sit on a jury, including:

- members of the Privy Council of Canada or the Executive Council of Ontario;
- members of the Senate, the House of Commons of Canada or the Assembly;
- judges and justices of the peace;
- barristers and solicitors and students-at-law;
- medical practitioners, veterinary surgeons, and coroners;
- law enforcement, including sheriffs; wardens; superintendents; jailers or keepers of prisons, correctional institutions, or lockups; sheriff's officers; police officers; firefighters who are regularly employed by a fire department; and officers of a court of justice;
- those who have a physical or mental disability that would seriously impair their ability to complete the duties of a juror; and
- those who have been convicted of an indictable offence, unless they have subsequently been granted a pardon.

Civil juries are also not available in some types of actions. In Ontario, civil juries are prohibited under the *Courts of Justice Act*, RSO 1990, Chapter C.43, s 108, including:

- injunctions or mandatory orders;
- partition or sale of real property;
- dissolution of a partnership or taking of partnership or other accounts;
- foreclosure or redemption of a mortgage;
- sale and distribution of the proceeds of property subject to any lien or charge;
- some trusts law;
- some actions including deeds;
- specific performance of a contract;
- declaratory relief; and
- other equitable relief and actions against a municipality.

Civil juries are dealt with differently depending on the province. In Quebec, civil juries are prohibited, Alberta and Saskatchewan allow civil juries for cases above a certain amount of money, and Ontario and British Columbia seem to be the provinces that most allow these forms of trial, but there are a significant number of excluded actions as noted.[11]

A review of the civil jury system done in Ontario in 2007 found that in "2005–2006, there were 6,839 civil trials heard. Of these trials heard, 1,598 or 23% were jury trials. The vast majority of these jury trials involved litigation arising from motor vehicle accidents (1,186 or 74% of civil jury trials heard)."[12] Most of the civil juries that are formed are in Ontario, but still few trials are being heard this way, and judges are often limiting their use in trials involving smaller amounts of money.

Some suggest that civil juries should be abolished, but this has not been done in Canada, even though there is some evidence that jury trials take longer, court resources are used to form a jury, and juries require instructions at the end of trial. However, proponents say that justice is served in a jury panel of other citizens, and there is less of a threat of judicial bias and political elements entering into a jury trial than may be found in a trial decided with a judge alone.[13] Is a civil jury a relic of the past? When would you want a civil jury? What kind of action? Why would you not want a civil jury?

Damages and Remedies

Many clients think that their issues have been resolved as soon as the defendant has been found liable. But the question may be, what now? Many people think that the

11. WA Bogart, "'Guardian of Civil Rights ... Medieval Relic': The Civil Jury in Canada," 62 *Law and Contemporary Problems* 305.
12. Coulter A Osborne, *Civil Justice Reform Project* (Toronto: Ministry of the Attorney General, 2007), online: <http://www.attorneygeneral.jus.gov.on.ca/english/about/pubs/cjrp/090_civil.asp>.
13. Lori Hausegger, Matthew Hennigar, and Troy Riddell, *Canadian Courts: Law, Politics and Process* (Don Mills, ON: Oxford, 2009) at 327.

TECHNOLOGY OF THE FUTURE?

Will e-trials be the wave of the future? Courtroom 807 in Toronto is outfitted for electronic trials. It was first wired in 1997, costing $250 000, but does not cost any more than a traditional courtroom to operate. Flat screens sit at each desk, on the judge's bench and the witness box. The documents referred to in trial can be displayed by the court registrar. The hope is that one day an electronic filing system could transfer all of the documents in the case directly to the trial. Some estimate that court time could be cut by 25 percent, and there is an increase in e-discovery, where a paperless system is becoming more common.

Courtesy of the Ministry of the Attorney General for Ontario

A Canadian e-courtroom

Today, an e-courtroom is estimated to cost as little as $1500 to set up. These types of courtrooms would allow witnesses to testify from around the world. Testimony in courtroom 807 in Toronto has come from Pakistan, Australia, China, and various prisons around Ontario.

Some criticize having witnesses testify remotely. Some say that the lawyers and judges need to look witnesses in the eye to determine the credibility of their evidence, and to allow witnesses to be comfortable. Others say that it is difficult to get documents to witnesses who might not have access to technology. However, many more point to the benefits, including access to justice in remote areas, and allowing individuals not to have to be in the same room for security reasons. This method of trials could shorten hearings and free up more court resources.[14]

Is this the future of trials in Canada?

plaintiff is given a cheque as he or she leaves the court, and the matter is over. However, this is far from the truth. The court has to formally award damages, and put a dollar value on what the plaintiff has lost. **Special damages** refer to those losses that are tangible. Losses such as missed wages, lost property, receipts for medical equipment, and other losses are relatively easy to value. However, **general damages** involve something much less clear. General damages can include things like pain and suffering, loss of future wages, and loss of earning ability. These are things that are extremely difficult to put a dollar figure on.

Unlike courts in the United States, Canadian courts have been particular in setting a limit on the general damages one can receive in a personal injury case. In the cases *Thornton (Next Friend of) v Prince George School District No. 57* [1978] SCR No 7 (SCC), and *Arnold v Teno*, [1978] SCJ No 8 (SCC), and *Andrews v Grand and Toy Alberta Ltd.* [1978] SCJ No 6, the Supreme Court found that general damages should be capped at $100 000, or approximately $275 000 to $300 000 in current dollars. Contrary to much of the public sentiment that litigants are suing for frivolous reasons, judges and jurors seem to be quite critical of those who bring suits wrongly.[15]

zimmytws/Photos.com

How does the court decide the appropriate damages due to a plaintiff?

14. Luigi Benetton, "E-trials Seen as 'Essential' for Justice in the Future," *Lawyers Weekly*, online: <http://www.lawyersweekly.ca/index.php?section=article&articleid=1396>.
15. Lori Hausegger, Matthew Hennigar, and Troy Riddell, *Canadian Courts: Law, Politics and Process* (Don Mills, ON: Oxford, 2009) at 346.

A judge may also award something called **punitive damages** to deter others from acting in a manner similar to the defendant, and to punish and denounce the defendant's actions, which may have included uncaring and calculated behaviour. Punitive damages seek to punish actions that are particularly offensive not only to the parties, but also to society in general. Punitive damages are absolutely an exceptional remedy in Canada today, and until recently did not occur in Quebec. In the case of *Whiten v Pilot Insurance Co.*, [2002] 1 SCR 595 (SCC), the Supreme Court upheld an Ontario jury case awarding $1 million for punitive damages, and subsequent cases have suggested that this is the absolute exception to the rule, and most punitive damages will be much less.[16]

Aggravated damages are somewhat related, and often confused with punitive damages, but they are only appropriate when the defendant's behaviour is so outrageous it needs to be separately compensated. This is an extraordinary remedy. For example, consider if the defendant (Mr. Jameson) punched the plaintiff (Mr. Williams) in the face from behind with absolutely no provocation. Mr. Jameson broke Mr. Williams's orbital socket and nose, shattered his teeth, and caused injuries to his face. After the fight, Mr. Jameson then spit on his body and used a racial slur as Mr. Williams lay on the ground, injured and in pain. Mr. Jameson prevented onlookers from coming to the aid of Mr. Williams, and the victim suffered life-threatening internal injuries because he was denied assistance for a prolonged period of time. In this situation, the court may award aggravated damages because of the outrageous behaviour of Mr. Jameson. Aggravated damages address matters such as humiliation, indignity, shame, and fear. On the other end of the spectrum, a judge may also award **nominal damages** in very small amounts (such as $1 or $100) simply to show support for the party and award something in recognition of the violation of that person's rights.

The court also has the power to order remedies outside of traditional damages in the form of money. Specific remedies will be discussed in Chapter 4 ("Contract Law") and Chapter 5 ("Tort Law"), but these may include the return of property or compensation in the form of personal action. The following case box illustrates an example of forfeiture by the state.

THE *CIVIL FORFEITURE ACT* IS NO JOKE! *BRITISH COLUMBIA (DIRECTOR OF CIVIL FORFEITURE) v RAI*, [2011] B.C.J. NO. 241.

The court may have the option to seize property as compensation, rather than monetary damages.

© iStockphoto.com/Alex Slobodkin

In this British Columbia case, new legislation in the province was tested for the first time. Under the *Civil Forfeiture Act*, SBC 2005, c 29, the government applied to seize two homes worth nearly $1 million. Mr. Rai owned three homes in Vancouver, and rented the properties to people he knew. When the homes were searched in May 2008, police found 2254 marijuana plants, with a value of between $282 000 and $507 000.

Mr. Rai was not charged with a crime for growing marijuana, but this new provincial legislation says that it does not matter if the individual actually *knew* that the properties in question were involved in criminal activity, that person is subject to severe consequences. The court found that Mr. Rai preferred to remain wilfully blind rather than to confirm that these illegal operations were taking place. The legislation allowed the government to seize the $24 000 that he received in rent for these homes. In addition, even though the court found that Mr. Rai was a "very hardworking family man" who had changed his rental practices, the government still seized two of the three homes. These homes now belong to the B.C. government, and not Mr. Rai.[17]

Should the government be able to seize your home if you were not sure what was going on in your rental property?

16. Lori Hausegger, Matthew Hennigar, and Troy Riddell, *Canadian Courts: Law, Politics and Process* (Don Mills, ON: Oxford, 2009) at 329.
17. Gary Oakes, "B.C. Landlord's Home Seized for Housing Marijuana Grow-Op," *Lawyers Weekly*, online: <http://www.lawyersweekly-digital.com/lawyersweekly/3040?pg=9#pg9>.

Costs

Most commonly, costs are awarded to the successful party, including the lawyer's fees. The unsuccessful party does not have to pay all of the fees of the other party, but there are scales provided for in the RCP. Usually the losing party will have to pay a third to a half of the costs of the *other side's* lawyer. To add insult to injury, not only have you lost the case (and you might have to pay damages to the other party), but you have to pay your own lawyer 100 percent of the fees *and* you may have to pay the other lawyer as well. Even the successful party is still responsible for a significant amount of that party's own lawyer's costs. Civil litigation is an expensive process.

Small Claims Court

The small claims court hears cases in which the damages contested are under a certain monetary limit. The small claims system is just a truncated version of the normal civil law process. The plaintiff initiates the action by filing a document, stating the nature of the complaint (and adds all relevant documentation at this stage, eliminating the need for a discovery); the claim is served on the defendant; the defendant responds; a pre-trial conference is heard; and a court appearance date is scheduled. Different provinces have different monetary limits (see Table 3.3).

Lawyers are often not present in small claims court, since the amounts contested and the legal costs awarded are relatively small, and there is very rarely any expert testimony. Thus, parties can represent themselves with the assistance of websites and publications issued by the court. The judge takes a more active role questioning and cross-examining witnesses, and judgment is typically made on the spot. The purpose of having this parallel system is to reduce the cost of civil litigation by diverting those smaller trials out of the clogged civil law system. Typical small claims matters involve unpaid bills, unpaid wages, consumer debts, and some minor personal injury cases.

Appeals

It has been estimated that 1 to 9 percent of civil trials are **appealed** by the unsuccessful party on the decision as a whole, or in relation to the amount or kind of damages awarded.[18]

Table 3.3 Monetary Limits to Actions in Small Claims Court

Alberta	$25 000
British Columbia	$25 000
Manitoba	$10 000
New Brunswick	$30 000
Newfoundland	$25 000
Northwest Territories	$10 000
Nova Scotia	$25 000
Nunavut	$20 000
Ontario	$25 000
Prince Edward Island	$8 000
Quebec	$7 000
Saskatchewan	$20 000
Yukon	$25 000

18. Lori Hausegger, Matthew Hennigar, and Troy Riddell, *Canadian Courts: Law, Politics and Process* (Don Mills, ON: Oxford, 2009) at 333–34.

Appeals can be made based on questions of law but rarely a question of fact, so only if an error has occurred, then an appeal may be granted. The costs of appeals can be prohibitive for most individuals as transcripts alone can run into the thousands of dollars. The terminology shifts in an appeal; the appellant launches the appeal and the respondent replies to the action. Parties must seek the approval of the Supreme Court in order to be heard at the highest level. The appeal court may uphold the decision, order a new trial, or overturn the decision.

Enforcement

It is important to remember that a judgment by a court is not worth the paper it is written on unless you can actually enforce that judgment against the other party. Most lawyers warn that you cannot "get blood from a stone," and all of these steps mean nothing without recovery at the end of the trial. The process of actually getting the money requires that the victor take steps to get the money awarded. This may be difficult if the defendant is hiding money, is bankrupt, or has other creditors also fighting for the remaining funds.

If the person has money or assets, then the successful party can take steps to **garnish** wages or bank accounts. In a garnishment, the successful party can apply to the employer of the unsuccessful party to take off some of the paycheque each pay period (approximately 20–30 percent, depending on the province). This can also be applied to investments and bank accounts until the debt is paid. However, it is important that you have the information about the other party's employer, bank account, and so forth.

The successful party may also obtain a **writ of seizure and sale** from the court, which is filed with the sheriff's office. The debtor is then prohibited from selling his or her property or assets in the same way that a lien operates. When or if the party tries to sell any property, the successful party will have to be paid back for the amount owed before that sale is completed. It is important to remember that each of these enforcement methods comes with filing fees and money paid to the sheriff for services.

COURT OF EQUITY

There is one additional element to the modern-day civil court that must be examined—the **court of equity**. Until the late nineteenth century, there were two separate legal systems—common law and the court of equity, which was created to supplement the common law. This second parallel system of law was created to address situations where an obvious injustice was found within the common law system. However, it was soon found to be too cumbersome to have two court systems, and lawyers did not know what court to start a lawsuit in, so the courts eventually merged. However, we retain some of the good parts of the court of equity.

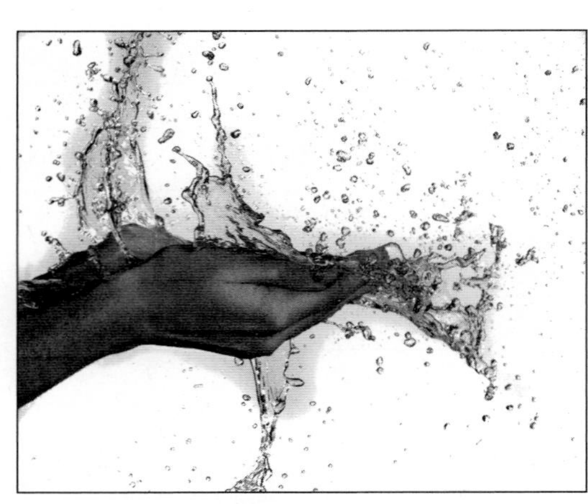

The doctrine of clean hands means that a court may not help settle a dispute if the party seeking assistance has engaged in wrongful conduct.

Chepko Danil Vitalevich/Shutterstock

Some students would look at the court of equity, and think that it would always give an "equitable" decision. However, equity did not just mean a fair decision, but rather a different type of law. We owe a debt to the system of equity for principles such as *subpoenas* (which will be examined in Chapters 9–12), discovery, and the principle of coming to court with **clean hands**. This doctrine of clean hands says that the court will not assist you if you come to the court with wrongdoing of your own. If you are the cause of the conflict or controversy, the court will not lower itself to come to your aid. For example, if you come to court and say that you were participating in an illegal pyramid scheme and one of the other participants broke the contract, the court will say that you engaged in wrongful conduct and it will not help you. Does Serena Van der Woodsen (see page 75) have clean hands? The case of *Miller v Carley* (see the following case box) provides an example of (un)clean hands.

MILLER v CARLEY, 2009 CANLII 39065 (ONT SCJ)

In an interesting case that really shows the principle of coming to the court with clean hands, the parties in this case were fighting over a lottery ticket that ended up being a $5 million winner. The judge in the case, J.W. Quinn, took an interesting approach to his judgment, which began with the statement, "after a busy day conducting illegal drug transactions, the Plaintiff, the Defendant and a mutual friend stopped at a corner store where the Defendant purchased some 'scratch' lottery tickets." The judge said that although this is simply a fight over a ticket, if the "ticket were a child and the parties vying for custody, I would find them both unfit and bring in Family and Children's Services." The plaintiff said he gave the defendant the $10 for the ticket; therefore, he argued, he is entitled to a share of the winnings.

The judge went through a long discussion of every stop the plaintiff and defendant made that day, the drug deals that they completed, and the 14 witnesses who testified at trial. The judge noted that 11 of the 14 witnesses had "a variety of credibility issues," meaning that he did not believe more than three-quarters of the witnesses.

At the end of the case, the judge concluded that the plaintiff had failed to satisfy the onus on a balance of probabilities that he gave $10 for the ticket, and was therefore not entitled to a share of the $5 million. Therefore, the court refused to provide assistance to this shifty plaintiff. There is little question with the tone and substance of this case that the plaintiff did not have clean hands.

Should the court help the plaintiff regardless of his illegal dealings?

Was the concept of clean hands an excuse in order to deny assistance to a drug dealer?

Another principle of equity is that an individual will not "suffer a wrong and be without a remedy." The court of equity will find a solution to your problem. If you entered into a contract to buy Lindsay Lohan's ankle bracelet from her house arrest (the police had given the bracelet to Lindsay to keep as a memento), you have entered into a contract for a specific thing. The common law court would have said that you had a contract, it was not fulfilled, you need a **remedy**, so here is $5000 for not receiving the item. However, you say that you do not want $5000—you want *that particular* ankle bracelet. The court of equity would step in and order something called **specific performance,** which would force the person selling the item to give you that bracelet. Not a similar bracelet—that particular bracelet. The common law system could not do this historically, but we retain this useful tool today.

Another principle that comes out of equity is a remedy called an **injunction**. Again, if one person violated a contract and the only thing that the plaintiff could receive at common law is damages (usually money), the court of equity would step in and order someone to stop his or her wrongful behaviour. Therefore, you could stop that seller from the last example from promising to sell that bracelet online to other people. Injunctions can also be issued to halt construction until an environmental assessment is completed, or to stop someone from developing a property. Equity can also issue a **declaratory order,** which states that someone is right in the dispute. For example, in a property dispute, the court could declare who owns the land, and the parties would know, once and for all, who is the owner. If the person does not comply with any of these remedies, the parties can go back to court to find them in **contempt of court** and make the party obey the order with the threat of a fine, jail, or possibly both.

Today, the systems are merged, so you take the best parts of equity (specific performance, injunction, declaratory orders, and many others) and add them to the system of the common law to make the best of both worlds.

CONCLUSION

It is difficult to tell the future directions of the civil law system; however, one of the pressing issues facing Canadians is being able to afford to use the legal system. Access of all Canadians to the justice system is something that seems not to be guaranteed. The Chief Justice of our Supreme Court, Justice McLachlin, said to the *National Post* that:

> access to justice is quite simply critical. Unfortunately, many Canadian men and women find themselves unable, mainly for financial reasons, to access the Canadian justice system.... Those with some income and a few assets may be ineligible for legal aid and therefore without choices. Their options are grim: use up the family assets in litigation; become their own lawyers or give up. The result may be injustice.[19]

A comprehensive review of the civil law in Ontario was completed by the Ontario Civil Legal Needs Project in May 2010, and it had some sobering conclusions. It found that almost 80 percent of Ontarians believe that the legal system works "better for the rich than the poor" and that although individuals were satisfied with their lawyers, they would prefer to solve their own legal problems.[20]

The report concluded that:

> low- and middle-income Ontarians experience many barriers to access to civil justice, including the real and perceived cost of legal services, lack of access to legal aid and lack of access to information and self-help resources. Once again, the poorest and most vulnerable Ontarians experience the greatest barriers. Our survey and focus groups revealed that communities and groups that tend to experience a higher rate of barriers include members of equality-seeking communities (particularly persons with disabilities and people whose first language is neither French nor English), people with limited literacy, people living in remote or rural communities (particularly in Northern Ontario), older people and women. This finding suggests that the civil justice system needs to have multiple, diverse and integrated access points and service responses. It also suggests that strategies should be developed to improve economic and geographic access to lawyers and legal services.[21]

Research, such as this Civil Legal Needs Project, need to be completed in other provinces as well.

A similar project completed in Alberta in 2009 found that "at any time 45–52% of Canadians, including Albertans, are likely to be experiencing a significant legal problem but many do not successfully access legal assistance." The report also concluded that

> access to legal services, including private lawyers, is not equitable for all Albertans. (a) There are few legal services outside of major centres, particularly those offering legal advice and representation. (b) In underserviced areas, most existing services do not currently have the capacity to adequately serve their catchment areas. (c) Residents of northern Alberta have fewer legal services distributed across greater distances that often pose formidable access barriers.[22]

It is clear that access to justice will continue to be an issue throughout Canada.

Many people say that access to justice would be improved by reducing lawyers' fees (which can be extremely expensive), in addition to court filing fees, photocopy fees, transcript costs, expert witnesses costs, and so on. As noted earlier, those who are unsuccessful in the civil law system might be on the line for hundreds of thousands of dollars of fees if they lose their case. This is a gamble that many Canadians are not willing to take, and thus their access to justice is severely limited. The search for answers to fix this system, which is in serious need of reform, will need to continue.

LEARNING OUTCOMES SUMMARIZED

1. Understand what parliamentary supremacy is.

The concept of parliamentary supremacy says that an elected group of representatives (Parliament) should be the supreme lawmakers, and no one person is above that power.

19. From Katie Rook, "Justice comes at too high a price: McLachlin," National Post, 9 March 2007, online: <http://www.canada.com/nationalpost/news/story.html?id=54c6a41b-4d85-460f-a21f-524087fbcf2e&k=18398>. Material reprinted with the express permission of: **National Post**, a division of Postmedia Network Inc.

20. Ontario Civil Legal Needs Project, Listening to Ontarians (Toronto: Ontario Civil Legal Needs Project Steering Committee, 2010) at 9.

21. *Ibid* at 46.

22. Glynnis Lieb et al, "The Alberta Legal Services Mapping Project: Final Report for the Calgary Judicial District" (Edmonton: Canadian Forum on Civil Justice, 2009), online: http://cfcj-fcjc.org/docs/2011/mapping-final-en.pdf.

This notion is fundamental to the common law system, and judges should simply interpret and enforce the laws of Parliament, even if they do not agree. If the courts make the wrong decision, it is up to Parliament to fix the legislation so it does not happen again.

2. Discuss what is meant by the court's assertion that you must come with "clean hands."

This doctrine says that the court will not assist you if you come to the court with wrongdoing of your own. If you are the cause of the conflict or controversy, the court will not lower itself to come to your aid. For example, if you come to court and say that you were completing a drug deal with your dealer, and then the dealer assaulted you, the court will say that you engaged in wrongful conduct, and it will not help you because you got yourself into that situation.

3. Describe what is meant by the phrase "distinguishing the case."

A judge can find a way to avoid following a precedent by distinguishing the case. A judge may find key differences in law or procedure or in the facts of the case suggesting that it should not be followed in this particular matter. Distinguishing a case is very much an art, but it can give flexibility to the system to circumvent a particular precedent. It can also become a battle of the precedents, as one side might present several cases about why a certain principle applies, while the other side has one more case showing that it does not apply. The court must look at the level of court in the precedent cases, determine how persuasive the argument is, and determine whether or not it applies to the particular case at hand.

4. List the main perspectives of statutory interpretation.

These perspectives are (1) the literal rule, (2) the absurdity rule, (3) the mischief rule, (4) the contextual analysis rule, (5) the plausible meaning rule, and (6) the modern interpretation rule.

5. Identify the purpose of a pre-trial conference.

Parties are subject to a pre-trial conference before trial. The lawyers and parties meet informally (sometimes formally), often in the judge's chambers, with a judge who is not going to hear the trial, to explain why a settlement cannot be reached. Judges will question the merits of the case, point out weaknesses, and may pressure both sides to come to an agreement. Pre-trial conferences are a tool used to discourage people from proceeding to trial, but they may be dependent on the judge and his or her opinion of the case. Some judges are proactive in encouraging settlement, and other judges are not motivated to bring the parties together. The parties may be convinced to settle if a judge is telling them that their case may or may not have any chance of success.

SELF-EVALUATION QUESTIONS

1. At a discovery, what can a lawyer do if he or she wishes to consult with the client and/or other documentary evidence before answering a question?
2. Identify what the courts may award as an equitable remedy.
3. What types of remedies can the court award at the end of a trial?
4. Which of the following statements is true about the hierarchy of courts in Canada?
   (a) The Supreme Court is the highest authority in Canada.
   (b) The Superior Court is the highest authority in Canada.
   (c) The Court of Appeal is an appellate court.
   (d) Both (a) and (c) are true.
   (e) Both (b) and (c) are true.
5. What is an originating process? How does litigation begin?
6. What is a headnote? What are the dangers of relying on a headnote?

Contract Law

"The 'ultimate power' to refuse to enforce a contract may be justified, even in the commercial context. Freedom of contract, like any freedom, may be abused. Take the case of the milk supplier who adulterates its baby formula with a toxic compound to increase its profitability at the cost of sick or dead babies. In China, such people were shot. In Canada, should the courts give effect to a contractual clause excluding civil liability in such a situation? I do not think so."[1]

—The Honourable Mr. Justice William I. C. Binnie, Supreme Court of Canada

Learning Outcomes

After completing this chapter, you should be able to:

1. Define what is meant by the term "contract."
2. Discuss the elements of a contract.
3. Identify the fundamental rules of contract.
4. Analyze how to discharge a contract through breach.
5. Assess legal remedies resulting from a contractual breach.

INTRODUCTION TO CONTRACT LAW

As functioning members of society, we enter into contracts every day. From parking in an underground garage to buying a ticket for a concert, contracts are everywhere and perform important functions in commerce. They help to protect our property, prevent fraud, and ensure that people live up to the deals that they make. Contract law is a dichotomy between two ideals: the freedom of choice and the protection of society. Individuals should be free to choose, but the law also needs to restrain our conduct to protect society. Contract law provides the rules that guide our voluntary relationships. Problems arise, however, when there are variances in the power differences between parties, in financial resources, and in our own susceptibilities to human frailties.

1. *Tercon Contractors Ltd. v British Columbia*, 2010 SCC 4 (SCC).

Feng Yu/Shutterstock

Whether written or unwritten, we enter into contracts every day.

Contracts come in various forms. Although most people think a contract is only a contract if written and signed, contracts can be oral and accepted with something as informal as a nod or handshake, and courts, when they feel warranted, go to some lengths to reconstruct the actions surrounding an agreement.

BASIC PRINCIPLES OF CONTRACT LAW

Contract law determines which relationships form contracts and which do not, using the rules that we have created. The law of contracts is largely a "common law" study; most of our law of contracts comes from the rules and principles derived from precedent, which comes from case law—first from England, and then from our own Canadian examples. However, there are increasing legislative sources that guide how individuals should form contracts, such as the *Sale of Goods Act* (discussed later in the chapter).

However, the law of contracts is universal. It governs the sale of an apple at your local market just as well as the multi-million-dollar deal between international corporations. The law of contracts is concerned with the exchange of goods and services for money and/or for other goods and services. What generally distinguishes the law of contracts from other areas of civil law is that people *voluntarily* enter into contracts rather than have rules imposed on them by law. (In Chapter 5, you will learn about tort law, which *dictates* rules for people, such as the duty not to interfere with the bodily integrity of others.) If disputes are not settled by the parties through negotiation, parties rely on civil litigation and allow the courts to resolve their differences.

Many contracts are signed, but not all.

Yari/Shutterstock

Almost anyone can draft or enter into a contract, and the courts do not want to impose a rigid form of a contract that everyone must adhere to. Rather, the court looks at the actions of the parties, what they said, and if they made any written record of what they were agreeing to. At the most basic level, the court is looking for an offer by one party that was unequivocally accepted by the other. Courts are generally not concerned about the fairness of a contract, nor about determining the fairness or appropriateness of the bargain struck. The main goal of the court is to enforce the clear **intention** of the parties. However, the courts are showing a greater willingness to interfere when faced with unfair or **unconscionable** contracts. This

zimmytws/Shutterstock

Much of contract law is derived from precedent.

happens frequently with consumer protection issues, where a considerable body of law has been developed to protect people who are taken advantage of by unscrupulous merchants. The general rule is that if the contract is already done, the court will not undo it, but if it is not done yet, the court will not help to enforce it.

DEFINITION OF CONTRACT

A **contract** may be defined as an agreement that is recognized by law between two or more persons, which gives rise to rights and/or obligations that the courts *may* enforce. A contract usually starts with a **promise**, but it is important to remember that not all promises are contracts. There are multitudes of cases examining what kinds of promises make an agreement and what the courts recognize as a contract. If something goes wrong, the question is whether the court will interfere to make the parties bound by what they promised to each other. What is clear is that the court wants the parties to have the ability to be free to contract with each other, as this is one of the fundamental principles of law. Our society has decided that we want people to make bargains with one another, and we do not want anyone to step in and say that we should be unable to negotiate with one another. Unless there is evidence of something fundamentally wrong with the circumstances, courts are reluctant to intercede. However, upon evidence of unfair dealings, especially with vulnerable populations, courts have shown a willingness to protect those in need of assistance.

Contracts consist of various statements, promises, and stipulations. These are called the **terms** of the contract. Terms may be expressed (stated) or implied (unstated). The terms determine each party's rights and obligations and the remedies available if the terms are broken. The language in the contract must be reasonably clear. If it is not, the courts could dispose of the contract or deem the term unenforceable. When terms are not explicitly stated, the courts may use evidence of custom within the locality or business to determine the rights and obligations of the parties (e.g., is 5 percent commission on the sale of a house and 10 percent on the sale of a water access cottage the standard in the current market?). The normal method of enforcement is an action for financial damages for breach of contract, though in some cases the court may compel performance by the party in default.

Bilateral Contacts

What you traditionally think of as a contract is probably a **bilateral contract**. A bilateral contract is one where there are promises made by each of the parties to the other, which they are both bound to perform. Thus, this is a contract where the **offeror** and **offeree** trade promises. For example, I agree to sell you my car and you agree to pay me $10 000. We both receive a benefit from the contract.

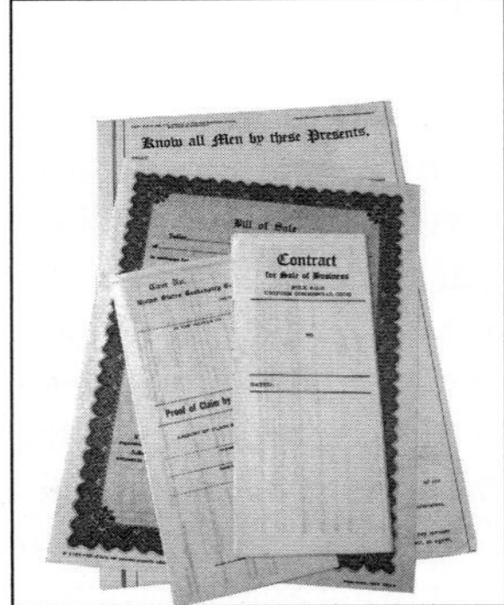

Comstock/Photos.com

What is a contract?

Unilateral Contracts

In **unilateral contracts**, one party promises to do something in exchange for the *act* of the other party, not a promise. Offering a reward for a lost laptop is an example of a unilateral contract. Here an offer is accepted by doing the act, or series of acts, per the contract. Only one person makes the promise to pay the reward, while the other person just performs and begins to look for the lost laptop. This is an offer that is made to the world at large, not contracting with anyone in particular, but asking anyone to enter into the contract by acting. A unilateral offer can be accepted by more than one person, but there must be action. I cannot accept the contract by simply promising that I will go out and look for the laptop in the future.

The court has found difficulties in this type of contract, as someone might put a great deal of effort into looking for the laptop but that person is ultimately unsuccessful. Thus, the concept of a **subsidiary promise**[2] has been developed. A subsidiary promise is an implied promise that the offeror cannot revoke once the individual begins looking, in good faith, and continues to perform. The court might attempt to assist the offeree by implying into the contract that there was a promise not to revoke the offer while the offeree was trying to complete the requisite actions. An example of this is the case of *Errington v Errington and Woods,* [1952] 1 KB 290 (CA), in which a father bought a house for his son and daughter-in-law to live in. The father told the daughter-in-law that the deposit on the home was a gift, but they had to pay the monthly mortgage payments. He said that once the payments were complete, the house would be theirs. Before the couple could finish the payments, the father died, and his widow sued to recover the house, saying there was no contract. However, the court found that this promise by the father was a unilateral contract—the house in return for the payments. When the couple started paying the mortgage in good faith, they were accepting the contract with the father by their performance of the terms and the house would be theirs when they completed the payments. Individuals must be careful about what they promise because a contract can be formed, and these promises must be honoured. This was the lesson learned in the case of *Goldthorpe v Logan* (see the following case box).

GOLDTHORPE v LOGAN, [1943] 2 DLR 519 (CA)

Ms. Goldthorpe had hair on her face that she wished to get removed by electrolysis, and she saw an advertisement posted by Ms. Logan, which "guaranteed" the results of her hair-removal process. Ms. Goldthorpe went for a consultation, and was told by the registered nurse, an employee of the company, that her face could be "cleared," as the hair would be guaranteed to be removed permanently. Even though Ms. Goldthorpe submitted herself to several treatments, the hair continued to grow as it had before the procedure, and Ms. Goldthorpe sued Ms. Logan. At the trial, the judge said that there was no binding contract in place. However, Ms. Goldthorpe appealed that decision to the court of appeal, asking the court to decide whether a guarantee or promise is an offer that, if accepted by the client, creates a contract enforceable in law. The court found that the advertisement was a message from Ms. Logan to every member of the public who was willing to accept the terms and conditions, and she made no effort to limit her liability by making this wide promise.

The court of appeal found that the law was in place to protect those who were the victims of an "extravagant promise." The court held that the "strong cannot disregard any undertaking binding in law, however lightly given, and the weak unfortunate person, however gullible, can be sure that the courts of this country will not permit anyone to escape the responsibility arising from an enforceable promise." This decision was a message from the court that the strong cannot take advantage of the weak and then seek to get out of their contracts. Thus, the court found that Ms. Goldthorpe accepted the offer in the advertisement, and this was communicated by her conduct of submitting to the electrolysis sessions. Ms. Logan was, therefore, responsible for the contract she had entered into and was liable for the resulting monetary damages when the treatments did not work.

Written Contracts

Contracts do not need to be in writing, but a document in writing makes for good evidence of the agreement. The requirement that some agreements *must* be in writing comes from the *Statute of Frauds* from 1677. The original rationale was to have some agreements in

2. See JE Smyth, DA Soberman, and AJ Easson, *The Law and Business Administration in Canada* (Toronto: Pearson Prentice Hall, 2007) at 106.

writing because by the seventeenth century there were concerns that individuals could fraudulently assert that agreements had been made that did not exist, and at this time there was no opportunity for the parties to testify about the contract. In addition, jurors were still able to decide cases on the basis of their personal knowledge, so perjury was endemic and the citizenry was very litigious.[3] Written contracts eliminated costly court time weighing one person's word against another's.

Today, the *Statute of Frauds* is incorporated into various other statutes, but there are several general categories of contracts that must still be in writing. These include guarantees and indemnities where one individual is responsible for the debt of another, contracts that are not to be performed within one year, contracts for property, promises in consideration of marriage, some promises of an executor to a will, and various other statutes often require matters to be in writing to be enforceable. In many jurisdictions, the *Sale of Goods Act* requires that goods over a certain value (over $50 in many provinces) be evidenced in writing. For example, in Alberta the *Sale of Goods Act,* RSA 1980, c S-2, s 6 says that "a contract for the sale of any goods of the value of $50 or more is not enforceable by action ... unless some note or memorandum in writing of the contract is made and signed by the party to be charged or his agent in that behalf." This requirement is similar to what is required in other provinces,[4] but many provinces have made detailed reforms to the legislation, while Manitoba has repealed these provisions completely. With today's technology, amendments are being made to allow for the validity of electronic documents rather than having a contract in written form that is signed by hand (as will be discussed when we look at e-commerce at the end of this chapter).

Written documents are taken seriously, and the court often gives weight to hard evidence, which includes written agreements. Written documents will carry more weight than a person's sworn testimony.

One individual cannot change the terms of the contract once the agreement is made unless both parties agree. Yet, in today's society, we often have no opportunity to negotiate many of the agreements we enter into as most contracts do not allow us to negotiate the terms and conditions (e.g., riding a bus, signing up for a cell phone or a credit card, purchasing software). **Standard form contracts** are written beforehand and have standardized clauses and conditions, and clients have no room to negotiate or discuss the terms. In practice, we often do not read the contract and have no idea what the terms and conditions are, but we are nonetheless bound.

Even when in writing, there can still be disputes that the contract is incomplete, that other terms should be included, that there are implied terms, or that there are different meanings that the parties could ascribe to the terms. Although the courts have used this flexibility to consider the factors surrounding the contract and what was truly intended by the parties, this practice has led to some uncertainty in the law of contract. Primarily, the courts will start at the most basic level: does the agreement have all of the ingredients of a contract?

INGREDIENTS TO A CONTRACT

Simply because parties decide that they are going to enter into a contract, it does not mean that it will be legally enforceable unless the parties follow basic rules. There are three basic ingredients to a contract:

1. *Consensus*: including an offer and an unqualified acceptance.
2. *Consideration*: both parties must provide valuable consideration.
3. *Intention*: both parties must intend to be legally bound.

3. Ontario Ministry of the Attorney General, *Ontario Law Reform Commission, Report on Amendment of the Law of Contract* (Toronto: ON, Ministry of the Attorney General, 1987) at 73.

4. *Sale of Goods Act*, RSA 2000, c S-2, s 4; *Sale of Goods Act*, CCSM c S10 s 4; *Sale of Goods Act*, RSNB 1973, c S-1, s 3; *Sale of Goods Act*, RSNL 1990, c S-6 s 4; *Sale of Goods Act*, RSNS 1989, c 408, s 5; *Sale of Goods Act*, RSNWT 1988, c S-2, s 7; *Sale of Goods Act*, RSNWT (Nu) 1988, c S-2, s 7; *Sale of Goods Act*, RSPEI 1988, c S-1, s 4; *Sale of Goods Act*, RSO 1990, c S.1 s 3; *Sale of Goods Act*, RSS 1978, c S-1, s 4; *Sale of Goods Act*, RSY 2002, c 198 s 3.

Consensus

The most important qualification to a contract is that a consensus must be reached between the parties. It forms the foundation upon which the agreement is based, as there must be a **consensus *ad idem*** or a "meeting of the minds" by both parties to the contract. The courts are concerned with the degree of shared understanding between the parties, but this standard is much more objective than it first appears. The test used is the **reasonable person** test—what would a reasonable person who was prudent and careful in his or her dealings have understood the contract to be? The courts will not allow a person to escape from a contract by claiming not to have to read it or not to have understood. Failure to read the contract or misunderstanding its content, when the meaning would be clear to others, will not provide an excuse to avoid the obligations set out in the agreement. The purpose of contract law is to protect the reasonable expectation of the parties. Consensus is comprised of an offer, an acceptance, and communication.

Offer

An offer is defined as a tentative promise or statement of willingness by one party to enter into a contract with another party on certain terms and conditions. The offeror makes the offer, and the offeree is the person to whom the offer is being made. The offeror sets out the terms including things like price, length of time to complete, and so forth, and the offeree accepts them. Thus, a contract is formed. There is an understanding that if the offer is accepted, the parties will enter a legally binding contract. An offer may be expressed, or it may be implied by conduct. It may be addressed to one person or to a group (e.g., an offer of a reward). However, an offer is not just about the intention inside of a person that he or she wants to form a contract, but rather it is the outward indications to show this intention so that the other party also knows that he or she is entering into a contract. An "agreement to agree" sometime in the future is also not a contract. Conduct of the parties can also be an offer. For example, at an auction when a purchaser lifts a hand to make a bid, the auctioneer nods to indicate that there has been an offer and this offer is accepted when the auctioneer announces that the item is sold.

ADVERTISEMENTS—INVITATIONS TO TREAT Before an offer is made and accepted, attempts are often made to attract the attention of the other party to invite him or her to enter into a contractual relationship. Store windows are designed to attract people to the business and the goods that are creatively displayed are meant to attract attention. These displays are referred to as **invitations to treat** and must be distinguished from offers because an invitation has no legal effect. It would be absurd to think that every time you looked into a store window you were accepting a contract. There still has to be an offer by the offeror and an acceptance by the offeree to make a binding agreement.

TERMINATION OF AN OFFER An offer can be terminated in six general ways:

1. *Refusal*. Offers that are refused by the offeree cannot later be accepted. If the offeree simply says "no" without a counteroffer, the entire deal comes to an end
2. *Lapse of time*. When a person states that his or her offer will be open for a specific period of time, the offer will end when that time has lapsed.
3. *Lapse of reasonable time*. When there is no specific period of time for the offer, the courts will determine a reasonable amount of time for the offer to be open. The court will look at the subject matter of the goods and/or services and what is reasonable in that market and what mode of communication was used by the offeror. Stock prices vary by the minute so offers are usually good for a brief period of time, as are perishable goods, while real estate offers may be good for several months.
4. *Failure of a condition*. There may be a failure of one of the conditions surrounding the offer. For example, in the case of *Re Reitzel and Rej-Cap Manufacturing Ltd.* (1985), 53 OR (2d) 116 (HC), there was a serious change in the conditions of the contract. The parties had negotiated the sale of a property for $300 000 and the deal was to

close at 11:59 p.m. on August 29. On the morning of August 28, there was a fire that destroyed the property. Instead of saying that one of the conditions of the sale had failed as the building no longer existed, the plaintiff accepted the defendant's offer to buy the building because he wanted to collect on the insurance money. The defendant thought that the contract had clearly been compromised by the fire, and had not even thought to revoke the offer. The court found that there was no contract because the deal was for the land and building, not the land and insurance money. Once the subject matter of the offer had changed, there was no offer and could be no acceptance. Death of one of the parties may also be seen as a failure of a condition surrounding the offer, but it is possible in certain circumstances that the estate to continue with the contract.

5. *Revocation.* The offeror is in control of the offer, and generally he or she can revoke an offer any time before it is accepted. The problem with non-instantaneous methods of communication is that the **revocation** and the acceptance could pass in the mail (as with the post box rule, discussed shortly). The revocation must be communicated by the offeror to the offeree, but the offeror can revoke the offer any time prior to acceptance. If the offeror revokes the offer, the offeree cannot accept because there is no longer an offer. The most important element is that the revocation must reach the offeree before that person has an opportunity to accept the offer.
6. *Counteroffer.* Lastly, the introduction of new terms is considered a termination of an offer. A **counteroffer** is a whole new deal; the offer must exactly match the acceptance, so you cannot accept the original offer when a new deal is on the table. A counteroffer means that the original offer has been rejected and is now void. If I offer to sell you my house for $150 000, and you offer $145 000, you have rejected the original offer and it no longer exists. If I in turn refuse the $145 000 and you change your mind because you really want the house and you agree to pay the original offer of $150 000, there is no acceptance. I have no obligation to sell you the house for $150 000 because that offer no longer exists; it was destroyed the moment the counteroffer was made. Your statement that you will pay $150 000 is actually a new offer, which I can then accept or reject. The exchange of documents to represent this counteroffer and the resulting negotiations is sometimes called "battle of the forms."

Acceptance

Acceptance is the second basic ingredient to a contract. The acceptance indicates that the expressed terms and conditions are acceptable and that the individual is willing to be bound by them. The offer contains the terms of the agreement; the acceptance merely indicates a willingness to be bound. Acceptance is quite simple and involves only an indication on the part of the offeree that he or she is willing to be bound by the terms set out by the offer. There are two other requirements: (1) the acceptance must be unqualified; and (2) it be communicated to the person who made the offer.

It is important that the acceptance is clear and unconditional. Acceptance must also be communicated by the purchaser and received by the seller. There are exceptions, as in the case of unilateral contracts and rewards where action is taken to be acceptance. Usually, an acceptance can be written, verbal, or by conduct (or a combination thereof), but it must be communicated. An offer may be accepted at any time until it is revoked, but an offer may be revoked at any time before it is accepted.

One of the first questions a court will consider is how the contract has been formed. Courts again use the reasonable person test and will ask whether a reasonable observer would assume that an agreement had been made and whether it appeared that the offer was accepted. It is also important to remember that the place where the contract was made can be of considerable importance when it has to be determined which jurisdiction applies to the contract. For example, suppose you were selling your condominium in Toronto to someone in Edmonton. Should the contract be governed by the laws of Ontario or Alberta? The general rule is that the communication is completed where it is received by the offeror.

If the offer was received on the telephone by the person in Edmonton, then Alberta law would govern in this case.

Although the concept of acceptance seems uncomplicated, it may be difficult to determine just when the parties have exchanged a matching acceptance to the offer that has been made. The courts have often said that the acceptance has to exactly match the offer or there will be no contract, but the courts have also been willing to have a flexible approach in deciding if the two sides match.

Communication

Communication of the offer is also very important and is the final ingredient to the contract. To be a valid offer, it must be communicated to the other party either orally, in writing, or by conduct. Courts will examine what was reasonable in the circumstances. Only the group or person to whom the offer is made may accept the offer. Identical offers that cross in the mail do not make a contract, and one cannot be responsible for work done without one's knowledge. Every individual is entitled to discuss and then accept or reject that offer, and then communicate that decision. The courts have found that one cannot accept the terms of a contract by silence; it must be by words or action. In *Brogden v Metropolitan Railway* (see the following case box), the court asked whether there was silence in this case or whether there was action to accept a particular offer.

BROGDEN v METROPOLITAN RAILWAY (1877) 2 APP CAS 666 (CA)

The plaintiffs drafted a contract for the supply of coal per week at a defined price. The defendants received the contract, added the name of an arbitrator that they could consult if there was an issue, and signed and returned the agreement to the plaintiffs. This change in the document made a new contract. However, when this document was received by the plaintiffs, they simply put the agreement into a drawer. Coal was ordered and delivered per the terms of the contract until there was a dispute between the parties. The defendants said that the plaintiffs had never accepted their offer and, therefore, there was no contract. The court found that a contract could not be accepted by silence, but there was more than silence in this case. The parties had placed and fulfilled orders on the basis of the agreement, and the defendants should be bound by its terms because of this conduct.

This case stands for the principle that there are "equivalents to acceptance" and that things like the "shipment of goods requested, acceptance of delivery, payment of money, 'receiving printed forms without objection' and abandonment of legal right to object to the transaction" are an acceptance.[5] There are many means of communication that are not traditional in nature. The offeror is called the "master of the offer" and can insist that the communication of acceptance is done in a very specific way because he or she is not obligated to make an offer at all. As Waddams has noted, the offeror may insist on acceptance "by return of wagon, or she may require acceptance to be addressed at a particular place, or require an acceptance written in red ink on parchment."[6] The offer may specifically identify a type of communication that is required so that an equivalent is not needed.

POST BOX RULE An important exception to the communication principle is what is called the **post box rule**. There is a great deal of case law dealing with the method by which acceptances are communicated: post, fax, email, and so forth. When traditional methods of communication are employed, such as what we now refer to as "snail mail," and where it is appropriate to respond by mail, the acceptance is deemed to be effective at the time and place it is posted. Thus, acceptance happens at the

5. SM Waddams, *The Law of Contracts*, 4th ed. (Toronto: Canada Law Book, 1999) at 68.

6. *Ibid* at 72.

Paul Vasarhelyi/Photos.com

The *post box rule* is an important exception to the communication principle.

moment the offeree puts the envelope into the mailbox. This rule does not apply to other forms of communication, such as a letter of revocation, which has to be received by the offeree to be effective.

There are some real problems with this rule because the offeree has all of the advantages. There is the legal fiction that the offer was accepted when it went into the mailbox, but the other party has no idea if it has actually been placed in the box. However, in law it is still deemed to be accepted. Again, the offeror is the master of the offer, so if the offeror says that mail is acceptable, the he or she has to live by these rules. Historically, there was a fear that many people would be victimized by fraud if the offer was deemed communicated when it reached the offeror because the offeror could simply say that he or she never received the document in the mail. There was a belief that there was more reliability in saying that there was acceptance when the letter entered the mailbox than to trust someone on the other end who had a motive to lie. The postmark is proof of the mailing date if the acceptance is received, but if the offeror does not specifically say that the acceptance has to be received to be completed, the offeror takes the risk that Canada Post might misplace the letter.

Consideration

The second ingredient of a contract is **consideration**, which is a tool that the courts use to see if they should enforce a promise. This is a requirement that both parties to an agreement pay a price and that both parties receive a benefit; a contract is not a gift but an exchange, and if there is no bargain, there is no contract. One party pays $500 and gets a car; the other person no longer has a car but now has $500. In this case, the money is the consideration for the transfer of goods, but price is not limited to a payment of money, but rather refers to anything of value being exchanged for the promise of the other party. This valuable consideration may consist of a "right, interest, profit, or benefit accruing to the one party, or some forbearance, detriment, loss or responsibility given, suffered, or undertaken by the other."[7] The parties must show that there was a benefit or detriment to the parties. Whether consideration has been exchanged is a fundamental issue in contracts and is an absolute requirement before the court will step in to settle a dispute.

The only situation where you do not need consideration is when the contract is under **seal**. The contract under seal is one of the most historic ways to create an enforceable promise and dates back to a time when signets on a ring or stamp would be pressed into wax to certify a contract. This is a method of formalization that was designed to make a party pause before entering into this formal arrangement, and is also formal proof that the promises were made and that they were intended to be relied upon. In a time with low literacy rates, a seal "made people aware of the significance of what they were doing and provided excellent evidence of what it was that they had agreed to."[8] This practice survives today in some limited circumstances around deeds and guarantees. Today, the courts have found that if the parties are going to go through the pains of putting a contract under seal, they have some sort of benefit, and this eliminates the need for consideration.

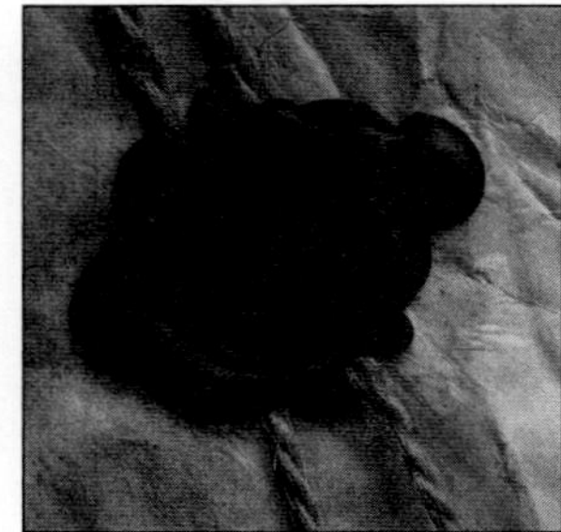

Leigh Prather/Shutterstock

When a contract is under seal, consideration is not needed.

General Rules Governing Consideration

There are four fundamental rules of consideration:

1. Consideration must be sufficient but not necessarily adequate and specific.
2. A gratuitous promise is not consideration.
3. Consideration is distinct from motive, but discharge of a moral or legal obligation is generally not sufficient.
4. Consideration may be present or future, but not past.

7. *Currie v Misa* (1875), LR, 10 Exch. 153 at 162.
8. Angela Swan, *Canadian Contract Law,* 2nd ed (Markham, ON: LexisNexis, 2009) at 135.

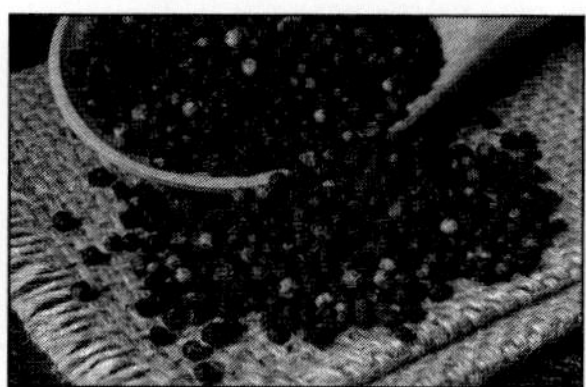
Marie C Fields/Shutterstock

Two parties could legally exchange a Bentley for a peppercorn as this is sufficient consideration.

CONSIDERATION MUST BE SUFFICIENT BUT NOT NECESSARILY ADEQUATE AND SPECIFIC The requirement that consideration be sufficient means that what is exchanged must have some value, but it does not have to be adequate; therefore, it does not have to be equal in value. For ease of comparison, value is usually based on economic value. Providing that consideration has some value, the courts will not concern themselves with its adequacy. If you wish to sell your 2013 Bentley for $5, that is sufficient consideration, because consideration can be as little as a "peppercorn." You can rent your house for a dollar a month and the courts will not interfere. People are free to make foolish deals, and the courts will not protect individuals from making a bad deal, nor will the courts step in just because one side made a substantial profit from the deal. If one person were to agree to pay $500 per month to another in exchange for tenderness and affection, that would not have value and would not be consideration. However, in the case of *Hamer v Sidway* (1891), 124 NY 538, 27 NE 256 (CA NY), the court found that there was consideration in the effort that it took for an individual to "refrain from drinking, using tobacco, swearing, and playing cards or billiards" until he was 21 years of age. When a transaction is obviously one-sided, it may be an indication of some other problem such as duress or unconscionability (discussed later in this chapter), which would call the validity of the contract into question.

Consideration must also be specific. It is not sufficient for a person to say, "I will pay you some money for your computer." The amount must be specific: "I will give you $500 for your computer." This can get complicated in a market where the value can constantly shift, and even more difficult when a party uses action as consideration.

BANK OF NOVA SCOTIA v MACLELLAN (1977), 78 DLR (3D) 1 (NSSC APP DIV)

In this case, the defendant made a deal with her bank: she would help the bank to find her debtor ex-husband and would pay a portion of the debt (she was jointly liable for the whole debt), if the bank promised not to pursue her for the rest of the amount owing. The appeal court in Nova Scotia said that this promise was consideration. The court said that although the promise was "slight and of little real value, [it] is enough to meet the legal test of consideration." The result seems to be that if the courts wish to find consideration, they may base that finding on even the weakest of facts.

Is turning in your ex-husband really enough to form consideration? Why or why not?

A Gratuitous Promise Is Not Consideration

After the agreement is made, there is an obligation on the purchasers to pay the amount agreed upon. But, a **gratuitous promise** is unenforceable. A gratuitous promise is a one-sided promise in which only one of the parties commits to do something. If I said, "I am going to give every one of my students 100 percent in this course," the promise is unenforceable since consideration flows in only one direction. However, gratuitous promises can be made enforceable by affixing a seal to the document containing the agreement. The seal makes a legally binding obligation without showing that there was consideration.

It is sometimes difficult to tell if there is a one-sided promise. If I say that I will give you $300 to paint my house, but half-way through you demand an additional $100 (even if I agree), one cannot enforce that promise. You were already obligated to paint the house—there was consideration there. After that additional promise was made, you were still obligated to paint the house.

There are similar problems with debt. The issue comes from a case called *Foakes v Beer* (1884), 9 App Cas 605 (HL). If you owe me $1000 and I agree to take $50 in monthly installments until the debt is paid off, there was no consideration when I agreed to take less, and there was no benefit to me other than getting money that you already owed. Case law says that this agreement to accept partial payment is not binding; you still owe me the full $1000 in one payment. However, legislation has replaced the common law to say that if a creditor agrees to take less to satisfy the debt, creditor cannot sue for the difference because he or she agreed to that alternative amount. For example, in Ontario s 16 of the *Mercantile Law Amendment Act* RSO 1990, c M.10 says that: "part performance of an obligation either before or after a breach thereof when expressly accepted by the creditor in satisfaction or rendered in pursuance of an agreement for that purpose, though without any new consideration, shall be held to extinguish the obligation." Thus, statute overrides the common law, and taking partial payments may be a new contract between the parties, even though there is no new consideration.

Consideration is not sufficient in cases where people simply perform what they are legally bound to do either because of their statutory duty (e.g., a promise to pay someone to testify in court when they already are required by *subpoena* to attend) or because of a pre-existing contractual duty. There is no consideration because there is no true bargain, and thus no real exchange. The consideration cannot be against public policy because we do not want people getting a benefit from something they were already required to do and, thus, such agreements are not binding. The only exception is when someone can show that he or she did something beyond a pre-existing duty, which would constitute a new contract.

However, as seen in the case of *Ward v Byham*, [1956] 1 WLR 496, the courts are willing to find consideration for a pre-existing duty if they want to help a vulnerable party. In this case, a mother brought an action to get the father of her child to pay child support for their "bastard child." The court found that although the mother had a pre-existing duty to support and care for her child, it also found that the father had a benefit from that duty—he did not have to support the child himself. The father had made a unilateral contract that he would pay for the support if the mother could prove that the child would be "well looked after and happy." Since the mother performed this promise, the court found there was consideration, even though this was a pre-existing duty.

Consideration Is Distinct from Motive, but Discharge of a Moral or Legal Obligation Is Generally Not Sufficient

The consideration also cannot be illegal, and an agreement in which someone agrees to perform an illegal act is not binding. When a person agrees to kill your neighbour in exchange for $5000 and does so, that person will not be able to enforce the claim for the $5000 in court. The court says that you have to come to court with **clean hands**. The Canadian principle was stated in the Saskatchewan case of *Miller v F Mendel Holdings Ltd.* (1984), 30 Sask R 298 (QB), that help will be refused to "any party who, in the matter of his claim, is himself tainted with fraud, **misrepresentation**, illegality or impropriety by reason of which his opponent has suffered a detriment of a kind rendering it unjust that the order sought should be made." Thus, to say that you are deserving of help from the court, you have to come to them without being in the wrong.

For example, in the Ontario case of *Dunlop v Major,* [1998] OJ No 2553 (Ont CA), the plaintiff, Mr. Dunlop offered to help Mr. Major with his career as an entertainer and song writer in country and western music. Mr. Dunlop paid to produce a master tape, and later entered into a contract to decide how future profits would be shared. Mr. Major said that the contract should not be enforced because it was the product of threats to Mr. Major and his family if he did not sign the agreement with Mr. Dunlop. Although the lower court awarded Mr. Dunlop $90 922, the court of appeal said that the contract was obtained by "grossly reprehensible activities in his dealings with the appellant," even before the contract was negotiated. Therefore, Mr. Dunlop was not able to go to the court to enforce a contract because he did not have clean hands, and the court was not going to assist him in getting money from Mr. Major.

At common law, agreements to perform certain types of acts have been declared to be against public policy, and while the acts involved are not illegal as such, contracts dealing with these activities are treated as if there is no contract. The willingness of courts to declare a contract as immoral or contrary to public policy can be difficult. For example, in the case of *Pearce v Brooks*, [1861–1873] All ER Rep 102 (C Ex), the defendant Mrs. Brooks hired a carriage from Mr. Pearce for use in the course of her occupation. Mrs. Brooks did not pay the amount agreed upon, and Mr. Pearce sought the help of the court to enforce that contract between them. However, the main issue that drew the attention of the court was that Mrs. Brooks was a prostitute, and the carriage was going to be used in "carrying on her immoral vocation." The plaintiffs knew that she was a prostitute, would use the carriage in her work, and that they would be paid with the profits from prostitution. Even though prostitution itself was not illegal, the contract was found to be contrary to public policy. The court found that there was no reason to make a distinction between an "illegal and immoral act" and where "people choose to enter into immoral contracts they must take the consequences, and cannot apply to the court for assistance in enforcing such contracts." The court found the contract immoral and thus unenforceable. However, the *motive* behind the contract has been found to be irrelevant as in the following case.

WILLIAMS v CARWARDINE (1833), 4B & AD 621, 110 ER 590 (KB)

In this case there was a reward posted by the defendant for information leading to the arrest and conviction of a murder suspect. The plaintiff, Mary Williams, was the last person to see the deceased (who was described as a "lusty man") alive, but Ms. Williams came forward with the information only after she had been brutally beaten and thought she was dying. The defendant felt that Ms. Williams was only motivated by her conscience, and not to help bring to justice the person who had committed this murder. He thought Ms. Williams did not deserve the reward because she did not come forward sooner. However, the court found that the plaintiff knew of the reward, she gave information leading to the arrest of the suspect, and she came within the terms of the advertisement. The court found that there was a contract with the person who performed the terms of the advertisement, and the plaintiff's motivation was completely irrelevant.

Difficulties also arise when both of the parties have done something wrong. Courts have generally followed the Latin maxim *in pari delicto, potior est condition defendentis*, or where "both parties are equally in the wrong, the position of the defendant is stronger." This means that the court is not going to help out a plaintiff who is also in the wrong. Illegal and public policy contracts fall into various categories including contracts to commit a crime or tort, contracts to avoid jurisdiction, contracts to obstruct justice, aiding the enemy, contracts to promote litigation, and contracts in restraint of trade. Not only does a contract have to be legal, it must also be possible. A contract with a psychic to bring your dead dog

YOU DECIDE

Brucker v Marcovitz, [2007] SCJ No 54 (SCC)

The parties were married in 1969 and divorced in 1981. As a part of the divorce proceedings, the parties negotiated an agreement that they would appear before the rabbinical authorities to seek a Jewish divorce (or "*get*") to allow the wife to remarry under Jewish law. Without a *get*, the wife would be unable to remarry in the religion. The two parties entered into the contract voluntarily, and intended it to have legal consequences. The husband refused to provide the *get* for 15 years, and the wife sought damages for breach of agreement. The husband said that a *get* was not valid under Quebec law, and that he had a right to freedom of religion. Although the trial court allowed damages for breach of contract, the court of appeal disagreed and overturned the judgment. What did the Supreme Court of Canada do?

back to life would not be legally enforceable since this is an impossible task. The entire contract does not have to be unenforceable. In limited circumstances if just parts of the agreement are illegal, only those parts of the agreement that are offensive or illegal will be void.

Consideration May Be Present or Future, but Not Past

Lastly, consideration may be present or future, but not past. Since consideration involves the exchange of commitment between parties, both parties must be required to do something by the agreement. This requirement is satisfied when both parties promise to make payment or payment in kind (e.g., services) at the same time (the present) or at a future time (e.g., when I get paid). So, the party may say, "I will pay $1000 when you are done the job," which is future consideration, or "I will pay you $1000 now," which is present consideration. But, the statement "because you painted my house, I will give you $1000" is past consideration and is not enforceable. The courts do not enforce a contract if the services have already been provided in the past and the recipient, out of gratitude, agrees to make some payment. "Thanks for painting my house. I'm going to give you $1000 when I get paid" is past consideration and will not be enforced. The courts have said that "past consideration is no consideration."[9] Past consideration was the issue in *Eastwood v Kenyon* (see the following case box).

EASTWOOD v KENYON (1840), 113 ER 482 (QB)

The plaintiff paid for the education of Sarah, his young ward, whose father died when she was young. The plaintiff borrowed money for Sarah's education, but Sarah later promised to repay him with interest on that loan. Sarah later married and her new husband also promised to pay the loan. Sarah's husband failed to pay the amount, and the guardian sued him on his promise. The court found that past consideration is not consideration at all, and that the new husband's promise to pay back the loan was simply moral and not legal. The commitment was made years after the consideration was given and, thus, was unenforceable.

PUTTING IT ALL TOGETHER—*BEACOCK v WETTER*, [2006] BCJ NO 1416 (BCSC)

The case of *Beacock v Wetter* incorporates parts of all of the elements needed to form a contract. Ms. Wetter owned a house in Port Coquitlam, British Columbia, which she rented to Mr. Beacock for $950 a month. Mr. Beacock moved his family into the house and paid the agreed-upon rent, but it was Mr. Beacock's evidence that Ms. Wetter agreed to a rent-to-own agreement where he would purchase the house for $200 000 at some time in the future in installments of extra $500-per-month payments for the next year and a half. Mr. Beacock made substantial improvements to the house, which he alleged to be in the amount of approximately $23 000. However, the $200 000 purchase price was not paid, the extra $500 per month was not received, and Ms. Wetter sought to evict the family from the property after their discussions had broken down about the purchase of the property. Eventually, Mr. Beacock sued Ms. Wetter for damages for not fulfilling the terms of the "contract" to sell him the house and to compensate him for all of the improvements he had made. The court had to examine whether there was a contract for the sale of the property, whether the defendant breached the contract, and whether Mr. Beacock was entitled to go through with the contract for sale, or whether he should receive damages to compensate him for the sale that did not go ahead.

9. There are some exceptions to this general rule under limited circumstances. See also *Pao On v Lau Yiu Long*, [1980] AC 614 (PC).

The court set out what is required in a contract including the "making of a definite offer by the promisor, that is unconditionally accepted by the promise, and for which consideration (something of value) has been provided by the promise to the promisor." The court said that a contract is incomplete if the terms are not agreed upon, or the contract is too general or uncertain to qualify as a contract. The court found that there was no evidence of a definite offer, acceptance, or consideration and that there was no meeting of the minds. The court held that a contract "requires certainty" and it was clear that there was no consideration which requires that something of benefit passes from the promise to the promisor. In the alternative, there was no evidence of a seal. The court found that Mr. Beacock was not to be permitted to enforce the sale of the house, nor for the improvements he had made because there simply was no enforceable contract. Mr. Beacock appealed this decision to the B.C. Court of Appeal in 2008, but the appeals court came to the same decision that there was no meeting of the minds, no consideration, and thus no contract.

Intention

The last element that must be present for a contract to exist is that there is an intention to enter into a legal relationship. Statements made in anger, such as "I am going to hire a bounty hunter to kill you" or as a joke, "I will give you a million dollars if you eat this worm" will not be held up by the courts to be a contract under the reasonable person test. The court will ask what would a reasonable person, in the position of the promisee, have thought of the conduct of the promisor? Did that person intend to enter into legal obligations?

People make agreements all the time but they are not legally binding; they agree to play soccer or to meet for dinner, but these agreements are not commercial relationships but rather they are friendships and domestic relationships and thus, there is no intention to be legally bound and no legal contract. To enforce these contracts, the wronged party would have to show persuasive evidence that the parties intended to be bound. It is not practical to delve into the mind of the promisor to see that he or she had a secret intention not to be bound, so these elements have to be made on an objective basis. Similarly, many people do not realize that they have entered into complex legal realities, not realizing that an oral contract was enforceable, or not realizing that the remedies could be costly if they breach that contract. Ignorance of the law is no excuse.

Agreements made by "honour" are also not enforceable. Famously stated by Justice Vaisey, "a gentleman's agreement is an agreement which is not an agreement entered into between two persons, neither of whom is a gentleman, with each expecting the other to be strictly bound, while he himself has no intention of being bound at all."[10] The courts will not step in to enforce these types of agreements.

A person must *intend* to agree to a contract before it is considered legally binding.

diego cervo/Photos.com

Where commercial transactions are involved, just the opposite is true. The court presumes there is an intention to be legally bound and the parties would have to present evidence to show that there was no intent to enter into a contractual relationship. One situation where there is difficulty telling if there was an intention to enter into a contractual relationship is with advertisements. Advertisers and sellers often exaggerate the quality and features of their products in order to make a sale. Advertisers beware—one of the most famous of all contracts cases, *Carlill v Carbolic Smoke Ball Company* (see the following case box), deals with product embellishment.

10. Cited in RE McGarvie, CL Pannan, and PJ Hocker, *McGarvie, Cases and Material on Contract*, 4th ed (Sydney: The Law book Co. Ltd., 1979) at 16.

CARLILL v CARBOLIC SMOKE BALL COMPANY, [1893] 1 QB 256 (CA)

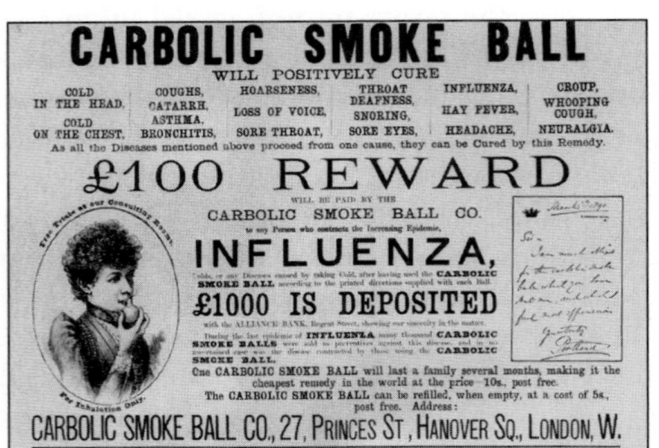

An ad for the Carbolic Smoke Ball, guaranteeing its effectiveness.

Illustrated London News/Hulton Archive/Getty Images

In 1893, the Carbolic Smoke Ball Company advertised that if you bought its "medical preparation" called the "Carbolic Smoke Ball," it would guarantee that you would not contract the flu. To show how confident the company was in its product, a £100 reward would be paid by the company to "any person who contracts the increasing epidemic influenza, colds, or any disease caused by taking cold, after having used the ball three times daily for two weeks according to the printed directions supplied with each ball." The money was deposited with a particular bank, named in the advertisement, in order to show "our sincerity in the matter." Ms. Carlill bought the product and did exactly as the directions instructed, but she still contracted the flu and sued the company. The trial court said that Ms. Carlill was entitled to the money, but the company appealed. The court had to examine whether the defendant's advertisement and the plaintiff's use of the product per the instructions constituted a contract that was enforceable. The company said that the offer was too vague and for an indefinite period of time, and that the advertisement was a mere "puff" rather than intent to be bound by a contract.

The court found that an ordinary person reading this advertisement would be induced to buy the product through a unilateral offer to the world at large. The court said that the specificity with which the company said that a defined amount of money was to be kept at a particular bank for payment if the person contracted the flu was not intended to be a "puff" but rather it was "intended to be understood by the public as an offer which was to be acted on." The acceptance was fulfilled by Ms. Carlill buying the smoke ball, and using it as directed as "performance of the condition is sufficient acceptance without notification of it." Consideration was also fulfilled as there was "inconvenience" to Ms. Carlill as she had to use the smoke ball several times a day for several weeks. The appeal was dismissed, and Ms. Carlill was entitled to her reward. There was a clear intention to enter into legal relations through this unilateral agreement, which always has the risk of not knowing that someone has accepted your offer until the other party performs. Today, this case would be more likely dealt with by regulations in place to protect consumers, rather than by case law.

CAPACITY

To form a contract, the person entering into the agreement has to have certain characteristics, and those individuals we view as vulnerable are in need of protection in contract law. Some groups are said to lack **capacity**, such as minors and those who are mentally disordered, so the law provides that they may not enter into legally binding contracts in certain situations. Many have criticized this paternalistic perspective that some should be protected from themselves and argue that everyone should have the right to contract freely.

Minors

In Canada, each province and territory is responsible for setting the age of majority, and anyone under the age of majority is a **minor child**. The age of majority is 18 years old in Alberta, Manitoba, Ontario, Prince Edward Island, Quebec, and Saskatchewan; and it is 19 years of age in British Columbia, New Brunswick, Newfoundland and Labrador, Nova Scotia, the Northwest Territories, Nunavut, and the Yukon. This age may vary according to other federal and provincial legislation.

A minor child's capacity to enter into a contract is restricted. One class of contract is for "necessaries," or what we now call "necessities." When a minor contracts to purchase necessities, which are goods like food, clothing, shelter, and services (such as medical treatment, education, and apprenticeship and employment matters), the minor is bound by the agreement and can be sued if he or she fails to honour that contract. These items must be true necessities and must have already been delivered and received. This is logical because if a minor was not able to enter into any contracts, they would not be able to go to the corner store and buy a chocolate bar. This ability to contract is even more important for those approaching the age of majority who increasingly look after their own affairs (such as paying tuition, renting an apartment, etc.). A contract that would not have been valid when the party was a minor can be affirmed later in time when the person does reach that age.

Interestingly, in the case of *Mosher v Benson*, [2008] NSJ No 464 (NS Small Claims), the court interpreted what constitutes a necessary. Mr. Mosher was 17 years old when he purchased a car and later sought to void the transaction for what he claimed was an inflated price. Since there was no evidence that this car was a necessary to the minor, the contract for the car was **voidable** at the option of the minor, and he wished to return the vehicle for the return of the full sale price.

While the child is free to enter the contract, the adult that the child is bargaining with cannot enforce the contract against the minor. If the child does not pay for the computer, the owner can go to court to have the product returned but cannot enforce payment. If the child has paid for the computer (the contract has been performed), then the court will only get involved when there is clear evidence that the child has been cheated.

Guardians may be put in place to assist young people who have not reached the age of majority, or the contracts made by the minor may be **void** or voidable. A void contract is one that is treated as if it never existed. However, a voidable contract is one where the party in control may make it binding or not binding on their preference. Consider the situation where a 16-year-old buys something that is not a necessity, but the adult contracted with finds out the other party is a minor and wants to rescind the contract. That adult is bound to fulfill the terms if the minor wishes it to be so. Thus, adults have to contract with minors at their own risk, and the court will question whether the minor paid a reasonable price for the goods. If it was unreasonable, the minor may not be obligated to pay.

Statute now governs much of the law on minors and contracts. See, for example, the British Columbia *Sale of Goods Act*, RSB. 1996, c 410. Section 7 provides that:

> **Capacity to buy and sell**
>
> 7(1) In this section, "necessaries" means goods suitable to the condition in life of a person, and to the person's actual requirements at the time of the sale and delivery.
> (2) Capacity to buy and sell is regulated by the general law concerning capacity to contract and to transfer and acquire property.
> (3) Despite subsection (2), if necessaries are sold and delivered to a person who because of mental incapacity or drunkenness is incompetent to contract, that person must pay a reasonable price for them.[11]

Mental Disorder

Those with serious mental disorders are also given protection in contract law, but the disorder must be serious enough that the individual did not understand the nature of the agreement. The purpose of this provision is, again, the protection of those who might not be in a position of equal bargaining power. The person with the disorder must show that the other party knew or ought to have known of this disability. The court will look at whether the deal was unconscionable. If the deal is fair, it will be enforced; if it is not,

11. See also *Sale of Goods* Act, RSA 2000, c S-2, s 4; *Sale of Goods Act*, CCSM c S10 s 4; *Sale of Goods Act*, RSNB 1973, c S-1, s 3; *Sale of Goods Act*, RSNL 1990, c S-6 s 4; *Sale of Goods Act*, RSNS 1989, c 408, s 5; *Sale of Goods Act*, RSNWT 1988, c S-2, s 7; *Sale of Goods Act*, RSNWT (Nu) 1988, c S-2, s 7; *Sale of Goods Act*, RSPEI 1988, c S-1, s 4; *Sale of Goods Act*, RSO 1990, c S.1 s 3; *Sale of Goods Act*, RSS 1978, c S-1, s 4; *Sale of Goods Act*, RSY 2002, c 198 s 3.

it may not be enforced. The party must also show that he or she **repudiated**, or sought to void, the agreement in a reasonable time after becoming sane (if this ever happens). A party is not permitted to decide at a time in the future that he or she no longer wishes to be bound by the contract after that person has benefitted from it for some time.

Intoxication

Intoxication by drugs and/or alcohol is treated similarly to mental disorder. The person trying to void the contract must have been so intoxicated that he or she did not understand the nature of the agreement, and moreover must show that the person he or she was dealing with knew or ought to have known that the individual was intoxicated. Again, the individual must make prompt and positive steps to repudiate the contract as soon as he or she is sober, as was done in case of *Watmough* et al *v Cap's Construction Ltd* (see the following case box).

WATMOUGH ET AL *v CAP'S CONSTRUCTION LTD*. 1976 CANLII 268 (AB QB)

In this case the defendant refused to deliver a piece of construction equipment to the plaintiff after they had signed an agreement. The defendant returned all cheques that the plaintiff had given him for the sale, and alleged that the he was incapacitated by alcohol and disease when the contract was signed. The defendant called evidence that he was so intoxicated that he had the agreement read to him twice, and that the plaintiff was fully aware that he was drunk and that the plaintiff had even asked the defendant to "be sober" when they were finalizing the deal. The defendant had obvious signs of mental deterioration on the witness stand and the court found that the defendant was not capable of entering into a binding contract on the day in question, and that the deal was not fair and reasonable. The court dismissed the plaintiff's claim, and the equipment remained with the defendant.

CONSENT

Each of the parties to a contract must understand to what they are agreeing to be bound. Four different issues can arise: mistakes, misrepresentations, undue influence, and duress. Statements made by the parties in the course of negotiations leading up to the contract may be classified as **representations**. Representations are statements that induce the contract but are not part of the contract (e.g., this will help you reduce your costs and increase business). If representations are false, then the remedy may include an action for misrepresentation. A term is an undertaking and implies a legal obligation. The word "condition" is used to describe an important term in the contract and is one that, if it is not met, voids the contract (e.g., a conditional offer on a house contingent on financing, a house inspection, or selling one's own house). A **warranty** denotes a term that is less important than a condition. It usually only allows one party to claim damages if there is a breach but does not discharge the person from the contract.

Mistakes

Mistakes often occur when a person has a mistaken belief about the subject matter or the content of the agreement. There are three main types of mistakes. First, there are common mistakes that are shared by both parties and can be fixed through rectification (e.g., a typo that can be fixed). Second, there can be a misunderstanding between the parties about the terms of the agreement. The court will ask what a reasonable person thought they were purchasing. Lastly, there is a one-sided, or unilateral, mistake where only one person knows there has been a mistake, but does nothing to remedy the problem. As long as that person did not actively contribute to the error, there is no remedy. The operative principle is ***caveat emptor*** or "let the buyer beware." Only where there is a special relationship of trust between the parties, where one party is clearly relying on the other to disclose information, is there an obligation to disclose the error (e.g., an insurance policy). If one can prove that there has been a unilateral mistake, the contract is void and unenforceable.

Misrepresentations

Although parties must accept the consequences of the contracts they negotiate, a misrepresentation is a false statement of fact that induces a person to enter into a contract that he or she would not otherwise enter. The seller cannot actively mislead the purchaser or provide false information about a **material fact**, or this will be considered as misrepresentation, which is a wrongful act. A misrepresentation may void the contract depending on whether it was an innocent misrepresentation or a fraudulent misrepresentation. If a seller is simply innocently repeating what he or she has been told about a product, then the buyer is entitled to **rescission**, which will put the parties back in the situation they were in before the contract.

However, if the victim has been induced to enter the agreement through a fraudulent misrepresentation, he or she may ask the court to rescind, or undo, the contract and/or sue for damages because the seller was trying to defraud the buyer. The buyer must prove that he or she has suffered a loss that requires compensation. Sometimes rescission is not possible, as when the item has been given to a third party or it has been destroyed. Courts will also award damages if a statement was made negligently. Thus, even though the person making the statement thought it was true, he or she can be held responsible.

Undue Influence

The use of **undue influence** is considered wrongful conduct and may affect the validity of the contract. Undue influence often occurs in situations in which one person has power over another or is in a position of higher authority and/or a position of trust. If a person is unduly influenced to enter into a contract because of the dominating influence of another with whom he or she has a **fiduciary** relationship, the contract may be declared void by the court. This has been found in relationships of parent/child, lawyer/client, priest/member of the congregation, and doctor/patient. Even if there is no special relationship, the weaker party can show evidence that the stronger person took unfair advantage. If a party is induced to sign a contract by his or her priest, or if a lawyer forces a client to settle a matter in order to receive fees, there may be a fiduciary relationship that might have to be examined.

Duress

The largely accepted modern definition of contractual **duress** comes from Lord Scarman in the 1983 British case of *Universe Tankships Inc. of Monrovia v International Transport Workers Federation*, [1983] 1 AC 366, 400 (HL), who said there are two elements to contractual duress including "(1) pressure amounting to compulsion of the will; and (2) the illegitimacy of the pressure exerted."[12] One must first examine the actions of the complainant and explore the pressure, as the defendant must have acted in such a way that it was clear that there was pressure that guided his actions, and that pressure was wrongful. It is the combination of these factors that forms duress. As a result of coercion in this context, contracts are not binding and are voidable at the option of the person who was coerced. *Cummings v Ince* is an outrageous example of contractual coercion (see the following case box).

CUMMINGS v INCE, (1847) 116 ER 418 (QB)

This case dealt with the forcible confinement in a "private lunatic asylum" of a mother by her two married daughters and their husbands. After the daughters had forcibly committed

12. Universe Tankships of Monrovia v International Transport Workers' Federation, [1983] 1 AC 366, 400 (HL).

their mother to the institution, they said that they would not pursue the finding of lunacy against her if she would sign over certain title deeds to property. Mrs. Cummings alleged that the contract that was the result of this deal was not binding as it was obtained by duress. Her lawyer's clerk testified that he believed that she only agreed to sign over the property because of her fear of being committed to a lunatic asylum. The court found that *even if* her confinement was legitimate, it was a "restraint on her will, which prevented any contract made under that duress from binding her." Justice Denman noted that "she was induced to resign them by fear of personal suffering brought upon her by confinement in a lunatic asylum by the act of the defendants," and that the contract that resulted was not of her own free will. The court found that Mrs. Cummings was induced to sign the documents so she would be released from the lunatic asylum, and concluded that this was certainly a case of duress. This confirmed the verdict of the lower court that the contract was found void for duress.

ISSUES AFFECTING THE CONTRACTUAL RELATIONSHIP

Exclusion Clauses

An exclusion clause inserted into a contract aims to exclude, or financially limit, one party's liability. Historically, the courts have sought to control the use of such clauses. Exclusion clauses do not protect parties from a serious or **fundamental breach** of the contract, even when the clause states that it does. This is especially so in the case of death or personal injury or negligence; one cannot **contract out** of the law. Generally, people who sign contracts with exclusion clauses are bound by them whether or not they read and/or understand them. Legislation also controls exclusion clauses in order to protect consumers and the general public.

Governments recognize the disparity in power and wealth between consumers and businesses and have passed legislation to protect consumers, as there is an imbalance in bargaining power. This usually requires companies to clearly notify clients about any waivers or limits to liability. For example, parking garages have to have a sign notifying clients that they are not responsible for theft of the contents of vehicles. Airlines will take responsibility for only so much of the value of lost or stolen luggage. Courier companies will insure packages only up to certain amounts, and additional insurance must be purchased beyond that limit. Courts have held that if you wish to impose restrictions on the client, you better make sure you bring it to the client's attention. With contracts in highly regulated industries, an individual is likely bound by the contract.

Privity

The rule of **privity** means that, in general, a person who is not a party to a contract, or what is called a third party, can neither sue or be sued on a contract. If you are a stranger, you are not allowed to have legal rights regarding other people's contracts. However, there are some exceptions, including contracts dealing with land. Privity **runs with the land**, which means that those people who rent still have rights, even though they do not own the land. Another exception to the privity principal is a trust. A trust involves a person entering a contract with another to hold money or property to be eventually paid out to a third party, often a family member. The trust allows the beneficiary to enforce the agreement even though the individual is not a party. Life insurance is treated in a similar way, since the beneficiary can force the insurance company to honour the contract even after the death of the insured. Another exception to the privity rule is the agency. An agent is a go-between, entering into contracts with a third party on behalf of a principal. The agent is not a party to the agreement. The contract is between the principal, the person the agent is acting for, and the third party (e.g., real estate agents or insurance agents).

What Does a Proper Contract Look Like?

You walk into the campus bookstore. You see the book that you need for your legal studies course on the shelf with the very reasonable price on the back of the book. You go to the cash register and put the book on the counter. By this action, you are telling the person working at the bookstore that you wish to purchase that book. The store clerk starts entering the price into the cash register. This is offer and acceptance. You offered to buy the book, and the clerk accepted that offer by starting the procedure to sell the book. You give your money to the clerk, and the clerk puts this money in the register, and gives you the book and a receipt. There has been consideration because something of value (here, something at least the value of a peppercorn) is exchanged between the parties. You have the capacity to enter into the contract as you are of age and free of a mental disorder, which would affect your capacity to buy the book. The clerk did not hold a gun to your head or threaten your family if you did not buy the fantastic legal studies book, and you did not berate the clerk into giving you the book for free. There was no other social policy reason to stop this contract, and it is (currently) not illegal to buy the book. Success! You have completed a contract.

DISCHARGING THE CONTRACT

A contractual relationship can be brought to an end in four different ways: performance, agreement, frustration, and breach.

Performance

When a contract is fully performed, the contract comes to an end. However, some contractual obligations may be ongoing, even though it seems that the performance of the contract has been completed (e.g., warranties). One must adhere to all of the rules for the contract to be performed. For example, there are rules about how to satisfy a debt, as only certain types of currency are allowed. The form of payment is dictated under the *Currency Act*, (RSC, 1985, c C-52) which allows a person to refuse payment (performance) under certain conditions (e.g., making the entire payment in nickels and pennies). According to the *Currency Act*, s 8, payment can only be made in the following denominations: $40 if the denomination is toonies; $25 if the denomination is loonies; $10 if the denomination is dimes or quarters; $5 if the denomination is nickels; and 25 cents if the denomination is pennies. Also, if one party attempts to perform the contract but the other party *refuses* payment or performance, the court has found that the party refusing then cannot go to the court to sue the person who attempted to perform.

Agreement

The second way a contract can come to an end, or be modified, is by agreement of the parties. If both agree to change or end the contract, that brings an end to the rights and obligations. The contract may explicitly provide how a contract can come to an end. This may be through something called a **condition precedent**—for example, subject to the sale of my home within 30 days, I will enter into a contract to buy another home. The deal to purchase the house is contingent on selling the old house. If this does not happen, the purchaser has no obligation to go forward with the sale. **Condition subsequent**, on the other hand, is that a contract may end when something happens. For example, I will continue to work at the business until it is sold. Contingent on something that might happen sometime in the future—the contract will end.

Frustration

The third major way a contract can come to an end is through **frustration**. Historically, a person entering into an agreement was bound to perform its terms no matter the circumstances. The results were often unfair, and so the doctrine of frustration was developed. A contract can be discharged by frustration when some outside event takes place that makes performance of the contract illegal or impossible. The outside event cannot be either party's fault, it cannot be within the control of either party, and it cannot be anticipated by either party.

Frustration can arise in three situations:

1. The contract becomes impossible to perform (e.g., the house burns down).
2. A change in law renders it illegal (e.g., an outbreak of war).
3. There occurs a radical change in circumstances, leading to the requirement of something radically different.

The effect of frustration is to discharge the contract. Benefits received beforehand must be paid for, and deposits can be recovered. But, if the frustration is self-induced, then the contract is not discharged (e.g., you cannot burn down your own house). What if something happened that no one could foresee? See *630393 Saskatchewan Ltd. v Antonishen* in the following case box.

630393 SASKATCHEWAN LTD. v ANTONISHEN 2003 SKPC 94 (SASK PROV CT)

Frustration was an issue in this case because the defendant, Ms. Antonishen, placed her mother in a personal care home for the fee of $3000 per month. In less than 48 hours of being placed in the home, the defendant's mother became ill and was rushed to the hospital, never to return to the care facility. The nursing home plaintiff sued the defendant for the fee of $3000, claiming that the contract that the defendant had signed said that she had to give the home "30 days written notice" of a termination of the agreement, or she was responsible for the entirety of the fees. There was no provision for dealing with a situation where the patient was taken out of the facility in such a short period of time. The defendant claimed there was frustration of the contract as neither party could have anticipated what happened.

The court cited Saskatchewan case law in that "when, without the default of either party, a supervening act occurs for which the contract has not made sufficient provision that so significantly changes the nature of the outstanding contractual rights and obligations from what the parties could have reasonably contemplated at the time of its execution ... it would be unjust to hold them to the terms of their contract in new circumstances." The court concluded that there had been frustration of the contract, and used the provisions under the *Frustrated Contracts Act* to apportion the expenses.[13] For the administrative and service charges incurred by the facility, the court ordered damages in the amount of $700 for the few hours the defendant's mother was in the home, and not the $3000 requested.

Breach

The final way a contract can come to an end is through **breach**. If one of the parties has not fulfilled his or her obligations, the victim is entitled to treat the contract as finished and can sue for breach and seek to recover damages. This breach may take place either through incomplete or incompetent performance of the contractual obligation or through refusal to perform. When refusal to perform is involved, the act is referred to as repudiation. **Anticipatory breach** is when repudiation takes place before performance is required under the contract. For example, I was under contract to walk your dog starting September 1, but I am not going to do it even though it is just July 1 now, and I have no justification for not performing. Breach can take various forms. Students must be aware that student loans are very important contracts, and there are severe consequences when there is a breach. (See the case of *Wang v HMTQ* in the following case box.)

13. See *Frustrated Contracts Act*, SS 1994, c F-22.2, s 6; *Frustrated Contracts Act*, RSA 2000, c F-27, s 4; *Frustrated Contracts Act*, RSNB 1973, c F-24, s 3; *Frustrated Contracts Act*, RSPEI 1988, c F-16, s 3; *Frustrated Contracts Act*, RSNL 1990, c F-26, s 4; *Frustrated Contracts Act*, RSY 2002, c 9, s 5; *Frustrated Contracts Act*, RSO 1990, c F.3, s 3; *Frustrated Contracts Act*, RSNWT (Nu) 1988, c F-12, s 4; *Frustrated Contracts Act*, RSNWT. 1988, c F-12, s 4; *Frustrated Contract Act*, RSBC 1996, c 166, s 7.

WANG v HMTQ, (2006) BCSC 2001 (SCBC)

Mr. Wang brought an action against the province of British Columbia for discontinuing his student loans (in addition to allegations of conspiracy, deceit, discrimination, fraud, and slander). In all, Mr. Wang was suing the province for $1 496 200. Mr. Wang applied for a student loan in B.C. for his education at Dalhousie University for the 2002–03 school year. The loan agreement is a contract between the parties, and the province alleged several breaches by Mr. Wang. First, he was alleged to have misrepresented how long he would be in school. Second, he took a leave of absence for the fall 2002 semester. Third, he failed to advise the loan office that his circumstances had changed, and finally, he failed to use the loan for tuition, but rather used it to pay for his expenses, and those of his wife and child still in British Columbia. In fact, the province alleged that it was owed $2912 for the semester that Mr. Wang did not attend school. The court found that Mr. Wang had breached his contract in all four ways alleged by the province, and he was responsible for paying back the loans he received when he was not in school. The court found the cancellation of the contract by the province was justified in the circumstances, as Mr. Wang had breached numerous contractual terms. Mr. Wang's action for $1 496 200 was wholly unsuccessful and, in fact, he was liable for paying back the $2912 to the province.

REMEDIES

Rescission

Where a contract has been breached there are several possible remedies. One of the most basic things that an individual can ask a court to do is to rescind the contract. This means that the parties are placed in the position they were in prior to the contract.

Damages

The most common remedy is monetary compensation, or what are called damages. Damages are ordered by the court to compensate the victim monetarily for the wrong perpetrated by the defendant, but they are not meant to punish person who has breached the contract. Rather, such a payment is designed to put the victim as near as possible to the position he or she would have been in had the contract been properly performed. Only those losses that could be reasonably foreseen at the time of the contract will be compensated for, and it is important to note that you have a responsibility to **mitigate** your losses by trying to limit the amount that was lost. If the court sees that you knew that there was a problem with the contract and continued to spend money or ignore the situation, the court is not going to compensate you for sitting back and watching the damages add up. For example, if your tenant in a building decides to leave in the middle of a tenancy agreement, you must not just sit back and leave the unit empty, but instead try to find another tenant to limit the losses that will be suffered. Damages can be classified as general damages (or those that are difficult to attribute monetary value to, like loss of income and future earnings, or things like pain and suffering) or special damages (for out-of-pocket expenses). Special damages are most common in contractual cases (see Chapter 5).

Quantum Meruit (Quantity and Merit)

A claim for ***quantum meruit*** is a claim for reasonable remuneration, or what some have termed "as much as one deserves." When services are requested without agreement on a specific price and those services are performed, there is a legal obligation to pay a reasonable price. When you take your car into a mechanic, you are obligated to pay a reasonable amount for the services you have requested, even though you may not have agreed on a price. The law will protect workers and tradespeople when clients refuse to pay their bills, but it can also protect individuals in agreements they were not sure they were entering into. In *Gill v Grant*, [1998] BCJ No. 1705 (BCSC), the plaintiff lived in a house that was owned by his wife's aunt, and they made major renovations to the home, as well as paying rent to cover the mortgage cost. The plaintiff's wife died, and there was a dispute about who should benefit from the sale of the house. The court found that if one has a contract that has no clause specifying the payment for the services, the courts are able to "award reasonable remuneration to the person who has rendered services." The court found that Mr. Gill was entitled to the **fair market value** of the materials and labour that he had expended to renovate the home.

The *Sale of Goods Act* in most provinces has similar provisions, providing a reasonable price for goods sold when no specific amount has been agreed upon. The Ontario *Sale of Goods Act*, RSO 1990, c S.1 states, at s 9(2), that when a price is not determined, "the buyer shall pay a reasonable price, and what constitutes a reasonable price is a question of fact dependent on the circumstances of each particular case."[14] Similarly, all other provinces and territories in Canada have a similar provision in their individual *Sale of Goods Act* legislation providing for an investigation of the circumstances of the dealings between the parties in order to determine what is a reasonable price.

Specific Performance

As a secondary remedy, the courts may also order the party in breach to finish the agreement through what is known as **specific performance**. This remedy is only available when damages are inadequate. It is most commonly used in relation to the breach of contract for the sale of land. Since land is often unique, damages are not usually enough to compensate the individual. However, this also applies to specific goods. If you purchased a one-of-a-kind painting, you can go to the court for this remedy so that you will get this exact painting. There are situations where specific performance is not appropriate, such as where performance will impose undue hardship. Specific performance is not available for personal service, as it cannot be specifically enforced; for example, the judge is not going to come to your house to sit on the couch to watch the painters to make sure that your living room is painted per the contract.

Injunction

An **injunction** is the opposite of specific performance and can be used to make a person stop what he or she is doing if it is inconsistent with the terms of the contract. This is an enforcement of a negative term or a promise not to do something in the contract. If an employee has signed a contract not to work for a competing company for six months, the previous employer can go to the court to order the employee not to work for another company for that period of time. This can also be used in patent law to ensure that someone is not wrongfully acting on a patent.

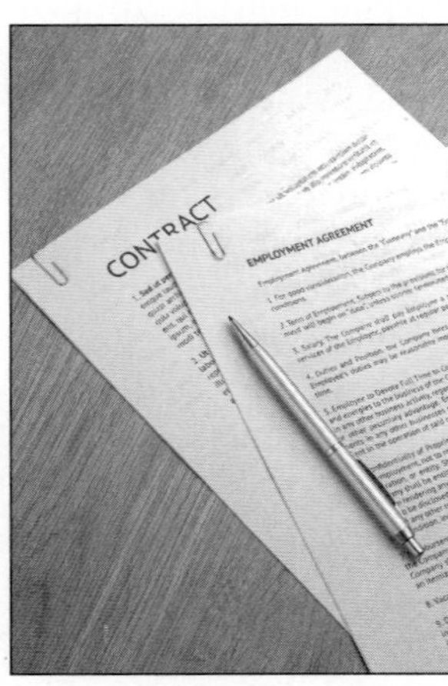

Svetlana Lukienko/Shutterstock

An employment agreement may include a provision that prevents the employee from leaving the company to work for a competitor.

EMERGING ISSUES IN CONTRACT LAW: ONLINE CONTRACT FORMATION

There are so many questions raised by electronic contracts in the business environment and what has now become known as e-commerce. Statistics Canada reports that e-commerce continues to grow every year, with the 2007 numbers up 26 percent to an estimated $62.7 billion a year.[15] It has been queried whether electronic data interchange and contracts formed by email are enforceable. Are encrypted electronic signatures and "I agree"

14. See also See also *Sale of Goods Act*, RSA 2000, c S-2, s 10; *Sale of Goods Act*, CCSM c S10 s 10; *Sale of Goods Act*, RSNB 1973, c S-1, s 9; *Sale of Goods Act*, RSNL 1990, c S-6 s 10; *Sale of Goods Act*, RSNS 1989, c 408, s 11; *Sale of Goods Act*, RSNWT 1988, c S-2, s 12; *Sale of Goods Act*, RSNWT (Nu) 1988, c S-2, s 12; *Sale of Goods Act*, RSPEI 1988, c S-1, s 10; *Sale of Goods Act*, RSS 1978, c S-1, s 10; *Sale of Goods Act*, RSY 2002, c 198 s 9.

15. Statistics Canada, 2008, online: <http://www.statcan.gc.ca/daily-quotidien/080424/dq08424a-eng.htm>.

boxes really components of a valid contract? Are user agreements and automated confirmations binding? Many commentators say that the differences between traditional contracts and those formed in the new age of technology are negligible. Some commentators say that there is a "cyberspace fallacy" that urges us to treat online contracts as somehow special.[16] However, many of the concepts discussed in this chapter apply to online methods as much as they do to the traditional contract.

It is quite evident that the principles learned in *Carlill* are just as relevant to Internet advertising as they were to the handbill produced on the Carbolic Smoke Ball. If one clicks the appropriate box to accept the terms of an agreement online, we have learned that a contract can be formed if you are said to have consented. Joseph Savirimuthu argues that this is simply "old wine in new bottles" but it is important to not allow "online methods of communications [to] become passive conduits."[16] It is important to recognize the new methods and the limitations and flaws related, but there is something to be learned from the traditional conception. A contract does not lose its fundamental components simply because the contract is online, and this is clearly something that early framers did not wholly anticipate. The court found in *National Bank of Canada v Chace*, [1996] OJ No. 3251 (Ont SCJ), that, just like the traditional rules, virtually instantaneous means of communication still provide that acceptance must be communicated to the offeror and be accepted in that place for a contract to be formed.

The post box rule simply is slightly reframed in that if there is non-immediate communication used, perhaps it should be deemed to be effective when it leaves the control of the person accepting the contract. This takes into account other forms of communication frequently used in today's marketplace, such as mail, couriers, and so forth. However, it is important to note that these rules may not be a complete account of the considerations required to determine if there is truly consent in our emerging cyber world. It seems that the Canadian courts have not yet fully determined if there should be an electronic post box rule, but it will likely take into consideration the technology used and the intention of the parties. Many questions, including when the message is sent (is it sent when you hit the "send" key, when it was stored, or when it leaves the sender's system?), will need to be addressed by the courts. Perhaps the answer is not to eliminate centuries of rules, but to learn what is needed to alter those rules for our new everyday realities. There are few cases on contracts formed by email in Canada at this time, but there are many issues that may face this type of communication of acceptance where the server is down, or where the technology fails for some reason.

The Ontario Superior Court of Justice had an early opportunity to discuss some of these issues in *Rudder v Microsoft Corp.*, [1999] OJ No. 3778 (Ont SCJ). The plaintiffs claimed that while reading the Microsoft Network member agreement, certain provisions were not visible on the computer screen without scrolling ahead, and were therefore not binding. The court found that scrolling down was not "materially different from a multi-page written document which requires a party to turn the pages," and that this membership agreement "must be afforded the sanctity that must be given to any agreement in writing." Although there has been little Canadian case law on the subject of electronic documents, it seems that great pains have been taken to eliminate some of the risk by being clear what is an advertisement, whether an order will constitute an offer, what time the offer must remain open, whether automatic acknowledgments are confirming the offer rather than creating a contract, and by specifying precise methods needed for communication. It seems that with instantaneous communications the acceptance should be complete when it is received by the offeror's system, or when reasonable time has passed when it could be read.

One of the other electronic contracts cases that has been heard was the Ontario Superior Court of Justice case of *Kanitz v Rogers Cable Inc.* [2002] OJ No 665 (Ont SCJ). The court found that changes to the user agreement were sufficiently brought to the attention of

16. Joseph Savirimuthu, "Online Contract Formation: Taking Technological Infrastructure Seriously" (2005) 2:1 UOLT. 105 at para 4.

the plaintiffs, and there was adequate notice given as to the change in the arbitration provision. The court said that the clause was in the same font and print type as the other provisions of the contract, and it was not "tucked away in some obscure place designed to make it discoverable only through dogged determination. The clause is upfront and easily located by anyone who wishes to take the time to scroll through the document for even a cursory review of its contents." So again, it was found that electronic contracts had to adhere to similar principles of a traditional contract.

Legislation now governs many of the potential issues related to e-commerce. In June 1999, the Uniform Law Conference of Canada adopted the *Uniform Electronic Commerce Act* (UECA). This legislation was designed to be adopted by all provincial and territorial governments, except the Northwest Territories,[17] to provide a similar approach to e-commerce. All Canadian provinces and territories have now adopted the provisions of an international convention.[18] Most provinces have similar legislation (see the Food for Thought box). Although the legislation is quite detailed, it does not say which rules apply to the communication of an acceptance or what court has jurisdiction. There has been some reluctance to thoroughly regulate Internet contracts, which might be explained by the constant change and growth in these methods of contract. The federal government has also adopted equivalency between electronic and paper documents in the *Personal Information Protection and Electronic Documents Act* (*PIPEDA*), SC 2000, c 5.

EXAMPLE: CREDIT CARDS

A good indication about where contract law is going to be important in the near future is with credit cards. In September 2009, Canada's Minister of Finance and Governor General approved regulation under the *Credit Business Practices* to:

- mandate an effective minimum 21-day, interest-free grace period on all new credit card purchases when a customer pays the outstanding balance in full;
- allow consumers to keep better track of their personal finances by requiring express consent for credit limit increases; and
- limit debt collection practices that financial institutions use in contacting a consumer to collect on a debt.[19]

These changes were introduced to ensure that access to credit is fair and transparent, and to urge credit card companies to provide clear information in credit contracts and application forms through a summary box that will set out key features, such as interest rates and fees.

CONCLUSION

The main function of contract law is to "protect reasonable expectations engendered by promises."[20] Contract law is the basis of most business relationships. It is impossible to understand consumer laws, corporate law, real estate law, or the legal obligations between employers and employees without knowing what constitutes a valid contract. It is also important to understand the principles of contract law to protect oneself in consumer and personal relationships. It is always a good idea to be cautious in commercial transactions. Consult a lawyer, clearly state the terms in writing, and you will save your friendships and prevent lawsuits. The overriding principle in commercial relationships is still *caveat emptor,* or let the buyer beware.

---

17. Northwest Territories is currently drafting a provision. See <http://www.justice.gov.nt.ca/Consultation/documents/ELECTRONICCOMMERCEACT-FinalDraft.pdf>.
18. See Electronic Transactions Act, SA 2001, c E-5.5; Electronic Transactions Act, SBC 2001, c 10; The Electronic Commerce and Information Act, CCSM c E55; Electronic Transactions Act, SNB 2001, c E-5.5; Electronic Commerce Act, SNL 2001, c E-5.2; Electronic Commerce Act, SNS 2000, c 26; Electronic Commerce Act, S Nu 2004, c 7; Electronic Commerce Act, 2000 SO 2000, c 17; Electronic Commerce Act, RSPEI 1988, c E-4.1; Electronic Information and Documents Act, 2000, SS 2000, c E-7.22; Electronic Commerce Act, RSY 2002, c 66. Quebec's provisions are substantially different and beyond the scope of this text.
19. PC 2009-1528, September 9, 2009, online: <http://www.gazette.gc.ca/rp-pr/p2/2009/2009-09-30/html/sor-dors257-eng.html>.
20. SM Waddams, *The Law of Contracts*, 4th ed (Toronto: Canada Law Book, 1999) at 105.

FOOD FOR THOUGHT...

LEGISLATION: ONTARIO, *ELECTRONIC COMMERCE ACT*, 2000 SO 2000, C 17

Formation and operation of electronic contracts

19. (1) An offer, the acceptance of an offer or any other matter that is material to the formation or operation of a contract may be expressed,
    (a) by means of electronic information or an electronic document; or
    (b) by an act that is intended to result in electronic communication, such as,
        (i) touching or clicking on an appropriate icon or other place on a computer screen, or
        (ii) speaking.

...

Legal recognition of electronic contracts

(3) A contract is not invalid or unenforceable by reason only of being in electronic form.

Involvement of electronic agents

20. A contract may be formed by the interaction of an electronic agent and an individual or by the interaction of electronic agents.

Errors, transactions with electronic agents

21. An electronic transaction between an individual and another person's electronic agent is not enforceable by the other person if,
    (a) the individual makes a material error in electronic information or an electronic document used in the transaction;
    (b) the electronic agent does not give the individual an opportunity to prevent or correct the error;
    (c) on becoming aware of the error, the individual promptly notifies the other person; and
    (d) in a case where consideration is received as a result of the error, the individual,
        (i) returns or destroys the consideration in accordance with the other person's instructions or, if there are no instructions, deals with the consideration in a reasonable manner, and
        (ii) does not benefit materially by receiving the consideration.

Time of sending of electronic information or document

22. (1) Electronic information or an electronic document is sent when it enters an information system outside the sender's control or, if the sender and the addressee use the same information system, when it becomes capable of being retrieved and processed by the addressee.

...

Presumption, time of receipt

(3) Electronic information or an electronic document is presumed to be received by the addressee,
    (a) if the addressee has designated or uses an information system for the purpose of receiving information or documents of the type sent, when it enters that information system and becomes capable of being retrieved and processed by the addressee; or
    (b) if the addressee has not designated or does not use an information system for the purpose of receiving information or documents of the type sent, when the addressee becomes aware of the information or document in the addressee's information system and it becomes capable of being retrieved and processed by the addressee.

Places of sending and receipt

(4) Electronic information or an electronic document is deemed to be sent from the sender's place of business and received at the addressee's place of business.

LEARNING OUTCOMES SUMMARIZED

1. Define what is meant by meant by the term "contract."

A contract may be defined as an agreement between two or more persons, recognized by law, which gives rise to rights and/or obligations which the courts *may* enforce.

2. Discuss the elements of a contract.

There are three basic ingredients to a contract: consensus (including an offer and an unqualified acceptance), consideration (both parties must provide valuable consideration), and intention (both parties must intend to be legally bound) .

3. Identify the fundamental rules of contract.

There are four fundamental rules of contract: (1) consideration must be sufficient but not necessarily adequate and specific; (2) a gratuitous promise is not consideration; (3) consideration is distinct from motive, but discharge of a moral or legal obligation is generally not sufficient; and (4) consideration may be present or future, but not past.

4. Analyze how to discharge a contract through breach.

A contract may come to an end through breach if one of the parties has not fulfilled the obligations, and the victim is entitled to treat the contract as finished and can sue for breach and seek to recover damages. This breach may take place either through incomplete or incompetent performance of the contractual obligation or through refusal to perform. When refusal to perform is involved, the act is referred to as repudiation. Anticipatory breach occurs when repudiation takes place before performance is required under the contract.

5. Assess legal remedies resulting from a contractual breach.

Damages in contracts may include rescission of the contract, damages, *quantum meruit*, specific performance, and injunctions.

SELF-EVALUATION QUESTIONS

1. Why do some contracts have to be in writing? What is the origin of this rule?
2. What was the key legal issue identified in the case of *Goldthorpe v Logan?*
3. Why can consideration be present or future but not past? Provide an example.
4. If I offer a payment of $500 if you find my missing pug dog, what kind of contract is this?
5. How can a gratuitous promise be made enforceable?
6. When is the remedy of specific performance available?

Tort Law

Over the centuries, tort has proved to be infinitely flexible and even the ancient rules are capable of being adapted to meet modern problems. The tort of negligence, which has emerged relatively recently as a tort in its own right, has been developed through case law to cover many important situations in life. By far the greatest number of tort actions arise out of road traffic accidents—a situation that would have been unimaginable in the Middle Ages.[1]

Learning Outcomes

After completing this chapter the student should be able to:

1. Identify the general categories of tort.
2. Define negligence.
3. List the six elements to prove a negligence action.
4. Assess class actions in Canada.
5. Identify legal remedies resulting from a tort.

DEFINITION OF A TORT

The word **tort** originally comes from the Latin term "*tortus*," which means twisted or curved, and has now come to be known in law as the French word for injustice or a "wrong."[2] In particular, it deals with civil law wrongs (rather than criminal wrongs), other than breach of contract, that one person commits against another, resulting in damages. Civil law, also known as private law, involves actions between parties that are not really of interest to the rest of society, and it simply compensates particular individuals for what has happened to them. The wrong done to the individual can be to his or her bodily integrity, dignity, property, or livelihood. Examples include assault, battery, malicious prosecution, infliction of nervous shock, false imprisonment, some privacy issues, trespass, and nuisance, and also includes manufacturers' liability, medical liability, and occupiers' liability.

1. Vivienne Harpwood, *Modern Tort Law*, 6th ed (London: Cavendish, 2005) at 484.
2. Robert M Solomon et al, *Cases and Materials on the Law of Torts* (Toronto: Carswell, 1996) at 1.

Tort law deals with civil, rather than criminal, wrongs.

© Peter Carroll / Alamy

Within certain circumstances, the person who causes the harm must compensate the victim. **Unintentional torts** such as negligence are the major cause of action in tort, but **intentional torts** are also litigated within distinct categories of wrongs. As was said in the case of *Ratych v Bloomer* (1990), 30 CCEL 161, the purpose of tort law is to "restore the injured person ... to the position he enjoyed prior to the injury, rather than to punish the tortfeasor whose only wrong may have been a moment of inadvertence."

Basic Principles

Tort law deals with situations in which one party has caused harm or injury to another party or his or her property. The person who begins the action is called the **plaintiff**, and the person who is defending the action is termed the **defendant**. A tort action is an attempt to use the civil law to bring a private action to seek compensation for the injuries suffered. Tort liability is premised on a lesser degree of proof than in criminal law; the standard is that of a **balance of probabilities.** Some behaviours are governed by statute and do not require the plaintiff to prove that the defendant was at fault, but simply committing the act makes the person guilty. Unlike contracts, in which parties agree when they can sue each other for breach, torts are governed by general principles of law that apply to everyone equally. It is important to note that there are some torts that relate to property, but property law has also largely become a separate class of civil action. One fact situation could result in a tort action, an equitable remedy, a breach of contract, and a criminal charge (see the Food for Thought box).

One of the first steps in an action is to determine whether the **cause of action** is a tort, and if so, what kind of tort has been committed, because there are several categories of wrongs and each has its own definition and requirements. Generally, Canadian law wants to compensate victims of intentional acts, negligent acts, acts deemed to be wrongful on the surface, and some special torts that have particular requirements. In addition, it must be decided who is going to be sued for the tort, and those people must be capable of compensating the victim. Tort cannot compensate victims for all of the losses that are remotely stemming from the wrongful act, so the courts must determine the amount of compensable damages owed to the victim.

Differences between Crime and Torts

Criminal cases also involve a wrong, but these behaviours are considered more serious because they threaten all of society, and they are dealt with as a public matter. Crimes are offences against the public or state (e.g., *R v Smith*), and the purpose is to punish the accused. The object of punishing criminal law offenders is the protection of society through incapacitation, deterrence, and/or rehabilitation. The interests of victims are largely ignored and they are relegated

FOOD FOR THOUGHT...

What is an example of a situation that could give rise to a tort action, an equitable remedy, a breach of contract, and a criminal charge? Consider the following situation.

Mr. Ashley was an employee of We-Make-Widgets.com, and has an employment contract. The contract specifies a "morals code." The code provides that the employees must not engage in any forms of violence in the workplace (putting aside whether this code would stand up in court). Mr. Ashley comes to work on February 23, 2012, and gets into a fight with his boss, Mr. Night. Mr. Ashley throws the first punch, which lands on Mr. Night's face, causing severe trauma to his nose. What may happen?

Can Mr. Night sue in tort?

Can Mr. Night file a police report and pursue a criminal charge?

Did Mr. Ashley violate his employment contract?

What equitable remedy could be pursued against Mr. Ashley?

to the role of witnesses in the criminal process, as criminal law is designed to punish an offender and to deter others from acting in a similar manner, with most of the focus on the offender.

Conversely, the object of the tort system is to compensate victims for negligence or intentional acts that cause harm between two individuals (e.g., *Jones v Smith*). Tort law looks more to the victim and what losses they need to be compensated for by another who has committed a tortious act. Whereas the state pays for criminal prosecutions, a tort action is wholly financed by the person who suffered the wrong. It is in the best interest of all of the population to stop criminal actions, but there is much less priority given to those who have suffered other kinds of losses. Individuals may spend hundreds of thousands of dollars in the civil law system without seeing any monetary compensation at the end of the matter.

There is an overlap between torts and many crimes. Being assaulted with a baseball bat is both assault in the criminal system and battery in the civil law system. Similarly, breaking into someone's property can be both criminal break and enter and trespass to land from a civil context. One act can be pursued in both criminal and civil court, but this is rarely done. The main reason is cost and the fact that the offender is unlikely to have money to pay for damages.

One of the most famous American examples of someone being liable for civil damages and facing criminal charges is the case involving former football star and actor O.J. Simpson. Mr. Simpson was accused of the 1994 stabbing death of his ex-wife Nicole Brown Simpson and her friend Ronald Goldman, who were found dead in front of her condominium in Brentwood California. On October 3, 1995, a jury found Mr. Simpson not guilty of the two counts of murder. However, the families of Ms. Brown Simpson and Mr. Goldman started a civil law wrongful death case against Mr. Simpson, and on February 4, 1997, the jury found Mr. Simpson liable for the deaths and awarded the plaintiffs US$8.5 million in compensatory damages. Although Mr. Simpson was found liable in civil law for the deaths, he was not found criminally guilty of murder. We may again see this type of high-profile case in both of the criminal and tort law systems with the conviction of Dr. Conrad Murray of the 2009 death of Michael Jackson, and now Jackson's family intends to sue Dr. Murray and Anschutz Entertainment Group (AEG). The family of Mr. Jackson alleges in their wrongful death tort case that the entertainment company pushed Mr. Jackson to stage a comeback tour when he was physically unfit to do so.[3]

In Canada, one may have to stop the civil action while the criminal action proceeds, and there can be long delays to seek assistance in both systems. The parties may apply to the court for a **stay of proceedings** of the civil matter until the criminal prosecution is completed, and there may be a practical reason to do so. The standard of proof is much different in the two types of actions. Conviction in criminal cases requires a higher degree of proof—that is, proof **beyond a reasonable doubt**. Tort liability is premised on a lesser degree of proof, that of a balance of probabilities. The standard of proof in a criminal context is much more difficult to achieve because of the potential loss of freedom and the punishment that will result. The plaintiff in a civil case must just show that there is more of a likelihood that the event happened than not. Some quantify this as the plaintiff proving it on a 51 percent basis. Just because there is a finding of guilt in a civil trial does not mean automatically that there will be a criminal conviction on the same facts, but there is a good chance of a civil win if there is a criminal conviction, because the standard is so much higher in the criminal realm. This may be a reason to delay proceeding with the civil litigation until the criminal matter is completed to have access to this finding.

CATEGORIES OF LIABILITY IN TORT

There are four general categories of tort: negligence, strict liability, intentional torts, and other unique torts.

3. CBS News, "Michael Jackson Wrongful Death Case Refiled," online: <http://www.cbsnews.com/stories/2010/11/30/entertainment/main7104925.shtml>.

Negligence

Negligence is the failure to take reasonable care to prevent foreseeable harm to another; it is about the **tortfeasor's** relationship with the victim. If you have a habit of juggling chainsaws when you walk to class, it is a foreseeable possibility that you could harm a fellow student who comes in contact with your chainsaw. The key to negligence is there must be a relationship between the parties. Historically, the first cases applied to those in a public calling such as "apothecaries, surgeons, common carriers, and innkeepers, who were alleged to have breached the standards of customary practice."[4] Negligence refers to actions that are inadvertent rather than wilful or deliberate. This is the branch of tort law that deals with conduct that falls below a standard of behaviour that society considers acceptable, and applies to a wide range of conduct. The classic statement of duty in negligence comes from the case of *Donoghue v Stevenson,* [1932] AC 562 (HL), where Lord Atkin said that a person owes a duty of care to one's "neighbour":

> [Y]ou must not injure your neighbour; and the lawyer's question, Who is my neighbour? receives a restricted reply. You must take reasonable care to avoid acts or omissions which you can reasonably foresee would be likely to injure your neighbour. Who, then, in law is my neighbour? The answer seems to be persons who are so closely and directly affected by my act that I ought reasonably to have them in contemplation as being so affected when I am directing my mind to the acts or omissions which are called in question.

Today, this concept of duty continues in that one has a duty of care to certain others. A person is negligent if he or she fails to do what a reasonable person would have done in the standards of the community (or industry, or profession, etc.). The standard of conduct expected is quite high. The overwhelming number of actions in civil court deal with negligence, and they all take on a single framework.

Figure 5.1 Proving Negligence

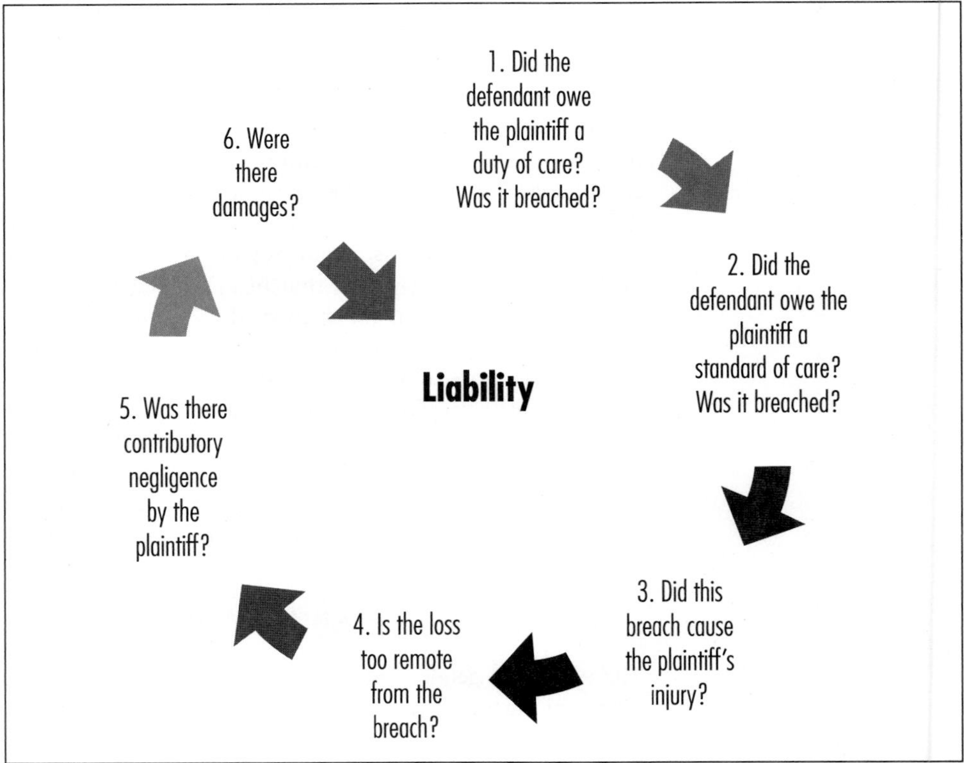

4. Robert M Solomon et al, *Cases and Materials on the Law of Torts* (Toronto: Carswell, 1996) at 210.

Conditions for Torts to Be Successful

There are six elements that must be analyzed for a negligence suit to be successful: (1) duty of care, (2) standard of care, (3) injury and causation, (4) remoteness, (5) contributory negligence, and (6) damages. Figure 5.1 outlines the six elements that ultimately lead to liability in negligence. If any of these steps is absent, liability cannot be found.

1. Duty of Care

The first element is referred to as a **duty of care** and the court must decide whether or not the plaintiff owed a legal duty to the defendant to be careful, and then must examine the nature of that duty. People are responsible for their inadvertent conduct when they anticipate that their conduct may cause injury to others, and they are required, in law, to maintain a standard of vigilance and to act in a careful manner. One has a duty not to act in a manner that would foreseeably hurt someone else. If there is a duty of care of the defendant to the plaintiff, the court must ask if that duty of care was breached. Fault is determined by a reasonable foreseeability test in which the courts examine the defendant's actions and attempt to determine whether or not that person acted in a prudent fashion. What would a reasonable person have done in the circumstances? This element is important in law because it allows judges to regulate how far negligence is to be extended. If there was no duty of care that the court can identify, the action cannot proceed to the next step. The case of *Donoghue v Stevenson* changed the face of what we consider a duty to others (see the following case box).

DONOGHUE v STEVENSON, [1932] AC 562 (HL)

This case is the classic example of duty of care and reasonable foreseeability, and it changed the course of tort law as it allowed negligence as a tort. A friend of the plaintiff (Donoghue) bought her a bottle of ginger beer, which she proceeded to drink. Her friend stopped her from drinking when he saw a decomposed snail coming out of the bottle. The plaintiff sued the manufacturer for shock and severe gastroenteritis as a result of consuming the product. However, the case had difficult issues. The plaintiff could not sue the pub where the bottle was purchased, because a friend of the plaintiff bought the product, not the plaintiff herself. She could not sue the servers at the pub because they had done nothing careless. The problem in this case was that the manufacturer of the beverage sold the drink to the distributer, who sold the product to the plaintiff's friend. There was no direct relationship between the plaintiff and the defendant, and until this time, you had to show a precise relationship between the parties. In a case of negligence, the court had to show that the plaintiff was injured by the breach of a duty owed to him or her by the defendant, who had a responsibility to take reasonable care to avoid that injury. The question was whether the defendant manufacturer owed a duty of care to the plaintiff. The defendant said that the bottle had passed through so many hands that the manufacturer could not possibly be responsible.

The court found that it was reasonably foreseeable that allowing a snail to be in the bottle would cause harm to the person who discovered the decomposing snail. The court said that the manufacturer must put effort into safely making a product, as the manufacturer owes a duty to the person consuming the product to take reasonable care. So, for the first time, the court found that a person/company owes a duty of care to those who can be reasonably foreseen to be affected by their actions (in this case, negligently allowing a snail to get into a bottle of ginger beer).

Rene Mansi/Vetta/Getty Images

Who should be held responsible for the snail in the ginger beer?

The case of *Donoghue v Stevenson* has been applied to many cases beyond manufacturer liability to any case in which an act or omission causes physical injury to another. The court must ask the question of whether a reasonable person in the circumstances of the defendant could have foreseen the injury to the victim by the defendant's actions. If the answer is yes, there is liability; but if it is no, there is no liability. However, sometimes it is difficult to decide if that duty of care is owed to the plaintiff. In Canadian law it seems that the plaintiff must prove that the defendant's conduct gave rise to a duty of care, and that duty was owed to the plaintiff. This is what has become known as the **foreseeable plaintiff test**, and it was examined in *Palsgraf v Long Island Ry. Co.* (see the following case box).

PALSGRAF v LONG ISLAND RY. CO. (1928), 248 NY 339 (NYCA)

Long Island Railway, 1900

The American case of *Palsgraf* raises interesting issues about foreseeability and who is a foreseeable plaintiff. In this unique case, Ms. Palsgraf was on the railway platform after buying a ticket. Another train stopped while Ms. Palsgraf was on the platform, and two men ran to the train to catch it before the train left. One of the men, who was carrying a package covered in newspaper, jumped on the train, but looked like he was going to fall. An employee of the train station reached down to help him aboard, and another guard on the platform pushed him from behind. In this motion, his package fell onto the railway tracks. It was carrying fireworks, and exploded. The shock of the explosion tipped over some scales at the other end of the platform where Ms. Palsgraf was standing and she was injured. She sued the railway company for negligence.

The court found that even if there was negligence by the railway personnel, it was not negligence in relation to the plaintiff, who was standing a long distance away. Nothing indicated that there were explosives in the package, and the court found that proof of "negligence in the air, so to speak, will not do" but that "[n]egligence, like risk, is thus a term of relation. Negligence in the abstract, apart from things related, is surely not a tort, if indeed it is understandable at all." Therefore, Ms. Palsgraf was not a foreseeable plaintiff and the railway company was not liable to her.

This principle of the foreseeable plaintiff has been referenced as recently as 2002 in the Supreme Court of Canada case of *Whiten v Pilot Insurance Co.*, [2002] SCJ No 19 (SCC), saying that the "liability of the defendant and the right of recovery of the plaintiff do not exist independently ... not only must the contractually bound defendant perform the promised act, but that performance is owed to a particular plaintiff." A consideration of duty of care is whether the duty is owed to the plaintiff from the defendant. Again, this is a legal pressure valve to control what actions are allowed and which are not based on what is in the best interests of society.

2. Standard of Care

Once the court has established that there is a duty between the parties, it must also determine the standard of care required of the particular defendant. Most often, the defendant is expected to conform to the standard of a reasonable person, and the court will examine whether or not the defendant's behaviour fell below the standard and constitutes fault. The court must ask what a reasonable person in the same circumstances would have done. If a defendant falls below that standard, the court asks if he or she was negligent. While the first step of duty of care is made up of legal and public policy rules, the standard of care is whether the defendant was negligent on the facts. Duty of care is based on legal issues, and standard of care is based on facts. There are two stages to the standard of care: first, what standard of care the defendant is required to meet and what factors are to be considered to see if it was breached; and second, on the facts of the case, can the plaintiff prove that there was a breach of the standard of care? The latter is usually decided by the judge hearing the particular evidence of the case.

THE REASONABLE PERSON One of the big questions asked regarding standard of care is what a reasonable person would have done. The court has found that a reasonable person is an imaginary person who is not perfect, just careful and considerate of others. However, there are constant debates over who this person is. Is this person male or female? What are this person's race, religion, and beliefs? Although clarity on these issues is difficult, what is known is that this person is reasonable in the circumstances of the case—a reasonable doctor if the case involves a doctor, a reasonable truck driver if that is the subject of the case. If you fall beneath this standard of a reasonable person in the circumstances, you are responsible for negligence. Justice Major in *Stewart v Pettie*, [1995] SCJ No 3, adopted the definition of the reasonable person from a lower court in that:

> [h]e is not an extraordinary or unusual creature; he is not superhuman; he is not required to display the highest skill of which anyone is capable; he is not a genius who can perform uncommon feats, nor is he possessed of unusual powers of foresight. He is a person of normal intelligence who makes prudence a guide to his conduct. He does nothing that a prudent man would not do and does not omit to do anything a prudent man would do. He acts in accord with general and approved practice. His conduct is guided by considerations which ordinarily regulate the conduct of human affairs. His conduct is the standard "adopted in the community by persons of ordinary intelligence and prudence."

This test is designed as objective standard and does not take into account what the person may have been thinking about, or how aware he or she was of the danger, or any psychological or physical differences. It is a relatively high standard, but it has been the test for a long time, and it provides a uniform test that can be applied without worrying about the actual thoughts of the defendant. The requirement that it be in relationship to the particular circumstances of the defendant allows for some malleability of the concept.

FOOD FOR THOUGHT...

Interestingly, the standard of a reasonable person adopted by the Supreme Court is quite markedly male, described by the pronoun "he." Should there be specific reasonable persons that are male or female? What about transgendered?

FORESEEABLE RISK In determining whether there was a reasonable standard of care, the court must see that the defendant avoided foreseeable risk to others. The court will also look at the likelihood that damage will occur and how severe the harm will be if it does occur, but the court will also weigh any social utility of the act (was the act done in pursuit of some higher goal? Did the individual push the child to save him from a speeding car?) The court will ask if this is something that happens 30 times a week and it will use a different standard than if it was something that has not happened in the last 50 years. If the expense is prohibitive with respect to the risk, then the courts will not hold the defendant responsible for not implementing costly precautions. However, if there are inexpensive and practical safety measures that could have been taken, the court will maintain that standard. An example of social utility is police on a high-speed chase. The police are allowed to put innocent bystanders at risk in a way that we would not allow of a private citizen because we feel, in certain circumstances, this should be allowed. The court is permitted to ask what situations we will allow some degree of risk needed for the functioning of society, or what standards could be in place in the case of an emergency.

Legislation often determines the standards of certain individuals or groups, but industry standards are also often used to determine liability. Did the defendant live up to industry standards? (Is it common for a lab technician to check the calibration of their devices once a day? Once a month?) Do industry standards meet the standard of care expected of the community? The same applies to professional liability, where the court will look to the customs of that business or trade to see what is expected. Standards also vary with circumstances, relevant legislation, profession, and so on. Doctors, lawyers, and police officers are held to a higher standard than the ordinary public because they are trained in their field and the public can reasonably expect a higher degree of competence and care.

FAILURE TO ACT The standard of care may also involve a failure to act. The common law distinguishes between injuries caused by "misfeasance" (positive action that is actionable because one acted, but acted improperly) and "nonfeasance," which is a failure to act. Generally, a failure to act is not a tort unless there is a statutory obligation to act. The exception is where there is a special relationship or legislation that requires one to act. Duty often attaches to one's position or role within an organization. In general, citizens do not have a duty to assist people in distress, such as a drowning person or someone in a car accident. However, people in positions of trust and responsibility are often required to act, so to not act would be considered negligence. For example, a teacher must report suspected child abuse or neglect; a police officer must help injured people; a lifeguard must try to save a drowning person. The common law has also imposed a duty to rescue if the individual innocently or negligently created the situation that he rescues the person from, the rescuer worsened the plaintiff's situation, denied other help offered, or induced the individual to rely on them to the person's detriment.

Those living in Quebec have a legislated positive duty to help, and this is provided in their *Charter of Human Rights and Freedoms.* Chapter I section 2 provides that:

> Every human being whose life is in peril has a right to assistance ...
>
> Every person must come to the aid of anyone whose life is in peril, either personally or calling for aid, by giving him the necessary and immediate physical assistance, unless it involves danger to himself or a third person, or he has another valid reason.[5]

This "Good Samaritan" law requires citizens to help others in distress and, at the very least, expects them to call 911 for assistance. Although other provinces and territories have not adopted a positive duty to help another, many jurisdictions have passed laws that prevent lawsuits against people who attempt to aid or rescue others unless their actions are highly unreasonable.[6] For example, Nova Scotia's legislation under the *Volunteer Services Act*, RSNS 1989, c 497, provides at s 3 that:

> **Emergency assistance to person**
>
> Where, in respect of a person who is ill, injured or unconscious as a result of an accident or other emergency, a volunteer renders services or assistance at any place, the volunteer is not liable for damages for injuries to or the death of that person alleged to have been caused by an act or omission on the part of the volunteer while rendering services or assistance, unless it is established that the injuries or death were caused by gross negligence on the part of the volunteer, and no proceeding shall be commenced against a volunteer which is not based upon his alleged gross negligence.

Although the question is largely unanswered in Canadian law, it seems that an individual who has voluntarily begun a rescue attempt is under no duty to continue unless it would worsen the situation of the victim. The *Criminal Code*, RSC 1985, c C-46, addresses this problem in s 217 saying that "every one who undertakes to do an act is under a legal duty to do it if an omission to do the act is or may be dangerous to life." Therefore, under criminal law, only someone who "undertakes" to save someone is liable to continue with that act. Some have speculated that a lifeguard who is employed to save people has undertaken that duty. The specifics of failure to act will continue to be formed by the case law. The following case box looks at a twist on the traditional failure to act in the context of a contract with a taxi company and the tort that results.

5. *Charter of Human Rights and Freedoms*, RSQ c C-12.

6. *Emergency Medical Aid Act*, RSA 2000, c E-7; *Good Samaritan Act*, RSBC 1996, c 172; *The Good Samaritan Protection Act*, CCSM c G65; *Civil Code of Quebec*, LRQ, c C-1991, s 1471; *Emergency Medical Aid Act*, RSNL. 1990, c E-9; *Emergency Medical Aid Act*, RSNWT 1988, c E-4; *Volunteer Services Act*, RSNS 1989, c 497; *Emergency Medical -Aid Act*, RSNWT (Nu) 1988, c E-4; *Good Samaritan Act*, 2001, SO 2001, c 2; *Emergency Medical Aid Act*, RSS 1978, c E-8; *Emergency Medical Aid Act*, RSY 2002, c 70.

WARE'S TAXI LTD. v GILLIHAM, [1949] SCR 637 (SCC)

In this case, five-year-old Carol Ann Gilliham fell out of the appellants' taxi when being taken from school to her home according to an agreement between the school and the company to transport the children. There was a standard push-button lock on the car door that was not defective, but the testimony at trial was that Carol Ann or one of the other children opened the door. The court found that the taxi company was "under a duty to exercise reasonable care in their conveyance" of the children. The driver of the taxi had picked up seven or eight children from school[7] and had warned Carol Ann not to touch the door, but a block later the door opened and Carol Ann fell out and sustained injuries.

The court found that the button and handle were an "allurement" to the children, and a "reasonable man, assuming an obligation to transport these children ... would foresee the possibility of these small children meddling or playing with the ... handle and foresee the danger or peril consequent upon their doing so and would take such precautions as would either prevent them playing ... [or] remove the possibility of dangerous consequences ensuing." As no safety devices had been installed or procedures put in place, and there was little supervision, especially in the back seat, the taxi company was found to be negligent, and breached the standard of care. The failure of the taxi company to act to enforce safety made them responsible.

3. Injury and Causation

It is also a crucial element of negligence to show the damage or injury the victim sustained and prove that the injury was directly caused by conduct of the defendant. Damage or injury must be present for liability for negligence to be imposed, but today the courts recognize mental distress as well as physical injury in negligence cases. Mere anger, anxiety, or fear might not be enough, but if the plaintiff can show a history of psychological injury, he or she might be successful.

For causation to be proved, there must be a sufficiently close causal connection between the action and the injury, and the test used is called the **but for test**. The plaintiff must show that but for the defendant's conduct, the injury or loss would not have taken place, proved on a balance of probabilities. The defendant does not have to be the sole cause of the injury, just one cause. While this might seem straightforward, causation is often indirect and difficult to evaluate in law. If the harm caused was reasonably foreseeable, then it is not too remote from the behaviour of the defendant and the defendant is therefore liable. The facts of the case must be examined. If you push a person and he falls, one might foresee injury, but if one person is pushed and falls onto a landmine, it might not have been foreseeable that he would have been blown to pieces. Can the Toronto subway system be just as dangerous? Consider the case of *Kauffman v T.T.C.* in the following case box.

KAUFFMAN v T.T.C., [1959] OJ NO 657 (ONT CA)

In this case, the plaintiff was using an escalator at the St. Clair subway station in Toronto. Two young people went first, followed by a man. When the youths were involved in a scuffle, they fell back against the man, who in turn fell back into the plaintiff. Ms. Kauffman suffered injuries from this incident and sued the T.T.C. for installing the new moving handrail without testing the

7. That's a shocking number of children by today's standards, and there was no mention if seat belts were installed in the car.

friction. The T.T.C. had installed a handrail that was round, corrugated, and metal clad, instead of the black rubber kind used for many years. The plaintiff alleged that she would have had a more secure grip if the rubber handrail had been installed rather than the slippery metal one.

Although the plaintiff alleged that when a handrail is inadequate and a person falls at the top of the escalator, the rest of the riders are going to fall like a "row of dominoes," the court found that there was no evidence that the parties involved attempted to grasp the handrail and were unable to hang on because of the type selected by the defendant. Therefore, the "but for" test fails; you cannot say that but for the acts of the T.T.C., the defendant was injured. Ms. Kauffman failed to prove that the T.T.C. caused her injuries, and the Supreme Court affirmed this decision.

4. Remoteness of Damages and the Thin-Skulled Plaintiff Rule

A defendant is not responsible for every outcome; if the damages are too remote in law to be recoverable, the plaintiff will not be able to receive damages. There are times that a loss is so unexpected that it is unfair to find the defendant legally responsible. The court asks if the damages are too remote from the negligence to allow the plaintiff to claim damages, and limits the damages to those that are foreseeable, natural, or directly caused by the negligent act. Like duty of care, remoteness is a legal tool to limit how much someone can claim in negligence. There must be some connection in space, time, or probability. Just because the claim is unusual, does not automatically exclude the claim.

For example, in *Smith v Leech Brain & Co.*, [1962] 2 QB 405, the plaintiff was working with a tank of molten metal when a piece flew up and burned his lip. It is a principle of tort law that the person who is committing the wrong "takes his victim as he finds him" as "it is no answer to the sufferer's claim for damages that he would have suffered less injury, or no injury at all, if he had not had an unusually thin skull or an unusually weak heart." The plaintiff happened to have a pre-existing condition that caused this burn on the lip to turn into cancer, and the plaintiff died. But for the burn, the cancer might never have developed. The court found that the defendant company could have foreseen the type of injury that actually happened to the plaintiff: the burn to the lip. The court found that the damage from that burn is particular to the victim, and Mr. Smith had damage that included death. Thus, the company is liable for the full extent of the damages for that specific defendant and the defendant's particular vulnerabilities.

AlexKalashnikov/Shutterstock

Damages can be increased or reduced depending on whether the plaintiff is found to have contributed to the accident, and in what proportion.

YOU BE THE JUDGE—WHAT SHOULD THE OUTCOME BE?

Mr. Smith was replacing an empty bottle of water in a water cooler and he saw a dead fly and part of another dead fly in the unopened replacement bottle. He became obsessed with the event and with the health of his family, who had been drinking water from that company for years. Mr. Smith developed a major depressive disorder along with phobias and anxiety. He sued the bottled water company for damages for his psychiatric disorders, and for loss of income.

Should Mr. Smith be allowed to claim for damages?

Does seeing a dead fly lead to this kind of injury?

5. Contributory Negligence

In order to prove negligence, there must also be no prejudicial conduct, called **contributory negligence**, on the part of the victim, or the damages may be reduced. The conduct of the plaintiff often becomes an issue in torts, since that person's behaviour may contribute to his or her own victimization. The principle of contributory negligence suggests that the plaintiff contributed to the victimization through his or her own negligence and is disqualified from seeking compensation, or the damages awarded will be reduced. If a person is found to have been 50 percent at fault, then the court may apportion blame by half and reduce any damages by the same amount. There are many cases in which the behaviour of both the plaintiff and defendant are partially responsible for the injuries, and rewards are adjusted down because of the principle of contributory negligence. Most provinces have legislation that governs the **apportioning** of loss between the parties where both are at fault.[8] The burden is on the defendant to prove that the plaintiff was contributorily negligent and responsible for his or her own injuries. The standard that the court will use is that of a reasonably prudent person, but many judgments are relatively arbitrary. See the following case box, which deals with *Wickberg v Patterson*.

WICKBERG v PATTERSON (1997), 145 DLR (4TH) 263 (ALTA CA)

Mr. Wickberg was injured when his motorcycle struck the rear of a truck driven by Mr. Patterson. Mr. Patterson was backing up his truck between the shoulder and the driving lane to assist a driver who was in the ditch. Mr. Wickberg was a novice motorcyclist and was distracted by the driver in the ditch and struck Mr. Patterson's truck. At trial, the court said Mr. Wickberg was solely responsible for his own motorcycle injuries, so he appealed to the Alberta Court of Appeal.

The appeal court found that Mr. Patterson stopped in the driving lane for his own convenience, as he did not want to get stuck in the mud of the soft shoulder, he had no flashers on, and since he was parked, there were no brake lights to warn other drivers. Mr. Patterson created a hazard on the road and, therefore, he was a cause of the appellant's injuries. However, Mr. Wickberg was inattentive, and made no attempt to swerve or stop, also causing his injuries, and he was accountable for contributory negligence. Based on the negligence of both and the *Contributory Negligence Act*, each party was liable for 50 percent of the damages to Mr. Wickberg.

8. *Negligence Act*, RSBC 1996, c 333; *Negligence Act*, RSO 1990, c N.1; *Contributory Negligence Act*, RSNS 1989, c 95; *Contributory Negligence Act*, RSS 1978, c C-31; *Contributory Negligence Act*, RSA 2000, c C-27; *Contributory Negligence Act*, RSY 2002, c 42; *Contributory Negligence Act*, RSPEI 1988, c C-21; *Contributory Negligence Act*, RSNL 1990, c C-33; *Contributory Negligence Act*, RSNB 1973, c C-19; *Contributory Negligence Act*, RSNWT 1988, c C-18; *Contributory Negligence Act*, RSNWT (Nu) 1988, c C-18; *Tortfeasors* and *Contributory Negligence Act*, CCSM c T90.

6. Damages

Anyone who has suffered a loss because of the defendant's negligence is awarded damages. Damages are intended to put the plaintiff in the position that he or she would have been if the negligent act had not happened. Aggravated and punitive damages, to punish the defendant for bad conduct, are limited in negligence law. Damages can be awarded for injury, fatality, and property issues. Insurance also plays a role in tort law damages, as most individuals would turn to their insurance if property is damaged, but insurers have something called **subrogation** rights. The insurance company has the right to reclaim some of the money that it has given to the policyholder by starting a tort action against the wrongdoer who negligently injured the plaintiff.

The court will hear evidence of what damages have been suffered by the plaintiff, and will take in available evidence of how the plaintiff's life has changed since the injury. In a recent Canadian case, evidence was adduced from the social networking site Facebook. In *Terry v Mullowney,* [2009] NJ No 86 (Nfld & LSC), before the Newfoundland and Labrador Supreme Court, Mr. Terry claimed over $1.3 million in damages after he had been injured in two motor vehicle accidents. He claimed that he had not been able to do mechanical work under the hood of a car since after the first accident, that he had soft tissue damage to his neck and back, and that the symptoms of his previously diagnosed "thoracic outlet syndrome" had been exacerbated. Mr. Terry said that there were profound effects on his social and personal life caused by the accidents.

Based on the evidence, the court found that Mr. Terry had exaggerated his injuries, and his memory was unreliable. There was surveillance video of the plaintiff doing work under the hood of a car. However, in a new development, the court also examined Facebook. The defendants produced as evidence printouts from Facebook proving that Mr. Terry had a "rather full and active social life" as the pictures and information showed that he had hosted parties, gone to cottages, drank alcohol "frequently," smoked marijuana daily, and "appeared to have a number of friends with whom he communicated and socialized on a regular basis." When Mr. Terry realized that this information was publically available on the Internet for months after the accident, he shut down his account because "he didn't want any incriminating information in court."

The judge drew an **adverse inference** against Mr. Terry because he took down this account. Mr. Terry alleged that he had a social life for the few months he was on Facebook after the accident, and then from 2001 to 2007, he had little or no social life. The judge found that "without this evidence, I would have been left with a very different impression of Mr. Terry's social life." This case shows the importance of damaging evidence that can be obtained from the Internet. Mr. Terry was awarded a total of $40 000, far less than the $1.3 million in damages alleged. Facebook users beware; this is a developing area of the law. Even if the privacy settings are set so that the public cannot see private information on Facebook, there is some indication that the court may, in the future, allow orders to compel the production of private material on Facebook, especially at the time of the injury.[9]

Putting It All Together

Many courts use this formula of negligence to examine a particular case, focusing on duty of care, standard of care, injury and causation, remoteness, contributory negligence, and damages. These all come into play in *Walford (Litigation guardian of) v Jacuzzi Canada Inc* (see the following case box).

WALFORD (LITIGATION GUARDIAN OF) v JACUZZI CANADA INC. (APPEAL TO SCC DENIED APRIL 2008) 2007 ONCA 729 (ONT CA)

Correena Walford was 15 years old when she went down the slide her parents had just installed beside their four-foot, above-ground, backyard pool, hit her chin on the bottom of the pool, and broke her neck. Coreena's parents had owned at least three backyard pools at different

9. See *Leduc v Roman* [2009] OJ No 681 (Ont SCJ).

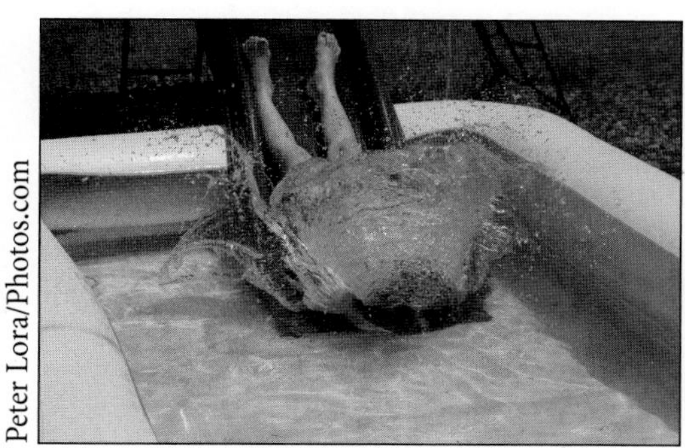
Peter Lora/Photos.com

Sliding down head first—who is at fault for injuries?

times, but the most recent pool was the "Mardi Gras" pool they bought second-hand and installed in 1994 before the 1996 accident. This pool was four feet deep, and the Mardi Gras instruction booklet that came with the pool showed a child on a slide installed at the end of the pool. Correena's mother had been a customer of Pioneer Pools for two years, and bought her pool supplies at their store, and a representative had come to see their pool to assist with a new vinyl liner and an algae problem.

Mrs. Walford said that she relied on the expertise of the store's staff to keep her pool in working order, and to advise her on pool-related matters. She called Pioneer about the slide for her four-foot-deep pool, and the store said that it would have to order one from the manufacturer for a cost of $1000. Mrs. Walford subsequently saw a classified ad for a 10-foot pool slide for $350. Mrs. Walford phoned Pioneer and spoke with a female employee about the used slide. The employee said that she could not see a problem with the used slide.

Mrs. Walford bought the used slide, but it was quite old and had some broken parts. After picking up the slide, Mrs. Walford drove directly to Pioneer Pools to speak with the store manager. The store manager inspected the slide, and again told her that there would be no problem. Mrs. Walford purchased three metal legs from the store for installation, and went to another Pioneer Pools location to buy other supplies. She asked the male employee at the other location whether the slide could be installed in a four-foot pool, and he said that it would be "okay."

Mrs. Walford testified that she relied on the expertise of the Pioneer Pools employees, and if anyone had said it was not safe to use the slide, she would not have installed the slide. Mrs. Walford was conscious of safety issues, and had strict rules around the pool, including no pushing, no running, having only one person going down the slide at a time, having no one under the slide when someone was coming down, and only using the slide feet first. Although Correena went down feet first the first time she went down the slide, the second time she crouched over her knees. Correena entered the water head first and hit her chin on the bottom of the pool, severely and permanently paralyzing herself.

The trial judge dismissed the Walfords' claim for negligence and failure to warn against the respondent pool store that sold Correena's mother fittings for the slide and assured her that installing the slide was okay. Even though the trial judge found against the Walfords, he found that Correena's injuries were assessed at over $5 million to take care of her for the rest of her life. One of the main issues of liability was whether the pool store breached a duty of care to the appellants by telling the mother that it was "okay" and that there would be "no problem" with installing the slide on their four-foot-deep above-ground pool, without warning Mrs. Walford of the potential for catastrophic injury, and if so, whether that breach caused or contributed to the damage that Correena suffered.

You be the judge. Go through the analysis for negligence with emphasis on the duty of care, standard of care, injury and causation, remoteness, and contributory negligence. Damages are already determined.

INTENTIONAL TORTS

Unlike torts of negligence, intentional torts involve actions that are wilful, deliberate, and conscious. While negligence is a relatively new creation, intentional torts have a long history, and are quite specific in their application to defined fact patterns and damage. Through intentional torts, one need only intend the act and not the harm that results for the defendant to be liable, but the conduct is almost always intentional and voluntary or the product of a conscious mind. Conduct is intentional if the consequences are substantially certain to happen if the defendant continues to act in a certain way. Thus, if a bomb is planted at a nursery school attached to a governmental building, the defendant may say that he or she did not wish to hurt the children, but intent will be imputed to that individual if the consequence was certain or substantially certain to follow the act.

This is also the case with what is called **transferred intent**. If the defendant intended to shoot one party, but accidentally missed and hit a bystander, the defendant is still liable for the injuries to the bystander, even though he or she did not intend to shoot that particular person. This also applies if the individual intended to commit one type of tort, and unintentionally committed another, as the intent from the first tort is transferred to the actual tort committed. The main types of intentional torts are (1) trespass to another (including assault and battery), (2), intentional infliction of nervous shock, and (3) false imprisonment.

1. Trespass to Another

The first category of intentional torts comprises those that originate with the direct interference with another person.

Battery

Battery, which is the most common trespass to the person, is the direct and intentional physical interference with another person, which is harmful or offensive to the reasonable person and is exercised without consent. There must be a direct touch to the individual, although this element is slowly evolving to involve actions beyond a direct touch. This tort recognizes the right to have your person secure from unlawful interference, and can be proven even if there is no damage, which is something that cannot be done in cases of negligence.

Battery can range from shooting a person with a gun, to spitting on a person, to pushing away someone coming towards you. If the touch is not harmful or offensive, it is not battery, but the line is transitory. For example, a kiss that can potentially be unwanted, upsetting, or offensive can be battery. The burden of proof that the conduct was unintentional or negligent falls to the defendant to prove. The tort of battery has regained popularity in recent history, especially for those wishing to find compensation for historical abuse, and abuse within institutions. Using battery, victims may get compensation for the unwanted touching of those who abuse them. Many times the goal is not monetary compensation for the wrong, but rather to find an individual responsible for this unwanted violation.

Assault

Assault is the intentional creation in the mind of another of a reasonable apprehension of immediate physical contact. Unlike battery, an assault in civil law refers to an attempt at injury where no physical contact takes place, but rather there is a threat of immediate danger. The key element is the plaintiff's reasonable belief in the threat. Assault can include things like shaking a fist, the swarming of a crowd, or pointing a gun at someone. If the plaintiff threatens but does not act, there is an assault but not battery, but threats about future violence are not enough to form an assault because there is no immediate danger.

Assault actions without a battery are rare, and damages are minimal because of the lack of physical touch. One may have an assault without a battery, a battery without an assault, or both at the same time. Assault without battery could involve yelling obscenities and shaking of one's fist without ever touching the plaintiff. If there is a surprise attack from behind, there is a battery but no assault because the person did not see it coming. If the accused threatens that he or she is going to beat you up right now and then does so, there is assault and battery. The courts have ruled that it is the state of mind of the victim that determines whether or not a threat has occurred. This may be particularly important when a homophobic statement is made, as in *Spencer v Rozon* et al (see the following case box).

SPENCER v ROZON ET AL, 2000 BCSC 674 (BCSC)

The case of *Spencer v Rozon* et al is an example of both battery and assault. In this case the plaintiff, Mr. Spencer, and his friend, Mr. Krause, were on their way home after an evening of nightclubbing. The plaintiff had been drinking, but Mr. Krause was completely sober. Mr. Spencer had to relieve himself, and went to some bushes beside a parking lot. After Mr. Spencer zipped his pants, he heard the term "Fag" shouted from a dark-coloured jeep. Mr. Krause yelled back "Bitches" to the car. The jeep did an immediate U-turn, and three men got out, including the defendant (Mr. Rozon) and his friend (Mr. Cowick).

Although Mr. Spencer and Mr. Krause said they did not wish to fight, the men began to violently punch the plaintiff and his friend. The plaintiff was knocked to the ground and was kicked in the head until he lost consciousness, and then the defendants drove away without knowing if he was dead or alive. Mr. Spencer's nose was broken and hemorrhaged severely. He had massive facial bruising and bruises throughout his body; he also suffered from other facial fractures, memory impairment, and a mild personality disorder. He had trouble breathing, three of his teeth were damaged, and his reading speed decreased to the bottom 1 percent of the population. The defendants pleaded guilty to two criminal law counts of common assault, received a sentence of 12 months' probation and a $500 fine.

In addition to the criminal charges, the plaintiff also sued the defendant in the civil law for the injuries he sustained. Although the court found the defendant had committed the torts of assault and battery, this case is representative of many when no distinction is made between the two terms; rather they are used in tandem. There was an assault with the use of the homophobic slur that was used, and the immediate U-turn of the vehicle and the subsequent beating comprised the battery.

Mr. Spencer was delayed entry into an MBA program because of his injuries, which resulted in a loss of $100 000. The attack also impacted his earning capacity by $10 000. Mr. Spencer was reimbursed for counselling sessions, as well as non-pecuniary damages of $75 000, with an additional $25 000 for aggravated damages. There were no punitive damages, simply because the judgment awarded was already sufficient to punish the defendants and prevent them from acting in the same way in the future.

2. Intentional Infliction of Nervous Shock

Torts do not simply impose liability for physical harm but also for psychological harm. There are three elements to proving that someone has psychologically injured the plaintiff. First, there must be outrageous or extreme conduct and a severe impact on the mental well-being of the plaintiff. This can include shocking news about family, criminal wrongdoing, harassment, and stalking. Many of these cases have a single shocking episode, but it can be a pattern over a longer period of time. Second, the plaintiff must prove the creation of a mental illness or disorder. Courts are now more willing to take severe emotional distress as damage to the individual. Third, the plaintiff must show that he or she did not have a predisposition to shock. This last element is becoming less important to the test.

In the classic 1897 case of *Wilkinson v Downton*, [1897] 2 QB 57, the defendant played a practical joke on Ms. Wilkinson, sending a message saying that her husband was in an accident and both of his legs had been broken. The message he sent said she was to come immediately to take him home. None of this was true, but the situation put the plaintiff into shock, causing vomiting and long-term psychological consequences. Ms. Wilkinson had no predisposition to this type of condition, and the court awarded her damages because of this incident.

3. False Imprisonment

The tort of false imprisonment was originally a remedy for wrongful incarceration, but now it governs situations where an individual's movement is limited. The restraint must be complete, even if it is just for a short period of time, and, again, it is actionable even if no damage occurred. Interestingly, there can also be false imprisonment by psychological means, and it may exist whether or not the individual is aware of their imprisonment. Confinement may be through physical boundaries, restraint, or by the authority of the person restraining the plaintiff. The plaintiff must only show that there was direct imprisonment, not that there was lack of authority or consent.

The traditional example is arrest by a police officer where a person is restrained and put in the control of another. For false imprisonment, the individual must attempt to escape the restraint. The common law has kept the tort fairly narrow in that the restraint must be total and not partial because of the multitudes of cases that could arise if the imprisonment was not direct and a total restriction. Police do have the ability to detain someone if they believe the individual has committed an indictable offence, but there are limits to their powers. Once the plaintiff has made the case for false imprisonment the onus shifts to the defendant to show that the arrest or imprisonment was justified. The right not to be arbitrarily detained or imprisoned is entrenched in section 9 of the *Canadian Charter of Rights and Freedoms* (discussed in Chapter 10). The following case box looks at the factors of false imprisonment.

NICHOL v LONDON (CITY) POLICE SERVICE, [2003] OJ NO 1857 (ONT SCJ)

Ms. Anne Nichol sued the London, Ontario, police for false imprisonment after she was wrongly arrested in place of her roommate, Ms. Mary Katherine Pitt. Constable Hassan came to Ms. Nichol's home to arrest Ms. Pitt. Ms. Nichol attempted to tell the officer that she was not Ms. Pitt, and that her roommate had gone to the police station to turn herself in for an outstanding warrant. Constable Hassan refused to listen to Ms. Nichol, and would not allow her to get her identification to prove who she was. The officer just kept responding, "I know who you are, Mary—I've been after you for months." Ms. Pitt was ignored and she was placed in handcuffs and arrested. In the police car, Constable Hassan looked through her purse and quizzed her on the identification, believing that she was just impersonating Ms. Nichol. When Ms. Nichol correctly stated her birthday, Constable Hassan said, "you're good, Mary." The officer called Ms. Nichol's place of work and asked for a physical description of Ms. Nichol, alerting them to the fact that her roommate was impersonating her.

Ms. Nichol was taken to the police station, and was left in the police car, handcuffed, for approximately one hour. The court found that even if the defendant acted in error in arresting Ms. Nichol, it did not excuse him from liability. The onus was on the defendant to show that there was a lawful justification, and Constable Hassan was unable to do this. The court found that the officer had "made up his mind that the person who answered the door ... was Mary Katherine Pitt." Ms. Nichol was immediately handcuffed, even though the officer had no concern for his safety, and it was not a situation of urgency. Ms. Nichol was polite and cooperative at all times, had no criminal record, and she was embarrassed to be taken out of her home in handcuffs in front of her neighbours. She was also humiliated by the call to her employer saying that someone was in custody for impersonating her. The court found for the plaintiff and awarded her $2000 in damages.

Nuisance torts can be public or private.

© Pat Tuson / Alamy

UNIQUE TORTS

Nuisance

Besides negligence and the specific intentional torts, there is a catch-all category of torts that include other wrongs not specifically falling in the other categories. Nuisance is one of these categories. There are two types of torts regarding nuisance. The first is private nuisance, which protects individuals from the substantial and unreasonable interference with the use, enjoyment, and comfort of their land. Public nuisance deals with the protection of the public to exercise the rights that are given to all citizens, like the right to use public highways. Any use of the land for things such as crack houses or brothels that disrupt the neighbourhood may be a public nuisance. If there is some special damage to the plaintiff that is not suffered by the general public, the individual can seek damages.

Private nuisance is more common, and secures property from indirect physical or intangible interference. This typically refers to behaviour that is ongoing and not limited to a single act and with something that is inadvertent or indirect, and does not permit the enjoyment of one's property. Most frequently, this type of tort deals with issues such as smoke, water seepage, noxious smells, machinery noise, and loud music. Private nuisance is not actionable unless there is unreasonable interference; it must be something not expected on that particular property, and the plaintiff has suffered damage. If you move beside an active pig farm and then complain of noxious smells, the courts will say that this was to be expected on that particular property. The court will examine the nature of the wrong and the extent of the interference alleged. Often the courts will issue an injunction against the person requiring him or her to desist from the offending behaviour.

A defence to a nuisance lawsuit is for the defendant to argue that the actions are lawful and reasonable. Nuisance is distinct from trespass to land, which is a distinct tort of entering into another person's land without permission or legal authority. Trespass is always an intentional tort, but nuisance can be intentional or unintentional, and trespass involves the possession and use of property, while nuisance is the quality of that use. Although injunction is a common remedy for nuisance, damages are also possible, as in the case of *Kenny v Schuster Real Estate Co.* (see the following case box).

KENNY v SCHUSTER REAL ESTATE CO., [1990] BCJ NO 1420 (BCSC)

Fedor Kondratenko/Shutterstock

Can the smell of French fries become a nuisance?

Ms. Kenny brought an action against the owners of a restaurant that was under her condominium. When she moved in, she made inquiries if the restaurant produced certain types of foods, and she was told that they did not deep fry or cook food on premises and that they only served light meals. Within five years, the restaurant installed an exhaust fan directly below her patio deck and underneath her dining and living room windows, and the restaurant did serve the types of fried food that they had ensured her that they did not. The fan was noisy could be heard from anywhere in the condo, Ms. Kenny would have to elevate her voice, and it created unpleasant odours in her condo which were described as a "deep fat frying type of odour." Ms. Kenny sold her condominium at a lower price, and was forced to pay the resulting real estate commission. The court found that the noise and smell from the fan was an actionable nuisance because there was a substantial and unreasonable interference with her use of the property.

The facts of the situation have to be examined because what can be nuisance in one case may not be in the next. The testimony of her neighbours was also vital to determining if there was a nuisance. In this situation there was a drop in the value of the property, and there was a causal connection between the defendant's conduct, installing the fan, and the drop in price. Damages were also awarded as a result of inconvenience to the plaintiff (within reason). The court found that the fan was a "gross interference" with the comfort and enjoyment of the condo, and the court awarded non-pecuniary damages in the amount of $7500, the amount of the commission, moving costs, and legal fees in the amount of $25 557. The defendant appealed the amount of the award to the court of appeal, but the appeal was dismissed.

Defamation

Another unique tort is **defamation**, which refers to the publication of a false statement about another person that defames or reduces esteem or respect in the eyes of others. This statement can be intentional or unintentional, and is measured on an objective basis of a reasonable person. Typically, the statement suggests that the person has done something illegal, dishonest, shameful, or otherwise discrediting. Damages can be sought if the injury to reputation is significant; otherwise, only nominal damages are possible. Innuendo can be defamation when the statement is indirect but is made to people who have sufficient information to know who the defendant is and what is alleged. The test is whether a reasonable person acquainted with the plaintiff would understand who the statement was referring to.

Defamatory comments must be heard or read by a third party to be liable, and this is referred to as having been **published** or **broadcast**. Publication does not have to be to a large group of people; publication to one person is still defamation. This statement heard by the third party must bring the defamed person into contempt or ridicule, and the more severe the statement, the more serious the tort. The court has found that almost all unflattering comments can be defamatory.

Libel is written defamation and slander is oral in nature, but several provinces, including Alberta, Manitoba, New Brunswick, Prince Edward Island, and Newfoundland and Labrador, have eliminated this distinction.[10] Slander can also include sounds, physical gestures, or facial expressions, and may be unintentional, even in the context of a private conversation. If you put yourself in a situation where your comments may be heard, you are subject to defamation. Libel is more permanent in its visual form, and has found to be in all kinds of publications, including cartoons, pictures, video, billboards, drawings, and so forth. Again, if you write defamatory statements about another person in a diary and someone reads that material, you could be liable. Libel is considered more serious because of the permanence of such a written or visual statement.

The media are offered greater protection against defamation in the United States than in Canada and can often avoid an action by printing a retraction and an apology. Legislation and court judgments often provide the media with these protections in order to protect freedom of speech and the freedom of the press. Typically, the media in the United States can only be sued for defamation if they were malicious in their actions and knew that what they published was false. In Canada, the media are offered far less protection and they must exercise due care before they print statements that may be regarded as defamatory. Damages may be lessened if there is a printed retraction or apology.

In practice, the Canadian media must check their sources and they often give the victim a chance to respond to the allegations. The media must also be able to prove that the statement is true if brought to court, and there is no onus on the plaintiff to prove his or her innocence. Truth is an absolute defence in Canada but the obligation is on the media outlet to prove that the statement was true. However, truth might not be a defence if a person continues to make false statements that he or she believes came from an authoritative source. There may be a new tortfeasor every time the information is published.

Mistake is not a defence, and it is also not a defence to say that one did not mean to defame another. If a media outlet mistakenly thought a statement was true, it does not have a valid defence, and it must ensure its source. Some countries require that publishing the information requires that there also be some public benefit, and a common defence is what is called **fair comment.** There is a right to openly and honestly criticize elements in our society. As long as the statements are not malicious and are fair, there is room for criticism. Public figures can be publicly evaluated and criticized under this principle in the defence of freedom of speech in an open society. These comments refer to opinions and not to facts. For example, we have all read reviews of restaurants, plays, sports teams, athletes, and politicians. Today, most provinces have specific legislation on defamation.[11]

10. See *Defamation Act,* RSA 2000, c D-7; *Defamation Act,* CCSM c D20; *Defamation Act,* RSNB 1973, c D-5; *Defamation Act,* RSNL 1990, c D-3; *Defamation Act,* RSPEI 1988, c D-5.

11. *Defamation Act,* RSA 2000, c D-7; *Defamation Act,* CCSM c D20; *Defamation Act,* RSNB 1973, c D-5; *Defamation Act,* RSNL 1990, c D-3; *Defamation Act,* RSNS 1989, c 122; *Defamation Act,* RSPEI 1988, c D-5; *Defamation Act,* RSY 2002, c 52; *Defamation Act,* RSNWT 1988, c D-1; *Defamation Act,* RSNWT (Nu) 1988, c D-1.

YOU DECIDE

Many people watch the CW Network's drama *Gossip Girl*. What is the liability of the illusive *Gossip Girl* for some of the untrue statements that she makes and transmits to hundreds of people through email? How will defamation extend to deal with new technology?

FOOD FOR THOUGHT...

HOW DOES DEFAMATION COINCIDE WITH THE CHARTER?

Section 2 (b) of the *Charter of Rights and Freedoms* provides that "[e]veryone has the following fundamental freedoms: (b) freedom of thought, belief, opinion and expression, including freedom of the press and other media of communication." How can the tort of defamation and the *Charter* both exist at the same time?

HENDERSON v PEARLMAN ET AL, [2009] OJ NO 3444 (ONT SCJ)

In this case, the plaintiff sought an injunction and damages for Internet defamation. The plaintiff ran a fraud awareness website called crimes-of-persuasion.com. He was a businessman, a chartered financial planner, and an author, and had never been arrested or charged with any criminal act. None of the seven defendants in the action lived in Ontario, but all were engaged in promotion in the talent and modelling industry, and were the subject of negative comments in the plaintiff's publication. The plaintiff alleged that the defendants defamed him through misinformation on various websites and newsgroups targeted at Ontario, where the plaintiff lives. The argument was that by having links on their website to defamatory sites, the defendants were acting together to defame him.

In particular, the information on the Internet said that the plaintiff:

> is a career criminal who is wanted by the FBI for endangering the welfare of a minor; that he is working with a group of criminals, that he lured a minor to a hotel room to do coke; that his books were plagiarized material, that his consumer fraud awareness website is a scam to lure victims; that he is a perverted individual; that he writes nothing but lies; that he has a long criminal record; that he is an extortionist; that he was convicted of shoplifting and selling stolen goods; and that Canadian authorities have made him take down his website.

One of the defendants had emailed the plaintiff to say that his life will never be the same as he will be hunted like a dog, that there are people that despise him, and that they will continue with lawsuits just to keep him spending money on lawyers.

Justice Hennessy cited the decision in *Barrick Gold Corp. v Lopehandia* (2004), 71 OR (3d) 416 (CA), saying that the:

> internet represents a communications revolution. It makes instantaneous global communication available cheaply to anyone with a computer and an internet connection. It enables individuals, institutions, and companies to communicate with a potentially vast global audience. It is a medium which does not respect geographical boundaries. [In addition to] heralding a new and global age of free speech and democracy, the internet is also potentially a medium of virtually limitless international defamation.

The court found that the statements made about the plaintiff were clearly defamatory, and that this material was posted on the Internet where, as stated in *Barrick*, "the truth rarely catches up with a lie." The court found for the plaintiff that a permanent injunction should be ordered to prohibit the defendants from posting these comments. In addition, the court granted $10 000 in damages against each of the seven defendants for a total of $70 000.

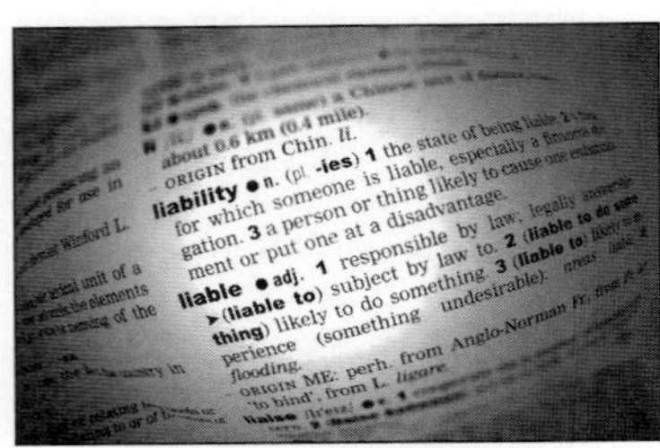

A defendant can be found liable without necessarily being found at fault.

SPECIAL CATEGORIES OF TORT

Strict Liability

In law, **absolute liability** was created in order to find a defendant liable if he or she causes the plaintiff's loss, without having to prove that the conduct was intentional, negligent, or blameworthy. In absolute liability, no defences are available. Absolute liability is almost exclusively found in provincial regulatory offences (as will be discussed in Chapter 9). No modern torts are based on absolute liability, but rather a related concept of **strict liability**.

Some behaviour governed by statutes does not require the plaintiff to prove that the defendant was at fault; simply committing the act makes the person guilty. These are known as offences of strict liability, or those without intent or negligence. You are guilty of doing that and you are given an opportunity to prove that you acted with **due diligence,** but no fault has to be established. Because of this lack of fault, strict liability does not play a significant role in tort liability. Canadian judges are much more apt to apply the formula discussed in negligence and to embrace a strict standard of care in negligence rather than ignore whether there was fault on the part of the defendant. An example of strict liability is that manufacturers can be sued if their products are defective and result in injuries. The onus is generally on the manufacturer to show that it used due care in producing the product and warned consumers of any dangers (see Chapter 7).

Vicarious Liability

Vicarious liability involves situations in which a person is held responsible for the actions of others—for example, those under that person's employ. It must be proven that the employee acted while under the **course of employment** and that there was a special relationship of master/servant between the parties. The employer can be strictly liable for the actions of the employees, regardless of fault on the part of the employer. The tort may be committed by others without the employer's knowledge or consent, but the court may rule that the employer is also partly responsible and can be sued. Employees are not relieved of liability just because their employer is vicariously liable. Often, an action will name both the employee and the employer, and then have the option of collecting against either; however, the employer is usually in a better position to satisfy the judgment, and usually ends up paying the entire amount. Generally, parents are not responsible for the actions of their children, but some jurisdictions have passed legislation that makes parents civilly responsible for certain behaviours.[12] See the following case box, which looks at *MO v EN*.

MO v EN, [2004] BCJ NO 2350 (BCPC)

British Columbia is one of the provinces to adopt legislation to ensure the liability of parents for the actions of their children. The court in this case looked at the B.C. *Parental Responsibility Act,* s 6, which provides that if a child "intentionally takes, damages or destroys property of another person, a parent of the child is liable for the loss of or damage to the property experienced as a result by an owner and by a person legally entitled to possession of the property." However, s 9 provides that there is a defence for parents if they can show that they provided "reasonable supervision over the child at the time engaged in the activity that caused the property loss, and made reasonable efforts to prevent or discourage the child from engaging in the kind of activity that caused the property loss."

12. *Parental Responsibility Act*, SBC 2001, c 45; *Parental Responsibility Act*, 2000, SO 2000, c 4; *The Parental Responsibility Act*, 1996, CCSM c P8.

In this case, an "immature" 14-year-old boy stole a computer from another child. This boy was charged and convicted of the theft in young offender court; however, there was no restitution ordered to the family whose computer was stolen. The mother of the child who lost the computer, Ms. MO, sought to recover the cost of the stolen computer using the *Parental Responsibility Act*, and sued the offender's mother, Ms. EN. The court found that there was no question that the computer was stolen by Ms. EN's son, and that the other family deserved damages for their loss. However, the court took into account that this was an isolated incident in the young person's life, that he had performed the 50 hours of community service required, and that no drugs or alcohol were involved. The court ordered damages paid in the amount of 50 percent of the cost of the computer under the *Parental Responsibility Act* in the amount of $924.92, less $200 for the depreciation of the computer, to be paid in $100 payments on the 15th of each month, until the judgment was satisfied, to be paid by the offender's mother.

Occupiers' Liability

The common law generally imposes a duty on owners of land, or the occupiers, to ensure that anyone who comes onto that land is not subject to injury. Occupiers were those people who were in control of the land. Over time, there became an active duty to protect those who were invited, as well as trespassers, from harm. The duty involves taking steps to warn and also to fence off the danger. The duty usually falls to the occupiers because they live on or control the premises and are in a better position to determine any dangers. This involves occupiers clearing their steps of snow and ice and putting out signs if a floor is wet. Schools must put up barriers or signs if the floors have been recently washed and are slippery, and stairs must have guardrails. There must be an operating fire alarm system and adequate fire exits, and people who have pools must have adequate fencing to ensure that children do not drown. Generally, the law requires that people who own or occupy property take due care to ensure that no one suffers injury or harm when on that property.

There are classes of people who may fall under occupier's liability, including invitees, licensees, and trespassers. Invitees are those who are on the property for something other than a social visit, including those making deliveries or repairs. They have the highest standard of care, as each of the parties is benefiting from their attendance. Licensees are those entering for a social purpose; therefore, there is a lesser standard. Trespassers have no legal right to be on the property. These individuals can range from a lost child, who has wandered onto the property, to someone who is breaking into the property for an illegal purpose.

20TH CENTURY FOX / THE KOBAL COLLECTION

The person who occupies a property is usually responsible for ensuring the safety of those on the property.

Negligence law is similar to occupier's liability, although it remains a separate category because the court has to look at the relationship between the occupier and the visitor. There is a relationship of proximity between the parties with a duty and a standard of care. However, some of the more ancient roots of the duty were updated in the 1975 case of *Veninot v Kerr-Addison Mines Ltd.*, [1975] 2 SCR 311 (SCC), where the Supreme Court lessened the standard of care owed a trespasser. If someone knows that there are trespassers, or knows that trespassing is likely, that individual must act with "common humanity" to prevent the injury of these persons from the dangers within their knowledge. This standard allows the court to tailor the standard to the personal characteristics of the trespassers, including whether they were children, why they came on the property, the cost of preventative measures, and so forth. Today, six provinces have replaced the common law with statute, and most of the law of occupiers is governed by legislation.[13] For example, in Ontario, s 3 of the *Occupiers' Liability Act*, RSO 1990, c O.2 provides that:

Occupier's duty

3.(1)An occupier of premises owes a duty to take such care as in all the circumstances of the case is reasonable to see that persons entering on the premises, and the property brought on the premises by those persons are reasonably safe while on the premises.

13. *Occupiers' Liability Act*, RSA 2000, c O-4; *Occupiers' Liability Act*, RSBC 1996, c 337; *The Occupiers' Liability Act*, CCSM c O8; *Occupiers' Liability Act*, SNS 1996, c 27; *Occupiers' Liability Act*, RSO 1990, c O.2; *Occupiers' Liability Act*, RSPEI 1988, c O-2.

(2)The duty of care provided for in subsection (1) applies whether the danger is caused by the condition of the premises or by an activity carried on on the premises.

New Brunswick has gone one step further in abolishing occupiers' liability and allowing the law of negligence to govern. However, the legislation adopted by most provinces has attempted to replace the common law with a duty of reasonable care to visitors. Although most provinces have seen this as an improvement on the common law, there are the new problems of statutory interpretation, and determining where the line is between negligence, occupiers' liability, and other areas of law.

One can also face tort and criminal liability for not only keeping an unsafe property, but also by setting up any type of "trap" to injure those on the property. Section 247 (1) of *Canadian Criminal Code* provides that it is an offence to set "traps likely to cause bodily harm," which is punishable by indictable offence with a potential life imprisonment if the trap causes bodily harm, or if the owner permits a trap to be set that could cause bodily harm or death.

CLASS ACTIONS

Historically, each plaintiff had to bring his or her own action, as each of them did not have standing to represent anyone else in their action, although the courts of equity allowed one plaintiff to represent others in some circumstances. Class actions (also called class proceedings) are used so that one individual, called the representative plaintiff, can bring an action on behalf of a group of people with similar actions. As a group, the class can receive a decision from the court that applies to all of the individuals involved. The *Rules of Civil Procedure* and the *Class Proceedings Act* for each province dictate how one may bring a class action in that province.[14] Under this system, one lawyer can handle the claims of many individuals, and the matter will be heard by one judge who is familiar with the claims of all plaintiffs. Many think this was a positive step in Canada to save time, money, and the resources of the court. Those who might not be able to afford litigation on their own are allowed access to the justice system, and actions may be brought that may have been far too complex for one plaintiff to prove.

Quebec was the first province to enact class action legislation in 1978, Ontario enacted legislation in 1993, British Columbia in 1995, and Saskatchewan and Newfoundland brought in legislation in 2002, Manitoba in 2003, and Alberta in 2004, and New Brunswick and Nova Scotia brought in legislation in 2006 and 2008, respectively. The representative plaintiff must go to the court to certify the action as a class proceeding by telling the court the nature of the action, what they are requesting in damages, how a person can opt out of the class action, and a timeline of when this will occur. The representative plaintiff goes through the action almost like he or she is the only one involved, but the other members may be required to participate in some form at a time in the action. Another benefit for many plaintiffs is that they will not have to be subject to discovery, or testify at trial, and the defendant may be more willing to settle when there are many plaintiffs pooling information and resources.

Once the matter is certified as a class action, people must be notified that they can join the class action, and this is often done in newspapers and publications (now it is sometimes done online). Lawyers who do this work often work on a **contingency fee.** The money that is awarded at the end of the matter (if there are damages) are split between the members of the class action who have not opted out of the proceeding, and there is also a fee for the lawyers because they have worked for free up until this time. Class actions are increasing in Canada for a variety of actions, with more than "200 having been initiated from 1992 to 2001 in Ontario and 75 across Canada in the first seven months of 2007 alone," with the main categories of defendants being "big businesses, including pharmaceutical and medical-product manufacturers, financial institutions, communications conglomerates, and computer and electronics manufacturers."[15] Even with this growth, class actions are a small proportion of all civil litigation. However, many

14. *Class Proceedings Act*, SA 2003, c C-16.5; *Class Proceedings Act*, RSBC 1996, C 50; *The Class Proceedings Act*, CCSM c C130; *Class Proceedings Act*, SNB 2006, c C-5.15; *Class Actions Act*, SNL 2001, c C-18.1; *Class Proceedings Act*, SNS 2007, c 28; *Class Proceedings Act*, 1992, SO 1992, c 6; *An Act Respecting the Class Action*, RSQ c R-21; *The Class Actions Act*, SS, 2007, c 21

15. Lori Hausegger, Matthew Hennigar, and Troy Riddell, *Canadian Courts: Law, Politics and Process* (Don Mills, ON: Oxford, 2009) at 342.

FOOD FOR THOUGHT...

Canada has a shameful history of treatment of our First Nations peoples. Between the seventeenth and late-twentieth centuries, Native children (including status Indians, Inuit, and Métis individuals) were taken from their homes and forced into residential homes run by various Christian and missionary groups (including Protestants, Catholics, Anglicans, and Methodists) and operated on behalf of the Canadian government. Starting in 1867, these schools were mandatory. Within these facilities the children were not allowed to speak their own languages, practise their religion, or even retain any of their culture. These children were subjected to horrific sexual, physical, and emotional abuse for many decades. The survivors (although some disapprove of this word) of this system were able to tell their histories with the use of class action proceedings. One survivor described the lasting effects of this abuse, saying that:

An Aboriginal residential school in Resolution, Northwest Territories

> I was deprived of the love and guidance of my parents and siblings for five years. I lost my Native language and Aboriginal culture and was removed from my family roots. The enormity of the loss of both my culture and my connection with my family feels overwhelming and the effects irreversible. I lost my identity as a Native person. I live with a sense of not knowing who I am and how I should be in the world. I lost the friendship and support of my friends and community. I suffered a loss of self-esteem.[16]

These homes were only phased out in 1969 after the profound damage had already been ingrained for generations of First Nations peoples, but some schools were still in operation until 1996 in Saskatchewan.[17] In 1989 non-Aboriginal residents of the Mount Cashel Orphanage in Newfoundland made allegations of sexual abuse by Christian Brothers who operated the school. This litigation began the class action process for residential school survivors.

Plaintiffs from the residential school litigation have used class actions and other tort claims to allege negligence, wrongful confinement, breach of fiduciary duty, breach of Aboriginal treaty rights, depriving these individuals of the necessities of life, and infliction of mental suffering, among other claims, against the churches and government.[18] A class-action **settlement** for $2 billion, which was described as one of the most complicated in Canadian history, was settled by December 2006 and approved by seven courts in Alberta, British Columbia, Manitoba, Ontario, Quebec, Saskatchewan, and the Yukon. The average payment to each survivor is estimated at $25 000, but those who alleged physical or sexual abuse could receive up to $275 000, and some churches have been found liable for millions of dollars.[19] Prime Minister Steven Harper formally apologized to these victims in 2008, and in 2009 Pope Benedict XVI stated the "sorrow" at what had happened to these survivors.[20]

Is there any amount of money that can compensate for the horrific abuse and loss of culture suffered by these individuals?

Why was this system allowed to operate for so long?

Is there more that the churches or the government should do for these individuals?

Does the mistreatment of First Nations people continue today? For example, Howard Lorne Tennenhouse was disbarred by the Law Society of Manitoba after pleading guilty to overcharging nearly $1 million in legal fees from more than 50 residential school survivors (see http://aptn.ca/pages/news/2012/02/21/lawyer-disbarred-pleads-guilty-to-taking-nearly-1-million-from-residential-school-survivors/).

16. Zoe Oxaal, "'Removing That Which Was Indian from the Plaintiff': Tort Recovery for Loss of Culture and Language in Residential Schools Litigation" (2005) 68 *Saskatchewan Law Review* 367 at para 1.
17. JR Miller, "Troubled Legacy: A History of Native Residential Schools" (2003) *Saskatchewan Law Review* 357.
18. Zoe Oxaal, "'Removing That Which Was Indian from the Plaintiff': Tort Recovery for Loss of Culture and Language in Residential Schools Litigation" (2005) 68 *Saskatchewan Law Review* 367 at para 1.
19. *Ibid* at para 8.
20. CBC News, "A Timeline of Residential Schools, the Truth and Reconciliation Commission," online: <http://www.cbc.ca/news/canada/story/2008/05/16/f-timeline-residential-schools.html>. For more information on the topic, see the report of the Truth and Reconciliation Commission of Canada, *Canada, Aboriginal Peoples, and Residential Schools: They Came for the Children* (Winnipeg: Truth and Reconciliation Commission of Canada, 2012), online: <http://www.attendancemarketing.com/~attmk/TRC_jd/ResSchoolHistory_2012_02_24_Webposting.pdf>.

Kzenon/Shutterstock

Self-defence is an example of a complete defence.

criticize the underpinnings of this system, which is governed by provincial statue, for making different rules for each area that is litigated. Some would like to see a Canada-wide system of class actions, which may be difficult to implement, but could be beneficial for large Canada-wide groups (see the Food for Thought box).

DEFENCES TO TORTS

There are a number of defences to torts. The defendant may be able to prove that there was no negligence (there was not a duty of care, etc.) and that the plaintiff contributed to his or her own injuries (contribution), but there are also defences that reduce the liability of the defendant. These include consent, illegality, and voluntary assumption of risk.

Consent—Defence to Intentional Interference with the Person

There are a number of defences to torts of intentional interference with the person after the tort has been proven. Most defences, including self-defence, defence of a third person, defence of property, discipline, legal authority, illegality, and consent are **complete defences**. Provocation and contributory negligence are **partial defences**, and mistake and duress fall somewhere along the defence continuum. One of the more common defences, and the one that will be highlighted here, is consent. There are some circumstances where one can **consent** to a fight, which would normally be battery under tort law. The court must examine if the plaintiff consented to the act giving rise to the tort action. This can be done verbally, in writing, by participation, or by the surrounding circumstances. For example, in a boxing match the parties consent to hit each other repeatedly. The law of tort has recognized that the consent extends to the normal risks of that sport or event. This is difficult to apply in certain circumstances.

It could be said that we consent to battery every day when we get our hair cut, get body piercings, engage in sexual acts, or go to the dentist or chiropractor. Our action of going to the chiropractor and lying down on the table may be proof that consent was freely and voluntarily given. Consent can be revoked if one no longer wants to give consent. However, it may be difficult to stop some actions once they have begun. If you are on a sunset cruise, one consents to going out into deep waters and not coming back for a period of time. Thus, consent is given for a temporary false imprisonment. Consent can be given in limited circumstances for violence where the parties have consented to a fight. However, the court will look at exactly what was consented to, or if the fighting continued when one person was unconscious on the ground.

Contact sports also involve consent to a tort, but again the court will examine whether the rules of the game were violated by serious harm not within the course of the sport. For example, NHL player Steve Moore sued fellow player Todd Bertuzzi (as well as Bertuzzi's team, the Vancouver Canucks) for hitting Moore from behind and driving his face into the ice, causing him severe injury in March of 2004 (see *Moore v Bertuzzi*, [2007] OJ No 5113 (Ont SCJ)). Mr Bertuzzi was charged criminally with assault causing bodily harm, and he had a multi-game suspension by the NHL. Mr. Moore sued in tort for general and specific damages as well as aggravated and punitive damages for the three fractured vertebrae that he suffered which ended his NHL career. Although the $19 million action was started in 2007, it has yet to be resolved. Mr. Moore argues that this action was outside of the rules of the sport, and that Mr. Bertuzzi should be made to pay for this action.

One also consents to medical treatment because the treatments performed can be battery unless the patient's consent is given. Problems arise when medical treatment other than what was consented to is performed, when the patient decides to revoke consent, when the patient is a minor, or suffers from a mental disorder. In medical treatment, the other major issue before the court is when patients refuse treatment for themselves or their children for religious reasons (e.g., Jehovah's Witness patients who refuse blood transfusions).

Sexual relationships also involve battery unless there is express consent. Again, the courts have had to determine whether there was consent, and what was consented to. Consent cannot be obtained through coercion or blackmail or when a person is under undue duress. In situations in which there is an imbalance of power, consent is often seen as having been extorted from the plaintiff (see the following case box, which looks at *Norberg v Wynrib*).

NORBERG v WYNRIB, [1992] SCJ NO. 60 (SCC)

In *Norberg v Wynrib*, Ms. Norberg was addicted to painkillers, and she had gone to an elderly doctor to get prescriptions. The doctor confronted her about her drug use and said that he would continue her prescriptions if she had intercourse with him. After a year of this arrangement, Ms. Norberg got treatment and sued the doctor for the tort of battery. Dr. Wynrib used the full defence of consent. This case went to the Supreme Court of Canada, which ruled in her favour, arguing that the defence of consent did not apply because of the power differential between her and the doctor. Consent requires autonomy and free will and hers was impaired by drug usage and dependency on both drugs and the doctor. The court found that the weaker party was unable to choose freely, and consent is thus legally ineffective because of this "power dependency" relationship. This inequality must first be proved and then it must be shown that this inequality was exploited. The Supreme Court awarded the defendant $45 000 in compensatory damages and an additional $25 000 in punitive damages, along with her costs.

Illegality (*Ex Turpi Causa Non Oritur Actio*)—Defence to Intentional Interference with the Person

One defence that is only permitted in limited circumstances is illegality (or what was called in the Latin, *ex turpi causa non oritur actio*). Intentional interference with the person may be defeated by the illegality or immorality of the plaintiff when the tort occurred. After *Norberg v Wynrib*, the court said that the defence would only be available in limited circumstances. It is the concept of clean hands in that the court does not want the plaintiff to profit from his or her own wrongdoing or undermine the justice system. This defence was used in the Supreme Court of Canada decision in *Hall v Hebert*, [1993] SCJ No 51 (SCC), where the plaintiff and defendant had been drinking when they decided to start the stalled muscle car they were driving by doing a "rolling start." The parties were both intoxicated and lost control of the car. The plaintiff had significant head injuries and sought to collect from the defendant. The court found that a person should not profit from his or her own wrongdoing, but in this case the plaintiff was not profiting, he was only receiving damages for the injuries he sustained, which put him back in the position he would have been prior to the injuries. Although the court allowed the possibility of this defence in the future, illegality can only be used when it comes to loss of income or punitive damages. Compensatory damages may be permitted, but allowing the individual to collect a windfall from doing something illegal would bring the administration of justice into disrepute.

Voluntary Assumption of Risk—Defence to Negligence

The courts and legislation generally exempt liability when the victim consents to the actions of the defendant in negligence. The court is guided by the Latin maxim *volenti non fit injuria*, or there is "no injury to one who consents." The modern cases that deal with the voluntary assumption of risk largely involve drunk drivers and the negligent injuries to their passengers who consented to get into the car. Today, this defence is quite rare, and the court must find that the person not only knowingly participated but they gave up claims against those other parties. To find that the injured party voluntarily assumed the risk, he or she must know and communicate to the defendant the legal and physical risks of the activity. With the apportionment of loss available through contributory negligence, the court has become more unwilling to find that a plaintiff voluntarily assumed the risk (however, see the following case box).

DUBE v LABAR, [1986] SCJ NO 29 (SCC)

The Supreme Court noted that this case was a rare case of voluntary risk. Both the plaintiff and the defendant had been drinking the night before the accident, and both had been taking turns driving the car. The defendant turned to look at the passengers, and the plaintiff tried to grab the wheel, but the car overturned. The court found that this was a situation where the plaintiff not only had knowledge of his risk, but made an express acceptance of the risk of harm without recourse to law, inferring that the defendant took no responsibility for the plaintiff's safety. The court found that there was understanding on the part of both parties that there would be no responsibility to take due care for the safety of the plaintiff. This was really a joint venture where the parties had a common purpose, and it was not available to the plaintiff to try to claim against the defendant.

DAMAGES

It is a fundamental principle of torts that there cannot be liability unless the plaintiff suffered some sort of loss because of the defendant's wrongful act. All of these rules do not matter unless you can say that the individual hurt you in a definable way, and remembering that you take your victim as you find him or her under the thin skull rule. If a defendant is found by the court to be responsible for the plaintiff's injury, the defendant can be liable for damages. Damages consist of a financial award or compensation to redress the harm or loss suffered by the plaintiff.

Special damages can be calculated precisely (e.g., the cost of repairing a car). **General damages** are awarded when it is difficult to precisely determine loss or injury. This includes things like pain and suffering, which are often determined by a schedule that has been worked out by insurance agencies and lawyers. **Punitive** or **exemplary damages** are rare in Canada and are meant to punish the defendant and to make an example of him or her. The use of punitive or exemplary damages has the intention of deterring both the specific offender and others in the future. **Aggravated damages** (often confused with punitive damages) are designed to compensate for the humiliation and loss of dignity caused by the *outrageous* behaviour of the defendant. Aggravated damages could inflate the amount of general damages or may be a separate award. Other judgments include an injunction in which the court orders that the defendant cease his or her wrongful conduct (e.g., harassing phone calls). The judge can also order the defendant to return wrongfully held goods to their rightful owner, which is called **replevin**. Replevin is used when those goods are so specific that the return of those exact items is crucial.

The case of *Spencer v Rozon* et al (see page 129) is a good indication of the types of damages that can be obtained in a Canadian civil court. For this severe beating of Mr. Spencer, the judge found that Mr. Spencer was entitled to special damages, including past wage loss, which could be precisely determined by looking at how much work was missed, and also for the injuries inflicted that delayed his entry into an MBA program for two years, for a total loss of $100 000. Mr. Spencer was also entitled to be reimbursed for twice-monthly psychological counselling sessions for the next year (special damages). In general damages, the court found that there was a decrease in his overall earning capacity in the amount of $10 000. Aggravated damages were assessed at $100 000. No punitive damages were awarded, only because the amount of the rest of the award was sufficient to punish the defendant.

Michael D Brown/Shutterstock

Multiple parties may be held responsible for damages.

Joint Tortfeasors, Several Tortfeasors, and Joint and Several Tortfeasors

In some special situations, several people may be responsible for the damages of the plaintiff. **Joint tortfeasors** are those who combine mentally together for a common purpose. All of the actors may have contributed to the loss suffered by the plaintiff, and an action may be brought against these joint wrongdoers. Each province has legislation that says that the plaintiff can recover the full amount of the damages from *any* of the defendants that are found responsible. It does not matter if you are a major or minor contributor to the injury, you are just as liable, as simply being in that relationship makes one liable. In this situation, proof of a single tort is enough to find liability where the individuals have a special relationship or a common venture or enterprise.

Several tortfeasors are those who act in the same event, but who have not acted in common with each other. They are responsible for the same damage, but not necessarily the same tort. There will be a separate action against each of the tortfeasors, and each will only be responsible for the damage he or she caused.

However, the parties can also be liable together or individually. For example, if an employee harms the plaintiff outside of his or her employment, but the employer is also negligent towards the plaintiff, the employee and employer will be considered **joint and several tortfeasors**, in that they can be considered both jointly *and* individually liable.

There are four categories of joint tortfeasors: an individual who encourages others to commit a tort; an employee and an employer who are joint within the scope of their employment; a principal and his or her agent (someone who you have authorized to do work for you); and lastly, a catch-all category of tortfeasors, which can be called "guilt by participation."

Again, the case of *Spencer v Rozon* is useful as an example. Mr. Rozon and his co-defendant were examined by the court to determine if they were joint tortfeasors. To determine whether they were, the court asked if they acted in concert with one another. The finding of the court was that they were acting in concert in this vicious attack with the common purpose of beating the plaintiff. The judge noted that they fit the test for joint tortfeasors in that they were acting "in pursuance of a common end, being thus identified with each other, [and] are accordingly responsible for the entire result." Thus, Mr. Rozon and his co-defendant were found jointly liable for all of the damages sustained by the plaintiff, meaning that Mr. Spencer could pursue the award from one or both of the defendants.

Joint liability means that the judgment can be enforced against all, one, or some individuals responsible for the plaintiff's loss. Legislation in most provinces has changed so that the plaintiff can sue each tortfeasor jointly until satisfaction. This means that the plaintiff can decide who he or she wants to enforce a judgment against. Parties are always looking for those with "deep pockets," or who is actually going to be able to afford to pay for the damage done. For example, if I know that one of the tortfeasors is a multi-millionaire, and the other four are students at the local university, I am going to try to enforce my judgment against the multi-millionaire for the entire amount. Once the millionaire has paid the full amount of the judgment, all of the defendants are off the hook for the amount owed. However, the millionaire can start his own action against the four university students to get them to pay their share of the judgment. **Double recovery** is not allowed. Often courts will state how much each of the defendants contributed to the loss so that when they are splitting the loss between them it is clear how much was contributed by each member. It is always open to the defendants to sue another person that they feel was also responsible for the loss in another action.

CONCLUSION

Tort law is both a mix of private law and public interest. It is used by individuals to address a private wrong but it is created by governments and courts based on societal values

FOOD FOR THOUGHT...

Have the worries over tort litigation gone too far? There are calls to ban those under the age of 18 from using tanning beds in several communities across Canada. Other regions are calling for the posting of warning signs on tanning beds to warn of the risks of cancer. The Canadian Cancer Society supports this proposed bylaw, saying that "indoor tanning causes cancer. It's the cause of melanoma, a deadly form of skin cancer ... certainly for people under 18, we do not think they should be put in the position where they could be making a costly mistake that would affect their health in the future."[21]

Do you think that this warning and ban are in reaction to the possible tort litigation that could follow the use of tanning beds?

Should everyone be able to choose if they wish to partake in this type of activity?

Is a ban going too far?

regarding right and wrong, fair play, and justice. Tort law and civil courts allow people to obtain justice, without taking the law into their own hands, for wrongs against their person. There are many emerging issues in this field, and with the advent of social networking technology, some of these matters may become even more contentious. Matters of evidence are evolving with the technology, and future cases will dictate the methods used.

LEARNING OUTCOMES SUMMARIZED

1. Identify the general categories of tort.

There are four general categories of tort: negligence, strict liability, intentional torts, and other unique torts.

2. Define negligence.

Negligence involves the failure to take reasonable care to prevent foreseeable harm to another and judges whether an individual has fallen below a standard of behaviour that society considers acceptable.

3. List the six elements to prove a negligence action.

These six elements are (1) duty of care, (2) standard of care, (3) causation, (4) remoteness, (5) contributory negligence, and (6) damages.

4. Assess class actions in Canada.

Class actions allow a representative plaintiff to bring an action on behalf of a group of people with similar actions in order to get a decision for all members of the class. The *Rules of Civil Procedure* and the *Class Proceedings* Act for the province dictate how one may bring a class action in a particular province. One lawyer may be retained to represent several of the litigants. Complex matters that could not be efficiently and economically viable for many individuals can now be brought on a more universal scale to allow many plaintiffs access to justice. It has been suggested that one Canada-wide system of class actions could be beneficial so that plaintiffs would not need to manage different rules in various provinces.

5. Identify legal remedies resulting from a tort.

Damages are frequently awarded to redress the harm or loss suffered by a plaintiff. Special damages can be calculated precisely but general damages are awarded when it is difficult

21. CBC News, "Tanning Bed Ban Would Be First in Canada," online: <http://www.cbc.ca/news/health/story/2011/01/11/bc-tanning-bed-bylaw.html>. Reproduced by permission of CBC.

to precisely determine the injury and resultant losses. Elements like pain and suffering are often determined by a schedule that has been worked out by insurance agencies and lawyers. Punitive or exemplary damages, which are rare in Canada, are meant to punish the defendant and to make an example of the offender. Aggravated damages are designed to compensate for the humiliation and loss of dignity caused by the *outrageous* behaviour of the defendant. Other judgments can include an injunction in which the court orders that the defendant cease his or her wrongful conduct (e.g., harassing phone calls). Replevin can also be awarded to have the defendant return wrongfully held goods to their rightful owner.

SELF-EVALUATION QUESTIONS

1. Identify the elements needed to prove a negligence action and give an example of each.
2. Outline a defence to negligence and give an example.
3. Describe how *Donoghue v Stevenson* was a pivotal case in the law of torts.
4. Give an example of both misfeasance and nonfeasance.

CHAPTER 6

Family Law

Family law is a changing and dynamic field. In the twenty-first century, Canadian families will encounter new challenges. Marriage and the family are no longer synonymous. The traditional nuclear family of the 1950s, with its breadwinning husband, homemaking wife, and their two or more children, is a minority group. Two-income families, with or without children, high divorce and remarriage rates, and the increasing incidence of unmarried cohabitation, whether involving opposite or same-sex couples, have fostered new family structures and radical legal reforms. At the same time, there has been increased recognition of the inherent limitations of the law in regulating marriage and family.[1]

Learning Outcomes

After completing this chapter, you should be able to:

1. Identify the historic grounds for divorce.
2. Analyze the role of the common-law marriage in Canada today.
3. Evaluate the changes in law regarding same-sex marriages.
4. Identify the areas of family law governed by federal and provincial legislation.
5. Assess the role of bigamy and polygamy in Canada.
6. Classify who has capacity to marry.

FAMILIES IN CANADA

Family law deals with the relationships among individuals in **conjugal** and other family relationships. The boundaries of this type of law seem straightforward, but defining what comprises "family" today is difficult. Who is family to you? Would others question your definition of your family? Is your conception of family based on law, or religion, or neither? In the 2006 Canadian census, the government defined family as "composed of a married

1. Julien D Payne and Marilyn A Payne, *Canadian Family Law*, 3rd ed (Toronto: Irwin Law, 2008) at xxiii.

zimmytws/Shutterstock

A marriage contract comes with legal obligations and consequences.

couple or two persons living common-law, with or without children, or of a lone parent living with at least one child in the same dwelling."[2]

Although there are religious and cultural aspects to the institution of marriage and the definitions of families, family law most closely relates to contract law. Getting married is one of the most important and financially significant contracts that one will enter into in a lifetime. However, because of the subject matter and the importance placed on families in Canadian society, there are other ramifications beyond mere contract. One of the most significant issues of the past few decades is which relationships should be given legal recognition, and whether extending the concept of family and marriage in Canada is wise. In particular, should those who live together without the benefit of marriage be given the same rights as married spouses? Should same-sex couples be included in this regime?

By the 1970s, family law rules began to expand, particularly in the realm of unmarried opposite-sex couples who lived together. The provinces began to recognize cohabitees as spouses when it came to tax laws and statutory benefits. However, by the 1990s, couples brought challenges under the *Charter of Rights and Freedoms* to eliminate remaining differences in treatment between those in traditional and non-traditional relationships.[3] These issues will be examined in this chapter.

DEFINING MARRIAGE

Historically, marriage has been an unequal partnership. In most countries, wives and children were legally considered the economic and social possessions of their husband or father. In the nineteenth century, women and children had the legal status of **chattels.** Today, marriage is an important contractual relationship with rights and responsibilities. However, marriage is much more than a contract between two persons; it is a status that is given to individuals by the state. There are a whole host of laws that suddenly come into effect upon marriage. Not only are there benefits that the state gives to those who marry, but there are also obligations and consequences that are given to, and expected of, those persons. Marriage is a public affair rather than a private personal matter and must

2. Statistics Canada, "2006 Census: Family Portrait: Continuity and Change in Canadian Families and Households in 2006," (20 November 2009), online: <http://www12.statcan.ca/census-recensement/2006/ref/dict/fam007-eng.cfm>.
3. Berend Hovius, *Family Law: Cases, Notes and Materials,* 6th student ed (Toronto: Thomson Carswell, 2005) at 9.

Figure 6.1 Percentage of Married Canadian Couples Compared to Those Divorced, Separated, Widowed, and Single

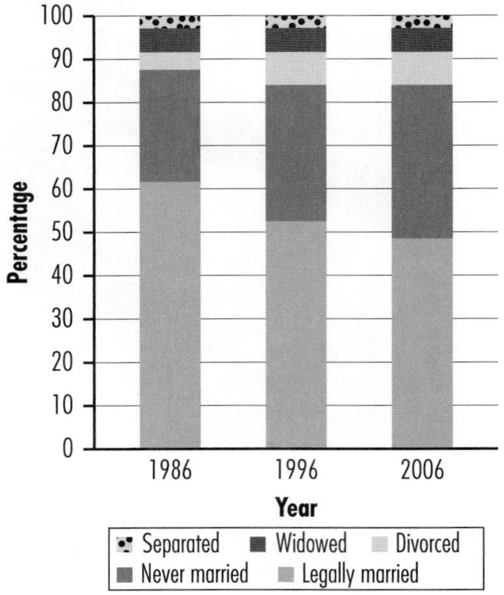

Source: Statistics Canada, 2006 Census: Family portrait: Continuity and change in Canadian families and households in 2006. <http://www12.statcan.ca/census-recensement/2006/as-sa/97-553/figures/c7-eng.cfm>. Reproduced and distributed on an "as is" basis with the permission of Statistics Canada.

be publically registered. A person cannot be married secretly, as marriage becomes part of government record.

In 2006, Statistics Canada did a study of families in Canada, surveying 8 896 800 individuals.[4] Although the largest group of those surveyed who were *in relationships* were married (68.6 percent), this number has been declining. Those in common-law marriages increased almost 19 percent over the last period studied. Statistics Canada also surveyed same-sex couples and found that 16.5 percent were married, and 83.5 percent were common-law couples. The number of same-sex couples had increased by 6 percent. Figure 6.1 shows that for the first time in 2006, there were more unmarried people (including those divorced, widowed, separated, and never married) aged 15 and over than married people.

FEDERAL AND PROVINCIAL POWERS

As examined in other areas of law, there is a division of powers given by the Constitution, which gives powers to federal or provincial/territorial government to pass legislation (see Chapter 8). The federal government has the ability to pass legislation on divorce, including the divorce action itself, the division of property, and the custody of children. Specifically, s 91(26) gives the federal government powers over "marriage and divorce." The federal government also has the power to dictate who can be married, capacity to marry, and annulments. The *Divorce Act*, RSC, 1985, c 3 (2nd Supp) D-3.4, is in effect when married parties seek a divorce. The act sets out the rights and obligations of those persons who are or were married. Since this is federal legislation, divorces from one province or territory are recognized throughout the country. If divorce were a provincial matter, there would be no guarantee that being divorced in one province would extend to all others.

However, the provincial government is responsible for laws *prior* to the actual divorce, including the creation of a marriage, documents on the breakdown of marriage, separation,

4. Statistics Canada, "2006 Census: Family Portrait: Continuity and Change in Canadian Families and Households in 2006: Highlights" (20 November 2009), online: <http://www12.statcan.ca/census-recensement/2006/as-sa/97-553/p1-eng.cfm>.

Table 6.1 Levels of Government in Family Law

Issue	Level of Government
Cohabiting couples	Provincial legislation
Married but have not applied for divorce	Provincial legislation
Property issues	Provincial legislation
Married and have applied for divorce	Federal legislation
Custody issues	Federal legislation

spousal and child support, division of property, adoption, and some custody issues. In particular, s 92(12) provides that the provinces have control over the "Solemnization of Marriage." These provincial powers include those things that happen before the actual marriage, including who can officiate, parental consent, how many witnesses are required, and other formalities. Provinces also have control over "Property and Civil Rights" according to s 92(13). This includes spousal support, child support, and other property rights. Issues at the beginning and end of the relationship are under provincial control. Since these are the responsibilities of the province, the formal requirements of marriage may differ slightly between provinces.

In summary, the law is a bit confusing when it comes to family law and the federal and provincial governments, but certain general principles apply. If individuals are not married but are cohabiting, provincial legislation applies. If they are married, provincial legislation applies until the moment that they apply for divorce. However, at the time of divorce, federal law applies. There may be an overlap between federal and provincial legislation if the couple is seeking a divorce. For example, custody and support are sought under federal legislation, but if the couples wish to deal with property issues, those issues come under the provincial legislation. Table 6.1 outlines family law issues and when provincial or federal legislation is applicable.

COURTS IN FAMILY LAW

There are specific courts that deal with family law cases including divorce, matrimonial property, custody, and related matters. Many jurisdictions have created **unified family courts**. The concept was first introduced in 1974 to allow a single court for those wishing to have family law matters heard before specialized judges with full access to community services. These courts were first introduced in Hamilton, Ontario, in 1977; Saskatoon, Saskatchewan, in 1978; Fredericton, New Brunswick, in 1979; St. John's, Newfoundland, in 1979; and later in the Richmond, Surrey, and Delta districts of British Columbia.[5] Judges for these courts were appointed and paid by the federal government.

These courts have the ability to deal with all aspects of family law in one court system, thus preventing some of the conflicts about the level of courts to hear a particular matter. Today, New Brunswick, Newfoundland and Labrador, and Prince Edward Island have permanent and province-wide family courts, and more unified courts are emerging in Saskatchewan and Nova Scotia.[6] Many have argued that the unified family court simplifies matters for divorcing couples, and allows decisions in the best interests of the children of the relationship without skipping from court to court. For example, in Ontario the unified court is known as the "Family Court of the Superior Court of Justice," which can be found in approximately 17 cities in Ontario. This branch will hear all family issues including divorce, division of property, child and spousal support, custody and access, adoption, and child protection applications, regardless of whether the issue falls under provincial or federal law.

5. Department of Justice Canada, "Unified Family Court, Summative Evaluation" (March 2009), online: <http://www.justice.gc.ca/eng/pi/eval/rep-rap/09/ufc-tuf/ufc.pdf>.

6. Julien D Payne and Marilyn A Payne, *Canadian Family Law,* 3rd ed (Toronto: Irwin Law, 2008) at 19.

Other cities in Ontario have either a family court within the Ontario Court of Justice or the Superior Court of Justice. The Ontario Court of Justice hears matters including custody, access, child and spousal support, adoption, and child protection applications, but does not hear matters of divorce or property. The Superior Court of Justice can hear matters including divorce, annulment, division of property, child and spousal support, and custody and access. Depending on the case, lawyers can decide if all of the matters under contention will be heard by a particular court.

ENGAGEMENTS

Engagements are a special type of contract entered into before marriage, and there may be an exchange of gifts as a representation of the couple's commitment to marriage. However, sometimes the engagement does not go as planned, and the parties can agree not to proceed with the marriage. At one time in Canadian history, individuals could sue for breach of promise of marriage if one party did not want to continue with the contract for marriage. Most provinces no longer allow you to sue for breach of promise of marriage, including Ontario, British Columbia, and Manitoba, and it has been abolished in Scotland, England, Australia, and many U.S. states. In Ontario, the *Marriage Act* RSO 1990, M.3, provides in s 32 that "no action shall be brought for a breach of a promise to marry or for any damages resulting therefrom." The following case box looks at what happens to the engagement ring.

WHAT HAPPENS TO THE RING?

Normally, gifts are unconditional. Once you give the gift, it is no longer yours, and you do not have a right to ask for it back. However, if you have been given (or have given someone else) an engagement ring and you decide to call off the marriage, what happens to the engagement ring? An engagement ring is usually considered a **gift in contemplation of marriage**. Unless there is a specific statute in your province, the rule from case law is that the party who is at fault forfeits the ring. However statutorily, in Ontario, s 33 of the *Marriage Act,* RSO 1990, M.3, provides that it does not matter if the donor was at fault in determining who gets the ring. Section 33 states that:

discpicture/Shutterstock

An engagement ring is usually a gift in contemplation of marriage.

Recovery of gifts made in contemplation of marriage

33. Where one person makes a gift to another in contemplation of or conditional upon their marriage to each other and the marriage fails to take place or is abandoned, the question of whether or not the failure or abandonment was caused by or was the fault of the donor shall not be considered in determining the right of the donor to recover the gift.

The legislation attempts to eliminate a dispute regarding some "fault" elements by the courts, but even with legislation, the case law is unclear.

The court must examine all of the details of the case. In *Rakus v Piccolo,* [1989] OJ No 2435 (Ont Gen Div), the court concluded that the engagement ring was a gift *without* the condition of marriage. The woman had left her job and moved to another city, but her receiving the ring was not conditional on marriage, but simply a gift. In that case, the court found that the woman could keep the ring, regardless of the fault of the parties. However, in *McArthur v Zaduk,* 2001 CanLII 28143 (Ont SCJ), the court took a different approach and examined if Mr. Zaduk had asked for the ring back. The court found that since he did not ask for the ring, he is stopped from demanding the ring later on. The court found that this lack of demand may suggest that the ring was not conditional on marriage, but rather it was an unconditional gift. This, in addition to the fact that Mr. Zaduk broke off the engagement because Ms. McArthur was unfaithful, led the court to conclude that he was not entitled to the ring, and he had to return it to Ms. McArthur.

Similarly, in *Marcon v Cicchelli* (1993), 47 RFL (3d) 403 (Ont Gen Div), the court found that although the fault of the parties would not be considered per s 33 of the *Marriage Act*, the court would only look at who had broken the engagement. In this case it was the man who called things off; therefore, he could not have the ring back. Beware that giving someone an engagement ring might mean that you never get that ring back, and that if you are given a ring it is not automatic that you get to keep it if the court decides that this was a gift conditional on marriage.

MARRIAGE

Capacity to Marry

Although the requirements of marriage are technically within federal powers, there is little statute law, and instead the provinces have legislated their own requirements. If there is a formality that is not fulfilled at the time of marriage, the marriage contract may be void. To marry, each person must have the legal capacity to appreciate the nature and quality of the legal commitment and must do so freely without the influence of drugs, alcohol, or illness. A person must comprehend the responsibilities of marriage at the time of the ceremony, and a marriage will remain valid even if this ability no longer exists after the marriage is complete.

Consent

Marriage is intended to be a binding contract that may endure for life. If **consent** is coerced or affected by alcohol or drugs, then the marriage can be declared void. To invalidate a marriage, the person's impairment must be such that he or she does not understand the ceremony of marriage and the duties and responsibilities that arise. A marriage can also be invalidated if one of the parties was pressured into entering into marriage. Duress involves the exertion of pressure or fear, but not necessarily violence. Marriages may also be set aside if there was fraud that induced a person to marry, or if there was a mistake as to the identity of one of the participants or about the nature of the ceremony. Mistaken beliefs as to the partner's wealth, religion, or habits are not a reason to have a marriage declared void.

Prohibited Degrees

Individuals are also prevented from marrying someone who is related by **consanguinity** or adoption. In 1990, the Canadian government enacted the *Marriage (Prohibited Degrees) Act*, SC 1990, c 46, which states that "no person shall marry another person if they are related lineally, or as brother or sister or half-brother or half-sister, including by adoption." Before 1990 there were additional prohibitions, including a restriction on individuals marrying their divorced husband's brother or nephew, or a divorced wife's sister or niece. These prohibitions are no longer in force. This means that cousins may marry each other, and a man can marry his mother-in-law or a woman can marry her father-in-law.

Non-Consummation

The requirement to **consummate** a marriage is still a requirement for a valid marriage in Canada, although it has been abolished in Australia and other Commonwealth countries. This is a historical requirement based on the assumption that the purpose of marriage is procreation. If one of the parties wishes to invalidate the marriage, a permanent inability to have intercourse is a reason, but this must be an inability and not simply a refusal. As can be imagined, many have questioned the definition of "intercourse," which has been defined in the case law as some penetration of the vagina by the penis. The inability to consummate does not have to be complete, and a person can use his or her own inability as a ground to invalidate the marriage. Premarital intercourse cannot qualify as consummation, although it is evidence of the party's ability to have sex.

The requirement of consummation has given rise to a host of issues, and the definition of intercourse has required that there is a judicial determination of a person's sex. In the English case of *Corbett v Corbett,* [1970] 2 All ER 33 (PDA), the court examined a marriage between a man and another person who had been registered as a male at birth but had a sex reassignment surgery. The marriage was held to be void under the laws at the time in England for non-consummation in the traditional manner.

Even with the recognition of same-sex marriage, the definition of intercourse requiring opposite-sex partners has not been resolved. Theorists have concluded that inability to consummate a marriage with a same-sex couple will not be used as a reason to invalidate a marriage because the partners clearly knew that they could not fulfill this requirement before marriage. Section 4 of the *Civil Marriage Act,* SC 2005, c 33, provides that "for greater certainty, a marriage is not void or voidable by reason only that the spouses are the same sex." However, some have used this antiquated notion of an inability to consummate under the definition as a reason for abolishing this historical requirement. However, non-consummation was an issue in *Gajamugan v Gajamugan* (see the following case box).

GAJAMUGAN v GAJAMUGAN (1979), 10 RFL (2D) 280 (ONT HC)

Mr. and Mrs. Gajamugan went through a formal civil marriage and a religious ceremony. On the wedding night, they attempted to have intercourse for the first time. Mr. Gajamugan testified that as soon as he touched Mrs. Gajamugan's face with his hand he had a "mental revulsion" to the marks on her face. He testified that he was not able to penetrate his new wife after this happened. Sexual intercourse was attempted two more times; each was unsuccessful. The court accepted Mr. Gajamugan's allegation that his inability to consummate was a permanent mental condition. The court declared the marriage was void.

Were the marks on her face something that was apparent before the marriage? Should Mr. Gajamugan have known this would be the result before going through the marriage ceremony?

Prior Marriage

One must be unmarried in order to enter into a marriage. A marriage is void if one of the parties had a prior marriage that is still in force and that the prior marriage did not get dissolved by divorce or death of the partner. If one loses contact with a spouse, there are methods by which a person can declare a person presumed dead (usually after seven years), or one may divorce the spouse with an uncontested divorce. Under the *Declarations of Death Act,* SO 2002, Chapter 14, a person can get a declaration that his or her spouse is dead if:

(a) the individual has been absent for at least seven years;
(b) the applicant has not heard of or from the individual during the seven-year period;
(c) to the applicant's knowledge, after making reasonable inquiries, no other person has heard of or from the individual during the seven-year period;
(d) the applicant has no reason to believe that the individual is alive; and
(e) there is sufficient evidence to find that the individual is dead.

This section is most often used for benefits under a life insurance policy. However, if someone deemed dead reappears, the new marriage be invalid, but the parties will not be tried for bigamy.

Bigamy and Polygamy

A legal marriage (or a divorce) in one jurisdiction is generally recognized as valid in another jurisdiction. However, some types of marriages are prohibited. In Canada, **bigamy** is defined as being married and nonetheless going through the process of being married again, and thus being married to more than one person at the same time. Section of the *Criminal Code* provides that bigamy is an offence punishable by up to five years imprisonment. **Polygamy** is also against the law under s 293 of the *Criminal Code*, which provides that:

> **293.** (1) Every one who
> (*a*) practises or enters into or in any manner agrees or consents to practise or enter into
> (i) any form of polygamy, or
> (ii) any kind of conjugal union with more than one person at the same time, whether or not it is by law recognized as a binding form of marriage, or
> (*b*) celebrates, assists or is a party to a rite, ceremony, contract or consent that purports
>
> to sanction a relationship mentioned in subparagraph (*a*)(i) or (ii), is guilty of an indictable offence and liable to imprisonment for a term not exceeding five years.

Currently, there have been few successful prosecutions of polygamy in Canada since the late-nineteenth century, but this may change in the future, as polygamous marriages become more open in North America.[7]

A subsequent marriage is void whether or not there is a charge of bigamy or polygamy under the *Criminal Code*. However, Canada does recognize polygamous marriages that were validly entered into in a country where polygamy is legal. Although polygamous marriages may not be recognized for the purposes of seeking a Canadian divorce, they may be recognized for spousal and child support and custody, for the purposes of inheriting property, and for marriage contracts and separation agreements.[8] The following box deals with polygamous marriage.

FAMILY FIRST?

Polygamy in Canada. A Student's Perspective—An Excerpt of an Essay by Shelley Chornaby, Student University of Waterloo, Winter 2011*

"The most important thing is family."

—Bill Hendrickson, HBO's *Big Love*

Canadian society prides itself on being diverse and open to all cultures and families, but is Canada really open? Polygamy is one of the few types of families that are prohibited by the *Canadian Criminal Code*. Polygamy is often considered wrong because it involves an individual who chooses to be married to more than one spouse, but does this constitute classifying polygamy as a crime? Are people who practise polygamy offenders that society needs to fear? What makes polygamy a crime?

Polygamy has a long history that can be traced back to ancient times. Many well-known biblical figures such as Abraham, David, and Solomon practised polygamy.[9] Polygamy was also contemplated by the Catholic Church as becoming integrated into its practices during a period where religion played a prominent role in society. While polygamy was practised worldwide, laws against its practice were often not enforced.[10] In 1820, polygamy gained many more followers because of a man named Joseph Smith Jr.

---

* Reproduced by permission of Shelley Chornaby.

7. Julien D Payne and Marilyn A Payne. *Canadian Family Law*, 3rd ed (Toronto: Irwin Law, 2008) at 28–29.
8. *Ibid* at 28–29.
9. Nicholas Bala et al, *An International Review of Polygamy: Legal and Policy Implications for Canada* (Ottawa, ON: Status of Women Canada, 2005) at 2.
10. Jessie Embry, *Mormon Polygamous Families* (Salt Lake City, UT: University of Utah Press, 1987) at 3–5.

Smith was the founder of Mormonism and the LDS (Church of Jesus Christ of Latter Day Saints), and at the age of 24, he found an ancient gold bible, which he was translating into what would become known as *The Book of Mormon*. This text is considered scripture to many followers; it continues to be used in branches of the LDS Church, and contains material on polygamy, and some followers have adopted this lifestyle.

In Canada, polygamy became an unaccepted and illegal practice in 1892 when the *Criminal Code* prohibited entering into or living in a state of polygamy within Canada. However, in 1985 the Law Reform Commission noted that "polygamy provisions in the *Criminal Code* should be repealed [as] polygamy is a 'marginal practice which corresponds to no meaningful legal or sociological reality in Canada.'"[11] Even though Canada has expanded its definition of marriage to include common-law couples and same-sex couples, polygamy is still recognized as a criminal offence.[12]

Should polygamy be classified as a crime? A crime is defined as "the breach of a legal duty treated as the subject-matter of a criminal proceeding" but crime "does not necessarily follow that this act is either good or bad; the punishment follows the violation of the law and not necessarily for any moral transgression."[13] Many polygamists maintain ordinary lifestyles and voluntary marriages. These families seek the best for all the individuals involved and only want what is the best for the family. What is criminal about that ideal? If that ideal is considered criminal, would the monogamous family also not be criminal? There are 850 societies that practise polygamy worldwide, thus making Canada part of the minority of countries that have declared polygamy a crime.

The Canadian government believes that polygamy breaches a legal duty not only harming the individuals involved, but also society as a whole. Polygamists assert that no crime is committed and they are only following their spiritual path. Since polygamy can be tied to religion, should Canada not recognize the Mormon faith (or others that recognize plural marriage) as it has done with many other religions within the country? Some provinces within the country have recognized polygamous relationships in certain circumstances and many provinces are aware that polygamous relationships are taking place. If polygamous relationships are such harm to the good of Canadian society, why not stop these unions from continuing to take place? Governments could be hesitant to act upon polygamous practices because of the uncertainty of the validity of the constitutional laws surrounding polygamy. If prosecutors are hesitant to prosecute cases of polygamy, why have legislation that prohibits the practice? Legislation is needed to prevent the misuse of polygamous relationships and ensure equality within the relationship.

The show *Sister Wives* has created debate about whether polygamy should be legal.

Bryant Livingston/© TLC/Courtesy: Everett Collection/The Canadian Press

With successful television shows such as HBO's *Big Love* and TLC's *Sister Wives*, polygamy has resurfaced as a controversial issue within the modern world. These television shows have not only generated debate, but they have introduced a new generation to the practices of polygamy. Polygamy is really about family. Polygamists seek to grow their family in hopes to achieve "the highest degree of celestial kingdom-life in the presence of God where they would be able to create worlds, continue to produce spirit progeny to people them, and become like God."[14] Why does Canadian society have trouble accepting the principles of polygamy in comparison to other religions? Is it because many people have a different idea of what a family entails? Should society regulate the family? Society often loses track of what is important. Family provides stability, love, and peace within a society. No family is perfect, and no family will ever be perfect regardless of what religion is practised. The family should be celebrated, not criminalized.

Do you agree with Shelley Chornaby that "no family is perfect, and no family will ever be perfect regardless of what religion is practised." Discuss this opinion.

Consider the following You Decide box.

11. Nicholas Bala et al, *An International Review of Polygamy: Legal and Policy Implications for Canada* (Ottawa, ON: Status of Women Canada, 2005) at iii.
12. *Ibid* at 3.
13. Clarence Darrow, *Crime: Its Cause and Its Treatment*. (New York: Kaplan, 2009) at 1.
14. Jessie Embry, *Mormon Polygamous Families* (Salt Lake City, UT: University of Utah Press, 1987) at 3–5.

YOU DECIDE

THE CANADIAN PRESS/Jonathan Hayward

A family in Bountiful, British Columbia

The town of Bountiful, British Columbia, has become a safe haven for polygamous families in Canada since its creation over 50 years ago by the Fundamentalist Church of Jesus Christ of Latter Day Saints. These polygamous families choose to live a private life in the area near Creston, British Columbia, which is remote, isolated, and rural.[15] Although the community has only about 1000 inhabitants, these individuals are believed to be the descendants of only six men, and this has brought much attention from the Canadian government.[16] In 2009, the government of British Columbia sought action against William Blackmore and James Oler, two residents of Bountiful. Although these charges were stayed, the government decided that reference was needed to test the limits of s 293 of the *Criminal Code in Reference re: Criminal Code of Canada (BC),* [2011] BCJ No. 2211 (BCSC). British Columbia Attorney General Craig Jones said that "polygamy is incompatible with individual freedom" and that a polygamous society "consumes its young" and should be criminally prosecuted.[17]

The Ministry of the Attorney General for British Columbia said at the start of the reference that "British Columbians and Canadians deserve and want to know whether valid laws are in place that prohibit polygamous relationships, particularly when those relationships involve minors. I am asking the court for its direction so the justice system, in B.C. and in Canada, can address the serious social harms that can result from the practice of polygamy."[18] After 42 days of hearings, Justice Robert Bauman, Chief of the Supreme Court of British Columbia, found that the *Criminal Code* section does violate the religious freedoms of those fundamentalist Mormons who wish to practise polygamy, but found that the harm to women and children outweighed the violation of freedom of religion.[19] Evidence was heard about the general ill effects of polygamy

15. Angela Campbell et al, *Polygamy in Canada: Legal and Social Implications for Women and Children* (Ottawa, ON: Status of Women Canada, 2005).

16. Josh Visser, "Polygamist Bountiful, B.C. Thrives, Despite the Law," CTV News, online: <http://www.ctv.ca/CTVNews/Specials/20080425/bountiful_polygamy_080425/>.

17. Jeremy Hainsworth, "Polygamous Society 'Consumes Its Young,' Says Crown" (15 April 2011) *The Lawyers Weekly,* online: <http://www.lawyersweekly-digital.com/lawyersweekly/3046?pg=14#pg14>.

18. Ministry of Attorney General of B.C. (October 22, 2009), online: <http://www2.news.gov.bc.ca/news_releases_2009-2013/2009AG0012-000518.htm>.

19. *National Post,* "B.C. Supreme Court Rules Polygamy Ban Is Constitutional, but Flawed" (November 21, 2011), online: <http://news.nationalpost.com/2011/11/23/b-c-supreme-court-rules-polygamy-law-is-constitutional/>.

(also called polygyny) on women and children, including a summary of research by Dr. Rose McDermott who concluded that polygamous:

> women sustain more physical and sexual abuse. They have more children, are more likely to die in childbirth, and live shorter lives than their counterparts in more monogamous societies. In polygynous societies, women are more subject to sex trafficking and female genital mutilation while receiving less equal treatment than men, and encountering more discrimination under the law. In addition, girls are less likely to be educated, restricting a key component allowing for upward mobility and economic independence. In societies with high rates of polygyny, up to half of the boys are ejected from their primary communities, with incalculable effects on them. Moreover, the average individual in a polygynous society has fewer liberties than the average individual in a state which prohibits polygyny. A polygynous state spends more on average on defense, leaving fewer resources available for building domestic infrastructure, including projects devoted to health and education. This is quite a diverse set of effects, confirming the wide-ranging consequences of polygyny in societies in which women live as enforced second class citizens.

The court in the reference found the evidence of Dr. McDermott to be "compelling" and Justice Bauman concluded that the "law seeks to advance the institution of monogamous marriage, a fundamental value in Western society from the earliest of times. It seeks to protect against the many harms which are reasonably apprehended to arise out of the practice of polygamy."[20]

Do you agree?

Should government time and resources be spent on this matter? Is this an urgent matter which should dictate the immediate apprehension of children in the community? See the full case at *Reference re: Criminal Code of Canada* (BC), [2011] BCJ No 2211 (BCSC).

Age

Historically, marriages of those under the age of seven were not permitted, and age requirements are still important today, as most jurisdictions prohibit marriages under a certain age. The age at which a person can marry is a federal power under s 91(26) of the Constitution, and Canada has adopted the requirements of the common law in England that the age of marriage is 12 years old for females, and 14 years old for males. However, marriage licences are within the provincial realm, and the provinces have made it difficult for a young person to obtain a marriage licence because of the requirement of parental consent for those who are underage, and all provinces have required a higher minimum age for marriage than provided at common law. Allowing those who are very young to marry and consummate their marriage could lead to charges of sexual assault, so the provinces attempt to regulate marriage ages.

The minimum age at which a person can marry varies from province to province, with a range of 16–19 years. In many provinces those under age 18 need parental consent, and persons under age 16 need a court order, usually granted because the woman is pregnant. A court order can be sought if parental consent is unreasonably withheld, and the court will examine whether the parental consent is rightfully withheld. If young people marry and consummate the marriage, then the marriage is valid. There are several categories of age consent across Canada, as shown in Figure 6.2.

Worldwide, the age of marriage also differs by sex. Certain countries have different age requirements for men and women (see Figures 6.3 and 6.4). It seems that society accepts that there should be a minimum age to marry, but what about a maximum age? Should there be an upper age limit on marriage, which would prevent the old and infirm from marrying? The case of *Feng v Sung Estate* deals with this issue (see the following case box).

20. *Reference re: Criminal Code of Canada* (BC), [2011] BCJ No 2211 (BCSC) at para 640 and 1350.

Figure 6.2 Marriage Ages in Canada

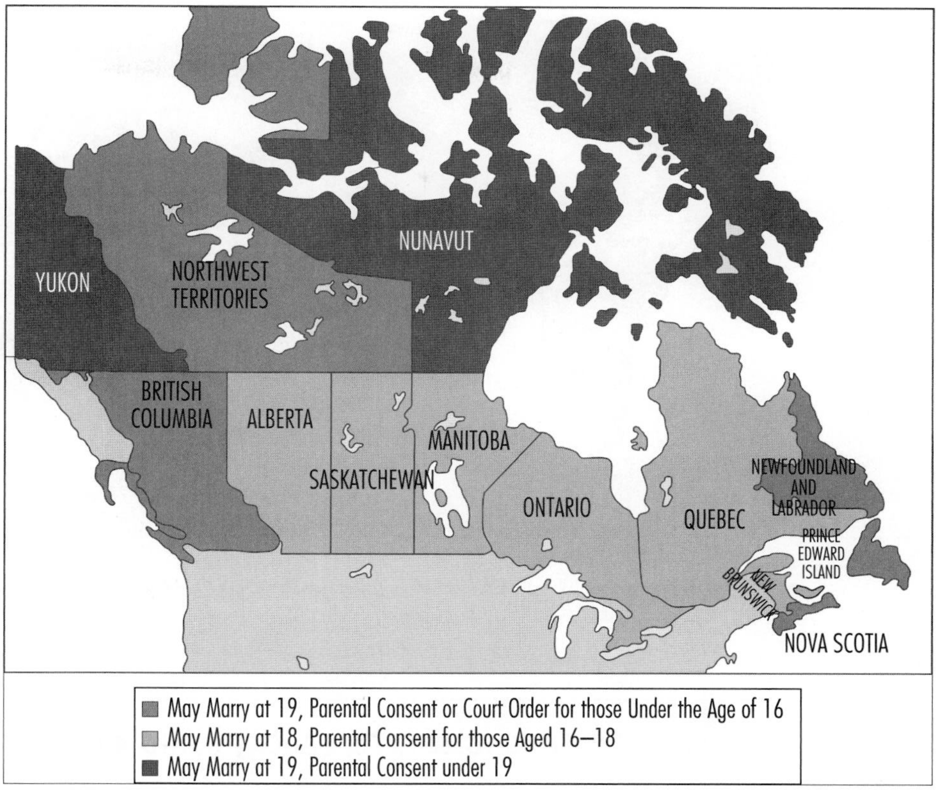

YUKON
NORTHWEST TERRITORIES
NUNAVUT
BRITISH COLUMBIA
ALBERTA
SASKATCHEWAN
MANITOBA
ONTARIO
QUEBEC
NEWFOUNDLAND AND LABRADOR
PRINCE EDWARD ISLAND
NEW BRUNSWICK
NOVA SCOTIA
May Marry at 19, Parental Consent or Court Order for those Under the Age of 16
May Marry at 18, Parental Consent for those Aged 16–18
May Marry at 19, Parental Consent under 19

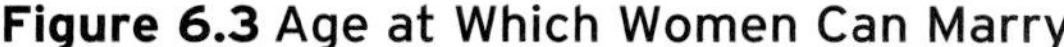

Figure 6.3 Age at Which Women Can Marry

Legal Age to Marry - Women
No age limit
13 and less than 13
14–15
16–17
18–19
20 and above

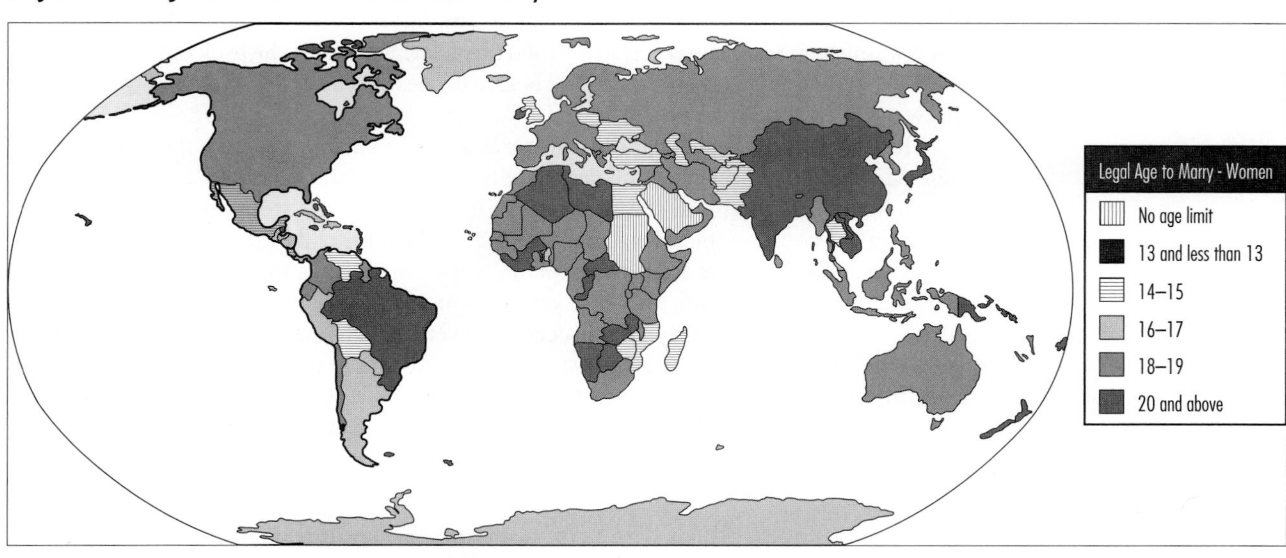

Source: ChartsBin statistics collector team 2009, Minimum Legal Age to Marry—Women, ChartsBin.com, <http://chartsbin.com/view/sr6>.

Figure 6.4 Age at Which Men Can Marry

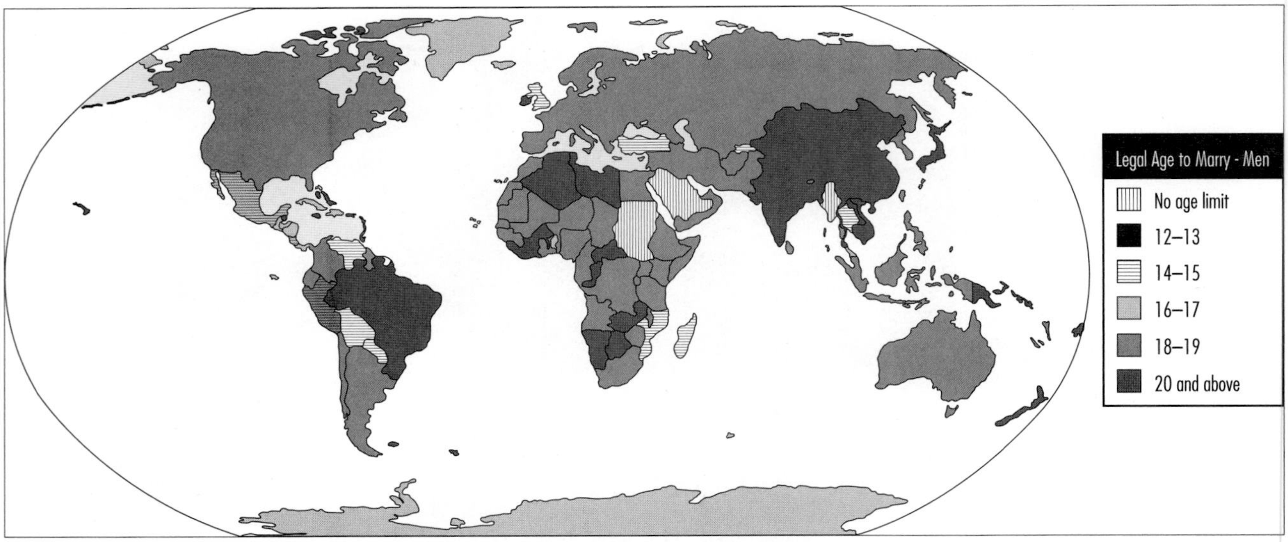

Source: ChartsBin statistics collector team 2009, Minimum Legal Age to Marry—Men, ChartsBin.com, <http://chartsbin.com/view/1o4>.

FENG v SUNG ESTATE, [2004] OJ NO 4496 (ONT CA)

By some accounts, Mr. Sung was a lonely and depressed 70-year-old man, whose wife had recently died. Mr. Sung met Ms. Feng four months after his wife's death. She was 47 years old, and became his housekeeper. Ms. Feng said that they developed a romantic relationship, and began a sexual relationship a few months after their relationship began. However, evidence entered at trial proved that Mr. Sung was, in fact, impotent after he was diagnosed with lung cancer, and could not have a sexual relationship.

Mr. Sung married Ms. Feng without telling his five children. Mr. Sung attempted to form a prenuptial agreement (marriage contract) that would limit the money going to Ms. Feng, but Ms. Feng took back the retainer amount from the lawyer, and the agreement was not finished. Ms. Feng received $30 000 from Mr. Sung, and she took out an additional $26 500 from his account in the six days before his death. The children sought to show that this was not a valid marriage.

The court found that, even though it was a valid marriage in form, the marriage was void. Ms. Feng had pressured the very ill Mr. Sung into marriage, used duress to get him to marry her, and told him she would leave if he did not go through with the marriage. Mr. Sung did not have the strength to resist her and tell his children because he was dying. The court found that he lacked the mental capacity to enter into a marriage, and that Ms. Feng married Mr. Sung simply to get his money.

The court of appeal affirmed this decision, even though it found that marriages should not be lightly set aside. Mr. Sung was very ill with terminal cancer, he was on massive amounts of medication, and he was too weak to pick up a pen to sign his discharge papers from the hospital. The court affirmed that Mr. Sung lacked capacity to marry Ms. Feng, and that the trial judge was in the best position to determine his capacity. Therefore, Ms. Feng was not his spouse, and she would not inherit his money under his will.

Should someone who is dying ever have the capacity to marry?
Was this just an action by children who did not want their new stepmother to inherit their father's money?

Non-Compliance with Formalities

Most provinces provide for specific requirements in a marriage ceremony, including the need for a licence, or the "banns" of marriage (announcement of marriage in a religious context), who can officiate, the requirement of witnesses (often two), registration of the marriage, and the specific things that need to be said at the ceremony. Even if all formalities are not precisely done the marriage is not void unless there is something that absolutely invalidates the marriage. For example, in Ontario under s 31 of the *Marriage Act,* RSO 1990, c M-3, says that if the parties went through the wedding ceremony "in good faith and intended to be in compliance with this Act are not under a legal disqualification to contract such marriage and after such solemnization have lived together and cohabited as a married couple, such marriage shall be deemed a valid marriage, although the person who solemnized the marriage was not authorized to solemnize marriage, and despite the absence of or any irregularity or insufficiency in the publication of banns or the issue of the licence." Thus, as long as the parties entered into the marriage in good faith, the marriage will be valid even if there are small technical issues.

Change of Name

The last name given to children in Canada recognizes the child's biological parents whether or not they are married, or in a common-law or same-sex relationship. Most provinces require the parent(s) to register the child within 30 days after birth, but a single mother can sign the documentation alone. The parents can choose any name as long as they agree, or if they do not agree the child's last name will be a hyphenated combination of both surnames in alphabetical order. If the mother is the only signer to the birth certificate, she gets to choose the last name. This name can be amended at a later time if the parents agree, or the father may enter an application with the court to establish paternity and ask for a change in the child's name. Many provinces will look at the best interests of the child in naming, and consider the wishes of the child (in some provinces for children as young as seven), and written consent is needed for a child from age 12 to 17.

Spouses can also apply to have a name changed at the time of marriage, but it is not a legal requirement. Women are much more likely to change their name to their spouse's name, or create some hybrid of their names. The rules governing these changes are found under a province's *Change of Name Act.*[21] Many provinces have made it much easier to change one's name through a simple administrative process, which costs relatively little. An adult may change his or her name relatively easily, but changing the name of a child can be much more complicated.

One parent wishing to unilaterally change a child's name is a provincial matter under s 92(13) of the *Constitution Act*; thus, it is a provincial responsibility. Each province is a bit different with the treatment of child name changes. For example, in Alberta under the *Change of Name Act,* RSA 2000, c C-7, a person must get the consent of the child to change his or her name if the child is over the age of 12. In addition, the Alberta legislation provides that you may only change your child's name to certain proscribed names:

> **Change of child's surname**
>
> 5 (1) Subject to section 7(2)(c) and (4), the surname of a child may be changed only to a surname that
> (a) is the surname or maiden surname of the mother,
> (b) is the surname of the father,
> (c) is the surname of the spouse or adult interdependent partner of the mother or of the father, or
> (d) consists of not more than 2 of the surnames referred to in clauses (a) to (c), combined or hyphenated.
>
> (2) If a person referred to in subsection (1)(a) to (c) has a hyphenated or combined surname, only one of the names of that surname shall be used.

Provinces are now also allowing a woman to give her child her name only if both parents consent. The bottom line is that if there is a dispute, many provinces allow

21. *Name Act,* RSBC,1996, c 328; *The Change of Name Act,* 1995, Chapter RSS, Chapter C-6.1; *The Change of Name Act,* CCSM c C50; *Change of Name Act,* RSO 1990, Chapter C.7; *Change of Name Act,* RSNB, Chapter C-2.001; *Change of Name Act,* RSNS 1989, c 66; *Change of Name Act,* RSPEI, Chapter C-3.1; *An Act to Provide for a Change of Name Act,* 1990, RSN Chapter C-8.1; *Change of Name Act,* RSY 2000, c *28; Change of Name Act, RSNWT (Nu) 1988, c C-3.*

for the child to have both of the parents surnames, hyphenated, and in alphabetical order.

Domestic Contracts—Marriage Contracts and Cohabitation Agreements

"Domestic contract" is a term that refers to **marriage contracts**, **cohabitation agreements**, and separation agreements (discussed later in the chapter), or what is termed in the United States as a "prenuptial agreement." Domestic contracts are a tool used by many couples to ensure that they agree on the division of assets if they separate or divorce. Historically in Canada, domestic contracts were severely limited in law because they were thought to undermine the stability of marriage, were thought contrary to public policy, and were considered immoral through the discussion of separation and divorce before marriage. However, these attitudes have changed significantly in the last few decades—not only between opposite-sex couples, but also for same-sex couples.

Today, the governing family legislation in each province and territory allows a couple who marries or cohabits to construct a marriage or cohabitation agreement, which can include a separation agreement. If the parties enter into a cohabitation agreement and later marry, the agreement may automatically become a marriage contract. For example, s 53(2) of the Ontario *Family Law Act,* RSO 1990, c F.3, provides that if the "parties to a cohabitation agreement marry each other, the agreement shall be deemed to be a marriage contract."

Cohabitation agreements also apply to common-law spouses who do not have the same automatic right to share in property when they separate, so more details can be set out in a contract. New Brunswick, Newfoundland and Labrador, Ontario, Prince Edward Island, and the Yukon have specific legislation allowing unmarried opposite-sex couples to enter into cohabitation agreements, and these agreements will override the prevailing legislation. For example, in Ontario the *Family Law Act,* RSO 1990, c F.3, s 2(10) states that a "domestic contract dealing with a matter that is also dealt with in this Act prevails unless this Act provides otherwise." Thus, the parties can resolve their issues in a way they agree rather than being bound by statute. In Ontario, cohabitation agreements can be entered into before or during cohabitation; in New Brunswick, Newfoundland and Labrador, Prince Edward Island, and the Yukon, the parties must be already cohabitating when they enter into the agreement.[22]

These agreements are contracts outside of provincial and territorial legislation, which usually provides that spouses are entitled to an equal share of marital property when they separate. Through contract, the parties can take property outside of legislation and decide between them how to divide property. The **matrimonial home** is something that is excluded from agreement. A domestic contract cannot limit the spouse's right to live in the home or share in its value, but the spouses may also be responsible for the obligations that flow from a matrimonial home. These contracts must be in writing, dated, signed by the parties, and witnessed, and any changes must be in writing. Like a separation agreement, the parties can agree on key issues to lead to an easier procedure upon separation or divorce.

A marriage agreement is used by those who are married or are planning to be married, while a cohabitation agreement is the equivalent when the parties are not married. The subject matter of a cohabitation agreement or marriage contract can include all types of issues, such as the division of property, career issues, the raising of children, and so forth. However, the courts are highly reluctant to issue orders directing spouses to behave in a particular way. A principle of contract law is that a contract for personal service will not be specifically enforced, and the courts do not want to enforce this type of requirement. The inclusion of such things as an agreement not to have children, not to have sex, or to end the marriage at a certain time period is difficult to enforce, and the courts will likely not entertain these agreements.

Marriage contracts typically will protect property that each person has brought into the marriage and dictate how to divide property acquired during the marriage. One of the parties may bring much more money or assets into a marriage, and these assets can be protected through this contract. Couples with children may also want to specifically divide assets so that their children can inherit the property instead of a former spouse. The court

22. Julien D Payne and Marilyn A Payne, *Canadian Family Law*, 3rd ed (Toronto: Irwin Law, 2008) at 51.

will not enforce a contract that completely waives child support rights and obligations, as this is almost always contrary to the needs and best interests of the children.

Marriage contracts can be disputed the same as any other contract on such grounds as fraud, duress, and misrepresentation. They can also be disputed on the grounds of improvidence (manifest unfairness) and non-disclosure of assets. Courts have ruled that both parties to a domestic contract must enter it in good faith. Legislation may also provide that a domestic contract or provision may be set aside if the parties did not truthfully disclose their financial situation, or one of the parties did not understand the consequences or responsibilities under contract. Although the aim is to allow parties to agree on matters before they are in the midst of a bitter battle on the breakdown of their relationship, the parties may not be in a position to know what their requirements will be on separation. It is important that both parties seek **independent legal advice** from their own lawyer to make sure that their rights are protected as individuals, which is separate from advice the couple may receive jointly.

There are several areas that cannot be included in a domestic contract, including provisions dealing with child custody and welfare, except in British Columbia and the Yukon. Courts can overrule these provisions and change them if it is in the best interests of the child (including child support agreements). The courts will enforce domestic contracts, but if one of the parties was not truthful in the agreement, if the contract is unfair, or if the contract is completely one-sided, the court may wish to override the contract. The court will not allow one powerful party to take advantage of the other, and the children, who must be protected. The parties should be free to contract, but the parties must also be protected (see the following box).

WHAT CAN YOU PUT IN A DOMESTIC CONTRACT?

Although Canadian domestic contracts usually focus on the division of the matrimonial home and the property of the marriage, U.S. prenuptial agreements potentially allow for all kinds of provisions. Whether or not they are enforceable is another matter. What are some outlandish provisions?

- Lona Smith and Zack Schiffman, among other things, agreed that every gift given would be accompanied by written documentation verifying that it was a gift not to be divided upon divorce. In the event of a divorce, Zack would have to pay for a personal trainer, dermatologist, and any plastic surgery that Lona wished for herself. The negotiation took 737 days, many drafts of the agreement, five terminated lawyers, screaming fights, and two cancelled wedding dates. The couple did eventually get married.
- Other couples require "lifestyle" clauses including limiting a wife's weight to 120 pounds with a $100 000 penalty if this is not maintained, and a $500 fine for each pound gained.
- Some have required "intimacy" clauses, which say the number of times a couple will have sex (and some have attempted to stipulate sexual positions).
- Some U.S. agreements have stipulated that in-laws may only stay for a limited number of days.
- Some have tried to say that the couple will have children in a certain period of time.
- One wife required her husband to pay $10 000 each time he was rude to her family.
- Some have requested random drug tests with monetary penalties for a failed test.
- Some of the most contentious issues surround who will get custody of the family pets.[23]
- Famed American divorce lawyer Raoul Felder says that it is more common to see provisions in prenuptial agreements that stipulate that a spouse will not smoke, or a plan to get pregnant.
- Felder states that one agreement said that a wife would not have sex with her husband unless he lost 50 pounds.[24]
- One couple allegedly had the provision that the husband could not watch more than one football game on Sundays during football season.
- Celebrities are among those most rumoured to have unique prenuptial requirements. Although not confirmed, it was rumoured that Katie Holmes and Tom Cruise had an agreement that Holmes would receive US$3 million for each year they were married if they divorced, but if they reached 11 years, the prenuptial agreement would no longer

23. Shanna Hogan, "Conditional Love: Despite Critics, Prenuptial Agreements More Popular and Outrageous than Ever" (March 2008), *Times Publications*, online: <http://www.shannahogan.com/?page_id=123>.

24. Michelle Andrews, "Prenuptial Agreements to Lose Weight, Have Sex" (28 August 2008) *U.S. News & World Report*, online: <http://health.usnews.com/health-news/blogs/on-health-and-money/2008/08/28/prenuptial-agreements-to-lose-weight-have-sex_print.html>.

be in effect, and Holmes would receive half of everything. The couple recently split (well before the 11 year mark), but the terms of the agreement were kept confidential.

- Jack Welch (a very wealthy U.S. CEO) and Jane Beasley Welch had an agreement that the prenuptial agreement would be void after ten years of marriage. It is said that instead of a few million that she was entitled to under the prenuptial agreement, Mrs. Welch was left with approximately US$130 million (unconfirmed settlement) when he allegedly unfaithful after 13 years of marriage.
- It is rumoured that Keith Urban and Nicole Kidman have an agreement that if Urban, who has issues with illegal drugs, relapses, he will not receive any of Kidman's estimated US$150 million fortune.[25]

Remember, just because a clause is in an agreement, it does not mean that the court will agree to enforce that term.

COMMON-LAW MARRIAGES

People who cohabitate and share their lives with each other, but are not formally married, often perceive themselves as being in a "common-law marriage"; but the term is a misnomer. There was once a power, for example during war, where countries would recognize the marriages of people who could not practically seek the approval and the formalities of the state. This is not what is meant by the modern term. Marriages are legally binding contracts, but common-law marriages are also legally binding contracts without a marriage ceremony, although the legal obligations and responsibilities on common-law spouses are less. Common-law relationships are not the same as marriages in Canada, even though we have extended certain rights to those couples. Although the federal government is responsible for marriages under the Constitution, there is no power of the federal government to deal with people who are not married. This has led to some problems when it comes to same-sex couples. However, there was eventually recognition of these types of relationships.

By July 2000, the Canadian government passed the *Modernization of Obligations and Benefits Act,* SC 2000, c 12, to amend 60 statutes to reflect the rights of same-sex and opposite-sex cohabitating couples. Some provinces, for example, do not give support rights to unmarried partners. Depending on the legislation and the particular situation, most provinces recognize common-law relationships after the couple has cohabited for two to three years, or for a substantial time and have a child.

However, some provinces, like Ontario, have not extended spousal property rights and succession rights to same-sex or opposite-sex unmarried couples. When married parties separate, they immediately have the right of dividing the property they own, but this right is not extended to many common-law couples. This means that there may be no recognition of the status of the parties as a couple when a party disputes the division of property or when one member of the couple dies without a will. Although matters are becoming much more equal between married and unmarried couples, there are still important differences. The *Charter* has generated claims by cohabitating parties to get benefits once reserved only for married couples, including pension benefits, insurance rights, and tax advantages. These challenges are slowly eroding the bars to benefits that unmarried spouses once faced, but there is still more work to be done.[26]

There are various reasons for living in a common-law relationship:

- one of the parties is still married to someone else;
- there is a religious issue between the parties;
- one or both of the parties sees marriage as an antiquated and patriarchal relationship;
- the parties do not want to assume the legal and social responsibilities of marriage;
- there is less of a stigma on unmarried couples than in the past;
- the parties wish to try living together before getting married;

25. MyWedding.com, "Ten Craziest Prenuptial Agreements," online: <http://www.mywedding.com/blog/planning/lifestyle/just-for-fun/ten-craziest-prenuptial-agreements/>.

26. Julien D Payne and Marilyn A Payne, *Canadian Family Law,* 3rd ed (Toronto: Irwin Law, 2008) at 49

- the parties may lose some benefits such as support payments from a previous spouse if they remarry; and
- the parties see the relationship as a convenience rather than a legal contract.

Some provinces, including Manitoba and Saskatchewan, have much broader legislation on the rights of unmarried couples. After two to three years as common-law spouses, many of the rights and responsibilities are conferred on the couple.

There are more common-law couples in Quebec than anywhere else in Canada (see Figure 6.5). Over one-third of couples in Quebec are in common-law unions, which is higher than in many countries in the world (see Figure 6.6). Ontario only has 10 percent common-law couples, and has the highest rate of married couples at almost 74 percent.

SAME-SEX MARRIAGES

Between 2003 and the present, most provinces changed their definition of spouse and marriage. The traditional definition of marriage as the "voluntary union for life of one man and one woman to the exclusion of all others" that was established in 1866 was contrary to s 15 of the *Charter,* as it excluded same-sex partners, so the Canadian government introduced

Figure 6.5 Percentage of Canadian Couples Who Are in Common-Law Relationships, 2006

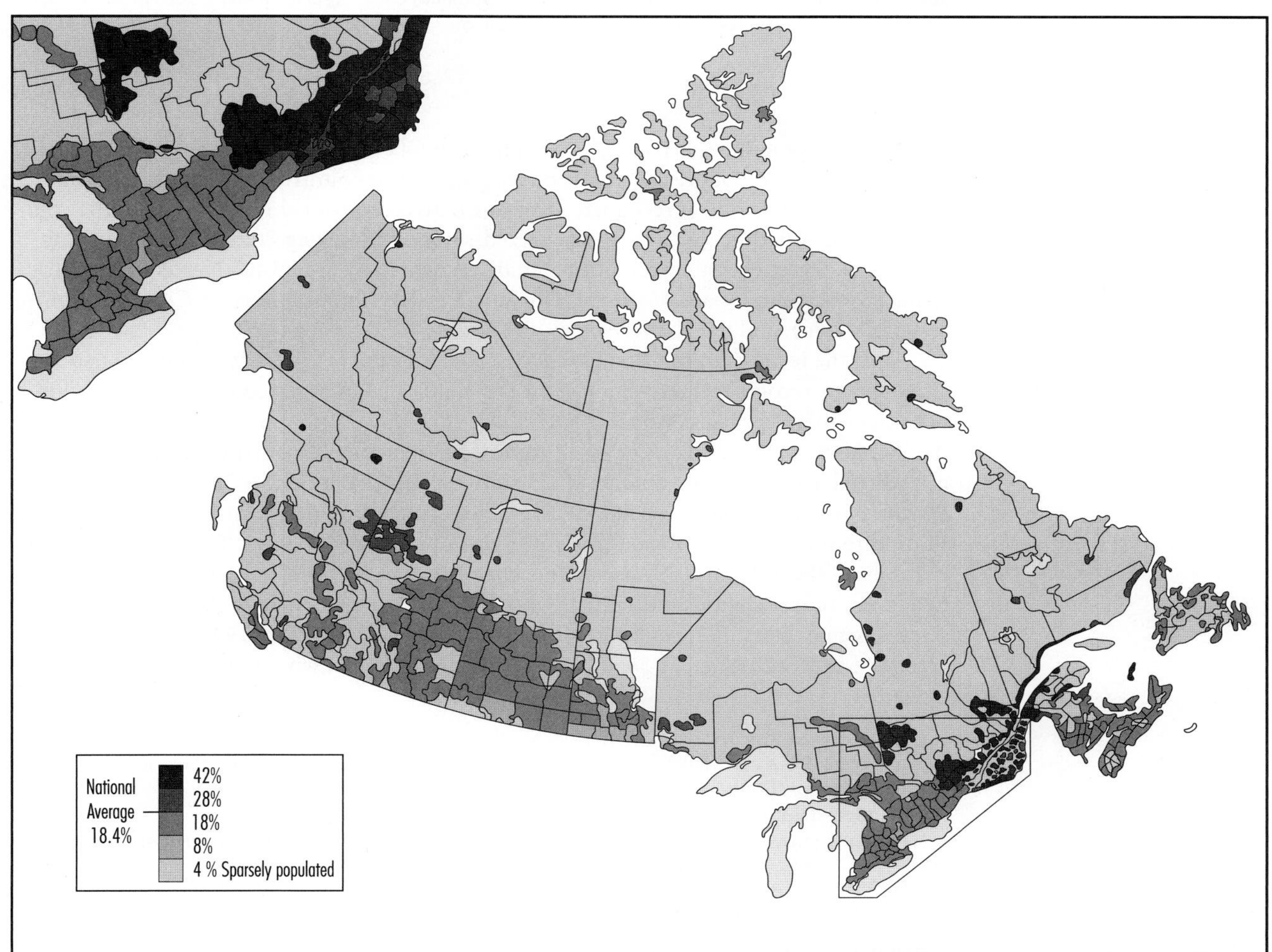

Source: Statistics Canada, Percentage of couples who are common-law by 2006 Census Division (CD), http://www12.statcan.gc.ca/census-recensement/2006/as-sa/97-553/maps-cartes/Family2006ec_NatCommLaw.pdf. Reproduced and distributed on an "as is" basis with the permission of Statistics Canada.

Figure 6.6 Common-Law Couples in Quebec, Canada, and Other Nations

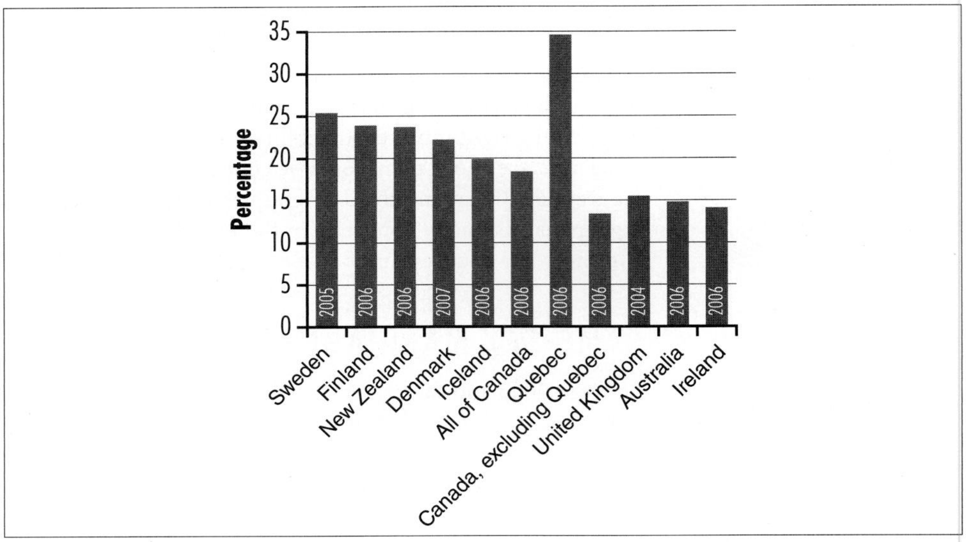

Source: Statistics Canada, 2006 Census: Family portrait: Continuity and change in Canadian families and households in 2006. http://www12.statcan.ca/census-recensement/2006/as-sa/97-553/table/t8-eng.cfm. Reproduced and distributed on an "as is" basis with the permission of Statistics Canada.

legislation to redefine marriage. At the time of publication, same-sex marriage is legal in some countries (see Figure 6.7) to various degrees (some countries only recognize domestic partnerships, while others recognize same-sex marriages from abroad). Some of the countries and jurisdictions that have recognized same-sex marriage include several states in the United States (but they are not federally recognized), Argentina, Nepal, South Africa, Hungary, Belgium, Spain, Portugal, Norway, Sweden, Iceland, Mexico City (but not the rest of Mexico), and the Netherlands.

After the legislation in Canada was passed, a number of provincial statutes had to be amended to recognize these changes in the status of same-sex couples. These included provincial marriage legislation. In 2005, the federal government passed the *Civil Marriage Act,* SC 2005, c 33, giving same-sex couples the right to marry. Provincially, legislatures introduced legislation to amend their statutes. In Ontario, the *Spousal Relationships Statute Law Amendment Act,* SO 2005, c 5, was created to alter more than 70 provincial statutes to recognize the obligations and rights of same-sex couples. To avoid some of the criticism of those against this legislation, the provinces added elements to their legislation to address those religious individuals who did not wish to partake in the solemnization of same-sex marriages. For example, the Ontario *Marriage Act,* RSO 1990, c M-3, s 20(6) as amended by SO 2005, c 5, s 39, provides that an individual who may perform a marriage ceremony is:

> not required to solemnize a marriage, to allow a sacred place to be used for solemnizing a marriage or for an event related to the solemnization of a marriage, or to otherwise assist in the solemnization of a marriage, if to do so would be contrary to,
> (a) the person's religious beliefs; or
> (b) the doctrines, rites, usages or customs of the religious body to which the person belongs.

Therefore, if an individual believes it is against his or her religious beliefs to acknowledge same-sex marriage, or the beliefs of that person's religion, he or she cannot be forced to officiate over a same-sex marriage.

More married same-sex couples are in Ontario, Quebec, and British Columbia (see Figure 6.8), and half of all same-sex couples in Canada live in Montreal, Toronto, and Vancouver. Some believe this is because Quebec, Ontario, and British Columbia were the first three provinces to legalize same-sex marriages.

Figure 6.7 Countries That Permit Same-Sex Marriage

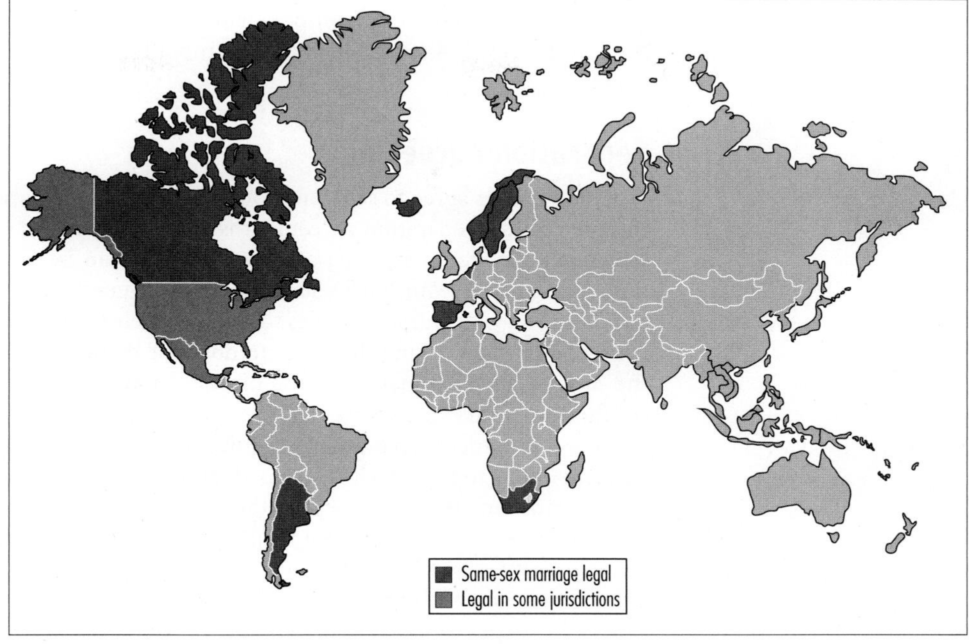

Source: Same-sex marriage around the world", CBC News, May 29, 2009, http://www.cbc.ca/news/world/story/2009/05/26/f-same-sex-timeline.html; <http://www.seattleglobalist.com/2012/02/02/ten-countries-that-were-ahead-of-washington-on-same-sex-marriage/1001>.

Figure 6.8 Same-Sex Couples by Marital Status

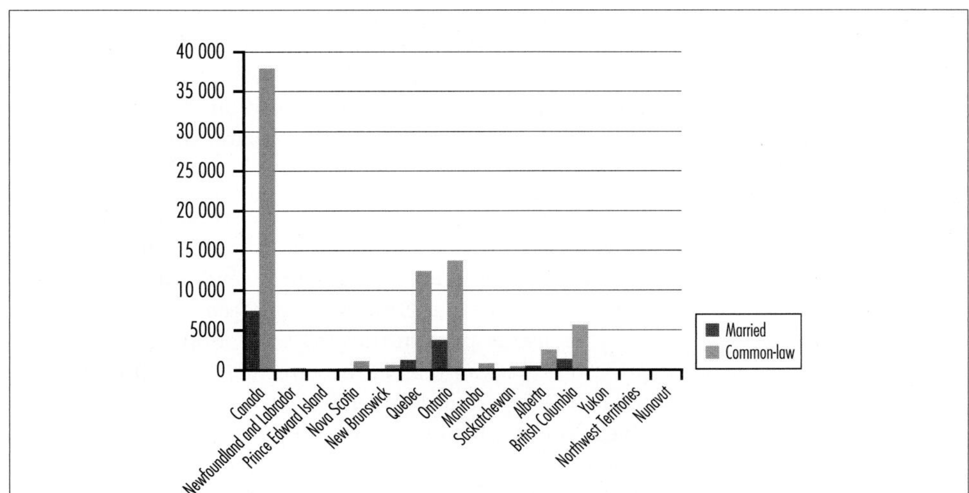

Source: Statistics Canada, 2006 Census: Family portrait: Continuity and change in Canadian families and households in 2006. <http://www12.statcan.ca/census-recensement/2006/as-sa/97-553/table/t9-eng.cfm>. Reproduced and distributed on an "as is" basis with the permission of Statistics Canada.

SEPARATION

When a relationship breaks down, the first step is **separation,** which is a status between marriage and divorce. The parties agree not to live as partners, but rather to live "separate and apart." Living separate and apart is a phrase from legislation that represents an often physical separation of the couple and indicates that they do not intend to live together in the future. Separation does not end the marriage, as the couple is still legally married. Most provinces have their own legislation that governs separation. For example, Ontario has the *Family Law Act,* RSO 1990, c F.3; Alberta has the *Family Law Act,* SA 2003, c F-4.5; and British Columbia has the *Family Relations Act,* RSBC 1996, Chapter 128.

Separation Agreement

Once the parties agree to separate, couples will often seek a separation agreement through their lawyers. A separation agreement is a written contract between the spouses in which they agree to live apart. Separation agreements can be entered into by opposite-sex or same-sex couples who have cohabited and are currently living separate and apart. The courts strongly encourage couples to sort out their issues and settle them before coming to court, rather than asking the judge to do it for them. A separation agreement means that the couple can settle matters in the most economical and efficient manner and minimize conflict and legal expenses.

Most provinces have formal requirements for a separation agreement; usually, the agreement has to be in writing, signed, and in some provinces (such as Ontario) there is also a requirement that the separation agreement is witnessed. It is always wise for each party to have independent legal counsel that can advise them on their individual rights. Some provinces (such as Alberta) make this legal advice mandatory so that each individual ensures that their rights are protected. A separation agreement is voluntary—you cannot be forced to sign any agreement, but the agreement does not need court approval. It is similar to any other contract. The separation agreement will typically include the following elements:

- a division of assets;
- provisions for spousal support;
- provisions for child support;
- provisions for custody and access to children;
- matters to the upbringing and education of the children;
- use of the matrimonial home;
- agreement about how to live separate and apart;
- how to pay ongoing debts;
- provisions for mediation or arbitration of disputes;
- anything else the couple wishes to agree upon; and
- a reopening clause.

If there is a valid and enforceable separation agreement, those terms will prevail over other legislation that may apply in the situation. However, when it comes to the custody and access of children, a judge can always decide not to follow the separation agreement if it is not in the best interest of the children.

It is also important that the separation agreement has a **reopening clause.** This is a provision that can reopen the agreement and discuss the matters further if certain things happen. A separation agreement may be reopened if one of the parties becomes ill or disabled, loses a job, or gets a promotion and/or raise; if one of the parties is hiding money; or if other life-altering events occur. Again, primary concern is with the best interests of the children, and these issues can always be reopened. Any of these issues brings into question the fairness and validity of the agreement, and the issues can be revisited. A court can also override a separation agreement if one of the parties is waiving his or her rights to support and it would be **unconscionable** to do so, or if there are other obvious injustices. Like any other type of contract, a separation agreement may be set aside if it was made under fraud, duress, misrepresentation, or coercion, or if a party failed to disclose significant assets or debts. Like any contract, the parties can pursue legal remedies for breach of contract if there is a misrepresentation or if the contract is not followed.

Figure 6.9 Divorce by Province, 2001–2005

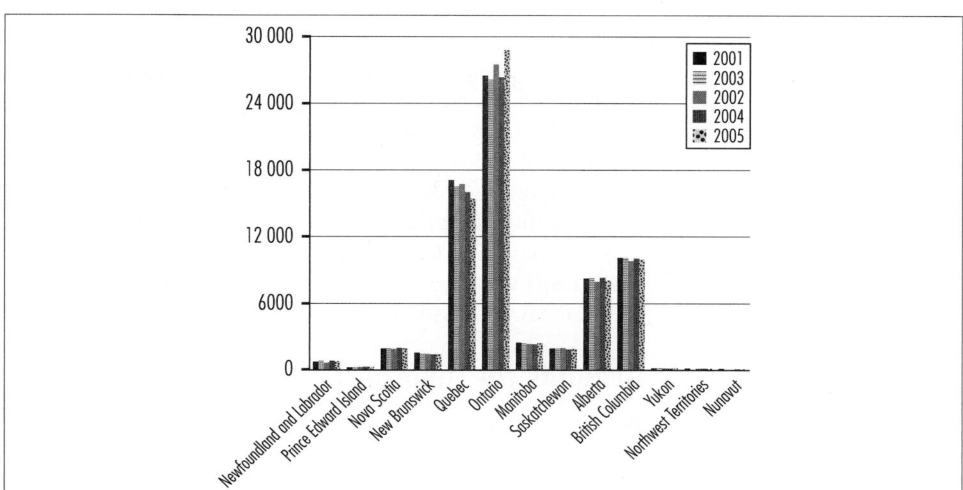

Source: Statistics Canada, Summary Tables, 2008: <http://www.statcan.gc.ca/tables-tableaux/sum-som/l01/cst01/famil02-eng.htm>. Reproduced and distributed on an "as is" basis with the permission of Statistics Canada>.

DIVORCE

Termination of a relationship is generally governed by the province under s 92(13) of the Constitution, but the exception to this rule is divorce, which comes under federal jurisdiction. This means that there may be some overlap between the provinces and the federal government when dealing with the process of divorce. Federally, divorce is governed by the *Divorce Act*, RSC 1985, c 3 (2nd Supp), where a court in each province and territory has jurisdiction to hear matters under the act.

Divorce is a phenomenon that will be experienced by many Canadians. The 2008 data on divorce was released by Statistics Canada, which showed that 43.1 percent of marriages end in divorce before their 50th wedding anniversary.[27] However, as is shown in Figure 6.9, divorce actually dropped in some provinces from 2001 to 2005.

Yet, some dispute the divorce statistics that are collected in Canada. The Institute of Marriage and Family Canada (IMFC) says that a crude divorce rate per 100 000 of the population should be used instead of the figures of Statistics Canada. The IMFC alleges that divorce rates are decreasing from a high of 362.3 per 100 000 people in 1987 to 220.7 per 100 000 in 2005. The IMFC says that the percentage of marriages that will end before the 30th wedding anniversary is between 36.1 and 37.9 percent, much lower than the 43 percent alleged by Statistics Canada. The IMFC says that there is a difference in these rates because 20 percent of divorces are repeat divorces for at least one member of the couple.[28] People are required by law to obtain a divorce if they wish to remarry, as only a divorce will legally end a marriage. You may also obtain a divorce in Canada even if you have been married outside the country.

zimmytws/Shutterstock

According to Statistics Canada in 2008, approximately 43 percent of Canadian marriages end in divorce.

History

Historically, Canada saw significant changes to the legal rights and obligations of marital partners in the late 1970s and early 1980s. Before 1968,

27. Joanna Smith, "Statistics Canada to Stop Tracking Divorce Rates" (20 July 2011) *Toronto Star*, online: <http://www.thestar.com/news/canada/politics/article/1027273--statistics-canada-to-stop-tracking-divorce-rates>.

28. Institute of Marriage and Family Canada, "Canadian Divorce Statistics" (2 June 2010), online: <http://imfcanada.org/default.aspx?go=article&aid=1182&tid=8>.

divorce law varied in Canada from province to province, and in Newfoundland and Quebec there was no judicial divorce and individuals were forced to lobby for the passage of a private act of Parliament to dissolve their marriage.[29] Individuals during this time period had to point to the party who was at fault for the dissolution of the marriage; simply being unhappy in marriage was not a sufficient ground. In the 1970s, Canada instituted a "no-fault" regime that dictated that the reason for divorce was not important.

In 1970, the state of California was the first jurisdiction in the Western world to institute no-fault divorce. The new law permitted either party to divorce on the terms of irreconcilable differences on the breakdown of marriage. Within a decade, all but two U.S. states had adopted some form of no-fault divorce. The goal of these new laws was to eliminate the sham testimony heard in "fault" divorces and restore dignity to the courts. It would also facilitate fair and equitable economic settlements.

Grounds for Divorce

Before 1967, one could seek a divorce in Alberta, British Columbia, Manitoba, the Northwest Territories, Saskatchewan, and the Yukon by a husband proving the wife's adultery. A wife could petition on the grounds of adultery, rape, sodomy, bestiality, or bigamy. The eastern provinces had their own divorce act prior to Confederation, which applied until 1968. Adultery was a ground for divorce in these provinces. In New Brunswick and Prince Edward Island, frigidity or impotence was accepted as a ground, and Nova Scotia also allowed for cruelty.

The 1968 *Divorce Act* retained some of the fault grounds for divorce including adultery, bigamy, homosexuality, imprisonment, alcohol or drug addiction, whereabouts unknown, non-consummation, and desertion. However, the new federal act brought in the concept of permanent marriage breakdown, and living separate and apart. If the parties could show that there was a three-year separation or a permanent marriage breakdown, the parties could seek a divorce without pitting the spouses against one another in court. Eventually, the three-year waiting period was considered too long, and this was eventually reduced to one year in 1985.

Today, the *Divorce Act,* RSC, 1985, c 3 (2nd Supp.) D-3.4, s 8 allows couples to obtain a divorce on the grounds that there has been a breakdown of the marriage. This section specifies that:

> **8.** (1) A court of competent jurisdiction may, on application by either or both spouses, grant a divorce to the spouse or spouses on the ground that there has been a breakdown of their marriage.
>
> **Breakdown of marriage**
>
> (2) Breakdown of a marriage is established only if
> (*a*) the spouses have lived separate and apart for at least one year immediately preceding the determination of the divorce proceeding and were living separate and apart at the commencement of the proceeding; or
> (*b*) the spouse against whom the divorce proceeding is brought has, since celebration of the marriage,
> (i) committed adultery, or
> (ii) treated the other spouse with physical or mental cruelty of such a kind as to render intolerable the continued cohabitation of the spouses.
>
> **Calculation of period of separation**
>
> (3) For the purposes of paragraph (2)(*a*),
> (*a*) spouses shall be deemed to have lived separate and apart for any period during which they lived apart and either of them had the intention to live separate and apart from the other; and
> (*b*) a period during which spouses have lived separate and apart shall not be considered to have been interrupted or terminated
> (i) by reason only that either spouse has become incapable of forming or having an intention to continue to live separate and apart or of continuing to live separate and apart of the spouse's own volition, if it appears to the court that the separation would probably have continued if the spouse had not become so incapable, or

29. Berend Hovius, *Family Law: Cases, Notes and Materials,* 6th student ed (Toronto: Thomson Carswell, 2005) at 141.

(ii) by reason only that the spouses have resumed cohabitation during a period of, or periods totalling, not more than ninety days with reconciliation as its primary purpose.

Breakdown of marriage is only established if the spouses have lived separate and apart for at least one year preceding the divorce petition, or there is adultery or cruelty. An individual can start an application before the 12-month waiting period has expired, but one must wait for 12 months to make the final application. This ground for divorce is overwhelmingly the most common method of divorce in Canada.

Separate and apart means that one person in the marriage decides that he or she no longer wishes to live as a conjugal couple and disengages from the marriage sexually, socially, financially, and physically. One of the spouses typically moves out of the home. However, the court has had to determine if one can live separate and apart while still sharing the same home, as in the case of *Rushton v Rushton* (see the following case box).

RUSHTON v RUSHTON (1969), 1 RFL 215 (BCSC)

Mr. and Mrs. Rushton were married in 1936. By 1960, they lived separate lives but lived in the same suite in an apartment building. By 1965, sex had entirely stopped, and the husband lived in one room of the apartment and the wife in another, with no contact between them. Mrs. Rushton shopped and cooked only for herself, and Mr. Rushton bought his own food and cooked for himself. Mr. Rushton did his own laundry, and Mrs. Rushton provided no household services for her husband.

Mr. Rushton paid his wife a sum of money each month to maintain her standard of living. The couple testified that they only lived in the same apartment because they were caretakers of the apartment building and had to be (or appear to be) husband and wife to live in the caretaker's apartment. The court found that this living situation did qualify as separate and apart. The court found that to live separate and apart there must be a "withdrawal from the matrimonial obligation with the intent of destroying the matrimonial consortium, as well as physical separation." The court found that there must be a withdrawal from the matrimonial obligation with the intent of ending the marriage and not just physical separation. The Rushtons had this intent to end the marriage.

Why would other couples still live together although they wished to divorce? Is this now more of an issue given the current economic realities?

Subsequent cases have looked at what factors are important in a determination of the spouses living separate and apart. The court has identified that there are certain factors that must be examined, including whether there was sexual contact, whether the couple socialized together, whether they had any communication, and whether they had separate bedrooms. The court would discuss various family issues in order to obtain a complete picture of the couple.

Reconciliation

Section 9(1) of the *Divorce Act* requires that lawyers draw it to the attention of their clients that the act has reconciliation as one of its aims, and to inform the parties of counsellors who might be able to help save their marriage unless it would be clearly inappropriate to do so. In addition, the court must also verify whether there appears to be any possibility of reconciliation between the parties under s 10 of the act, and inform the parties of the possibility of mediation. If the court believes there is a possibility of reconciliation through mediation, it must adjourn the divorce and assist the parties to find a counsellor who may be able to help.

However, s 8(3)(b)(ii) of the *Divorce Act* states that parties will no longer be able to state that they are living separate and apart if the "spouses have resumed cohabitation during a period of, or periods totalling, not more than ninety days with reconciliation as its primary purpose." This reconciliation could be one period of more than 90 days, or over several times that equals more than 90 days. If they are together for more than 90 days, the clock calculating one year separate and apart starts over at day one. However, some spouses struggle with what constitutes reconciliation. Consider the case of *Rogler v Rogler* (see the following case box).

ROGLER v ROGLER (1977), 1 RL (2D) 398 (ONT HC)

Mr. and Mrs. Rogler had separated in 1973 and started divorce proceedings in 1976. The question in this case was whether the parties had their period of separation interrupted, and if they had reconciled and restarted the one year separate and apart. Mr. Rogler would come over to Mrs. Rogler's home "now and again" from 2:00 a.m. to 4:00 a.m. They would have sex because she thought it was the "right thing to do in the sight of God," since they were still married. The parties did not live together any other time. They did not eat meals together, and there were no other "services" provided to the other spouse.

The court found that the time period of living separate and apart was not interrupted. They found that there was no intention to reconcile, and there are many more factors than sex that have to be accounted for to interrupt the time period and count as reconciliation. There were no other physical, mental, or moral supports. The divorce was granted.

To use the modern parlance, is there a situation where a "booty call" or a series of interactions could interrupt the time period of separate and apart?

Adultery

The *Divorce Act* s 8(2) also provides for divorce if the spouse against whom the divorce proceeding is brought has, since celebration of the marriage, committed **adultery**. This allows for immediate divorce without the standard one-year waiting period. However, there is no definition of adultery in the act, but rather the definition of adultery comes from the common law and ancient British cases. As antiquated as it sounds, in *Maclennan v Maclennan* [1958] Sess. Cas. 105 (Scotland Ct. Sess.), the court uses the definition, "1. For adultery to be committed there must be two parties physically present and engaging in the sexual act at the same time. 2. To constitute the sexual act there must be an act of union involving some degree of penetration of the female organ by the male organ." There may also be adultery if the parties are separated but not legally divorced. However, Justice Donald at the British Columbia Court of Appeal in *McPhail v McPhail*, 2001 BCCA 250, noted:

> as it usually takes a year to bring a contested matter to trial a divorce can usually be given on the ground of one-year separation. In those circumstances a cruelty allegation is unnecessary and will likely prolong the hostility between the parties. A cruelty finding bears a stigma; it should be avoided when no useful purpose is served.

In order to use adultery as a ground for divorce, the person accusing the adultery must prove that the act occurred. This adultery evidence may be difficult to prove, and it may take more than one year to get court dates and evidence (and there can be exorbitant legal fees). Most find it much simpler to wait for one year separate and apart.

Cruelty

Like adultery, cruelty is the only other modern ground for divorce that results in an immediate divorce without a waiting period. The test comes from the case of *Knoll v Knoll*, 1 RFL 141 (Ont CA) that:

> if in the marriage relationship one spouse by his conduct causes wanton, malicious or unnecessary infliction of pain or suffering upon the body, the feelings or emotions of the other, his conduct may well constitute cruelty which will entitle a petitioner to dissolution of the marriage if, in the court's opinion, it amounts to physical or mental cruelty "of such a kind as to render intolerable the continued cohabitation of the spouses."

This element is subjective and dependent on the individual alleging cruelty, and the impact upon him or her. This is something beyond mere incompatibility but something that has a grave impact on the individual. This cruelty can be either mental or physical, although physical cruelty may be easier to prove to a court. Some elements that have been found to be mental cruelty have been alcoholism, refusal to have sex, psychiatric disorders, and constant criticisms.[30] Again, it may be quicker, less expensive, and less traumatic to wait for one year separate and apart.

Condonation and Connivance

Condonation is a term that is not defined formally, but again comes in through the common law as a bar to divorce based on the grounds of adultery or cruelty. This is the principle that if you know that your spouse has cheated on you, and you accept that fact and forgive your spouse and continue with the marriage, you cannot later use adultery as the grounds for divorce. A definition is found from the Newfoundland case of *Watkins v Watkins* (see the following case box).

WATKINS v WATKINS (1980), 14 RFL (2D) 97 (NFLD TD)

Mr. Watkins petitioned for divorce based on his wife's adultery. However, after filing the paperwork, the couple had sex. Mrs. Watkins said that this amounted to condonation because her husband must forgive her infidelities if he had sex with her, and her husband should not be granted a divorce on this basis.

The judge said that there are three elements to condonation: "(a) knowledge of the matrimonial offence; (b) an intention to forgive; and (c) the restoration into the marriage of the guilty spouse." The court found that even if Mr. Watkins suspected his wife was cheating, he did not know the extent of her infidelities, and there was no intention on his part to forgive what she had done, and there was no intention to continue with the marriage. The judge said that this did not amount to condonation and the parties had sex "solely with a view to personal satisfaction."

Should this old principle still be part of modern divorce cases?

Connivance is term that has been established in the case law that deals with a bar to divorce based on adultery or cruelty. Unlike condonation, connivance, where the person filing for divorce and complaining that the spouse is guilty of misconduct, is actually consenting to, or wilfully contributing to the offence to the extent of a "corrupt intention." Thus, this is some active contribution to the marital wrong by the innocent party by, for example, pushing the spouse to go out and have an affair.

The *Divorce Act RS*, 1985, c 3 (2nd Supp) D-3.4, s 11(1)(c) says that it is the duty of the court:

> (*c*) where a divorce is sought in circumstances described in paragraph 8(2)(*b*), to satisfy itself that there has been no condonation or connivance on the part of the spouse bringing the proceeding, and to dismiss the application for a divorce if that spouse has condoned or connived at the act or conduct complained of unless, in the opinion of the court, the public interest would be better served by granting the divorce.

Thus, the court must ensure that neither of these principles is a factor in the divorce. Both of these factors are discretionary bars to divorce; a judge can decide to still grant the divorce regardless of the existence of condonation or connivance if the judge feels it is justified.

30. Dwight L Gibson et al, *All About Law*, 5th ed (Toronto: Thomson Nelson, 2003) at 405.

WHAT ABOUT PRIVACY IN FAMILY LAW EVIDENCE?

The state of evidence surrounding family law matters is still largely undecided. It seems as if it is not "clearly unlawful" for individuals to take information from a spouse's email account as long as it is not used for an illegal activity.[31] There do not seem to be many repercussions for a spouse that "snoops" without permission. There is no statutory provision relating to spouses, and no clear way for someone to punish those who have gone into their email. However, a court may exclude evidence if it was improperly obtained. This test for the judge is weighing the **probative value** against the **prejudicial effect.** In addition, if evidence is collected in unclear ways, the judge may give the other party additional costs to discourage unethical collection of electronic evidence. (See *Antle v NCC Financial Corp.*, [2009] BCJ No 718 (BCSC), where special costs were ordered against the employer, saying that they had "acted reprehensibly by intercepting ... private emails.")

The case of *Eizenshtein v Eizenchtein* (2008), 62 RFL (6th) 182 (Ont Sup Ct), is a good example of evidence and privacy in family law matters. In this **acrimonious** divorce, the wife sought to enter into evidence emails between her husband and his lawyer. These emails talked about legal strategy, and were discovered by the husband's girlfriend who used his computer. When the husband and the girlfriend broke up, the girlfriend sent all of these damaging emails to the wife. Although these emails were excluded because of solicitor–client privilege, the judge did not mention the way that these emails were obtained.

Do you think that courts will eventually allow this evidence in family law cases?

Would you use damning emails against your spouse in a family law matter?

Procedures for Obtaining a Divorce

The process of getting a divorce is quite uncomplicated so long as it is **uncontested**. This means that the couple agree on the conditions of custody, support, and the division of property before they intend to divorce. The person wanting to start the process fills in a document called a **Petition for Divorce**. The person who files for divorce is the **petitioner**, and the other spouse is the **respondent**. The couple often consult legal counsel to assist with the technicalities. However, as discussed, no-fault divorce laws have shifted the focus of the legal process from the moral questions of fault and blame to economic issues. Approximately 90 percent of divorce actions are settled without going to court.

The petition contains information about you, your marriage, your children, your financial situation, and that of your spouse. The petitioner must also supply a copy of the marriage certificate and a fee. The petition is filed in court and a copy is served on the spouse. The spouse has up to 30 days to reply in most provinces. If the spouse does not reply, then the petitioner may apply for an "undefended divorce." An affidavit will be prepared setting out the facts on which the court will grant a divorce. A judge will read the documents and if they are in order, will make the divorce order usually within four weeks. The divorce order usually becomes effective 31 days after it is issued by the court, and the spouse seeking the divorce is required to mail a copy of the divorce documents to the other spouse. A judge will not refuse a divorce to a couple simply because one spouse wants to remain married. If the parties cannot agree on matters such as custody and support, this is a contested divorce, which will take longer, but a divorce will still be granted as soon as these issues are resolved. However, custody and support are never final and can be changed by the parties on specific grounds at any time.

ANNULMENTS

If the parties do not wish to divorce, they may seek a legal **annulment,** which declares that the marriage never existed, rather than simply coming to an end in divorce. A marriage may be annulled if the marriage was void from the start because of the age of the bride or

31. Katherine Cooligan, "You've Got Mail: Snooping Emails, Privacy Law, and Admissibility of Evidence" (2011), Ontario Bar Association, at 26.

groom, if the marriage was not consummated, if consent was coerced, because one person did not understand the nature of the ceremony (often because of a language barrier), or because the marriage was not performed by an authorized person. An annulment is a declaration in law that a legitimate marriage has not occurred; therefore, there is no need to seek a divorce. The court will issue a document called a **decree of nullity,** which says that the marriage did not exist.

Annulments can be denied if the parties are colluding with each other to fabricate or suppress evidence, or if the parties are insincere in seeking the assistance of the court. Some faiths, including the Roman Catholic faith, the Jewish faith, and the Islamic faith (among others), may seek a religious annulment of their marriage. However, it is important to note that this does not legally end a marriage. If the parties wish a legal termination of marriage, they must seek a legal annulment or a divorce, as the religious annulment will not be legally recognized. A marriage can be annulled even if there are children of the union, and most religions still recognize these children as "legitimate" children of the relationship. In law, some provinces have gone so far as to recognize children as legitimate regardless of the status of their parents' marriage. The *Civil Code of Québec*, SQ, 1991, c 64 at s 381 states that:

> 381. The nullity of a marriage, for whatever reason, does not deprive the children of the advantages secured to them by law or by the marriage contract. The rights and duties of fathers and mothers towards their children are unaffected by the nullity of their marriage.

THE DIVISION OF PROPERTY AFTER THE DIVORCE

Historically, division of property at divorce was straightforward because married women could not own their own property, but rather the property became that of the husband as they were one person under the law. Although married women eventually obtained legal status to own property, husbands were often the breadwinners and would take whatever they had paid for during the marriage. This resulted in a huge disparity for women upon divorce, and homes were often only in the name of the husband. Until the 1970s, the law did not recognize the economic contribution of women in their roles as mother and working in the home in the accumulation of family wealth.

Today, the rights and obligations in marriage are considered equal under the law. Spouses have identical rights and obligations owed to each other. With the case of *Murdoch v Murdoch,* [1975] 1 SCR 423, the public was outraged that the Supreme Court had found that a woman who had been an equal partner in her husband's business would walk away with almost nothing. Even though Mrs. Murdoch was a homemaker and did hard physical labour on the family's ranch, she was not entitled to a share in the property originally bought with his money. After this case, all provinces and territories brought in legislation to deal with the equal division of property between the couple on divorce.[32]

Property rights differ from province to province but in all cases, marriage creates a statutory right to share in the value of property acquired during marriage. In Ontario, the *Family Law Act,* RSO 1990, Chapter F.3, Part I, provides for the division of property, which is equalized between both parties, with few exceptions. The basic principle under the *Family Law Act* is that "net family property" should be divided equally between the spouses unless an equal distribution would be unfair. The legislation also recognizes the work of those who have child-care responsibilities and those that work within the home. However, there are some provinces and territories that distinguish between family and business assets that may be treated differently. It is important to note that common-law and same-sex partners may not have the same rights under current law.

32. See other provinces including the *Matrimonial Property Act,* RSA 2000, c M-8; *Family Relations Act,* RSBC, 1996, c 128; *Marital Property Act,* CCSM c M45; *Marital Property Act,* SNB 1980, c M-1.1; *Family Law Act,* RSNL 1990, c F-2; *Matrimonial Property Act,* RSNS 1989, c 275; *Family Law Act,* SNWT 1997, c 18; *Family Law Act (Nunavut)* SNWT 1997, c 18, *Family Law Act,* SPEI 1995, c 12; *Civil Code of Quebec,* SQ 1991, c 64; *Matrimonial Property Act,* 1997, c M-6.11; *Family Property and Support Act,* RSY 1986, c 63.

Matrimonial Home

The home in which the parties live during the course of their marriage is called the **matrimonial home**. The term matrimonial home is usually defined by statute. In Ontario under the *Family Law Act,* RSO 1990, Chapter F.3, the matrimonial home is defined in s 18(1) as "every property in which a person has an interest and that is ... occupied by the person and his or her spouse as their family residence is their matrimonial home." Both spouses have the right to possession of the matrimonial home under s 19 of the *Family Law Act* in Ontario. On separation, the court may decide which spouse may live in the house (often the spouse with custody or the majority of custody of the children). After this period, the spouses may divide the proceeds from the sale of the home through an equalization depending on whether the spouse is on deed, or there may be an agreement of one spouse to buy the other's interest in the home.

SPOUSAL SUPPORT

Historically, spousal support originates from ecclesiastical law in England, when the church had jurisdiction over various marital issues. Later the concept of **alimony** developed in the common law as a right that women only could exercise over their husbands after separation. In Ontario prior to 1978, a wife had to apply through the *Deserted Wives' and Children's Maintenance Act,* RSO, 1937, c 211, to show that there was desertion by her husband and he failed to support her. However, adultery by the wife was an absolute defence and the husband would no longer be responsible to support his wife. A wife could get support if the parties had a valid marriage, they were living separate and apart, and the husband was guilty of adultery, cruelty, or desertion.

Many provinces and territories abolished alimony in 1978 and replaced it with the concept of spousal support. This is a gender-neutral term because either spouse can claim support. Support is paid by one spouse to the other upon the breakdown of marriage to compensate the other for financial losses suffered and to assist the spouse until he or she can be self-sufficient. Spousal support is not designed to punish the other spouse, and it is not automatic as the spouse must apply for support.

The court can order a spouse to pay support either under provincial legislation or the *Divorce Act,* which is federal legislation. Only a "spouse" can seek an order under the *Divorce Act,* but under the provincial legislation, there is an extended definition. For example, under the Ontario *Family Law Act,* a man and a woman who are not married but have cohabited for not less than three years, or are in a relationship of some permanence and have natural or adopted children, can qualify for support. This also applies to same-sex couples (see the following case box).

M v H (1999), 46 RFL (4TH) 32 (SCC)

Ms. M and Ms. H were same-sex partners who shared living expenses, financial responsibilities, and started an advertising business. Ms. M assumed more of the duties at home, including entertaining clients. The economy faltered, and the business was struggling. Their relationship broke down, and Ms. M suffered severe financial hardship in becoming financially independent because she had spent much of her life supporting the business from home. Ms. M filed for a partition of their home and property and she sought support.

Ms. M said that the definition of "spouse" in the *Family Law Act,* RSO 1990, c F.3, infringed s 15 of the *Charter* because it did not include same-sex couples. The argument at the Supreme Court was that it was unconstitutional to define spouse as a man and a woman. Same-sex couples should be treated the same as heterosexual couples.

The court found that denying same-sex partners the same rights given to unmarried heterosexual partners (who had cohabited for a period of time) was unjustified and was discrimination on the basis of sexual orientation, contrary to s 15 of the *Charter.* This decision forced legislative change with the striking down of the *Family Law Act* section as being discriminatory. The court gave the Ontario government six months to rewrite Ontario laws to include same-sex spouses.

Although *M v H* was an Ontario case, the court sent a message that all of the provinces and territories should recognize same-sex spouses, so that their legislation would not be struck down as violating the *Charter*. Federally "common-law partners" was defined as two persons of either opposite or same sex who cohabit for at least one year. Ontario changed the definition of "spouse" in some legislation, but it is important to look at the particular piece of legislation in a particular province or territory to see the definition for the purposes of that act. In the *Family Law Act,* Ontario has taken out the words "a man and a woman" in the definition of "spouse," and the phrase was replaced by "two persons."

Support Under the *Family Law Act* (1990)

All provinces have similar statutes which deal with both child and spousal support. For example, in Ontario the purposes of spousal support are set out in the *Family Law Act,*[33] which states that an order for spousal support should:

(a) recognize the spouse's contribution to the relationship and the economic consequences of the relationship for the spouse;
(b) share the economic burden of child support equitably;
(c) make fair provision to assist the spouse to become able to contribute to his or her own support; and
(d) relieve financial hardship, if this has not been done by orders under Parts I (Family Property) and II (Matrimonial Home).

This is an individualized standard, and spousal support has to be determined on an individual basis. There has been no attempt to make a mathematical formulation in spousal support like there is in child support. Flexibility is the most important element in looking at each case separately. In determining the amount of support that should be awarded, the courts will look at a wide variety of factors, including the applicant's financial needs, future and present earning ability, the time needed to upgrade job skills, length of time that one spouse cared for children and worked within the home, age, physical and mental health, capacity to become financially independent, the length of time couple was married or cohabited, their accustomed standard of living, the respondent's income and ability to afford support payments, and the obligation of the respondent to provide support for any other person (e.g., new family, ailing parents, etc.). A spouse's misconduct is not a factor in awarding support. Spousal support can be ordered in one lump sum, or weekly, monthly, or yearly payments.

Similarly, federal spousal support under s 15.2(6) of the *Divorce Act* similarly sets out the policy objectives of an order for spousal support. The order should:

(a) recognize any economic advantages or disadvantages to the spouses arising from the marriage or its breakdown;
(b) apportion between the spouses any financial consequences arising from the care of any child of the marriage;
(c) in so far as is practicable, promote the economic self-sufficiency of each spouse within a reasonable period of time.

The federal legislation provides that the court must take into account the length of time the couple cohabited, the functions performed by each, and agreement they had regarding support. The *Family Law Act* and the *Divorce Act* both place the primary obligation on spouses to support themselves to the extent that this is possible and practical.

The *Divorce Act* introduced the idea of economic self-sufficiency for women following the divorce and property settlement. The courts promoted a "clean break" model and tended to award the spouse, often the wife, support for a maximum of three

---

33. Other provinces' legislation includes the *Domestic Relations Act,* RSA 2000, c D-14; *Family Relations* Act, RSBC 1996, Chapter 128; *Family Maintenance Act,* CCSM c F20, *Family Services Act,* SNB 1980, c F-2.2; *Family Law Act,* RSNL 1990, c F-2; *Family Law Act,* SNWT 1997, c 18; *Family Maintenance Act,* RSNS 1989, c 465; *Family Law Act,* SNWT (Nu) 1997, c 18; RSPEI 1988, c F-2.1; *Civil Code of Quebec,* SQ 1991, c 64; *Family Maintenance Act,* 1997, SS 1997, c F-6.2; *Family Property & Support Act,* RSY 2002, c 83.

years, after which she was on her own and required to get a job and support herself. The goal of economic self-sufficiency has been heavily criticized by women's groups because it often places an unreasonable and unrealistic expectation on the wife to support herself after decades out of the workforce outside of the home, and raising children and taking care of the home. The case of *Moge v Moge*, [1992] 3 SCR 813 (SCC), recognized that the clean break model should be rejected, and other factors should be taken into account.

Beginning in the early 1990s, courts began awarding much greater spousal support and for much longer periods of time. Case law increasingly recognized the problem that women faced in the workplace and began to give less weight to the principle of economic self-sufficiency if it was unlikely to be realized. The courts have ruled that the objective of self-sufficiency is a goal "only insofar as is practicable." Proper compensation is often judged to be long-term support.

Under the law, spouses are entitled to be compensated for contributions made to the marriage and for losses sustained as a consequence of the marriage. Contributions include supporting a spouse through school, raising children, working in a family business, and so forth. Losses include lower educational attainment, forgone income and promotions in the workforce, the lack of a pension plan, among other factors. The ultimate goal of spousal support is to reduce or alleviate economic disadvantages that one spouse may suffer because of the marriage breakdown. Clearly, support orders are limited in what they can accomplish by the ability of the respondent to pay. The elements that can be taken into account have extended even further in the last few years, as in the case of *Leskun v Leskun* (see the following case box).

LESKUN v LESKUN, [2006] SCJ NO 25 (SCC)

Mr. and Mrs. Leskun met at the Toronto Dominion (TD) bank where they both worked, and married in 1978. Mrs. Leskun worked at TD through most of the marriage, but she moved for her husband's work and school, and they moved to British Columbia in 1993 because of his work. Mr. Leskun then moved to Chicago in 1998 for his job, but Mrs. Leskun stayed with their daughter in British Columbia. Mrs. Leskun eventually went on medical leave, and found out her work position was going to be eliminated. Mr. Leskun came home from Chicago to discuss Mrs. Leskun's employment options, but instead told her that their marriage was over, he was having an affair with a woman he met at work, and he wanted to marry the new woman. Mrs. Leskun was devastated.

At the time of separation, Mrs. Leskun was 53 years old with no job or a way to support herself. Her medical conditions became worse and she could not work. Mrs. Leskun was supporting their 19-year-old daughter, who had become pregnant and had no support from the baby's father. Mrs. Leskun's father, brother, and sister-in-law died at the same time during this period. Mr. Leskun was 45, earned more than $200 000 a year, but said that his new family took most of this income. They had $61 500 in RRSPs, and $65 000 in the family home. Mrs. Leskun had cashed in her RRSPs and pension to send her husband to school. At trial, the court said that Mrs. Leskun was not disadvantaged by the marriage, and she should be able to support herself, even though Mrs. Leskun had no way to maintain the standard of living that she was accustomed to. The court ordered spousal support of $2250 per month.

Mr. Leskun stopped paying in April 2003. He invested in his own business in Chicago, and acquired more than $1 million in assets after trial, with debts of $500 000. Mrs. Leskun remained unemployed and could not even find part-time employment. Even after Mrs. Leskun requested more support, the judge said that Mr. Leskun had to keep paying the same amount. The judge commented that Mrs. Leskun was "consumed by bitterness over the end of her marriage and what she sees as the betrayal and duplicity of her former husband; and her inability to move on in the work force is unfortunate in the long run for her, no matter how justified her feelings may be." Mrs. Leskun appealed.

By the time the case went to the court of appeal in 2004, Mrs. Leskun was still unemployed, but Mr. Leskun now said that he was also unemployed. The court of appeal found that Mrs. Leskun was "bitter to the point of obsession with his misconduct and in consequence has been unable to make a new life. Her life is this litigation." The court of appeal found that when observing a spouse's inability to achieve self-sufficiency, it is permissible to consider the "emotional devastation of misconduct by the other spouse." The court ultimately found that Mrs. Leskun should continue to receive spousal support because she was now 57 years old, had family difficulties and medical problems, and was unable to move on.

This case went to the Supreme Court in 2006, where it drew a distinction between taking the "*blameworthiness* of misconduct into account in assessing the entitlement of an aggrieved spouse to receive support, versus considering the *result* of that misconduct in assessing entitlement." Mr. Leskun's lawyers argued that by taking into account the fact that a spouse was so bitter as to be unable to work, the court would be opening floodgates to the extent of a "legal tsunami," where everyone would want to review their support, leading to fault in the *Divorce Act* and a huge "weakening ... of the Canadian economy."

The Supreme Court found that there is a "distinction between the emotional consequences of misconduct and the misconduct itself. The consequences are not rendered irrelevant because of their genesis in the other spouse's misconduct." Thus, the court can consider the emotional situation of the spouse, just because her bitterness came out of an affair does not mean that it does not count as a bar to self-support. The circumstances are important; it does not matter how those consequences came about. If she was having these problems because of a car accident, these factors would be relevant, and just because it is emotional and not physical does not matter.

Although the Supreme Court said that it was not in the game of assigning blame, and it could not get to the bottom of every spousal dispute, and support cannot be awarded just to punish someone, some immoral action cannot be taken into account to determine the amount of support. However, this is not like tort, where the goal is to put the person in the position he or she would have been if the wrong had not occurred. The court found that the wrongdoer cannot use his or her misdeeds as a shield to avoid support payments arising from those actions.

Mrs. Leskun was 57 years old, and in a 20-year marriage, she cashed in all of her assets to send her husband to school. The emotional impact of their marriage breakdown made her medically unfit to work, her daughter was a single mother, and her relatives had all died at the same time. Some say that her emotional state would have been "irrelevant had Ms. Leskun not carried the torch of her betrayal so boldly."[34] The Supreme Court found that the appeal should be dismissed, and that Mrs. Leskun should continue to be supported.

Should a spouse be entitled to long-term support if he or she is unable to work?

Reopening Support Awards

Under provincial legislation in Canada, a support order can be changed if there is a material change in the circumstances of either party. In such cases, the support order could be discharged, suspended temporarily, increased or decreased, and varied in any way the court deems reasonable. Either side can ask to have a support order revisited by the court. It is common in separation agreements for lawyers to include a reopening clause that gives either spouse the right to renegotiate changes to the terms of the contracts if material circumstances should change significantly (through illness, loss of job, a promotion and salary increase, etc.).

Men generally seek finality and a clean break. Women are typically the ones who will seek to reopen support provisions because they are struggling financially. The change in circumstances typically must be a consequence of the marital breakdown and not caused by some external agents or causes, but the financial crisis has been recognized by courts in Canada (see the following case box, dealing with *Serra v Serra*).

34. John-Paul Boyd, "Tsunami in a Teapot: *Leskun v Leskun*" (2007) 40 *UBC L. Rev* 293 at 308.

SERRA v SERRA, [2009] OJ NO 432 (ONT CA)

This case involved an appeal by the husband from an order requiring him to pay his wife approximately $4 million upon their divorce. The parties were married in 1976, separated in 2000, and divorced in 2003. The husband operated a profitable textile business, and the wife was unemployed and lived at the parties' condominium in Florida for six months of each year.

The parties lived a luxurious lifestyle because at the time of separation, the husband's business was valued between $9.5 million and $11.25 million. However, by the time of trial, the value had decreased to between $1.875 million and $2.6 million because of a downturn in the Canadian textile industry. At trial, the husband argued that this type of payment based on the value of the business at the time of separation would be unconscionable. It would have required him to make an equalization payment of $4 129 832, an amount that exceeded his total net worth. However, the trial judge said that he would not take into account the decline in the value of the assets and ordered the large equalization payment.

On appeal, the court said that the payment to the wife should be reduced to $900 000. Mrs. Serra had the option of accepting the transfer of the husband's one-half interest in the Florida condominium, or receiving three installments of $300 000. The courts said that a reduction in the value of assets could be taken into account if the equal division of net family properties would shock the conscience of the court. In this case, the trial judge made a mistake by not taking into account the downturn in the textile business, because Mr. Serra did whatever he could to save the business but he had no control over the market. The payment had to reflect the length of the marriage, the wife's role in the business, and the downturn in the business. Mrs. Serra should not have to take the entire hit for the downturn in business, but the payment should be reduced.

Support Obligations Enforcement

There are enforcement mechanisms to allow a person to collect on the amounts of spousal and child support ordered by the courts. The enforcement of support is regulated by the provinces and territories. The parties register with the local agencies that monitor payments, and they will take steps to get the money. Ontario and other provinces have a system for the automatic deduction of support from the paycheque of a spouse ordered to remit. Employers will take this money and send it to the enforcement office to be paid to the spouse. Examples of enforcement legislation can be found in Ontario's *Support and Custody Orders Enforcement Act,* SO 1996, Chapter 31; in British Columbia's *Family Maintenance Enforcement Act,* RSBC 1996, Chapter 127; in Alberta's *Maintenance Enforcement Act,* RSA 2000, c M-1; and in Nova Scotia's *Maintenance Enforcement Act,* SNS 1994-95, c 6.

Although the provinces mainly deal with enforcement, there is also federal legislation called the *Family Orders and Agreements Enforcement Assistance Act,* RSC, 1985, c 4 (2nd Supp), which can be used to find people who have defaulted on their support orders, or to take federal payments to individuals to use for their back support payments (such as employment insurance cheques, income-tax refunds, CPP payments, and interest from savings bonds), or to refuse benefits like passports to those who are behind in payments.

Remarriage and Support

It is common for support payments to be reduced or terminated when the recipient remarries or cohabits with another. However, this is not automatic. The fact that the applicant is cohabiting with another person does not necessarily mean that he or she is financially independent, and the amount should not automatically be reduced or eliminated. Self-sufficiency should not be presumed, but rather it must be proved.

Even in the case of remarriage in which the new spouse does not have sufficient income to support the new partner, the former spouse may still be required to continue payments. However, there are some conflicting cases. In some cases the courts say that the primary responsibility is owed to the first family, but other courts have said that the new family should take precedence, and other courts have taken a position that no preference should be given to either family. The trend is that each case will be determined individually.

Child Support

Parents have an obligation to contribute to the needs of their children, even if they have more children in subsequent relationships. The federal *Divorce Act,* RSC, 1985, c 3 (2nd Supp.) D-3.4, governs couples with children who are divorced or planning to divorce. Provincial or territorial legislation applies if the parents are not married, separated, or planning to separate but do not have an intention to divorce. The Child Support Guidelines were created in 1997 in Canada to establish fair child support on an objective and efficient basis. By determining the income of the spouse who does not have custody of the child, the number of children, and the province in which the parent lives, couples can find out exactly how much child support is required (see http://www.justice.gc.ca/eng/pi/fcy-fea/lib-bib/legis/fcsg-lfpae/index.html and Table 6.2).

There are both federal and provincial guidelines. If one qualifies under the *Divorce Act,* then the federal guidelines apply, but if one qualifies under the provincial legislation (like the Ontario *Family Law Act*), then provincial guidelines apply. These are legally binding rules that must be followed. A person who is not a biological parent of the child, but has knowingly stood in the place of a parent, can still be responsible to support that child. What

Table 6.2 Federal Child Support Table, Newfoundland and Labrador, Two Children

Income ($)		Monthly Award ($)		
From	**To**	**Basic Amount**	**Plus (%)**	**Of Income Over**
0	10 819	0	–	–
25 000	25 999	354	1.32	25 000
30 000	30 999	436	2.04	30 000
35 000	35 999	517	1.38	35 000
40 000	40 999	584	1.46	40 000
45 000	45 999	651	1.36	45 000
50 000	50 999	720	1.40	50 000
58 000	58 999	833	1.40	58 000
74 000	74 999	1055	1.34	74 000
79 000	79 999	1123	1.36	79 000
84 000	84 999	1190	1.28	84 000
89 000	89 999	1255	1.34	89 000
94 000	94 999	1319	1.30	94 000
99 000	99 999	1383	1.26	99 000
107 000	107 999	1486	1.26	107 000
123 000	123 999	1692	1.26	123 000
128 000	128 999	1756	1.18	128 000
133 000	133 999	1817	1.26	133 000
138 000	138 999	1878	1.26	138 000
143 000	143 999	1940	1.24	143 000
148 000	148 999	2001	1.22	148 000

Source: Federal Child Support Guidelines, Table: Federal Child Support, SOR/97-175 http://laws.justice.gc.ca/eng/regulations/SOR-97-175/page-20.html#docCont Department of Justice Canada. Reproduced with the permission of the Minister of Public Works and Government Services, 2012.

WHAT ABOUT SPERM DONORS?

In the case of *Pratten v British Columbia (Attorney General)*, [2011] BCJ No 931 (BCSC), the British Columbia Supreme Court struck down portions of the province's *Adoption Act*, RSBC 1996 Chapter 5. Ms. Pratten brought the case as one who was conceived from an anonymous sperm donor, but the B.C. government permitted the destruction of her insemination documents, thus depriving her of information on the donor and her medical and psychological history. Even though Ms. Pratten could not get access to her information, she won her battle to give other children conceived in this way the same rights as adopted children to learn about biological parents. Ms. Pratten said that she did not know anything about one-half of her makeup and feared having a sexual relationship with a part sibling, and worried about her future children who would have no medical history and information.

It is unknown how big an impact this might have on family law, health law, estate law and many other areas. If an anonymous donor had 25, 50, or 150 kids born from his donation (which is thought to have happened in the United States,) would all of those children have rights to the estate of their biological parent?

Could donors seek paternal rights over their biological children?

Should it be "donor" beware?

is the responsibility to children (or a family) that you did not know existed? Consider the case of sperm donors in the above box.

An additional amount of child support can be requested because of school, illness, medical and heath expenses not covered by insurance, extracurricular activities of the children, and post-secondary education expenses. The amount can also be reduced if it would create an undue hardship for the parent who is paying. Parents must support their children until they reach the age of majority (18 or 19, depending on the province) but may be ordered to continue support for education if the children are enrolled full-time. The case law has found that this support usually extends only for the first post-secondary degree or until the child turns 23 (whichever comes first). This can also be reflected in the legislation. For example, in s 31 of the Ontario *Family Law Act*, a parent has an "obligation to provide support for his or her unmarried child who is a minor or is enrolled in a full time program of education, to the extent that the parent is capable of doing so." Under the federal *Divorce Act* s 15, parents have a responsibility to support their children if they are under the age of majority, or if illness, disability, or another cause prevents the children from providing the necessaries of life for themselves.

If the child between 16 and the age of majority leaves home, the parent is no longer obligated to provide support. It is interesting to note that there is also provincial legislation that requires

FOOD FOR THOUGHT...

HOW MANY PARENTS CAN YOU HAVE? *AA v BB*, [2007] OJ NO 2 (ONT CA)

In this case, the court had to decide how many parents a child can have. AA and CC were female same-sex partners who wanted to have a child (DD). They sought the help of BB, who was a friend of the family, to provide the sperm to CC to conceive a child. BB also wanted to maintain a parental relationship with the child. All of the parties wanted AA (who was not biologically related to the child) to be a parent of the child and have all of the rights and obligations as a mother. However, if AA sought to adopt DD, the parental rights of BB would be lost and this would not be in the best interest of the child.

Although denied in the trial court, the court of appeal recognized AA as DD's mother. Legislation did not contemplate a child having two legal mothers, but given the changing nature of families, this was a relationship that needed to be recognized. The legislation did not seek to *exclude* a child having two mothers; it was simply something not considered. Thus, DD had three parents—his biological parents (BB and CC) and his adoptive mother (AA).

Could a child have more than three parents? Can you imagine a situation where this would be true?

iStockphoto/Thinkstock

Child custody is one of the most difficult areas of family law to govern.

adult children to be responsible for their parents. In the *Family Law Act* in Ontario, s 32 provides that "every child who is not a minor has an obligation to provide support, in accordance with need, for his or her parent who has cared for or provided support of the child, to the extent that the child is capable of doing so." Very few cases have got to court with this legislation, but this is an important area to pay attention to in the future.

CHILD CUSTODY

Upon divorce, the court can decide who has **custody** of the children and who may have **access** to the children. Even though the couple does not wish to continue a relationship with each other, the relationship with the children of the marriage continues despite divorce. This is one of the most difficult areas of family law to govern. The key consideration in every decision is what is in the **best interests of the child**. A parent's conduct in the course of marriage is not a factor in custody and access unless there has been abuse or violence in the home.

The court will look at the health of the parent, the relationship between parent and child, the home situation, the support available from an extended system of friends and relatives, scheduling, the goal of keeping siblings together, and if the child is old enough—his or her wishes. Although historically the custody of children (and especially young children) was given to mothers, this is no longer a reality given the changing roles in many families. Mediation can be important in these situations, and community supports like those offered at local groups like Community Justice Initiatives (CJI) can be essential. CJI offers programs like "family group decision making" which allows the parties to sit down together and take into account the wishes of the children and those who support the children at the broadest level.

Community Justice Initiatives
http://www.cjiwr.com/family-group-decision-making.htm

Custody refers to the rights and obligations of a parent towards a child, including the child's physical day-to-day control, the rights to determine the education of the child, the right to choose religious upbringing, decisions about medical care, and other issues such as extracurricular activities. **Joint custody** is a term used to describe any situation where both parents take a significant role in the raising of the child, or the child spends much time with both parents. There can be joint physical custody, where the child spends equal time physically with both parents. Joint legal custody is more common, where both parents have legal custody and decision making, but only one has care and control and the other has liberal access. In practice, this arrangement will require the agreement of both parents.

Shared parenting or co-parenting is a term that is used for parents with joint custody but where the child resides with each of the parents for significant time, and both play a meaningful role with the child. A new term that is being used is **parallel parenting,** where one parent can decide on some issues, and the other parent decides on other issues. **Split custody** once referred to situations where one child lived with one parent (the son with the father) and the other with the other parent (daughter with the mother). This is something that is largely avoided today. But what happens if the parents cannot agree on these issues? Consider the case of *Bruni v Bruni* in the following case box.

WHAT HAPPENS WHEN THE PARTIES SIMPLY HATE EACH OTHER? *BRUNI v BRUNI*, 2010 ONSC 6568 (ONT SCJ)

There are certain cases that come through the court system where all legal issues are almost impossible to sort out because the parties hate each other and make every step difficult. An example is the case of *Bruni v Bruni.* Justice Quinn heard this case in 2010, and had a great commentary on the state of marriage, separation, divorce, custody and access.

Brian A Jackson/Shutterstock

Sometimes the divorcing couple is unable to agree on almost any issue involving their children.

In an entertaining decision, Justice Quinn began the long judgment with the phrase "Paging Dr. Freud, Paging Dr. Freud." At the conclusion of the decision Justice Quinn admitted that the "parties repeatedly have shown that they are immune to reason. Consequently, in my decision, I have tried ridicule as a last resort." Some parties, like the Brunis, may be unable to agree on almost any issue to do with their divorce and the custody of their children. The family court may not be the right tool for dealing with these types of cases, and Justice Quinn noted that this is "yet another case that reveals the ineffectiveness of the family court in a bitter custody/access dispute." Justice Quinn remarked that if only the "wedding guests, who tinkled their wine glasses as encouragement for the traditional bussing of the bride and groom, could see the couple now."

Mr. Bruni alleged that he was under duress when he was forced to sign a separation agreement, and was told that he had to waive his right to independent legal advice. The court also noted the misuse of the criminal justice system, as on "fourteen occasions, within eighteen months, the parties drew the police into their petty disagreements—a sad commentary on their inability to get along and a shocking abuse of the Niagara Regional Police Service." Mr. Bruni regularly drove by his ex-wife's house and gave her the finger, and on several occasions yelled "jackass, loser." He also created a false Facebook account to post things in the name of his ex-wife, so that others would think she was posting that material. Mr. Bruni would send her text messages saying the "game is just starting. Prepare yourself for a long winding road," "Busted! Always look in your rear view mirror," "Blood isn't always thicker than water," and "Loser! Homewrecker!" Mrs. Bruni would send text messages calling him a "dickhead." Although the judge altered some of the terms of the separation agreement, the case is more of a commentary on the sad state that many couples can get to during a bitter divorce. Although Justice Quinn suspended the hearing and required the couple to seek counselling, this method was still not effective, and the court had to rule on a host of issues.

When it came to the custody of the children, the separation agreement said that custody of would be with the mother, with "reasonable access to the children" by the father. However, the mother ended these visits a few years into the process until the father gave the mother $2500 to purchase a new washing machine, and then continued to be irregular because the parties could not cooperate and agree on parenting.

Is this a case where mediation should be essential? What happens if the parties still do not agree?

If parties are this much at odds, should they be able to make custody and access decisions?

Do you think it is appropriate for a judge to use ridicule to try to get the couple to reflect how they are acting?

CONCLUSION

Family law is a difficult and involved area of law and there are increasing number of couples who will need the family law system. Unfortunately, Statistics Canada announced on July 20, 2011, that it was going to stop publishing data on the national marriage and divorce rates in order to save $250 000 a year. Marriage statistics will still be collected by the provinces and territories, and divorces will still be recorded by the federal justice department, but the data will no longer be combined.[35] This is an area of law that is only going to grow, and the bitter fights associated will only get more destructive.

35. Joanna Smith, "Statistics Canada to Stop Tracking Divorce Rates" (20 July 2011), *Toronto Star*, online: <http://www.thestar.com/news/canada/politics/article/1027273--statistics-canada-to-stop-tracking-divorce-rates>.

LEARNING OUTCOMES SUMMARIZED

1. Identify the historic grounds for divorce.

Before 1967, a husband could seek a divorce in many provinces by proving the wife's adultery. A wife could only petition on the grounds of adultery, rape, sodomy, bestiality, or bigamy. The eastern provinces had their own divorce act prior to Confederation, which applied until 1968. Adultery was the grounds in these provinces, but in New Brunswick and Prince Edward Island frigidity and impotence were also grounds. Nova Scotia also allowed for cruelty. The 1968 *Divorce Act* retained some of the fault grounds for divorce, including adultery, bigamy, homosexuality, imprisonment, alcohol or drug addiction, whereabouts unknown, non-consummation, or desertion.

2. Analyze the role of the common-law marriage in Canada today.

Marriages are legally binding contracts, but common-law marriages are also legally binding relationships without a marriage ceremony, although there are fewer legal obligations and responsibilities for common-law spouses. The *Modernization of Obligations and Benefits Act* amended 60 statutes to reflect the rights of same-sex and opposite-sex couples. Most provincial legislation recognizes common-law relationships after the partners have cohabited for two to three years or for a substantial time and have a child.

However, some provinces (such as Ontario) have not extended spousal property rights and succession rights to same-sex or opposite-sex unmarried couples. When married parties separate, they immediately have the right of property division, but this right is not extended to many common-law couples. This means that there may be no recognition of the status of the parties as a couple when one party disputes the division of property or one member of the couple dies without a will.

3. Evaluate the changes in law regarding same-sex marriages.

Most provinces changed their definitions of "spouse" and "marriage" in the last decade. The traditional definition of marriage as the "voluntary union for life of one man and one woman to the exclusion of all others" that was established in 1866 was contrary to s 15 of the *Charter,* as it excluded same-sex partners, so the Canadian government introduced legislation to redefine marriage.

Legislation had to be amended to reflect this change, and in 2005, the federal government passed the *Civil Marriage Act,* giving same-sex couples the right to marry. Provincially, the legislatures introduced legislation to amend their statutes. In Ontario, the *Spousal Relationships Statute Law Amendment Act* changed more than 70 provincial statutes to recognize the obligations and rights of same-sex couples. To avoid some of the criticism against this legislation, the provinces added elements to their legislation to address those religious individuals who did not wish to partake in the solemnization of same-sex marriages.

4. Identify the areas of family law governed by federal and provincial legislation.

The division of powers is dictated by the Constitution, which gives the power to pass legislation. The federal government has the ability to pass legislation on divorce, including the divorce action itself, the division of property, and the custody of children. The federal government has power over who can be married, capacity to marry, and annulments. The federal legislation, *The Divorce Act,* applies when the parties who are married seek a divorce. The act sets out the rights and obligations of those persons who are or were married. This makes sense so that divorces are recognized across all the provinces.

Provincial governments are responsible for laws *prior* to the actual divorce, including the creation of a marriage, documents on the breakdown of marriage, separation, support and maintenance of children and spouses, division of property, adoption, and custody.

These provincial powers include matters before the actual marriage, including who can officiate, parental consent, how many witnesses are required, and other formalities. Provinces also have control over spousal support, child support, custody, and other property rights. The law is a bit confusing when it comes to family law, but certain general principles apply. If individuals are not married but living together, provincial legislation applies. If they are married, until the moment they apply for divorce, provincial legislation applies, but at the time of divorce, federal law applies. There may be an overlap between federal and provincial legislation if the couple is seeking a divorce. Custody and support are sought under federal legislation, but if couples wish to deal with property issues, that comes under provincial legislation.

5. Assess the role of bigamy and polygamy in Canada.

A legal marriage (or a divorce) in one jurisdiction is generally recognized as valid in another jurisdiction. However, some types of marriages are prohibited. In Canada, bigamy is prohibited. Bigamy is defined as being married and nonetheless going through the process of getting married again, or being married to more than one person at the same time. Polygamy (married to several others) is also against the law under s 293 of the *Criminal Code.*

However, Canada does recognize polygamous marriages that were validly entered into in a country where polygamy is legal. Although polygamous marriages may not be recognized for the purposes of seeking a Canadian divorce, they may be recognized for spousal and child support and custody, for the purposes of inheriting property, and for marriage contracts and separation agreements.

6. Classify who has capacity to marry.

Although the requirements of marriage are within the federal powers there is little statute law, and provinces have legislated their own requirements. If there is a requirement that is not fulfilled at the time of marriage, the marriage contract may be void. To marry, each person must have the legal capacity to appreciate the nature and quality of the legal commitment and must do so freely without the influence of drugs, alcohol, or illness. A person must comprehend the responsibilities of marriage at the time of the ceremony, and a marriage will remain valid even if this ability no longer exists after the marriage is complete.

SELF-EVALUATION QUESTIONS

1. How is reconciliation defined in Ontario?
2. Can a separation agreement be reopened if circumstances change?
3. What were the historic grounds for divorce?
4. What factors does the court look to when determining spousal support in either the provincial legislation or the *Divorce Act*?
5. What are the current legal grounds for divorce in Canada?
6. What is the difference between condonation and connivance?

CHAPTER 7

Administrative Law

What is administrative law? It is the law that governs bureaucrats and tribunals. These include any governmental or quasi-governmental authority that has powers derived directly or indirectly from statute. Some obvious examples include immigration and unemployment insurance authorities, parole boards, professional discipline bodies, municipal councils and boards, university committees, and utilities regulatory bodies. Administrative law also governs discipline committees of private associations and clubs. The list appears endless. These organizations have in common the power to make rules and decisions that affect people. Administrative law prescribes the rules by which these authorities are expected to operate and, when these rules are not complied with, provides the complaint procedure and the remedies.[1]

Learning Outcomes

After completing this chapter, you should be able to:

1. Discuss what remedies are available after judicial review.
2. Assess privative clauses and how they can be used to avoid judicial review.
3. Discuss the pros and cons of administrative tribunals.
4. Identify the three branches of government in Canada and their respective roles.
5. Pinpoint the differences between a tribunal and a court.

INTRODUCTION

Administrative law is everywhere. Most of us do not think, "Holy cow! There is administrative law in action" on a day-to-day basis, but it is in the background working for our benefit. I do not know many people who truly get excited about administrative law (excluding, of course, my friend Ken, but he is a special case), but it is a much-needed system. Previous

1. Sara Blake, *Administrative Law in Canada* (Toronto: Butterworths, 1992) at 1.

chapters have noted that there are many day-to-day matters that the legal system regulates, but the administrative law system, in addition to the matters discussed at the opening of the chapter, regulates matters such as obtaining a driver's licence, immigration issues, taxation maters, Worker's Compensation claims, and landlord and tenant issues. It is extremely difficult for the traditional court system to keep up with all of these diverse issues. And as seen in Chapter 3, there may be a huge time span between the beginning of litigation and the time when parties finally have a resolution.

As we have learned, Canada has a highly regulated, formal, and complex system populated with lawyers hired to protect their clients' rights. The clogged court system was in great need of relief, so it was necessary to implement another system of justice that would act like a court, but function outside of the court system. As noted in Chapter 1, administrative law is **public law** and deals with the relationships between individuals and the state. Administrative law has been defined as a "body of rules and principles which governs the exercise of powers granted by statute," and the institutions that operate in this fashion are governed by the principles of administrative law.[2]

Government departments and agencies are established through legislation and they run programs and perform other government business outside of the court system. Their function is to implement administrative processes and ensure they are run efficiently, fairly, and according to law. Typically, these agencies regulate themselves, and hear and resolve conflicts with citizens.

Our government has three branches: (1) the legislative branch, which includes the elected Members of Parliament (federal and provincial) and the appointed Members of Senate who create, debate, and repeal statutory laws; (2) the judicial branch, which consists of the courts, which hear legal cases; and (3) the executive branch, which consists of government departments that are responsible for implementing laws and social policies and ensuring compliance through **boards**, **commissions**, and **tribunals** (also called authorities, committees, bodies, and agencies). These terms are almost interchangeable, and will be used together in this chapter to refer to these administrative bodies. Figure 7.1 illustrates the three branches of the Canadian government.

Often disputes arise between citizens and government agencies and the civil servants who are making decisions in these departments. A federal example of this would be immigration officers. The government has seen fit to give a great deal of power to these officers to decide who can and cannot stay in the country. The *Immigration and Refugee Protection Act*, SC 2001, c 27, s 4, states that the Minister of Citizenship and Immigration is responsible for the administration of the act, and s 6 states that the Minister may "designate any persons or class of persons as officers to carry out any purpose of any provision of this Act, and shall specify the powers and duties of the officers so designated." An individual may take issue with a finding made by

Figure 7.1 The Three Branches of Power

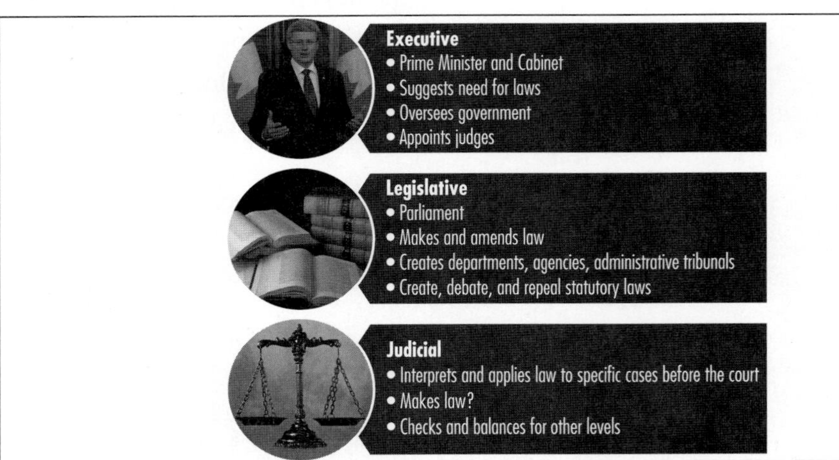

Top: THE CANADIAN PRESS/Sean Kilpatrick
Middle: Linda Macpherson/Shutterstock
Bottom: MilousSK/Shutterstock

2. Law Society of Upper Canada: Bar Admissions Course, *Public Law: Introduction and Overview*, Chapter 2 (Toronto: Law Society of Upper Canada, 2002).

Provincial tribunal examples include the following:
Alberta Human Labour Relations Board
http://www.alrb.gov.ab.ca/
British Columbia Securities Commission
http://www.bcsc.bc.ca/
Manitoba Pensions Commission
http://www.gov.mb.ca/labour/pension/
Nova Scotia Alcohol and Gaming Commission
http://www.gov.ns.ca/lae/agd/liquor.asp
Yukon Forest Commission
http://www.emr.gov.yk.ca/forestry/

a designated officer who makes decisions, and may have to appear before the Immigration and Refugee Board to resolve that dispute. Most agencies have developed these kinds of boards or **administrative tribunals** that function to help resolve disputes and have set up rules to deal with these matters. The tribunals may be created by federal, provincial, or municipal governments.

Many statutes have been written to make room for bodies to administer the law outside of the formal legal system. The tribunals that administer the system may physically look like formal courts, but they are actually a part of the executive branch of government and not the judicial branch like ordinary courts. Although these bodies are not within the court system, their decisions are binding on the parties. A decision by a tribunal may have even more impact on an individual than a criminal law conviction. For example, the License Appeal Tribunal in Ontario is an adjudicative agency under the *License Appeal Tribunal Act*, SO 1999, c 12, Schedule G. The tribunal can affirm a suspension of a driver's licence under the *Highway Traffic Act*, RSO 1990, c H.8., which may have much more effect on an individual than other relatively minor consequences under the *Criminal Code*, RSC 1985 c C-46, especially for someone who makes a living from driving.

It is important that administrative tribunals do not go beyond their jurisdiction, or act in a way that is ***ultra vires***, a Latin term that means beyond the power of the body, or acting beyond the given jurisdiction. The tribunal must adhere to the **jurisdiction** that has been granted to it by statute, and that statute must be followed exactly. These powers cannot be redelegated to someone else unless the statute specifically provides for that action.

Jurisdiction refers to the authority of a body to make decisions or take action with reference to certain specific areas of control, such as the right of the Parole Board to award or deny parole to an inmate. Despite the powers given to these tribunals, citizens still have recourse to the courts if they feel they have been treated unjustly or if the tribunal did not have jurisdiction. A tribunal must look to the legislation that created the tribunal, to regulations that may apply, to general legislation that may apply to that area of law, and to rules, guidelines or notices created in that area of law. Those seeking help from a tribunal must make sure that they are asking the correct board for help. If they are approaching the wrong tribunal for the resolution of a problem, their matter will likely be dismissed immediately, regardless of the money and time spent, as seen in *Glover v Canada Pension Plan* (see the following case box).

GLOVER v CANADA PENSION PLAN, 2010 HRTO 1364 (HUMAN RIGHTS TRIBUNAL OF ONTARIO)

Examples of federal government tribunals include the following:
The Parole Board of Canada
http://www.pbc-clcc.gc.ca/index-eng.shtml
The Immigration and Refugee Board of Canada
http://www.irb.gc.ca/eng/pages/index.aspx
The Commission for Public Complaints Against the RCMP
http://www.cpc-cpp.gc.ca/
The Canadian Human Rights Commission
http://www.chrc-ccdp.ca/default-eng.aspx

The applicant, Ms. Glover, applied to the Ontario Human Rights Tribunal alleging that there was discrimination by two separate government bodies, and she wanted the Ontario tribunal to assist her. She said that she had suffered discrimination in her employment with a school board in British Columbia, and she also faced discrimination by the Canada Pension Plan for denying her a disability pension.

However, the tribunal quickly dealt with this application, saying that the Ontario Human Rights Tribunal is created by provincial statute, and only applies to those bodies that are given jurisdiction over by the province of Ontario. The tribunal had no jurisdiction over the British Columbia school board that the applicant identified, and the tribunal also had no jurisdiction over the Canada Pension Plan, because the Canadian Human Rights Commission has jurisdiction over matters that involve the federal government. The tribunal completely dismissed the application at that time.

Do you think the tribunal should have given some relief to the applicant? Should it matter how much time and money that the applicant has spent simply to be dismissed?

The government **delegates** certain powers to each tribunal, including a specific jurisdiction and authority. These agencies or tribunals can set standards and regulations that persons or corporations are required to follow. These bodies often have significant powers and a variety of punishments, including ordering fines, sending people back to prison, decertifying professionals, revoking licences, terminating the employment of individuals, and deporting them out of the country.

Administrative tribunals are established to provide an impartial body that is intended to ensure that the government's authority is exercised in a fair and non-discriminatory way. Typically, members of these tribunals have specialized knowledge, training, education, and/or experience. Ideally, the members should have autonomy from the department and not be unduly influenced by authorities. See the following box for how to become a tribunal member.

HOW DO YOU BECOME A TRIBUNAL MEMBER?

Each tribunal is individualistic about how you become a member and what kinds of issues will be adjudicated. Take the example of the Environment and Land Tribunals Ontario (ELTO), which brings together five Ontario tribunals and boards that look after matters related to land use planning, environmental and heritage protection, property assessment, and land valuation. Included are the Assessment Review Board, which hears property assessment appeals under several pieces of legislation and hears appeals on property tax matters; the Board of Negotiation, which conducts voluntary mediation in the event of a dispute over the value of land taken by the government; the Conservation Review Board, which hears disputes on issues of cultural heritage or interest; the Environmental Review Tribunal, which hears matters under environmental and planning statutes; and the Ontario Municipal Board, which hears matters of municipal planning, financial and land matters, zoning bylaws, and subdivision plans through numerous Ontario statutes.

But who are the people making these important decisions? Many Ontario tribunals are subject to the *Adjudicative Tribunals Accountability, Governance and Appointments Act*, 2009 SO 2009, c 33, sch. 5 s 14, which states how someone is appointed to an adjudicative tribunal. The provision says that:

Adjudicative tribunal members to be selected by competitive, merit-based process

14. (1) The selection process for the appointment of members to an adjudicative tribunal shall be a competitive, merit-based process and the criteria to be applied in assessing candidates shall include the following:
   1. Experience, knowledge or training in the subject matter and legal issues dealt with by the tribunal.
   2. Aptitude for impartial adjudication.
   3. Aptitude for applying alternative adjudicative practices and procedures that may be set out in the tribunal's rules.

Tribunal-specific qualifications

(2) If a member of an adjudicative tribunal is required by or under any other Act to possess specific qualifications, a person shall not be appointed to the tribunal unless he or she possesses those qualifications.

Publication

(3) The responsible minister of an adjudicative tribunal shall make public the recruitment process to select one or more persons to be appointed to the tribunal and in doing so shall specify,
   (a) the steps intended to be taken in the recruitment process; and
   (b) the skills, knowledge, experience, other attributes and specific qualifications required of a person to be appointed.

Thus, after making the position public, a panel must select the most qualified candidate who has the expertise to sit on that particular panel, and each administrative tribunal may add some qualities to the list to select the best person for the particular position.

What kind of skills do you need to be on this type of tribunal? What will be added to this general posting? See the following box with a job posting from the ELTO website, which states what is required.

ENVIRONMENT AND LAND TRIBUNALS ONTARIO[3]

Members may be assigned to carry out their adjudicative responsibilities alone or, occasionally, as part of a panel.

As an Adjudicator:

- Is familiar with and applies the relevant procedures and, as appropriate, uses an expert, active adjudication approach rather than a more-traditional adversarial model with a passive adjudicator.
- Understands and applies the relevant law and policies.
- Maintains impartiality and open-mindedness while also maintaining control of the hearing process.
- Respects cultural diversity and needs for accommodation.
- Treats every person who uses or seeks to use tribunal services with the utmost fairness, respect and courtesy, and conducts all matters with a view to facilitating access to justice.

Key Duties

- Manages the hearing process with a view to timely resolution of disputes.
- Makes rulings before and during a hearing to ensure the fair, proper and expeditious conduct, control and completion of the matter.
- Reviews and analyzes all evidence and submissions thoroughly and provides clear, concise, well-reasoned decisions which reflect a solid grasp of the issues and the relevant law and policies. When sitting as a member of a panel, participates frankly and openly in panel discussions and works cooperatively with other panel members in sharing ideas, concerns, knowledge and expertise.
- Participates in initial training and stays current in the field by engaging in ongoing professional development and by keeping informed of leading case law from tribunals and courts in Ontario and elsewhere.

Integrity and Fair Practices

- Ensure equal access, fair treatment and fair and proportionate process in accordance with the tribunal's rules and procedures.
- Deal with conflict and diverging interests while maintaining decorum, due process, and professional and respectful interactions among all participants.
- Recognize and deal appropriately with situations that may involve an issue of bias or conflict of interest.
- Act with integrity and honesty, with all actions being guided by the best interests of ELTO and the public.

Qualifications

- Understanding of the justice system, administrative law and human rights law, as well as the concepts of fairness, natural justice and proportionality.
- Demonstrated analytical, conceptual, problem-solving, decision-making and writing skills.

You will note that this position does not require the member to be a lawyer.
Should you be a lawyer to be an adjudicator on a tribunal?

What kinds of people would apply for this position?

Take a look at the biographies of ELTO members at **http://www.pas.gov.on.ca/scripts/en/bios.asp?minID=36&boardID=682&persID=117263#1.**

FAIRNESS AND THE RULES OF NATURAL JUSTICE

Generally, the tribunal's purpose is to hear **grievances** from citizens against government departments and resolve these conflicts according to certain principles that are consistent with the law. This includes a duty to observe **natural justice.** It is the role of the tribunal to decide whose interests will prevail. If the powers given to the tribunal are not used properly, the person can allege that the tribunal did not act in accordance with the rules of natural justice. The rules of natural justice are the rules of fair play—the

3. © Queen's Printer for Ontario, 2011. Reproduced with permission.

right to a fair hearing, the right to be allowed to cross-examine a witness, the right to be notified of the hearing, but importantly, the right to know and answer the case against the individual, and the right to an unbiased decision maker. These issues are important because a person should be given the opportunity to defend his or her interests and provide information so that the decision-maker can make an informed ruling. This is extremely important inside a prison as shown in *Cardinal and Oswald v Director of Kent Institution* (see the following case box).

CARDINAL AND OSWALD v DIRECTOR OF KENT INSTITUTION, [1985] 2 SCR 643 (SCC)

Mr. Cardinal and Mr. Oswald were prisoners at the Matsqui Penitentiary in British Columbia when they took a guard hostage at knifepoint and held him for five hours. The pair were charged with crimes in relation to this kidnapping, and they were transferred to the Kent Institution, which was a maximum-security prison. Both were placed in **segregation** away from other prisoners. The Segregation Review Board at the prison recommended that they be released from segregation, but the prisoners were not allowed out of their solitary confinement by the director of the institution. Mr. Cardinal and Mr. Oswald appealed this decision saying that they did not have a fair hearing.

The Supreme Court said that the director of the prison should have adhered to the rules of natural justice. The prisoners should have been notified of the reasons for the decision, and they should have had the right to a fair hearing. The court found that the prisoners should have made representations and had the ability to state their case. The director had a duty to hear the prisoners and understand why the inmates had been involved in the hostage taking and anything else that was relevant. The right to a hearing is a fundamental right of the prisoners. The Supreme Court found that:

> the denial of a right to a fair hearing must always render a decision invalid, whether or not it may appear to a reviewing court that the hearing would likely have resulted in a different decision. The right to a fair hearing must be regarded as an independent, unqualified right which finds its essential justification in the sense of procedural justice which any person affected by an administrative decision is entitled to have.

The court found that the right of natural justice includes the right for the prisoners to be heard.

Do you think that prisoners should have more/fewer rights than other citizens? Should the same administrative principles apply?

Certain provinces have specific statutes that deal with procedure in administrative tribunals. For example, Ontario has the *Statutory Powers Procedure Act,* RSO 1990, c S.22, which codifies the rules of natural justice. This type of legislation governs tribunals, and s 3(1) says that there are formal rules for tribunals that have the statutory power of decision-making where there is a hearing. Alberta has similar legislation with the *Administrative Procedures Act,* RSA 2000, c A-3, as does Quebec with the *Administrative Justice Act* RSQ, c J-3. Even if the legislation does not apply to a particular body, the rules of natural justice may still be used.

Tribunals also have a **duty to act fairly** when dealing with parties before them. Defining what is meant by fairness is difficult. However, as was said in *Maxwell v Stable,* [1974] QB 523 at 539, "like defining an elephant, it was not easy to do, although fairness in practice has the elephantine quality of being easy to recognize."

What is fair will depend on the circumstances. In one type of tribunal, written submissions may be enough evidence, while in another the duty of fairness dictates that an individual should be able to orally submit his or her position to the tribunal. Tribunals are given latitude to decide what procedures are fair in the particular context of the case, but this procedure must be applied uniformly to all of the matters that appear before them.

Certain considerations will be taken into account, including the effect of the decision. The more serious the consequences of the decision, the more procedural protections must be followed. The tribunal or reviewing court will look at the nature of the decision, if it applies to a community or individual, or if it was based on broad social policy. It will also consider the tribunal's mandate, what was entrusted to it by statute, whether the procedural problems were fixed at a later point in the proceedings, whether there were problems at one stage or all stages, and what the statute provided for in regards to procedure. Finally, was the tribunal relieved from compliance with normal rules because of rules that are specific to that tribunal? All of these factors have to be carefully considered (see the following case box).

KNIGHT v INDIAN HEAD SCHOOL DIVISION NO. 19, [1990] 1 SCR 653 (SCC)

Mr. Knight was employed by the school board under a contract for employment. Mr. Knight was dismissed, but he asked the tribunal to find that he was owed a duty of fairness prior to being dismissed. This case went to the Supreme Court, where there was a discussion of fairness. The Supreme Court found that not all administrative bodies are under a duty to act fairly, but there are elements that must be considered.

First, the finality of the decision is an important matter to consider in order to determine if the individual was owed a duty of fairness. In this case, the decision was final, as Mr. Knight lost his job. Second, what was the relationship between the board and the employee? Mr. Knight was under contract, and could be terminated by the board when they decided to no longer employ him. Third, it must be observed if the decision had an important impact on the individual. Again, a loss of employment was a significant decision for Mr. Knight. The nature of the decision, the relationship between Mr. Knight and the board, and the impact on him all led to the conclusion that there was a duty to act fairly on the school board in these circumstances. The court said even though he was just a contract employee, Mr. Knight should have been given notice of the reasons why the board was not satisfied with his performance, and he should have an opportunity to be heard before the board. This decision was an extension of fairness to employees, even if they are simply on contract.

Should the board be able to use its discretion to terminate a contract employee whenever it decides it is the best time? Does this impact contract law?

DIFFERENCES BETWEEN A TRIBUNAL AND A COURT

There are some similarities and differences between tribunals and courts. While courts interpret and apply the law, administrative tribunals may also regulate the law. Courts are bound by *stare decisis,* while tribunals are not, although tribunals attempt to be consistent with their own decisions. Tribunals are often more informal and flexible than courts, they often do not have strict rules of procedure, and tribunal decisions can be made on public policy rather than strictly on law. Tribunal members usually come with a wealth of experience and knowledge in a particular area, while a judge may have no expertise in the field of law being decided on.

The courts maintain a supervisory role and will overrule a tribunal if there has been some violation of due process or if the judgment is contrary to the *Charter of Rights and Freedoms.* One of the operational variables relevant to administrative tribunals is the issue of **due process** or procedural fairness. This means that the procedures followed are relevant, lawful, fair, and impartial. In addition, the complainant has the right to be given relevant information, representation, and the opportunity to participate.

However, some tribunals can look very much like courts, and their decisions are similar to what is seen in civil litigation. There may not be strict rules of evidence like you would have in a court case, but many of these traditions are carried forward into administrative law, as seen in the following case box, which deals with a tribunal decision on immigration.

MALONG v THE MINISTER OF CITIZENSHIP AND IMMIGRATION, (2009) IAD FILE NO.: VA7-02330

This case concerned an appeal by Mr. Malong regarding the refusal of a permanent resident visa application of his spouse, Ms. Gumabao, who applied under the family class for immigration to Canada. The couple were married on November 5, 2005, and Ms. Gumabao was interviewed at the Canadian Embassy in the Philippines on August 28, 2007. The application was denied pursuant to section 4 of the *Immigration and Refugee Protection Regulations,* SOR 2002-227. The visa officer concluded that the marriage was not genuine, and was entered into with the primary purpose of gaining status under the *Immigration and Refugee Protection Act,* SC 2001, c 27. Section 4 of the Regulations provides that:

> 4. (1) For the purposes of these Regulations, a foreign national shall not be considered a spouse, a common-law partner or a conjugal partner of a person if the marriage, common-law partnership or conjugal partnership
> (*a*) was entered into primarily for the purpose of acquiring any status or privilege under the Act; or
> (b) is not genuine.

Mr. Malong was unable to describe how the relationship started and how it transformed from a friendship into a romantic relationship and marriage. Ms. Gumabao was unable to give sufficient information about her spouse. Testimony was heard from three witnesses, including the couple and Mr. Malong's sister, and documents and pictures were entered into evidence in addition to an affidavit from Ms. Gumabao's sister. The burden of proof of proving there was a valid marriage was on the applicant, and sufficient evidence was not provided to prove that there was a valid marriage for the purpose of the act.

Mr. Malong was found not to be a credible witness. The tribunal found that he did not come to this appeal with "clean hands." Both he and Ms. Gumabao's knowledge about what they identified as an important issue (religion), knowledge of financial affairs, and testimony on children was different. Ms. Gumabao's sister was unable to accurately say whether the wedding reception was held at a home or a restaurant. They were also unable to describe the appellant's relationship with his adopted son. Because of this lack of candour about the marriage, the tribunal concluded that this marriage was not genuine, and could not be considered a valid marriage under the Regulations.

The single tribunal member, Renee Miller, concluded that the marriage was entered into primarily for the purpose of acquiring status or privilege under the *Immigration and Refugee Protection Act.* Thus, the decision to refuse permanent status to Ms. Gumabao was affirmed.

Does the evidence in this case sound much like a civil litigation matter?

ADVANTAGES AND DISADVANTAGES OF THE ADMINISTRATIVE SYSTEM

Pros of the Administrative System

A significant benefit of administrative tribunals is that they are (largely) not governed by the strict procedures or rules of evidence that the courts must follow. Most tribunals combine both formal and informal characteristics in their hearings and members are allowed a degree of **discretion** in making decisions. Members are also allowed to use their expertise, which is often considerable, and this experience can assist with decisions. Financial cost and efficiency are often considerations in moving cases through the administrative law system. Costs can be reduced when there is an expert panel ready to hear matters in a flexible way, and to deal with recurrent matters. These safeguards are beneficial to individuals, as their individual rights are respected by the government. There are different types of tribunals—ones that are administrative, judicial or quasi-judicial types of tribunals, and legislatives. For example, some tribunals will just issue licences, and at the other end some tribunals can actually write legislation. The system can be flexible to account for these huge differences, tribunal to tribunal.

As discussed in Chapter 3, the traditional justice system has huge financial, emotional, and psychological costs, and it takes a significant amount of time, which can be greatly reduced in an administrative system. The traditional system takes power away from those who have been wronged—to the point that they do not feel part of the system—and often neither party is satisfied at the end of the process. It is the aim of the tribunal system to avoid this disconnect and to allow the parties to participate. In addition, the rights of natural justice and the right to a fair and impartial hearing attempt to respect all who appear before a tribunal. Finally, the decision-making process is largely open to the public, making it an accessible system, and decisions can be appealed through the courts if these principles are not maintained.

Cons of the Administrative System

There are also problematic issues with the administrative justice tribunals, especially when they do not use strict rules of procedure. Not having these strict rules of procedure can be a pro of the system as evidence can be entered without the huge procedural journey found in other types of law, but this can also be a disadvantage. Evidence may be entered that would not be allowed in a court, and many suggest that the evidence should stay out of the decision.

Often there no transcripts taken of the proceedings, and this has a huge impact on precedent. How is one matter to be tried like another under the rule of precedent if this material does not exist? If detailed records are not kept about the matter, it cannot be used in subsequent hearings in the same way that material can be used in the traditional court system. This makes consistency much more difficult in the administrative law realm. The lack of formality is a positive attribute of the tribunal, but this may also be frustrating for the players who are used to the procedure of court. Some believe administrative tribunals should be more formal, as they may deal with important issues of law.

Many decisions in administrative law concern an element of discretion, but this discretion is not absolute. Discretion should only be used to follow the policies and objectives of their governing legislation. Tribunals may be reviewed in situations where the tribunal has misused discretion. Improperly using discretion can be alleged on various grounds, including (1) **bad faith**, (2) acting for an improper purpose or motive, (3) taking account of irrelevant factors, (4) failing to take account of relevant factors, (5) undue fettering of discretion, and (6) acting under the dictation of someone without authority.

Abuse of Discretion

Administrative tribunals are given a wide ability to use their discretion as long as they do so in a fair way. Tribunals have discretion as to whether a case comes within particular legislation and what the policy implications may be. If a tribunal is accused of operating in bad faith, the parties may be asked to prove that the tribunal was using improper considerations, or elements such as discrimination. One of the most blatant forms of bad faith occurred in the case of *Roncarelli v Duplessis* (see the following case box).

RONCARELLI v DUPLESSIS, [1959] SCR 121 (SCC)

The Canadian Press

Premier Maurice Duplessis

This case began in 1946 at a time when the Quebec government was allegedly attacking the civil liberties of those in the Jehovah's Witness faith. Mr. Roncarelli was a Jehovah's Witness who posted bail for other Witnesses who had been imprisoned for various charges, including giving out pamphlets, a practice contrary to municipal bylaws. Unrelated to his religious beliefs, Mr. Roncarelli also had a liquor licence for his business.

The premier of Quebec, Mr. Maurice Duplessis, instructed the manager of the liquor commission to revoke Mr. Roncarelli's licence and said that he would never get another one for his business. The Supreme Court found that this decision was simply to punish Mr. Roncarelli "for having done what he had a right to do in a matter utterly irrelevant to the *Liquor Act.*" The court found that revoking Mr. Roncarelli's liquor licence was a "gross abuse of legal power expressly intended to punish him for an act wholly irrelevant to the statute, a punishment which inflicted on him, as it was intended to do, the destruction of his economic life as a restaurant keeper within the province."

The court went on to discuss what good faith would be in the circumstances, saying that it means

> carrying out the statute according to its intent and purpose; it means good faith in acting with a rational appreciation of that intent and purpose and not with an improper intent and for an alien purpose; it does not mean for the purposes of punishing a person for exercising an unchallengeable right; it does not mean arbitrarily and illegally attempting to divest a citizen of an incident of his civil status.

The Supreme Court found in favour of Mr. Roncarelli, saying that he was entitled to damages for the tribunal's "abuse of power."

The court found that Premier Duplessis took over the power given to the manager of the liquor commission. He dictated the actions of the manager of the commission, and required him to use his power for an improper purpose or for irrelevant considerations. The Supreme Court found that Premier Duplessis interfered with the religious freedoms of Jehovah's Witnesses, and said that there was no such thing in administrative law as "absolute and untrammeled 'discretion,'" but that discretion is only to be used in good faith in discharging a public duty. This case established the parameters within which discretion can be used.

Are there recent examples of bad faith?

Bad faith can also include a refusal to exercise discretion. A refusal to follow a statutory purpose is also not permitted. A tribunal has a duty to follow that legislation, and refusing to do so contradicts the purpose of the system. For example, refusing to consider giving a licence for a particular trade would completely hinder the purpose of the legislation and would completely bar that individual from that profession.

Bias

The rules of natural justice provide that decisions must not be biased, and no one should be a judge in his or her own case. **Bias** is the inability of a tribunal member to be neutral on the issue at hand. If a tribunal member is biased, he or she may be disqualified from hearing a matter, or if the bias is discovered after the hearing, the decision made may be **quashed**. One of the most common grounds of bias is that the decision-maker would get some monetary benefit from the decision, and is interested in the outcome. This is true for situations involving relatives, friends, or business associates, and a member of the tribunal may not hold private interviews with parties or witnesses. Bias is unacceptable, but even the appearance of bias may also be enough to disqualify a member. The parties do not even have to prove that the bias actually prejudiced a party.

The reasonable apprehension of bias is a key phrase in administrative law. The tribunal will ask whether that magical reasonable person would have understood that there was unfairness in a particular situation. The phrase was defined by the Supreme Court in *Committee for Justice & Liberty v Canada (National Energy Board)* [1978] 1 SCR 369 (SCC), which stated the proper test to be applied is that a decision must be a

> reasonable one, held by reasonable and right minded persons, applying themselves to the question and obtaining thereon the required information. In the words of the Court of Appeal, that test is "what would an informed person, viewing the matter realistically and practically—and having thought the matter through—conclude."

The reason why the appearance of bias is treated so harshly is that there is great difficulty in proving that a person is actually biased. It is also important because of the aphorism from Chief Justice Hewart in *R v Sussex Justices, Ex Parte McCarthy,* [1924] 1 KB 256: "justice should not only be done, but should manifestly and undoubtedly be *seen to be done*." Tribunal members should not prejudge a case, because the reputation of the tribunal is fundamental.

If a decision is found to have been made through a lens of bias, the decision will likely be discarded, and the member will be disqualified from hearing the case. This can be true for things like improper conduct at the hearing, including derogatory language or comments. If a member even suspects that there could be the reasonable apprehension of bias, he or she should abstain from the hearing completely. Bias was the key issue in *Baker v Canada (Minister of Citizenship & Immigration)*, as shown in the following case box.

BAKER v CANADA (MINISTER OF CITIZENSHIP & IMMIGRATION), [1999] 2 SCR 817 (SCC)

Ms. Baker was a citizen of Jamaica and was being **deported** from Canada. Even though she had lived in Canada for 11 years, she had never become a citizen, although her four children were born in Canada. Ms. Baker suffered from mental illness. She applied to gain permanent residency on humanitarian and compassionate grounds because it would be in the best interest of her children for her to stay in the country. She was denied her request, and she did not receive the official decision or any notes. Ms. Baker asked that this decision be reviewed by the court on the grounds of bias of the immigration adjudicator.

The immigration officer, who played a significant role in the decision to deport, wrote specific comments (that were not disclosed to the applicant) about the immigration system and why individuals stayed in Canada, while referring to stereotypes about Ms. Baker. He made a link between Ms. Baker's mental illness, her training as a domestic worker, the fact that she had several children, and that she would be a strain on the Canadian social welfare system. He concluded that "Canada can no longer afford this kind of generosity."

The decision was reviewed by the Supreme Court and it was concluded that the officer was making conclusions based on the fact that she was a single mother with mental disabilities, rather than on the relevant evidence presented. The Supreme Court found that a reasonable member of the community would conclude that there was bias by the officer, and that this qualified as a reasonable apprehension of bias. The decision to deport was set aside and sent back to immigration to have the application reviewed by a different immigration officer.

Do you think that an immigration officer should be allowed to consider the broader implications of this decision to stay in Canada?
Was there bias in this decision?
If the decision allowed these extrinsic matters, would it form a precedent that decisions based on elements outside of the jurisdiction of the tribunal were permitted? What would the impact be?

Other Issues in Administrative Law

Another common critique of the administrative system is that members of the tribunal may feel it is their duty to uphold the policies or reputation of the department, which pays their salaries and promotes them, against the needs or rights of individuals. Others say that taking matters out of the judicial branch, which is slow, to put it in a governmental tribunal in the executive branch, which can also be slow, is not a much improved system. There are still delays and the process may take a significant amount of time. Some say that parties are allowed to use the lack of technicality to manipulate the system for their own needs. The lack of formality also may lead to a loss of predictability of future matters.

APPEAL

The decision of a tribunal may not be the final word on a matter. There are rights of appeal built in to the statutes of many administrative bodies. Depending on what is set out in the legislation, the parties may be entitled to a new hearing without reference to the previous decision, a new hearing with some **deference** to the body who heard the matter, or a review of the decision without oral argument, which looks for errors made by the body on the record. Each tribunal is different, and the legislation of that particular body must be examined. Consider for a moment the Environmental Review Tribunal discussed earlier. One of the pieces of legislation that it might make a decision under is the *Safe Drinking Water Act*, 2002, SO 2002, c 32 at s 129. Under this act a "Director" makes the decision, and the act provides what to do if one wants to appeal a decision of the Director, and sets out what is a "reviewable decision". One may appeal to the tribunal as the legislation provides that:

> **Right to appeal to Tribunal**
>
> **129.** (1) Within 15 days after being served with a notice of a reviewable decision, the person notified may require a hearing by the Tribunal by written notice served on the Director and the Tribunal.
>
> And s **132 (2)** provides that:
>
> The Tribunal may do any or all of the following on a hearing in relation to a reviewable decision:
>
> 1. Confirm, vary or revoke the decision.
> 2. Direct the Director to take such action as the Tribunal considers necessary for the purposes of this Act.
> 3. Substitute its opinion for that of the Director.

However, the legislation may also provide what happens if you want to appeal this matter beyond the tribunal and into the court system. As is the case of civil litigation, the review must be on the rules, procedure, and evidence used to get the result, not simply because a party was unsuccessful. Some tribunals will ask those seeking appeal to be granted leave, or permission to appeal, and there must be a substantial element that was not correctly decided. Common grounds of appeal are jurisdiction (in that the tribunal did not have the power to hear the case or was *ultra vires* so that the decision should be overruled), a question of law that was used by the tribunal, and a question of evidence. There may be significant rules and procedures about the time and the place to make an appeal, but there may be broad powers to review a decision. Appeal rights are usually required to be exhausted within the administrative system before an appeal is made to the court system.

To whom the appeal is made is also an important question. As discussed, an appeal may be made to the tribunal itself, to another tribunal, to the Superior Court, to the **Divisional Court** (in some provinces), to the Court of Appeal or the Federal Court of Appeal, and ultimately to the Supreme Court. The grounds on which a party may appeal (and if the party may appeal at all) may be set out in the governing legislation. There may also be general statutes that may dictate how an appeal is to be completed, such as the *Federal Court Act,* RSC, 1985, c F-7, which may provide for appeals from certain tribunals. The legislation itself may also state the procedure. For example, the *Environmental Protection Act*, RSO 1990, c E.19, says right in the legislation how one can appeal a tribunal decision when it comes to environmental compliance approvals under Part II.1 of the act at s 20.16:

Appeal from decision of Tribunal

20.16 (1) A party to a proceeding under this Part before the Tribunal may appeal from its decision,
(a) on a question of law, to the Divisional Court; and
(b) on a question other than a question of law, to the Minister.

Appealing to the court system is called judicial review.

JUDICIAL REVIEW

If one is still unsatisfied after all appeals have been exhausted to the particular tribunal, the parties can apply for **judicial review,** where the court system can review what was done. All previous appeal possibilities must be sought before going to court, as the court will often dismiss the case if the parties have not pursued these options. The parties must come to the court with clean hands, must not have waived or acquiesced to the errors made, and must not have taken too long to seek this remedy. Specific legislation, such as the *Judicial Review Procedure Act*, RSBC 1996 c 241 in British Columbia, may dictate the procedure.[4]

The courts will ensure that the tribunal made the decision in a reasonable manner. There must be evidence of the tribunal's justification of the decision, including statutes and regulations, and evidence that relevant legislation in the territorial jurisdiction was followed. The decision-maker has to be properly appointed, with proper delegation and proper notice, and the courts will inquire whether there was an infringement of the rules of natural justice. If all of these things seem to have been done, the courts are reluctant to interfere, giving deference to the tribunal with its expertise. The entire point of the administrative law system is to have decisions taken out of the courts, and to have a panel with special skills that can save time and money by hearing these cases. Having every decision reviewed by the courts would negate this aim.

Having the courts review a decision of a tribunal should be the last resort, but the courts do serve an important function to act as a supervisor so that the government can ensure that power is not being used arbitrarily. Judicial review is a complex procedure, and it tends to be narrow, so only in cases where rights have been absolutely infringed upon will the court step in. If the answer is that something was not done properly at any of these levels, the court can review the decision and apply a remedy. Provinces may expressly provide for judicial review by having specific legislation to deal with the procedure. Usually, courts recognize and try to rectify errors of jurisdiction, errors of law, and errors of fact in judicial review. The court will determine if there was a standard of correctness, or a standard of unreasonableness. This can apply to Canadian universities, as seen in the following case box.

KHAN v THE UNIVERSITY OF OTTAWA (1997), 2 ADMIN LR (3D) 298 (ONT CA)

Ms. Khan failed her evidence exam in her second year at the University of Ottawa law school. She was graded on the basis of three exam booklets, but Ms. Khan insisted that she had handed in four booklets. She appealed her grade to the Faculty of Law Examinations Committee, and then to the Senate Committee at the University of Ottawa, but both appeals were dismissed, as she had not established that a fourth book actually existed, and in fact she had written "1 of 3," "2 of 3," and "3 of 3" on the books submitted. At the next level, the Divisional Court rejected her appeal, saying that if there was "any denial of natural justice in the proceedings before the Examination Committee ... such defect was cured in the proceedings before the Senate Committee." Thus, even though Ms. Khan was not permitted to present her case before the Faculty of Law Examinations Committee, these problems were

4. *Judicial Review Procedure Act*, RSBC 1996 c 241; *Judicial Review Procedure Act*, RSO 1990, c J.1; *Judicial Review Act*, RSPEI 1988, c J-3; *Alberta Rules of Court; Saskatchewan Queen's Bench Rules.*

rectified before the Senate Committee with their processes, and natural justice had been adhered to.

Ms. Khan appealed to the Court of Appeal for Ontario on the grounds that she was denied procedural fairness. Ms. Khan argued that at the Examinations Committee level she had no opportunity to appear, she was not told of any concerns, and she had no ability to answer any questions. Because Ms. Khan's credibility was in question (whether she was lying about the existence of a fourth book), the Court of Appeal said that she should have had an opportunity to appear before the committee. In her appeal to Senate, the Court of Appeal found that she was also denied procedural fairness because she was not given an opportunity to appear at that level as well. The Court of Appeal disagreed with the Divisional Court that any defects in procedure were cured by the hearing in the Senate. Ms. Khan also was denied procedural fairness at the Senate level.

The Court of Appeal was convinced that Ms. Khan did not have a hearing that adhered to procedural fairness. The court allowed the appeal, set aside the decision of the Divisional Court, quashed the decisions of the Senate Committee and the Examinations Committee, and awarded Ms. Khan costs in the matter. The matter was sent back to the Examinations Committee for the oral hearing that it should have had afforded to Ms. Khan from the beginning of the matter.

Do you think that Ms. Khan should get the chance to go back to the Examinations Committee for a hearing?
Do you think she would get a fair hearing from the Examinations Committee?

Privative Clauses

Some statutes will attempt to contract their way out of judicial review by a court by drafting sections indicating that their decision is not reviewable by the courts and no remedies can be ordered by the courts. One must be careful to ensure that there is not a **privative clause** in the governing legislation of a particular matter. An example of this in Alberta is the *Worker's Compensation Act,* RSA 2000 c W-15. This legislation provides in s 13.1(1) that the "decision of the Appeals Commission on the appeal or other matter is final and conclusive and is not open to question or review in any court." The legislation is clear that there is no possibility of judicial review so that their decision is the final one without running to the courts. These clauses have not been totally accepted by the courts, but it does send a clear message to the judiciary that there must be deference to the tribunals, and the courts should only set aside a decision that is completely unreasonable. Courts may still find a way to interpret that clause to say it is ambiguous so that they have the power to review, but it will be difficult.

The Supreme Court has also said that there is such thing as a full privative clause, which means the decisions of the tribunals are final, and usually words such as "final and conclusive" will be used. Thus, the courts will look at the nature of the problem under review, the words within the statute (including privative clauses), the purpose of the tribunal's enabling statute, and the expertise that a tribunal may have. These factors will be evaluated to decide a standard of review in this particular situation.

A party may be denied judicial review if he or she had procedural fairness at one step in the process. If the party had fairness at one level, then this cured the problems of unfairness at other levels. However, if that fairness was missing, the courts system may send the decision back to the original decision-maker to rehear the case (as can be the case in the court system as well).

REMEDIES

When it is appropriate for a court to intervene, a court may decide to quash a decision of a tribunal, *prevent* a tribunal from taking action, or *require* a tribunal to take an action. The court may define the rights and powers of a tribunal and, rarely, may even be able to order damages against it. The court can use ***writs*** to remedy the situation caused by the tribunal. Although there is no absolute right to a remedy, where appropriate there are seven main *writs* and remedies available: (1) quashing the decision of the tribunal; (2) prohibition, or stopping the tribunal from acting; (3) *mandamus*, or forcing an official to act; (4) *certiorari*; (5) *habeas corpus*; (6) declaratory judgment; and (7) damages.

1. Quashing the Decision of the Tribunal

A court may find that a tribunal did not have jurisdiction, did not use a fair procedure, or the decision was made in bad faith, and for this reason the decision should be quashed. In quashing the decision, the court may give guidance to the tribunal about what should have occurred, but the court may not substitute its decision for that of the tribunal. However, the court can order the tribunal to revisit the matter in light of these comments, or have the matter heard by a new panel. This remedy serves to function as if the tribunal never made a decision so the panel can take back the case and make a conclusion all over again.

2. Prohibition—Stopping the Tribunal from Acting

Usually a court will only take such a drastic step as a **prohibition** if the tribunal lacks the authority to make the decision. Prohibition may be in the form of an **injunction** that can be enforced by holding the non-compliant party in contempt of court. A prohibition may occur in a situation where the parties are facing a lengthy trial by a disqualified decision-maker, and they would like to stop the trial before it even starts. A prohibition cannot be made after the final decision has been handed down. See the discussion of *certiorari* on this page for an example of a prohibition.

3. *Mandamus*—Force an Official to Act

Mandamus is the Latin term for "we command." This is a remedy that will force a decision-maker to make a proper decision if that person is not currently completing his or her duties. If an official has a power and must exercise that power, an order of *mandamus* will force him or her to act. A federal court example of this remedy is found in *Almrei v Canada (Minister of Citizenship and Immigration)*, [2011] FCJ No 781 (Fed Ct), where Mr. Almrei had applied for permanent residence in Canada, and had asked the government for the status of that application. Mr. Almrei continued to seek information on the status, and none was forthcoming, so he filed an application for *mandamus* in the federal court to force the Minister to make a decision on his application. The Minister would then be forced to respond and fulfill these duties.

4. *Certiorari*

Certiorari is a remedy used to access the record of the proceedings to be certain that there was not an error made by the tribunal. The consequence of this finding is an error that would lead to the quashing of the decision of the government administrator, usually because there was no jurisdiction. This may require a tribunal to deliver the written form of the decision so it may be reviewed and possibly set aside. This order can only be made *after* a final decision has been made. In the case of *Paul v British Columbia (Forest Appeals Commission)*, [2003] SCJ No 34 (SCC), Mr. Paul had cut down several trees but an official in the British Columbia Ministry of Forestry seized four logs. Mr. Paul said that s 96 of the *Forest Practices Code of British Columbia Act*, RSBC 1996, c 159, did not apply to him as an Aboriginal person. The Forest Appeals Commission found that it had jurisdiction to decide this issue on Aboriginal rights, but Mr. Paul moved under the Judicial Review Procedure Act, RSBC 1996, c 241 for an order of *certiorari* to review and ultimately quash the decision of the commission. He also requested an order of prohibition to prevent the commission from deciding an issue of Aboriginal rights. Mr. Paul was ultimately unsuccessful, but this was a good examination of the remedies available.

5. *Habeas Corpus*

A writ of ***habeas corpus*** is an ancient writ that was sent to the government (or rulers) from the court saying "let me have the body (alive)" of the person named in the application.[5] This document called those responsible to produce the individual so that the validity of that person's detention could be determined. Today, this *writ* is used where a person is improperly detained in criminal matters, immigration, child custody, and mental health issues, but it is very infrequently used. An example is the case of *Cardinal and Oswald v Director of Kent Institution,* [1985] 2 SCR 643 (SCC) discussed on page 188. In that case, the prisoners argued that they should be able to use *habeas corpus* to free them from segregation in a prison, and that they should be able to go back to the general prison population because they did not have a fair hearing with the Segregation Review Board. The court found that they had a right, on the basis of *habeas corpus,* to be released into the population.

6. Declaratory Judgment

Also called a declaratory order or declaration, a declaratory judgment is a statement of the court that sets out the legal standing of the parties and/or confirms the law that applies. Although there is almost no way to enforce a **declaration**, it is usually respected and used in administrative law to determine if the tribunal had the power to take the actions that it did. A declaratory judgment can be a flexible remedy to establish the position of the parties, the powers of the tribunal, and the rights of those involved on questions of law. See the case of *McIntosh* below for a declaratory order.

7. Damages

The court has the power to award punitive or exemplary damages where a tribunal may have acted maliciously. This is a remedy not often used, but it can be a tool in administrative law, and damages were awarded in *Roncarelli v Duplessis* (see page 192). There must be a gross misuse of powers for a tribunal to have to pay damages when it was simply using its statuary powers. *McIntosh v Metro Aluminum Products Ltd. and Zbigniew Augustynowiczm* provides an example of abuse of power justifying damages from the party involved (see the following case box).

MCINTOSH v METRO ALUMINUM PRODUCTS LTD. AND ZBIGNIEW AUGUSTYNOWICZ, 2011 BCHRT 34 (B.C. HUMAN RIGHTS TRIBUNAL)

Mr. Augustynowicz entered into a consensual sexual relationship with one of his employees, Ms. McIntosh. During their relationship, the parties both exchanged sexually explicit texts. The relationship ended, but Mr. Augustynowicz continued to send texts, which became more offensive over time. Ms. McIntosh eventually left her job and filed a complaint against Mr. Augustynowicz and the company, Metro Aluminum, under s 13 of the *Human Rights Code* RSBC 1996, c 210, alleging discrimination in employment based on sex (sexual harassment). The onus was on Ms. McIntosh to show, on the balance of probabilities, that she was discriminated against on the basis of sex.

After Ms. McIntosh told Mr. Augustynowicz not to text her anymore, he continued with messages such as "how about a bj," "any horny girlfriends," "can I date your daughter," "don't be such a bitch," "screw you, I had enough of your crap. Stay with your queer boyfriend," "need hookers," and "I need a nooner," among others. The tribunal defined sexual harassment as "unwelcome conduct of a sexual nature that detrimentally affects the work environment or leads to adverse job-related consequences" and that "undermines his/her sense of personal dignity." One of the big issues in this matter was whether the texts were unwelcome.

5. David J Mullan, *Administrative Law* (Toronto: Irwin Law, 2001) at 406.

The tribunal said that the test was objective: "would a reasonable person, taking into account all the circumstances, know that the comments were unwelcome." The tribunal took the following considerations into account from the case of *Mahmoodi v University of British Columbia* (1999), 2001 BCSC 1256 (BCHR): the complainant did not have to object to the unwanted attention unless the other party would have no reason to suspect it was unwelcome; behaviour can be tolerated but still unwelcome; whether something is unwelcome may be subtly communicated; and the tribunal must look at the power differential and understand that lack of cooperation would result in disadvantage in the workplace.

The tribunal found that Ms. McIntosh was subjected to sexual harassment as Mr. Augustynowicz was in a position of power, was responsible for her employment, and should have maintained a workplace free of sexual harassment. The tribunal found that the parties were allowed to enter into a sexual relationship, but once Ms. McIntosh said that the texts were no longer welcome, her boss should have known that they were impacting their working relationship. The tribunal found that she was subject to discrimination that adversely affected her work conditions and led her to leave the company on stress leave. The tribunal gave the following remedies:

1. an order that Mr. Augustynowicz cease all discriminatory conduct;
2. a declaration that the conduct was discriminatory; and
3. damages of $14 493.80 for lost wages, $2900.85 for her costs, and $12 500.00 for damages for loss of "dignity, feelings and self-respect."

Do you think that Mr. Augustynowicz was responsible for these damages? Should Ms. McIntosh have received more/less in damages?

CONCLUSION

Although there is tension about what issues should be exclusively within the realm of administrative tribunals and what should be decided in the courts, the two systems work in relative harmony in Canada today. Although the courts maintain their position as the overseer of the system on guard for offences against the individual rights of the person, the administrative system needs room to be able to shape public policy and do the job it has been tasked with. It is only when tribunals go outside of their jurisdiction that the courts should be able to step in. Many tribunals have found that the court's review of their decision has resulted in praise from the courts for their professionalism and expertise. The administrative justice system is, and likely will remain, one of the most common ways that Canadians have contact with the justice system.

LEARNING OUTCOMES SUMMARIZED

1. Discuss what remedies are available after judicial review.

The remedies are (1) quashing the decision of the tribunal; (2) prohibition, or stopping the tribunal from acting; (3) *mandamus*, or forcing an official to act; (4) *certiorari*; (5) *habeas corpus*; (6) declaratory judgment; and (7) damages.

2. Assess privative clauses and how they can be used to avoid judicial review.

Some statutes will attempt to contract their way out of review by a court saying that their decision is not reviewable by the courts. These clauses have not been totally accepted by the courts, but they do send a clear message that there must be deference to the tribunals, and the courts should only set aside a decision that is completely unreasonable. Courts still find a way to interpret that clause to say it is ambiguous so that they have the power to review.

The Supreme Court has also said that there is such thing as a full privative clause, which means the decisions of the tribunals may be final. Thus, the courts will look at the nature of the problem under review, the words within the statute, the purpose of the tribunal's enabling statute, and the expertise that a tribunal may have, before choosing a standard of review.

3. List the pros and cons of administrative tribunals.

A benefit of administrative tribunals is that they are not governed by the strict procedural rules of the court. Most tribunals combine both formal and informal characteristics in their hearings, allowing members a degree of discretion in making decisions, and the members are also allowed to use their expertise. Financial cost and efficiency are maximized when there is an expert panel ready to hear matters in a flexible way. The rights of natural justice and the right to a fair and impartial hearing lead to the respect of all who appear before a tribunal, the decision-making process is open to the public, and decisions can be appealed through the courts if these principles are not maintained.

There are also problematic issues with the administrative tribunals, especially when they do not use strict rules of procedure. Evidence may be entered that would not be allowed in a court. Often there are no exact transcripts taken of the proceedings, and this has a huge impact on precedent, as records are not kept about the matter, and it cannot be used in subsequent hearings. This makes consistency much more difficult in the administrative law realm. The lack of formality can be frustrating for the players who are used to the procedure of court. Many decisions in administrative law concern an element of discretion, but this discretion is not absolute. Improperly using discretion can be alleged on various grounds, including (1) bad faith, (2) acting for an improper purpose or motive, (3) taking account of irrelevant factors, (4) failing to take account of relevant factors, (5) undue fettering of discretion, and (6) acting under the dictation of someone without authority. If a tribunal is accused of operating in bad faith, the parties may be asked to prove that the tribunal was using improper considerations or elements such as discrimination.

4. Identify the three branches of government in Canada and their respective roles.

Our government is often described as having three branches: (1) the legislative branch, which includes the elected Members of Parliament and the Members of Senate, who create, debate, and repeal statutory laws; (2) the judicial branch, which consists of the courts; and (3) the executive branch, which consists of government departments that are responsible for implementing laws and social policies.

5. Pinpoint the differences between a tribunal and a court.

While courts interpret and apply the law, administrative tribunals may also regulate the law. Courts are bound by *stare decisis,* while tribunals are not, although tribunals attempt to be consistent with courts' decisions. Tribunals are often informal and flexible, without specific rules of procedure, and tribunal decisions can be made on public policy rather than strictly on law. Tribunal members usually come with a wealth of experience and knowledge in a particular area, while a judge may have no expertise in an area of law being decided upon.

The courts maintain a supervisory role and will overrule a tribunal if there has been some violation. One of the operational variables relevant to administrative tribunals is the issue of due process or procedural fairness. This means that the procedures followed are relevant, lawful, fair, and impartial. However, some tribunals can look much like courts, and their decisions are similar to what we have seen in civil litigation. There are no strict rules of evidence like you would have in a court case, but many of these traditions are carried forward into administrative law.

SELF-EVALUATION QUESTIONS

1. What factors will the courts consider in deciding whether an administrative tribunal's decision is subject to judicial review?
2. What are the arguments for having a legal system that includes administrative tribunals?
3. Which branch of the government are administrative tribunals are part of? What are the other two branches and what are their roles?
4. In the case of *Roncarelli v Duplessis*, why did the court find that Mr. Roncarelli was entitled to damages?
5. Identify the pros and cons of administrative tribunals.
6. Discuss how disputes between citizens and governmental agencies are resolved.

CHAPTER

8

Constitutional Law

A constitution tends to be regarded in the modern day as a badge of nationhood. As such, it may reflect the values that a country regards as important and show how they are to be protected. In Canada, these values are manifested in constitutional features such as the vesting of the highest law-making authority into the hands of democratically elected representatives, the non-partisan administration of law and certain executive functions of the state, and a charter of rights.[1]

Learning Outcomes

After completing this chapter, you should be able to:

1. Discuss how constitutional law guides our Canadian legal system.
2. List the actors and discuss the powers of the three branches of government.
3. Evaluate how a constitutional issue comes before the courts.
4. Discuss how a court determines if a body is within its mandate.

INTRODUCTION

> The role of the judiciary is, of course, to interpret and apply the law; the role of the legislature is to decide upon and enunciate policy; the role of the executive is to administer and implement that policy.[2]

Some have said that the rules found in the Canadian Constitution are the most fundamental laws of our system because they govern how the state can act at its most basic level. A Constitution is a body of law, which establishes a framework for a government and is the supreme law of the country. Constitutional law is the system of written (and unwritten) principles that defines what power we give to our government while still protecting individuals and certain groups. Constitutional law is formed from **conventions**, statutes, proclamations, and court decisions.

1. Patrick Fitzgerald, Barry Wright, and Vincent Kazmierski, *Looking at Law: Canada's Legal System,* 6th ed (Markham: ON: LexisNexis, 2010) at 40–41.
2. Justice Dickson, *Fraser v Canada (Treasury Board),* [1985] 1 SCR 441 at 491.

The three branches of government include the executive (technically the Queen, but the powers lie with the Cabinet); the legislative, including the House of Commons, the Senate, and the Governor General; and the judicial, which is composed of the judges who interpret and apply the Constitution to actual cases. The separation of powers in this way allows the system to run efficiently in that the **rule of law** is maintained. The rule of law dictates that the law is supreme over both the individual and the government, as the power of the government must find its root in a legal principle. Although the Constitution includes political as well as legal rules, the legal aspects will be the focus of this chapter.

Constitutional law is that which overrides all other laws in Canada. Mr. Justice Dickson said in the case of *Canada (Director of Investigation & Research, Combines Investigation Branch) v Southam:*

> A statute defines present rights and obligations. It is easily enacted and as easily repealed. A constitution, by contrast, is drafted with an eye to the future. Its function is to provide a continuing framework for the legitimate exercise of governmental power.... It must, therefore, be capable of growth and development over time to meet new social, political and historical realities often unimagined by its framers. The judiciary is the guardian of the constitution and must, in interpreting its provision, bear these considerations in mind.[3]

Each level of government is assigned duties, and none is able to control the activities of the others.

It is important to recognize after a review of the administrative law system that the Canadian government does not have unlimited power. As discussed, Canada is a federal state, but the power is divided between the federal, provincial, and territorial governments and governed at the most basic level by what we call the *Constitution Act 1982.* Originally, the British Parliament created the *British North America Act,* or what was commonly called the *BNA Act,* which came into force in 1867. This legislation created the Dominion of Canada and the provinces of Ontario, Quebec, New Brunswick, and Nova Scotia, which still depended on Great Britain for decisions on international treaties, and for the high court called the Privy Council.

Table 8.1 The Unwritten Parts of the Constitution

Category	Elements or Illustrations
Constitutional enactments before 1867	*The Royal Proclamation of 1763* Provincial constitutions of Nova Scotia, Prince Edward Island, New Brunswick, Newfoundland, British Columbia
Constitutional conventions	Principles of responsible government Conventions regulating federal–provincial relations
Judicial decisions	Interpretations of the *Constitution Acts* Common law doctrines defining powers of the Crown, Parliament, or state officials
Organic statutes	*Supreme Court Act* *Canada Elections Act* *Financial Administration Act* *Citizenship Act*
Prerogative orders	*Letters Patent* of 1947 constituting the office of the governor general
Aboriginal agreements	*James Bay and Northern Quebec Agreement Inuvialuit Final Agreements* *Yukon First Nations Final Agreements* *Nisga'a Final Agreement*

Source: From Patrick J *Monahan, Constitutional Law,* 3rd ed © 2006 Irwin Law (Toronto). p. 178. Reproduced by permission.

3. *Canada (Director of Investigation & Research, Combines Investigation Branch) v Southam,* [1984] 2 SCR 145 at 155.

When the remainder of the ten provinces and three territories were created, all decided to be bound by the division of powers that were first developed in 1867. In 1982 we renamed this legislation the *Constitution Act, 1867*. Canadians' constitutional rights are not set out in just one piece of legislation, but in the *Canada Act 1982, Constitution Act 1982,* and 24 other acts and orders, mostly comprising the *Constitution Acts 1867–1975* (formerly the *British North America Acts 1867–1975*) and any amendments to this legislation.[4] There are also parts of the Constitution that are unwritten, and Table 8.1 outlines these elements.

PRIVY COUNCIL AND THE SUPREME COURT

As discussed in Chapter 3, the Supreme Court of Canada was created in 1949 giving Canadians more freedom by having their own courts without going to the British Privy Council. On December 23, 1949, a federal bill abolished the right of appeal to Britain, and replaced it with the right of appeal to the newly formed Supreme Court of Canada. It was important to the separation of powers that the judiciary be a separate and independent branch of government as protected in the *Constitution Act, 1867.* In order for judges to rule against the government in any law that is not consistent with the Constitution, judges must be completely free to make their decisions. Judicial salaries are constitutionally protected, and they are also immune from legal action that may arise during the course of their duties.

PARLIAMENTARY SUPREMACY

Canada adopted the British concept of **parliamentary supremacy**, as explained in Chapter 3, which meant that only Parliament can make laws and that no one individual should be above those laws. Thus, Parliament can make or repeal any laws on all topics. It then follows that the court must follow this properly formed legislation, however unseemly it may be. However, s 52 of the *Constitution Act, 1982* provides that if a law is inconsistent with the Constitution it is of "no force and effect." Thus, the Canadian notion of parliamentary supremacy is unique in that the Constitution must be acknowledged as the supreme law of Canada.

FOOD FOR THOUGHT...

Consider the case of *R v Tse,* [2012] SCJ No 16 (SCC). The Supreme Court of Canada has declared emergency wiretapping without a warrant under s 184.4 of the *Criminal Code* unconstitutional. The court struck down the provision, but gave the government 12 months to bring the section into conformity with the *Charter of Rights and Freedoms*. Thus, although the section has been struck down, Parliament has been given enough time to redraft the provision to make sure that it does conform to the Constitution. Section 184.4 will not exist in its current form 12 months from the ruling of the Supreme Court. What form it will take will be up to Parliament.

CONVENTIONS AND PREROGATIVE POWERS

Even though principles such as the rule of law and the independence of the judiciary are cornerstones of our system, many of these operate by way of conventions. Conventions are important to constitutional law, and although they may lie outside of the legal documents, they may be recorded elsewhere. One of the most germane conventions that apply in this circumstance is the role of judges and courts in the government and their independence from the executive and

4. Patrick Fitzgerald, Barry Wright, and Vincent Kazmierski, *Looking at Law: Canada's Legal System*, 6th ed (Markham: ON: LexisNexis, 2010) at 40 and 50.

legislative branches of government. It has been noted that conventions are important because they "clothe the legal framework of the formal Constitution and provide a large measure of flexibility; the operation of the Constitution can be significantly changed without having to directly amend the Constitution Acts or other legal aspects of the Constitution."[5] A convention is a rule that officials apply that is somewhere on the continuum between custom and constitutional law. **Prerogative powers** are the privileges accorded to the **Crown**, but there are few surviving powers, as they are mostly defined by statute. Some remaining powers are the Crown's power to dissolve Parliament, to make treaties, to issue passports, to grant honours or awards, to take actions in an "emergency," and to appoint ambassadors.[6]

AMENDMENT

Canadians wanted to be truly independent, and in 1981, the government agreed on a way to change our own Constitution with what was called an **amending formula.** This document was completed on April 17, 1982, and the *Constitution Act, 1982* now contained the amending formula and the *Canadian Charter of Rights and Freedoms* (discussed further in Chapter 10).

Constitutional law and the division of powers have remained stable because of the amending formula that is required to make a change in the law, as there must be consent from Parliament to change the Constitution. Once that is established, two-thirds of the provinces must agree on the changes, and these seven provinces must contain at least 50 percent of the population of Canada. Practically, this formula would mean that either Quebec or Ontario would have to agree, as together they house more than 50 percent of Canada's population. If a maximum of three provinces find the change unacceptable, these provinces have the ability to "opt out." The result will be the changes will not apply in those jurisdictions.

STRUCTURE OF THE *CONSTITUTION ACT, 1982**

The Constitution has a defined structure, and is divided into seven parts including:

Part I: *Canadian Charter of Rights and Freedoms*
s. 1: Guarantee of Rights and Freedoms
s. 2: Fundamental Freedoms
s. 3–5: Democratic Rights
s. 6: Mobility Rights
s. 7–14: Legal Rights
s. 15: Equality Rights
s. 16–22: Official Languages of Canada
s. 23: Minority Language Educational Rights
s. 24: Enforcement
s. 25–31: General
s. 32–33: Application of Charter
s. 34: Citation
Part II: Rights of the Aboriginal Peoples of Canada
s. 35
s. 35.1
Part III: Equalization and Regional Disparities
s. 36
Part IV.1: Constitutional Conferences
s. 37
Part V: Procedure for Amending the Constitution of Canada
ss. 38–49
Part VI: Amendment to the *Constitution Act*, 1867
ss. 50–51
Part VII: General
ss. 52–61

Prime Minister Pierre Trudeau and Queen Elizabeth II at the1982 signing of the Constitution in Ottawa

Tim Clark/The Canadian Press

* *Canadian Charter of Rights and Freedoms*, http://laws.justice.gc.ca/eng/Charter/

5. Bernard W Funston and Eugene Meehan, *Canada's Constitutional Law in a Nutshell,* 2nd ed (Toronto: Carswell, 1998) at 38.

6. Patrick J Monahan, *Constitutional Law,* 3rd ed (Toronto: Irwin Law, 2006) at 59–60.

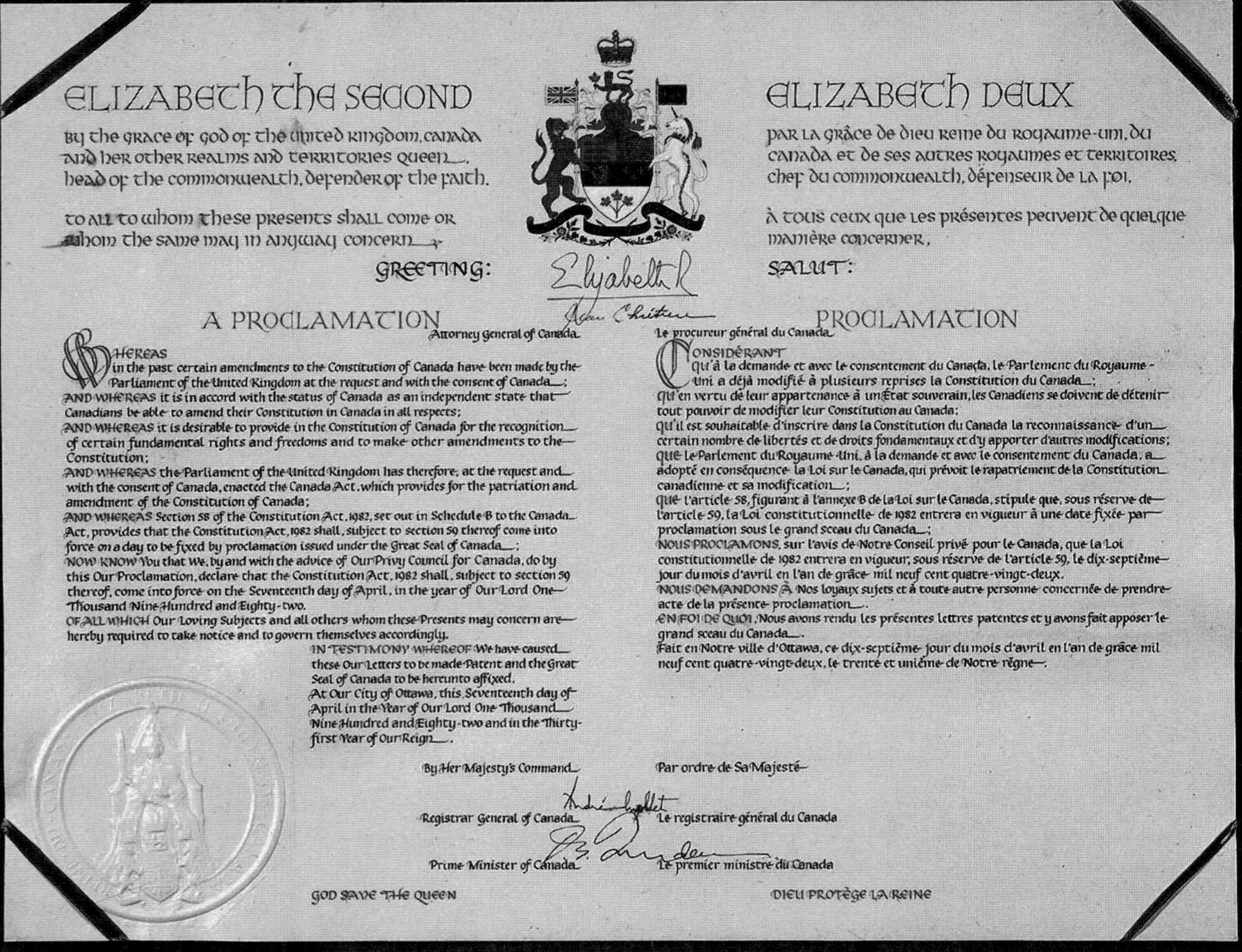

ELIZABETH THE SECOND

BY THE GRACE OF GOD OF THE UNITED KINGDOM, CANADA AND HER OTHER REALMS AND TERRITORIES QUEEN, HEAD OF THE COMMONWEALTH, DEFENDER OF THE FAITH.

TO ALL TO WHOM THESE PRESENTS SHALL COME OR WHOM THE SAME MAY IN ANYWAY CONCERN,

GREETING:

A PROCLAMATION

Attorney General of Canada

WHEREAS in the past certain amendments to the Constitution of Canada have been made by the Parliament of the United Kingdom at the request and with the consent of Canada;

AND WHEREAS it is in accord with the status of Canada as an independent state that Canadians be able to amend their Constitution in Canada in all respects;

AND WHEREAS it is desirable to provide in the Constitution of Canada for the recognition of certain fundamental rights and freedoms and to make other amendments to the Constitution;

AND WHEREAS the Parliament of the United Kingdom has therefore, at the request and with the consent of Canada, enacted the Canada Act, which provides for the patriation and amendment of the Constitution of Canada;

AND WHEREAS Section 58 of the Constitution Act, 1982, set out in Schedule B to the Canada Act, provides that the Constitution Act, 1982 shall, subject to section 59 thereof come into force on a day to be fixed by proclamation issued under the Great Seal of Canada;

NOW KNOW You that We, by and with the advice of Our Privy Council for Canada, do by this Our Proclamation, declare that the Constitution Act, 1982 shall, subject to section 59 thereof, come into force on the Seventeenth day of April, in the year of Our Lord One Thousand Nine Hundred and Eighty-two.

OF ALL WHICH Our Loving Subjects and all others whom these Presents may concern are hereby required to take notice and to govern themselves accordingly.

IN TESTIMONY WHEREOF We have caused these Our Letters to be made Patent and the Great Seal of Canada to be hereunto affixed.

At Our City of Ottawa, this Seventeenth day of April in the Year of Our Lord One Thousand Nine Hundred and Eighty-two and in the Thirty-first Year of Our Reign.

By Her Majesty's Command

Registrar General of Canada

Prime Minister of Canada

GOD SAVE THE QUEEN

ELIZABETH DEUX

PAR LA GRÂCE DE DIEU REINE DU ROYAUME-UNI, DU CANADA ET DE SES AUTRES ROYAUMES ET TERRITOIRES, CHEF DU COMMONWEALTH, DÉFENSEUR DE LA FOI.

À TOUS CEUX QUE LES PRÉSENTES PEUVENT DE QUELQUE MANIÈRE CONCERNER,

SALUT:

PROCLAMATION

Le procureur général du Canada

CONSIDÉRANT

qu'à la demande et avec le consentement du Canada, le Parlement du Royaume-Uni a déjà modifié à plusieurs reprises la Constitution du Canada;

qu'en vertu de leur appartenance à un État souverain, les Canadiens se doivent de détenir tout pouvoir de modifier leur Constitution au Canada;

qu'il est souhaitable d'inscrire dans la Constitution du Canada la reconnaissance d'un certain nombre de libertés et de droits fondamentaux et d'y apporter d'autres modifications;

que le Parlement du Royaume-Uni, à la demande et avec le consentement du Canada, a adopté en conséquence la Loi sur le Canada, qui prévoit le rapatriement de la Constitution canadienne et sa modification;

que l'article 58, figurant à l'annexe B de la Loi sur le Canada, stipule que, sous réserve de l'article 59, la Loi constitutionnelle de 1982 entrera en vigueur à une date fixée par proclamation sous le grand sceau du Canada;

NOUS PROCLAMONS, sur l'avis de Notre Conseil privé pour le Canada, que la Loi constitutionnelle de 1982 entrera en vigueur, sous réserve de l'article 59, le dix-septième jour du mois d'avril en l'an de grâce mil neuf cent quatre-vingt-deux.

NOUS DEMANDONS À Nos loyaux sujets et à toute autre personne concernée de prendre acte de la présente proclamation.

EN FOI DE QUOI, Nous avons rendu les présentes lettres patentes et y avons fait apposer le grand sceau du Canada.

Fait en Notre ville d'Ottawa, ce dix-septième jour du mois d'avril en l'an de grâce mil neuf cent quatre-vingt-deux, le trente et unième de Notre règne.

Par ordre de Sa Majesté

Le registraire général du Canada

Le premier ministre du Canada

DIEU PROTÈGE LA REINE

The Canadian Press

Proclamation of the *Constitution Act, 1982*

DIVISION OF POWERS

The Constitution lists the powers of the federal, provincial, or territorial governments and which level of government is permitted to legislate in that area. Section 91 outlines the powers of the federal government, s 92 lists the powers of the provincial and territorial governments, and s 93 gives power to the provinces and territories over education (see the following box).

91. It shall be lawful for the Queen, by and with the Advice and Consent of the Senate and House of Commons, to make Laws for the **Peace, Order, and good Government of Canada**, in relation to all Matters not coming within the Classes of Subjects by this Act assigned exclusively to the Legislatures of the Provinces; and for greater Certainty, but not so as to restrict the Generality of the foregoing Terms of this Section, it is hereby declared that (notwithstanding anything in this Act) the exclusive Legislative Authority of the Parliament of Canada extends to all Matters coming within the Classes of Subjects next hereinafter enumerated; that is to say, —

91. 1. Repealed.
1A. The Public Debt and Property.
2. **The Regulation of Trade and Commerce.**
2A. Unemployment insurance.
3. **The Raising of Money by any Mode or System of Taxation.**
4. The borrowing of Money on the Public Credit.
5. **Postal Service.**
6. The Census and Statistics.
7. **Militia, Military and Naval Service, and Defence.**
8. The fixing of and providing for the Salaries and Allowances of Civil and other Officers of the Government of Canada.
9. Beacons, Buoys, Lighthouses, and Sable Island.
10. Navigation and Shipping.
11. Quarantine and the Establishment and Maintenance of Marine Hospitals.
12. Sea Coast and Inland Fisheries.
13. Ferries between a Province and any British or Foreign Country or between Two Provinces.
14. **Currency and Coinage.**
15. Banking, Incorporation of Banks, and the Issue of Paper Money.
16. Savings Banks.
17. Weights and Measures.
18. Bills of Exchange and Promissory Notes.
19. Interest.
20. Legal Tender.
21. Bankruptcy and Insolvency.
22. **Patents of Invention and Discovery.**
23. **Copyrights.**
24. Indians, and Lands reserved for the Indians.
25. **Naturalization and Aliens.**
26. **Marriage and Divorce.**
27. **The Criminal Law, except the Constitution of Courts of Criminal Jurisdiction, but including the Procedure in Criminal Matters.**
28. **The Establishment, Maintenance, and Management of Penitentiaries.**
29. Such Classes of Subjects as are expressly excepted in the Enumeration of the Classes of Subjects by this Act assigned exclusively to the Legislatures of the Provinces.

And any Matter coming within any of the Classes of Subjects enumerated in this Section shall not be deemed to come within the Class of Matters of a local or private Nature comprised in the Enumeration of the Classes of Subjects by this Act assigned exclusively to the Legislatures of the Provinces.

92. In each Province the Legislature may exclusively make Laws in relation to Matters coming within the Classes of Subjects next hereinafter enumerated; that is to say, —

1. Repealed.
2. **Direct Taxation within the Province in order to the raising of a Revenue for Provincial Purposes.**
3. The borrowing of Money on the sole Credit of the Province.
4. The Establishment and Tenure of Provincial Offices and the Appointment and Payment of Provincial Officers.
5. The Management and Sale of the Public Lands belonging to the Province and of the Timber and Wood thereon.
6. **The Establishment, Maintenance, and Management of Public and Reformatory Prisons in and for the Province.**
7. **The Establishment, Maintenance, and Management of Hospitals, Asylums, Charities, and Eleemosynary Institutions in and for the Province, other than Marine Hospitals.**

8. Municipal Institutions in the Province.
9. Shop, Saloon, Tavern, Auctioneer, and other Licences in order to the raising of a Revenue for Provincial, Local, or Municipal Purposes.
10. Local Works and Undertakings other than such as are of the following Classes:
    (*a*) Lines of Steam or other Ships, Railways, Canals, Telegraphs, and other Works and Undertakings connecting the Province with any other or others of the Provinces, or extending beyond the Limits of the Province:
    (*b*) Lines of Steam Ships between the Province and any British or Foreign Country:
    (*c*) Such Works as, although wholly situate within the Province, are before or after their Execution declared by the Parliament of Canada to be for the general Advantage of Canada or for the Advantage of Two or more of the Provinces.
11. The Incorporation of Companies with Provincial Objects.
12. **The Solemnization of Marriage in the Province.**
13. **Property and Civil Rights in the Province.**
14. **The Administration of Justice in the Province, including the Constitution, Maintenance, and Organization of Provincial Courts, both of Civil and of Criminal Jurisdiction, and including Procedure in Civil Matters in those Courts.**
15. The Imposition of Punishment by Fine, Penalty, or Imprisonment for enforcing any Law of the Province made in relation to any Matter coming within any of the Classes of Subjects enumerated in this Section.
16. Generally all Matters of a merely local or private Nature in the Province.

93. In and for each Province the Legislature may exclusively make Laws in relation to **Education**, subject and according to the following Provisions:—

(1) Nothing in any such Law shall prejudicially affect any Right or Privilege with respect to Denominational Schools which any Class of Persons have by Law in the Province at the Union:

(2) All the Powers, Privileges, and Duties at the Union by Law conferred and imposed in Upper Canada on the Separate Schools and School Trustees of the Queen's Roman Catholic Subjects shall be and the same are hereby extended to the Dissentient Schools of the Queen's Protestant and Roman Catholic Subjects in Quebec:

(3) Where in any Province a System of Separate or Dissentient Schools exists by Law at the Union or is thereafter established by the Legislature of the Province, an Appeal shall lie to the Governor General in Council from any Act or Decision of any Provincial Authority affecting any Right or Privilege of the Protestant or Roman Catholic Minority of the Queen's Subjects in relation to Education:

(4) In case any such Provincial Law as from Time to Time seems to the Governor General in Council requisite for the due Execution of the Provisions of this Section is not made, or in case any Decision of the Governor General in Council on any Appeal under this Section is not duly executed by the proper Provincial Authority in that Behalf, then and in every such Case, and as far only as the Circumstances of each Case require, the Parliament of Canada may make remedial Laws for the due Execution of the Provisions of this Section and of any Decision of the Governor General in Council under this Section.

Even though the Constitution sets out what is a federal and what is provincial power, there are often disputes between the levels of government about whether one level of government has exceeded its jurisdiction. Table 8.2 outlines the important federal (under s 91) and provincial powers (under s 92).

It is important to note that the "peace, order, and good government" (POGG) clause gives the rest of the legislative power that is "left over" to the federal government. This was purposely done at Confederation to avoid leaving residual (or left over) powers to the local state government, as was done in the United States. As Sir John A. Macdonald stated in the Confederation debates in 1865: "we have expressly declared that all subjects of general interest not distinctly conferred upon the local governments and local legislatures shall be conferred upon the General Government and the Legislature—We have thus avoided that great source

Table 8.2 *Constitution Act, 1982*, Division of Powers

Federal Government—Section 91 of the *Constitution*	**Provincial Government—Section 92 of the *Constitution***
Peace, order, and good government of Canada	
2. The regulation of trade and commerce	2. Direct taxation within the province in order to the raising of a revenue for provincial purposes
3. The raising of money by any mode or system of taxation	6. The establishment, maintenance, and management of public and reformatory prisons in and for the province
5. Postal service	7. The establishment, maintenance, and management of hospitals, asylums, charities, and eleemosynary institutions in and for the province, other than marine hospitals
7. Militia, military and naval service, and defence	12. The solemnization of marriage in the province
14. Currency and coinage	13. Property and civil rights in the province
22. Patents of invention and discovery	14. The administration of justice in the province, including the constitution, maintenance, and organization of provincial courts, both of civil and of criminal jurisdiction, and including procedure in civil matters in those courts
23. Copyrights	
25. Naturalization and aliens	
26. Marriage and divorce	
27. The criminal law, except the constitution of courts of criminal jurisdiction, but including the procedure in criminal matters	
28. The establishment, maintenance, and management of penitentiaries	

FOOD FOR THOUGHT...

The division of powers in constitutional law is not perfect. Paul Atkinson notes that:

> Most people would expect the federal government to look after sea coasts, as they do because of power 12, but some may wonder why federal government employees look after the buoys and lighthouses on Lake Winnipeg, Lake Superior or Great Bear Lake. The federal government has been assigned "Beacons, Buoys and Lighthouses" in enumerated power 9 and are responsible for "Navigation and Shipping" due to power 10 in section 91.... By the way, why are the highways of Ontario being patrolled by the Ontario Provincial Police, while R.C.M.P. officers are performing the same function in Manitoba? It is because "The Administration of Justice in the Province" has been assigned to provincial government in enumerated power 14, section 92. Each province has the legal authority to choose the police service it desires to help enforce provincial statutes.[7]

What other inconsistencies do you find?

of weakness which has been the sources of the disruption of the United States."[8] In Canada, POGG has been used in situations where there is a "gap" not covered by the division of powers, where it is a national concern but is not provided for in the division, and where there is a national emergency not otherwise provided for.

7. Paul Atkinson, *The Canadian Justice System: An Overview*, 2nd ed (Markham, ON: LexisNexis, 2010) at 13–14.

8. *Confederation Debates*, February 6, 1865, cited in Patrick J Monahan, *Constitutional Law*, 3rd ed (Toronto: Irwin Law, 2006) at 102.

As we have seen, it is inevitable that there may be some overlap in powers. Patrick Monahan examined a survey of provincial and federal legislation and found that the only exclusive federal spheres were "military defence, veterans' affairs, the postal service, and monetary policy."[9] Similarly, the only areas of provincial matters that were exclusive were "municipal institutions, elementary and secondary education, and some areas of law related to property and other non-criminal matters."[10] To expect these areas to be what has been described as "watertight compartments" is not so realistic.[11]

TERRITORIAL POWERS

It is also worth noting that the territories of Yukon, Northwest Territories, and Nunavut have a different status than the provinces. All three territories were created by federal statutes: *Yukon Act,* SC 2002, c 7; *Northwest Territories Act,* RSC 1985, c N-27; and *Nunavut Act,* SC 1993, c 28. This legislation dictates the powers that can be controlled by territorial governments, which takes the language from ss 92 and 93 of the *Constitution Act,* but these powers may be taken away by the federal government without using the amending formula that would be used with a province.

CONSTITUTIONAL ISSUES AND THE COURTS

Much of the time it is up to the courts to interpret whether an area is within the jurisdiction of the federal or provincial government. Practically, this is difficult to do. For example, how do judges

> decide whether pornography and prostitution—censorship and anti-soliciting rules— fall within the domain of criminal law? Does the federal government's power over trade and commerce embrace activities such as Sunday shopping or television advertising aimed at young children? Or are all these issues really about "property and civil rights" in the province, and more matters of a "merely local or private nature"?[12]

Sometimes the overlap works quite well. As will be seen in Chapter 12, s 91 gives the federal government the responsibility for the "establishment, maintenance, and management of penitentiaries," but s 92 gives the provinces power over the "establishment, maintenance, and management of public and reformatory prisons." The practical difference is that those serving a sentence of two years or more will serve their time in federal penitentiaries, while those serving less than two years will be in a provincial institution.

However, there are times when the division is not tenable, and the parties will request the assistance of the courts. There are various ways that a constitutional issue can come before the courts. The first is through a factual dispute with the government or an individual who alleges that a statute is unconstitutional because it is outside the powers of the legislating body. The courts may also hear these issues if a party to a legal dispute contends that the interpretation of the legislation makes it beyond the powers of that level of government (see the discussion of *ultra vires* powers on page 211). The last way that it may come before the courts is by way of a **reference**. The federal government may ask the courts for an opinion regarding federal or provincial legislation. Although these decisions are technically non-binding, governments traditionally treat them as if they were, and these decisions have been helpful in a variety of situations. Some criticize this use of the justice system when no real parties are involved, but others have noted that this is an effective tool for the functioning of the system. The Governor in Council has jurisdiction to order a reference, but the Supreme Court has the discretion to refuse to hear a reference if there is not enough material in the record, or there is

9. Patrick J Monahan, *Constitutional Law,* 3rd ed (Toronto: Irwin Law, 2006) at 105.

10. *Ibid* at 105.

11. *Ibid* at 105.

12. David Beatty, *Constitutional Law in Theory and Practice* (Toronto: University of Toronto Press, 1995) at 21.

no foundation to the reference, or it would be otherwise inappropriate. An example of a reference occurred when the government was deciding whether to extend marriage to same-sex couples (see the following case box).

REFERENCE RE SAME-SEX MARRIAGE, [2004] 3 SCR 698 (SCC)

The court was faced with the general question of whether the existing common law definition of marriage would remain "voluntary union for life of one man and one woman, to the exclusion of all others" or shift to the voluntary union of two persons to the exclusion of all others. This was not a particular case with one individual seeking individual rights but something that more broadly applied to many individuals in Canada. Pursuant to s 53 of the *Supreme Court Act*, the Governor in Council referred the following questions to the Supreme Court:

> 1. Is the annexed Proposal for an Act respecting certain aspects of legal capacity for marriage for civil purposes within the exclusive legislative authority of the Parliament of Canada? If not, in what particular or particulars, and to what extent?
>
> 2. If the answer to question 1 is yes, is section 1 of the proposal, which extends capacity to marry to persons of the same sex, consistent with the Canadian *Charter of Rights and Freedoms*? If not, in what particular or particulars, and to what extent?
>
> 3. Does the freedom of religion guaranteed by paragraph 2(a) of the *Canadian Charter of Rights and Freedoms* protect religious officials from being compelled to perform a marriage between two persons of the same sex that is contrary to their religious beliefs?
>
> 4. Is the opposite-sex requirement for marriage for civil purposes, as established by the common law and set out for Quebec in section 5 of the *federal law–Civil Law Harmonization Act*, No. 1, consistent with the Canadian *Charter of Rights and Freedoms*? If not, in what particular or particulars and to what extent?

The court heard arguments on all of these questions and decided that "Question 1 is answered in the affirmative with respect to s 1 of the proposed legislation and in the negative with respect to s 2. Questions 2 and 3 are both answered in the affirmative. The Court declined to answer Question 4." The result? The beginning of same-sex marriage in Canada, thanks to a reference case.

INTRA VIRES AND *ULTRA VIRES*

One of the most fundamental parts of constitutional law is determining whether a body is acting within its mandate. The language of the Constitution is not always sufficient to determine the proper method of interpretation, and the POGG portion of the legislation gives the federal government residual power for those areas not specifically mentioned. The courts must determine if legislation is ***intra vires***, or within the jurisdiction, or ***ultra vires***, or outside of the jurisdiction of a particular branch of government. (See *Reference Re Firearms Act* on page 213 for an example of *intra vires*.)

DOUBLE ASPECT AND THE PARAMOUNTCY DOCTRINE

One area of the powers can have a "double aspect," meaning that it may be a federal matter from one perspective and a provincial matter from another perspective. If both aspects are of equal importance and it is possible to operate without conflict, they can be upheld as double aspect. Thus, Parliament may define the rights that will operate federally, and the legislature will have regulations to structure the matter from a provincial viewpoint.

Conversely, if laws conflict and the law cannot comply with both elements, the court has developed a system of federal paramountcy to be used where the federal legislation trumps the provincial. This means that the provincial aspect will be inoperable, and this may only affect a certain portion of the legislation. If the federal legislation eventually ceases to exist (if it is struck down or repealed), the provincial counterpart can again be activated. However, if it is possible for citizens to comply with both laws, both may be allowed to apply concurrently, but if they are in conflict, the federal law will prevail. An example of this conflict was seen in *Law Society of British Columbia v Mangat* (see the following case box).

LAW SOCIETY OF BRITISH COLUMBIA v MANGAT, [2001] 3 SCR 113 (SCC)

In this case, the provincial legislation provided that those who appear on behalf of others at the Immigration and Refugee Board be licensed under the provincial *Legal Profession Act,* SBC 1998 Chapter 9. However, the federal *Immigration Act* said that non-lawyers could represent refugees. The Supreme Court found that the provincial legislation conflicted with the purpose of the federal legislation. Thus, the court found that provincial laws could not operate where they were in conflict with federal legislation, and the federal *Immigration Act* prevailed.

INTERJURISDICTIONAL IMMUNITY DOCTRINE

Related to paramountcy is the interjurisdictional immunity doctrine. This doctrine governs what happens if there is an overlap between federal and provincial jurisdiction in the essential core of a constitutional power. Thus, provincial legislation may not apply if there is federal legislation to govern this core principle. Paramountcy is only triggered when there is both a valid piece of provincial and federal legislation, but for interjurisdictional immunity, there need not be a law in conflict, and there may not even be any federal legislation. Despite the lack of federal legislation, the provincial law would be inapplicable. Interjurisdictional immunity only works to invalidate provincial law and not federal legislation. As noted in *DFS Ventures Inc. v Manitoba (Liquor Control Commission)*, "the effect of the provincial law would be to ... affect a vital part of a federally-regulated enterprise"; thus, the federal law should be the only legislation to apply in these situations.[13]

MUNICIPALITIES AND DELEGATION

Although the Constitution provides for the federal and provincial/territorial division of powers, municipalities are also given responsibilities by the provinces. There is also the ability of the bodies to use "delegation" in order to request that one level of government assume the responsibility for an area of public policy. Cities, towns, townships, counties, villages, and hamlets may be delegated certain responsibilities, including the ability to pass bylaws. Regulations about noise complaints, garbage, special speed safety zones around schools, and building permits are also given to the municipalities, and they regulate these issues through municipal bylaws.

CRIMINAL LAW

As we have discussed, constitutional law is the link between civil and criminal law. Responsibility for criminal law was divided in the Constitution between the federal

13. *DFS Ventures Inc. v Manitoba (Liquor Control Commission)*, 2003 MBCA 33 (CA).

government, which enacts criminal law and procedure under 91(27), and the provinces under s 92(14), which gives the provinces power over the "administration of justice in the province." Thus, provinces are responsible for the policy, laying charges, and prosecuting offences in provincially run courts, while the federal government defines what is strictly illegal under the *Criminal Code*. The *Criminal Code* is federal legislation, but municipal bylaws and provincial offences like traffic violations are the responsibility of the province, and they may differ province to province.

There have been many cases that attempt to distinguish between what should be a federal or provincial criminal matter. In the Supreme Court case of *Reference Re Validity of x. 5(a) of Dairy Industry Act (Canada),* Justice Rand found that there must be three factors to justify federal criminal legislation: the prohibition of a certain activity, a penalty if there is an offence, and it must be enacted for a "criminal ... public purpose," including "public peace, order, security, health, morality."[14] In this case, there was federal legislation against the manufacture and sale of margarine. Although the legislation provided the prohibition and penalty, it did not have a criminal public purpose and was not valid federal criminal legislation because it really fell within the civil rights of an individual in economic trade, and therefore was within the provincial sphere. The result is that there is much shared responsibility for criminal matters in both the federal and provincial realms. It has been noted that the provincial governments as well as the federal government may pass

> laws proscribing and punishing pornography, sharp and unethical business practices, as well as socially unacceptable behaviour in public places (for example, reckless driving on highways). The Sunday shopping, television advertising, marketing board, and labour relations cases show that trade and commerce has also become an area of joint jurisdiction. On other matters that are not expressly allocated by the constitution, such as the environment and communications, we have already seen that the courts have opted for a concurrent approach as well.[15]

Courts are often asked to determine which level of government should be responsible for a certain area of law, as was the case in *Reference Re Firearms Act (Canada),* which is outlined in the following case box.

REFERENCE RE FIREARMS ACT (CANADA), [2000] 1 SCR 783 (SCC)

In 2000, the Supreme Court heard a reference about the *Firearms Act,* SC 1995, c 39. In 1995 the federal government amended the *Criminal Code* by enacting legislation called the *Firearms Act,* which required individuals to get a licence and register guns. The province of Alberta alleged that the Canadian government could not pass gun legislation, and sent the reference to the Alberta Court of Appeal. A majority of the appeal court upheld the ability of the Canadian government to pass the legislation, so the Alberta government appealed to the Supreme Court to ask if Parliament had the constitutional authority to pass such a law. The federal government argued that it has constitutional power under s 91(27) or the "peace, order and good government" provision, while the province said that the law was within the "property and civil rights" provision in s 92(13). Thus, the Supreme Court had to decide what was the real subject of the matter, or the **pith and substance** of gun control.

The Supreme Court found that gun control did, in fact, come within the federal powers because the pith and substance of the legislation was to keep the public safe by controlling firearms; this was not simply a matter about the regulation of property. Although the

14. *Reference Re Validity of s 5(a) of Dairy Industry Act (Canada)*, [1949] SCR 1 at 50.

15. David Beatty, *Constitutional Law in Theory and Practice* (Toronto: University of Toronto Press, 1995) at 45.

provinces might have some regulation of guns, it is primarily a federal concern, and the federal government was not unnecessarily going beyond its jurisdiction. Since the federal government rightly had a prohibition backed by a penalty for non-compliance, the Supreme Court found this was a valid criminal law purpose and therefore was *intra vires* the federal government.

CONCLUSION

The fact remains that there is much unresolved business in the Canadian Constitution. Do the provinces have too much or too little power? Will constitutional change be possible without new amendment processes? Perhaps, most importantly, the future of Canadian constitutional law also lies in attempts to accommodate the self-determination of groups, including many Aboriginal peoples and Québécois, who consider themselves nations within the Canadian state. Should other cultural practices be formally recognized, and how can they be accommodated within a common citizenship?[16]

The Canadian Constitution has proven to be flexible and has largely functioned in sync with the changes inherent in modern society. This flexibility has largely stemmed from the judicial interpretation of its provisions, and most anticipate that our Constitution will continue to evolve in the coming years. Determining how the government exercises its powers must continue to be monitored and delegated between the federal and provincial/territorial systems.

LEARNING OUTCOMES SUMMARIZED

1. Discuss how constitutional law guides our Canadian legal system.

The rules found in the Canadian Constitution are the most fundamental laws of our system because they govern how the state can act. A Constitution is a body of law that establishes a framework for a government and is the supreme law of the country. Constitutional law is the system of written (and unwritten) principles that defines what power we give to our government, while still protecting individuals and groups. Constitutional law is formed from conventions, statutes, proclamations, and court decisions.

2. List the actors and discuss the powers of the three branches of government.

The powers of the three branches of government include the executive (the Queen but the powers lie with the Cabinet); the legislative (including the House of Commons, the Senate, and the Governor General); and the judicial (including judges who interpret the law). The separation of powers in this way allows the system to run efficiently in that the rule of law is maintained.

3. Evaluate how a constitutional issue comes before the courts.

There are various ways that a constitutional issue can come before the courts. The first is through a factual dispute with the government or an individual who alleges that a statute is unconstitutional because it is outside the powers of the legislating body. The courts may also hear these issues if a party to a legal dispute contends that the interpretation of the legislation makes it beyond the powers of that level of government. The last way that it may come before the courts is by way of a reference.

4. Discuss how a court determines if a body is within its mandate.

This is one of the most important parts of constitutional law, and it necessitates a reading of the governing legislation to see what is allowed. The language of the Constitution is not

16. Patrick Fitzgerald, Barry Wright, and Vincent Kazmierski. *Looking at Law: Canada's Legal System,* 6th ed (Markham: ON: LexisNexis, 2010) at 59.

always sufficient to determine the proper method of interpretation, and the POGG portion of the legislation gives the federal government residual power for those areas not specifically mentioned. The courts must determine if the matter is *intra vires* (within the jurisdiction) or *ultra vires* (outside of the jurisdiction).

SELF-EVALUATION QUESTIONS

1. When was the Supreme Court of Canada formed, and where would Canadians appeal before this time?
2. What is a federal state, and how is the Canadian system divided? What were the original provinces that comprised the Dominion of Canada?
3. How is the Constitution amended?
4. What is is the interjurisdictional immunity doctrine?

CHAPTER

9

Criminal Law

Learning Outcomes

After completing this chapter, you should be able to:

1. Evaluate the role of each of the parties in a criminal matter.
2. Analyze the elements of a criminal offence.
3. Understand the different types of parties to an offence.
4. Review the concepts involved in inchoate offences.
5. Identify regulatory offences and the difference between strict and absolute liability.

INTRODUCTION

For as long as there has been crime, there have been debates about what causes someone to act in a criminal manner. Criminal law is different from civil law, as discussed in the first part of this text, and often concerns different moral and ethical issues. Unlike in the study of criminology, the criminal law student does not ask why someone acted, but rather how to deal with that person after the crime has been committed. However, it is sometimes difficult to focus on the legal issues without a view to the moral realities. The famous British case of *R v Dudley & Stephens* demonstrates this issue (see the following case box).

R v DUDLEY & STEPHENS (1884), 14 QBD 273 (CCR)

On July 5, 1884, Thomas Dudley, Edward Stephens, Edmond Brooks and a young cabin boy named Richard Parker were on an English yacht, 1600 miles from the Cape of Good Hope near South Africa. Each of these individuals was forced to evacuate the yacht to a life raft after a storm. The four sailors went 20 days without rescue as they drifted thousands of miles from land. There was no supply of water and only two cans of turnips, which were consumed after three days. On the fourth day, they caught a small turtle, but this was

THE ILLUSTRATED LONDON NEWS

REGISTERED AT THE GENERAL POST-OFFICE FOR TRANSMISSION ABROAD.

No. 2370.—VOL. LXXXV. SATURDAY, SEPTEMBER 20, 1884. WITH EXTRA SUPPLEMENT } SIXPENCE. BY POST, 6½D.

THE LOSS OF THE YACHT MIGNONETTE.—FROM SKETCHES BY MR. EDWIN STEPHENS, THE MATE.

The way in which they stowed themselves in the dinghy.

Sailing before the wind: How the dinghy was managed during the last nine days.

How the dinghy was managed in the heavy weather: with the stern sheets up aft, and the "sea anchor," made of the water-breaker bed and the head-sheets grating.

The Illustrated London News, September 20, 1884, Courtesy of John Weedy, www.iln.org.uk.

Newspaper reporting on the case of *R v Dudley & Stephens*

the last thing they ate until the 20th day at sea. The only water was the little rain they had caught, and they were forced to drink their own urine and turtle blood.

On the 18th day, they had been seven days without any food, and five without water. Mr. Brooks, Mr. Dudley, and Mr. Stephens discussed what they should do, as they would not survive much longer without food and water. Mr. Dudley and Mr. Stephens suggested that they should sacrifice one life to save the rest and that they would need to eat one of the survivors on the lifeboat. Mr. Stephens and Mr. Dudley agreed, but Mr. Brooks objected. The cabin boy was unconscious from famine and thirst, so he was not consulted. On the 20th day, Mr. Dudley and Mr. Stephens wanted to draw straws, and the person with the shortest straw would be the one to be consumed. The cabin boy could not consent because he remained unconscious, and Mr. Brooks refused to participate. So in the end, they never drew straws. Instead, Mr. Dudley and Mr. Stephens reasoned that they had families, while the cabin boy did not. Since he would likely die before the others, the cabin boy should be consumed if no ship was in sight, but Mr. Brooks did not participate.

Mr. Dudley told Mr. Brooks that he should go to sleep while the boy was killed. The cabin boy was lying on the bottom of the boat, helpless and weakened by hunger and thirst. He did not resist, but also did not consent to being killed. On day 20, Mr. Dudley put a knife to the cabin boy's throat and killed him with only Mr. Brooks's dissent. All three men "fed upon the body and blood of the boy for four days." Mr. Dudley was reported to have said, "I can assure you I shall never forget the sight of my two unfortunate companions over that ghastly meal ... like mad wolfs who should get the most ... we could not have our right reason."[1] Some reports say that Mr. Stephens ate very little, while the bulk was consumed by Mr. Brooks and Mr. Dudley.

On day 24, the fourth day after killing the cabin boy, the castaways were picked up by a passing ship—they were alive, but very weak. Mr. Dudley and Mr. Stephens returned to England, and were charged with murder. The court found that it was unlikely that the men would have survived without eating the cabin boy, as they would have all died of famine before help arrived. It was also found by the court that the boy "probably" would have died before the others because he was so weak, and that the parties acted as they did because there was no "reasonable prospect of relief." Mr. Brooks was not charged with murder.

The Trial

Mr. Dudley and Mr. Stephens used the defence of **necessity**. Justice Coleridge, the judge in this case, stated that that Mr. Dudley and Mr. Stephens were "subject to terrible temptation, to sufferings which might break down the bodily power of the strongest man, and try the conscience of the best." However, the court found that saving their own lives was not a defence, and it was not permitted to select the "weakest, the youngest, the most unresisting" and end his life. According to the law, the two sailors were guilty of homicide because the "deliberate killing of this unoffending and unresisting boy was clearly murder."

The jury refused to say whether Mr. Dudley and Mr. Stephens were guilty or not guilty, and instead left a **special verdict** for the judges in the case to decide. Mr. Dudley and Mr. Stephens were found guilty of murder, but the court said that if the law was too severe, the court would leave it to the monarchy to exercise the **Royal Prerogative of Mercy** if appropriate and the Crown could exercise this right to intervene and grant them immunity. Mr. Dudley and Mr. Stephens were taken from the prison to a place of execution, where the court ordered them to "suffer death by hanging; and that [their bodies] be afterwards buried within the precincts of the prison in which you shall have been confined before your execution. And may the Lord have mercy on your souls."

The Aftermath

Mr. Dudley and Mr. Stephens were, in fact, given a royal prerogative of mercy and instead of death, their sentence was reduced to life imprisonment. However, the authorities

1. AWB Simpson, *Cannibalism and the Common Law: The Story of the Tragic Last Voyage of the Mignonette and the Strange Legal Proceedings to Which It Gave Rise* (Chicago: University of Chicago Press, 1984).

exercised their discretion and released Mr. Dudley and Mr. Stephens after six months' imprisonment.[2]

Some authors have reported that both Mr. Dudley and Mr. Stephens assumed that they would be promptly pardoned for their crime, and the news of the six-month sentence was a shock. Mr. Stephens wrote 23 letters to the **Home Office,** reflecting his distress at this sentence. Soon after his release, he returned to his maritime career, but he apparently never fully recovered, and died in 1914 at the age of 66. Mr. Dudley emigrated to Australia to begin a new career, but the stigma of the trial barred him from taking up a position as ship's master again. He died in 1900 of the bubonic plague.

What would you have done if you were Mr. Dudley or Mr. Stephens?
Were Mr. Dudley and Mr. Stephens justified in killing the cabin boy?
What considerations would you take into account?
Is murder ever justified?
How should the legal system respond?
Was it wrong that Mr. Brooks was not charged with murder, as he also ate the cabin boy?
Mr. Stephens did not physically murder the boy. Should he be as responsible as Mr. Dudley, or as free as Mr. Brooks?
Did Mr. Dudley suffer a harsher punishment and more legal scrutiny than Mr. Stephens?
What would you do if you were the judge?

SOURCES OF THE CRIMINAL LAW

The difficult moral issues of the criminal law are seen in many forms. When we open the morning newspaper, we are led to believe that criminal activity is rampant. However, not all things that we consider immoral are crimes. The purpose of criminal law is for social order, not necessarily moral order. For example, some think that sex outside of marriage is morally wrong, but it is not criminally actionable unless a party is underage, there is no consent, or in such situations where there may be lewd behaviour in public. Thus, certain situations may be immoral, but they are not necessarily criminal.

To examine the criminal law in more depth, it is important to see where its power comes from. The power to prosecute criminal matters comes from what is called the **division of powers** in the *Constitution Act,* which provides that lawmaking is the responsibility of the federal government under s 91, and the provinces' powers are discussed under s 92. The *Criminal Code* is a federal document. Only the federal government has the power to enact criminal legislation. The provincial and territorial governments also have the authority to make legislation when it comes to certain other matters. For example, provincial governments can legislate driving **offences** (such as driving while your licence is suspended under the *Highway Traffic Act*) and other provincial offences, which are sometimes called "quasi-criminal" matters, within their own jurisdictions.

There are also ancient principles that guide the criminal law. What we call an offence is important—an act is only a crime if Parliament has deemed it a crime. An individual can only be punished if, at the time of the action, the act was criminal. The state cannot apply the law retroactively to an action that was previously legal. This has become an issue arising with technological advances. For example, cyber-bulling is becoming an important issue, but this is something that was not specifically anticipated in the legislation. Individuals are being charged under harassment or defamatory libel under the *Criminal Code,* which was not designed for this exact purpose, and new provisions may need to be drafted. Conversely, things that were once considered criminal are no longer defined that way. For example, homosexuality was previously an offence, and abortion was a crime. Until 1972 attempted suicide was an offence, but it was removed, leaving only the offence of "counselling or aiding suicide" under s 241 of the *Criminal Code.*

2. See R Cairns-Way and RM Mohr, *Dimensions of Criminal Law,* 2nd ed (Toronto: Emond Montgomery, 1996) at 955.

Similarly, the punishment for an offence could change. For example, Canada had capital punishment for some crimes, but this was eliminated when the state no longer sanctioned this punishment. On July 14, 1976, the first step towards the abolition of the death penalty proceeded through Bill, C-84, which passed by a narrow margin (with the exception of certain offences under national defence). In 1998, Parliament fully removed the death penalty with the passing of *An Act to Amend the National Defence Acts*, SC 1998, c 35.

It is important to remember that through the **rule of law,** all people are equal, and no one is above the law. The law must be certain and not vague. If it is too vague, a court can say that it is **void** because people could not tell if their actions were criminal. If there is ambiguity in the legislation, the uncertainty is decided in favour of the accused. This is important because the state could draft this legislation in any way it wished, so the benefit of the doubt favours the accused when there is a question about what the statute says.

When studying Canadian criminal law, the *Canadian Criminal Code* will be the most important document, but there are others like the *Controlled Drugs and Substances Act,* SC 1996, c 19, that function in conjunction with the criminal law. For example, drug trafficking would come under s 5 of the *Controlled Drugs and Substances Act,* but the money made from those offences might be forfeited under s 462.37 of the *Criminal Code.*

There are two primary sources of criminal law in Canada: (1) legislation or statute law, and (2) **common law**, the judicial decisions that have interpreted the legislation.

Legislation

"Bad laws are the worst sort of tyranny."

—Edmund Burke, Speech at Bristol, 1780

Legislation is the process of making written law by a branch of the government. As we have discussed, the Parliament of Canada has jurisdiction under the *Constitution Act, 1867* to enact criminal law and create crimes. Pursuant to s 91(27), federal Parliament has jurisdiction in the field of "criminal law and the procedures relating to criminal matters." The primary source of Canadian criminal law is the *Criminal Code,* which was drafted (but never enacted) in England. Canadians took this document and enacted the *Code* in 1892, revised it in 1955, and amended it frequently over the last few decades.

Crime consists of conduct that is prohibited because it has a negative impact on the public, and the law dictates what penalty can be imposed when the law is violated. The *Criminal Code* consists of the many rules and is called **substantive criminal law** because it talks about specific crimes and defences (summary, indictable, and hybrid, as will be discussed). Criminal procedure consists of other documents like the *Canada Evidence Act,* RSC 1985, c C-5, the *Constitution Act,* and the *Canadian Charter of Rights and Freedoms,* being Schedule B to the *Canada Act 1982* (UK), 1982, c 11, which tempers what can be accomplished under criminal law.

Common Law

Although legislation is essential in the criminal law, the common law is also important. There are many areas of the law that are not codified in the criminal code. Necessity is a defence under our criminal law, but there is nothing in the *Criminal Code* that discusses this particular justification. Section 8 (3) of the *Criminal Code* provides that if the common law creates a justification or an excuse, that concept continues to be in force as long as it is not inconsistent with the *Criminal Code.* This creates what we call a **common law defence**. The result is that common law defences (like the defence of necessity in *R v Dudley & Stephens*) can continue to grow through case law. New defences can be created when they are seen as needed in our system. However, other than contempt of court, there are no common law *offences*. If the government wants some conduct to be illegal, it must draft legislation that formally makes it against the law.

Civil Law and Criminal Law

As discussed in Chapter 3, there are many differences between the two distinct areas of law. A case involving assault and battery can be both a civil and a criminal matter, but the results are very different. A civil matter will involve procedural matters, including the filing of a statement of claim and a statement of defence (usually by trained lawyers). The victim has control of the civil law matter, the plaintiff usually seeks damages in the form of money, and the case is proven on a balance of probabilities. **Tort** is a private wrong while crime is a public matter, and the purpose of the criminal law is to protect society from dangerous conduct. For example, consider if Mr. Singh assaults Mr. Manni by punching him in the face. Mr. Manni decides to sue in tort for damages resulting from the injuries he suffered, including the medical expenses, loss of his income, and his pain and suffering. In criminal law, Mr. Manni would go to the police, they would consider charges under the *Criminal Code,* and the state would prosecute Mr. Singh for his actions.

In a criminal court, the case is heard by a provincially or federally appointed judge with or without a jury, and the case is brought in the name of the state (*Regina v Chapman* or *R v Chapman*). The Crown attorney employed by the state will prepare the case (largely without the input of the victim), and the accused will plead "guilty" or "not guilty." The victim will have little control over the matter, and the injured person often gets no personal benefit, as the convicted individual will either face incarceration by the state, after being found guilty beyond a reasonable doubt, or will have to pay a fine, which often goes to the state and not the victim (although there are some provisions for reparation, as will be seen in Chapter 12). The injured party in criminal law is deemed to be the state, not just the person physically or psychologically impacted by the crime. The only role that the criminal victim may have is as a witness, and the victim may not even be able to take that role if he or she is severely injured or deceased.

The differences between the two systems are reflected by the different terms used. In a civil trial there is a plaintiff and a defendant, while in a criminal proceeding there is the state and an accused. In a civil matter, the defendant is found liable and collects damages after the judgment, while the accused in a criminal trial is found guilty and will be convicted and punished. The maxim that it is "better to let nine guilty persons go free than convict one innocent person" is a cornerstone of the criminal system. If the wrong judgment is given in a civil trial, only a few individuals will feel its impact, but in a criminal trial the fundamental basis of our system is brought into question for all if one innocent person is found guilty. Table 9.1 outlines the differences between the civil and criminal law.

Originally, crimes were divided into treason, felonies, and misdemeanors (terms which are still used in the United States). Today, Canadian criminal offences are divided into summary, indictable, and hybrid offences. **Summary conviction** offences are those crimes that are considered less serious than indictable offences. Section 787 of the *Criminal Code* provides that:

> 787. (1) *Unless otherwise provided by law*, everyone who is convicted of an offence punishable on summary conviction is liable to a fine of not more than five thousand dollars or to a term of imprisonment not exceeding six months or to both.

Table 9.1 Differences between Civil and Criminal Law

Civil Law	Criminal Law
Private matter	Public matter
Focus on the individual	Focus on society
File a statement of claim and defence	Police collect information to give to Crown, this is disclosed to the defence
Plaintiff and defendant	State (Crown) and accused
Plaintiff has control of the matter	Victim does not have control of the prosecution
Found liable for damages	Found guilty and convicted (and punished)
Damages usually in the form of money	Punishment often in the form of imprisonment

An example of a summary offence is s 177 of the *Criminal Code,* "Trespassing at Night," which states:

> 177. Every one who, without lawful excuse, the proof of which lies on him, loiters or prowls at night on the property of another person near a dwelling-house situated on that property is guilty of an offence punishable on summary conviction.

Indictable offences are more serious and may have more serious consequences. They are punishable by sentences of two, five, ten, fourteen years or **life in prison** (25 years). An example of an indictable offence is murder, which, under s 235 of the *Criminal Code,* states that:

> 235. (1) Every one who commits first degree murder or second degree murder is guilty of an indictable offence and shall be sentenced to imprisonment for life.

Those charged with an indictable offence may have a choice of court.

The *Criminal Code* also defines **hybrid** offences, which may be tried as indictable or summary offences at the choice of the Crown, and may depend on factors such as future plea negotiations, or if the Crown thinks it can get a conviction for an indictable offence. Until the Crown elects that a hybrid offence will be tried as an indictable or summary offence, it proceeds as an indictable offence in accordance with the *Interpretation Act,* RSC 1985, c I-21, s 34(1). An example of a hybrid offence is s 218 of the *Criminal Code,* "Abandoning a Child," which says that:

> s 218 Every one who unlawfully abandons or exposes a child who is under the age of ten years, so that its life is or is likely to be endangered or its health is or is likely to be permanently injured,
>
> (*a*) is guilty of an indictable offence and liable to imprisonment for a term not exceeding five years; or
>
> (*b*) is guilty of an offence punishable on summary conviction and liable to imprisonment for a term not exceeding eighteen months.

Note that although s 218 (b) is a summary offence, it is specifically provided in the legislation that imprisonment may be up to 18 months rather than the standard six months. Hybrid offences are sometimes also referred to as "dual procedure" offences or "Crown option" offences, as the prosecutor is in full power of how this offence proceeds. Table 9.2 provides some examples of the types of offences in Canada.

Election between summary or indictable offences on the part of the Crown is also important because it may determine what institution an individual is sentenced to given the seriousness of the crime. Section 743.1 of the *Criminal Code* provides that those sentenced to more than two years must serve their sentence in a penitentiary, which is a federal institution and is often much more punitive than a provincial institution.

STRUCTURE OF THE CRIMINAL LAW COURT SYSTEM

The Adversarial System

The system of criminal law (in addition to civil law) follows the **adversarial system**, in which disputes are resolved by an impartial decision-maker after hearing the evidence of both sides. This tradition has evolved over time to include antagonistic parties who are both arguing over the guilt or lack of guilt of the accused. At one point in history, the parties would physically fight one another to determine the winner.

Today in criminal law, the opposing sides are the state (represented by the Crown attorney) and the individual accused (represented by the defence lawyer). The Crown has the burden of proving that the individual committed the crime **beyond a reasonable doubt**. Beyond a reasonable doubt was defined in the criminal case of *R v Lachance,* [1963] 2 CCC 14 (Ont CA) as the "burden cast upon the Crown is to prove all essential ingredients of the crime charged beyond a reasonable doubt, viz. 'outside the limit or sphere of' or 'past' a reasonable doubt." Thus, the Crown does not have to prove that the evidence is certain

Table 9.2 Types of Criminal Offence in Canada

Offence name	Description	What the *Code* says	Example
Summary offences	Less serious than indictable	787. (1) Unless otherwise provided by law, everyone who is convicted of an offence punishable on summary conviction is liable to a fine of not more than five thousand dollars or to a term of imprisonment not exceeding six months or to both.	s 177 trespassing at night, s 174 nudity
Indictable offences	More serious than summary	235. (1) Every one who commits first degree murder or second degree murder is guilty of an indictable offence and shall be sentenced to imprisonment for life.	s 235 first- or second-degree murder s 99 weapons trafficking
Hybrid offences	Offences which can be tried as either of the above, at the choice of the Crown.	s. 218 Every one who unlawfully abandons or exposes a child who is under the age of ten years, so that its life is or is likely to be endangered or its health is or is likely to be permanently injured, (*a*) is guilty of an indictable offence and liable to imprisonment for a term not exceeding five years; or (*b*) is guilty of an offence punishable on summary conviction and liable to imprisonment for a term not exceeding eighteen months.	s. 218 abandoning a child s. 264 uttering threats

and there is no chance of error, but that the evidence is so complete and convincing that reasonable doubts are erased from the minds of the judge or jury.

Our adversarial system places a great deal of emphasis on playing by the rules. This is something that we call "due process." Section 1 (a) of the *Canadian Bill of Rights*, RSC 1970, App. III, states that due process means the court system must act "according to the legal processes recognized by Parliament and the Courts in Canada." Our system emphasizes and prioritizes the procedural fairness rather than a search for the "truth." *How* you establish guilt might be just as important as the truth.

Role of the Parties

Crown Attorneys

From the Crown: Mark T. Poland, Assistant Crown Attorney, Waterloo Region Crown Attorney's Office

The role of the Crown in Canada is, put simply, to act on behalf of an Attorney General, in order to prosecute cases that have been placed before the courts by persons (mostly police officers), who claim to have reasonable grounds to believe that an offence contrary to Canadian law has occurred.

Diagram of the Superior Court of Justice

The role of the prosecutor, at least in common law jurisdictions, has evolved significantly, and has over hundreds of years adopted a progressively more public character. In the English common law tradition, while crimes against the sovereign were addressed by the Crown's representative, crimes against individual persons were generally understood to be private matters. In the result, most prosecutions were conducted by private individuals in order to address the alleged personal wrongs. As one can imagine, such prosecutions often became expressions of vengeance and private rancour.[3] In an effort to remedy this situation, Henry VIII proposed the prosecution of penal statutes by a group of Crown-appointed prosecutors.[4] The proposal was not immediately accepted, and the process of conversion of the private prosecution scheme into a public prosecution system was incremental and slow to evolve. In fact, it was not until the early part of the nineteenth century that prosecutors began to appear even in the most significant criminal cases such as murder.[5]

In most jurisdictions in Canada today, criminal cases are prosecuted by Crown counsel. Crown counsel are provincially appointed lawyers who act as agent for the Attorney General of the province. In order to understand the evolution of the role of the Crown in modern prosecutions, one requires an understanding of two basic concepts: the prosecutor's authority and how that authority is exercised.

The modern prosecutorial authority in Canada is not defined clearly in a single source. Instead, it exists as an amalgam of four primary sources: historical convention, the Constitution, legislation, and, perhaps somewhat surprisingly, to a significant degree in convention and the common law.

The *Constitution Act, 1867* is the backbone of our modern federal state. It provides a separation of legislative authority between the provinces and the federal government. Unfortunately, the division of powers in sections 91 and 92 of the *Constitution Act, 1867*, does

3. For an excellent discussion of the historical roots of criminal prosecutions, see Brian A Grosman, *The Prosecutor: An Inquiry into the Exercise of Discretion* (Toronto: University of Toronto Press, 1969). See also Phillip C Stenning, *Appearing for the Crown* (Toronto: Brown Legal Publications, 1986) at 241 –242.

4. Brian A Grosman, *The Prosecutor: An Inquiry into the Exercise of Discretion* (Toronto: University of Toronto Press, 1969) at 11.

5. David JA Cairns, *Advocacy and the Making of the Adversarial Criminal Trial 1800 –1865* (Oxford: The Hambledon Press, 1998) at 3.

not readily define the modern prosecutorial authority. In fact, the Constitution muddies the waters by granting broad jurisdiction over criminal law issues to the federal state in s 91(27), while reserving "the administration of justice" as part of the exclusive legislative competence of the province in s 92(14).

In order to conduct a solid analysis of the prosecutorial function in the Canadian justice system, one has to look prior to the birth of Canada at Confederation. Prior to 1867, the original colonies existed as nominally independent "new world" entities, which reported to Great Britain. Criminal prosecutions in the colonies were conducted by County attorneys, who were appointed by the colony's Attorney General. Notwithstanding that in 1867, Confederation reserved the criminal law power to the federal state, the "provincially appointed" County attorneys continued to prosecute crime by convention, as a function of executing the administration of justice in the provinces.

Of course, certain modern realities did not exist in 1867. One example includes the state control of drugs and substances. The use of the penal sanction to regulate drug possession and trafficking falls within the federal head of powers. Unlike the "traditional" criminal law, drug laws were not drafted until well after 1867.[6] Accordingly, drug offences were not prosecuted by the provincial County attorneys as a matter of convention. This convention-based division continues to this day, as federally appointed lawyers prosecute drug cases, while provincial Crown attorneys continue to prosecute all *Criminal Code* offences from theft to murder.

Apart from convention, it is clear that specific legislation, both federal and provincial, continues to both give rise to and regulate the conduct of prosecutorial authority. For example, in the federally enacted *Criminal Code*, there are a number of offences and procedures that require the consent of an "Attorney General" in order to be validly commenced or executed.[7] Similarly, provincial legislation regulates the employment, conduct, and responsibilities of the provincial Crown attorneys.[8]

The legislative and conventional roots are flushed out by common law powers affecting prosecutorial authority, which often bear importantly on the issue of how prosecutorial authority is to be exercised. The best example of this is captured in the common law conception of the role of the prosecutor as a quasi-judicial or "ministerial" actor, whose loyalty lies to the administration of justice as a whole, and not to any particular interest captured within the adversarial contest that plays out before the court. This conventional and common law direction is perhaps best expressed in the case of *Boucher v The Queen,* [1955] SCR 16 (SCC):

> [The prosecutor's] … functions are quasi-judicial. He should not so much seek to obtain a verdict of guilty as assist the judge and jury to render the most complete justice…. The role of the prosecutor excludes any notion of winning or losing; his function is a matter of public duty than which in civil life there can be none charged with greater personal responsibility.

Earlier cases like *R v Chamandy* (1934), 61 CCC 224 (Ont CA), suggested that the Crown prosecutor's function as an advocate at the bar was overtaken by the prosecutor's obligation to serve the administration of justice. More recent cases, however, like *R v Savion and Mizrahi* (1980), 52 CCC (2d) 276 (Ont CA), posit a more clearly bipolar role where Crown counsel must act concurrently as a strong advocate for a trial interest, and also as a "minister of justice," which is otherwise described as a "public officer engaged in the administration of justice." The role of the Crown prosecutor has not only been described as quasi-judicial or ministerial, but other authorities have focused on the prosecutor's duty as an "officer of the court." This line of cases does not seem to add much to the special responsibilities borne by a prosecutor, since defence counsel bears no such public duty, yet he or she is similarly considered to be an officer of the court.[9]

6. *The Controlled Drugs and Substances Act*, SC 1996, c 19, and its predecessors including the *Opium Act*, SC 1908, c 50, the *Food and Drugs Act*, RSC 1985, C.F-27, and the *Narcotics Control Act*, RSC 1970, c N-1.
7. See the *Criminal Code of Canada*, RSC 1985, c C.46, at ss 136(3) (Giving Contradictory Evidence), 318(3) (Advocating Genocide), 473(1) (Possibility of trial by judge alone for s 469 offence).
8. See *Crown Attorneys Act*, RSO 1990, c C.49.
9. See Phillip C Stenning, *Appearing for the Crown* (Toronto: Brown Legal Publications, 1986) at 241 242.

The exercise of the prosecutorial authority is not only addressed by legislation and common law. It is also controlled through the Attorney General's delegation of authority to his or her agents. While the Attorney General is a member of the cabinet, who presides at the pleasure of the government of the day, the exercise of the prosecutorial function in individual cases is carried out by permanent, appointed civil servants who act as the Attorney General's agents. These agents include the individual Crown counsel who appear in the criminal courts on a daily basis. These individual Crown prosecutors must exercise their judgment and discretion in individual cases in a manner that is independent of political influence or interference. The Attorney General's control over his or her agents is not generally exercised in individual cases, but rather is expressed in formal written directives or policies that guide the exercise of prosecutorial discretion in all cases.

These policies and directives are control measures which are, "in essence, the instructions of the Attorney General to his agents, the Crown Attorneys."[10] Provincial prosecution policy manuals contain guidance to individual Crown counsel and Crown attorneys on important subjects such as the provision of advice to police services. They also express guidance and set out mandatory factors to take into account when deciding whether to prosecute or withdraw charges for specific types of cases, such as firearms offences, sexual assaults, and domestic violence. They are specifically designed, and explicitly attempt to ensure that the prosecutorial authority is exercised only in pursuit of the public interest, and in a manner that is "fair, dispassionate and moderate."[11]

Crown Attorneys: A Summary

With this history of the Crown position, it is important to keep in mind that the ultimate burden of proof is on the Crown, with all of the resources of the state, to prove that the accused committed the crime. The Crown is required to present all evidence, even if it brings its case (and conviction) into question. The Crown must disclose all of its evidence to the defence. The Crown attorney, also called the prosecutor, has the discretion to consult with police and decide whether to lay charges, or what charges to pursue. If evidence is found that supports the case of the accused but hurts their argument, the Crown must disclose this evidence even after the trial has begun. The Crown's duty is to protect the public interest, which includes not only the community and the victim, but also the accused, and must present all credible evidence that is available. Defence lawyers often negotiate with the Crown to have charges dropped or sentences lowered (see Chapter 10 for a further discussion).

Criminal Defence Lawyers

The role of the defence lawyer intersects with the general duties of lawyers under the Rules of Professional Conduct. However, the Rules of Professional Conduct in Ontario specifically speak to the role of a defence lawyer in Rule 4.01(1) commentary saying that they have:*

> a duty to raise fearlessly every issue, advance every argument, and ask every question, however distasteful, which the lawyer thinks will help the client's case and to endeavour to obtain for the client the benefit of every remedy and defence authorized by law. The lawyer must discharge this duty by fair and honourable means, without illegality and in a manner that is consistent with the lawyer's duty to treat the tribunal with candour, fairness, courtesy and respect and in a way that promotes the parties' right to a fair hearing where justice can be done. Maintaining dignity, decorum, and courtesy in the courtroom is not an empty formality because, unless order is maintained, rights cannot be protected.

A criminal defence lawyer must represent the individuals who are being prosecuted by the Crown with all of the resources that the state has, with the (often) little money and resources that the defendant may have. Many times this individual has done something that many would

* The Commentary following subrule 4.01(1) The Lawyer as Advocate, Advocacy, of the *Rules of Professional Conduct*, in effect since November 1, 2000, located on the Law Society's website at http://www.lsuc.on.ca/media/rpc_4.pdf.

10. Excerpt from the Nova Scotia Public Prosecution Service, Director of Public Prosecutions Directives, distributed 1 Feb 11, http://www.gov.ns.ca/pps/ca_manual.htm.

11. Excerpt from the Ontario Ministry of the Attorney General, Crown Policy Manual, http://www.attorneygeneral.jus.gov.on.ca.

find reprehensible, but it is the obligation of defence lawyers to represent every one of their clients to the best of their abilities, regardless of the charge. This dedication to individuals who have been accused of serious crimes is what often brings reproach from the public to defence lawyers. The obligations of confidentiality can be particularly important for the defence lawyer and the client (see Chapter 2). Defence counsel must be conscious of their responsibilities to their clients, the justice system, and the community as a whole.

An accused can represent him- or herself at the lower court hearings, but many individuals secure a lawyer through legal aid. As will be seen in this chapter and the next, there are a multitude of procedural and evidential matters that an individual must understand to navigate the criminal justice process.

Judges

> The idea of justice and the rule of law are both ideals—part of Western society's dream—never fully attainable. So is the concept of the impartial tribunal. No judge can free herself from her background and surroundings. In a sense no judge who is not an automaton can be completely impartial. But we consider the ideal of sufficient value to attempt the creation of tribunals that are as impartial as humanly possible. . . . It is all part of an attempt to preserve, so far as we can, the real and apparent impartiality of the judge.[12]

Just as in the civil realm, we adopt the paradigm that judges of the criminal court can be impartial and make decisions independent of their own beliefs. Judges in Canada are appointed by either the federal, provincial, or territorial jurisdictions (see Chapter 2). To become a judge, a lawyer must practise law for at least ten years in most provinces.

Judges are in control of what happens in their court room, and they can decide who can observe in their court and who should be excluded. Although the Supreme Court of Canada's hearings are televised, lower courts are not, and cameras are not permitted. Criminal court judges must decide whether evidence is admissible, and their decisions form the basis of what is appealed to a higher level of court. If there is no jury, the judge determines guilt and sentence.

Justices of the Peace are appointed to preside over certain matters within the court. These duties include things such as reviewing **summons** and **warrants**, receiving an **information,** administering **oaths** for **affidavits**, and more. They may also preside over the first appearance of the accused where the charge is read, and administer other administrative matters. Justices of the Peace can also administer trials, including those that involve municipal matters and provincial matters, such as traffic court matters. A Justice of the Peace does not need to be a lawyer, and some provinces (such as Saskatchewan) provide that practising lawyers may not be appointed.[13]

Jury

Being on a jury is an opportunity for individuals to engage in the legal process, but many citizens know little about the function of a jury. Juries are expected to understand and retain all of the evidence properly presented to them at trial and to affirm legal precedent while following the rules given to them by the judge. The juror must take in the facts and make a decision. This gives them the title of **trier of fact**. Often it is difficult for a jury not to take in irrelevant elements like the likeability of legal counsel, empathy (or lack of it) for the accused, or evidence that was ruled **inadmissible** by the judge.

Anyone trying to influence a jury can be found to have "obstructed justice." Section 139 of the *Criminal Code* defines obstruction as:

> (1) Every one who wilfully attempts in any manner to obstruct, pervert or defeat the course of justice in a judicial proceeding ...

---

12. SM Waddams. *Introduction to the Study of Law*, 7th ed (Toronto: Carswell 2010) at 8. Reprinted by permission of Carswell, a division of Thomson Reuters Canada Ltd.

13. *The Justice of Peace Act*, RSA 1998, c s 6; *Provincial Court Act*, RSBC 1996, c s 30, s 31; *Justice of Peace Regulation*, CCSM 2006, c C275, s 5, s 11; *Provincial Court Act*, RSNB 1973, c s 4, s 8, s 13; *Justices Act*, RSNL 1990, c s 7; *Justice of the Peace Act*, RSNWT 1988, c J-3, s 4; *Justice of Peace Act*, RSNS 2000, c s 7; *Justice of the Peace Act*, SNWT 1998, c 34, s 2, s 7; *Justice of Peace Act*, RSO 2009, c s 13, s 15, s 17; *Provincial Court Act*, RSPEI 1988, c s 14; *Courts of Justice Act*, RS 1992, c s 106, class 2, s160, s 181; *Justice of Peace Act*, SS 1988 C.J-5.1, s 13, s 15; *Territorial Court Act*, RSY 2002, c s 79.

(*b*) influences or attempts to influence by threats, bribes or other corrupt means a person in his conduct as a juror; or

(*c*) accepts or obtains, agrees to accept or attempts to obtain a bribe or other corrupt consideration to abstain from giving evidence, or to do or to refrain from doing anything as a juror.

Thus, allowing a jury to do its job without any undue influence is a key part of our system, and anyone who violates this principle may be charged with an indictable offence.

There is a specific process that must be completed when selecting jurors. Individuals may be dismissed pursuant to s 632(a) of the *Criminal Code* if they have a personal interest in the trial; if they have a relationship with the judge, lawyers, witnesses, or accused; or if they would face "personal hardship" if they completed their duty. Jurors are notified to be in court on a certain day and are selected from pools of citizens summoned randomly from electoral rolls in a province or community (students may be called to serve in the community in which they are registered to vote). The names of the jurors are placed on cards, which are selected by the clerk of the court. Both the Crown and the defence lawyer have certain **challenges for cause** that they can make to object to a particular juror. There are several reasons for challenging (for cause) a potential juror including:

- the person's name is not on the panel;
- a person is not "indifferent between the Queen and the accused" (i.e., he or she has some sort of bias);
- the person has been convicted of an offence and sentenced to a term of more than one year;
- the person is not a Canadian citizen; or
- the person is physically unable to perform the necessary duties.

The defence lawyer gets the first opportunity to challenge the first juror, and then the prosecutor and defence are called on alternatively.

Each lawyer can either challenge or say that he or she is "content." If both sides are content with a particular juror, that individual is sworn in and takes a seat in the jury box. This process is repeated until 12 jurors have been selected, or until more cards must be drawn. The number of challenges are dependent on the crime that has been charged. In the 1990s, the Ontario Court of Appeal and Supreme Court ruled that there may be a grounds on which to challenge a juror based on racial biases. The trial judge decides if such questions can be raised. This issue has been raised in the context of Aboriginal jurors in *Nishnawbe Aski Nation v Eden,* as discussed in the following case box.

NISHNAWBE ASKI NATION v EDEN, [2011] OJ NO 988 (ONT CA)

In a recent case of the Ontario Court of Appeal, the court looked at the issue of a properly formed representative jury in the context of a **coroner's inquest**. Justice Laskin found that "to function properly, a jury must have two key characteristics: representativeness and impartiality. A representative jury is one that corresponds, as much as possible, to a cross-section of the larger community. And a representative jury enhances the impartiality of a jury." This led the court to find that a new inquest should be held because the jury on the former panel was not representative, because in 2000 the federal Department of Indian and Northern Affairs decided to stop providing band electoral lists to the Provincial Jury Centre, and thus there was a lack of Aboriginal representation on the jury. Another inquest was ordered.

Some have argued that there should be no jury trials in Northwestern Ontario until the Ontario government deals with the problem. Do you agree or disagree? Should jury trials in Canada not be ordered until there is Aboriginal representation?

Table 9.3 Names of the Provincial Courts in Canada

Provincial Court of British Columbia	Newfoundland Provincial Court
Provincial Court of Alberta	Provincial Court of Prince Edward Island
Provincial Court of Saskatchewan	Provincial Court of Nova Scotia
Provincial Court of Manitoba	Provincial Court of New Brunswick
Ontario Court of Justice	Territorial Court of the Northwest Territories
Court of Quebec	Territorial Court of Yukon
Nunavut Court of Justice (which is a Unified Court that hears matters at all levels)	

THE CANADIAN COURT SYSTEM

Provincial Inferior Courts

There is a distinct hierarchy to the courts involved in the criminal justice system. At the first level is the provincial courts (see Table 9.3).

These courts are called provincial inferior courts and are staffed by Justices of the Peace (formerly called magistrates), who have jurisdiction over minor criminal offences. These courts are under the control of a higher court, where individuals may appeal these decisions. Under this level of court are also youth court and family court.

The criminal division of the provincial courts hears all summary conviction offences, some indictable offences, and those under provincial statutes, such as traffic court. Under s 553 of the *Criminal Code*, power is given to these provincial courts for specific offences, such as keeping a gaming house or driving while disqualified. This court also hears preliminary hearings.

Provincial Superior Courts—Trial Division

Each province has a trial court. Courts under this heading are listed in Table 9.4. Section 469 of the *Criminal Code* provides that some offences must be tried by the provincial superior court of justice. These include crimes such as treason, murder, and other serious crimes. Other indictable offences can be tried in this higher level of court at the choice or election of the accused. Trial can be before a superior court judge sitting alone, or a superior court judge and jury. This court hears appeals from the provincial court criminal division and family law courts if they were started at the lower level.

Provincial Superior Courts of Appeal

Each province also has a court of appeal where the court hears cases from the superior court of justice (trial division). These courts are listed in Table 9.5.

Ontario Court of Appeal (Osgoode Hall)

Mary Lane/Shutterstock

Appeal courts are responsible for reviewing the decisions of the lower courts. They read information and arguments from the lawyers instead of hearing the evidence of witnesses. The goal is to apply the law to the facts as they were described at trial. Appeal judges use **deference** to the trial judge on the facts because it was that trial judge who actually heard the witnesses and saw their mannerisms and reactions in court. However, there might be situations where the facts were clearly used in an incorrect way that the court of appeal might interfere. While trial courts resolve individual arguments based on facts, the appeal court applies legal rules and makes sure that the law is applied evenly from case to case. A case may be appealed as a right of the individual rather than by **leave of the court**, which is required at the Supreme Court level.

Table 9.4 Superior Trial Courts in Canada

British Columbia Supreme Court	Supreme Court of Prince Edward Island (Trial Division)
Alberta Court of Queen's Bench	Supreme Court of Nova Scotia
Saskatchewan Court of Queen's Bench	New Brunswick Court of Queen's Bench (Trial Division)
Court of Queen's Bench of Manitoba (General Division)	Nunavut Court of Justice
Ontario Superior Court of Justice	Supreme Court of the Northwest Territories
Superior Court of Quebec	Yukon Supreme Court
Supreme Court of Newfoundland and Labrador (Trial Division)	

Table 9.5 Courts of Appeal

British Columbia Court of Appeal	Supreme Court of Prince Edward Island (Appeal Division)
Alberta Court of Appeal	Nova Scotia Court of Appeal
Saskatchewan Court of Appeal	Court of Appeal of New Brunswick
Manitoba Court of Appeal	Court of Appeal for the Northwest Territories
Ontario Court of Appeal	Court of Appeal of the Yukon Territory
Court of Appeal of Quebec	Nunavut Court of Justice (Unified court)
Supreme Court of Newfoundland (Appeal Division)	

The Supreme Court of Canada

The Supreme Court has been the highest level of court in Canada since 1949 (see Chapter 3). The court is comprised of eight justices and one chief justice, and it may hear a case in panels of three, five, seven, or all nine members. If there is an appeal on a question of law from the provincial courts of appeal, the case may be filed with the Supreme Court. The court only gives leave to appeal to select cases that have particular significance to the population.

The *Supreme Court Act*, RSC 1985 c S-26, states that an application for leave to appeal may be granted if the Supreme Court of Canada finds that the case (1) raises an issue of public importance, and (2) should be decided by the Supreme Court of Canada. The case must raise an issue that goes beyond the immediate interests of the parties to the case. Leave applications are usually heard by three judges of the court. As many as 600 applications are made each year, but only approximately 80 are actually heard by the Supreme Court.

ELEMENTS OF A CRIMINAL OFFENCE

A criminal offence has several elements, including

- an act or omission (***actus reus***) in violation of a law;
- criminal intent (***mens rea***);
- union of the *actus reus* and *mens rea*; and
- there must be a punishment provided in law.

The Crown must prove an offence through proving both the *actus reus* (the voluntary act or omission that is the basis of the criminal offence) and the *mens rea*. The *mens rea* is the basis for liability in criminal law and focuses on the mental state of the accused in that the defendant had intention, recklessness, or wilful blindness.

Actus Reus

The *actus reus* is the physical action that constitutes a crime with evidence of that unlawful conduct. For example, the *actus reus* of theft under s 322(1) is that someone without the right "takes ... to his use or to the use of another person ... anything, whether animate or inanimate." If it is shown on security cameras that I went to a store and took an iPad and put it in my bag, I have committed the *actus reus* of theft.

The Crown will have to prove that the *actus reus* occurred beyond a reasonable doubt. There must be some transgression that triggers the criminal justice system; it is not enough to simply think about acting, there has to be an actual act. As Lord Blackburn said in *Brogden v Metropolitan Railway Co.*, (1877) 2 AC 666, "the thought of a man is not triable, for the Devil himself knows not, the thought of a man." The criminal justice system needs *actus reus* because it is impossible to prove a purely mental state.

Crimes are divided into two categories: ones that are ***mala in se,*** which is "evil in itself" or ***mala prohibita,*** which is a "prohibited evil" that the law says is wrong. The first step in analyzing a crime is to look at the *actus reus* and the voluntariness requirement.

Voluntariness

To satisfy the *actus reus* element, there must be a willing mind. In situations such as the defence of automatism (discussed in Chapter 11), you are not consciously willing your actions, it is not voluntary and thus there is no *actus reus.* The Crown has the onus of proving that the act was voluntary, as *actus reus* has its own mental element. The act or omission must be one that a person is physically capable of doing and a product of conscious control. There is a presumption that all acts are voluntary unless the accused formally says that the act was not voluntary.

An action can be involuntary if it is a reflex or convulsion or a bodily movement during unconsciousness or sleep. Someone cannot be convicted of dangerous driving if he or she had a heart attack or epileptic seizure while driving. This is the mental element of the *actus reus.* However, the courts are reluctant to extend this concept of involuntary action too far, as can be seen in *R v Ryan,* discussed in the following case box.

R v RYAN (1967), 40 ALJR 488 (AUS HC)

In the Australian case of *R v Ryan,* the court faced a situation with a 20-year-old man who had read a novel where the hero had robbed a gas station, tied up the attendant, and stole money in order to play the lottery. In the book, the hero won the lottery, paid back the gas station, and gave the balance to his deserving parents. Mr. Ryan decided to emulate his hero and went into a service station, tied up the attendant, and held up the employee with a sawed-off rifle, which was loaded and cocked. The attendant made a sudden move during the course of the robbery, and Mr. Ryan alleged that he involuntarily squeezed the trigger. Mr. Ryan was convicted of murder.

This case went to the High Court of Australia, where a review of involuntary actions was undertaken. The court found that there was a complex course of acts done by Mr. Ryan, including loading the rifle, cocking it, taking it to the station, and pressing the trigger. The court said that "reflex action" is a term that can be used "imprecisely and unscientifically." The court found that Mr. Ryan was conscious of the situation he found himself in, and that it could "not be said that his action was involuntary so as to make the homicide guiltless." Mr. Ryan's conviction for murder was upheld.

Causation

Causation is also an element of the *actus reus.* The Crown has to show that the event was "caused" by the accused's conduct. This is usually obvious, but sometimes with minimal actions there might be a question of causation. There are specific crimes where causation is an element. For example, s 222 of the *Criminal Code*, which deals with homicide, states that a "person commits homicide when, directly or indirectly, by any means, he causes the death of a human being." One must break down the elements of the section to its component elements. The homicide must be a human-to-human killing (not the killing of animals or plant material), it may be by direct or indirect action, the person must "cause" the death, and it is understood from this section that it must be voluntary.

One of the most important questions is whether there was causation—a direct line from the actions (the **but-for test**) to the injury. For example, if you are shot in the foot with a gun and it is likely that you will survive, but you go into surgery with an incompetent doctor who cuts off your arm and you bleed to death (exclusively because your arm was cut off), which is completely unrelated to the gun shot, did the original shooter *cause* the death of the victim? The court will look at the substantial and integral cause of the death. The You Decide box illustrates what a difficult inquiry the integral cause of death can be.

Example of *Actus Reus*—Section 88 *Criminal Code* (Possession of Weapon for Dangerous Purposes)

When starting an analysis of the *actus reus,* one must start by examining the *Criminal Code* provision in question. An example is possession of a weapon for dangerous purposes, which says:

> 88. (1) Every person commits an offence who carries or possesses a weapon, an imitation of a weapon, a prohibited device or any ammunition or prohibited ammunition for a purpose dangerous to the public peace or for the purpose of committing an offence.

From this short section one can establish the elements of the *actus reus* that the Crown has to prove:

1. Was the weapon voluntarily "carried"? (Was it in the trunk of a car? Is that carrying?)
2. What is possession? Was there possession in the particular situation?
3. Was it a "weapon"? (Was it just an old-fashioned ice pick used for ice?)
4. Was it "dangerous" to the public?
5. Was it for the "purpose of committing an offence"?

YOU DECIDE

Mr. Brar went over to Mr. Luu's house. Mr. Brar was angry because his cat had been harmed by the cat of Mr. Luu. Mr. Brar threatened the cat and Mr. Luu, and provoked Mr. Luu into a fight. Mr. Luu went upstairs to get his shoes, and his wife, Mrs. Luu said to Mr. Brar, "my husband has had strokes; stop this nonsense" and "my husband is not a young man, he's had three strokes." Mr. Brar did not listen, and went outside, took off his coat, and waited for Mr. Luu. Mr. Luu got his shoes and walked 65 feet to where Mr. Brar was waiting. They had a brief encounter, and Mr. Luu was thrown or pushed to the ground. Two hours later, Mr. Luu had a heart attack and died.

The evidence at trial was that Mr. Luu was a very sick man. He had diabetes, high blood pressure, a history of strokes, and he had at least one previous heart attack. Mr. Luu was on disability leave from work, and he was inactive and overweight. He could not perform household duties such as vacuuming, taking out the garbage, bringing in groceries, or walking even a short distance. Medical experts testified that there was an "acute plaque rupture" in his heart that caused his death, but that there was an "80 to 90 percent probability that the plaque rupture may have occurred even if the physical assault had never taken place." The expert said that he did not "think the actual dropping of the body, the actual fall, the trauma of the fall, had much bearing on the matter."

Did Mr. Brar cause the death of Mr. Luu? See *R v Shanks,* [1996] OJ No 4386 (Ont CA)

Is this like the concept of the "thin skull rule" in civil law?

Omission or a Failure to Act

In limited circumstances, one can be convicted of a crime for *failing* to act in certain situations. Criminal liability arises when the law imposes a duty to act, and therefore failure to act can be an offence. The general rule is that an accused cannot be convicted on the basis of an omission unless that person is under a legal duty to act.

The *Criminal Code* provides some duties for Canadian citizens. For example, in s 129 (b) of the *Code,* it provides that there are "offences relating to public or peace officer" where the individual:

> (*b*) omits, without reasonable excuse, to assist a public officer or peace officer in the execution of his duty in arresting a person or in preserving the peace, after having reasonable notice that he is required to do so ... is guilty of
>
> (*d*) an indictable offence and is liable to imprisonment for a term not exceeding two years, or
>
> (*e*) an offence punishable on summary conviction.

Thus, an individual must assist the reasonable requests of a police officer. Similarly, individuals have duties if they create a dangerous situation like in s 263:

> Duty to safeguard opening in ice
>
> (1) Every one who makes or causes to be made an opening in ice that is open to or frequented by the public is under a legal duty to guard it in a manner that is adequate to prevent persons from falling in by accident and is adequate to warn them that the opening exists.

Duties can arise from statutes and common law rules with defined categories (e.g., parent/child, master/servant, doctor/patient, prison official/inmate).

Duty to Provide the Necessaries of Life

Other duties imposed on individuals are those imposed on parents and caregivers. Under s 215 of the *Criminal Code,* a parent, foster parent, guardian, or head of a family has a duty to provide necessaries of life to a child under the age of 16, to a spouse, or to someone who is detained, aged, ill or mentally disordered, who is unable to provide themselves with the necessaries. This means that these categories of individuals must provide medical care and goods and services to keep their dependants alive. This seems to be an objective basis—what a reasonable parent/guardian/spouse would understand that dependant would need.

If the person is injured or dies because of an omission, one can be charged for causing death by criminal negligence, causing bodily harm by criminal negligence, or manslaughter. If you have caused the circumstance of the dangerous situation, the court has found that you should take some steps to rectify the situation.

Duty to Rescue

The duty to rescue has already been established from a civil law point of view. As discussed in Chapter 1, Quebec has its own code under s 2 of the *Quebec Charter of Human Rights and Freedoms.* Those living in Quebec have a legislated positive duty to help, and this is provided in Quebec's *Charter of Human Rights and Freedoms*, RSQ c C-12. Chapter I s 2 which provides that:

> Every person must come to the aid of anyone whose life is in peril, either personally or calling for aid, by giving him the necessary and immediate physical assistance, unless it involves danger to himself or a third person, or he has another valid reason.

There is no offence of failing to rescue, but if there is failure to perform a duty imposed by law (as in Quebec), those individuals might be convicted of manslaughter by criminal negligence or criminal negligence causing death. One must find the duty to find the responsibility. No other provinces have this positive legislated duty outside of the common law.

To prove a criminal offence, the Crown must prove beyond a reasonable doubt

1. that a "voluntary" act or omission was "caused" by the "accused's conduct" (*actus reus*); and
2. this act or omission was "accompanied by a certain state of mind" (*mens rea*).

The Elements of an Offence—*Mens Rea*

In the criminal law there is a requirement that a "guilty mind" accompany the act that constitutes a crime. However, there is no single type of fault that is applicable in all circumstances, and there may also be more than one mental element in a particular crime. In addition, the guilty mind does not necessarily mean that the accused had a malicious intention. The only thing that links all offences and the *mens rea* element is what is specifically stated in the *Criminal Code*. As Justice Stephen said in the case of *R v Tolson*, (1889), 23 QBD 168, "the full definition of every crime contains expressly or by implication a proposition as to a state of mind. Therefore, if the mental element of any conduct alleged to be a crime is proved to have been absent in any given case, the crime so defined is not committed." If you cannot find the mental element, you do not satisfy the requirements of the offence.

The first step in analyzing the *mens rea* of any particular offence is to go to the *Criminal Code* and read the specific *mens rea* requirements for the particular crime. For example, if the accused has committed murder (causing the death of a human being), one must look at s 229 of the *Criminal Code:*

> Culpable homicide is murder
>
> (a) where the person who causes the death of a human being
>
> i. means to cause his death, or
>
> ii. means to cause him bodily harm that he knows is likely to cause his death, and is reckless whether death ensues or not.

Thus, if you do not foresee the consequences of your actions it cannot be murder because it is an essential element of the *mens rea* that the person foresees the likelihood that there will be a death or bodily harm or there is recklessness. One must always ask what mental elements were involved. Did the accused intend the consequence, did he think that he may cause the death, did he never consider the possibility of death or did he actually believe that death would ensue? Although these answers may be in the *Criminal Code*, many mental states are established by decisions of various cases interpreting the legislation.

It is important to note that the Crown must prove all mental elements, other than voluntariness, which is an element of the *actus reus*, in order to obtain a conviction of a criminal offence. Persons are assumed to intend the natural consequences of actions; one cannot always say that they did not anticipate that something would happen. The court will look at the circumstances surrounding the act to see if they can conclude if there was *mens rea*.

There is a question as to why the criminal law has this mental element. The answer is that the system must make sure that only those who are "morally blameworthy" are convicted of true crimes. In *Reference Re Section 94(2) of the Motor Vehicle Act*, [1985] 2 SCR 486, Justice Lamer said that "it has from time immemorial been part of our system of laws that the innocent not be punished. This principle has long been recognized as an essential element of a system of justice which is founded upon a belief in the dignity and worth of the human person and on the rule of law." Justice Lamer said that this is a fundamental principle of justice and enshrined in the *Charter of Rights and Freedoms* that those who are morally innocent must not be punished.

There are also some exceptions, including s 16 of the *Criminal Code*, which says that those who suffer from a mental disorder and who do not appreciate the nature and quality of the act or omission, or if they do not know that it was wrong, are not responsible (see Chapter 11). In addition, s 13 of the *Criminal Code* says that children under the age of 12 cannot be held criminally responsible for their actions. One must always look to the particular offence and what is required, and make sure that the individual is not excluded from liability because of a special exception.

Motive

Motive was defined by Justice Martin in the Court of Appeal of Ontario in *R v Malone* (1984) 11 CCC (3d) 34, as the "emotion or inner feeling such as hate or greed which is likely to lead to the doing of an act. The word 'motive' is also used, however, to refer to external events, for example, a previous quarrel, which is likely to excite the relevant feeling." Thus, motive is the reason why the person may have committed the act. However, good motives do not excuse the criminal actions, but motives may be taken into account on sentencing (e.g., if one killed a terminally ill relative to end that person's suffering).

Most of the time it is not relevant that you stole laptops to feed your starving children, it only matters that you stole the item. However, at times motive does impact culpability. As will be discussed in Chapter 11, some full or partial defences do involve motive. If you deliberately assault someone to save your life, your motive is relevant to establish a defence of self-defence, and the person acting out of self-defence is entitled to a full acquittal. So, although motive is always evidence of a mental element, it is not relevant to the primary examination of criminal responsibility. Showing that there is a lack of motive is important for the accused to present to the court, and a presence of motive may be a factor in the Crown's case as an important evidentiary tool, but it should not be confused with *mens rea.*

Objective *Mens Rea*

There are two distinct tests for *mens rea* in Canada: subjective or objective. The objective standard is what is expected from society, and the court will examine whether there was a marked departure from the standard of care expected of a "reasonable person." The Crown has to prove that the accused person's conduct fell below the standard of what a reasonable person's conduct would be if in the same circumstances. We assume that everyone is aware of that standard and should have known to be careful in the circumstances, whether he or she knew something was a crime or not, and to avoid the risk. The test is that reasonable persons, in the same circumstances as the accused, would have understood that their conduct was creating a risk of illegal consequences and should avoid this action. There may be an onus on the Crown to prove an objective test of intention like "reasonable care" or "reasonable steps." However, not all objective *mens rea* crimes are strictly objective—they may also allow the details of the personal characteristics of the accused, the particular activity, and the particular knowledge of the individual in certain circumstances.

Subjective *mens rea* is what was actually going on in the mind of this particular accused at the time in question, as opposed to objective *mens rea,* which is what should have been in the person's mind if the accused acted reasonably. This test recognizes that those with subjective *mens rea* are more blameworthy than those with objective *mens rea* because actual subjective knowledge or intent is seen as morally blameworthy. Murder is the most serious of crimes; therefore, the courts dictate that there must be the high standard of subjective *mens rea*. Table 9.6 outlines the differences between objective and subjective *mens rea.*

EXAMPLE—DANGEROUS DRIVING Dangerous driving is an example of an offence that has been shown to have an objective *mens rea.* The Crown must show the accused was operating a motor vehicle in a manner that is dangerous to the public, and as a result the accused's driving conduct fell below the standard of the reasonable driver acting in the same circumstances. Thus, the question is whether the accused's driving conduct constitutes a marked departure from the standard of care of a reasonable driver in the same circumstances (thus with some subjective elements).

In the case of *R v Hundal,* [1993] 1 SCR 867, the court established that dangerous driving is a **modified objective test**. The trial judge took into account the busy downtown

Table 9.6 Comparison of Objective and Subjective *Mens Rea*

Objective *Mens Rea*	Subjective *Mens Rea*
What is expected of a reasonable person	What was in that particular accused's mind
Accused's actions fell below that standard of a reasonable person	Accused fell below a standard for that particular person
Some subjective elements of the reasonable person in that situation	All subjective elements of that actual offender
Less blameworthy	More blameworthy
Not used for the most serious crimes	Used for the most serious crimes

traffic, the weather, and the working order of the vehicle, and still found that there was a marked departure from the standard of a reasonably prudent driver.

Many are critical of an objective standard. It appeals to some because of the idea that there might be some sort of "scientific method" to quantify *mens rea,* but many others say that true objective *mens rea* is impossible. There is always some element of the observer when trying to determine what was in the mind of an actor; we bring our own understandings and perspectives to our judgment of others. Dictating that one must adhere to a reasonable standard of action to avoid criminal penalty is, for some, a fallacy. Subjective *mens rea,* on the other hand, does not ask what a reasonable person would have done, but instead what that particular individual did, even though he or she knew or took the risk to commit a prohibited action. Many courts have endorsed a subjective/objective standard, or modified objective test, where the question becomes would a reasonable person, having the same knowledge of the relevant circumstances as the accused, have taken the risk of violating the law.

EXAMPLE—NEGLIGENCE Negligence is conduct that creates an unreasonable risk of harm. It, too, is measured on an objective basis, and does not look at the subjective knowledge of the individual. The question is whether the accused person exercised reasonable care. Section 219 of the *Criminal Code* states that:

> Every one is criminally negligent who
>
> (a) in doing anything, or
>
> (b) in omitting to do anything that it is his duty to do, shows wanton or reckless disregard for the lives or safety of other persons

Negligence refers to indifference to the consequences of an act and implies inadvertence. This means that the accused was *not* thinking when it was necessary to do so. However, if it is an omission, you have to show that the accused had a legal duty to act. For negligence, you must show that there was a marked departure from the standard of the reasonable person acting prudently in the circumstances facing the accused. Consider these questions in *R v Barron* in the next case box and ask whether there was a marked departure from a reasonable person.

R v BARRON, [1985] OJ NO 231 (ONT CA)

Mr. Barron was 16 years old and invited several friends over to his home where they became intoxicated. Mr. Barron and his friend Roberto decided to go upstairs and strip down to their underwear and Mr. Barron suggested that they "streak" in front of the girls downstairs. When they got to the top of the stairs, Roberto hesitated and said, "No, I don't want to do it."

The accused said, "Come on, Roberto, let's go," and gave his friend a slight push on the back. Roberto lost his balance, fell down the stairs, and eventually died of head injuries.

Although the trial court found that this act was a "slight push involving minimal force," the judge said that Mr. Barron had a wanton and reckless disregard for the life and safety of his friend and found him criminally negligent. However, the Ontario Court of Appeal entered an acquittal and said that it was not a marked and substantial departure from the standard of a reasonable person, but rather this slight push was only a momentary inadvertence. The appeal court said that the combination of the momentary inadvertence and the minimal force in this particular case did not amount to criminal negligence and acquitted Mr. Barron using this modified objective test.

Subjective *Mens Rea*

In subjective *mens rea,* one must take into account the personal circumstances of the accused. Was the individual a battered wife for ten years? Did the accused grow up in an abusive family and have limited education? This standard measures what was actually in the mind of the accused when he or she committed the act. This is the standard used for most crimes. The Crown has to show that the accused had the *mens rea* to deliberately intend to bring about the consequences *or* the accused subjectively realized his or her conduct might produce those consequences whether or not the accused actually knew the risk. Whether one should use an objective or subjective standard (or one of the many subjective states) is an inquiry for each provision of the *Criminal Code.* Again, there is no one-size-fits-all standard in *mens rea.*

Another avenue attempted by an accused is to say that he or she did not have the requisite elements of the offence because the accused did not have the requisite subjective *mens rea* for the *particular* crime. *R v Ladue,* discussed in the following case box, was a case where subjective *mens rea* was argued for a specific crime.

R v LADUE, [1965] 4 CCC 264 (YT CA)

Mr. Ladue was charged with offering an indignity to a human corpse under s 167 of the *Criminal Code* (now s 182), which provides that "Every one who ... (*b*) improperly or indecently interferes with or offers any indignity to a dead human body or human remains, whether buried or not ... is guilty of an indictable offence and is liable to imprisonment for five years."

Mr. Ladue visited his friend Veronica's apartment where he found her on the couch in a state that Mr. Ladue took to be asleep. He had sexual relations with Veronica who, at the time, was in fact dead. Mr. Ladue's defence was that he was so drunk that he did not know that Veronica was dead. In his own defence, he tried to explain his behaviour by saying that the dead woman was a drug addict and was often found in a comatose state.

However, in affirming the conviction of Mr. Ladue, the court of appeal noted that there was an "insuperable difficulty" in Mr. Ladue's defence. The court found that even if he was intoxicated, Mr. Ladue did not argue that he had Veronica's consent to engage in sexual relations with her. So, the court concluded that "if the woman was alive he was raping her. Therefore, it is impossible for him to argue that, not knowing her to be dead, he was acting innocently. An intention to commit a crime, although not the precise crime charged, will provide the necessary *mens rea.*" Thus, Mr. Ladue could not say that he did not have the *mens rea* for one offence by saying he instead had the *mens rea* for another crime. Many critics say that this was an extension of the *mens rea* concept simply to prevent Mr. Ladue from escaping liability. The following You Decide box illustrates that whether an objective or subjective standard should be used may not always be an easy decision.

YOU DECIDE

Mr. Lamb is 25 years old and has a Smith & Wesson revolver that he is showing his friend. It is an old-fashioned gun that has a five-chambered cylinder, which turns each time the trigger is pulled. The evidence was that Mr. Lamb had no intention to do harm to anyone. He pointed the revolver at his friend and pulled the trigger. Mr. Lamb thought that there was no bullet in the revolver, but he did not understand that the chamber would turn and a bullet would be inserted into the chamber. The gun fired, and his friend was immediately killed. Evidence at trial was presented that both Mr. Lamb and the deceased were treating the whole episode as a joke.

Should the court use an objective or subjective standard in analyzing the *mens rea* of Mr. Lamb?

See *R v Lamb,* [1967] 2 QB 981 (CA).

Subjective *Mens Rea*—Forms of Intent

One of the most important elements of our justice system is that to find a person guilty he or she must have some sort of intention. We have different levels of culpability for an individual who deliberately planned to kill someone, another for someone who accidentally killed someone through recklessness, another for someone who was simply blind to whether they killed someone or not, and another for someone who killed another through no fault of his or her own. However, there is often a variety of fault elements in one offence and one can be at fault for several of reasons. As Morris Manning and Peter Sankoff note, it is not "uncommon for one to *intentionally* commit an act, with full *knowledge* of various relevant circumstances, while being *reckless* as to the possible consequences."[14] There are three forms of subjective *mens rea*: (1) intention/knowledge, (2) recklessness, and (3) wilful blindness. The first type of subjective *mens rea* is intention or knowledge.

INTENTION/KNOWLEDGE Many of the offences in the *Criminal Code* require *mens rea* to be that the accused "intended" a consequence or had actual knowledge of what he or she had done. The court will ask: Did the accused desire the consequences? Did he or she have a purpose to bring about the consequences? Did the accused foresee it as virtually certain? For example, under s 155 (1), incest is prohibited in that:

> Every one commits incest who, *knowing* that another person is by blood relationship his or her parent, child, brother, sister, grandparent or grandchild, as the case may be, has sexual intercourse with that person.

Simply consulting the *Criminal Code* provision on incest informs the reader that the *mens rea* required is actual knowledge of the circumstances. Sometimes the meaning of intention will be identified in the *Code,* but more often the meaning will come from judicial interpretation of various sections.

Similarly, in s 265 of the *Criminal Code,* someone commits assault when "without the consent of another person, he applies force *intentionally* to that other person, directly or indirectly." Thus, to commit assault someone has to apply the force with intention to fulfill the *mens rea* requirement as he or she committed the act and intended to commit the act. Other terms in the *Criminal Code* have also been found to imply intent. Intent has been found with the use of the words "wilfully" or "means to."

"Fraudulently" and "planned and deliberate" are words that have special meanings in the *Criminal Code* in that the Crown must prove a higher standard. Murder under s 231(2) is a special case, where for first-degree murder the killing must be "planned and deliberate." After it is found that the person acted intentionally, the Crown must decide whether it was first- or second-degree murder depending on the intent. Sometimes first-degree murder can be found when the act is not planned and deliberate, but when it happens to a police officer or other named officials, or in conjunction to other offences, such as aggravated

14. Morris Manning and Peter Sankoff, *Manning, Mewett & Sankoff: Criminal Law.* 4th ed (Markham ON: Lexis Nexis, 2009).

sexual assault. Mental illness can also be an issue in *mens rea*, even if a full defence of not criminally responsible by means of mental disorder (NCRMD) is not successful (see Chapter 11). Some individuals can show that mental illness prohibited them from acting with intention and they may be found NCRMD.

INDIRECT INTENTION Someone can have indirect intention because he or she might not directly want something illegal to happen, but that person may break the law getting to that result. In the case of *R v Buzzanga and Durocher,* [1979] OJ No 4345 (Ont CA), Justice Martin stated that "as a general rule, a person who foresees that a consequence is certain or substantially certain to result from an act which he does in order to achieve some other purposes, intends that consequence." If the accused is virtually certain that something will occur, then he or she is presumed to intend the logical result of their actions. For example, if you blow up a building simply because you do not like the paint colour in the lobby, you will not be excused from the crime of murder because that was not the result you wanted.

TRANSFERRED INTENT Transferred intent is an ancient common law principle that takes the guilty mind toward one person, and shifts it to correspond to the act against another person to get the *actus reus* and the *mens rea* to occur at the same time. In other words, it takes the *mens rea* of an offence to an intended victim and transfers it to the *actus reus* of the same offence to another victim. This is often used in situations where *mens rea* lacks an *actus reus* and the *actus reus* lacks a *mens rea.* The accused may intend to hit one person but that intention can be transferred to the assault that was actually committed against someone else. There have been several cases where the accused meant to kill one person, but killed another by accident or mistake. The common law says you may transfer the *mens rea* element from the intended victim to the actual victim. However, a difficult situation can arise if the action you wished to commit led to a completely different crime. The case of *R v Fontaine* in the next box illustrates this principle.

R v FONTAINE, [2002] MJ NO. 363 (MAN CA)

Mr. Fontaine attempted to commit suicide. He deliberately drove his car, which was filled with passengers, into a parked trailer. Mr. Fontaine survived, but one of the passengers was killed. The question for the court was whether the intent to cause your own death could be transferred to the death of someone else. However, suicide is not illegal. The Manitoba Court of Appeal found that a person could not be convicted of murder if he or she only intended to kill him- or herself. Intent cannot be transferred from suicide (which is not a crime) to murder, as murder is the most serious crime that we have in our code. One cannot transfer the intent from a non-crime to a crime.

RECKLESSNESS AS SUBJECTIVE *MENS REA* Recklessness is a type of subjective *mens rea* that is sufficient in some offences. Recklessness occurs when an individual understands the risk as a consequence of his or her actions, even though that person does not foresee the consequences as certain. Justice McIntyre said in the leading case of *R v Sansregret* [1985] 1 SCR 570, that recklessness is "the attitude of one who, aware that there is danger that his conduct could bring about the result prohibited by the criminal law, nevertheless persists despite the risk. It is, in other words, the conduct of one who sees the risk and takes the chance." In the hierarchy of the forms of *mens rea,* recklessness is considered a lower form of culpability than intent or knowledge, but it still involves someone who is morally blameworthy because he or she knew the risk and proceeded anyway.

The situation in *Sansregret* is an example of recklessness. The accused broke into his ex-girlfriend's house. In order to prevent injury to herself, the girlfriend had sex with the accused so that he would agree to leave her home. Mr. Sansregret was charged with sexual assault, but he said that his girlfriend had consented to the sexual conduct. The court found that the accused was reckless to the victim's consent to a sexual act, and that she was not actually consenting but only acting to protect herself from harm, and this recklessness was sufficient *mens rea* for a sexual assault conviction. So, the standard is that either the accused had actual knowledge or was reckless as to the victim's consent, which will lead to a conviction for sexual assault. There is both a subjective element in that the accused actually foresaw the risk, and also an objective element as the court will ask whether a reasonable person would have assumed such a risk in the same circumstances.

It was not explicit in the legislation at the time whether recklessness could be a standard of *mens rea* permitted in sexual assault, so the case of *Sansregret* actually led to a change to the *Criminal Code* s 273.2 in 1992. It now provides that:

> It is not a defence to a charge under section 271, 272 or 273 that the accused believed that the complainant consented to the activity that forms the subject-matter of the charge, where
>
> (*a*) the accused's belief arose from the accused's
> (i) self-induced intoxication, or
> (ii) recklessness or wilful blindness; or
>
> (*b*) the accused did not take reasonable steps, in the circumstances known to the accused at the time, to ascertain that the complainant was consenting.

The *Code* now provides that consent is not a defence to sexual assault if the accused is reckless in obtaining consent. Today, either actual knowledge or recklessness are standards of *mens rea* for which you can be found guilty of sexual assault.

Sometimes the *Criminal Code* specifically mentions recklessness, as in s 229 (a)(ii) for culpable homicide, where it says that "(*a*) where the person who causes the death of a human being ... [and] (ii) means to cause him bodily harm that he knows is likely to cause his death, and is reckless whether death ensues or not." However, the Supreme Court has suggested that words like "wilfully" or "with intent" exclude a standard of recklessness. Although sexual assault is one of the most common examples of recklessness, there are other applications.

WILFUL BLINDNESS *Mens rea* also exists where the person is virtually certain something is the case but the person "shuts his or her eyes" to the possibility. In the case of *R v Harding*, [2001] OJ No. 4953, the Ontario Court of Appeal found that the accused must have "(1) a subjective realization (2) of the likely result of his actions and (3) deliberately avoid[s] actual knowledge while engaging in or pursuing an activity."

Wilful blindness is different than recklessness. In *Sansregret* the court found that:

> wilful blindness arises where a person who has become aware of the need for some inquiry declines to make the inquiry because he does not wish to know the truth. He would prefer to remain ignorant. The culpability in recklessness is justified by consciousness of the risk and by proceeding in the face of it, while in wilful blindness it is justified by the accused's fault in deliberately failing to inquire when he knows there is reason for inquiry.

In a standard of recklessness, you know the danger but decide to do it anyway (i.e., you do not care); wilful blindness means that you know you need to ask at least one last question but you refuse to do it because you do not want to know the truth. The court has found that wilful blindness can be the equivalent of actual knowledge in some offences, but in the case of *R v Malfara* (see the following case box), the court questions whether a suspicion can be wilful blindness.

R v MALFARA (2006), 211 OAC 200 (ONT CA)

Mr. Malfara was offered $50 to deliver a parcel he was told contained "clothing" to a particular prison. The contents of the package, in fact, contained marijuana. The trial judge in the case said that being asked to take an unknown package to jail "should have alerted

Mr. Malfara of a suspicion that there may be more to the parcel than clothing and required on his part to make an inquiry as to what was in the package." The trial judge said that this suspicion should have "alerted Mr. Malfara" and thus, he was wilfully blind when he took the items to the jail. However, the Court of Appeal said that the "question is not whether the accused should have been suspicious, but whether accused was *in fact* suspicious." The court found that the *suspicion* that the package may contain something more than clothing did not support a finding of wilful blindness. The verdict was quashed and a new trial ordered.

Contrast this case with the case of *R v Oluwa* (see the following case box).

R v OLUWA (1996), 107 CCC (3D) 236 (BC CA).

Mr. Oluwa was accused of importing a pound of heroin into Canada in his stomach after the first portion of a flight from Tokyo bound for Mexico City. The accused said that he did not know that the plane had a 90-minute stopover in Canada, where he was arrested when the heroin was detected. This stop was not printed on his ticket. Mr. Oluwa argued that he could not have imported a substance "into Canada" because he did not have the *mens rea* for the crime because he did not know he was stopping in Canada. The majority of the B.C. Court of Appeal rejected this argument and said that even "if [the accused] did not know his flight would stop in Canada ... he was wilfully blind to that fact. His lack of knowledge, if any, resulted from his wilful failure to obtain information which was readily available and which was of significant importance to him."

Many are critical of this decision because Mr. Oluwa must have had some reason to believe the plane would stop somewhere other than Mexico, but there was no proof that Mr. Oluwa had any idea the plane would stop in Canada. Many say that Mr. Oluwa may not meet the test for wilful blindness, but the court simply did not want him to go free when he clearly admitted that he was importing a controlled substance—just not to Canada.

Why were there different results for Mr. Malfara (see page 240–241) and Mr. Oluwa?

Actus Reus and *Mens Rea* Must Occur Simultaneously

After establishing that the accused had the *actus reus* and *mens rea,* there is a further important step—the two elements must be said to have occurred at the same time. *R v Fagan* considers what is meant by "at the same time" (see the following case box).

R v FAGAN, [1968] 2 ALL ER 442 (QB DIV)

Mr. Fagan was parking his car on a city street. Constable Vickers told him to park closer to the curb and guided him into the space. One of the rear wheels of Mr. Fagan's car came to rest on the Constable's foot. At that moment, the car engine stopped but the evidence did not make it clear whether this was because the engine stalled or because Mr. Fagan switched off the ignition. Vickers said "get off, you are on my foot." Mr. Fagan made a snide remark and left the car on the Constable's foot for a period of time until he turned on the car and moved off of his foot. Mr. Fagan was charged with assaulting a police officer in the execution of his duty.

Mr. Fagan's lawyer argued that, when the car wheel came to rest on the constable's foot, Mr. Fagan performed the *actus reus* of an offence of assault but at the time he had no *mens rea*. When he had the *mens rea*—that is, when he finally decided to leave the wheel on the foot—he was not committing any *actus reus*, as it was merely an omission and not an act. Mr. Fagan did not *act*; instead, he *failed* to act.

The defence contended that there was no "coincidence" of *mens rea* and *actus reus* as they did not occur simultaneously. The defence further argued that criminal liability would have been more feasible if Mr. Fagan's foot had been squashing the policeman's foot because that would have required a continuing willed pressure. The pressure of the car was not an act.

The Court of Appeal did not accept this submission and convicted Mr. Fagan on the basis that the *actus reus* was an ongoing one. When Mr. Fagan decided that he would not immediately accede to the policeman's request, he committed *mens rea* as well. The court said that the act was "continuing" from the time the car came to rest on the foot until the time that the wheel was removed.

There have been many cases where counsel has tried to say that there was no *actus reus* at the time when there was *mens rea* (or vice versa). However, it seems clear from the case law that there will be a bending of the rules to make the two elements occur at the same time to get a just result. The court may say that a series of events are all "part of the same transaction" and that if the *mens rea* occurs at any one of these events, the accused can be convicted.

After proving the *actus reus*, *mens rea* and the coincidence of the two, there must be a punishment provided in law for any criminal offence. This will be examined further in Chapters 11 and 12.

PARTIES TO AN OFFENCE

Introduction

There are many who may fall under criminal liability, and not just individuals. Section 2 of the *Criminal Code* defines that "'every one', 'person' and 'owner', and similar expressions, include Her Majesty and an organization." Therefore, individuals, the Crown and corporate organizations are subject to criminal laws. In common law, there were also various types of parties to a crime including the **principal,** who committed the offence; the **aider,** who enabled someone else to commit the criminal act; the **abettor,** who encouraged another person to commit a crime; and the **counsellor,** who did something to incite another to commit a crime. All of these terms were established in the common law, but now the *Criminal Code* defines these roles. The most important section is 21, which defines the parties to an offence:

> 21. (1) Every one is a party to an offence who
>
> (*a*) actually commits it;
>
> (*b*) does or omits to do anything for the purpose of aiding any person to commit it; or
>
> (*c*) abets any person in committing it.

It is important to know the differences in these terms because they may be important on sentencing, and the different terms still have some influence on how culpable a judge may see an individual. Section 21 merely states that more than one actor may be liable for committing a particular crime, and that someone who assists the principal may be *equally* culpable for the same offence.

Aiding and Abetting

As seen in the *Criminal Code* provision just mentioned, aiding and abetting are almost always used together, but they do have a slight distinction. Aiding is helping *without* encouragement or instigation, and abetting means promoting or instigating a crime to be committed. Abetting was defined in *R v Greyeyes,* [1997] SCJ No 72 (SCC) as "encouraging, instigating, promoting or procuring the crime to be committed" and this must have an effect of encouraging the principal. There are situations where someone assists with a crime without communication that would encourage, and some that would encourage without actually helping. The aider and abettor does not need to know all of the details of the crime, but just the type of crime that was aided. The distinction between aiders and abettors is still important because there are some crimes to which a particular defence might not be available.

Most commonly, a person who aids or abets is one who encourages or supplies a weapon, acts as a lookout, or drives the "getaway" car. It is also important *when* this assistance was given. To aid or abet, the assistance must have been rendered *before* or *during* the course of the offence. Helping *after* the offence makes one an accessory after the fact. For an example of aiding and abetting, see the following case box on *R v Kulbacki*.

R v KULBACKI, [1965] MJ NO 9 (MAN CA)

Mr. Kulbacki was a 20-year-old man who owned a motor vehicle. He sat in the front passenger seat while a 16-year-old female drove his car at speeds over 90 miles per hour on a rough municipal highway. He said or did nothing to prevent the driver from proceeding in a dangerous way. The court found that the owner of the car omitted to do something to stop the dangerous driving, which assisted in the commission of the offence because he did "by his lack of action, encourage her to violate the law." The Manitoba Court of Appeal upheld the conviction of the accused, saying only that every passenger would not be an aider and abettor, but in this case the accused had authority over the car and/or the driver.

Compare this case with *R v Laurencelle* in the following case box.

R v LAURENCELLE (1999), 28 CR (5TH) 157 (BC CA)

Mr. McCarron was kidnapped by four men and taken to a nearby house. His captors threatened and assaulted him, and convinced him to give his bank card and PIN number so that they could withdraw money from his bank account. The accused, Ms. Laurencelle, arrived home the first night to find someone kept as a prisoner in her house. The accused's only contact with the victim was to bring him water on several occasions, and to take the tape from his hands so that he could smoke a cigarette. She also attempted to comfort the prisoner, and it was clear to the victim that she was afraid of the principal perpetrator. There was no evidence that the accused received any goods or cash from the money taken from the victim.

The trial judge found that Ms. Laurencelle made the "wrong decision," as she did not leave the home where Mr. McCarron was being held, even though she was "free to go at any time," but rather she allowed the kidnappers to stay in her home. In reversing the decision, the British Columbia Court of Appeal found that there was no evidence that the accused "allowed" the kidnappers to stay in her home, nor did she have a duty to leave or to make the kidnappers leave. The court found that her "acts of kindness" did not amount to aiding and abetting with the offence of confinement. The court allowed the appeal and set aside the conviction and acquitted Ms. Laurencelle.

Compare and contrast this case with *R v Kulbacki* (page 243). Why were the results different?

Counselling

Counselling is found in s 22 of the *Criminal Code,* which states that:

> 22. (1) Where a person counsels another person to be a party to an offence and that other person is afterwards a party to that offence, the person who counselled is a party to that offence, notwithstanding that the offence was committed in a way different from that which was counselled.
>
> (2) Every one who counsels another person to be a party to an offence is a party to every offence that the other commits in consequence of the counselling that the person who counselled knew or ought to have known was likely to be committed in consequence of the counselling.
>
> Definition of "counsel"
>
> (3) For the purposes of this Act, "counsel" includes procure, solicit or incite.

Counselling is a much debated concept in Canadian criminal law because there has been little interpretation by the courts. To be convicted of counselling, one must intentionally solicit another person to commit a criminal offence. The person counselled may not actually commit an offence but simply help another party. The person must "procure, solicit, or incite" but these words have been given little meaning. However, the court has found that the individual must actually be encouraged by the counselling. The counsellor will be liable for *every* offence that the person commits as long as the counsellor knew, or ought to have known, that other offences could result from their counselling.

Counselling involves less participation than aiding and abetting, and counselling does not require participation or assistance with the crime. In *R v Hamilton,* [2005] SCJ No 48, Justice Fish of the Supreme Court said that "the *actus reus* for counselling will be established where the materials or statements made or transmitted by the accused *actively induce* or *advocate*—and do not merely *describe*—the commission of an offence." The court has consistently found that the accused must do or say something, as mere acquiescence will not be enough to form the crime. Justice Fish went on to say that the *mens rea* of counselling is that the accused either "intended that the offence counselled be committed, or knowingly counselled the commission of the offence while aware of the unjustified risk that the offence counselled was in fact likely to be committed as a result of the accused's conduct." Thus, knowing there is a *risk* that the person counselled will commit a crime is enough to form the offence.

Counselling is also found in another section of the *Criminal Code* in situations where the offence is *not* committed. Section 464 states that where no crime has been committed, the counsellor is guilty of an indictable offence and liable to the same punishment as one who attempts a crime. If a summary offence is committed, the counsellor is liable to the same punishment for conviction of that summary offence.

Accessories After the Fact

Being an accessory after the fact is a serious offence and holds a maximum of 14 years imprisonment. Section 23 of the *Criminal Code* provides that:

> 23. (1) An accessory after the fact to an offence is one who, knowing that a person has been a party to the offence, receives, comforts or assists that person for the purpose of enabling that person to escape.

Passively not reporting a crime is not necessarily an offence, but actively assisting a person who has committed an offence is a crime. This is often a situation such as hiding or otherwise helping the offender to escape. To be an accessory, the crime *must* have been committed (unlike in counselling). The accessory must have knowledge or wilful blindness that the party he or she is helping has committed a criminal offence, and be aware of the circumstances of the person who has offended. The key element is helping the accused to escape.

Historically, it was said that a husband and wife could not be an accessory to a crime because they were seen as "one person in law, and are presumed to have but one will."[15] However, s 23 (2) of the *Criminal Code,* which used to provide that a husband or wife could not be an accessory after the fact for allowing their spouse to escape, was repealed in 2000.[16] In modern society, can you be an accessory if you do not monitor your Facebook friends? See the following box.

IF YOU ARE ESCAPING FROM THE LAW—DO NOT POST IT ON FACEBOOK

Although 26-year-old Maxi Sopos had fled to Mexico when he learned that federal agents were investigating the fraud scheme that he was part of, he did not let this affect his Facebook postings. In Seattle, Mr. Sopos had persuaded young accomplices to lie about their income to buy cars, and then he would take the fraudulently received money and go to Las Vegas or support a friend's business. After he learned that agents were investigating the scheme, he rented a car and drove to Mexico. Mr. Sopos updated his Facebook page from Cancun to tell his friends that he was "living in paradise" and "loving it." In a post that no one could miss (all in caps) he made the statement that "LIFE IS VERY SIMPLE REALLY!!!! BUT SOME OF US HUMANS MAKE A MESS OF IT ... REMEMBER AM JUST HERE TO HAVE FUN PARTEEEEEE." However, the biggest mistake that Mr. Sopos made was to allow his friends on Facebook to be public, and he added an American friend he met in Mexico who just happened to be a member of the American justice department. This agent said that he had met Sopos in Cancun nightclubs, but had no idea he was a fugitive, and had no wish to be accused of being an accessory after the fact. Authorities contacted this agent who let them know exactly where he was. Mr. Sopos was arrested and could face up to 30 years in prison.[17]

INCHOATE OFFENCES–ATTEMPTS

Inchoate offences are those offences in which the crime is incomplete. These offences serve as a preventative measure to stop a crime from occurring, with the rationale that police need to be able to intervene and prevent serious crimes, and society has a strong interest in having these crimes stopped before they cause harm. In *R v Chan* (2003), 178 CCC (3d) 269 (Ont CA) the court said that "inchoate crimes are a unique class of criminal offences in the sense that they criminalize acts that precede harmful conduct but do not necessarily inflict harmful consequences in and of themselves." An attempt is a key example of punishing an individual *before* the harmful conduct. The *Criminal Code* states that:

> 24. (1) Every one who, having an intent to commit an offence, does or omits to do anything for the purpose of carrying out the intention is guilty of an attempt to commit the offence whether or not it was possible under the circumstances to commit the offence.
>
> (2) The question whether an act or omission by a person who has an intent to commit an offence is or is not mere preparation to commit the offence, and too remote to constitute an attempt to commit the offence, is a question of law.

Attempts are for those acts that go beyond mere preparation. The court in *R v Cline* (1956), 118 CCC 18 (Ont CA), looked at those who have made a serious attempt, and found that "when the preparation ... [is] fully complete and ended, the next step done by the accused for the purpose and with the intention of committing a specific crime constitutes an *actus reus* sufficient in law to establish a criminal attempt to commit that crime." The court has found that when determining if an attempt is beyond mere preparation, one must

15. *William Hawkin's Pleas of the Crown*, Vol 1 (London: Professional Books, 1716).

16. Repealed, 2000, c 12, s 92.

17. Alexandra Topping, "Fugitive Caught after Updating His Status on Facebook: Maxi Sopos Told His Facebook Friends, Including a Former Justice Department Official, He Was Living in Paradise in Mexico" (14 October 2009), Guardian.co.uk, online: <http://www.guardian.co.uk/technology/2009/oct/14/mexico-fugitive-facebook-arrest/print>.

look at elements such as temporal distances, geographical distances, and the remaining acts to be completed.

Attempts—*Actus Reus*

The *actus reus* of an attempt is difficult to prove. The *mens rea* in each of these cases will be complete, but not the *actus reus.* Historically, the court would look if the conduct was "too remote" from the crime to be convicted. The question became where to draw the line between acting and not acting.

The *Criminal Code* specifies that one must examine if the act or omission is "mere preparation to commit an offence, and [therefore] too remote to constitute an attempt to commit the offence" and that it is a "question of law." A judge must determine whether this element has been fulfilled. There is no universal test, so it must be examined on a case-by-case basis by looking at all the circumstances. In *R v Deutsch* (see the following case box), the court had to look to what was *preparation* and what was a *crime.*

R v DEUTSCH, [1986] SCJ NO 44 (SCC)

In this case, Mr. Deutsch sold franchises and was charged under s 212(1)(a) of the *Criminal Code* for attempting to procure women to have sex with other persons. Three women were interviewed for secretary/sales positions with his company, and Mr. Deutsch told them they could make up to $100 000 a year with some extra work. He also told the women that the secretary/sales assistant would be expected to have sexual intercourse with clients or potential clients of the company if it was necessary to complete the contract. The accused did not make offers of employment during the interviews. All three women said they were not interested, but then an undercover officer went to interview as an applicant. Again, Mr. Deutsch did not offer the officer a job.

The court asked whether this was enough to satisfy the *actus reus* of attempting to procure women, which must be beyond mere preparation. At trial, the judge said that the relationship to procurement was too remote. If the accused had made the job offer, the trial court said that this would have crossed the line into an attempt. However, the Ontario Court of Appeal ordered a new trial, and said that Mr. Deutsch had indeed committed an attempt to procure. The Supreme Court upheld the decision of the Court of Appeal. The highest court said that there are no general criteria for an attempt but rather it is a "common sense judgment." The court said that there was an element of *actus reus* even if there were other events to follow, or if it occurred over a period of time. The court stated that the act of Mr. Deutsch telling the candidates that they would have sex with clients was an "important step" in the commission of the offence, and therefore found him guilty of the attempt.

Attempts—*Mens Rea*

Mens rea is of primary importance in attempts. Section 24 of the *Criminal Code* provides that there is a need for "intent to commit an offence." In many cases, the attempt requires a degree of *mens rea* that is greater than would be required for the completed offence. For example, in murder one can be "reckless" as to whether death ensues or not pursuant to s 229(1)(ii). Oddly enough, recklessness is not enough in an attempt.

For example, in the case of *R v Ancio,* [1984] 1 SCR 225, in the Supreme Court of Canada, the court said that for attempted murder nothing less than actual intent to kill will suffice. Many have noted the illogical conclusion that this is a higher standard of culpability for attempted murder than required to actually *commit* murder. The explanation is that in an attempt, the individual has not actually committed the full crime. If the justice system is going to accuse someone of having the intent to do so, there must be a really clear intent before imposing this very severe penalty for not actually committing a criminal offence. Thus, *mens rea* is extremely important, and the bar is set high in an attempt to prevent wrongful convictions. *R v Sorrell & Bondett* (see the following case box) was a case close to the line where the *mens rea* was in question.

R v SORRELL & BONDETT (1978), 41 CCC (2D) 9 (ONT CA)

Mr. Sorrell and Mr. Bondett were accused of robbing "Aunt Lucy's Fried Chicken" in Montreal. Mr. Sorrell was carrying a concealed Smith & Wesson revolver, and pleaded guilty to that offence. However, the trial judge acquitted the parties of robbery on the grounds that the Crown had not proved the *mens rea* element of "guilty knowledge."

The store was closing early one night, and the staff was cleaning up with the doors locked. Two men in balaclavas approached the store and went to one of the customer entrances. One of the men knocked on the window. The store manager turned from where he was mopping the floor and said, "sorry we are closed," and returned to cleaning up. The men turned toward each other and made a "gesture of surprise," and walked away from the store. The men said nothing to the staff. The manager called the police and the two men were apprehended a few blocks away, and the balaclavas and the gun were found along their path.

Although the trial judge found that he was satisfied beyond a reasonable doubt that these were the two men that knocked on the window of the store, he made no such finding with the necessary intent (*mens rea)* to commit robbery. He found that the acts had advanced beyond mere preparation and constituted an attempt, but the intent was missing. The Court of Appeal affirmed that there was no evidence of intent other than the elements of the *actus reus.* The court found that there was no evidence "in the form of statements of intention, or admissions by the respondents showing what their intention was" as neither of the men chose to testify on their own behalf. The Court of Appeal affirmed the acquittal of both men because of the lack of *mens rea* for robbery.

Attempting the Impossible

Section 24 (1) of the *Criminal Code* says that one commits an offence "whether or not it was possible under the circumstances to commit the offence." Thus, if you intend to commit a crime, it is not important whether you could actually successfully *complete* that crime. An example of this is *R v Scott,* [1964] 2 CCC 257 (Alta CA). Mr. Scott was charged with attempting to steal cash under $50. He put his hand in the back pocket of Mr. Dodd, and Mr. Dodd caught him and turned him over to the police. However, Mr. Dodd's wallet had no cash inside. Mr. Scott was convicted at trial, and this was upheld by the Alberta Court of Appeal.

The judge said that it was clear that Mr. Scott attempted to steal from Mr. Dodd. The court said that although the pickpocket could not be convicted of the crime of theft unless there was money in the wallet, the situation with attempts was different. There was intent to steal from Mr. Dodd, and Mr. Scott did an act toward completing that crime; therefore, Mr. Scott was guilty of an attempt at an impossible crime, which is still a crime.

Yet, the Supreme Court has also distinguished between impossible crimes and "imaginary crimes." If an accused attempts to do something that he or she believes is a crime but no crime exists, that is not an attempt. If someone thinks that duty is payable on some items brought across the border from the United States to Canada, but in fact no duty is payable, that person cannot be charged with an attempt to commit an "offence" that is not really an offence at all.

Punishment for Attempts

The *Criminal Code* sets out maximum penalties for attempts. Under s 239 of the *Criminal Code,* if one commits attempted murder, the sentence is life imprisonment plus a mandatory minimum if the crime was committed with a firearm. If a crime normally carries a punishment of life imprisonment for an indictable offence, the maximum is 14 years for an attempt under s 463(a) of the *Criminal Code.* If the attempt involves any other indictable offence it is punishable by one-half the longest term that might have been imposed if the crime had been completed. For example, if the maximum sentence is ten years, an individual would receive five years for an attempt of that same crime.

If the offence is punishable by summary conviction, one receives the same maximum sentence as if the crime was completed (which is usually a short period of time)—a maximum $5000 and/or six months in prison. If it is a hybrid offence, the sentence depends on how the accused was tried. If the offence was tried as an indictable offence, the maximum penalty is one-half of the sentence of the completed offence.

TRUE CRIMES AND REGULATORY OFFENCES

Introduction

Section 91 of the *Constitution Act* says that Parliament has the authority to decide what acts are crimes. A crime committed in Newfoundland is the same as in all the other provinces or territories. However, provinces still have some right to pass laws. We call these offences **quasi-criminal offences.** These types of non-criminal offences (that is non-*Criminal Code* offences) carry a penalty similar to that of a criminal offence, but they are subject to less complex court procedures than are criminal offences. For example, traffic offences fall under the *Highway Traffic Act* of each province and usually carry a fine as a consequence of violating these quasi-criminal laws.[18]

As we have discussed, only the federal government has the power to create crimes. However, the provinces are permitted to legislate regarding regulatory offences. The term regulatory offence was established in *R v Wholesale Travel Group Inc.,* [1991] 3 SCR 154 (SCC) as describing a wide range of offences created by statute to regulate in the areas of health, convenience, safety, and the general welfare of the public. However, these offences often do not have the element of *mens rea* as an essential element to be proven by the Crown. Usually, the Crown must establish an offence with both the *actus reus* and *mens rea,* which are proven beyond a reasonable doubt, but this category of offences is treated differently.

Regulatory Offences

A regulatory offence is a non-criminal charge that regulates conduct in the public interest for areas such as securities regulations and trade. Regulatory offences are often dealt with at administrative tribunals and not in a court setting. Many statutes have been written to make room for bodies to administer these areas outside of the formal legal system. These tribunals may look as if they are courts, but they are really part of the executive branch and not the judicial branch of the government. Even though these tribunals are not in a formal court system, their decisions are binding on the parties. These tribunals are not permitted to go beyond their jurisdiction, and the rules of natural justice must be followed (see Chapter 7).

18. *Traffic Safety Act,* RSA 2000, c T-6; *Motor Vehicle Act,* RSBC 1996, c 318; *Highway Traffic Act,* CCSM c H60; *Highway Act,* RSNB 1973, c H-5; *Highway Traffic Act,* RSNL 1990 c H-3; *Motor Vehicles Act,* RSNWT 1988, c M-16; *Motor Vehicle Act,* RSNS 1989 c 293; *Motor Vehicle Act,* RSNWT (Nu.) 1988, c M-16; *Highway Traffic Act,* RSO 1990, c H.8; *Highway Traffic Act,* RSPEI 1988, c H-5; *Highway Safety Code,* RSQ c C-24.2; *Traffic Safety Act,* SS 2004, c T-18.1; *Motor Vehicles Act,* RSY 2002, c 153.

These tribunals have specific jurisdictions and their authority comes from laws (statutes) in which the government delegates, or hands over, certain powers to government agencies. These agencies or tribunals can set standards and regulations that persons or corporations are required to follow. These bodies often have significant powers and can levy fines, send people back to prison, decertify professionals, revoke licences, terminate people from jobs, deport them out of the country, and impose a wide variety of punishments.

Administrative tribunals are established to provide an impartial body that is intended to ensure that the government's authority is exercised in a fair and non-discriminatory way. Typically, members of these tribunals have specialized knowledge, training, education, and/or experience. Ideally, the tribunals should have autonomy from the department and not be unduly influenced by authorities. Their job is to hear complaints/grievances by citizens against government departments and resolve these conflicts according to certain principles and be consistent with the law.

True Crimes and Regulatory Offences

Some authors make a distinction between what they call "true crimes" and regulatory offences. True crimes are behaviours that are considered to be inherently wrong and harmful by the majority of the population. These include predatory crimes such as robbery and murder and, to a lesser degree, consensual crimes or **victimless crimes,** such as illicit drug usage or sales. Criminal offences carry more severe penalties, greater social stigma, and a criminal record if the accused is convicted.

Regulatory offences, on the other hand, are meant to control activities that are considered lawful such as business, trade, transportation, and various activities related to industrial production, environmental concerns, sales of food products, building regulations, game and fishing requirements, and various services. The objective of regulatory offences is to protect the public and societal interests from possible harm resulting from careless or possibly unscrupulous actions taken by business and industry. Generally speaking, regulatory offences are seen as less serious and less morally culpable than true crimes.

Although regulatory offences differ from true crimes, there are nonetheless serious penalties attached to them and they are often legislated by quasi-criminal statutes. The bodies that oversee the process are said to exercise quasi-judicial powers.

Offences of Absolute Liability

Originally, regulatory offences were treated as **absolute liability offences** and only the *actus reus* needed to be proven; *mens rea* was considered irrelevant to the charge. The idea was that simply showing that the act occurred was sufficient to attach liability. Thus, if a company was carelessly transporting plutonium in a tanker truck on unapproved transport routes, it would be guilty of a regulatory offence, even though the company might not have known, might have misunderstood, or did not care what the substance was. The regulatory body in charge for this transport would simply have to prove that the act had been completed—not what the company thought or believed—for an absolute liability offence.

Many see absolute liability offences as useful in preventing harm to the public welfare, and those entrusted with these tasks need to meet a high standard of care. Absolute liability offences eliminate many "loopholes" that individuals and/or corporations would use to avoid responsibility. Some argue that if you eliminate the loopholes, everyone will go above and beyond and take precautionary measures not to come within the regulatory regime. The argument is that absolute liability offences create administrative efficiency as it is far too much of a burden for the Crown to prove mental culpability. If the Crown had to prove *mens rea,* some say that hundreds of thousands of violators would avoid liability because the system simply could not function and the Crown could not prove full *mens rea* in every case. Some see this as a necessary tool for effective trade, commerce, and industry.

Others say that there is no sense of justice when it comes to absolute liability offences. They say that punishment is reserved for those who are morally culpable, and with the absolute liability system, moral blameworthiness does not enter the discussion. Many argue that with this system there is no freedom of choice; for most crimes you have to choose to break the law, but this regime takes that option away. Some say that there is no evidence that there is a higher standard of care when it is an absolute liability offence.

Until the case of *R v Sault Ste. Marie* (1978), 85 DLR (3d) 161 (SCC), absolute liability and strict liability were interchangeable, but this case (see the box on this page) changed the face of strict liability. Many started to believe that it was not fair that a company had no defence. The courts started to shift towards examining fault in addition to the *actus reus* for these crimes. The court system was increasingly uncomfortable with absolute liability, and felt that it was not a fundamental element of our system to deprive the defendant of a defence. There was a need for a flexible strategy, and the court found that there should be a middle ground between requiring the Crown to prove all *mens rea* beyond a reasonable doubt as in true crimes, and convicting on the grounds of *actus reus* alone as in absolute liability.

Offences of Strict Liability

In **strict liability** offences, there is still no necessity for the Crown to prove *mens rea*. However, unlike absolute liability where simply the act is proven and the person or group is automatically guilty, with a strict liability offence a certain defence is available. Once the Crown proves the *actus reus,* the burden of proof shifts to the accused entities to prove on the balance of probabilities that they were diligent. A certain defence (or explanation) is now available in the form of due diligence. The **due diligence defence** requires that the accused prove that he or she took reasonable care before proceeding, and this defence can be used as an explanation as to why the accused should not attract liability. The case of *R v Sault St. Marie* (see the following case box) changed the face of this type of liability in Canada.

R v SAULT STE. MARIE (1978), 85 DLR (3D) 161 (SCC)

The City of Sault Ste. Marie was charged under the *Ontario Water Resources Act* for putting waste materials into a body of water. It was an absolute liability offence under the act to put any kind of material in water that might impair the quality of the water. The City had a

© Jim Wark/age fotostock/First Light

The city of Sault Ste. Marie

contract with a private company to dispose of the city's garbage, and that company decided to dump the garbage on a site that was by a creek, resulting in water pollution.

The Supreme Court said that this was a public welfare case that should fall into the category of strict liability cases where the City was allowed to show due diligence. The court also found that the Crown does not have to prove *mens rea* because it would have been almost impossible to show actual knowledge of the parties, and only they have that information. The City was permitted to come forward with this information to show due diligence, but the burden was on the defendant to a standard of a balance of probabilities. The court said that it would be fair to allow the City to show what it had done to avoid the pollution. The Supreme Court found that there should be a new trial for the City to prove it had shown due diligence.

The due diligence defence requires that the accused prove that he or she took reasonable care before proceeding (e.g., selling cigarettes to a minor and checking their identification). Shifting the onus is clearly different from the standard established for true crimes; however, the Crown has the advantage of not proving all mental elements beyond a reasonable doubt, and the accused now has a defence that it can establish on a balance of probabilities.

Strict liability has come under scrutiny, but it has also survived a *Charter* challenge (see Chapter 10). Some of the Supreme Court justices found strict liability to violate s 11(d) of the *Charter* and the presumption of innocence, but that it was "demonstrably justified in a free and democratic society" under s 1. The court was split with some of the other judges saying that it did not violate 11(d) at all. If an absolute liability offence had a severe punishment (such as a prison sentence), the court would likely find that it would not survive a *Charter* challenge. It is a deeply entrenched part of our system that if liberty is taken from an individual, that person must be given the chance to defend him- or herself.

How Do You Tell whether Liability Is Strict or Absolute?

To determine whether an offence is strict or absolute liability, one must examine the legislation and the case law in a particular area of law. If the subject matter is concerned with public safety, it will more likely be absolute liability because the state wishes to absolutely enforce this important area of law. If the sentence is severe, the court is more likely to say that it is strict rather than absolute and the individual should have a chance to defend him- or herself. If it is a trivial penalty, it is more likely to be absolute because the impact on the public is less (and the punishment is not severe). One needs to look at the wording in the legislation because if terms like "mandatory and absolute" are used, it is likely not a strict liability offence. But, what responsibility does an individual or corporation have to ensure compliance? Consider the case of *Lévis (Ville) c Tétreault* (see the following case box).

LÉVIS (VILLE) c TÉTREAULT (2006), 36 CR (6TH) 215 (SCC)

An employee of Société de l'assurance Automobile du Québec (SAAQ) told a company that they would send a notice for registration when it was time to renew their fleet car insurance, but the notice was sent to the wrong address. One of the employees of the company, Mr. Tétreault, was driving and got pulled over for expired insurance. The company was charged with violating the *Highway Safety Code*, RSQ, c C-24.2, which prohibits operating a vehicle if the registration is not paid. Although the company and Mr. Tétreault were acquitted at trial and at the Court of Appeal for Quebec, the Supreme Court quashed the acquittals and imposed a minimum fine of $300.

The Supreme Court found that this is a regulatory offence which is usually strict liability, but a category of absolute liability still remains. The court found that passive ignorance is not a valid defence in Quebec regulatory law. Mr. Tétreault did not prove due diligence because he was passively waiting for the renewal notice, and he confused the date for expiry with the due date for paying fees. However, he took no steps to get further information. The company also knew of the date for payment, and should have inquired when no notice arrived. The company and Mr. Tétreault were both passive when there was a duty to do more, and therefore they were convicted.

CONCLUSION

Determining whether each of the elements of any particular crime has been committed is not an easy task. Rather, it is a complex process of legal acuity fought out between the police, the Crown, and the defence lawyer. This differs from public opinion that an accused either committed a crime or did not. After it has been established that a crime occurred, it is then up to the defence counsel to determine if all of the evidence has been collected in a way which respects the *Charter* and that the proper procedure has been followed (see Chapter 10). Then it is up to the defence counsel to craft a defence to a crime for the client if the accused wishes to excuse or justify his or her actions (see Chapter 11). Finally, if the accused is convicted, the court must determine a proper sentence for the crime and decide whether alternative measures should be considered (see Chapter 12).

LEARNING OUTCOMES SUMMARIZED

1. Evaluate the role of each of the parties in a criminal matter.

The defence lawyer's role is to represent the client, within the bounds of the law, and to raise fearlessly every issue, advance every argument, and ask every question, however distasteful, which the lawyer thinks will help the client's case. The Crown attorney is hired by the state and is an agent of the Attorney General. It is his or her job to prosecute criminal cases on behalf of the Crown. Criminal court judges must decide whether evidence is admissible, and their decisions form the basis of what is appealed to a higher level of court. Juries are expected to understand and retain all of the evidence properly presented to them at trial and to affirm legal precedent while following the rules given to them by the judge.

2. Analyze the elements of a criminal offence.

The elements of a criminal offence consist of an act or omission (*actus reus*) in violation of a law, criminal intent (*mens rea*), the union of *actus reus* and *mens rea*, and there must be a punishment provided in law for the offence.

3. Understand the different types of parties to an offence.

At the common law there were various types of parties to a crime, including the "principal," who commits the offence; the "aider," who enables someone else to commit the criminal act; the "abettor," who encourages another person to commit a crime; and a "counsellor," who does something to incite another to commit a crime. All of these terms were established in the common law, but now the *Criminal Code* defines these roles.

4. Review the concepts involved in inchoate offences.

Inchoate offences are those offences in which the crime is incomplete. An attempt is a key example of punishing someone before he or she has completed the harmful conduct.

5. Identify regulatory offences and the difference between strict and absolute liability.

Regulatory offences are non-criminal offences that carry a penalty similar to criminal offences, but that are subject to less complex court procedures than are criminal offences.

For example, traffic offences fall under the *Highway Traffic Act* of each province and usually carry a fine as a consequence of violating these quasi-criminal laws. For strict liability offences, there is still no necessity for the Crown to prove *mens rea*. However, unlike absolute liability, where simply the act is proved and the person or group is automatically guilty, in strict liability offences a certain defence is available. The court has found that there is no necessity for the Crown to prove *mens rea*, but rather once the Crown proves the *actus reus*, the burden of proof shifts to the accused, who is entitled to prove on the balance of probabilities that he or she was diligent and careful in his or her actions.

SELF-EVALUATION QUESTIONS

1. Identify the role of the *Constitution Act 1867* on jurisdiction over criminal law.
2. In the case of *R v Dudley & Stephens*, explain why Mr. Brooks was not charged with murder. Do you think that Mr. Brooks should have been charged? With what offence?
3. Discuss the difference between abetting and aiding.
4. List the penalties for accessories after the fact convicted of (a) an indictable offence, (b) a summary offence, or (c) a hybrid offence.
5. Who is required to make reasonable efforts to rescue a person who is in danger?
6. Discuss the duty to provide the necessaries of life.
7. In the case of *R v Sault Ste. Marie,* the court examined a situation where the city had hired a private garbage company to dispose of the city's garbage. Without the city's knowledge, the private company put the garbage by a creek, which caused pollution. What was the finding of the court?
8. What are the pros and cons of absolute liability?

CHAPTER 10

The *Charter*, Criminal Procedure, and Evidence

Learning Outcomes

After completing this chapter, you should be able to:

1. Discuss the test using s 1 of the *Charter* established by the Supreme Court of Canada in the *R v Oakes* case.
2. Assess what evidence the defence must raise in a preliminary hearing, and the reasoning behind this decision.
3. Identify what the Crown/defence can agree to in return for an accused pleading guilty.
4. Discuss the elements that have been found to potentially induce false confessions.

THE *CHARTER OF RIGHTS AND FREEDOMS*—INTRODUCTION

A discussion of criminal procedure necessarily begins with the *Constitution Act, 1982,* and the *Charter of Rights and Freedoms* (*Charter*), which was created under the Constitution. Indeed, the *Charter* comprises the first 34 sections of the *Constitution.* Many constitutional issues arise outside of the *Charter*, but for our purposes we will focus almost exclusively on the *Charter* in this chapter (see Chapter 8 for more constitutional information). As already discussed, there is a division of powers between federal and provincial governments through the *Constitution Act, 1982*. The introduction of the *Charter* in 1982 had a huge impact on Canadian law because it empowered judges to declare legislation invalid and not in force if it infringes on an individual's rights.

A constitution is comprised of rules for lawmakers. It defines the roles of different laws and how they work together, and provides mechanisms for how they can be changed. The purpose of a constitution is to provide some limits to the way a state can exercise their power. Our system was adapted from the British system through a piece of legislation called the *Constitution Act, 1867* (and before that, the *British North*

America Act). Before the *Charter*, **parliamentary supremacy** dictated that the parliament and statute law was above all judge-made law (common law or case law). However, in Canada, parliamentary supremacy has always been limited by the *Constitution Act, 1867*. The court can decide that something is beyond the federal or provincial government's power and can override Parliament. Section 52 of the *Constitution Act* says that the "Constitution of Canada is the supreme law of Canada, and any law that is inconsistent with the provisions of the Constitution is, to the extent of the inconsistency, of **no force or effect**."

Since the *Charter*, the court has taken on a more important role, by limiting the supremacy of Parliament and putting certain entrenched individual and group rights beyond the power of the federal or provincial government. Most of the legislation that we look at in this text is very precise in meaning and what is being defined; however, any discussion of the Constitution necessarily deals with broad, sweeping generalizations, and the court has to interpret what these concepts mean.

A variety of rights within the criminal law are provided for in the *Charter*. For example, s 7 of the *Charter* provides that "everyone has the right to life, liberty and the security of person and the right not to be deprived thereof except in accordance with the principles of fundamental justice." Each of these principles have then been interpreted by the courts. For instance, Canadian law has dictated that legal rights only begin after birth, so *life* does not include a fetus. This does not mean that a fetus has no moral value, just no legal rights under the *Charter* and Canadian law. Similarly, *liberty* has been interpreted as the right to carry on certain activities, and *security of person* has been interpreted in a variety of physical ways. We have defined *fundamental justice* as natural justice, the right to a fair trial, the right to be heard, and the right to state your case.

The *Charter* is about structuring a relationship between the state and individuals. Although there were cases dealing with these subjects before the *Charter*, the *Charter* was necessary to formalize these relationships. If the rights of those facing criminal sanction can be resolved in this way, then the rights of all Canadians are clarified. However, one should not conclude that the court overrides every issue that Parliament tries to draft; legislative alterations must be done in a measured way. Even when legislation is struck down and of no force and effect, it is possible for the legislature to address this problem and fix the section so that it does not violate the *Charter*. Striking down the entirety of the legislation is a last resort. Instead, courts can choose to "sever" the one offending part of the legislation by **reading down** or **reading in** words that are consistent with *Charter* rights.

The courts must be careful not to alter anything that would contravene the intention of the Parliament of Canada or of the particular province or territory. Some say that adding words that were not drafted by the legislators is not the proper place for a court, and that it is not the role of courts to interpret a statute so narrowly that the legislation applies in a way that the government did not intend. To further understand the *Charter* and the criminal law, it is important to look at the technical aspects of the criminal law. This is done through looking at what is called "criminal procedure."

CRIMINAL PROCEDURE

Search Warrant

Criminal procedure comprises the rules of the game. Those who work in criminal law are required to conduct themselves a certain way, and to adhere to specific steps. For example, the *Criminal Code* and some other federal statutes give the police and government investigators the power to **search and seize**. But that power is dependent on compliance with the *Charter*, which provides that everyone has the right to be "secure against unreasonable search and seizure." Under the *Controlled Drugs and Substances Act*, SC 1996, c 19, there are special rules when searching for drugs. Under s 11 of that act, if a judge is satisfied there are reasonable grounds to suspect a person has a controlled substance, the peace officer can get the permission of the court to search a person for the substances. Section 11(7) provides that if by "reason of exigent circumstances it would be impracticable to obtain" a warrant, there are powers to search without a warrant.

The Supreme Court of Canada has defined what is meant by "unreasonable search and seizure," and has concluded that it is reasonable if the search is authorized by law, the law itself is reasonable, and the manner in which the search was made is reasonable. This does not mean that every technicality must always be met to ensure that the search is reasonable, but if the illegality is substantial, then any search performed will necessarily be unreasonable.

When the police need to enter **premises** to gather evidence, they must go to a Justice of the Peace and report that they have "reasonable and probable grounds to search for evidence." If the justice is convinced by the information that there are reasonable grounds to search, they will grant a search warrant pursuant to s 487 of the *Criminal Code.* This inspection may be allowed in a situation where one needs to search a building, receptacle, or place (if an offence is suspected to have been committed and evidence must be gathered), or if there is evidence that will reveal the location of a person who has committed an offence. The officer must bring the seized item (or report on it) to the court. A search warrant can also be issued by telecommunications and electronic means. The following case box examines a search conducted in a Canadian high school.

R v AM, [2008] SCJ NO 19 (SCC)

The police accepted a long-standing invitation by the principal of a high school to bring "sniffer dogs" into the school to search for drugs. The police had no specific knowledge that drugs were at the school and would not have been able to obtain a warrant to search the school. All students were sent to their classrooms, and sniffer dogs were used in the gym where unattended backpacks were against one wall. Without obtaining a warrant to search the backpack, the police opened a backpack identified by the dog and found illegal drugs. The student who owned the backpack (referred to as "AM") was charged with possessing cannabis marijuana and psilocybin for the purpose of trafficking.

A sniffer dog at work

The accused brought an application to exclude evidence, arguing that his rights under s 8 of the *Charter* had been violated. The trial judge agreed and said there were two unreasonable searches—the search conducted with the sniffer dog in the gym and the search of the backpack. He excluded the evidence and acquitted the accused. The Court of Appeal upheld the acquittal.

The Supreme Court of Canada found that the common law powers of the police to investigate crime and bring perpetrators to justice included the use of sniffer dogs based on a reasonable suspicion. The majority of the court agreed that the dog's sniffing of AM's backpack amounted to a search, triggering s 8 of the *Charter*.

The court said while teenagers might have little expectation of privacy from searches performed by their parents, they expected the contents of their backpacks to be free from random searches by police. The defence argued that the air around the backpacks was not "public air space," as the Crown argued. The court found that by using the sniffer dog, the police were able to "see" through the backpack to the concealed contents of the bag although AM had a continuing expectation of privacy.

They said that a "well-educated guess" that drugs would be found in the school did not amount to a reasonable suspicion. Thus, while a warrantless sniffer-dog search could be conducted if the police had reasonable suspicion, in this case the sniffer-dog search violated s 8 of the *Charter*, and the evidence was excluded.

The court has given the police some latitude in the methods they use in searching a location, as seen in the case of *R v Cornell* (see the following case box), but compare that case with the next box (see page 258), where the police search a cell phone.

R v CORNELL, [2010] SCJ NO 31 (SCC)

Peter Power/The Globe and Mail/The Canadian Press

A specially trained tactical team can be called upon in potentially dangerous situations.

The Alberta Court of Appeal upheld an earlier conviction against Mr. Cornell for possession of cocaine for the purpose of trafficking. Police had properly obtained a search warrant, and determined that a "tactical team" (a special police team that is trained to enter in dangerous situations), would enter the home to prevent the destruction of evidence by the occupants of the house.

The tactical team rammed down the front door of Mr. Cornell's home without knocking or announcing their arrival, and nine police officers wearing masks and body armour entered the house with weapons drawn. The tactical team did not have the search warrant when they entered, but a detective had the warrant and entered the home four minutes after the tactical team. Evidence was provided that the team tore through the house looking for drugs and handcuffed Mr. Cornell's mentally challenged brother, who was the only person in the house.

The search caused damage, but the police discovered nearly 100 grams of cocaine in Mr. Cornell's bedroom. Mr. Cornell said the evidence was obtained illegally and should be excluded from his trial. The trial judge and the majority of the Court of Appeal held that Mr. Cornell's rights under s 8 of the *Charter* had not been infringed because the search was lawfully authorized and reasonable. Mr. Cornell appealed that judgment.

In a four-to-three decision, the Supreme Court agreed with the trial and appeal courts. The high court found that police should announce their entry unless they have reasons not to do so. There was evidence that the police believed that gang members were running a drug-operation out of this house, and they were fearful that less intrusive methods would have endangered the police officers, and would lead to the destruction of evidence. The court also found that not having the warrant with them immediately when they entered did not make the search unreasonable. Police must be given deference based on the information that they had at the time of the search. Thus, the court found the search was reasonable and the evidence was entered.

The minority decision held that state power was used in this circumstance in an unjustifiable way by wearing masks and armour when they did not have firm information that these procedures were warranted. Justice Fish said that "just as anonymity breeds impunity, so too does impunity breed misconduct—which, unsanctioned by legal consequences, tends to bring into disrepute our enviable system of justice."

Do you think this was a justifiable use of police power?
Are police wearing balaclavas no better than "armed bandits," as some have alleged?
Does it make a difference that the brother was "taken down" and handcuffed? The police testified that the brother's "emotional distress became apparent and the handcuffs were removed within minutes. The brother was comforted by one of the officers and received the help of a paramedic." Did these circumstances make the search reasonable/unreasonable?

THEY CAN SEARCH WHAT?! THE ULTIMATE INVASION—CAN POLICE SEARCH YOUR CELL PHONE?

Mr. Bradshaw was arrested for the robbery of a music store where cell phones were stolen. The accused was searched when he was arrested, and the police found and seized a cell phone. In order to identify the owner of the cell phone, the police opened the phone and searched the stored data. In the course of looking at the cell phone, a picture of Mr. Bradshaw holding a sawed-off shotgun was found, which had been stored the day after the music store robbery. The photo was downloaded to the police officer's cell phone, downloaded onto a computer, and printed. A warrant was then obtained to search the phone. Counsel for Mr. Bradshaw said that the picture should not be admissible because this was not a proper search, breached his s 8 *Charter* rights, and should be excluded.

What is the result? Should the evidence be excluded?

Because cell phones had been stolen, were the police entitled to conduct a warrantless inspection of the cell phone to see who the owner was?

See *R v Manley* 2001 ONCA 128 (Ont CA).

Exclusion of Evidence

The way that evidence is collected is extremely important in the Canadian justice system. The *Charter* is specific in that evidence must be disregarded if its inclusion would "bring the administration of justice into disrepute." Determining this is an important step in the exclusion of evidence, and if this is not respected, all of the evidences may be inadmissible, as seen in *R v Feeney* (see the following case box).

R v FEENEY (1997), 146 DLR (4TH) 609 (SCC)

Police were investigating a murder and were told that Mr. Feeney had been near the scene of the crime. When the police arrived at the place where he was said to be staying, his sister said he was sleeping in the trailer he rented behind the house.

The police knocked on the door and yelled "Police," but there was no answer. The officer drew his gun, entered the trailer and found Mr. Feeney sleeping. They asked the accused to come into the light, and realized he had blood on his shirt, which Mr. Feeney claimed was his own after he was hit with a baseball in the face. There were no injuries on his face. Mr. Feeney was arrested and was told about his right to counsel at that time.

At trial, the evidence was used to find Mr. Feeney guilty of second-degree murder. The B.C. Court of Appeal affirmed the conviction. The case was appealed to the Supreme Court. In a five-to-four decision, the court found that the officers did not have reasonable grounds to arrest prior to entering his home.

The court found that Mr. Feeney was not immediately told of his right to counsel when he was in his bed, and this was a violation of his *Charter* rights. In addition, the officer did not have grounds for arrest. The officer testified that he was "suspicious" that Mr. Feeney was the murderer, but he did not have the grounds to arrest. The court then did a s 24(2) analysis. Under this section of the *Charter*, if a judge is convinced that evidence was "obtained in a manner that infringed or denied any rights or freedoms guaranteed by this *Charter*, the evidence shall be excluded if it is established that, having regard to all the circumstances, the admission of it in the proceedings would bring the administration of justice into disrepute." Because this arrest was improperly executed, the evidence collected at the time of this arrest was excluded under s 24(2) of the *Charter* as the evidence would bring the administration of justice into disrepute.

Theorists call this the "fruit of a poisoned tree:" all of the evidence that comes from an illegal act must be discarded because it is all tainted. Do you agree that this evidence should be excluded?

The dissent at the Supreme Court said that police should be allowed to secure the scene before reading the rights to counsel. They also said that the officer had reasonable and probable grounds to arrest based on the information that Mr. Feeney was at the scene of the crime. Do you agree?

The *Criminal Code* was amended after this case to allow for a warrant through telephone or other telecommunication to enter into a dwelling place, and to allow entrance to a dwelling place to execute an arrest which may be done in "exigent circumstances." See s 487. Do you agree that a search without a warrant should be allowed in some circumstances? Compare this case to the case of *R v Harrison* in the following case box.

R v HARRISON, [2008] OJ NO 427 (SCC)

The accused and his friend were driving a rented SUV from Vancouver to Toronto, but they were pulled over in Ontario after a police officer noticed that the vehicle had no front licence plate. Only after putting on his roof lights to pull over the accused did he realize the SUV was registered in Alberta where vehicles do not require a front licence plate. The officer was informed by dispatch that the vehicle had been rented at the Vancouver airport, leaving the officer with no grounds to believe that any offence was committed.

The officer was suspicious (without concrete proof) of the pair in the SUV and he arrested the accused after discovering that his driver's licence had been suspended. The officer then searched the vehicle without a warrant. He found two cardboard boxes containing 35 kg of cocaine.

The trial judge found that pulling over the accused and detaining him was simply done on a "hunch" rather than reasonable grounds and therefore there was an arbitrary detention, which violated s 9 of the *Charter*. He also found that searching the car without a warrant was unreasonable and contrary to s 8 of the *Charter*.

The court then did a s 24(2) analysis to see if using this information would bring the administration of justice into disrepute. The court in this case found that the violations of the accused's rights were serious and the officer had no grounds for stopping the vehicle. However, he found that the evidence was extremely important to the Crown's case, and he admitted the cocaine into evidence because "the repute of the administration of justice would suffer more from its exclusion than from its admission." The accused was convicted of trafficking. The Court of Appeal, in a majority decision, upheld the trial judge's decision to admit the evidence and affirmed the conviction.

At the Supreme Court of Canada, Justices McLachlin, Binnie, LeBel, Fish, Abella, and Charron found that the *Charter* breaches were evident, but the issue was whether the cocaine was properly admitted into evidence. The justices found that one must consider three elements to determine if the admission of the evidence would bring the administration of justice into disrepute:

1. the seriousness of the *Charter*-infringing state conduct;
2. the impact of the breach on the *Charter*-protected interests of the accused; and
3. society's interest in the adjudication of the case on its merits.

The court found in this case the balance of these factors means that the evidence must be excluded. It found that the *Charter* breaches by the police represented a blatant disregard for the accused's rights. The court found that the unconstitutional detention and search were significant breaches. The drugs seized were also important, but not as important as maintaining the rights of each citizen.

The court said that "the price paid by society for an acquittal in these circumstances is outweighed by the importance of maintaining *Charter* standards. That being the case, the admission of the cocaine into evidence would bring the administration of justice into disrepute. It should have been excluded."

Do you think that the court should admit evidence of 35 kg of cocaine no matter what the method of collection?

Right to Be Informed of Offence

Historically, there was a common law duty on a person making an arrest to inform the accused of the reasons for the arrest, or the accused would have a justification to resist arrest. These rights are now formalized under the *Charter,* which provides in s 11(a) that a "person charged with an offence has the right *(a)* to be informed without unreasonable delay of the specific offence."

Arrest

The first step in a prosecution may be the arrest of an individual by a peace officer or, in some circumstances, a private citizen. The person charged has a responsibility to appear in court. Arrest is not defined in the *Criminal Code,* but the Supreme Court has defined it as touching a person's body with the goal of detaining them or verbally directing the person that he or she is under arrest. An arrest is not complete until the person is informed that that he or she being arrested and under what grounds.

Under s 495 of the *Criminal Code,* a peace officer may arrest a person who has committed an indictable offence without a warrant in limited circumstances. A **peace officer** is defined under s 2 of the *Criminal Code,* which includes many different people, as shown in Table 10.1. Peace officers cannot arrest an individual for a summary conviction offence.

The officer must know that the individual has committed an indictable offence, which means he or she must have witnessed the act, reasonably believes the offence has been committed, or is about to be committed. An officer can also arrest if he or she believes there is a warrant for the individual's arrest in that jurisdiction. There must be reasonable grounds for arrest on the basis of all the information available.

Table 10.1 Who Is a Peace Officer?

reeve	sheriff
deputy sheriff	sheriff's officer
justice of the peace	police officer
correctional officer (including a warden, deputy warden, instructor, keeper, jailer, guard and any other permanent employee of the prison)	
bailiff	customs officer
immigration and refugee officer	constable
fishery guardian	pilot in command of an aircraft
Canadian forces officer	mayor

Citizen's Arrest

Traditionally, s 494 of the *Criminal Code* permits a citizen to arrest without a warrant any person that the citizen finds:

(a) committing an indictable offence, or

(b) a person who, on reasonable grounds, he believes

(i) has committed a criminal offence, and

(ii) is escaping from and freshly pursued by persons who have lawful authority to arrest that person.

The *Code* also provides for an owner of land to arrest a person committing a criminal offence in relation to the landowner's property. Under these "Citizen's arrest" provisions, the individual must turn over the person who has committed the crime to a peace officer immediately. The case of *R v Chen* (see the following case box) deals with this issue of citizen's arrest.

R v CHEN, [2010] OJ NO. 5741 (ONT CJ)

Mr. Chen was the store owner of the Lucky Moose Food Mart in Toronto. On May 23, 2009, Mr. Chen and his family members (who were also employees) apprehended Mr. Bennett who they said had been stealing plants and returned to the store an hour after the original theft. Mr. Bennett eventually pleaded guilty to the theft. The issue in this case was that Mr. Chen and his two employees tied up the man and locked him in a delivery van.

The police responded to a 911 call that someone was being taken hostage and being put into a van. They came to the scene to find that someone was bound and placed in a van, and Mr. Chen was found with a box-cutter (a dangerous weapon), and he was charged and arrested for assault and forcible confinement. The Crown decided to proceed with these charges because Mr. Chen did not catch Mr. Bennett in the course of a crime. The police defended their actions as they saw an individual in distress who was bound and held captive in a van and a man with a weapon—and even if this was a citizen's arrest, there is an argument that there was excessive force by Mr. Chen. Mr. Chen said that he was just trying to protect his store, and police were often slow to respond.

Justice Khawly found that the defence

> held all the emotional cards. Think of this as a screenplay: A hard working, relatively newly arrived immigrant to our shores toils relentlessly to eke out a living for his family only to find himself preyed upon by one of the undesirables of our community. The big, cumbersome, ham fisted, sometime mean machine of the state swoops down to protectively cradle into its bosom this most despicable of thieves while lashing out in fury against this poor man whose only sin is attempting to protect his hard earned labour.

Since it was unclear what exactly happened on that day, the judge found that there was reasonable doubt and acquitted Mr. Chen and his employees of assault and forcible confinement. The judge commented that the case was more "not proven" rather than anything else.

Should a store owner be able to make a citizen's arrest? Do you see any issues with a citizen making an arrest?

Partly in reaction to the *R v Chen* case, Prime Minister Stephen Harper introduced a new piece of legislation called the *Citizen's Arrest and Self-Defence Act* in February 2011, and the legislation was adopted by the House of Commons on May 1, 2012. This legislation will expand the circumstances in which a citizen's arrest can be made. The Prime Minister's website states the purpose of this expansion of rights, saying:

> our government is committed to putting real criminals behind bars. Canadians who have been the victim of a crime should not be re-victimized by the criminal justice system. That's why we have introduced changes to the *Criminal Code* so Canadians know they have the law on their side and that our justice system targets criminals and not victims.[1]

The proposed changes will be made to s 494(2) and will further allow a private citizen to make an arrest within a reasonable period of time after he or she finds someone committing an offence, or an offence in relation to property. There will still be limits placed on the amount of force that will be allowed. These arrests will consist of "either actually seizing or touching a person's body with a view to detaining them; or by using words where the person submits to the arrest."

The legislation will also clarify that a citizen must consider whether a peace officer is available at the particular time to assist, and the citizen's personal safety or the safety of others will be compromised by this arrest. The citizen must have a reasonable belief about the criminal conduct and the identity of the individual, and he or she must turn over the alleged offender without delay. Private individuals must be careful to not cross a line that would make the citizen subject to a crime or tort.

Arrest and *Charter* Rights

Section 10 of the *Charter* provides that:

> Everyone has the right on arrest or detention
>
> (*a*) to be informed promptly of the reasons therefor;
>
> (*b*) to retain and instruct counsel without delay and to be informed of that right; and
>
> (*c*) to have the validity of the detention determined by way of *habeas corpus* and to be released if the detention is not lawful.

Section 10 of the *Charter* provides that on arrest everyone has the right to be informed promptly of the reason, to retain and instruct counsel and to be informed of that right, and to have the validity of that detention determined by way of ***habeas corpus.*** If the person is not informed of the reasons for the arrest, then the arrest is unlawful. Some leeway has been given to peace officers where the person being arrested has made it difficult to inform them of the reasons because the arrested person is resisting and not listening.

Section 9 of the *Charter* says that: "[e]veryone has the right not to be arbitrarily detained or imprisoned." Any detainment or imprisonment has to be supported in law if one is going to take away freedom from a citizen.

1. Prime Minister Stephen Harper, "*Citizen's Arrest and Self-Defence Act*" (17 February 2011), Prime Minister of Canada, online: <http://pm.gc.ca/eng/media.asp?id=3966>.

Those who arrest with a warrant have duties imposed on them as well. Under s 29 of the *Criminal Code* it is provided that:

> 29. (1) It is the duty of every one who executes a process or warrant to have it with him, where it is feasible to do so, and to produce it when requested to do so.
>
> (2) It is the duty of every one who arrests a person, whether with or without a warrant, to give notice to that person, where it is feasible to do so, of
>
> (a) the process or warrant under which he makes the arrest; or
>
> (b) the reason for the arrest.

The person arresting with a warrant must have the warrant available for inspection and to produce it when requested to do so.

The Right to Remain Silent at Arrest

Police officers have the right to investigate crime and to ask questions, but it has been a long-standing principle that to freely allow agents of the state (police) to compel statements or answers would be to deny the individual rights of persons who are innocent until proven guilty. The ability of the police to question is limited under the common law and the *Charter* for those persons who are not under arrest or detention. One that is not detained is not required to answer questions, but some provisions of the *Highway Traffic Act* and other legislation provide situations where citizens may be asked to reply to questions.

However, a police officer cannot compel a person to answer questions, or detain solely for the purpose of questioning. This is generally referred to as the "right to remain silent," which is as fundamental as our right to be presumed innocent. An individual does not have an obligation to make the case for the Crown. Our system has developed rules to govern the admissibility of statements if they were obtained in an unlawful way. Those who have been accused must be cautioned of this right to remain silent, that their statement can be used against them in a court of law, and that they have the right to have a lawyer present. It is important for the accused to realize that there may be no immunity against the use of the evidence discovered or derived from answers if they do choose to answer. Beware!

DEBUNKING THE MYTH

There is no specific *Charter* right to remain silent. Most think that this right comes under section 7 in that "everyone has the right to life, liberty and security of the person and the right not to be deprived thereof except in accordance with the principles of fundamental justice."

The Right to Retain Counsel

An individual has the right under s 10 of the *Charter* to retain and instruct a lawyer without delay. It has also been found that the individual must be informed of free legal assistance through legal aid or duty counsel, and he or she must be given an opportunity to contact counsel, including the use of a telephone in privacy, and the arrested person must make an effort to contact a lawyer. Questions arise if there are cognitive issues with the person being detained, especially if they are suffering from a serious mental disorder as in *R v Whittle* (see the following case box).

R v WHITTLE (1994), 32 CR (4TH) 1 (SCC)

Mr. Whittle was arrested for outstanding warrants against him. He was informed of his right to counsel, but the police officers noted "strange conduct," making them question whether the accused was mentally stable. While being held, the accused confessed to a murder and three robberies, and he was then arrested for those additional crimes. Again, the accused was informed of his right to counsel. Mr. Whittle said he understood his rights, but that he did not wish to retain a lawyer. After more evidence was revealed by Mr. Whittle, he agreed to a videotaped statement where he was once again informed of his right to counsel. The videotape stopped when the accused said he did wish to talk to a lawyer.

The lawyer advised the accused to remain silent, but the accused said he had to talk to the police in order to make the voices in his head stop. Mr. Whittle confessed to the murder and also made several odd comments, but he continued to talk to police despite being cautioned. It was later found that Mr. Whittle suffered from schizophrenia and was having auditory hallucinations at the time. A psychiatrist testified at trial that the accused was aware of the consequences, but he was driven to continue to talk by his mental illness.

The trial judge found that the statements were involuntary and were made without Mr. Whittle realizing the consequence. Therefore, the statements should be excluded as they violated Mr. Whittle's s 10(b) rights. The accused was acquitted, but the Court of Appeal set aside the acquittal and ordered a new trial. The Supreme Court affirmed this decision and said that the statements were **admissible**.

The Supreme Court said that the statements were voluntary and were not obtained in a manner that breached his rights under s 10(b) of the *Charter*. The court found that the accused had the mental competence to make the choices on the right to silence and the right to counsel. The accused could instruct counsel, and voices could not be the basis for exclusion of the statements.

Did this case present a violation of Mr. Whittle's s 10 and s 7 *Charter rights?*
Should the statements made in this case be inadmissible due to his schizophrenia?
Was Mr. Whittle actually aware of what he was saying?
Was he aware that what he was saying would be held against him?

Right to Be Tried Within a Reasonable Time

Section 11(b) of the *Charter* provides that a person tried with an offence has the right to be tried within a reasonable time. The time being referred to is between the charge and the end of the trial. The court must examine the length of the delay, any waiver of this right by the accused, the reason for the delay, and the prejudice that has resulted to the accused. As with other *Charter* elements, the burden is on the individual alleging the infringement to persuade the court that there has been an infringement (or breach of the individual's rights). These elements are taken extremely seriously, and if the rights are violated, there are serious ramifications (see *R v Askov* in the following case box).

R v ASKOV, [1990] 2 SCR 1199 (SCC)

The Supreme Court said in a nine-to-zero decision that a delay of almost three years in bringing charges to trial violated the s 11(b) *Charter* right of Mr. Askov to be tried within a reasonable time. The court found that the primary aim of this section is the protection of the individual's rights and the provision of fundamental justice for the accused, but there is also a societal interest to be met. Those who have broken the law should be brought to trial quickly and punished under the law. Those on trial must be treated fairly, justly, and swiftly, because some accused individuals might be incarcerated for the time leading to trial. The court found that the liberty of the accused person is fundamental.

However, the court noted that there are also benefits to the other parties in having a swift trial as memories of the event may fade, witnesses may die or become incapacitated, and victims may be impacted by having to wait years for a resolution. In addition, there is a societal interest because the respect for the system fades as the time passes without resolution for all of the parties involved.

In the unanimous decision, the charges against Mr. Askov were **stayed.** The court said that the institutional delay (a busy court system) could not excuse a violation of s 11(b) rights. The court said that to find if there was unreasonable delay one must consider the following:

1. the length of the delay;
2. the reason for the delay;
3. whether the accused waived his or her rights under s 11(b);
4. whether the accused was prejudiced by the delay (did something happen to the accused that hurt his or her case during this time lag).

These factors applied to Mr. Askov, and he was a free citizen.

This resulted in hundreds of criminal charges being stayed all across Ontario based on this precedent. Should other accused persons have benefitted from Mr. Askov not being tried within a reasonable period of time?

Limitation of Rights

It is important to remember that there are some limitations to *Charter* rights. First, the *Charter* only deals with interactions between the government and individuals, *not* between two (or more) individuals. However, it is often difficult to tell where the government ends and a person begins. It is a good rule that if there is a government function, it is likely that the *Charter* applies. The *Charter* also applies to government officials at governmental agencies. If these individuals are doing something that they are not authorized to do by statute, the *Charter* can be used. For example, police officers are a representative of the state, so they must adhere to the rights of all individuals, or they can be sanctioned using the tool of the *Charter.*

The *Charter* itself also provides for a limitation in s 1 which says that the "*Canadian Charter of Rights and Freedoms* guarantees the rights and freedoms set out in it subject only to such reasonable limits prescribed by law as can be demonstrably justified in a free and democratic society." Chief Justice McLachlin said in *Canada (Attorney General) v JTI-Macdonald Corp.,* [2007] SJC No 30 (SCC), that "most modern constitutions recognize that rights are not absolute and can be limited if this is necessary to achieve an important objective and if the limit is appropriately tailored, or proportionate." Thus, there is a balance between the infringement of an individual's rights and whether those rights should be limited for the good of society.

The *Charter* is not absolute. Sometimes the courts find that some action does violate the *Charter*, but we agree it is permissible. This does not mean we are taking these rights away, just that reasonable limits are imposed on them. For example, we value the freedom of expression, but we also limit expression through libel, slander, hate speech, and some pornography (child pornography in particular). It has been established that this limitation is reasonable. It is often difficult to agree when the limitations are permitted and when it is allowable to violate the *Charter.* One of the most fundamental cases on this principle came in *R v Oakes,* as discussed in the following case box.

R v OAKES, [1986] 1 SCR 103 (SCC)

Mr. Oakes was charged for possession of a drug for the purposes of trafficking under s 8 of the *Narcotic Control Act* (now repealed). Prior to this case, the onus was on the defendant to prove he or she was *not* going to **traffic** these drugs. This is contrary to the **presumption of innocence** and is called a **reverse onus.** In a seven-to-zero decision, the Supreme Court found this reverse onus was not justified in that requiring a rebuttal of a presumption of possession for the purposes of trafficking violated s 11(d) (the provision that says that all are presumed innocent until proven guilty) and was not justified by s 1.

The court found that there was a strong reason to try to prevent the sale of drugs, but it had to examine whether the section of the *Narcotics Control Act* could be "saved" under s 1 of the *Charter*. The burden of establishing that an infringement is justified is (almost always) on the Crown, and there must be a strong reason to override *Charter* rights.

The court in *Oakes* found that two central criteria must be satisfied to establish that a limit is reasonable and demonstrably justified in a free and democratic society, including

1. The reason why you are limiting a *Charter* right must be very important. The standard must be high to ensure that these principles of a free and democratic society do not get overridden. This must be something "pressing and substantial," which is important enough to take away a fundamental freedom from an individual.
2. If there is a really good reason to take away a right, there must be a "proportionality test." Proportionality has several elements:
   (a) The law must accomplish only what is stated.
   (b) It should impair the rights of the individual as "little as possible."
   (c) There must be a proportionate effect between the effects of the measures and the objectives you were trying to accomplish. The effects cannot be worse than the original problem. The more severe the effects of the measure, the more important the objective has to be.

The court then looked at the particular circumstance of Mr. Oakes. Parliament's concern about drug trafficking was substantial and pressing, and it was important that the Crown get convictions for drug trafficking. However, there was no connection between possessing some small amount of a drug, and trafficking the illicit drug. Just because you have drugs does not automatically mean that you are a drug dealer. Thus, the test fails right away because s 8 of the *Narcotic Control Act* is **overinclusive.** It violates the *Canadian Charter of Rights and Freedoms,* it is not saved by s 1, and is therefore of no force or effect.

The decision in *R v Oakes* is one of the most cited cases in the history of the *Charter,* and many have said that it has implications far beyond the case, while looking for a balance between the rights of the individuals and the ideals of a democratic nation. Table 10.2 outlines the procedure for launching a *Charter* challenge.

Table 10.2 The *Charter* Process

1	Individual, group or corporation identifies law or governmental agency which has violated rights
2	Is a *Charter* right being violated? Freedom of expression, right against unreasonable search and seizure, equality rights etc.? If yes, continue to 3. If no, analysis is over.
3	Is there a legal dispute, do the parties have standing, and do *Charter* rights apply? If yes, continue to 4. If no—analysis is done.
4	Is this a reasonable limit under s 1 of the *Charter*? If yes, it is a reasonable limit—case is over. If no, continue to 5.
5	If not a reasonable limit, then it is a violation and one must strike down the legislation, read in, read down. Evidence collected in violation must be excluded. Would the violation bring the administration of justice into disrepute? If yes, continue to 6.
6	Should there be a response from legislature to address this problem?

Confessions

A confession is defined by *Black's Law Dictionary* as a "criminal suspect's acknowledgement of guilt, usually in writing and often including details about the crime."[2] Police are trained to elicit confessions, and this function is considered an integral part of police enforcement. A confession has long been held as the key in any case, as the "introduction of a confession makes the other aspects of a trial in court superfluous," meaning that no person would confess to something he or she did not do. It has long been a principle of law that a confession is not admissible unless the Crown shows that the statement was voluntary and that it was not made in fear or in hope of some sort of advantage by someone in a position of authority, so that one can be sure that a statement is true and trustworthy.[3]

In the historical case of *Commrs. of Customs and Excise v Harz,* [1967] 1 A.C. 760, the court recognized that although many of the police officer's means to get an confession may be "so vague that no reasonable man would have been influenced by them, but one must remember that not all accused are reasonable men or women: they may be ignorant and terrified by the predicament in which they find themselves." The court has recognized that there is the potential for false confessions even if the inducements or threats seem inconsequential to those looking at the situation from the outside.

It is also important to remember that interrogations are inherently stressful. An English study examined the reactions of first-time offenders interrogated about sex crimes. The researchers found that the suspects had reactions including shivering, sweating, hyperventilation, trembling, incoherence, and frequent urination. Police officers try to persuade a suspect to confess because denial of the crime is considered an undesirable outcome. Moreover, the number of confessions an officer obtains is linked to his or her interviewing competence. This pressure put on officers to obtain confessions from suspects leads officers to resort to coercive interrogation tactics, which have the potential to lead to false confessions (see Chapter 13).[4]

Interrogation techniques focus on how to overcome denials and elicit confessions from suspects. Theorists have noted three main tactics used in police interrogations to obtain confessions:

- isolation as a means to increase the suspect's anxiety and desire to escape;
- confrontation, whereby the interrogator accuses the suspect of the crime using real or fictitious evidence to support the accusation; and
- minimization, where the investigator conveys sympathy and provides a moral justification for the crime to lead the suspect to expect leniency upon confession.[5]

Others discuss the technique of "maximization," in which interrogators convey to the accused a solid belief that the suspect is guilty and tell him that any attempt to deny guilt will fail. Interrogations are designed to be stress-inducing in order to obtain confessions from suspects. Other techniques include invading the suspect's personal space, keeping light switches, thermostats, and other control devices out of the suspect's reach, and using a one-way mirror to allow other officers to look for signs of fatigue, weakness, anxiety, and withdrawal, as well as misinterpreting the suspect's body language.[6] However, having an accused confess is an important part of police work.

---

2. Henry Campbell Black, ed, *Black's Law Dictionary*, 7th ed (St. Paul, MN: West Pub. Co., 1999) at 293.
3. CT McCormick, *Handbook of the Law of Evidence,* 2nd ed (St. Paul, MN: West, 1972) at 316, as cited in Saul M Kassin, "The Psychology of Confession Evidence" (1997) 52 *American Psychologist* 221 at 221.
4. Hollida Wakefield and Ralph Underwager, "Coerced or Nonvoluntary Confessions" (1998) 16 *Behavioral Sciences and the Law* 423 at 426.
5. Stephen Moston, "From Denial to Admission in Police Questioning of Suspects," in G Davies et al, (eds), *Psychology, Law and Criminal Justice: International Developments in Research and Practice* (New York: de Gruyter, 1996).
6. Saul M Kassin, "False Confessions: Causes, Consequences, and Implications for Reform" (2008) 17 *Current Directions in Psychological Science* 249.

Plea

Section 606 of the *Criminal Code* provides that an accused who comes before the court must plead either guilty or not guilty. The judge may accept a plea of guilty only if he or she is convinced that the accused person is acting voluntarily, that the accused understands that the plea is an admission of all of the elements of the offence, and that the accused is aware of the consequences. The judge is not bound by an agreement between the accused and the prosecutor; the judge may still substitute his or her own sentence, regardless of any deal that may be negotiated between the Crown and defence. Since this is a vital step in the criminal justice system, many lawyers have written instructions from their client confirming that they understand what they are declaring. If there is any question whether an accused person understands the process, the court may refuse to accept the plea, or the judge may make inquiries to satisfy that the individual is entering a plea unequivocally.

If the accused enters a plea of "not guilty," then the Crown must prove every element of the charge beyond a reasonable doubt, but the accused has to do nothing more than enter that plea, and watch the Crown meet its burden. There is no requirement that the defence enter anything more. The overwhelming majority of cases are resolved by the accused person entering a plea of guilty after plea bargaining.

DEBUNKING THE MYTH

There is no such thing as a plea of "innocent." Although recent cases (like the wrongful conviction case of Steven Truscott) have asked a court to comment on innocence, this is something that is currently impossible. A not-guilty plea is not an "innocence" plea; rather, it is putting the Crown to the onus of proving the case. An accused person may enter a guilty plea even when the trial has started. If the accused decides to change his or her plea from not guilty to guilty, the judge is required to discharge the jury and enter the verdict.

Plea Bargaining

Plea bargaining is also referred to as "pre-trial negotiations," "resolution discussions," "plea negotiation," and "plea agreements." The **Law Reform Commission of Canada** made a substantial review of plea bargaining in the late 1980s. It defined the practice as "an agreement by the accused to plead guilty in return for the prosecutor's agreeing to take or refrain from taking a particular course of action." There is no definition of a plea agreement in the *Criminal Code,* but more recently, the Director of Public Prosecutions of the province of Saskatchewan has defined it as "a proceeding whereby competent and informed counsel openly discuss the evidence in a criminal prosecution with a view to achieving a disposition which will result in the reasonable advancement of the administration of justice."[7]

Plea bargaining is typically a deal between the Crown and defence lawyer for a sentencing reduction in return for a guilty plea. It can occur at any stage in the process, but it normally happens early on after the charge but before trial. These discussions can range from a simple and informal discussion to an actual formal agreement between the parties. This practice is one of the most controversial and misunderstood parts of the criminal process, yet is also an accepted and widespread. Many believe that a deal should never be made with someone who may have committed a brutal crime.

Plea bargaining is made possible by the accused's right to plead guilty or not guilty and the Crown's discretionary powers with respect to the types, seriousness, and the number of charges pursued. In a plea bargain, the accused person relinquishes his or her right to a trial by pleading guilty in exchange for concessions by the Crown. There may be several things that the parties can negotiate through a plea agreement, including (but not

7. Victims of Violence, "Research—Plea Bargaining" (28 February 2011), online: <http://www.victimsofviolence.on.ca/rev2/index.php?option=com_content&task=view&id=378&Itemid=197>.

limited to) reducing the number of charges; withdrawal or stay of some of the charges, and promise not to pursue other charges; reducing the charge to a **lesser but included charge**; agreement to withdraw charge for the defendant entering into a **peace bond**; and a promise not to seek **prohibitions or forfeiture orders**. The following box outlines other elements that may be negotiated in a plea bargain.

The accused's motive for plea bargaining is usually to obtain a lesser sentence. However, the judge will not be involved in the plea negotiations and is free to impose a wide range of sentences, *regardless* of what has been agreed to. The sentence the accused expects is not guaranteed.

WHAT OTHER ELEMENTS MAY BE NEGOTIATED WITH THE CROWN IN A PLEA BARGAIN?

1. Promise not to charge friends or family.
2. Reducing the seriousness of a charge (e.g., murder to manslaughter).
3. Proceeding by summary conviction rather than by indictment.
4. Promise to make a specific sentence recommendation.
5. Promise not to oppose the defence counsel's sentence recommendations.
6. Agreement to enter a joint submission on sentencing.
7. Promise not to appeal the sentence imposed.
8. Promise not to ask for a more severe sentence.
9. A promise by the prosecutor to impose an intermittent sentence rather than continuous sentence.
10. An agreement on the types of conditions to be imposed in a conditional sentence.
11. An agreement to transfer charges from or to a particular province or territory.
12. Promise not to pursue a dangerous offender designation.
13. Promise to request a particular place of imprisonment or type of treatment.
14. Promise to seek a particular judge for sentencing.
15. Promise not to volunteer information or talk about circumstances that could be an aggravating factor.[8]

PROS OF PLEA BARGAINING The main reason that Crown attorneys engage in plea bargaining is to speed up the court system and prevent costly delays in court trials. This practice also lessens the cost of trials and lengthy appeals that could be made if the matter is not negotiated earlier in the process. Defence lawyers often agree to bargain because they realize that this will result in a lesser sentence for the accused. The judge will often take a guilty plea as a show of remorse and as a mitigating factor and reduce the sentence accordingly.

Plea bargaining also saves the police time and money since a guilty plea means that they are not required to testify and spend time in the courtroom. This bargain also provides closure for the police and signifies that they have done their job since the evidence is sufficient to obtain a conviction. In addition, the police may be able to get information on other persons who might be involved in criminal activity.

Victims and witnesses often support plea bargaining, since a guilty plea saves them the ordeal of testifying and the expense and stress that this entails. This is particularly true for young victims and victims of domestic abuse and sexual assault. Victims and parents of victims will sometimes pressure the Crown to bargain in order to avoid a trial and the trauma of having to testify.

Judges are aware that plea bargains occur and most will tacitly accept the practice. They will take steps, however, to ensure that the accused's rights have been respected and that the final outcome is consistent with the principles of justice. Judges are likely to choose a sentence in the range that is recommended by the Crown and defence unless there are compelling reasons to ignore their recommendations.

In practice, the vast majority of criminal defendants plead guilty to the charge(s). It is not known how many of these guilty pleas result from plea bargains, but some observers

8. Department of Justice. "Victim Participation in the Plea Negotiation Process in Canada" (15 May 2011) justice.ca <http://www.justice.gc.ca/eng/pi/rs/rep-rap/2002/rr02_5/d.html>

estimate that at least 90 percent are resolved through plea bargains. The Law Reform Commission was originally critical of plea bargaining several decades ago, but it has since come to the position that pretrial negotiations are necessary to ensure the smooth running of the courts. Many say that it is both morally and legally permissible because both parties voluntarily negotiate and benefit from the practice.

CRITICISMS OF THE PLEA BARGAINING PROCESS There are many who oppose plea bargaining because of the problems inherent in the process. Critics argue that the process of making deals with criminals that result in more lenient sentences brings the administration of justice into disrepute. Often, the accused person does not have a trial because of a plea negotiation, so some say this infringes on the right to due process that the individual is guaranteed. Some also see plea bargaining as having an element of secrecy and lack of supervision, because the deals often happen between the Crown and defence lawyer. Plea bargaining is also criticized as being an informal and hurried affair that often occurs just prior to the trial. In such situations, the defendant may not be made fully aware or appreciate what is happening, what his or her rights are, and the legal repercussions of a guilty plea and that it may victimize those that the system is charged with protecting.

Others say the plea-bargaining process takes away from deterring would-be criminals because they do not see the punishment that is given to the individual in a public setting. Others, from a social justice standpoint, say there is a real risk of false confessions and false pleas from those individuals who are simply afraid of going through the trial process. Some offenders may get a particularly lenient sentence if they know how the system works, and this can be especially true for experienced criminals who understand the system and for wealthy clients who can afford the best lawyers. Some say these realities hurt victims who are outraged that the Crown is bargaining with criminals, while the victim may not be involved in the process whatsoever.

Critics also accuse the police and the Crown of overcharging in order to put pressure on persons to make a deal for reduced charges. Defence lawyers are criticized for engaging in delay tactics that take up police and court time in order to put pressure on the Crown to make a good deal for their clients. Critics also contend that some defence lawyers will put a great deal of pressure on their clients to accept a deal that may not be in their best interests. Some fear that lawyers who do not like or believe their criminal clients or who are inexperienced may resort to unfair deals.

Others worry that because there is no guarantee of a sentence, the accused may receive a much harsher sentence than expected because the judge is not constrained to provide a sentence in the range recommended by the Crown and defence. Judges retain final authority over the **disposition** and can impose any sentence consistent with the law. Some accused persons later seek to overturn the plea deal they agreed to, as in the case of *R v Nevin* (see the following case box).

R v NEVIN, [2006] NSJ NO 235 (NS CA)

On appeal to the Nova Scotia Court of Appeal, Mr. Nevin sought to have his guilty plea withdrawn. The accused was caught with many rocks of cocaine, marijuana, a rifle, and cash. He pleaded guilty to the charges the day immediately following the charges. Mr. Nevin said that his plea was invalid because there were specific and detailed threats made against him and his family by police officers if he did not enter a guilty plea. Mr. Nevin stated that police threatened they would arrest his mother, his older sister, his younger sister (who was then 12 years old), and that they would have Children's Services take away his six-year-old niece. Mr. Nevin had minimal time to meet with his lawyer to consider his options, and his lawyer had little time to consider the validity of the search warrant before the plea. The plea was immediately entered and he received a sentence that day of two years for the drug charge, one month for the firearms violations, and a ten-year firearms prohibition.

The Crown decided not to introduce evidence that would contradict Mr. Nevin's allegations against the officers saying that they were "inherently implausible and should not be believed." At trial, Mr. Nevin had alleged that two police officers had their handguns drawn, and that one of the officers was high on drugs at the time of the arrest. There was no contradictory evidence provided by the Crown. The appeals court found that Mr. Nevin met the burden of demonstrating that his plea was invalid and involuntary. The court found that to allow the plea would be to allow a miscarriage of justice. The court ordered a new trial, and the Crown agreed not to seek a sentence of greater than what had already been imposed, as Mr. Nevin had already served the time in prison.

Are these allegations from someone who was a possible drug addict sufficient to withdraw a guilty plea?

Compare this case with *R v Brown*, which is discussed in the following case box.

R v BROWN, [2006] PEIJ NO 44 (PEI SUP CT APP DIV)

Mr. Brown was convicted for sexual assault and received a sentence of 15 months' imprisonment and three years' probation. Before sentencing, the accused sought to withdraw his guilty plea because he alleged that new evidence had become available. Mr. Brown stated that this new evidence raised a reasonable doubt about his guilt, and undermined the credibility of the victim, and that this new evidence could result in his full acquittal. However, the judge at sentencing denied the accused's motion to withdraw his plea as this new evidence was not enough to change the circumstances of the case.

The P.E.I. court of appeal found that this "new evidence" was not enough to withdraw his plea. The accused had agreed to a **statement of facts** and the new evidence did not materially contradict the evidence that existed when he entered his plea. The new evidence was only opinion, it would likely be inadmissible at trial, and it likely would not have hurt the **credibility** of the victim as alleged. Therefore, there was no error by the trial judge, and the plea and sentence should stand.

Most agree that plea bargaining is an essential element of the criminal justice system, but it is important to see both sides of the issue. Some theorists suggest that Canada should adopt a policy based on the method in the United States, where judges are given more responsibility for reviewing plea agreements to see if all parties have been represented properly. Canadian courts have been reluctant to do this. What is clear is that abolishing the practice completely would bring the system to a halt, but there must be safeguards to ensure that the negative aspects do not bring the administration of justice into disrepute. Discussion must be honest and frank and the deal must be an unequivocal agreement between the parties, and many say this must be done with more respect shown to the victims and offenders.

Election

Under ss. 536 and 560 of the *Criminal Code*, the accused may decide what kind of court and trial he or she wants. If the individual is accused of a summary offence, the case will be tried before a provincial court judge (appointed and paid for by the province). If it is an indictable offence, the accused can select a provincial court judge alone, a higher court judge alone, or judge and jury of the Superior Court of Justice. In some cases, there is no choice. For example, in a murder trial, the accused must be tried by judge and jury unless special exceptions are complied with. An accused may change his or her election, or if the accused refuses to elect, he or she will be deemed to have elected judge and jury.

Preliminary Inquiry

Under s 535 of the *Criminal Code*, the defendant accused of an indictable offence has a right to a **preliminary hearing**. Provincial court judges hold the preliminary inquires and hear evidence to determine if there is sufficient material to put the accused to trial. There must be some evidence of each element of the accused's offence. The purpose of this hearing is to prevent persons from being subject to trial where criminal punishment is not supported. The prosecution has to present evidence, and witnesses have to testify under oath to establish whether the Crown has a case.

The defence may call witnesses, but usually it is not in best interest for them to do so and reveal the defence. However, the defence may find it useful to test the evidence and to make witnesses testify under oath as to what they observed. The judge may also commit an accused to stand trial for additional offences that are revealed from the evidence at the hearing, but it is an opportunity for the defence to obtain a possible reduction of charges. After a preliminary hearing, the accused may be more willing to enter into a plea negotiation after he or she has seen the strength of the Crown's case. Although the preliminary hearing does not establish guilt, the Crown may decide to have a second preliminary hearing if it is unsuccessful, or the Crown may choose to proceed to trial despite the negative finding of the preliminary hearing. The *Criminal Code* has been amended to provide that the accused must request a preliminary hearing, and the issues to be heard must be very narrow.

Presumption of Innocence

The concept that a person is considered innocent until proven guilty is a common law principle that is also enshrined in the *Charter s* 6(1) in that a "person shall be deemed not to be guilty of the offence until he is convicted or discharged," and s 11(d), which provides that "any person charged with an offence has the right ... to be presumed innocent until proven guilty according to law in a fair and public hearing by an independent and impartial tribunal." Thus, no person is to be considered guilty of an offence unless convicted of that offence at a proper trial, and the person must be convicted on every element beyond a reasonable doubt.

In practice, this means that the accused does not need to reply to the charge, and an **adverse inference** cannot be made against those who choose not to respond. The rationale is that this protects an accused from all of the massive powers of the state and its resources. As seen in the Food for Thought box, technology can also be of assistance to those maintaining their innocence.

FOOD FOR THOUGHT...

PRESUMPTION OF INNOCENCE—BUT IT IS GREAT TO HAVE FACEBOOK EVIDENCE

Nineteen-year-old Rodney Bradford used Facebook in a positive way to keep him out of prison. Mr. Bradford was arrested for a mugging in Brooklyn, though he maintained that he was not guilty of the crime. Mr. Bradford was held for almost two weeks until his father checked his Facebook page and noticed that his son had made a "status update" one minute before the crime occurred 12 miles away. The Facebook records were obtained that proved that this update was made from a computer at his father's apartment, meaning that he could not have been at the scene of the crime. Although there was a suggestion that someone with the Facebook password could have posted this message, the prosecution found it unlikely that this teenager would have planned this elaborate scheme, and there were other witnesses who confirmed his whereabouts. It was this "electronic alibi" that finally cleared Bradford of all charges.[9]

Do you think that this is sufficient evidence that Mr. Bradford did not commit the crime?

9. *Time Magazine*, "Saved by a Status Update" (30 November 2009), online: <http://www.time.com/time/specials/packages/article/0,28804,1943680_1943678_1943652,00.html>.

Equality under the Law

It is important to remember that each individual is equal under the law. Section 15 of the *Charter* provides that "every individual is equal before and under the law and has the right to the equal protection and equal benefit of the law without discrimination and in particular without discrimination based on race, national or ethnic origin, colour, religion, sex, age, mental or physical disability."

CRIMINAL EVIDENCE

There are many preliminary evidentiary issues when it comes to the trial of an accused person. Adults (persons over the age of 18) who are alleged to have committed an offence will be the focus of the following evidentiary issues. Before even starting a criminal trial, a few preliminary matters must be examined.

Burden of Proof

In criminal law, the "ultimate" burden of proof is always on the Crown, who has the responsibility in law to prove each and every essential ingredient of the offence charged. If the evidence as a whole indicates a reasonable doubt, then the accused has the right to the benefit of that doubt and deserves an acquittal. **Reasonable doubt** means proof of guilt to the degree of moral certainty which excludes any reasonable possibility of innocence. The much accepted adage of 18th-century British judge William Blackstone is that "we would rather let ten guilty persons go free than punish one innocent person."[10] For this reason, there is a high standard to be met by the Crown seeking to take away the freedom of any individual.

There is also what is called the **evidentiary burden**. This burden can switch back and forth between the Crown and defence. This is not on proof beyond a reasonable doubt, but rather it is the requirement of putting an issue before the court by presenting evidence that suggests that certain facts exist. For example, if the defence wishes to exclude evidence because it violated the *Charter,* the burden will be on the accused to prove on a balance of probabilities that the violation of the *Charter* occurred. This burden is tactical in nature, rather than going to the ultimate burden.

Compellability

Accused persons will not be forced to testify against themselves at trial. This principle has been confirmed in the *Charter s* 11(c), which provides that an individual cannot be "compelled to be a witness in proceedings against that person in respect of the offence." You may be compelled to testify at someone else's trial, but you can refuse to incriminate yourself if the primary reason for calling you as a witness is to elicit self-incriminatory information. The lack of testimony in your own trial cannot be commented on by the Crown or judge. Section 4(1) of the *Canada Evidence Act,* RSC 1985, c C-5, allows one to testify on his or her own behalf, although that person is not compellable by the Crown. However, if the accused does testify, his or her evidence can be used if it benefits the Crown.

There is a specific procedure on how to deal with these questions. Section 5 of the *Canada Evidence Act* provides that "no witness shall be excused from answering any questions on the ground that the answer to the question may tend to criminate him, or may tend to establish his liability." Therefore, one must answer the questions that are properly posed, but these answers cannot be used against you for anything but to establish **perjury**. This is provided in s 5(2) in that "the answer so given shall not be used or admissible in evidence against him in any criminal trial or other criminal proceeding against him

10. William Blackstone, *Commentaries on the Laws of England* (originally 1765 and 1769) (Boston, MA: Beacon Press, 1962) at 420.

thereafter taking place, other than a prosecution for perjury in the giving of that evidence or for the giving of contradictory evidence." Thus, you may face a trial for perjury based on the answers given, but not for any other matter.

In addition, s 13 of the *Charter* provides that "a witness who testifies in any proceedings has the right not to have any incriminating evidence so given used to incriminate that witness in any other proceedings, except in a prosecution for perjury or for the giving of contradictory evidence." If witnesses think what they are going to say could be used against them, they can invoke the protection of the *Canada Evidence Act* (which is similar to "pleading the fifth" in the United States). One must still answer, but the information supplied cannot be used as evidence in a criminal proceeding except a trial for perjury.

Additionally, each province is a bit different with regards to evidence. All make the parties to a proceeding a competent witness, and most make the parties compellable in civil proceedings, although they cannot be made to testify against themselves in provincial prosecutions.[11] Others make the defendant a compellable witness in the prosecution even in a provincial offence.[12] Again, if one does testify, he or she must answer all proper questions.

Witnesses

In a perfect world, all witnesses would freely give testimony as to their knowledge. However, this is not always the case and there are formal steps to take to make sure the testimony is delivered before the court. The most basic method of compelling a person to testify is a ***subpoena.*** Section 698 of the *Criminal Code* provides that if there is evidence that the person *subpoenaed* will not attend, or that he or she is evading a *subpoena*, that person may be arrested and brought to give evidence. The witness may also be required to bring any written documents or other items referred to in the *subpoena*. The court must be satisfied that the person is likely to give "material evidence" that will assist in the trial.

Husband or Wife

A spouse is what is called an "incompetent witness," or a witness that is not required to testify, for both the Crown and defence. While this is an ancient practice, what is protected today is defined under s 4(3) of the *Canada Evidence Act* as "communications during marriage—no husband is compellable to disclose any communication made to him by his wife during their marriage, and no wife is compellable to disclose any communication made to her by her husband during their marriage." However, this does not include documentary evidence or the spouse's visual observations, which may still be compellable.

It is important to remember that a husband and wife can *voluntarily* testify if they so wish. An adverse inference may not be made under s 4(6) of the *Canada Evidence Act* in that the "the failure of the person charged, or of the wife or husband of that person, to testify shall not be made the subject of comment by the judge or by counsel for the prosecution."

Common-law spouses are not currently considered to be husband or wife. Spousal compellability applies only where there is a valid and current marriage, and where the parties are not separated. If the parties are separated without reasonable hope of reconciliation at the time of the trial, a spouse can be compelled by the Crown. The parties would go before the judge in a *voir dire* (hearing within a hearing, without the presence of a jury) to decide if their evidence should be given. The right not to call a spouse to testify occurs at the point of legal marriage, even if this marriage happens after the alleged offence.

If the marriage takes place after the offence but before trial, the spouse has a right not to testify. A divorce prior to trial, however, makes the spouse available. In the case of *R v Hawkins,* [1996] 111 CCC (3d) 129 (SCC), the parties were married after the witness testified at the preliminary hearing, but by the time they got to trial, the new spouse refused to testify. The court found that the wife was now not a competent or compellable witness,

11. *Alberta Evidence Act,* 4(3); British Columbia, *Evidence Act,* s 7; New Brunswick, *Evidence Act,* ss 5 and 9; Newfoundland, *The Evidence Act,* ss 2 and 4(a); Nova Scotia, *Evidence Act,* ss 45 and 48; Ontario, *Evidence Act,* s 8, and *The Provincial Offences Act,* ss 46(5); *Saskatchewan Evidence Act,* 35(1) and (2); and Yukon Territory, *Evidence Act,* s 8.

12. Prince Edward Island, *Evidence Act,* s 4; Northwest Territories, *Evidence Act,* s 4(2); *Manitoba Evidence Act,* s 4.

and she was not required to testify against him. However, the court allowed the testimony from the preliminary hearing to be **read in** at the trial. Many have speculated that if the opposing parties could establish that the marriage was a sham to render a witness not competent to testify, the partners could not invoke the spousal incompetency rule. It is also interesting to note that there does not appear to be other privileges, such as a parent child privilege.

There are exceptions to the spousal compellability rules. A husband or wife is a compellable witness for the prosecution for certain charges under s 4(2) and 4(4) of the *Evidence Act,* such as incest, corrupting children, sexual assault, and a number of sections in which the victim is a child under the age of 14. In these cases, the court has found that it is in the best interest of the child not to have a spousal exception.

Testimony

Witnesses can only testify to what is within their knowledge; to testify about what someone else told you is called **hearsay**. The court usually does not allow the admission of hearsay evidence because it is second-hand knowledge. Hearsay is defined as an "out-of-court statement that is offered to prove the truth of its contents."[13] An out-of-court statement may be admitted as proof that the statement was made, but not for the truth of its contents. Witnesses cannot give their opinion except in certain circumstances (such as an expert witnesses). If there is a question about what evidence should come into a trial, the parties have a *voir dire* to see if the evidence is admissible. Some question the role of privacy when it comes to evidence (see the following box).

WHAT ABOUT PRIVACY AND EVIDENCE?

When talking about evidence that can be presented at trial, one must ask about privacy concerns and technology. In an age where assessing what a person believes on a topic can be as easy as logging on to Facebook, criminal law is trying to catch up with this technology. Why would lawyers call someone to testify on the stand when they might have the answers they are looking for in black and white?

It may depend on how that information was gathered. Did someone secretly access someone else's email account? Did they have free access to a computer or their spouse? Sections 183 and 184 of the *Criminal Code* say that someone who "intercepts" communications is mainly used in the circumstances where there is formal "wiretapping" or investigative techniques used by the police. Section 342.1 provides that anyone who obtains "without colour of right ... any computer service" including the retrieval of data, may be subject to a criminal law offence.

Danilantiq/Shutterstock

How much privacy can we reasonably expect in the digital age?

An interesting case on this issue involved the criminal trial of Crinu Iliescu (unreported). Mr. Iliescu's criminal troubles were discussed in his civil trial against his former employer for wrongful dismissal, *Iliescu v Voicegenie Technologies Inc.*, [2009] OJ No 85 (Ont SCJ) affirmed by *Iliescu v Voicegenie Technologies Inc.*, [2010] OJ No 480 (Ont CA). After Mr. Iliescu was fired from his job, he "surreptitiously accessed" his previous employer's computer network and downloaded documents that he felt would assist him in his civil law claim. When Mr. Iliescu submitted this documentation to the court, the employer notified Toronto Police that their system had been unlawfully accessed by Mr. Iliescu and he was arrested and charged with "improper use of a computer under section 342.1(1)(a) of the *Criminal Code*. Mr. Iliescu was convicted at trial, but on appeal the charges were set aside (mainly because of charges of "malicious prosecution claims"), and a new trial was ordered. The Crown's office decided not to proceed with a second trial and withdrew the charges. Thus, evidence that is obtained in an illegal way may not simply be inadmissible in a civil law case, but the accused may also be arrested under the *Criminal Code*.[14]

13. David Paciocco and Lee Stuesser, *The Law of Evidence,* 2nd ed (Toronto: Irwin, 1999) at 67.

14. Katherine Cooligan, "You've Got Mail: Snooping Emails, Privacy Law, and Admissibility of Evidence" (2011) *Ontario Bar Association* 26

Trial

The trial process begins all the way back when one pleads not guilty to the specific charges that are contained in the **information** or **indictment**. Since many charges end with a plea bargain or withdrawal by the Crown, there are few trials in comparison to the charges laid. Many estimate that only about 10 percent of criminal cases come to trial. Preliminary matters are taken care of at the beginning of trial, including the admissibility of evidence, and then the trial begins.

In complex matters, the Crown may make an opening statement outlining the evidence it will present. Each witness of the Crown will be examined by the prosecution in what is called an **examination in chief**, and then **cross-examined** by the defence counsel.

If the Crown does not prove its case, the defence lawyer does not have to provide a defence, and the judge can dismiss the action for lack of evidence. If the Crown does make out a case where there is evidence on each element of the offence for which the trier of fact could convict, the defence can decide whether to call evidence. The defence may also make an opening statement and call witnesses who may be cross-examined by the Crown. If the defence calls evidence, then the defence makes the first closing statement. If the defence does not call evidence, then the defence make its submissions last.

The judge then instructs the jury on the key points of substantive law including the burden and the standards of proof and the use of the evidence. It is the jury members' recollection of evidence that will inform their decision. The lawyers may make submissions to the judge on what procedure should be reviewed with the jury before they make their decision, and then the judge may pass this information to the jury. If there is no jury, the judge reviews the evidence in order to make a decision.

The jury then makes a decision based on the facts that were deemed admissible evidence after applying all of the relevant tests. A judge alone makes a decision or adjourns the matter in order to review the evidence and provide reasons for the judgment. The judge will usually submit a written judgment and will sentence the accused (see Chapter 12).

Appeal

After the accused has been found guilty of the charges against him or her, there is an ability to appeal to a higher court. If the charge was indictable, the appeal is made to the court of appeal for the province or territory in which the original trial took place. If it is a summary offence, the appeal is made to the superior branch of the provincial court, as set out in s 812 of the *Criminal Code*.

A person convicted to an indictable offence may appeal the conviction, the sentence, or both. The conviction can be appealed "as a right" or automatically on any **question of law**. This means that an appeal is automatically allowed in these situations. The accused may also appeal the conviction on the grounds of mixed law and fact or a **question of fact** alone, with the permission of the higher court. The line between questions of law and questions of fact is not always easy to ascertain. For example, a question of fact would be whether Jimmy touched Billy, a question of law would be whether that touch amounts to assault under s 266 of the *Criminal Code*. To appeal to the Supreme Court of Canada, one must get **leave to appeal** from the court.

CONCLUSION

The *way* that evidence is collected is often even more important than *what* is gathered in our justice system. The Canadian criminal system has complex rules in place, using the guidance of the *Charter*, to ensure that the rights of the individual are not trammelled by the power of the state. This may lead to difficult negotiations about what crime fits the actions of the accused, and what proof there may be of a crime. Once this is established, it is the duty of defence counsel to craft a defence to a crime for his or her client if the matter is going to trial (see Chapter 11). Finally, if the accused is convicted, the court must determine a proper sentence for the crime, and decide if alternative measures should be considered (Chapter 12).

LEARNING OUTCOMES SUMMARIZED

1. Discuss the test using s 1 of the *Charter* established by the Supreme Court of Canada in the *R v Oakes* case.

Mr. Oakes was in possession of a prohibited drug, but at the time of the trial the onus shifted to the defendant to show that he was *not* going to traffic the drug. The court found that although there was a strong reason to try to prevent the sale of drugs, it needed to determine if this was enough of a reason to "save" the provision under s 1 of the *Charter*. There must be a strong reason to show that you should override *Charter* rights. The court found that two central criteria must be satisfied to establish that a limit is reasonable and demonstrably justified in a free and democratic society, including:

1. The reason to infringe a *Charter* right must be important and must be "pressing and substantial" to be important enough to take away a fundamental freedom from an individual.
2. If there is a really good reason to take away a right, there must be a "proportionality test." Step two of the test has several elements:

   a. The law must accomplish only what is stated.
   b. It should impair the rights of the individual as "little as possible."
   c. There must be a proportionate effect between the measures and the objectives it was trying to accomplish, they cannot be worse than the original problem, and the more severe the effects of the measure, the more important the objective has to be.

2. Assess what evidence the defence must raise in a preliminary hearing and the reasoning behind this decision.

The purpose of a preliminary hearing is to prevent persons from being subject to trial where criminal punishment is not warranted. The defence may call witnesses, but usually it is not in the defence's best interests to do so and reveal the defence, but they may wish to test their evidence. The justice may also commit an accused to stand trial for additional offences that are revealed from the evidence at the preliminary hearing, and it is also an opportunity for the defence to obtain a reduction in charges. The accused may be more willing to enter into a plea negotiation after he or she has seen the strength of the Crown's case. Although the preliminary hearing does not establish guilt, the Crown may choose to proceed to trial despite the finding of the preliminary hearing.

3. Identify what the Crown/defence can agree to in return for an accused pleading guilty.

1. Reducing charges.
2. Finding lesser but included charges.
3. Withdrawal or stay of some of the charges.
4. Promise not to charge friends or family.
5. Negotiation of a peace bond.
6. Reducing the seriousness of a charge.
7. Reducing crimes to summary offences rather than indictable.
8. Make sentencing recommendation.
9. No opposition to sentence recommendations.
10. Joint submission on sentencing.
11. No appeal of sentence.
12. No request of a severe sentence.

13. No prohibitions or forfeiture orders.
14. Intermittent sentence rather than a continuous sentence.
15. Negotiation on conditions imposed.
16. Negotiation to change the place where the charges proceed.
17. Not to pursue a dangerous offender designation.
18. Negotiation about the place or type of treatment.
19. Negotiation on sentencing judge.
20. Not to volunteer information or talk about circumstances that could be an aggravating factor.

4. Discuss the elements that have been found to potentially induce false confessions.

Police interrogation is a psychological process involving three components: isolation as a means to increase the suspect's anxiety; confrontation, whereby the interrogator accuses the suspect of the crime using real or fictitious evidence; and minimization, where the investigator conveys sympathy and provides a moral justification for the crime. Others discuss the technique of maximization where the interrogators convey to the accused a solid belief that the suspect is guilty. Interrogations are designed to be stress-inducing in order to obtain confessions from suspects. Other techniques include invading the suspect's personal space, keeping light switches, thermostats, and other control devices out of the suspect's reach, and using a one-way mirror to look for signs of fatigue, weakness, anxiety, and withdrawal, and body language.

SELF-EVALUATION QUESTIONS

1. The *Constitution Act 1867* says that the federal parliament has jurisdiction over which fields in relation to criminal law?
2. What may the accused in a criminal matter plead?
3. The *Charter of Rights and Freedoms* only addresses what disputes?
4. Describe the circumstances under which an individual may be punished by incarceration to a federal penitentiary.
5. In the case of *R v Feeney,* Mr. Feeney was found by police with blood on his shirt. The Supreme Court found that Mr. Feeney should not have been convicted. Discuss these reasons.

Criminal Law Defences

Learning Outcomes

After completing this chapter, you should be able to:

1. Discuss the elements involved in the defence of necessity.
2. Assess the different types of automatism.
3. Identify the elements of duress both statutorily and in the common law.
4. Discuss the remaining defence of intoxication after *Daviault*.
5. List the developing defences in Canada today, as identified in this chapter.

CRIMINAL LAW DEFENCES

It is important to note from the outset that there is no need for a defendant to launch a defence. There is no requirement that a criminal defendant must testify to what happened, or rebut evidence, or do anything after he or she has pleaded not guilty. The ultimate burden is on the Crown to prove all elements of the evidence. However, there are situations where a person convicted of a crime may tell the court that he or she should escape responsibility by using a criminal **defence**. Many of these defence fact situations fall within the ambit of **excuses**. An example of an excuse would be someone who completed the criminal actions but did so under duress because there was a gun to his or her head. Thus, even though the individual acted, he or she should be excused. There are also what are called **justification** defences. An example would be someone who admitted to breaking driving and related offences under the *Criminal Code* but did so to get an accident victim to the hospital. We consider justifications rightful rather than wrongful. Many in society are critical of defences in the criminal law.

Although the Crown always has the ultimate burden of proof (as we have discussed in previous chapters), the defence may have an **evidentiary burden** when it comes to a defence. Often the defence must meet the **air of reality** test. This test asks if a properly instructed jury *could* acquit the accused using a defence. Once a judge finds that there is some believability to the defence, the burden is then on the prosecution to prove the guilt of the accused beyond any reasonable doubt, including that the defence is inapplicable. For example, Mr. Bradshaw is accused of murder, but he says that he was simply defending himself. Mr. Bradshaw's lawyer must submit to the court that there is an air of reality that the accused was attempting to defend himself using self-defence, and he should not be convicted of murder. Once this is done, the Crown has the burden to prove that the crime was committed beyond a reasonable doubt, and to show that self-defence does not apply in this particular situation.

Ignorance or Mistake of Law

The maxim "ignorance of the law is no excuse" is codified in s 19 of the *Criminal Code*, which states that "ignorance of the law by a person who commits an offence is not an excuse for committing that offence." This **mistake of law** can include ignorance of the existence of a law or its meaning, ignorance to the scope of the law, and ignorance to the application of the law. The rationale for this section is that all Canadians have the responsibility to know the laws of the country, and they must govern their actions accordingly. However, there are also the concerns of the system over the fairness of treating accused persons with respect and giving them fair notice of all laws. If people are assumed to know the law, then the law must be clearly stated, and this is often not the case. How much of the law should you know? The following box looks at ignorance of the law.

IGNORANCE OF THE LAW IN THE NEWS

In May 2010, the RCMP learned that boys in grades 11 and 12 (16- to 18-year-olds) at a British Columbia high school had a Facebook competition challenging boys to see who could have sex with the most grade 8 girls (who were 13 years old). The authorities were alerted after administrators at a Surrey School District school read the postings on Facebook and talked to students. Although no victims came forward, a letter was sent to parents of the senior boys and another letter to the families of the grade 8 girls.

The RCMP visited the school to explain the *Criminal Code* to the boys and to tell them that having sex with someone under the age of 14 (depending on the age of the boys) may be a crime punishable by a maximum sentence of ten years under s 151 of the *Criminal Code*. A spokesman for the district said that the senior boys were "surprised by the information."[1]

If one of these 18-year-old boys was proven to have had sex with a 13-year-old girl, should ignorance of law be an excuse because he is a high school student?

See ss. 150 and 151 of the *Criminal Code*. Do you agree with these sections and the age limits proscribed?

Some say that s 19 of the *Criminal Code* is too broad, as there are many offences that include knowing the law as an element of the *actus reus* or *mens rea*, so individuals must be aware they are breaking the law. However, the accused is permitted to raise a mistake of fact as a valid defence.

Mistake of Fact

Mistake of fact is a defence that prevents an accused from forming the proper *mens rea* for the crime. It is mainly used by an accused who acts innocently under a flawed understanding of the facts. It is often difficult to tell what is a mistake of law, mistake of fact, or a mistake of both, but only a mistake of fact is a defence. There must be an *innocent* mistake of fact for a defence to be proven. The court found that there was no innocent mistake in *R v Kundeus* (see the following case box).

1. The Canadian Press, "Cloverdale Students Caught in Facebook Sex Contest" (21 May 2010), CTV News, online: <http ://www.ctvbc.ctv.ca/servlet/an/local/CTVNews/20100521/bc_sex_contest_100521/20100521?hub=BritishColumbiaHome>.

R v KUNDEUS, [1976] 2 SCR 272 (SCC)

The accused was charged with trafficking the illegal drug "LSD." Mr. Kundeus offered to sell "speed, acid, MDA or hash" to an undercover police officer. The officer asked to buy hash or acid (LSD), but the accused said that he only had "mescaline," a drug that is illegal to sell without a prescription. The drug was given to the officer, but when tested, the mescaline in fact contained LSD. The accused argued the defence of mistaken belief of fact. He did not know that he was selling LSD—he simply thought it was mescaline. This case went to the Supreme Court, which convicted Mr. Kundeus of trafficking LSD. The court said that any intention to traffic drugs (any illegal drug, including mescaline) was enough to form the *mens rea* of the offence, and the *actus reus* of selling LSD established the other element. Since the accused did not testify, the court found that there was no evidence of an honest belief that the substance was another drug, nor was there other evidence that he intended only to sell mescaline. Mr. Kundeus was convicted of trafficking LSD despite the alleged mistake of fact.

Should the court make assumptions from the lack of testimony on the part of the accused? Should there be no adverse inference drawn from a decision of Mr. Kundeus not to testify?
Do you think this case was wrongly decided? Why?

Although these defences go to one of the essential elements of the case, most defences are much more complex.

Necessity

The defence of necessity refers to situations in which crimes are in a sense involuntary; one is forced to do something he or she may otherwise not have done in reaction to the circumstances. Historically, necessity was a defence that the court resisted accepting. In the case of *Southwark London Borough Council v Williams* [1971] 1 Ch. 734, the court said that it had been reluctant to recognize necessity because, as Lord Denning said, "[n]ecessity would open a door which no man could shut," and the defence "would be an excuse for all sorts of wrongdoing." Lord Justice Edmund Davies stated in the same case that "necessity can very easily become simply a mask for anarchy." However, the door was opened to the defence.

Necessity is a **common law defence**, which means that it is not provided for specifically in the *Criminal Code* but rather it exists because of s 8(3) of the *Criminal Code,* which allows for common law defences to continue to exist. So, the way necessity has been interpreted comes directly from the case law on the subject.

Those using the defence of necessity say that the evil trying to be avoided is greater than breaking the law. A typical example is that of a mountain climber who breaks into an abandoned cabin for warmth when he would have frozen to death outside. The choice was death or to break the law (break into the property) to survive. Some say that the choice in these circumstances is no real choice at all. Although many of the cases deal with threats from nature, this does not necessarily have to be the case. Necessity is an excuse in urgent situations where the accused has no legal way out. The accused must attempt to resist that pressure before committing the crime.

As explored in Chapter 9, *Dudley & Stephens* (1884), 14 QBD 273 (CCR) is an example of necessity (sailors starving to death on a life raft decide to consume the young cabin boy, who was unconscious). Society is torn about how to deal with those individuals who fall victim to a situation of necessity. Although Dudley and Stephens were convicted of murder and sentenced to death, they were released from prison after six months. Many theorists have said that a very punitive sentence in *Dudley & Stephens* (a death sentence followed by a reduction to a sentence of imprisonment, to eventually commuting the sentence) was required in the case because seamen were seen as "rough" and had a "law unto themselves."[2]

2. See R Cairns-Way and RM Mohr, *Dimensions of Criminal Law,* 2nd ed (Toronto: Emond Montgomery, 1996) at 956.

The verdict in the case was a message to sailors that they were not above the law, and to other occupations, such as mining, that in the case of a cave-in there would not be a precedent that they could select the weakest member to kill and eat. How would you react if you found yourself in this type of situation? See the What Would You Do box.

WHAT WOULD YOU DO?

What would you do if you were on a lifeboat that was sinking under the weight of too many passengers?

© Classic Image/Alamy

A ship destined for Newfoundland strikes an iceberg. All of the passengers who do not escape to lifeboats sink with the ship. The captain and crew escape with some of the passengers onto two lifeboats, but one raft is not in good condition and begins to leak. Unfortunately, this is the boat with the most passengers crushed together. The occupants have buckets and cups and start bailing the water coming into the lifeboat, but it continues to fill with water. The crew realizes that the boat can only accommodate half the passengers onboard, even without a leak threatening all of their lives. The crew decides that the lives of everyone onboard are in jeopardy, and something must be done.

The crew on the leaky lifeboat asks the captain (who is on the other lifeboat) to take some of the passengers into the other boat or they would have to draw straws to see who should be thrown overboard. The captain replied that this plan to board his boat should only be the last resort. The two boats drift away from each other, and the captain and his lifeboat are rescued. The other boat remains at sea.

After 24 hours the crew decides they have to throw some of the passengers overboard. The crew decides that 14 male passengers and two females should be thrown overboard, excluding only two married men who had their wives onboard, and a small boy. The passengers are not consulted, and none of the crew goes overboard.

You are one of the crew members onboard. It is up to you to decide who will live and who will die. Do you agree that the male passengers should be thrown overboard? Do you think more of the women should be thrown over? What about the children?

What would you do? What should be the legal response?

See *United States v Holmes,* (1842) 26 F. Cas. 360 (No 15,383) (CCED PA).

Judge Macdonald observed in *R v Salvador* (1981), 21 CR (3d) (NSCA), that "the defence of necessity covers all cases where non-compliance with law is excused by an emergency or justified by the pursuit of some greater good." The leading modern Canadian case dealing with necessity was the British Columbia decision in *Perka,* as discussed in the following case box.

R v PERKA, [1984] SCJ NO 40 (SCC)

The accused was charged with importing and possessing narcotics in the amount of \$6–7 million for the purpose of trafficking in Canada. The marijuana, from Columbia, was supposed to be shipped to Alaska along the Pacific coast, but Canadian authorities ended up recovering 33.49 tons of marijuana in the form of 634 "bales" of cannabis.

At trial, the accused individuals used the defence of necessity by claiming that they did not plan to import drugs into Canada, since their destination was Alaska. They explained that because of mechanical problems made worse by the bad weather, they decided to flee to the Canadian shoreline for the safety of the ship and crew. When the ship attempted to land, it was grounded on a rock, and the captain ordered the crew to offload the marijuana.

The crew landed on the west coast of Vancouver Island. When the police arrived on the scene, most of the marijuana was onshore. The accused individuals argued that they were simply going to make repairs to the boat, load up their marijuana, and go about their way. Experts testified that the need to come to shore was imminent and lives may have been lost if they had not come ashore. The accused were acquitted at trial. The Court of Appeal set aside the acquittal and ordered a new trial.

The Supreme Court looked at necessity on the basis of what they called "moral involuntariness." It said that these actions should be measured on society's expectation of what you should resist doing. The court says that the defence only applies in circumstances of "imminent risk," where people are acting to avoid a direct and imminent peril. The act can only be called involuntary if it was inevitable, unavoidable, and where no reasonable opportunity for an alternative course of legal action was available. In addition, the harm done must be less than the harm the accused sought to avoid. The court said that the question should be if the wrongful act (landing on shore with 34 tons of marijuana) was the only option open to the actors, or if they had another choice (e.g., stay out in the water). If they had a choice, then the action was not involuntary.

The court said that in a situation where you should have known that there could have been an emergency requiring you to break the law, it is not permissible to say that your actions were involuntary. Conversely, just because you were involved in criminal or immoral activity when the emergency arose, does not necessarily mean the defence cannot be used.

Where there is evidence, or an air of reality, to a defence of necessity, the onus falls upon the Crown to prove beyond a reasonable doubt that the accused's act was voluntary; the accused bears no ultimate burden of proof. The Supreme Court said the test is whether this circumstance arose in an "urgent situation of clear and imminent peril when compliance with the law is demonstrably impossible." The case failed on the "legal way out" question—was there a reasonable, legal alternative to the peril. According to the Supreme Court, the trial judge did not properly put that question to the jury; therefore, there was an improper jury address, the acquittal was overruled, and a new trial was ordered. This case had the effect of limiting the defence to situations where there is no reasonable legal alternative to breaking the law.

There are three elements to the defence of necessity that came out of *Perka*:

1. there must be a clear and imminent peril or danger;
2. there must be an absence of a reasonable legal alternative; and
3. the harm inflicted must be less than that avoided (i.e., it must be proportional).

The defence of necessity is only available to persons who have committed an illegal act under pressure that no reasonable person could withstand. This three-part test from *Perka* was confirmed in the *Latimer* case, where it was used unsuccessfully in the "mercy killing" case involving Robert Latimer and his daughter Tracey (see the following case box).

R v LATIMER, [2001] 1 SCR 3 (SCC)

Robert Latimer was charged with murder for causing the death of his daughter Tracey, who had cerebral palsy and was in constant pain. Mr. Latimer argued that killing Tracey was a necessity as he had to end her suffering and prevent her from having future painful surgeries.

The trial judge decided not to instruct the jury on the defence of necessity because there was no air of reality (which meant that the jury could not consider this defence), and the Supreme Court affirmed this decision. The Supreme Court rejected the argument on the first step of the test. The court said that the peril had to be immediate: "it must be on

Laura and Robert Latimer

Kevin Frayer/The Canadian Press

the verge of transpiring and virtually certain to occur." This is measured using the modified objective test where necessity is only available where the person's beliefs were reasonable, in light of the circumstances, and then some subjective elements of what was in the person's subjective mind can be considered. In this case, the court said Mr. Latimer had no situation of imminent peril, as Tracey's situation was ongoing, rather than an emergency, and that further surgeries may have helped her condition.

For the second part of the test, the accused must show that there was no "reasonable legal alternative." If there is a legal way of resolving the peril, the accused must choose that alternative. Again, this is on a modified objective test, that the accused must believe reasonably that there was no other way than to break the law. The court found that Mr. Latimer could have continued with things as they were, and could have continued with surgeries even though he did not believe this was a viable or kind option.

The third part of the test is decided on a purely objective basis: was the harm inflicted more than the evil that the accused sought to avoid? The court in *Perka* used the example that it is clearly not proportional to blow up a city to avoid breaking a finger. The court found that the actions must be comparable or greater than the harm inflicted. Some question whether necessity could ever be a defence to murder. The court left this door open in *Latimer,* but found that necessity was not a defence in this case, as the test had not been met.

Thus, the court found that Mr. Latimer's daughter was not in "imminent peril," there were reasonable legal alternatives, and murder was not a proportional response to Tracey's condition. The air of reality was absent in this case, and Mr. Latimer could not use the defence of necessity, and was eventually convicted and served a lengthy prison sentence.

***Latimer* is clearly a very difficult case. Was it properly decided?**
Was this case simply a statement about the rights of the disabled?

Although it may seem that a defence of necessity might never be successful, there have been some cases where necessity was used. In the Alberta case of *R v Morris,* [1981] AJ No 561, 61 CCC (2d) 163 (Alta QB), the accused had been charged with the assault of his wife. They were coming home from the local pub, and the wife was extremely intoxicated and was putting the safety of the vehicle in jeopardy. The accused grabbed and restrained his wife simply because the car was moving, and he had no other legal alternative than to restrain her so that they did not hurt themselves or others. Thus, the assault charge was successfully challenged with the defence of necessity, and the husband was acquitted.

Another unusual case was the case of *R v Lotufo,* [2008] OJ No 2894 (Ont SCJ), where the accused was charged with the dangerous operation of a motor vehicle, failing to stop, and operating a motor vehicle while being pursued by a peace officer. These offences happened after the accused was approached by plain-clothes officers, who attempted to arrest him. There were no activated police lights on the car. It was a dark, raining, and late at night, and he had no idea that he was the subject of a police sting. The trial judge accepted that Mr. Lotufo did not know that these individuals were police officers, but rather strange men who were pointing guns at him. The court found it was not unreasonable to drive off in a dangerous manner to escape these men as he believed, reasonably, that his life was at risk. The Crown failed to prove beyond a reasonable doubt that the defence of necessity did not apply.

One can conclude by looking at these cases that, rather than becoming the "mask of anarchy," the defence of necessity has been attempted few times, and has been successful in even fewer cases.

Zdorov Kirill Vladimirovich/ Shutterstock

The traditional view of duress

Defence of Duress

The defences of duress and necessity are intertwined. Duress is a threat from another human being, while necessity is often a threat from the situation (as discussed, a choice between disaster and choosing to break the law). Both necessity and duress ask whether the person acted in a voluntary manner. In necessity, one can be said to have to choose between two evils. In duress, a person is faced with threats of death or grievous bodily harm from another person if he or she does not comply. Over time the defence of duress (also called compulsion, compulsion by threats, or coercion) was conceptualized as a full defence, as a "concession to human frailty."[3] Humans cannot make perfect decisions when their lives may be in jeopardy.

Like necessity, there is a common law defence of duress. However, it is very confusing because there is *also* a statutory basis to duress. The common law defence is slightly different and not as onerous as s 17 of the *Criminal Code,* but it is only available for offences that are not *excluded* under s 17. Section 17 of the *Criminal Code* provides that:

> 17. A person who commits an offence under compulsion by threats of immediate death or bodily harm from a person who is present when the offence is committed is excused for committing the offence if the person believes that the threats will be carried out and if the person is not a party to a conspiracy or association whereby the person is subject to compulsion, but this section does not apply where the offence that is committed is high treason or treason, murder, piracy, attempted murder, sexual assault, sexual assault with a weapon, threats to a third party or causing bodily harm, aggravated sexual assault, forcible abduction, hostage taking, robbery, assault with a weapon or causing bodily harm, aggravated assault, unlawfully causing bodily harm, arson or an offence under sections 280 to 283 (abduction and detention of young persons).

The common law defence says that there are six elements that must be fulfilled for a duress defence:

1. The threats must be of death or serious bodily harm.
2. The threats must be sufficiently serious that the accused believed he or she would be carried out.
3. The threats were of such a gravity that the reasonable person might have acted in the same manner.
4. There was no safe avenue of escape.
5. There must be proportionality between the threat and the reaction.
6. The defence is not available if the accused is put in the situation as part of a criminal organization.

After the case of *Ruzic* (see the following case box), most of the differences between the codified defence and the common law defence seemed to be eliminated. In the case of *R v Hibbert* [1995] 2 SCR 973, the Supreme Court made it clear that duress did not affect the *actus reus* or the *mens rea* of the offence, apart from exceptional circumstances. Thus, duress is usually considered a complete defence. The case that set the stage for the future of duress in Canada was the case of *Ruzic.*

R v RUZIC, [2001] SCJ NO 25 (SCC)

Marijana Ruzic was charged with unlawfully importing two kilograms of heroin (with an estimated street value of $1 million) into Canada on April 29, 1994, contrary to s 5(1) of the *Narcotic Control Act* (now *Controlled Drugs and Substances Act*, SC 1996, c 19), and was also charged with possession and use of a false passport, contrary to s 368 of the *Criminal Code.* The offences charged were not excluded offences under s 17 of the *Criminal Code.*

3. *R v Howe & Burke*, [1987] AC 417 at 432 (HL).

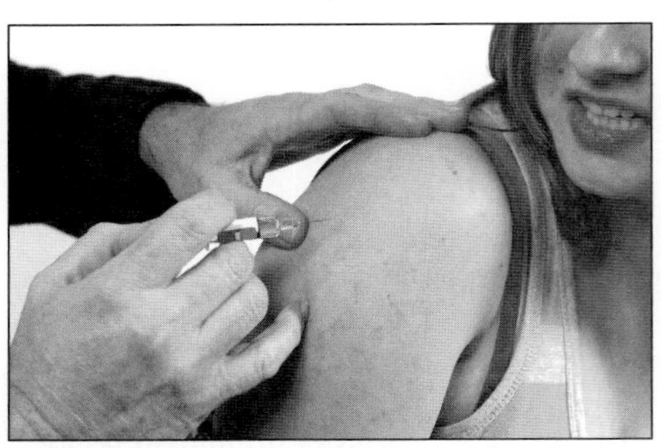
Ruzic claimed she was forcibly injected with heroin, among other abuses.

Patricia Hofmeester/Shutterstock

Ms. Ruzic testified that she was forced to bring the drugs to Canada or her mother would be harmed or killed in Belgrade in the former Yugoslavia. A man named Mirko Mirkovic knew personal information about the accused and approached Ms. Ruzic on several occasions. He claimed to know that Ms. Ruzic's mother was ill and that they lived together. Ms. Ruzic, who was only 21 years old at the time, was the sole caretaker for her mother, and she did not want to cause her mother concern by telling her about this situation.

Ms. Ruzic testified that she felt she could not seek the assistance of the police because of the authorities' potential involvement with criminal organizations in Yugoslavia and that "people die in the streets. We don't have a law; it's corruption. And the crime is very high and so people are afraid." Mr. Mirkovic showed Ms. Ruzic a knife and said that he liked to "cut people." He started sexually touching the defendant and telling her that he would like to have sex with Ms. Ruzic and her mother. The violence escalated, and Mr. Mirkovic burned the defendant with a lighter and injected her with a needle of a substance that she believed was heroin.

Mr. Mirkovic strapped three packages of heroin to Ms. Ruzic's body and told her she had to travel to Canada with the drugs or he would "do something" to her mother. Upon entering the country, Ms. Ruzic lied to Canadian Immigration officers, but eventually the packages of heroin were discovered in her possession.

Before *Ruzic,* courts had been restrictive with their interpretation and application of s 17 of the *Criminal Code,* and Ms. Ruzic would come under this codified provision. At trial, defence counsel argued that Ms. Ruzic did not meet the "immediacy" or "presence" requirements of s 17, and that s 17 violated s 7 of the *Charter* and that it was not saved by s 1 (because the threatener was not present with the threatened party, the threat was to a third party, and there was not an immediate threat to the victim). On the surface, Ms. Ruzic did not meet many of the requirements of the codified version of duress. The trial judge ruled that s 17 did violate the *Charter,* and instead instructed the jury on the *common law* defence of duress. Ms. Ruzic was acquitted of all charges using the common law defence of duress.

This case was appealed to the Supreme Court. Justice LeBel, writing for the unanimous court, said that the issues came down to "moral involuntariness." They said that a person who was being threatened like Ms. Ruzic should not be punished because she had no realistic choice whether or not to break the law. It is a principle of fundamental justice that only voluntary conduct that is a product of a free will and controlled body (that is not being controlled by someone else) should be convicted under the criminal law. The court said that labelling someone a criminal and taking away their liberty would infringe the principles of fundamental justice as defined in Canada as Ms. Ruzic did not have any realistic choice.

The court used this reasoning to strike down the "immediacy" and "presence" requirements of s 17 of the *Criminal Code.* As Justice LeBel noted in the decision "[t]he plain meaning of s 17 is quite restrictive in scope. Indeed, the section seems tailor-made for the situation in which a person is compelled to commit an offence at gun point." The fact is that not every case involves a gunman who is present and threatening immediate force. The defence is more nuanced than this typical example. Ms. Ruzic was acquitted of the charges and let go without punishment using the common law defence of duress.

Do you agree with this case?
Why might the court have accepted the testimony of Ms. Ruzic?

It is easier to acquit an offender who did not injure another person. Controversy, however, surrounds the defence, particularly where the threats involve the sacrifice of an innocent life to save another. Theorist Alan Brudner asks the question about a person who, with a "gun pointed at his head, kills an innocent child at the behest of a terrorist. Is he a victim who merely chose life over death? Or, is he the villain because 'his aversion to dying was greater than his aversion to killing?'"[4] These are difficult questions with no easy answers. One important step in the defence of duress is that the defence must have an air of reality. This was the issue in *McRae,* as discussed in the following case box.

4. Alan Brudner, "A Theory of Necessity" (1987) 7 *Oxford Journal of Legal Studies* 339 at 353.

R v McRAE, [2005] OJ NO 3200 (ONT CA)

The Ontario Court of Appeal case of *McRae* affirmed that the common law defence of duress (as set out earlier in the chapter). In this case, Mr. McRae (the accused) was charged with being an accessory after the fact to murder. Mr. McRae's cousin, Mr. Armstrong, picked up hitchhikers and took them to the McRae family cabin in northern Ontario. Mr. Armstrong killed two of the hitchhikers and their dog, and Mr. McRae assisted in destroying evidence and burning the remains of the victims. The issue on appeal was whether Mr. McRae was under duress when he disposed of the bodies. Mr. McRae said the only reason he helped was because he feared for his safety, and he had no safe avenue of escape. Although Mr. Armstrong did not verbally or explicitly threaten to kill Mr. McRae, he had already killed two people and he had a gun. The cabin was in an area with difficult terrain, which Mr. McRae believed would not allow him to escape. The trial judge said there was no air of reality to the defence.

The Court of Appeal reviewed this decision and said the situation that Mr. McRae found himself in could "reasonably be perceived as one of stark horror involving escalating levels of irrational violence." The higher court said that Mr. Armstrong's conduct, his instructions to Mr. McRae to assist, and the presence of the gun were capable of communicating a serious threat that he could be killed if he did not cooperate. The Court of Appeal found that the trial judge erred in finding that there was no air of reality to the defendant's duress defence. The court set aside the conviction and ordered a new trial.

Do you think that Mr. McRae fulfills the other elements of the common law defence of duress?

There is a question if any of the excluded offences in the codified version of duress should continue to exist. There was a successful constitutional challenge in the case of *R v Fraser* [2002] NSJ No 401 in the Nova Scotia Provincial Court in 2002, in which robbery was taken off of the list of excluded offences in the *Criminal Code*. However, the list remains as a part of s 17 today, and if you look at the current duress section, robbery is still listed. Many have said there is no reasonable way to use s 17 of the *Criminal Code*, and some courts have seemed to take for granted that s 17 is no longer in effect. In *R v MPD*, [2003] BCJ No 771 (BC Prov Ct), the court found that it would not address how s 17 of the *Criminal Code* violates the *Charter* because it "appears that is now settled law in Canada. I need only have consideration to the common law principles relating to duress." Thus, the present and future states of duress are quite uncertain.

Defence of Mental Disorder—Not Criminally Responsible by Means of Mental Disorder (NCRMD)

The Canadian defence of mental disorder is found in s 16 of the *Criminal Code of Canada,* which states that no one is responsible for any act or an omission that was committed when the accused suffered from a mental disorder. It is a fundamental part of the defence that the accused was incapable of "appreciating the nature and quality of the act or omission or of knowing that it was wrong." However, this is a defence that frequently causes public concern. More commonly known as the "insanity defence," the not criminally responsible by means of mental disorder (NCRMD) finding concludes that an accused who commits an act or omission cannot be held responsible if a mental disorder prevented the accused from understanding the nature or wrongfulness of his or her act.

Although some say that this type of defence has existed as far back as the 13th century, the mental disorder defence fully emerged in the eighteenth century during the English case of *Rex v Arnold*, 16 Howell's State Trials 695 (10 George I. A.D. 1724), with what was then described as the "wild beast defence." Edward Arnold was tried for maliciously and wilfully shooting at, and wounding, the Right Honourable Lord Onslow. Mr. Arnold believed that Mr. Onslow sent people to disturb him, and he believed that Mr. Onslow was an "enemy of God and country and should be destroyed." Even though the judge found the shooting was only malicious if

Mr. Arnold was sane, he was nevertheless found guilty, and sentenced to be executed. However, in recognition that Mr. Arnold may have been insane, the sentence was commuted to life in prison.

Clearly, a more refined approach was needed to determine whether an accused suffered from a mental disorder, but this was an early recognition of reduced culpability of those who were insane. In 1843, the "M'Naghten Rule" was established when Daniel M'Naghten attempted to assassinate British Prime Minister Robert Peel, as discussed in the following case box.

M'NAGHTEN'S CASE (1843), 10 CL & FIN 200

Daniel M'Naghten believed he was being persecuted by the government. He shot and killed Edward Drummond, the secretary to Prime Minister Sir Robert Peel, thinking that he was assassinating Sir Peel. At trial, Mr. M'Naghten said he could not control his actions, and many witnesses testified that he was mentally ill. The jury found Mr. M'Naghten not guilty on the grounds of insanity. The public was outraged that someone would be found not guilty on these grounds, and Parliament reviewed the decision. Judges were asked to attend the House, and the answers to questions posed to them formed what were called the "M'Naghten Rules," in which the accused must be suffering from "natural imbecility," "a disease of the mind," or a "specific delusion." These rules eventually formed the basis for s 16 of the *Canadian Criminal Code*. The terms "insane" and "insanity" were replaced with "mental disorder" and "suffering from a mental disorder" in later years.[5]

Mr. M'Naghten went to a mental hospital until the time of his death, but the law became concerned with the state of mind of the accused at the time of the offence. It was now important to examine if the accused could understand the nature and quality of the act or omission in question or did not realize it was wrong. If the accused cannot understand the act or know it was wrong, that person must be acquitted.

M'Naghten trial at the Central Criminal Court, 1843

5. Morris Manning and Peter Sankoff, *Manning, Mewett & Sankoff: Criminal Law*, 4th ed (Markham ON: Lexis Nexis, 2009) at 413.

Section 16 of the *Criminal Code* provides that:

(1) No person is criminally responsible for an act committed or an omission made while suffering from a mental disorder that rendered the person incapable of appreciating the nature and quality of an act or omission or of knowing that it was wrong.
(2) Every person is presumed not to suffer from a mental disorder so as to be exempt from criminal responsibility by virtue of subsection (1), until the contrary is proved on the balance of probabilities.
(3) The burden of proof that an accused was suffering from a mental disorder so as to be exempt from criminal responsibility is on the party that raises the issue.

Section 672.34 of the *Criminal Code* provides that if there is a finding of NCRMD, then the "judge or jury shall render a verdict that the accused committed the act or made the omission but is not criminally responsible on account of mental disorder." The accused is presumed not to suffer from a mental disorder; thus, the onus of proof lies on the party who raises the defence of NCRMD. In many cases, although the medical community may agree that the individual has a defined mental disorder, the accused is often found capable of understanding right from wrong from a legal perspective and of foreseeing the consequences of his or her actions and is, therefore, not eligible for the NCRMD defence.

Expert testimony of psychiatrists, psychologists, and other medical professionals has become important in the modern-day NCRMD defence. Since sanity is presumed in all cases, experts may be called to prove the defence on a balance of probabilities. However, legal insanity must be ultimately decided by the judge and jury, and not just the experts. A finding of NCRMD must take into account the ability to tell right from wrong from the subjective perspective of the accused, as in the case of *R v Oommen* (see the following case box).

R v OOMMEN, [1994] SCJ NO 60 (SCC)

Mr. Oommen suffered from psychosis of a paranoid delusional type. The delusions caused him to believe that members of a local union were conspiring to destroy him. The victim, Ms. Beaton, was a friend who asked Mr. Oommen if she could stay in his apartment for a period of time in exchange for cooking and cleaning. Mr. Oommen came to believe that Ms. Beaton was part of the conspiracy, and he believed that members of the union had surrounded his building to kill him. This convinced him that he had to kill his friend in order to save his own life. Mr. Oommen shot his friend where she lay sleeping on the floor.

At the second-degree murder trial, the accused raised the mental disorder defence. Psychiatrists testified that the accused had a general capacity to distinguish right from wrong, but on the night of the murder his delusions deprived him of that capacity and made him believe killing was necessary, given that, in his mind, the union had surrounded the building.

The trial court said because the accused had a general ability to tell right from wrong, NCRMD was inapplicable. This was the finding despite the fact that at the time of the killing the accused thought he was doing the right thing and he was unable to apply his knowledge of right and wrong to that particular situation. The Court of Appeal for Alberta allowed the accused's appeal and ordered a new trial.

The Supreme Court found that s 16 not only looks at a general intellectual ability to tell right from wrong, but the ability to apply this knowledge to the criminal act. Mr. Oommen honestly thought he was in danger and that the killing of the victim was justified. This deprived him of knowing right from wrong; he believed the killing was allowed. He was so disordered that he was unable to consider what was right and wrong in the way a normal person would reason. Thus, s 16 is not just about the intellectual ability to tell right from wrong, but the capacity to apply that knowledge to the situation. The highest court ordered a new trial.

Review Boards

A finding of NCRMD is not a full acquittal—the accused does not walk out of the courtroom as a free citizen. Although the accused is not held criminally responsible, the court acknowledges the potential danger the accused poses to the public and thus mental health orders can be made. Those who are acquitted on these grounds may be committed to a psychiatric institution and subjected to "state-determined psychiatric assessment, treatment, and detention."[6] This means that individuals are held for an indefinite term subject to periodic review. Those who agree with this method of punishment point to the interest of protecting the public.

The Alberta Review Board, **http://justice.alberta.ca/programs_services/about_us/Pages/ab_review_board.aspx**
The British Columbia Review Board **http://www.bcrb.bc.ca**
The Ontario Review Board **http://www.orb.on.ca/scripts/en/about.asp#membership**

A review board will decide if the offender shall be detained and/or treated in a psychiatric institution. A review board is established under s 672.38 of the *Criminal Code,* which provides that it shall be "established or designated for each province to make or review dispositions concerning any accused in respect of whom a verdict of not criminally responsible by reason of mental disorder or unfit to stand trial is rendered, and shall consist of not fewer than five members appointed by the lieutenant governor in council of the province." At least one member must be in the psychiatric profession, and another member must have mental health training and experience. The members are appointed by the Lieutenant Governor in Council for each province, even though the *Criminal Code* is a federal statute. The chairperson must be a federal court, superior court, district, or county court judge, or a person who has retired from or could be appointed as a judge (with ten years of experience as a lawyer). The Ontario Review Board sits in panels of five members.

The review board must consider what is consistent with the protection of the public and the needs of the accused, which could range from absolute discharge where he or she is not a threat to the safety of the public, discharge with conditions, or custody in a hospital with conditions. Those who are found NCRMD remain under the authority of a review board, which examines cases until offenders are no long deemed a public threat. However, depending on the case, this process can take years, and the NCRMD individual could be detained or subjected to conditional supervision longer than if he or she was found guilty of the original crime. Review occurs at least every 12 months and can continue indefinitely.

The public is rather skeptical of the NCRMD defence. Many believe this verdict is made too easy to use, that offenders are "getting off easy" without punishment, and that NCRMD offenders are likely to be recidivists. In reality, the NCRMD defence is difficult to argue successfully and there can be significant restrictions placed on the offender for a long period of time. For example, consider the case of *R v MLC* (see the following case box).

R v MLC, [2010] OJ NO 5310 (ONT CA)

Mr. MLC appealed a mental health review board's findings and its change of his restrictions to the Court of Appeal. Mr. MLC was a 32-year-old who was found not criminally responsible in relation to charges of assault with a weapon and sexual assault in 2004. His mental disorder was related to his drug use, but his behaviour issues were controlled by prescription medication until 2006. At this time he was permitted to live in the community with 24-hour supervision but was readmitted to the care of a hospital after he tested positive for cannabis. Mr. MLC again improved and went back to supervised accommodation with regular reporting to the hospital five days a week, but it was reduced to three days a week when he showed signs of stabilization.

In August 2009, the review board held its annual review of the patient and noted that Mr. MLC was doing better, and allowed discretion to the hospital to allow him to participate

6. R Cairns-Way and RM Mohr, *Dimensions of Criminal Law,* 2nd ed (Toronto: Emond Montgomery, 1996) at 487.

in community activities. The board decided to have another review after six months instead of one year to further evaluate the offender. However, in late 2009, Mr. MLC inappropriately questioned his case worker in a group setting, and there was a suspicion that he was again using illicit drugs so his reporting to the hospital was again increased to five days a week. After he reported several hours late to the hospital, he was readmitted and tested positive for cannabis and cocaine. Mr. MLC continued to make inappropriate sexual comments and was rude to staff. Even when he was no longer using illicit drugs, conditions continued to deteriorate, and his psychiatrist could not rule out a mental disorder as the cause. The review board found that Mr. MLC should return to the hospital and because he was a significant threat to the public, and he was committed as patient to the hospital. Mr. MLC appealed this finding.

The Court of Appeal found that the review board put reasonable restrictions on Mr. MLC, given the evidence. The review board was also entitled to impose indefinite terms of restrictions that were the least onerous and least restrictive necessary from the view of the public and Mr. MLC. Thus, the review board has significant powers to keep amending its orders to best serve the offender and the public, and to keep Mr. MLC confined to the hospital.

FOOD FOR THOUGHT...

Psychiatrist Thomas Szasz is a very vocal critic of mental illness and the law. In his article "Psychiatry, Ethics and the Criminal Law" (1958), 58 *Columbia Law Review* 183, Szasz says that:

> If the defense of insanity has been raised ... it is considered to be a "matter of fact" for the jury to decide whether the offender suffered from a "mental illness" ... This is unadulterated nonsense ... [the expression "mental illness"] denotes a *theory* (if it denotes anything) and not a fact. This would be true, of course, for any disease, and especially for a bodily disease ... Of course, it is quite possible for a group of people (a jury) to decide that someone is "crazy" or "mentally ill." But this is then *their theory* of why he has acted the way he did. It is no more—or less—a fact than it would be to assert that the accused is possessed by the devil; that is another "theory," now discarded. To believe that one's own theories are facts is considered by many contemporary psychiatrists as a "symptom" of schizophrenia.*

Do you agree? Disagree? Why?

Do lawyers and judges have the ability to identify mental disorders?

Automatism

Automatism is another common law defence that is not found in the *Criminal Code.* A definition of the term comes from *R v Stone,* [1999] SCJ No 27 (SCC), in that automatism is "a state of impaired consciousness ... in which an individual, though capable of action, has no voluntary control over that action." The defence is available for all offences, and once successful, the accused receives a complete acquittal. However, because the defence results in a full release, the courts have placed strict limits on how the defence is used.

Automatism concerns voluntariness, which in turn is part of the *actus reus.* Voluntariness is a key component of criminal liability, and as such, the courts will absolve when it is missing, that is, when someone does not voluntarily act. If someone grabbed your hand when you have a gun, and you shot a bystander, this act cannot be said to be voluntary. The applicability of automatism is broad and can include conditions an individual may

* From Thomas Szasz, "Psychiatry, Ethics and the Criminal Law" (1958), 58 *Columbia Law Review* 183-198. *Columbia Law Review* by ESTREICHER, SAMUEL; COLUMBIA UNIVERSITY Copyright 1958 Reproduced with permission of COLUMBIA LAW REVIEW ASSOCIATION, INC. via Copyright Clearance Center.

experience from concussions, hyperglycemia, sleepwalking, cerebral tumours, physical blows, arteriosclerosis, and some dissociative states. However, there are four main types of automatism.

1. Normal Condition or "Non-Insane" (Non–Mental Disorder) Automatism

The first type of automatism is what the law calls "normal" conditions, which includes sleepwalking and hypnosis, but not anything that would usually be considered a mental disorder. (Earlier courts used the old term "non-insane automatism," which would be referred to today as "non-mental disorder automatism.") These cases are extremely rare. One of the most notorious cases of automatism involved sleepwalking and the much publicized case of *R v Parks,* discussed in the following case box.

R v PARKS, [1992] 2 SCR 871 (SCC)

Ken Parks

Erik Christensen/The Globe and Mail/The Canadian Press

In this Supreme Court of Canada case, the court found that the Crown must establish the *actus reus* of the offence by proving that the act was voluntary. At the time of the offence Mr. Parks was having serious personal problems including the loss of his job because he was stealing company money. Mr. Parks had difficulty sleeping because of these problems, but one night after he had fallen asleep in his living room, he got up, put on his coat and shoes, and drove 23 kilometres to his in-laws' house. Some of the distance was on busy highways, and it took approximately 20 minutes. He parked in their underground parking garage, took a tire iron from his car, entered his in-laws' residence, and retrieved a knife from his in-laws' kitchen.

Mr. Parks strangled his father-in-law until he was unconscious and cut him on the head and chest with the knife (the father-in-law survived this attack). Mr. Parks also stabbed and hit his mother-in-law with a blunt instrument until she was dead. The accused then drove himself to the police station, where he was found with cuts on his hands and blood on his clothing. Mr. Parks was very agitated with the police and said, "My hands; I just killed two people. I killed them; I just killed two people; I've just killed my mother- and father-in-law. I stabbed and beat them to death. It's all my fault."

Mr. Parks had a good relationship with his in-laws before this incident, but he was charged with the murder and attempted murder of his relatives. There seemed to be no motive for the murders. At trial, the defence raised the defence of sleepwalking, and Mr. Parks was acquitted by the jury who believed the evidence of experts that Mr. Parks was sleepwalking during the episode. One of the keys to this finding was that Mr. Parks had an extensive history of sleepwalking that was medically documented. This case was appealed to the Supreme Court. The Supreme Court was careful to say that sleepwalking could, in some circumstances, be mental-disorder automatism, but it was not in this case. Because he raised the defence of automatism and not mental disorder, Mr. Parks was entitled to a full acquittal. Both the Court of Appeal and the Supreme Court agreed that the defence of automatism had been properly left with the jury, and Mr. Parks left the courtroom a free man.

Do you believe that someone who was sleeping could perform these complex actions and commit this brutal crime?

The bottom line for sleepwalking cases is that the courts, like the medical profession, are unsure about what to do with cases of sleep disorders. A more recent case from the Ontario Court of Appeal involves "sexomnia," and is discussed in the following case box.

R v LUEDECKE, [2008] OJ NO 4049 (ONT CA)

Mr. Luedecke had a history of sleepwalking, which is known as a "parasomnia." At 32 years old, he was a well-liked and hard-working man, who owned his own landscaping business. Mr. Luedecke was at a party and decided to sleep over on the couch because he had consumed a large quantity of alcohol throughout the evening (eight to twelve beers, a couple of drinks with rum and Coke, and several vodka drinks). Mr. Luedecke fell asleep beside a woman he did not know, and when the woman woke, she found that the accused was having non-consensual sex with her. Mr. Luedecke immediately admitted that he had non-consensual sex with the victim.

The accused was acquitted of sexual assault on the grounds of non mental-disorder automatism because he had engaged in "sleep sex," which is akin to sleepwalking. Mr. Luedecke had not slept in over 20 hours when he fell asleep, he was very intoxicated, he had been working hard, and he had a history of having sex with previous girlfriends when he was asleep. Expert witnesses said that there was no question that Mr. Luedecke was in a parasomniac state at the time of the sexual assault, and in a study in a sleep clinic Mr. Luedecke had all of the hallmarks of someone who was a sleepwalker. The expert witness looked at the brainwaves of the accused, the fact that he quickly cycled from deep sleep to a wakened state, and his history of sleepwalking, as well as evidence of sleepwalking in his family.

A new trial was ordered on appeal to determine whether there was a proper verdict of acquittal or whether it should have been one of not criminally responsible by means of mental disorder. The court of appeal found it more likely that a NCRMD defence could be established if there was an issue of social protection that needed to be addressed. Under NCRMD, the accused can have long-term restrictions on his or her liberty that might stop this from happening again. Thus, the court of appeal said almost all automatisms are the product of mental disorder and should receive a NCRMD verdict so that the accused can get individualized treatment for the condition. However, the court stressed that it did not find that the accused was mentally disordered; the law uses the concept of mental disorder much differently than the medical community. The court ordered a new trial that would be limited to the question of whether Mr. Luedecke's automatism should be considered NCRMD.

Do you think the fact that Mr. Luedecke was intoxicated changed the application of the automatism defence? How so?

Other sleep-related cases, such as *R v Romas,* [2002] BCJ No 3256 (BC Prov Ct), have found that the accused should be found NCRMD. Mr. Romas had a condition called "confusional sleep arousal," which is close to sleepwalking, but was deemed to be allowable under NCRMD and not automatism.

2. "Insane" or Mental-Disorder Automatism

After the case of *Parks,* Canadian courts have become much more reserved when it comes to the automatism defence, and particularly when an individual raises non-mental-disorder automatism because there is a complete acquittal if the defence is established. This became particularly true with the case of *R v Stone* (see the following case box). Before *Stone,* courts had recognized what was called "psychological-blow automatism." Other cases had argued that because of a psychological event on the accused, he or she was unable to act voluntarily, and therefore the accused should come under non-mental-disorder automatism. Psychological-blow automatism was all but ruled out by the Supreme Court in *Stone,* although it noted that there might be cases where something absolutely shocking happened to the accused and he or she could argue mental-disorder automatism.

R v STONE, [1999] 2 SCR 290 (SCC)

Mr. and Mrs. Stone were on a car trip to visit his sons from a previous marriage. Mrs. Stone insisted that she go on the trip, but objected to the accused seeing his sons after about 15 minutes. When they got back into the car, Mrs. Stone said she was going to leave him, would falsely report to the police that he was abusing her, would take the house and the kids, and he would be forced to support them. Mr. Stone recounted her statements "that she couldn't stand to listen to me whistle, that every time I touched her, she felt sick, that I was [lousy sexually] and that I had a small penis and that she's never going to [have sexual relations with] me again." Mr. Stone stabbed his wife 47 times after she had insulted and berated him in the car.

In his defence of automatism, Mr. Stone said he felt a "whoosh" sensation from head to feet and when he later focused, he saw his wife's lifeless body slumped in the seat. He put her body into the tool box in his truck, went home to get some things and clean up, got some money together, and then he bought a ticket to Mexico. While in Mexico, Mr. Stone said that he recalled stabbing his wife and the whooshing sensation that came over his whole body in the truck. He turned himself in to police back in Canada, and was charged with murder.

In a five-to-four decision, the court said that mental-disorder automatism was properly put to the jury and that non-mental-disorder automatism was not proven. Mr. Stone was found guilty of manslaughter and received a sentence of four years in prison, taking into account the 18-month pre-trial incarceration.

The Supreme Court found it will only be in rare circumstances that automatism is found to be non-mental disorder. The evidence of psychological-blow automatism would have to show that something very shocking happened to the accused to put him or her into a state of automatism. The court said that this might be possible if someone witnessed the murder of a loved one, or if there was a serious assault on a loved one, which left the possibility that this might be re-examined in the future. The court concluded that non-mental-disorder automatism would only occur where the average person would have become disassociated in the same circumstances.

The court said it was important in automatism to see if the accused is a continuing danger, and if triggered, is that behaviour likely to happen again with a risk to the public. The court said that policy concerns could be examined to see if an accused would be better treated under the mental-disorder regime under the *Criminal Code*. Mr. Stone's conviction and sentence was confirmed, although four of the judges dissented on the conviction and would have ordered a new trial.

Do you think the fact that Mr. Stone was not a very sympathetic accused influenced the decision? What if he had seen his wife kill his children?

Thus, it is uncertain what the state of mental-disorder automatism (and non-mental-disorder automatism) is after the case of *Stone*.

3. External Trauma

Some have alleged that a blow to the head can cause a state of automatism through a type of altered consciousness. *R v Bleta* (see the following case box) provides the perfect example of this type of automatism.

R v BLETA, [1964] SCR 561 (SCC)

Mr. Bleta was engaged in a fight on Dundas Street in Toronto. In the course of the fight, Mr. Bleta was knocked (or fell) to the ground and struck his head. The person who knocked Mr. Bleta to the ground began to walk away from the fight, but Mr. Bleta got up from the ground, pulled out a knife, and fatally stabbed him in the neck. Witnesses said that when Mr. Bleta got up from the ground he looked unfocused and was staggering, and a nearby police officer said he looked dazed.

At trial, Mr. Bleta advanced an automatism defence, saying that the blow to his head deprived him of voluntary control over his actions, and he was an automaton when he stabbed the victim. The jury accepted this defence, and the full acquittal was affirmed by the Supreme Court.

4. Involuntary Intoxication Induced by Alcohol or Drugs

There have been situations where the court has found that involuntary intoxication can amount to automatism. For example, if your drink was laced with drugs, you may not be responsible for your resulting actions.

In the case of *R v King,* [1962] SCR 746 (SCC), the accused was charged with impaired driving. The accused went to the dentist to get two teeth taken out. Before the procedure, he signed a form agreeing that he should not drive after the procedure, and he was verbally warned at the end of the appointment that he should have someone drive him home. Mr. King said he did not remember the warnings, and did not know he was impaired when he began to drive. Mr. King went into an automatic state while driving and caused an accident. The court said that although one would know voluntarily consuming alcohol might be dangerous, a patient might not know the effects of medication given by a medical professional, and thus Mr. King was acquitted. However, the courts have made a test to determine whether the intoxication was voluntary (and accused persons will not be acquitted under automatism) or involuntary (which may be excused).

In the case of *R v Daviault,* [1994] 3 SCR 63 (SCC), the Supreme Court said if there was extreme (yet voluntary) intoxication that is akin to automatism, the accused is entitled to be acquitted. *Daviault* involved a brutal sexual assault of an elderly and disabled woman by a man who had ingested a significant amount of alcohol. Many were outraged by the decision to allow a defence for someone who had perpetrated this terrible crime. By 1995 the legislature decided to fix this problem by amending the *Criminal Code* s 33.1 so that one cannot use *self-induced* automatism if it is a crime that "includes an element of an assault or any other interference or threat of interference by a person with the bodily integrity of another." This means that intoxication can still be a partial defence only in specific crimes (see *R v Chaulk* in the following case box). Section 33.1 has not been tested by the *Charter.*

R v CHAULK (2007), 223 CCC (3D) 174 (NS CA)

Chaulk is a case from Nova Scotia, where the defence of automatism was once again explored in the context of intoxication. At trial, Mr. Chaulk was acquitted of assault, threats of bodily harm, breaking and entering, and mischief by wilfully damaging property. Mr. Chaulk was causing a disturbance in his apartment building. Mr. MacDougall went outside his apartment to investigate, and saw Mr. Chaulk, who was naked and screaming at a female neighbour. Mr. MacDougall brought the neighbour inside his unit for safety and dialled 911. Mr. Chaulk broke down the door to Mr. MacDougall's apartment and threw Mr. MacDougall's belongings around the apartment. Mr. Chaulk said he would kill Mr. MacDougall and his children, and then lunged at Mr. MacDougall.

Mr. MacDougall was able to restrain Mr. Chaulk, but he was sweating profusely and babbling incoherently. Mr. Chaulk was taken to the hospital. At trial, Mr. Chaulk advanced a defence of non-mental-disorder automatism due to extreme intoxication. Mr. Chaulk alleged that he was given a "wake-up pill" by an acquaintance at a party, and he took the medication. Mr. Chaulk said his heart was pounding and things were "looking weird" and he had no further recollection until he woke up in the hospital. When interviewed in the hospital, Mr. Chaulk said that he had consumed a large amount of alcohol at the party, he had smoked marijuana, and was offered a "paper" with something on it that he thought was caffeine.

The court looked at the issue of self-induced intoxication and said that there was a three-part test: (1) The accused voluntarily consumed a substance that (2) he or she knew or ought to have known was an intoxicant, and (3) the risk of becoming intoxicated was or should have been within his or her contemplation. Using this test, the Court of Appeal found that Mr. Chaulk was voluntarily intoxicated, thus not falling within automatism, and the court overturned the acquittal and ordered a new trial.

Stone greatly limits automatism as a defence, and the offences that will fall under non-mental-disorder automatism will be restricted. The same can be said of mental-disorder automatism. Those who suffer a specific incidence of automatism are more likely to be successful in their defence, especially if the accused can point to one external event that caused the offence and that is unlikely to recur. Those that are likely to be successful in the future will likely have to prove that this event could have produced a dissociative state in an otherwise "normal person."

Defence of Intoxication

As in the case with automatism, self-induced intoxication is almost never a defence, but there are limited circumstances that intoxication can be used as a partial defence, as there may be incapacity to form intent. Although the defence is allowed to exist, the Supreme Court has said it will be successful only in rare and limited circumstances. The primary burden of proof is with the accused, who must prove on a balance of probabilities that he or she was in a state of extreme intoxication akin to automatism or insanity. Section 33.1 of the *Criminal Code* governs the law of self-induced intoxication in situations that involve an element of assault or interference (or threat of interference) with the bodily integrity of another person.

Intoxication has also been used as an element in a charge of first degree murder. If there is evidence of intoxication there may be reasonable doubt if the accused "planned" the murder with "deliberation." Even though this might not be a full defence to murder, a jury might be able to find that there was reasonable doubt about whether the accused has the elements of planning and deliberation that are required in first-degree murder.

Provocation

> *"It is impossible to read even a selection of the extensive modern literature on provocation without coming to the conclusion that the concept has serious logical and modern flaws."*
>
> —Lord Hoffman in *R v Smith,* [2000] 4 All ER 289

Historically, courts have recognized situations where provocation could occur within the context of a wholly shocking situation that caused a person to act in the heat of the moment in a violent rage. In the English case of *DPP v Camplin,* [1978] AC 705, the court identified some situations where one might be incited to kill another. For instance, Lord Diplock said one might be provoked in a spontaneous fight, or if a husband discovers his wife committing adultery, or if a father discovers someone sexually assaulting his child. Other aspects have been added to the defence over time, but interestingly, many of the modern cases involve men and sexuality.

Provocation is called an **affirmative defence**, or a defence in which all of the elements of the offence are present. These actors did the crime voluntarily and with the requisite *mens rea.* A successful provocation defence does not lead to a full acquittal, but the charge of first- or second-degree murder may be reduced to manslaughter. Many of the other defences that have been explored are a choice between the lesser of two evils. However, in provocation there is recognition by the court that the greater evil was selected by murdering another person, yet provocation is still a partial defence. Provocation is an important defence because those convicted of murder face a minimum sentence of life imprisonment without parole for at least ten years, while manslaughter has no mandatory minimum sentence. Section 232 of the *Criminal Code* provides that:

> 232 (1) Culpable homicide that otherwise would be murder may be reduced to manslaughter if the person who committed it did so in the heat of passion caused by sudden provocation.
>
> (2) A wrongful act or insult that is of such a nature as to be sufficient to deprive an ordinary person of the power of self control is provocation if the accused acted upon it on the sudden and before there was time for his passion to cool.
>
> (3) For the purposes of this section the questions
>
> a. whether a particular wrongful act or insult amounted to provocation, and
>
> b. whether the accused was deprived of the power of self-control by the provocation that he alleges he received, are questions of fact, but no one shall be deemed to have given provocation to another by doing anything that he had a legal right to do, or by doing anything that the accused incited him to do in order to provide the accused with an excuse for causing death or bodily harm to any human being.

There are three elements of provocation:

1. Provocation must be a wrongful act or insult such as to take away the control of a reasonable person.
2. The accused must act "upon the sudden"; he or she must act quickly in an act of passion without a significant lapse in time.
3. The accused must murder the person who provoked him or her (not another bystander).

There must also be an air of reality to the defence of provocation. The trial judge must be satisfied that there is some evidence that the wrongful act or insult alleged would have caused an ordinary person to lose control, and there is evidence that the accused *actually* lost his or her self-control because of that act or insult. *R v Thibert* (see the following case box) speaks to this subjective element in the context of an extramarital affair.

R v THIBERT, [1996] 1 SCR 37 (SCC)

The case of *Thibert* dealt with the air of reality test in provocation. The only issues before the Supreme Court were whether the trial judge was correct in leaving the defence of provocation to the jury, if he was satisfied that there was some evidence that an ordinary person would have lost self-control, and if there was evidence that the accused was, in fact, actually deprived of self-control.

The court found that asking if a reasonable person would have lost control is an objective test, but it also has subjective elements in looking at the age, sex, and other background factors. Mr. Thibert's wife was having an intimate relationship with a co-worker, and she had decided to leave Mr. Thibert. Mr. Thibert took his shotgun from its storage place and contemplated killing himself, Mrs. Thibert, and/or the man who was having the affair with his wife. He found the gun in a state that he believed was inoperable, but he put the gun in his car to use as a "final bluff" to get his wife to come back to him. Mr. Thibert went to his wife's workplace, and her boyfriend also came outside. Mr. Thibert took the gun out of the car. The boyfriend walked toward Mr. Thibert and said "[c]ome on big fellow, shoot me? You want to shoot me? Go ahead and shoot me." The boyfriend refused to stop coming toward the accused. Mr. Thibert testified that his eyes were closed as he tried to retreat inward and the gun discharged and the boyfriend was killed.

The majority of the Supreme Court said it was possible for a jury, looking at the past history of the deceased's relationship with Mr. Thibert's wife, to find that the behaviour was insulting.

The court said, given the possessive and affectionate behaviour of the deceased towards Mrs. Thibert and the taunting remarks, there was some evidence that the defence of provocation had an air or reality; therefore, the court ordered a new second-degree murder trial.

The dissenting judge thought that it was a dangerous precedent to say that an extramarital affair was conduct that could lead to a defence of provocation. Do you agree with this position?

FOOD FOR THOUGHT...

In the case of *R v Nahar* (2004), 181 CCC (3d) 449 (BCCA) in the British Columbia Court of Appeal, the accused appealed his conviction, arguing that the court should take into account his cultural background. Mr. Nahar came to Canada from the Punjab in 1995 and Mrs. Nahar joined him a few years later after an arranged marriage. There were ongoing problems in the marriage about the behaviour of Mrs. Nahar. The couple got into an argument one night, and when Mr. Nahar asked if his wife needed other men and if she was leaving and, she said, "Yes ... I will go. You can't do anything to me. You can't stop me." Mrs. Nahar pushed the accused out of the room. Mr. Nahar said he did not know what happened next, but it was alleged that he picked up a knife and punctured his wife's aorta and then her jugular vein in her neck. Both of these wounds were fatal. The accused appealed his conviction for second-degree murder and said that it was not clear that the trial judge took into consideration that he was raised in the Sikh culture, and the behaviour as identified by the accused would be "intolerable and embarrassing to a married man." The court of appeal found no errors by the trial judge and dismissed the appeal.

How much (if any) cultural background do you think should be considered in a case of provocation?

FOOD FOR THOUGHT...

Morris Manning and Peter Sankoff note that the law takes into consideration a murder that is committed when one is angry or in a rage, and there is an allowance made for these offenders. However, they note that no defence exists for "intentional killings motivated by compassion, hopelessness, confusion or love."[7]

Should we have more defences available for these offenders?

Self-Defence

Historically, self-defence has been recognized a situation in which the individual had "no choice" but to kill an adversary to protect him- or herself. Although the legal system does not encourage taking the law into your own hands, there are several sections where there is a justification for the reasonable use of force in certain circumstances. Sections 34 and 35 of the *Criminal Code* provide an allowance for defending yourself against assault, s 37 allows one to prevent an assault against yourself or someone under your protection, and ss. 38–42 provides for defence of property. When one thinks about self-defence, one often thinks of s 34:

> (1) Every one who is unlawfully assaulted without having provoked the assault is justified in repelling force by force if the force he uses is not intended to cause death or grievous bodily harm and is no more than is necessary to enable him to defend himself.
>
> (2) Every one who is unlawfully assaulted and who causes death or grievous bodily harm in repelling the assault is justified if

7. Morris Manning and Peter Sankoff, *Manning, Mewett & Sankoff: Criminal Law*, 4th ed (Markham ON: Lexis Nexis, 2009) at 748.

(*a*) he causes it under reasonable apprehension of death or grievous bodily harm from the violence with which the assault was originally made or with which the assailant pursues his purposes; and

(*b*) he believes, on reasonable grounds, that he cannot otherwise preserve himself from death or grievous bodily harm.

Section 34 provides for several requirements:

1. The person acting in self-defence was first unlawfully assaulted.
2. The actor did not provoke the assault (by blows, words, or gestures).
3. The actor did not intend to cause death or grievous bodily harm (a significant injury that interferes with the person's well-being in a serious way).
4. The actor used no more force than necessary (proportionality; see the Food for Thought box).

The accused has the evidentiary burden to raise the defence of self-defence, and then the burden shifts to the Crown to establish beyond a reasonable doubt that the accused did not act in self-defence. Section 35 of the *Criminal Code* also provides for self-defence in a situation where the individual starts the assault, but does not mean to cause death or grievous bodily harm.

The court must look carefully at the precise actions involved in each case to determine if there was, in fact, self-defence. As in *R v Kagan* (see the following case box), the court may have to re-create what actually happened at the time of the criminal act.

FOOD FOR THOUGHT...

IS THIS PROPORTIONAL?

In the case of *R v Nelson*, [1953] BCJ No 98 (BCCA), the importance of proportionality was discussed. There was a fight in a shipyard where the two parties worked. The victim was knocked down with a blow that fractured his jaw in several places. When the victim fell, he struck his head on the pavement, which caused a brain hemorrhage resulting in his death. Mr. Nelson raised self-defence. There was evidence that the deceased had thrown the first blow (which was said to be a slap in the face), and he had an iron bar in his hand, but he did not use the weapon. The accused was 29 years old, 6 feet in height, and weighed 170 pounds, while the victim was 59 years of age, 5 foot 10 inches and weighed 130 pounds. Mr. Nelson said that punching the deceased was simply self-defence. The conviction for manslaughter at the trial level was upheld by the court of appeal (with one dissent).

Was this proportionate force?

R v KAGAN (2009), 276 NSR (2D) 381 (NS CA)

Mr. Kagan was a first-year computer engineering student at Dalhousie University in Nova Scotia. He was assigned to a student residence with a roommate, Mr. Kinney. Mr. Kinney had originally said he was a non-smoker, but he did in fact smoke, and Mr. Kagan and Mr. Kinney would smoke marijuana together. However, the smoking issue bothered Mr. Kagan. Mr. Kagan was given the opportunity to move into a room by himself in the same building, and he eventually agreed to move. On the day of the move, Mr. Kinney alleges he was attacked by Mr. Kagan, was sprayed by "bear spray," and was stabbed in the back. Mr. Kagan alleged self-defence as he said Mr. Kinney had been aggressive and threatening.

Although the stories of the roommates differed, the court found that Mr. Kinney's recollection was more accurate. When Mr. Kinney came into the apartment, he was sprayed with bear spray. The spray completely incapacitated Mr. Kinney, who fled to the elevator when he thought he was punched in the back. It was later discovered that he was stabbed in the back and suffered a collapsed lung from the stabbing. This was a serious injury, and experts testified that there was a possibility of death from such a wound. Mr. Kagan said he was simply defending himself, and he was not sure how Mr. Kinney came to be stabbed in the back.

The Court of Appeal said that there was no evidence that Mr. Kinney was aggressive or violent on the day of the attack or any other. The court saw no air of reality to the self-defence claim, and the appeal by Mr. Kagan was dismissed.

Do you believe that roommates should be treated differently than other groups of people when it comes to violence?

The Battered Woman Syndrome

Before entering into any discussion of battered woman syndrome (BWS) in Canadian law, it is important to note that BWS is not a defence. BWS has been used in conjunction with already-established defences like self-defence and duress, but it is not itself a defence. Rather, in the context of self-defence, the understanding of BWS has led to a re-conceptualization of how courts assess the reasonable fear and reasonable response of a spouse claiming self-defence.

Clearly, the thread that runs through the research on battered women is that, historically, assaults of women by their spouses were considered a family matter and not a legal matter. It has been noted that wife abuse in North America has existed "since the founding of the Colonies. English Common Law and Christianity, foundations of this nation's culture, accepted wife abuse as the husband's prerogative. Marital violence was his privilege. In order to find a time in history when wife beating did not enjoy having custom and law on their side, it is necessary to go back . . . to pre-biblical times."[8] Although there have been many improvements in the law regarding women, violence against women continues to be the subject of many criminal matters.

LENORE WALKER In her seminal book, *The Battered Woman Syndrome,* American psychologist Lenore Walker coined the term "battered woman" in 1984 as she looked at the historical basis of this phenomenon. Walker was the first to develop the fundamental pattern of spousal abuse, which has been adopted by many working in the area of domestic violence. She describes a cycle which has three phases:

> (1) tension building, (2) the acute battering incident, and (3) loving-contrition. During the first phase, there is a gradual escalation of tension displayed by discrete acts causing increased friction such as name-calling, other mean intentional behaviors, and/or physical abuse ... The woman attempts to placate the batterer, doing what she thinks might please him, calm him down, or at least, what will not further aggravate him ... Often she succeeds for a little while which reinforces her unrealistic belief that she can control this man. It also becomes part of the unpredictable noncontingency response/outcome pattern which creates the *learned helplessness*. The tension continues to escalate and eventually she is unable to continue controlling his angry response pattern ... The second phase, the acute battering incident, becomes inevitable without intervention. Sometimes, she precipitates the inevitable explosion so as to control where and when it occurs, allowing her to take better precautions to minimize her injuries and pain ... Phase two is characterized by the uncontrollable discharge of the tensions that have built up during phase one ... The acute battering phase is concluded when the batterer stops, usually bringing with its cessation a sharp physiological reduction in tension ... In phase three which follows, the batterer may apologize profusely, try to assist his victim, show kindness and remorse, and shower her with gifts and/or promises. The batterer himself may believe at this point that he will never

---

8. Steven M Morgan, *Conjugal Terrorism—A Psychological and Community Treatment Model of Wife Abuse* (Palo Alto, CA: R and E Research, 1983) at 4, citing T Davidson, "Wifebeating: A Recurring Phenomenon Throughout History" in M Roy, ed, *Battered Women: A Psychological Study in Domestic Violence* (New York: Van Norstand Reinhold, 1977) at 233. Morgan notes, at 6, that in England "beatings were so common in some districts, they were known by the manner of beating administered there. Liverpool was known as the 'kicking district' because the husbands kicked their wives with hobnailed boots."

> allow himself to be violent again ... This third phase provides the positive reinforcement for remaining in the relationship, for the woman. Many of the acts that he did when she fell in love with him during the courtship period occur again here. Our research results demonstrated that phase three could also be characterized by an absence of tension or violence, and no observable loving-contrition behavior, and still be reinforcing for the woman. Sometimes the perception of tension and danger remains very high and does not return to the baseline or loving-contrition level. This is a sign that the risk of a lethal incident is very high.[9]

Although this model has been accepted by the legal and psychological disciplines, there has been criticism.

CRITICISM OF THE CYCLE OF VIOLENCE Researchers such as Regina Schuller and Sara Rzepa question this typology and note that the methodology of Walker's studies is flawed, as there may have been "leading questions" used in the interviews of battered women. They note it is possible that the questions interviewers used "conveyed the hypotheses to the women and thus provided them with responses that they might otherwise not have given ... [Additionally] they may have interpreted more consistency with the hypotheses than the responses in fact warranted."[10] Some say that Walker's research (which might not be sound) has misled the courts into making women sick instead of battered.

Not only the methodology but the term "battered woman syndrome" has been subject to scrutiny. It has been noted that the definition of this term is unclear in both the legal and psychological literature. Yet the impact of this syndrome, whether or not methodologically or definitionally precise, is hard to ignore. Theorists explain that BWS has been admitted with some frequency in courts in Canada, the United States, Great Britain, Australia, and New Zealand.[11] Despite this inconsistency and definitional imprecision, BWS has been accepted by the Canadian courts and is currently being used as a legal concept within the Canadian justice system.

It has been noted that counsel may have little choice but to use the term if they wish to have the jury hear experts on the intricacies of domestic violence. Often it is difficult for jury members, many who have not experienced this type of violence, to understand why a woman stays in an abusive relationship, and that the psychological violence experienced by women is often more debilitating than even extreme physical violence. The battered woman has been defined as

> a woman who is repeatedly subjected to any forceful physical or psychological behavior by a man in order to coerce her to do something he wants her to do without any concern for her rights. Battered women include wives or women in any form of intimate relationships with men. Furthermore, in order to be classified as a battered woman, the couple must go through the battering cycle at least twice [and if] she remains in the situation, she is defined as a battered woman.[12]

Today, this syndrome is also termed "intimate partner violence," which can include physical, psychological, emotional, or sexual abuse. Most recently, a particular type of battering termed "intimate terrorism"[13] has been identified, which theorists adopted from brainwashing literature. Lewis Okun compares woman battering to torture and use the term "conjugal terrorism" to depict the control and threats used to control victims. This lack of control and blind acceptance are characteristics of this debilitating condition which can be described as terror. Evan Stark has noted that a woman who is battered is different from others who are subject to violence. Many battered women today prefer the term

9. The Battered Woman Syndrome, 3rd Edition, Walker, 2009, Springer Publishing Company, LLC.
10. Regina Schuller and Sara Rzepa, "The Scientific Status of Research on Domestic Violence Against Women" in David L Faigman et al, eds, *Modern Scientific Evidence: The Law and Science of Expert Testimony* (St. Paul MN: West, 2002) 32 at 44.
11. Regina A Schuller and Gwen Jenkins, "Expert Evidence Pertaining to Battered Women: Limitations and Reconceptualizations" in Mark Costanzo, Daniel Krauss, and Kathy Pezdek, eds, *Expert Psychological Testimony for the Courts* (Mahwah, NJ: Lawrence Erlbaum, 2007) 203 at 203. Schuller and Jenkins also note at 208, that BWS is "not specifically listed in the *Diagnostic and Statistical Manual of Mental Disorders.*"
12. Lenore E Walker, *The Battered Woman* (New York: Harper & Row, 1979) at xv.
13. Michael P Johnson, "Conflict and Control: Gender Symmetry and Asymmetry in Domestic Violence" (2006) 12 *Violence Against Women* 1003 at 1003.

"battered woman survivor" and there is a growing literature on the "active efforts" of these survivors.[14]

BWS first entered the Canadian criminal law discourse through self-defence in *R v Lavallee* (see the following case box). Lavallee was 22 years old when she shot her abusive partner.

R v LAVALLEE, [1990] SCJ NO 36 (SCC)

Ms. Lavallee alleged that she lived in an atmosphere of constant violence over a significant period of time, and that she believed she had to kill her abuser to preserve herself from death or grievous bodily harm. Ms. Lavallee had been with her partner Mr. Rust for several years. She shot him in the back of the head as he was leaving her room after physically attacking her and threatening her with death. The couple was hosting a party, but Mr. Rust went upstairs with Ms. Lavallee, gave her the gun and told her he would kill her once all the guests had left.

Ms. Lavallee had been to the hospital several times for "severe bruises, a fractured nose, multiple contusions and a black eye" and said she had been severely battered by her spouse. In this case, the court concluded that expert psychological evidence was needed because it was difficult for the average person to understand the actions of a battered spouse, and why Ms. Lavallee would accept this kind of violence in her life. The court found that this evidence was necessary because it is "up to the jury to decide whether, *in fact*, the accused's perceptions and actions were reasonable."

Ms. Lavallee testified that she was terrorized to the point that she felt trapped, vulnerable, worthless, and unable to leave the relationship. The court used the research of Lenore Walker to explain that a battered woman goes through many cycles of abuse and she can predict when her abuser will attack; thus, she had a reasonable apprehension of death or grievous bodily harm at this point in the cycle of abuse, even though her abuser was leaving the room at the time when she fatally shot him. Ms. Lavallee was acquitted.

Compare this case to *R v Malott* (see the following case box).

R v MALOTT, [1996] OJ NO 3511 (ONT CA)

The case of Malott concerned another battered woman who shot her spouse, but in this case she also attempted to kill her spouse's girlfriend. The court again used expert testimony to understand why a woman might remain in this relationship, the violence she has sustained, her perception of danger, and how she felt she had to preserve herself. Ms. Malott was in a relationship for 19 years and had two children. She was continually abused physically, sexually, and emotionally. Ms. Malott alleged that police would not help her because her husband was a valuable informant for them.

Ms. Malott took a gun with her to run errands with her husband, and after driving to a medical appointment (where he was making her get prescription drugs for his illegal drug trade), she shot him, took a taxi to his girlfriend's house, and shot the girlfriend and stabbed her with a knife (she survived). Ms. Malott was found guilty of second-degree murder of her spouse, and attempted murder of the girlfriend.

The court found it was necessary that the jury be instructed on BWS and how it related to the law of self-defence; however, Malott's appeal was dismissed. In the dissent, Justice L'Heureux-Dubé and Justice McLachlin noted that the "utility of such evidence in

14. Elizabeth M Schneider, "Feminism and the False Dichotomy of Victimization and Agency" (1993) 38 *N.Y.L. Sch. L. Rev.* 387 at 390.

criminal cases is not limited to instances where a battered woman is pleading self-defence, but is potentially relevant to other situations where the reasonableness of a battered woman's actions or perceptions is at issue (e.g., provocation, duress or necessity)." This left the possibility of the use of BWS in provocation, duress, or necessity, and BWS has, in fact, played a fundamental role in the development of these defences in addition to self-defence.

Some courts are attempting to exclude this defence from offenders who might have some "prior fault," or somehow brought the violence on themselves. However, some have noted that the focus of BWS has been on self-defence and little attention has been paid to offences that do not involve harm to the batterer.

VIOLENCE AGAINST MEN Often when students hear about violence from women directed at men in a domestic situation they meet the topic with skepticism and amusement, and there are often comments that the man somehow "deserved it." Violence toward men by women seems to be one of the last socially acceptable forms of abuse. Men are traditionally seen as strong and the leader of the household, not those who would cower in the face of their spouse. Many find it hard to believe that a 100-pound woman could abuse a 250-pound man.

However, a 2008 Statistics Canada report found that 17 percent of spousal violence is committed against men, which accounts for violence against approximately 159 000 men in Canada. Spousal violence is defined as physical assaults, threats, or criminal harassment involving common-law or married couples. Many theorize that violence against men is underreported because many males are loath to report that they are experiencing violence in the home out of shame and traditional gender expectations.[15]

There is also the problem that there are not as many services for men as there are for women victims of domestic violence. There are few shelters for battered men, but there are some resources in Vancouver, Calgary, and Toronto and various locations worldwide. Switzerland opened two shelters in late 2009. Many advocates also say that the term BWS is too gender-specific, and should be changed to "battered spouse syndrome."[16]

CRITICISMS Socio-legal theorists Joanne Minaker and Larleen Snider argue that there is not a problem of underreporting of male violence. They say "just the opposite is true—that an over-recognition of male victimization by women has occurred." They say that "[a]lthough some men *are* emotionally, psychologically, or physically mistreated by their intimate partners, the bulk of the empirical evidence indicates that female partners are abused more frequently and suffer more serious injuries." They also say males who are abuse victims "are primarily victims of child abuse, and most of them were victimized by other males."[17]

Some say the incidence of female-to-male violence has been overstated, and what is described by men is really poor conflict resolution rather than the systematic violence that is experienced by battered women. Many sources still say women are still battered much more frequently, suffer greater injuries, are often more financially dependent on their spouses, and are much more likely to be killed by a partner.

SAME-SEX ABUSE Another under-studied subset of domestic violence is same-sex violence. J Michael Cruz states that "one in five gay men will experience violence or abuse within a romantic relationship. However, the actual prevalence of gay male domestic violence is unknown for various reasons."[18] Cruz goes on to say many find it difficult to define "violent behaviour" in the gay community, and others do not want to report their abuse to the police because they do not want to be made to expose their homosexuality.

---

15. Canadian Centre for Justice Statistics, *Family Violence in Canada: A Statistical Profile 2008* (Ottawa: Public Health Agency of Canada, 2008).
16. See "Battered Men: The Hidden Side of Domestic Violence," http://www.batteredmen.com/bathelpnatl.htm, for resources for male victims of domestic violence.
17. Joanne C Minaker and Laureen Snider, "Husband Abuse: Equality with a Vengeance?" (2006) *Canadian Journal of Criminology and Criminal Justice* 754.
18. J Michael Cruz, "Why Doesn't He Just Leave?": Gay Male Domestic Violence and the Reasons Victims Stay" (2003) *The Journal of Men's Studies* 1.

In addition, many lesbians feel they are outside of a feminist theory that attempts to explain male-to-female domestic violence as patriarchal oppression. Therefore, there may be an additional population who is being unserved in the current regime. More research is needed on all of these populations that come within the realm of BWS.

DEVELOPING DEFENCES

Brainwashing and Women Who Kill

The Canadian criminal justice system has attempted to separate those who are criminal from those who are excused. However, there are examples that fall on the continuum between free choice and implanted choice. One of these situations is the defence of **brainwashing**. Through s 8(3) of the *Criminal Code* we know that that common law excuses and justifications can continue to apply where they are not inconsistent with legislation. It has been suggested by some that the Canadian criminal law should allow for a new defence of brainwashing, especially in the context of the battered spouse. For the purposes of this discussion, brainwashing is defined as having

1. a forcible or violent element;
2. an abandonment of previous beliefs and an adoption and/or an implantation of new beliefs (recognizing that there is a continuum between adopting and implanting which is done in either a passive or active way);
3. new beliefs that are foreign to the brainwashee; and
4. the brainwashee keeps these beliefs until removed from the presence of the indoctrinator for a significant period of time.[19]

Although brainwashing—also called coercive persuasion, mind control, thought control, thought reform, menticide, and brain warfare—has not been fully recognized as a viable defence in North America, the use of the techniques and psychological bases for the phenomenon have been explored for decades. The term "brainwashing" is problematic because there is no specific magic to the process that people may experience. Rather, it is a short form for a psychological influence that may cause certain individuals to commit crimes. One of the best definitions is Richard Delgado's conceptualization that brainwashing is the "forcible indoctrination process designed to induce the subject to abandon existing political, religious, or social beliefs in favour of a rigid system imposed by the indoctrinator."[20] This type of violent conversion to a thought process foreign to the brainwashee's values and principles is most relevant to that experienced by the battered woman.

An analysis of the Karla Homolka and Paul Bernardo case may link brainwashing and the battered spouse. Ms. Homolka and Mr. Bernardo were incarcerated for the sexual assault and murder of three young women. Ms. Homolka successfully negotiated a plea agreement of 12 years imprisonment in return for her testimony against her husband. However, after the plea deal, videotapes were found showing Ms. Homolka actively participating in the sexual crimes against the young girls. The public sentiment immediately turned to horror that a woman, in particular, could be capable of these acts. The media portrayal of Ms. Homolka and her culpability in

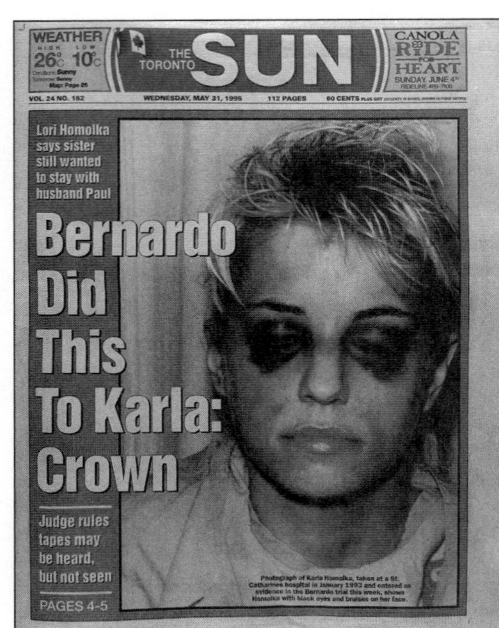
WEATHER HIGH 26°C LOW 10°C

THE TORONTO SUN

CANOLA RIDE FOR HEART SUNDAY, JUNE 4

VOL. 24 NO. 182 WEDNESDAY, MAY 31, 1995 112 PAGES 60 CENTS

Lori Homolka says sister still wanted to stay with husband Paul

Bernardo Did This To Karla: Crown

Judge rules tapes may be heard, but not seen

PAGES 4-5

Photograph of Karla Homolka, taken at a St. Catharines hospital in January 1993 and entered as evidence in the Bernardo trial this week, shows Homolka with black eyes and bruises on her face.

Karla Homolka

The Canadian Press

19. For a more in-depth discussion of this topic see Frances E Chapman, "Intangible Captivity: The Potential for a New Canadian Criminal Defense for Brainwashing and Its Implications for the Battered Woman" (2012) 28 *Berkeley Journal of Gender, Law & Justice* (upcoming publication).

20. Richard Delgado, "Ascription of Criminal States of Mind: Toward a Defense Theory for the Coercively Persuaded ("Brainwashed") Defendant" in Michael Louis Corrado, ed, *Justification and Excuse in the Criminal Law, A Collection of Essays* (New York: Garland, 1994) 1 at 6.

the deaths of her sister Tammy, Leslie Mahaffy, and Kristen French was overwhelmingly negative, painting Ms. Homolka as a willing and culpable participant in these crimes. But, was Ms. Homolka a victim of domestic violence and brainwashing?[21]

Some argue that Ms. Homolka was an example of an individual living under the control of her **sexual sadist** partner, Mr. Bernardo. This case is part of our collective awareness and has captured the attention of the public through books and movies, but it has not resolved the liability issue regarding the manipulated party. Much of the case material involves hypothesizing because Ms. Homolka did not go to trial for her crimes. Few people saw Ms. Homolka as a victim, although she agreed to be the key witness against her sadistic partner.

Ms. Homolka and Mr. Bernardo are not the only example of those in an intimate partnership who murder. There are many more examples of women who partner in this capacity, and there are other well-publicized cases that are just as horrifying. For example, Carole Bundy was married to a sexual sadist, Doug Clark, in the 1970s. Carole was herself a sex offender as a youth (as a peeping Tom), and eventually their "fantasies began to merge, becoming one shared daydream of immutable outlaw power."[22] Within one year, they killed seven women; one victim was beheaded. Bundy eventually killed alone after finding an ex-lover and removing his head with a "boning knife."[23]

Fred and Rosemary West were convicted of ten counts of murder. Fred West was the focus of tabloids in England until he killed himself in prison in January 1995. However, after his death, which was read as a sign that he was unable to live with himself, someone had to satisfy the public's need for vengeance. Rosemary West became the new focus. Similarly, Veronica Compton, the girlfriend of Kenneth Bianchi (the Hillside Strangler), killed in order to distract the police from her boyfriend; Judith Ann Neelley killed six victims with her husband Alvin; and Charlene Gallego killed ten individuals with a male partner.[24]

Cynthia Lynn Coffman abducted and strangled two women with her lover James Gregory Marlow. Tina Powell and Lafonda Foster shot five victims; they also stabbed, burned, mutilated, and ran over victims with a car. Gwendolyn Graham and Catherine Wood were lovers at a nursing home who suffocated six patients. Alton Coleman and Debra Brown killed eight. Kosta Fotopoulos took videos while his girlfriend Deidre Hunt shot an acquaintance four times and then planned a "hit" on Fotopoulos's wife. Raymond Fernandez and Martha Beck murdered at least 20 women over two years beginning in 1947. Nathan Leopold and Richard Loeb were lovers who killed 14-year-old Bobby Franks in 1924, deciding that they could perpetrate the perfect murder (noting that Leopold called Loeb "master" and referred to himself as "devoted slave").[25] Whether both parties in all of these cases were full participants or coerced subjects is something that is lost in the history of these crimes.

Although some view the science of brainwashing as an unsubstantiated relic of the past, such a conclusion fails to recognize certain realities of brainwashing that merit investigation. Indeed, these techniques may play an integral part in our lives—and in the law. It is important to recognize that "[m]ind-manipulation techniques are not merely the pet projects of white-coated, laboratory-housed, contract-funded intellectual recluses who fiddle with dials, pull levers, push buttons and throw switches."[26] These are techniques designed to be used on people. See the following Food for Thought box, which looks at Myra Hindley and Ian Brady.

---

21. Frances E Chapman, "Intangible Captivity: The Potential for a New Canadian Criminal Defense for Brainwashing and Its Implications for the Battered Woman" (2012) 28 *Berkeley Journal of Gender, Law & Justice* (upcoming publication).
22. See Patricia Pearson, *When She Was Bad: Violent Women and the Myth of Innocence* (Toronto: Random House, 1997) at 185.
23. *Ibid* at 186.
24. *Ibid* at 176–177.
25. Colin Wilson, *A Criminal History of Mankind* (London: Mercury, 2005) at 26.
26. Alan W Scheflin and Edward M Opton, *The Mind Manipulators: A Non-Fiction Account* (New York: Paddington, 1978) at 85.

FOOD FOR THOUGHT...

WHAT KINDS OF CASES WOULD FALL WITHIN A BRAINWASHING DEFENCE?

Myra Hindley and Ian Brady

Myra Hindley's dream was not to murder children. Yet, she did have dreams that all seemed to come true when she met Ian Brady at age 21. Ms. Hindley did not:

> fancy her suitors, until she met Ian Brady. He stood back from the world more coolly than she ... They were moving to the mundane beat of working-class Manchester, two anti-social souls fed up with the rules ... Up on the moors, they wove grandiose notions into the curtain they drew between themselves and the city below. Notions of power and risk, of transcending the rules. Hours spent planning bank robberies to extricate themselves from society once and for all. Joining forces, all that comes to matter is him, is her, everything else recedes in shades of gray. Freed from needing, they could invent their own codes of conduct, become Romeo and Juliet in *Lord of the Flies*, and play their own, private jokes upon the world.[27]

This partnership collapsed in October 1965 when police were alerted that the couple were hiding a corpse in their home. As police investigated, they found a trail of clues that led to suitcases left at the railway office in Manchester, and photographic and audio evidence that connected Mr. Brady and Ms. Hindley to a missing ten-year-old, Lesley Ann Downey, who had been missing since Boxing Day 1964. A search of the nearby moors resulted in the discovery of Downey and 12-year-old John Kilbride, in addition to the body of 17-year-old Edward Evans, who had been killed with an axe. Mr. Brady and Ms. Hindley were charged with the three murders, they were found guilty, and they were sentenced to life imprisonment.

Ms. Hindley was convicted of the sex killings of the three children with her psychopathic boyfriend. By all accounts, Ms. Hindley was a relatively innocent young woman who had no history of any wrongdoing before she met Mr. Brady.[28] Within a short period of time, Mr. Brady convinced Ms. Hindley to participate in a bank robbery, coerced her to take pornographic pictures, and eventually to take photographs kneeling (and sleeping) on the graves of the victims. The couple also recorded the screams of the children on audiotapes, which were played in court during the course of their trial. They were ultimately caught when they enlisted the help of a young man named David Smith to assist in their crimes, but Smith instead led police to the couple. There was a public outcry to prevent the release of Ms. Hindley up until her death in November 2002.

Ms. Hindley was absolutely vilified for her crimes. As Anne McGillivray explains "[n]o 'battering' or 'compliant victim' theory was offered for Ms. Hindley, as none existed in 1966."[29] It has been noted that few male serial killers "attract the virulent hatred Myra Hindley does (even Brady is not so viciously and constantly reviled)."[30] The accounts of Ms. Hindley's case clearly distinguished her crimes from Mr. Brady's as there was no language for when a woman kills. Theorists Deborah Cameron and Elizabeth Frazer say that Ms. Hindley personified the evil of the couple. The authors note this difference and conclude that there is a double standard. They note that somehow more is expected of women and the "disproportionate and irrational loathing with which Myra Hindley is widely regarded may be analysed as stemming from a similar set of attitudes toward women as those which we detect in so many sexual killings."[31]

However, little is said of Mr. Brady's coercion of Ms. Hindley and the abuse she endured. Pearson cites an advocate for Ms. Hindley who tried to secure parole for Ms. Hindley in 1993, telling the panel that she was "a victim: a normal human being who [went] through hell."[32]

27. Patricia Pearson, *When She Was Bad: Violent Women and the Myth of Innocence* (Toronto: Random House, 1997) at 176–177.
28. Colin Wilson, *A Criminal History of Mankind* (London: Mercury, 2005) at 27.
29. Anne McGillivray, "'A Moral Vacuity in Her Which Is Difficult If Not Impossible to Explain': Law, Psychiatry and the Remaking of Karla Homolka" (1998) 5 *International Journal of the Legal Profession* 255 at 277.
30. Deborah Cameron and Elizabeth Frazer, *The Lust to Kill: A Feminist Investigation of Sexual Murder* (Cambridge: Polity in Association with Basil Blackwell, 1987) at 25 and 147.
31. Deborah Cameron and Elizabeth Frazer, *The Lust to Kill: A Feminist Investigation of Sexual Murder* (Cambridge: Polity in Association with Basil Blackwell, 1987) at 25, that whatever "crimes she may have committed, Myra Hindley has offended against standards of femininity and has been punished accordingly."
32. Patricia Pearson, *When She Was Bad: Violent Women and the Myth of Innocence* (Toronto: Random House, 1997) at 179–180.

It was alleged that Ms. Hindley was used as a lure to kidnap the young girls. Mr. Brady kept detailed records of their crimes. She testified that Mr. Brady threatened to kill her family members, and he used the photos taken to blackmail her in continuing to commit crimes. Deborah Cameron and Elizabeth Frazer note that Ms. Hindley's coercion is documented in the photographic images. Although Ms. Hindley was not an "unwilling victim—unlike the unfortunate Lesley Ann Downey—she was not the *subject* of the photographs either ... In some of the pictures she is posed to display the marks of Brady's whip on her naked body. In these pictures Myra Hindley confirms the masculine transcendence of her sadist lover."[33]

Dr. Rachel Pinney visited Ms. Hindley in jail and was convinced of her innocence, and wrote about her experiences. Dr. Pinney described Ms. Hindley as "framed" and "hooked," and was convinced that she had no part in the torture or murder of the victims.[34] The case still leaves commentators no answer as to why this young girl could commit the worst criminal acts. While Ms. Hindley eventually wished to be released, Mr. Brady was labelled with a mental disorder while in prison. Researcher Catherine Mary O'Sullivan notes that "Brady faded from view, both because psychiatrists have labelled him insane, and because he never wants to be released; Hindley came into focus and was demonised. It is her wish for eventual freedom that is taken of evidence of her 'evil' nature, and proof that she was worse than her partner. The implication cast, therefore, is that at least Brady had the decency to go mad."[35]

One account of the case is that Ms. Hindley acted completely under the control of Mr. Brady. However, some believe that this theory leads to the conclusion that Mr. Brady's ideas would be adopted simply because a "superior man ... fills the otherwise empty mind of this female disciple with ideas which she accepts just because they are his, and not because of any independent assessment."[36] Yet, does it have to be a choice between whether a woman is freely choosing or else entirely vacuous, with nothing in between? Is there a continuum along which to situate these vulnerable offenders? Attitudes towards women have changed significantly since the 1960s, but the story of Ms. Hindley and Mr. Brady is by no means unique.

Although this graphic case may seem rare, there are numerous examples of intimate partnership crimes. While it has been established that a partner who strikes out against her batterer can be excused through self-defence,[37] this defence is inapplicable to a partner who commits crimes against innocent third parties. The difficulty with a potential new defence for these offenders is, as many theorists have argued, the distinction between what should be excused and what should not. Many have concluded that although certain acts can be excused, the "behavior that flows from conversion is not protected."[38] What excuse is available for the woman who was an accomplice or participant in murder, sexual assault, and torture, and who had thoughts implanted, making her believe that her actions were acceptable, or even necessary? Would Myra Hindley have a defence?

What do you think about this case? Should Ms. Hindley be excused? Should her relationship with Mr. Brady be examined? Do any of these background factors matter?

Should there be a defence of brainwashing?

Could this defence apply to Karla Homolka?

Entrapment

Another developing defence in Canada is entrapment. Entrapment is a defence where the accused says he or she committed the offence, but the police trapped the individual into the commission. Entrapment arises for a variety of reasons, but mainly these cases arise from undercover operations of the police. The tension in entrapment is the balance between the

33. Deborah Cameron and Elizabeth Frazer, *The Lust to Kill: A Feminist Investigation of Sexual Murder* (Cambridge: Polity in Association with Basil Blackwell, 1987) at 148.
34. Colin Wilson, *A Criminal History of Mankind* (London: Mercury, 2005) at 26.
35. Catherine Mary O'Sullivan, The Sacrifice of the Guilty: The Importance of Narrative Resonance in Understanding Criminal Justice and Media Responses to Aberrant Offenders (North York ON: Osgoode, 1996) at 283 n 55 [unpublished].
36. Deborah Cameron and Elizabeth Frazer, *The Lust to Kill: A Feminist Investigation of Sexual Murder* (Cambridge: Polity in Association with Basil Blackwell, 1987).
37. Carol Jacobsen, Kammy Mizga, and Lynn D'Orio, "Battered Women, Homicide Convictions, and Sentencing: The Case for Clemency" (2007) 18 *Hastings Women's Law Journal* 31.
38. Alan W Scheflin and Edward M Opton, *The Mind Manipulators: A Non-Fiction Account* (New York: Paddington, 1978) at 85.

police using methods in order to investigate crimes, and the need to protect individuals and the rule of law, so that citizens are not encouraged to commit crimes they otherwise would not have committed.

This concept has had a long history, beginning with one of the earliest American cases of *Sorrells v United States*, 287 US 435 (1932). The case involved an undercover police officer who induced the defendant to sell him liquor by using stories of wartime service. The court found that although there was a range of activity that the police had at their disposal for investigative purposes, a "different question is presented when the criminal design originates with the officials of the government, and they implant in the mind of an innocent person the disposition to commit the alleged offense and induce its commission in order that they may prosecute." The court concluded that the act was not the defendant's, but rather a "creature" of the police officer.

Legal theorist George Fletcher notes the similarities to duress, saying in "one case the actor is seduced by the wiles of a duplicitous police officer; in the other he is coerced by the threats of an overbearing will."[39] Similarly, in the 1973 case of *United States v Russell* (1973) 411 US 428, the court found that the "function of law enforcement is the prevention of crime and the apprehension of criminals. Manifestly, that function does not include the manufacturing of crime. Criminal activity is such that stealth and strategy are necessary weapons in the arsenal of the police officer." The court goes on to say that it is "only when the Government's deception actually implants the criminal design in the mind of the defendant that the defense of entrapment comes into play."

There have been many critics of entrapment both in the United States and Canada. Some argue that entrapment is an illegitimate police power because it interferes with intent and the voluntariness of the individual forcing him or her to commit crimes. The leading Canadian case of *R v Mack* (see the following case box) sets out the test, but the case was instead decided on a procedural assessment.

R v MACK, [1988] SCJ NO 91 (SCC)

Mr. Mack was charged with unlawful possession of a narcotic for the purpose of trafficking. The Supreme Court set out the test for entrapment in that:

(a) the authorities provide a person with an opportunity to commit an offence without acting on a reasonable suspicion that this person is already engaged in criminal activity or pursuant to a *bona fide* inquiry:
(b) although having such a reasonable suspicion or acting in the course of a *bona fide* inquiry, they go beyond providing an opportunity and induce the commission of an offence.

However, the Supreme Court in the Canadian case *R v Mack* found that some types of entrapment are legitimate law enforcement activities because:

> the police must be given considerable latitude in the effort to enforce the standards of behaviour established in the criminal law ... There is a crucial distinction, one which is not easy to draw, however, between the police or their agents—acting on reasonable suspicion or in the course of a *bona fide* inquiry—providing an opportunity to a person to commit a crime, and the state actually creating a crime for the purpose of prosecution.

Do you think that police should be able to entrap individuals?

The law of entrapment is not well established, and some think that entrapment might not be a defence to every crime in the *Criminal Code*. This defence will continue to evolve.

39. George P Fletcher, *Rethinking Criminal Law* (Boston: Little, Brown, 1978) at 542.

Prank

The prank defence is another evolving defence in the criminal law, although its foundation is not clear. The following case box looks at *R v Pake*. The case seems to confuse intent with motive, but the prank defence was used successfully.

R v PAKE, [1995] AJ NO 1152 (ALTA CA)

In this Alberta Court of Appeal case, Mr. Pake was charged with communicating with another person for the purposes of engaging in prostitution. The accused stopped his car on a corner in Edmonton and spoke with a female police officer who was posing as a prostitute. He asked her how much she charged, they agreed on a price, and she told him to drive around the corner. However, Mr. Pake drove off in the other direction.

Mr. Pake's defence at trial was that he was "just joking." He said he had no intention of completing the transaction—he was simply curious. Mr. Pake testified that he pulled up to the officer and said "Hi, how are you?" When the officer asked what she could do for him he said "I don't know. I don't have much money." When she asked him what he wanted he said "A lay," but followed this with "I'm a student. I only have $20.00."

At trial, the judge said whether or not the accused actually intended to carry out the bargain was immaterial once the communication was finished and the transaction was complete. On appeal, the judge held that the communication itself was not illegal. The purpose of the appeal was whether it was necessary for the Crown to prove the accused intended to complete the transaction at the time of the communication.

The court clarified that if the accused had a "change of heart" there would still be an offence because there would have been intent to commit the crime. However, if the accused said he never intended to go through with the sexual act, he never had the intent because he was "just fooling." The trial judge in the matter found that on the surrounding circumstances, it was simply a joke.

The Court of Appeal dismissed the appeal. The court said it was important to reduce street prostitution, but without the intention to engage in sexual services, there was no offence and it would be unworkable if everyone who spoke with a prostitute was convicted of a crime.

Do you agree? Was it easy for Mr. Pake to say that he was "just fooling?"

Double Jeopardy and *Res Judicata*

> *"The underlying idea, one that is deeply ingrained in at least the Anglo-American system of jurisprudence, is that the State with all its resources and power should not be allowed to make repeated attempts to convict an individual for an alleged offence, thereby subjecting him to embarrassment, expense and ordeal and compelling him to live in a continuing state of anxiety and insecurity, as well as enhancing the possibility that even though innocent he may be found guilty."*
>
> —*Green v US* (1957), 355 US 184

What is commonly called "double jeopardy" in the United States is called ***autrefois acquit*** in Canada. This refers to a common law principal that a person must not be put on trial twice for the same offence, and includes a claim by the defendant that he or she has lawfully been acquitted or convicted of the offence. This plea is heard by judge without a jury present, and the current charge must be the same or included offences. For example, in murder you cannot later be charged for manslaughter on the same facts (or assault causing bodily harm). The rationale for this principle of law is that society has an interest in the speedy and final conclusion of disputes. The accused has the right to be spared from numerous prosecutions by the state with all of its resources. We call this final decision ***res judicata***, and this principle allows an individual to feel he or she has a final conclusion on the matter that cannot be reopened. Section 11(h) of the *Charter* also provides a protection to an accused who has been pardoned for a crime through a royal prerogative. The section says "if finally acquitted of the offence, not to be tried for it again and, if finally found guilty and punished for the offence, not to be tried or punished for it again."

If a second prosecution is attempted, section 607 of the *Criminal Code* provides that "(1) An accused may plead the special pleas of (*a*) *autrefois acquit*." This defence was attempted in the case of *R v Ekman* (see the following case box).

R v EKMAN, [2006] SCCA NO 339 (SCC)

Mr. Ekman had a trial in which there was a question of whether his statement was admissible. When this statement was ruled inadmissible, he was acquitted. The ruling was overturned by the Court of Appeal, and a new trial was ordered. At the second trial, Mr. Ekman was acquitted of murder but convicted of attempted murder. The Crown appealed, and Mr. Ekman was convicted of first-degree murder at the third trial. Mr. Ekman appealed this decision to the British Columbia Court of Appeal, saying that the trial judge erred in saying that a defence of *res judicata* was not available to Mr. Ekman at the third trial.

The defence alleged that the third trial should not have occurred because in trial two, the Crown failed to prove that Mr. Ekman caused the death; therefore, the finding of first-degree murder in the third trial was inconsistent with that finding. The Court of Appeal said the second trial was completely set aside and a new trial was ordered on all issues. No issues were resolved in trial two; therefore, in trial three all options were available and *res judicata* did not exist as a defence. The case was appealed to the Supreme Court, but Mr. Ekman was denied the right to appeal without reasons.

CONCLUSION

After the jury has received all information from both the Crown and defence on the charge and the applicable defence, the judge and/or jury must reach a decision. If there is a jury, the judge then makes a **charge to the jury.** The charge involves the judge reviewing the facts, and discussing the application of the law to the case, including the defence. The judge will review concepts such as "beyond a reasonable doubt," and instruct the jury about how the evidence may be weighed. The lawyers may challenge the information given to the jury, and may direct the judge about what they would like to be said. The jury must then unanimously make the decision in the case, but they may return to the courtroom to ask for laws or facts to be reviewed by the judge. If the jurors cannot make a unanimous decision, they may inform the judge, and the judge may decide to give further instructions to the jury. If the jury can still not make a decision, this is called a **hung jury.** There may be a need to constitute a new jury to rehear the evidence and come to a unanimous decision.

If the defendant successfully uses a full defence, he or she is free to leave with no further restrictions. A partial defence may simply lead to a lesser sentence to be imposed by the judge. (See Chapter 12 which discusses sentencing.)

LEARNING OUTCOMES SUMMARIZED

1. Discuss the elements involved in the defence of necessity.

The required elements in a defence of necessity are (1) there must be a clear and imminent peril or danger, (2) there must be an absence of a reasonable alternative, and (3) there must be proportionality between the harm inflicted and the harm avoided (i.e., the harm inflicted must be less than that avoided).

2. Assess the different types of automatism.

The different types of automatism are (1) normal condition or "non-insane" (non - mental-disorder) automatism, (2) "insane" or mental-disorder automatism, (3) external trauma, and (4) involuntary intoxication induced by alcohol or drugs.

3. Identify the elements of duress both statutorily and in the common law.

Statutory elements:

- immediate threat of death or bodily harm;
- threatener is present;
- belief that the threats will be carried out;
- person using the defence must not be a party to a conspiracy or criminal association; and
- it is not applicable to list of excluded offences.

Common law elements:

- the threats must be of death or serious bodily harm;
- the threats must be serious and the accused must believe they would be carried out;
- the threats were such that a reasonable person might have acted in the same way;
- there is no safe avenue of escape;
- proportionality; and
- it is not available if the accused is a part of a criminal organization.

4. Discuss the remaining defence of intoxication after *Daviault*.

The Supreme Court identified in *Daviault* that if there was extreme (yet voluntary) intoxication that is akin to automatism, the accused is entitled to be acquitted. Because of the backlash from this finding (allowing someone to escape responsibility for a brutal crime because that person was drunk), the legislature amended the *Criminal Code* s 33.1 so that one cannot use self-induced automatism if it is a crime that "includes an element of an assault or any other interference or threat of interference by a person with the bodily integrity of another." The result was that intoxication can only be used as a partial defence in specific crimes.

5. List the developing defences in Canada today, as identified in this chapter.

The developing defences are brainwashing, entrapment, and prank.

SELF-EVALUATION QUESTIONS

1. What has the court found in relation to a "prank defence?"
2. What defences are not codified (written down) in the *Criminal Code*?
3. What are the different types of automatism?
4. In the *Parks* sleepwalking case, what did the court find in relation to *mens rea*?
5. In which Canadian case did the element of battered woman syndrome (BWS) first arise?
6. What is a partial defence?
7. After *Perka*, what three elements emerged as elements of necessity?

CHAPTER

12

Sentencing and Alternative Dispute Resolution

Learning Outcomes

After completing this chapter, you should be able to:

1. Analyze the purposes of sentencing.
2. Evaluate the similarities between denunciation and general deterrence.
3. Assess the appropriateness of restitution in the criminal law system.
4. List aggravating and mitigating factors in sentencing.
5. Discuss the benefits of alternative dispute resolution.

THE HISTORY OF PUNISHMENT AND SENTENCING

To understand our modern conceptions about crime and punishment, one must look at the historical reasons why we punish those who commit crime. The punishment phase of corrections in Canada was greatly influenced by English criminal law, and torture and public execution were common practice in Europe in the eighteenth century. For example, an individual was "dragged along on a hurdle (to prevent his head smashing against the cobble-stones), in which his belly was opened up, his entrails quickly ripped out, so that he had time to see them, with his own eyes, being thrown on the fire; in which he was finally decapitated and his body quartered."[1] **Capital punishment** was also adopted in Canada.

However, by the beginning of the nineteenth century, Canadian juries were increasingly reluctant to give the death penalty. Other options included of **banishment**, time in the local jails (or **gaols**), fines, and **corporal punishment,** but each of these alternatives had disadvantages. Many criminals returned before the expiry of their banishment order, and because enforcement was difficult, the punishment was ineffective. Common gaols were overcrowded and lacked classification, allowing the most hardened criminal to remain with the petty or young offender. Fines were seen as unjust because of

1. Michel Foucault, Discipline and Punishment: The Birth of the Prison (London: Penguin, 1977).

financial disparities, and corporal punishment was seen as degrading. Other alternatives, like the **pillory** and **branding,** were also used for public embarrassment, while transportation to penal colonies continued as an option.

New ideas about crime and punishment marked the beginning of the Canadian penal system in the early 1830s. Executions were no longer publically enacted, and it was discovered that the pain of losing one's freedom for a period of time could be effective in maintaining control. Thus, the **penitentiary** was created as the new face of punishment. Rather than public physical torture, it became a more "civilized" method of punishment within the walls of a penitentiary. Whether the penitentiary system was an improvement on the torturous past was questionable, as the first penitentiary was opened with the intent to break the souls of the men condemned to live there. Although public torture was eliminated, this was not to suggest it ceased to exist, even within this higher aim.

The Creation of the Kingston Penitentiary

The term "penitentiary" first came into common usage in the late 1780s, and referred to the institution as a "place for doing penance."[2] The punishment and penitence model of Canadian corrections began in Kingston, Ontario. Kingston Penitentiary, Canada's oldest penitentiary, began receiving inmates in 1835.[3]

The basis of Canadian corrections was built on the perception of a population out of control and society's desire to reform these sinners. Politicians HC Thomson and John Macaulay were set with the task of erecting a Canadian penitentiary. They visited American penitentiaries in New York and Connecticut, and Bridewell prison in Glasgow, Scotland. Upon the completion of this research, Thomson proposed to the legislature that a penitentiary be built on the model of the Auburn prison in New York. It would cost approximately £12 500 British and would, subsequently, be self-sufficient.

Previously, penitentiaries had been perceived as warehouses of the deviant, but eventually became viewed as institutions of possible salvation through discipline and labour. The Auburn penal model was established in New York between 1819 and 1823 and emerged as the "generally accepted model of most future prisons in the New World to present times."[4] The cells at Auburn were seven

Correctional Service of Canada Museum, Kingston, Ontario. Reproduced with the permission of the Minister of Public Works and Government Services Canada, 2013.

Kingston Penitentiary, 1892

Archives Canada/PA-030472

Kingston Penitentiary today

2. Jerald J Bellomo, "Upper Canadian Attitudes Towards Crime and Punishment (1832 1851)" (1972) *Ontario Historical Society*, 11 at 17.

3. See <http://www.mckendry.net/CHRONOLOGY/chronology.htm>.

4. Barbara Lavin McEleney, *Correctional Reform in New York: The Rockefeller Years and Beyond* (New York: University Press of America, 1985) at 5.

feet long, three-and-a-half feet wide and seven feet high, and were arranged back to back and in tiers five cells high. An outside wall surrounded the entire institution. This physical plan then became the model for many maximum security institutions worldwide.

Letters were not permitted and reading material consisted only of the Bible or a prayer book. The prisoners at American Auburn prisons were told to consider themselves dead to those outside of the prison. No visitors were allowed except for the individuals who paid an admission fee to view the criminals. Visitors paid 25 cents each, and numbered between 6000 and 8000 a year to come to a type of human zoo.

The Auburn system was most recognized for the strict and absolute rule of silence, sometimes dubbing it the "silent system." Inmates were not allowed to communicate with anyone, including other prisoners. The idea was that prisoners should not be allowed to contaminate others with their ideas. Visitors to these institutions noted the

> most profound silence, and nothing heard in the whole prison but the steps of those who march, or sounds proceeding from the workshops ... the silence within these vast walls ... is that of death.... We felt as if we traversed catacombs; there were a thousand living beings, and yet it was a desert solitude.[5]

Marching, posture, and eyes focused in front were all aspects of life in Auburn penitentiary, and inmates were separated by screens to prevent communication even while at work. These partitions made observing the inmates easy as it impossible to distinguish a guard monitoring the men from other prisoners. Solitary confinement was enforced at night, and inmates were not allowed to face one another even during meals.

Although the American system was the first to theoretically suggest the possible reformation of the offender, in practice there was a general pessimism about the offender's salvation, and instead an overwhelming focus on control and incapacitation. The penitentiary was designed to be a place where a man could repent for his sins without cost to the state. The overwhelming focus was on **retribution**; this was reconsidered in modern times.

SENTENCING PRINCIPLES

> Sentencing is of course an inexact science involving a blend of many factors with aims that often conflict and competing interests that not always can be harmonized.[6]

Today, punishment is seen as a much more reasoned process. Sentencing is defined as the judgment that a court pronounces after finding a criminal defendant guilty, or the punishment imposed on a criminal wrongdoer. Although this sounds straightforward, sentencing has become one of the more controversial elements of the criminal law. The courts must balance the needs of the offender, victims, and society. Historically, retribution was a large part of how sentences were rationalized. Retributive sentences adhered to the concept of ***lex talionis***, or retaliation in kind (an eye for an eye, a tooth for a tooth). A sentence such as this was seen to restore the balance or repay the debt to society.

Once offences began to be defined as crimes against the state or the people, the principle of retribution became popular through state-endorsed revenge, and the idea became that the punishment should fit the crime. Many persons see retribution as approximating what we conceive to be justice, and a retributive sentence requires that it be proportional to the seriousness of the offence. While there may be no way to undo the harm, we can subject the offender to an equivalent evil which allows victims to feel justice was done.

However, s 12 of the *Charter of Rights* states that "everyone has the right not to be subjected to any cruel and unusual treatment or punishment." This constitutional right

5. DJ Rothman, *The Discovery of the Asylum: Social Order and Disorder in the New Republic* (Hawthorne, NY: Little Brown, 1971) at 97.
6. Kenneth WF Fiske, "Sentencing Powers and Principles" in Joel E Pink and David C Perrier, eds, *From Crime to Punishment* (Toronto: Thomson Carswell, 2007) at 301.

created a real need for guidance for judges on how to sentence. In *R v Goltz,* [1991] 3 SCR 485 (SCC), **cruel and unusual punishment** was defined by the courts as punishment that is "grossly inappropriate to the crime." But judges needed more information on how not to violate this principle.

In September 1996, Bill C-41 came into force, creating a part of the *Criminal Code* dedicated to sentencing, and it was one of the most comprehensive reforms to sentencing in Canadian history. The fundamental principle stated in the new legislation was that the sentence be proportionate to the offence and the responsibility of the offender. This approach stressed the use of incarceration only where other methods are unavailable.

These principles became s 718 of the *Criminal Code,* which states that:

> 718. The fundamental purpose of sentencing is to contribute, along with crime prevention initiatives, to respect for the law and the maintenance of a just, peaceful and safe society by imposing just sanctions that have one or more of the following objectives:
> (a) to denounce unlawful conduct;
> (b) to deter the offender and other persons from committing offences;
> (c) to separate offenders from society, where necessary;
> (d) to assist in rehabilitating offenders;
> (e) to provide reparations for harm done to victims or to the community; and
> (f) to promote a sense of responsibility in offenders, and acknowledgment of the harm done to victims and to the community.

However, there is latitude given to judges to use their discretion. Section 718 provides that:

> 718.3(1) Where an enactment prescribes different degrees or kinds of punishment in respect of an offence, the punishment to be imposed is, subject to the limitations prescribed in the enactment, in the discretion of the court that convicts a person who commits the offence.

There are clear principles to be followed. A judge can consider a **pre-sentence report** prepared by a probation officer that includes interviews with the offender, his or her family, and those who are familiar with the situation of the accused. The Crown and defence lawyers can call evidence at the sentencing hearing to determine if this offender is deserving of one purpose of sentencing over another. The judge may inquire about the offender's background and upbringing, the convicted person may give evidence of his or her life circumstances, and the Crown may present the offender's previous criminal history (if any).

Judges often rely on precedent cases that dictate what should be done with the current offender. The judge may also hear **victim impact statements** from the victim or others impacted by the crime. This in-court statement can be particularly influential on the sentence of the accused, as it informs the court of the ongoing physical, social, emotional, psychological, or financial damage to those involved.

Denunciation

Denunciation is the first element listed in s 718 of the *Criminal Code.* Denunciation is used to express disapproval of the crime and emphasize society's condemnation of the behaviour. Denunciation has a symbolic value and performs two functions: it is an educative function to inform citizens about what society will not tolerate, and it supports societal values. Judges will often give an offender a lecture followed by a sentence that is relatively light but symbolic. For instance, a **suspended sentence** means the person does not serve the time in prison but rather in the community, and could be a sentence that expresses denunciation by making the offender adhere to societal rules. The court can separate the offender from the offence and condemn the crime but still express hope in the offender and give him or her a second chance. If a person violates these terms, under s 732.2 of the *Criminal Code,* he or she must come back to court to have the probation revoked, and the judge may impose any sentence that could have been imposed if the suspended sentence was not granted, in addition to punishment for the violation. Those sentencing decisions may be appealed, as in *R v Field* (see the following case box).

R v FIELD, [2011] AJ NO 122 (ABCA)

The Crown appealed the sentence of a young person who had pleaded guilty to two counts of dangerous driving causing bodily harm. Mr. Field was 18 years old when he lost control of his vehicle while street racing with a friend. He was driving approximately 140 km/h in a 60 km/h zone (80 km over the limit) when he jumped the median and crashed into a Jeep, which then struck two other vehicles. The Jeep driver was seriously injured, including ligament injuries and sprains to her cervical and lumbar spine, which required over a year of physical therapy. A passenger in Mr. Field's car had a dislocated shoulder, a sprained foot, and a cut requiring 35 stitches.

The pre-sentence report said that Mr. Field was a hard-working student and employee, and was recommended for community supervision. The Crown sought a 12- to 15-month custodial sentence, but the offender received a 90-day sentence to be served intermittently, 24 months probation, 200 hours of community service, and a two-year motor vehicle prohibition. The Crown said that this sentence did not meet the appropriate sentencing objectives.

The Alberta Court of Appeal agreed and said that the trial judge had understated the conduct of the accused, calling it a "stupid" and "foolish" decision, and did not look at the severity of the victims' injuries, but rather overemphasized Mr. Field's youth. The Crown argued that this was "thrill seeking" and not simply a momentary lapse. The court considered that the accused had been drinking the night before, had inadequate sleep, and even when the passenger expressed concerns about the racing, the accused ignored this warning.

The court found that this did not meet the proportionality principle in s 718 of the *Criminal Code*, and did not represent denunciation and deterrence given the blameworthy conduct involved in street racing. The court found that driving a vehicle is a privilege and not a right. The appeal court substituted a 15-month custodial sentence minus the 90 days already served, and a withdrawal of the probation order.

Do you think this was a fair sentence for an 18-year-old driver?

Deterrence—Specific and General

Deterrence theory is based on the principle of controlling others through the fear of punishment. **General deterrence** refers to harsh sentences aimed to deter other potential offenders from committing the same or similar crimes as the offender before the court. This theory assumes that would-be criminals will track what the court thinks about a certain crime, and will not make the same choice. From a philosophical perspective, one can ask if it is morally right to sentence one particular offender to an overly harsh sentence in order to deter other individuals contemplating an offence. **Specific deterrence** aims at deterring that specific offender from re-offending.

Critics argue that deterrence theory is based on a number of very tenuous assumptions:

- Offenders are completely rational, where in reality many choices to commit crime might be affected by poor impulse control or by drugs and alcohol.
- Offenders contemplate apprehension and are thus deterred by calculating the risk and their abilities accurately.
- Offenders understand the consequences if they are caught and consider what they would risk.
- Offenders know what the common sentences are in court if they were to commit this crime.

Is general deterrence effective? Consider the case of *R v Ramage* (see the following case box).

R v RAMAGE, [2010] OJ NO 2970 (ONT CA)

The Toronto Star/GetStock.com

NHL player Rob Ramage

Mr. Rob Ramage attended a funeral of a good friend and colleague, and then left to attend a NHL Alumni Association event. Both he and his passenger, Keith Magnuson, were past and present NHL players. Mr. Ramage's car crossed four lanes of the highway they were travelling on, and struck two oncoming vehicles. Mr. Magnuson was killed, and a driver of the other car was severely injured. Blood and urine samples were taken at the hospital, and they revealed that Mr. Ramage was over the legal limit for alcohol. Mr. Ramage was charged with impaired driving causing death, dangerous driving causing death, impaired driving causing bodily harm, and dangerous driving causing bodily harm.

The trial judge sentenced Mr. Ramage to four years' imprisonment and a five-year driving prohibition. The trial judge wrote in his reasons that his responsibility was to "impose a sentence on an offender who is an exemplary citizen, who has committed a serious crime with tragic consequences ... It is not an easy task but the message of general deterrence must be met." The defence made the argument that a conditional sentence within the community would still meet the principles of general deterrence and denunciation, but this was unsuccessful. The sentence was appealed.

The Court of Appeal gave deference to the trial judge, who had heard all of the evidence in the case and who felt that deterrence was the predominant concern in a case such as this one where his blood alcohol level was beyond the legal limit. A harsh sentence was needed to signal to society that there is no tolerance for drunk driving, even if you are a high-profile NHL player.

Even though Mr. Ramage was an "outstanding" member of the community, a dedicated father and husband, showed real remorse for his actions, and would "probably never forgive himself," along with the fact that Mr. Magnuson's family actually asked the sentencing judge for mercy in this case, a **custodial sentence** was still appropriate. This decision would have a profound impact on Mr. Ramage's ability to live and work in the United States, but this sentence was found to be fitting in the circumstances. The court found that there was no error in the sentence; therefore, the Court of Appeal agreed with the sentence of four years that was imposed.

Do you think four years was an appropriate sentence for Mr. Ramage?
Will this deter other impaired drivers?
Mr. Ramage served 10 months in jail and was released to a halfway house in early 2011. Is this an appropriate sentence?

Imprisonment

A custodial sentence is imposed on persons who are a threat to society because they have committed serious and/or violent offences or they have become a **recidivist** within the system. This is an expensive means of dealing with offenders and is considered to be highly coercive. Imprisonment is a common sentence which is meant to prevent the offender from re-offending and to protect society for the time the offender is incapacitated.

If an offender is sentenced to less than 30 days, he or she is often kept at a local detention centre. If an offender has a custodial sentence of less than two years' imprisonment, he or she will serve this time at a provincial correctional facility or jail. A sentence of over two years means a sentence at a federal penitentiary. There are some exceptions to permit those in federal penitentiaries to serve time in provincial prisons, particularly if this means they may be closer to family or for humanitarian reasons.

If the offender has multiple offences, the judge may rule that he or she can serve the sentence concurrently (at the same time) or consecutively (one sentence after the

Eddies Images/Shutterstock

Imprisonment is a costly method of dealing with serious offences.

other). It is most common for sentences to be served concurrently. Time may also be taken off for time served pre-trial, which is governed by s 719(3). Those deemed "dangerous offenders" may be kept indefinitely in a federal penitentiary, and other offenders can be designated "long-term offenders" under s 753.1 of the *Criminal Code,* and can face additional supervision for up to ten years when they are released into the community.

There are serious repercussions to imprisonment. One Canadian study dealing with violence in prisons showed that male prisoners are at a 14 times greater risk of being a victim of homicide in prison than in the community.[7]

Communities, families, employment, and economic and social interactions change over time, so prisoners may not fit within their previous roles when they are released back into society. Prisons are crowded and can have severe psychological repercussions, in addition to the physical and emotional injuries that may occur. There is also a significant stigma related to being imprisoned, and there may be impediments to travel, employment, and other parts of life. Other than the few exceptions noted earlier, almost all offenders are released back into the community at some time in their lives.

Because of these repercussions, judges are directed to consider all available sanctions other than imprisonment that are reasonable under the circumstances for all offenders, with particular attention to the circumstances of Aboriginal offenders. Offenders should not be deprived of their liberty if less restrictive sanctions are appropriate in the circumstances, and imprisonment should be treated as a final resort. Those who commit summary offences may only face a jail term of less than six months, but those convicted of indictable offences can receive sentences, depending on their crime, up to and including **life imprisonment**.

Government of Alberta, Office of the Solicitor General and Public Security
http: //www.solgps.alberta.ca/programs_and_services/correctional_services/adult_centre_operations/correctional_and_remand_centres/Pages/calgary_correctional_centre.aspx

Provincial Correctional Centres

Adult inmates/offenders awaiting trial without bail, and those serving sentences in provincial correctional centres are located throughout the province. Provincial correctional centres house inmates/offenders that are remanded in custody or serving a sentence of up to two years less one day. For example, in Alberta, the Calgary Correctional Centre and the Calgary Remand Centre are located in Calgary and house sentenced and remanded male and female inmates. The Edmonton Remand Centre located in Edmonton houses remanded inmates. A new Edmonton Remand Centre that is currently under construction will have the capacity to house up to 2000 inmates and is scheduled to open in 2013. Other provincial correctional centres in the province include the Fort Saskatchewan Correction Centre located in Fort Saskatchewan, the Lethbridge Correctional Centre in Lethbridge, the Medicine Hat Remand Centre in Medicine Hat, the Peace River Correctional Centre in Peace River, and the Red Deer Remand Centre in Red Deer. In some cases, the families of offenders/inmates may have difficulty commuting to some of the more remote locations for family visits.

Calgary Correctional Centre, Calgary, Alberta

Courtesy of Alberta Justice and Solicitor General

How many provincial offenders are incarcerated at any particular time depends on the province. There is a capacity of approximately 9700 offenders in Ontario's 31 correctional centres, detention centres, treatment centres, and jails (depending what type of detention is warranted in the situation). In comparison, the province of

7. Allan Manson, Patrick Healy, and Gary Trotter. *Sentencing and Penal Policy in Canada: Cases, Materials, and Commentary* (Toronto: Emond Montgomery, 2000).

Prince Edward Island has a total of three provincial institutions (two for adult offenders and one youth centre) for a total capacity of 132 offenders.[8]

Federal Penitentiaries

Today, there are relatively few federal penitentiaries spread throughout Canada, which can again cause geographical problems for offenders' families to be close to their loved ones serving federal sentences. Figure 12.1 shows the locations of some of these institutions. There are approximately 50 federal institutions spread across Canada in 2012, as outlined in Table 12.1.

It is very costly to house one person in federal custody. In 2010, the average cost of housing one woman per year was $211 093, and the average cost of all offenders in Canada is $113 974 per year. In contrast, it costs only $29 537 to supervise offenders in the community.[9] These amounts are listed in Table 12.2. Note that the numbers are on the rise from 2005 to 2010.

Figure 12.1 Federal Penitentiaries in Canada

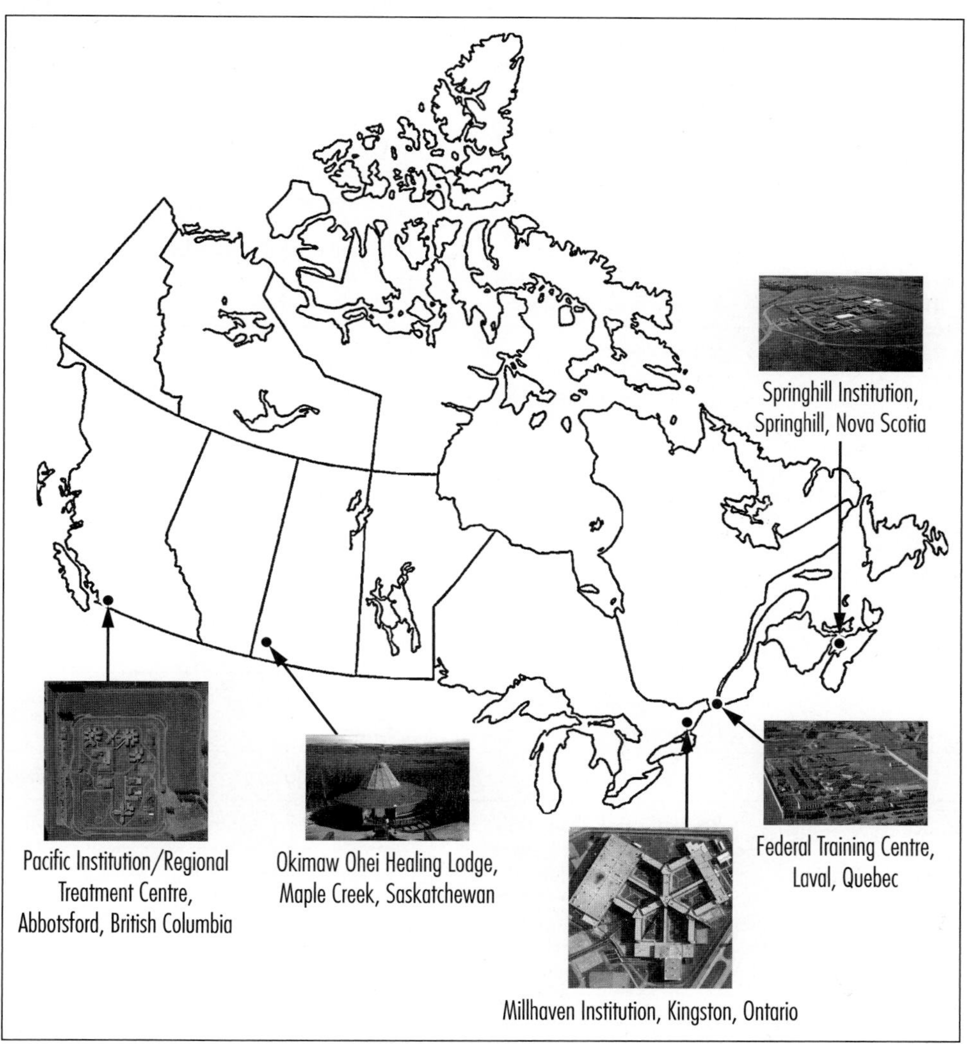

Source: © Institutional Profiles, Correctional Service of Canada. Reproduced with the permission of the Minister of Public Works and Government Services Canada, 2012.

8. Ontario Ministry of Community Safety and Corrections Services, http://www.mcscs.jus.gov.on.ca/english/corr_serv/adult_off/earned_rem/earned_rem.html, and Prince Edward Island Department of Environment, Labour and Justice, online: <http://www.gov.pe.ca/jps/index.php3?number=1027251&lang=E>.

9. Corrections Canada, "Corrections and Conditional Release Statistical Overview 2011," online: <http://www.securitepublique.gc.ca/res/cor/rep/2011-ccrso-eng.aspx>.

Table 12.1 Federal Institutions in Canada, 2012

	Region	Institution	Location	Security Level	Women, Aboriginal, or Psychiatric Institution
1	Atlantic	Atlantic Institution	Renous, New Brunswick	Maximum	
2	Atlantic	Dorchester Penitentiary	Dorchester, New Brunswick	Medium	
3	Atlantic	Nova Institution for Women	Truro	Multi-level	Women
4	Atlantic	Shepody Healing Centre	Dorchester, New Brunswick	Multi-level	Psychiatric
5	Atlantic	Springhill Institution	Springhill, Nova Scotia	Medium	
6	Atlantic	Westmorland Institution	Dorchester, New Brunswick	Minimum	
7	Quebec	Archambault Institution	Sainte-Anne-des-Plaines	Medium	
8	Quebec	Cowansville Institution	Cowansville, Quebec	Medium	
9	Quebec	Donnacona Institution	Donnacona, Quebec	Maximum	
10	Quebec	Drummond Institution	Drummondville, Quebec	Medium	
11	Quebec	Federal Training Centre	Laval, Quebec	Minimum	
12	Quebec	Joliette Institution	Joliette, Quebec	Multi-level	Women
13	Quebec	La Macaza Institution	La Macaza, Quebec	Medium	
14	Quebec	Leclerc Institution	Laval, Quebec	Medium	
15	Quebec	Montée St.-François Institution	Laval, Quebec	Minimum	
16	Quebec	Port-Cartier Institution	Port-Cartier, Quebec	Maximum	
17	Quebec	Regional Mental Health Centre	Sainte-Anne-des-Plaines, Quebec	Multi-level	Psychiatric
18	Quebec	Sainte-Anne-des-Plaines Institution	Sainte-Anne-des-Plaines, Quebec	Minimum	
19	Ontario	Bath Institution	Bath, Ontario	Medium	
20	Ontario	Beaver creek Institution	Gravenhurst, Ontario	Minimum	
21	Ontario	Collins Bay Institution	Kingston, Ontario	Medium	
22	Ontario	Fenbrook Institution	Gravenhurst, Ontario	Medium	
23	Ontario	Frontenac Institution	Kingston, Ontario	Minimum	
24	Ontario	Grand Valley Institution for Women	Kitchener, Ontario	Multi-level	Women
25	Ontario	Joyceville Institution	Kingston, Ontario	Medium	
26	Ontario	Kingston Penitentiary	Kingston, Ontario	Maximum	
27	Ontario	Millhaven Institution	Kingston, Ontario	Maximum	

(continued)

Table 12.1 (*continued*)

28	Ontario	Pittsburgh Institution	Joyceville, Ontario	Minimum	
29	Ontario	Regional Treatment Centre (in Kingston Penitentiary)	Kingston, Ontario	Maximum	Psychiatric
30	Ontario	Warkworth Institution	Campbellford, Ontario	Medium	
31	Prairie	Bowden Institution and Annex	Inisfail, Alberta	Minimum/ Medium	
32	Prairie	Drumheller Institution and Annex	Drumheller, Alberta	Minimum/ Medium	
33	Prairie	Edmonton Institution	Edmonton, Alberta	Maximum	
34	Prairie	Edmonton Institution for Women	Edmonton, Alberta	Multi-level	Women
35	Prairie	Grande Cache Institution	Grande Cache, Alberta	Minimum	
36	Prairie	Grierson Centre	Edmonton, Alberta	Minimum	
37	Prairie	Okimaw Ohci Healing Lodge	Maple Creek, Saskatchewan	Multi-level	Aboriginal Women
38	Prairie	Pê Sâkâstêw Centre	Hobbema, Alberta	Minimum	Aboriginal
39	Prairie	Regional Psychiatric Centre	Saskatoon, Saskatchewan	Multi-level	
40	Prairie	Riverbend Institution	Prince Albert, Saskatchewan	Medium	
41	Prairie	Rockwood Institution	Stony Mountain, Manitoba	Minimum	
42	Prairie	Saskatchewan Penitentiary	Prince Albert, Saskatchewan	Medium	
43	Prairie	Stony Mountain Institution	Winnipeg, Manitoba	Medium	
44	Pacific	Fraser Valley Institution for Women	Abbotsford, British Columbia	Multi-level	Women
45	Pacific	Ferndale Institution	Mission, British Columbia	Minimum	
46	Pacific	Kent Institution	Agassiz, British Columbia	Maximum	
47	Pacific	Kwìkwèxwelhp Healing Village	Harrison Mills, British Columbia	Minimum	
48	Pacific	Matsqui Institution	Abbotsford, British Columbia	Medium	
49	Pacific	Mission Institution	Mission, British Columbia	Medium	
50	Pacific	Mountain Institution	Agassiz, British Columbia	Medium	
51	Pacific	Pacific Institution/Regional Treatment Centre	Abbotsford, British Columbia	Multi-level	
52	Pacific	William Head Institution	Victoria, British Columbia	Minimum	

Table 12.2 The Cost of Incarceration

Categories	Annual Average Costs per Offender (current $)				
	2005–06	**2006–07**	**2007–08**	**2008–09**	**2009–10**
Incarcerated Offenders					
Maximum Security (males only)	113 645	121 294	135 870	147 135	150 808
Medium Security (males only)	75 251	80 545	87 498	93 782	98 219
Minimum Security (males only)	82 676	83 297	89 377	93 492	95 038
Women's Facilities	170 684	166 830	182 506	203 061	211 093
Exchange of Services Agreements	71 605	77 428	77 762	87 866	89 800
Incarcerated Average	**88 067**	**93 030**	**101 664**	**109 699**	**113 974**
Offenders in the Community	23 105	23 076	24 825	29 476	29 537

Source: *Corrections and Conditional Release Statistical Overview. Table: The cost of keeping an inmate incarcerated has increased.* <http://www.securitepublique.gc.ca/res/cor/rep/2011-ccrso-eng.aspx>. Correctional Service of Canada. Reproduced with the permission of the Minister of Public Works and Government Services, 2012.

In 2010–11, there were approximately 14 000 federal offenders in Canada. The number of incarcerated federal offenders increased in 2010–11 (see Figure 12.2).

Sixty-four percent of the federal offender population in 2011 were self-identified as Caucasian. Aboriginal offenders made up 18.5 percent of the federal inmate population,

Figure 12.2 Number of Incarcerated Federal Offenders

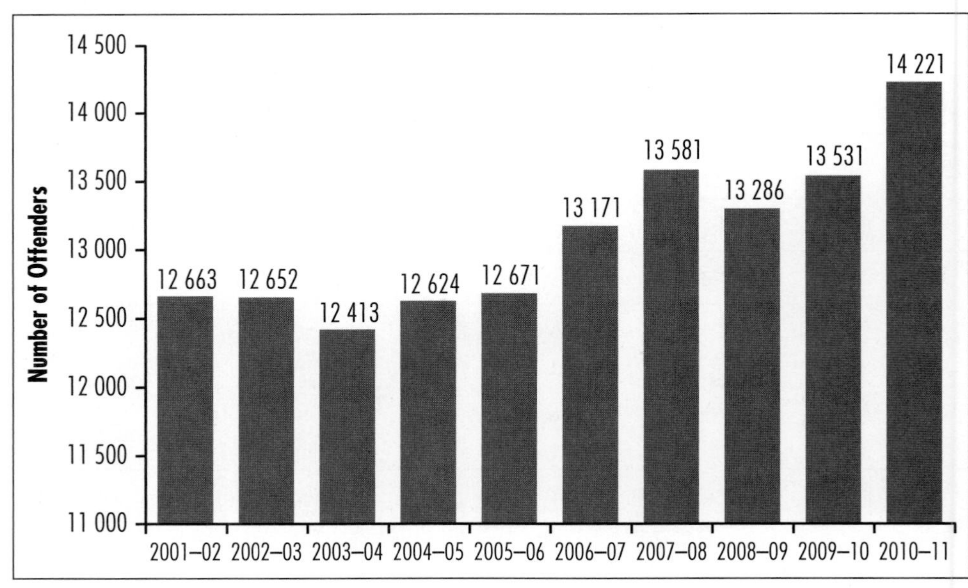

Source: *Corrections and Conditional Release Statistical Overview. Table: The number of incarcerated federal offenders increased in 2010-2011.* <http://www.securitepublique.gc.ca/res/cor/rep/2011-ccrso-eng.aspx>. Correctional Service of Canada. Reproduced with the permission of the Minister of Public Works and Government Services, 2012.

Figure 12.3 Ethnicities of Federal Offender Population

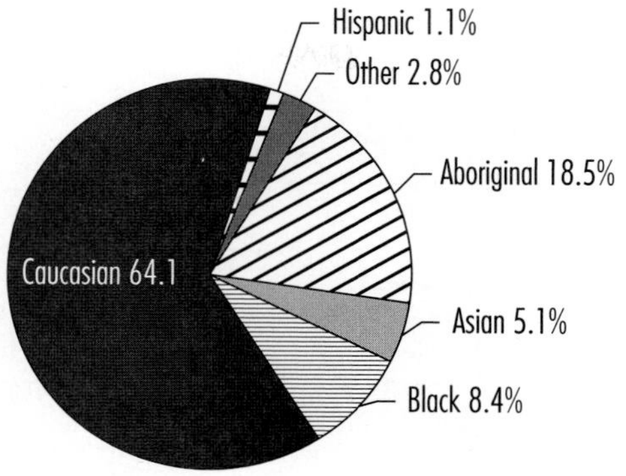

Notes:

These data are self-identified by offenders while they are incarcerated, and the categories are not comprehensive; therefore, the reader should interpret these data with caution.

"Aboriginal" includes offenders who are Inuit, Innu, Métis and North American Indian.

"Asian" includes offenders who are Arab, Asiatic, Chinese, East Indian, Filipino, Japanese, Korean, South East Asian and South Asian.

"Hispanic" includes offenders who are Hispanic and Latin American.

Source: *Corrections and Conditional Release Statistical Overview. Figure: 64% of federal offenders are Caucasian.* <http://www.securitepublique.gc.ca/res/cor/rep/2011-ccrso-eng.aspx. Correctional Service of Canada. Reproduced with the permission of the Minister of Public Works and Government Services, 2012>.

even though they comprised only 3.9 percent of the Canadian population in 2006.[10] Figure 12.3 outlines the ethnicities of the federal offender population.

In 2011, most federal offenders surveyed self-identified as Catholic (37.5 percent) or Protestant (19.5 percent), with those identifying "None" as their religion placing third (16.2 percent). Table 12.3 lists the religious affiliation of Canada's prison inmates.

There have been many surveys of the rates of incarceration worldwide. According to King's College in London, England, in 2010, the United States has the highest incarceration rate in the world at 743 imprisoned individuals per 100 000 residents (see Table 12.4). The Russian Federation is a distant second with 577 per 100 000, the England is 86th with 154 per 100 000, Scotland is 92nd with 149 per 100 000, Canada is 124th with 117 per 100 000, and Japan is 184th with 59 per 100 000. At the end of the list is Timor-Leste (formerly East Timor) at 216th with 20 imprisoned individuals per 100 000 residents (see Figure 12.4).[11] Many argue that incarceration is not working as there are so many recidivists in the United States despite their high rates of incarceration, and other methods must be pursued.

Intermittent Prison Sentences

This provision allows the court to impose an intermittent sentence of no more than 90 days on an offender with consideration of his or her age and character, the nature of the offence, the circumstances surrounding the crime, and the availability of local prisons that can accommodate this type of offender who needs to come in and out of the facility. This type of sentence allows offenders to serve the time on weekends and/or nights so that they can fulfill familial, educational, and employment responsibilities, without putting those opportunities in jeopardy. Offenders may still have to comply with conditions while they are not incarcerated, and possibly probationary conditions after their sentences have been served.

10. Statistics Canada, "Population Projections by Aboriginal Identity in Canada, 2011," online: <http://www.statcan.gc.ca/daily-quotidien/111207/dq111207a-eng.htm>

11. King's College of Law, London, International Centre for Prison Studies, "Prison Brief—Highest to Lowest Rates" (18 March 2010) King's College, http://www.kcl.ac.uk/depsta/law/research/icps/worldbrief/wpb_stats.php?area=all&category=wb_poprate.

Table 12.3 Religious Identification of the Offender Population

	Offender Population			
	2005-06		2010-11	
	#	%	#	%
Catholic	8 755	41.6	8 571	37.5
Protestant	4 328	20.6	4 446	19.5
Muslim	776	3.7	1 029	4.5
Native Spirituality	765	3.6	909	4.0
Buddhist	380	1.8	468	2.0
Jewish	155	0.7	164	0.7
Orthodox	106	0.5	106	0.5
Sikh	106	0.5	149	0.7
Other	1 363	6.5	1 539	6.7
None	3 257	15.5	3 709	16.2
Unknown	1 045	5.0	1 753	7.7
Total	**21 036**	**100.0**	**22 863**	**100.0**

Source: *Corrections and Conditional Release Statistical Overview. Table: The Religious identification of the offender population is diverse.* <http://www.securitepublique.gc.ca/res/cor/rep/2011-ccrso-eng.aspx>. Correctional Service of Canada. Reproduced with the permission of the Minister of Public Works and Government Services, 2012.

Table 12.4 Incarceration Rates of Selected Nations

Country	Number Detained per 100 000 Residents
United States	743
Russian Federation	568
United Kingdom	153
Canada	117
Japan	58
Timor-Leste (East Timor)	20

Source: Roy Walmsley, International Centre for Prison Studies, "World Population List" 9th ed. <http://www.apcca.org/stats/9th%20Edition%20(2011).pdf>

Even with this many offenders in Canada, very few attempt escape, as offenders have options of serving sentences in alternative ways. Figure 12.5 outlines the escape from prison of inmates in Canada.

Figure 12.4 Incarceration Rates Worldwide

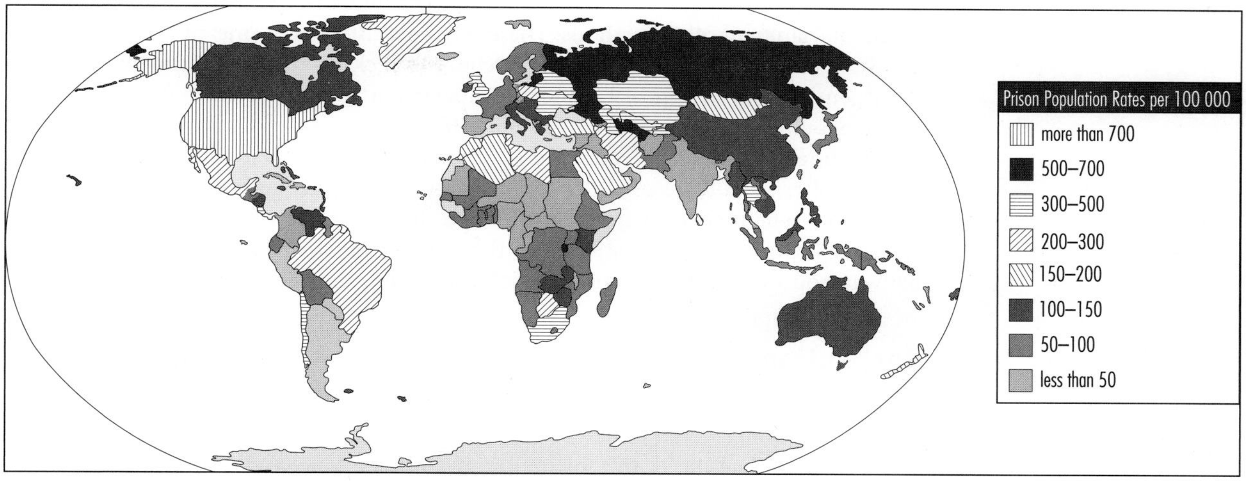

Prison Population Rates per 100 000
more than 700
500–700
300–500
200–300
150–200
100–150
50–100
less than 50

Source: ChartsBin statistics collector team 2010, World Prison Population Rates per 100,000 of the national population, ChartsBin.com, <http://chartsbin.com/view/eqq>.

Figure 12.5 The Number of Escapes of Federal Offenders

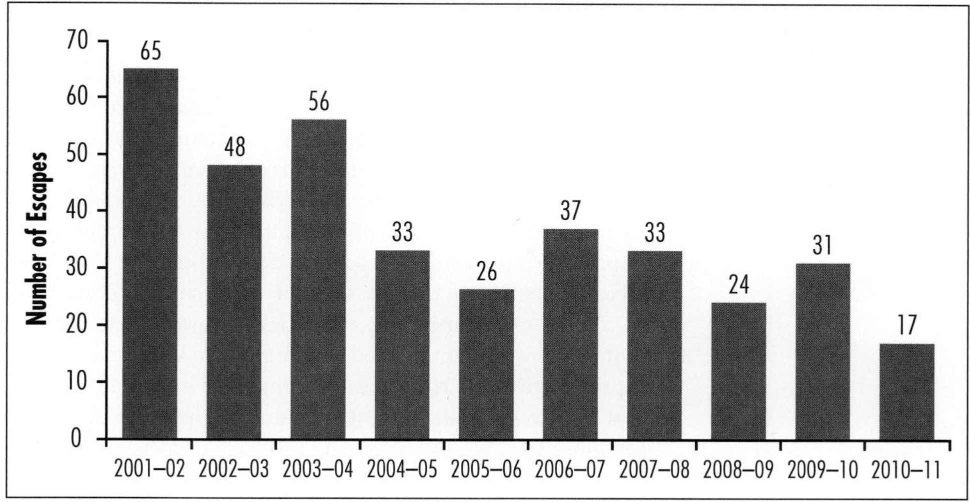

Notes:

- In 2010–11, there were 14 escape incidents involving a total of 17 inmates. Of these 17 escapees, 15 had been recaptured as of April 1, 2011.
- In 2010–11, all of the escapees were from minimum-security facilities.
- Inmates who escaped from federal institutions in 2010–11 represented less than 0.1 percent of the inmate population.

Source: *Corrections and Conditional Release Statistical Overview. Figure: The number of escapes has decreased.* <http://www.securitepublique.gc.ca/res/cor/rep/2011-ccrso-eng.aspx>. Correctional Service of Canada. Reproduced with the permission of the Minister of Public Works and Government Services, 2012.

Rehabilitation

In the past, some sentences were justified as rehabilitative but were actually highly punitive. Some sentences to mental institutions were indefinite, and individuals were spending more time in institutions than they would have if incarcerated in a penitentiary. However, rehabilitation is future-oriented and it focuses on the needs of the offender. The sentence is intended to help the offender to overcome impediments to become a contributing and law-abiding citizen. Many see rehabilitation as a lenient sentence, but it may also be more humanitarian than other methods. These types of sentences are meant to give the offenders another chance and may require the offender to seek psychiatric treatment such as anger management counselling, or help for alcoholism and other substance-abuse disorders.

Rehabilitative programs are often only effective if the offender is motivated and willing, as it is almost impossible to effectively treat people against their will. We nonetheless continue to offer these types of sentences out of hope for a change in the offender and a moral obligation to help people who wish to live productive and law-abiding lives. Rehabilitation can also include re-socialization into the community following imprisonment through halfway houses and programs such as job counselling and training.

Restitution and Victim Surcharge

Restitution as a form of punishment that comes from the English common law, when offences were considered to be private wrongs against individuals. The goal of sentencing was to compensate the victim for the harm that was done, and restitution was a sentence in which the offender had to repay the victim for losses or pay some equivalent amount. This payment is usually made in monetary payments, but in some cases young offenders or those with limited income have been ordered to provide services **in kind,** mostly for damaged or stolen property, or income lost because of a personal injury. Restitution is often used in addition to other sanctions, but the court must take into consideration the offender's financial resources. This type of order addresses the purposes of sentencing in ss. 718(e) and (f) of the *Criminal Code* to provide reparations to victims and promote a sense of responsibility.

A fine is a punitive measure paid to the state, although it can be ordered in conjunction with other sanctions. There are various maximum fines provided in the *Criminal Code.* A judge must take into consideration the offender's abilities to pay under s 734(2) of the *Code*, as non-payment could lead to imprisonment and can be a punitive sentence. For a summary offence, the highest fine permitted is $5000. For an indictable offence there is no limit, but there may be a fine option program that allows offenders to work through community service to pay down their fines. Those sentenced under the *Criminal Code* can also be ordered to pay a **victim surcharge** that goes to a victim assistance fund to assist victims of crime.[12]

There are other monies that might be available to the victims of crime. In April 2011, the Ontario government created the Vulnerable Victims and Family Fund, which provides funds for the victims of crime and the families of homicide victims. The government will cover the cost of travel to court appearances and will provide interpretation services and other services for those who are disabled. The province of Ontario has also provided $900 000 over three years to victims of crime through the **Victim/Witness Assistance Program**. Since 2003, the government of Ontario has invested $320.4 million for the **Victims' Justice Fund.**[13]

The Individual Offender and Offence

As for the individual offender, the *Criminal Code* outlines other facts that must be considered:

718.2 A court that imposes a sentence shall also take into consideration the following principles:

(a) a sentence should be increased or reduced to account for any relevant aggravating or mitigating circumstances relating to the offence or the offender, and, without limiting the generality of the foregoing,

(i) evidence that the offence was motivated by bias, prejudice or hate based on race, national or ethnic origin, language, colour, religion, sex, age, mental or physical disability, sexual orientation, or any other similar factor,

(ii) evidence that the offender, in committing the offence, abused the offender's spouse or common-law partner,

12. Government of Canada, Restitution Orders, http://publications.gc.ca/collections/Collection/J2-287-1999E.pdf.

13. Minister of the Attorney General for Ontario, "Supporting Vulnerable Victims and their Families" (10 April 2011), http://www.attorneygeneral.jus.gov.on.ca/english/news/2011/20110410-victims-nr.asp

(ii.1) evidence that the offender, in committing the offence, abused a person under the age of eighteen years,
(iii) evidence that the offender, in committing the offence, abused a position of trust or authority in relation to the victim,
(iv) evidence that the offence was committed for the benefit of, at the direction of or in association with a criminal organization, or
(v) evidence that the offence was a terrorism offence shall be deemed to be aggravating circumstances;

(b) a sentence should be similar to sentences imposed on similar offenders for similar offences committed in similar circumstances;
(c) where consecutive sentences are imposed, the combined sentence should not be unduly long or harsh;
(d) an offender should not be deprived of liberty, if less restrictive sanctions may be appropriate in the circumstances; and
(e) all available sanctions other than imprisonment that are reasonable in the circumstances should be considered for all offenders, with particular attention to the circumstances of aboriginal offenders.

Each offender must be individually assessed. Compare the cases of *R v Castro* and *R v Collins*, discussed in the boxes on this page.

R v CASTRO, 2010 ONCA 718 (ONT CA)

Mr. Castro ran a paralegal firm specializing in victims of motor vehicle accidents seeking settlements from insurance companies. Most of the clients were immigrants to Canada whose first language was Spanish (which was also Mr. Castro's first language). Mr. Castro began to take the settlement cheques for the clients, place them in his trust account, and then transfer them to his personal funds. When clients asked for their money, he told them no settlement had been reached. The accused had his licence suspended, and he stopped working as a paralegal.

At trial, Mr. Castro was convicted and as part of his sentence he was ordered to pay restitution in the amount of $141 752 to five clients who had lost money. The court cited s 718(1)(a) of the *Criminal Code*, which governs restitution where money has been taken from victims. Mr. Castro appealed the order for restitution.

The Court of Appeal reviewed the judge's reasons for the decision and found that when the judge considered restitution along with the other aspects of the punishment of the individual, he did take into account the offender's ability to pay, even given his submission that he was no longer able to work as a paralegal. The court found that the trial judge's sentencing order was reasonable and proper with the discretion of the sentencing judge who had taken into consideration the appropriate factors. Since Mr. Castro used his position to engage in breach of trust with vulnerable persons and the restitution was properly ordered.

R v COLLINS, [2011] OJ NO 978 (ONT CA)

In this case Ms. Collins appealed her sentence of 16 months' imprisonment and restitution of $96 000 for fraud. Ms. Collins was attempting to defraud a program called "Ontario Works" by providing identities for which false claims were created and cheques were obtained for individuals who did not exist. The accused processed 67 cheques for a total amount of $96 298, which went toward her gambling addiction.

The accused had no criminal record, but she had grown up in abject poverty and faced discrimination and alienation by the Canadian government, which put her father into a residential school and deprived her entire family of their rights as Aboriginals. Her mother grew up on a reserve in a home "riddled with substance abuse and violence." Ms. Collins had a difficult life, experienced racism throughout, and these circumstances led to a gambling addiction. Immediately prior to sentencing, she suffered three brain aneurysms, and she had a decline in memory, language, and processing. Ms. Collins appealed the sentence of 16 months' imprisonment and restitution in the amount of $96 000.

The appeals court found that the trial judge had erred, and the sentence was too punitive, given the Aboriginal heritage of the accused. The sentence was reduced to 10 months' imprisonment with two years' probation and a restitution order for $96 000. The court was bound under s 718.2(e) to recognize the impact of Canada's treatment of the Aboriginal population; however, a jail sentence and restitution was warranted, given the need for general deterrence and denunciation.

Do you think this is the right sentence, given the sentencing principles and purposes? Should Aboriginal status influence sentencing?

Aggravating Factors

In sentencing, the court must take into account factors that would cause the sentence to be increased under s 719.2 of the *Criminal Code*. Elements that have been found to be aggravating factors are evidence of hate against an identifiable group, terrorism, abuse of the offender's spouse or common-law partner or child, evidence that the offender was in a position of trust or authority in relation to the victim, and whether the individual was part of a criminal organization. Other aggravating factors can include the use of a weapon, violence, cruelty in the commission of the crime, injuries (physical and psychological), multiple victims and incidents, criminal record, lack of remorse, impeding the access of the victim to the justice system, economic losses, and the planning involved in the crime.

Mitigating Factors

Mitigating factors, or those that cause a reduction in sentence, must also be considered under s 718.2 of the *Criminal Code*. Several factors that have been considered include:

- Was this a first offence?
- Was the offence out of character?
- Was there prior good character?
- Was there impairment by drugs or alcohol?
- Did the offender enter a guilty plea to save the victim from testifying?
- Was there remorse?
- Were there personal problems to help account for the crime?
- Did the offender have a positive employment or schooling record?
- Were there indirect consequences to the offender?
- Had the offender enrolled in post-offence rehabilitation?
- Is there unrelated meritorious conduct?
- Was reparation or compensation made to the victim?
- Were there elements of provocation and duress?
- Was there a delay in prosecution?
- Was there a gap in the criminal record?
- Was there a lack of recidivism?
- Was this a test case?
- Did the accused have a disadvantaged background or childhood?

SENTENCING OPTIONS

Absolute and Conditional Discharge

A discharge results in a finding of guilt without a conviction being registered on an individual's record. A record of the discharge is kept and it can be used in sentencing if you are charged with criminal offences in the future. This option can be used for all offences in which there is no mandatory sentence or where the maximum sentence is less than 14 years.

An absolute discharge is effective immediately, and the court has to evaluate if it would be in the best interests of the offender and not contrary to the public interest. This sentence allows an individual to properly say that he or she does not have a criminal record and may avoid restrictions/difficulties with employment, travel, immigration, and so forth. Even if an offender receives an absolute discharge, this does not prevent him or her from appealing the finding itself under s 730(3)(a).

A conditional discharge has certain conditions attached (e.g., community service) that the offender must complete within a certain period of time before the discharge becomes permanent. Again, the court must consider if this is in the best interests of the offender and not contrary to the public interest (see *R v Aussem* in the following case box). This method is usually reserved for less serious offences, first-time offenders, and persons who are not a threat to the community or not likely to repeat. If the offender does not complete the conditions, under s 730(4), the court may revoke the discharge and sentence the offender to the sentence he or she could have been liable to at the time of sentencing. See *R v Aussem* (next box) for an example of a conditional discharge.

R v AUSSEM, [1997] OJ NO 5582 (ONT CJ)

Mr. Aussem was 22 years old at the time of the offence, and he was convicted of assault and assault with a weapon. Mr. Aussem was a hockey player and during a Junior A hockey game, he violently cross-checked a standing opponent from behind while he was skating at full speed, by striking him on the back of the neck with his stick. The victim was able to rejoin the team after one week, but there was potential for severe injury. The defence counsel requested a conditional discharge, while the Crown requested a sentence of 60 to 90 days in jail.

The court looked at the following factors to determine if a conditional discharge was appropriate: the fact that the victim had no long-term injuries, that Mr. Aussem showed remorse for his crimes, that he had no adult criminal record, that he had worked hard to capitalize on his hockey skills, and that he had missed opportunities in Europe because he had to stay in Ontario for his trial. The judge heard the suggestions of the Crown that general deterrence was important to send a message that this kind of violence in sport will not be permitted, but the judge also acknowledged that a punitive sentence for Mr. Aussem would not solve the problem of violence in hockey.

The judge entered a sentence of a conditional discharge including probation for 18 months during which Mr. Aussem was to complete 100 hours of community service related to amateur hockey, participate in anger management, and pay a contribution of $500 to an amateur league to be used for the promotion of less violence in the game of hockey. In addition, he was given the other common provisions on a conditional discharge, including keeping the peace, maintaining good behaviour, and notifying probation of any change in address.

Probation

Probation is an option that may be imposed alone, with a suspended sentence, or in addition to other sentencing options. Probation is available in most criminal cases except where there is a mandatory minimum sentence. This sentence is meant to be rehabilitative as the person serves the sentence in the community under supervision and with restrictions. Common requirements include keeping the peace and being of good behaviour, appearing in court as required, notifying court and probation workers of a change of address or employment, completing up to 240 hours of community service in a period of 18 months, going for substance abuse treatment, reporting to a probation officer, supporting dependents, refraining from owning a weapon, and any other reasonable conditions imposed by the court.

The maximum period of probation is approximately three years. The offender usually has to report to a probation officer or the police, meet curfews, attend school or seek or maintain employment, obtain psychiatric treatment, take counselling, make restitution, and so on. It is common that a community service order is part of a probation order. Courts have flexibility but usually make the conditions reasonable and appropriate to the offence. If an offender breaches probation, he or she may be sentenced to a term of up to two years in prison.

Suspended Sentences

The offender may be given a term of imprisonment but the sentence is suspended, often until the offender completes a period of probation. This sentence is often used for denunciation purposes in order to send a societal message that this behaviour will not be tolerated, and is often used along with probation. If a person fails to adhere to the probation order, he or she may be brought back into court and forced to serve the original prison sentence. The offender will still have a record of conviction.

Commonly Imposed Sanctions

A 2006–2007 study followed 250 000 cases in which the accused was found guilty to see what sentences were imposed. Although offenders could be sentenced for multiple reasons, the study looked at the most serious sentence imposed. Incarceration was ordered in 34 percent of the cases, probation in 28 percent, and fines in 26 percent of the cases (see Figure 12.6). A conditional sentence was imposed in only 4 percent of cases, but in another aspect of the study, probation was the most frequent sentence in youth cases, at 59 percent.[14]

Sentencing Disparity

Sentencing disparity has been identified as one of the major issues in the criminal justice system, and there is evidence that this remains a problem, even after the 1996 reforms. Divergent sentences among different offenders have been shown to influence how people see justice being done, and how offenders themselves feel when sentenced. As discussed earlier, the *Criminal Code* gives the judge an enormous degree of discretion in sentencing. Disparity can mean that there must be a "fit" sentence for a particular crime, which necessarily means that there will not be identical sentences, but many feel that there is a lack of certainty in sentencing when each case is examined individually.

Figure 12.6 Types of Sentence Imposed

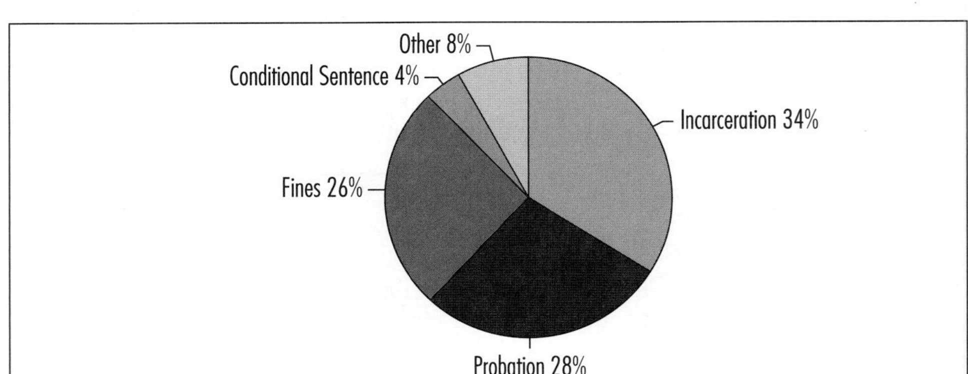

Source: Lori Hausegger, Matthew Hennigar, & Troy Riddell. *Canadian Courts: Law, Politics and Process.* (Don Mills, ON: Oxford, 2009) at 300.

14. Lori Hausegger, Matthew Hennigar, and Troy Riddell, *Canadian Courts: Law, Politics and Process* (Don Mills, ON: Oxford, 2009) at 300

There has been considerable variation across provinces, but there has been some reluctance to give sentencing guidelines for each and every offence. Some provinces have identified a "starting point" for sentences given to classes of offences (e.g., sexual assault in Alberta has a starting sentence to be used as a guide for judges). The Supreme Court has refused most appeals for sentence and left these decisions with the provincial judges. There is a general range of sentences that are appropriate for any particular offence when examining case law, but many advocate for a "fixed tariff" for offences. Ontario has not yet done this formally, but in some offences, the province has come close by saying it would consider the "usual range" in some cases.

However, many practitioners say that disparity is the "strongest virtue of a system that seeks to ensure the protection of society through fit sentences."[15] Many think that having individual sentences for individual offenders is the only way to make our system function in a balanced way.

Again, the sentencing judge must also look at a variety of aggravating factors, including the seriousness of the offence, current sentencing practices, prior criminal record, perceived likelihood of recidivism, the offender's record of employment, the victim impact statement, the judge's characteristics, and the case law provided which isolates an appropriate range of sentences.

Remand

Those who are held on "remand" are those who are incarcerated temporarily awaiting trial or sentencing. In 2011, Statistics Canada released a report showing the number of adults in remand surpassed those in sentenced custody in 2005–2006. Fifty-eight percent of adults in custody were there on remand, while only 42 percent were in sentenced custody. The numbers are attributed to higher admissions and longer periods spent awaiting sentencing or trial. Just ten years earlier, the proportions were 60 percent sentenced offenders and 40 percent remand (see Figure 12.7).[16]

Mandatory Minimums

Historically, the use of a mandatory minimum penalty has been used sparingly to allow courts to give sentences that fit the offender. Research has shown that forcing mandatory sentences on offenders creates a rigid system of sentencing, and does not allow judges to look at the individual circumstances of the accused.

However, there are approximately 30 offences in the *Criminal Code* that carry a mandatory minimum sentence. (This may change with the introduction of Bill C-10 introduced at the time of publication, and challenges to the constitutionality of mandatory minimums were working through the courts in 2012.) At least 16 of these offences were related to firearms and were

Figure 12.7 Prisoners Serving Sentences and Prisoners on Remand

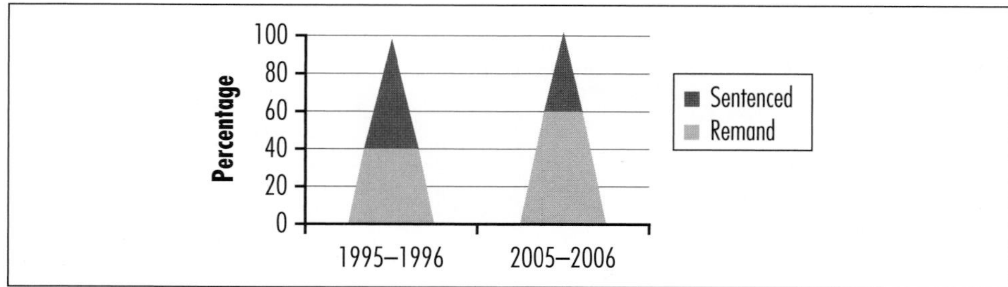

Source: Canadian Press. "Prisoners on Remand Far Outnumber those Serving Sentences, StatsCan Says" <http://www.citytv.com/toronto/citynews/news/national/article/131522-prisoners-on-remand-far-outnumber-those-serving-sentences-statscan-says>

15. Allan Manson, Patrick Healy, and Gary Trotter, *Sentencing and Penal Policy in Canada: Cases, Materials, and Commentary* (Toronto: Emond Montgomery, 2000) at 86.

16. "Prisoners on Remand Far Outnumber those Serving Sentences, StatsCan Says," http://www.citytv.com/toronto/citynews / news/national/article/131522--prisoners-on-remand-far-outnumber-those-serving-sentences-statscan-says.

introduced in Bill C-68 in 1995, but others include child prostitution and impaired driving. Judges have no discretion to reduce the sentences set under these provisions.[17] Table 12.5 outlines several examples of crimes requiring mandatory minimum sentences.

Sentencing Myths

Many in the population believe that people are "getting away with murder" in Canada because of our lax sentencing measures. However, Canada has many offences other than murder that have a possible sentence of 14 years or life imprisonment. These include high treason, treason, piracy, hijacking, endangering the safety of an aircraft or airport, commission of an offence for a terrorist group, criminal negligence, aggravated sexual assault, robbery, and various firearm offences.

An international comparison of time served in custody for someone serving a life sentence for first-degree murder reveals that Canadian standards far exceed the time spent in prison in other countries (see Figure 12.8). The average time spent in Canada for a life sentence is 28.4 years; in the United States, life in prison with parole is 18.5 years; in Australia it is 14.8 years; in

Table 12.5 Examples of Mandatory Minimum Sentences

Provision of the *Criminal Code*	Mandatory Minimum
S 47—Punishment for high treason	Minimum term of life in prison
S 103—Importing or exporting knowing it is unauthorized (object is a firearm)	Minimum term of three years for first offence, and five years for a second or subsequent offence
S 151—Sexual interference	Minimum punishment of 45 days for an indictable offence, and 14 days for a summary offence
S 163—Making child pornography	Minimum term of one year for an indictable offence, and 90 days for summary offence
S 220—Causing death by criminal negligence	Minimum term of four years in prison
S 235—Murder	Minimum term of life in prison
S 236—Manslaughter (with firearm)	Minimum term of four years in prison
S 244—Discharging firearm with intent	If restricted or prohibited firearm, minimum term of five years for first offence, seven years for a second or subsequent offence; all others have a minimum term of four years
S 272—Sexual assault with a weapon	If restricted or prohibited firearm, minimum term of five years for first offence, seven years for a second or subsequent offence; all others have a minimum term of four years
S 273—Aggravated sexual assault (with firearm)	If restricted or prohibited firearm, minimum term of five years for first offence, seven years for a second or subsequent offence
S 279—Kidnapping	If restricted or prohibited firearm, minimum term of five years for first offence, seven years for a second or subsequent offence; all others have a minimum term of four years
S 279.01—Trafficking in persons (if committing another crime in the commission of offence)	Minimum term of life in prison
S 344—Robbery	If restricted or prohibited firearm, minimum term of five years for first offence, seven years for a second or subsequent offence; all others have a minimum term of four years

17. Department of Justice, "Mandatory Sentences of Imprisonment in Common Law Jurisdictions: Some Representative Models" (8 January 2010), online: <http://www.justice.gc.ca/eng/pi/rs/rep-rap/2005/rr05_10/p2.html>.

Figure 12.8 Length of Life Sentences in Selected Countries

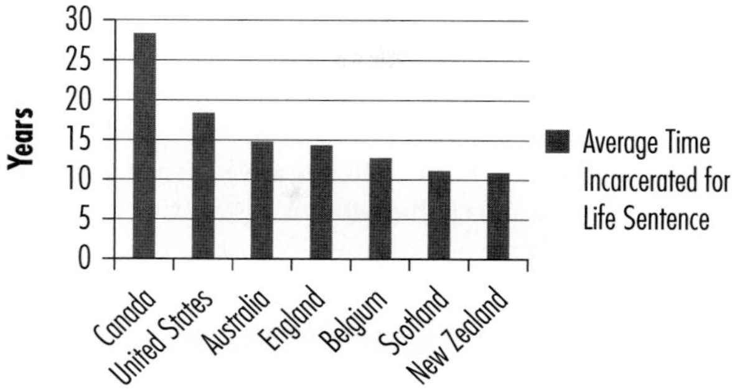

Source: Library of Parliament, "Bill C-36: An Act to Amend the Criminal Code" (11 September 2009) at 9–10, online: <http://www.parl.gc.ca/About/Parliament/LegislativeSummaries/bills_ls.asp?lang=E&ls=c36&Parl=40&Ses=2&source=library_prb>.

Belgium it is 12.7 years; in Scotland it is 11.2 years; and in New Zealand it is 11 years. The only exception is the US for those serving life without parole which averages 29 years.[18]

ALTERNATE MEASURES

Section 717 of the *Criminal Code* provides for "alternative measures" in sentencing if these measures are consistent with the protection of society. Alternative measures can include anything from a warning by a police officer after a traffic violation, to diverting a person to the mental health system rather than proceeding in a criminal court. There are also community programs that may provide services for those who have been taken outside of the criminal system, with the cooperation of Crown attorneys. The offender must agree that to participate in an alternative measure and must take responsibility for his or her crimes, and the Crown must be confident that a conviction could be secured. Many offenders do not warrant a full prosecution, and diversion is often a cost-effective alternative.

Such programs can occur at the pre-charge stage, when the police or Crown can choose to place someone into a program rather than proceed with a criminal charge; after the charge but before trial, when the charge may be stayed or withdrawn after completion of the diversion program; or at the sentencing stage, when the offender is placed into a program instead of a traditional sentencing procedure. This trend has led to courts becoming specialized in the fields of drug offences, mental health issues, and domestic violence. All of these measures seek to deal with the offender in the most appropriate way possible.

Restorative Justice

One last, and very important, piece of the criminal justice system is restorative justice. In the case of *R v Laliberté,* [2000] SJ No 138 (Sask CA), Justice Vancise succinctly defined what is meant by restorative justice in Canada:

> the creation of a positive environment for change, healing and reconciliation for offenders, victims and communities. It is a condemnation of criminal actions rather than perpetrators and an integration of offenders into the community rather than a stigmatization or marginalization of them. Within this framework the offender is encouraged to accept responsibility and to make reparations to the community. The restorative approach defines crime as a violation of one person by another and focuses on problem solving and the repair of social injury. It is a system in which the community is facilitator, where restoration is used as a means of reconciling the parties, and where the liability to the victim is recognized and redressed.[19]

18. Library of Parliament, "Bill C-36: An Act to Amend the Criminal Code" (11 September 2009) at 9 10, online: <http://www.parl.gc.ca/About/Parliament/LegislativeSummaries/bills_ls.asp?lang=E&ls=c36&Parl=40&Ses=2&source=library_prb.>

19. See also H Zerr, *Changing Lenses: A New Focus for Crime and Justice* (Scottsdale, PA: Herald Press, 1990); and D Van Ness, "Pursuing a Restorative Vision of Justice" at 1 30, *Justice: The Restorative Vision, New Perspectives on Crime and Justice,* Occasional papers of MCC Canada/U.S. February 1989.

Restorative justice focuses on the healing relationships between individuals who have been involved in the justice system. It includes the offender, victim, and larger community. Under restorative justice, the offender and victim play key roles in resolving the conflict rather than engaging an agent of the Crown to prosecute the offender with little input from the victim.

Section 718.2 of the *Criminal Code* provides that all available sanctions should be considered for all offenders; thus, there is a push to explore some of these alternative methods of resolution. Restorative justice programs are being established in communities across Canada.[20] But what is restorative justice? See the following box for a discussion with Chris Cowie of Community Justice Initiatives.

Community Justice Initiatives
http://www.cjiwr.com/

WHAT IS RESTORATIVE JUSTICE?

Talking With Executive Director Of CJI, Chris Cowie

Restorative Justice is a way of viewing justice that prioritizes the repairing of relationships and redressing of harm done to victims over retributive measures. Proponents of a restorative approach feel that justice has been served when one who commits an offence expresses sincere remorse directly to the victim and makes reparation of loss or damage in a way that is consistent with a victim's expressed desire. Restorative justice is achieved through programs, usually referred to as victim offender reconciliation programs (VORPs).

Community Justice Initiatives homepage

Courtesy of Community Justice Initiatives of Waterloo Region

Restorative justice attempts to redress the harm done to victims, offer support and responsibility to offenders, and to promote a sense of family and community. This can include programs such as Victim Offender Reconciliation. This type of program was first created in Kitchener-Waterloo, Ontario, by Mark Yantzi, and it has blossomed into the organization known as Community Justice Initiatives (CJI). Some of the work being done by this organization is the first of its kind in Canada, and the world. In this program, which is voluntary to all involved, trained mediators bring the offender and the victim together to facilitate discussion about what has occurred, and how healing can begin.[21]

Family group conferencing (FGC) is a method of facilitating victim offender reconciliation for young offenders. FGC is distinguished by its inclusion of support persons for both the victims and offenders in face-to-face meetings. Opportunities are provided for supporters, usually family members, of the young offender to communicate the impact of the crime on them and the family dynamic. Similarly, the victim's supporters can share their feelings regarding the impact of the crime. This provides the young person with a greater awareness of the impact of his or her crime and creates a liminal space in which a vague notion of community can become concrete for all present. The atmosphere created in FGCs is highly conducive to healing and reintegration.

Family conferences also employ restorative principles to assist families in making decisions about children. Conferences are not necessarily in response to a crime committed, but involve bringing together caregivers, social workers, and community and other members in the child's life to decide what works for that young person.[22]

Some victims' rights advocates say that victims may not want to meet with offenders who victimized them, and that they might feel pressure to meet with someone who had wronged them. Much attention must be paid to ensuring that this system is voluntary and that victims are not pressured to participate. However, the results show that offenders are staying out of prison, and up to 85 percent of offenders who participate in this type of program fulfill the conditions that they agree to. Offenders are said to have much more

20. Community Justice Initiatives of Waterloo Region, Kitchener, Ontario, http://www.cjiwr.com/. See also *Ottawa Citizen* (September 11, 2004) "How a Drunken Rampage Changed Legal History," online: <http://www.canada.com/ottawacitizen/story.html?id=68c9484e-7dfa-41a6-976a-fcd9b0a96424>.

21. Community Justice Initiatives of Waterloo Region, Kitchener Ontario, online: <http://www.cjiwr.com/>.

22. Chris Cowie, Community Justice Initiatives.

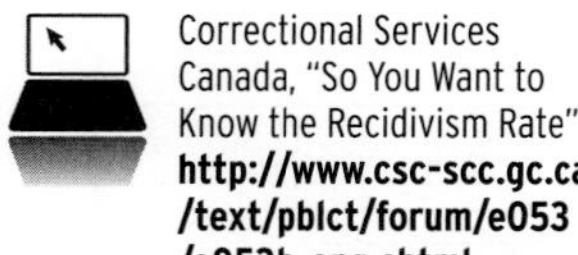

Correctional Services Canada, "So You Want to Know the Recidivism Rate" **http://www.csc-scc.gc.ca/text/pblct/forum/e053/e053h-eng.shtml**

ownership deciding how they can restore their victims (through money, services, etc.) and are much more likely to adhere to those promises.

Sentencing circles are another method that is common in Aboriginal communities, and they are spreading outside of that sphere. In a sentencing circle, the offender and his or her supporters, the victim and his or her supporters, community leaders, judges, lawyers, police, and other interested parties come together to decide how to deal with a particular case in order to maintain the principles of restorative justice. There may be a court-appointed judge in attendance but the judge's role is mainly as facilitator, as the members of the circle decide how best to hold the offender responsible for his or her actions.

These programs have been successful in getting offenders outside of the clogged criminal justice system. They have also led to more satisfaction from victims because their voices have been heard, and they have resulted in less recidivism and a greater commitment by all to the community. Again, there must be a focus on addressing power imbalances between offenders and victims, but training methods are being used to identify those who would benefit from restorative justice, and to manage expectations and beliefs even before a session begins. The Department of Justice has recognized the importance of these programs. Its website says that this method is important because the restorative justice process

> approaches crime as an injury or wrong done to another person rather than solely as a matter of breaking the law or offending against the state. Accordingly, it is concerned not only with determining appropriate responses to criminal behavior, but also with reparation—that is, actions that attempt to repair the damage caused by the crime, either materially or symbolically. Therefore, restorative justice encourages the victim and the offender to play active roles in resolving conflict through discussion and negotiation. Instead of taking over the process, and perhaps losing sight of the people who are directly affected, the state and legal professionals become facilitators in a system that encourages offender accountability, full participation of both victim and offender, and efforts to fix the damage that has been done. Thus, restorative justice is more than just a practice or a program—it is a philosophy, a way of looking at crime and a response to crime.[23]

It is with innovative programs such as these that the criminal justice system can address some of the wrongs of the past, and bring sentencing of offenders into the twenty-first century. However, advances in solutions outside of the traditional system are not limited to the criminal realm.

ALTERNATIVE DISPUTE RESOLUTION

It is not just the criminal justice system that is seeking alternative forms of resolution. Given the costs involved with civil litigation and many appearances before administrative tribunals, there is a great need for those seeking a less adversarial and less costly way to resolve their issues. Collectively, these methods are called alternative dispute resolution (ADR). ADR has been used in labour arbitrations for a long time in Canada, but the methods are being used in other commercial matters, in family law, and in many areas of law where there might be conflict.

In a typical civil litigation matter, the plaintiff and the defendant are giving up control of their conflict to other players—to judges, arbitrators, mediators, lawyers, experts, and so on. In civil litigation, it is a possibility that neither party may get the solution that they are seeking, and both parties may leave unsatisfied. ADR seeks to improve the individual satisfaction of the parties by tailoring the process to their needs—giving the power back to the parties in their matter by being a valuable actor in the solution. And there can be a resolution by reacting to conflict in a positive way. In addition to these goals of the individual, society also benefits from ADR in the form of social control as individuals are more likely to be committed to a solution that they have crafted and there is more social cohesion, as there is more solidarity between the parties and the community. However, ADR does not come in

23. Department of Justice, "Restorative Justice in Canada: A Consultation Paper" (May 2000), online: <http://www.justice.gc.ca/eng/pi/pcvi-cpcv/cons.html#principles>.

Figure 12.9 Continuum of Dispute Resolution

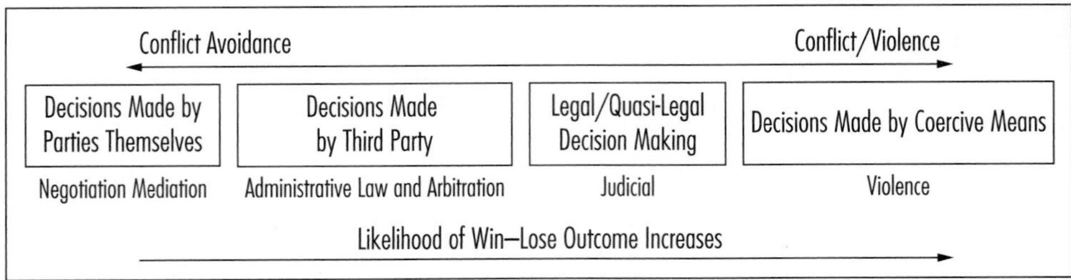

one size. There are different levels and goals of different types of ADR in the legal system, which are on a continuum from conflict avoidance to conflict (see Figure 12.9).

Negotiation

At one end of the spectrum is negotiation, which is the process of consensual dispute resolution. Negotiation is a voluntary process that can be formal or informal, and there is no third party to lead the discussion. The two parties who are in conflict sit down and try to talk to each other to discuss what is important to them. Lawyers are often involved in the negotiation process, and spend a majority of their time negotiating with various parties to see if litigation can be avoided. Law schools and universities offer entire classes on negotiation, and it can be an in-depth skill set.

The parties will themselves identify the issues, and discuss how to resolve them in a way that is beneficial to both parties. One side may be forced to concede some issues to find a compromise. This agreed solution may be formalized in writing and make the parties bound by that resolution, but the parties are empowered to find their own solution and to adhere to the deal that they make. Lawyers frequently engage in this type of negotiation to try to avoid the civil litigation system, if possible, where the parties would have to face a situation where one party wins, and the other loses.

The Advantages of Negotiation

There are pros and cons to each method of ADR, but negotiation has several positive aspects. First, it is a cost-effective method. The parties may be able to come to a resolution without hiring a lawyer, but if they do, the costs are going to be categorically less than taking the matter to litigation or before a tribunal. Because the parties sit down alone without outside parties, their privacy can be maintained, and they can control the process and guide it in a direction that they decide based on their priorities and the solutions they wish to find—not those forced upon them by a third party.

Negotiation can be the best solution if the parties must continue to have a business relationship, as the conflict is kept to a minimum. The parties can be well informed of what they have agreed to, and they will be much more likely to adhere to their agreement because they had a hand in coming to that conclusion. This method is frequently used in many areas of the law, but employment law often uses this technique after someone has been terminated from a job. A settlement needs to be reached that deals with the parties' needs upon that termination. Parties can negotiate how much severance pay they will receive, how long their benefits may continue, the return of company property, and so forth.

Litigation can often be avoided through negotiation.

Denisenko/Shutterstock

The Disadvantages of Negotiation

There are also disadvantages to negotiation. You cannot force anyone to take part in this voluntary ADR method, as there is no power to force anyone to sit at a table and talk to you. The parties may have differing levels of power in the relationship, and one party may be much more skilled at negotiating than the other. An employer may have more power than an employee, a corporation may have more power than a small supplier, or one spouse may have more power than another. This disparity can also apply to lawyers hired by either or both parties who may be motivated to find a resolution, or to encourage their client to abandon this stage and advance to litigation. In a situation with differing levels of power, negotiation may not be the best method of resolution.

The negotiated settlement is often not binding in court as it is a private contract. It will show the intentions of the parties, but there is much room for one party to say that he or she entered into this contract under duress or pressure. Parties cannot be forced to make a settlement, and there may be much money spent litigating the matter after negotiation, which takes away the benefit of lowered costs. The outcome negotiated may require compromise by one or both parties, and the individuals may still see this process as a lose–lose outcome. Although there might be a formal written agreement, the parties may have to seek the assistance of the court to enforce the agreement, which again could lead to significant costs.

Mediation

Mediation is a technique that emerged in Canada in the 1970s and 1980s as a way of solving disagreements that did not involve the formal justice system. Dispute or conflict resolution often involves the intervention of a third party, which can be done formally or informally. Mediation is a non-adversarial technique in which a neutral third party is placed between those in conflict to assist the parties in an agreement in a situation where they need more guidance than negotiation. A mediator has no authority over the parties and they can only use persuasion to influence the final outcome, as the mediator does not impose a decision on the parties. Mediation works best only if both parties are willing to work out a reasonable settlement of their dispute and are of equal bargaining power. Mediators may be legal professionals or others trained in the methods of mediation. Depending on the subject matter of the mediation, different qualifications may be needed.

ADR Institute of Canada
http://www.amic.org/

The underlying principle of mediation is cooperation. The goal is to seek compromises and to ensure the satisfaction of both parties. Mediation is typically done in a private setting to maintain the confidentiality of the discussions—known as a "closed" mediation. The information obtained in a closed mediation cannot be used in the future against either of the parties, and the mediator will not report to lawyers or judges on what happened in the mediation. There is also an option of an "open" mediation, where the mediator prepares a formal report that can be used in the court process at a later date.

The role of the mediator is that of a facilitator rather than a judge. Mediators are usually chosen because they have a particular expertise in the area, and authority on the particular subject. The mediator is trained to extract all relevant information, and can identify what concessions each party is open to. This agreement between the parties may turn into a contract that is much more enforceable in court. Before signing any agreement reached in mediation, individuals are often urged to seek legal advice to make sure that the agreement is beneficial to their needs.

Lawyers are often not present at mediation, but parties are free to seek the advice of a lawyer before entering into mediation, so they know their rights. Canada's *Divorce Act* requires that lawyers mention the possibility of using mediation to their clients, and some provinces have instituted mandatory mediation in family law matters. As of July 18, 2011, Ontario has instituted that all couples who are divorcing must attend a mandatory information session before their divorce will be processed, but mandatory mediation has been required in Toronto for several years. This process is more formalized than negotiation, but it is still not a fully binding process such as arbitration.

Advantages to Mediation

Like negotiation, mediation agreements are created by the parties so they are much more willing to abide by the decisions. Mediation has a lower cost than litigation, and it can be done fairly quickly in a few sessions. Sensitive topics, such as custody and child support issues, can be discussed openly in a private setting that allows the parties to speak freely in a way that will not necessarily be used against them in the future.

Either party can leave at any time if they feel that their needs are not being met, and if they feel that there is a power imbalance. The money saved in this process can go to other necessities, like the care of children, instead of coming to an agreement with a costly legal team. The parties are left to seek independent legal advice before they commit to an agreement. There is some evidence that couples who use mediation are less likely to litigate issues, are more satisfied with the results, and have better relationships with their ex-spouses. This can be beneficial to the children in family law matters.

Disadvantages to Mediation

Like negotiation, there is no guarantee that mediation will be successful, and the parties may still have significant lawyer's fees. There is a possibility that the agreement will not be enforceable in court, and will not be fully binding on the parties like a court order would be. The parties must have equal bargaining power for this method to work, and in family mediations it is common that one party will have more power in the relationship. Again, the parties have to be willing to participate or the matter will not be resolved, and in an open mediation these private conversations can be used in the future. Parties have to be willing to openly share information so that a resolution can be found, but this is often difficult for parties in conflict.

Arbitration

Arbitration is a more formal process, which historically has its origins in Greece and Egypt.[24] Today, arbitration is most often discussed in the context of labour law, which is how it first came to the Canadian system. Arbitration also involves a third party but, unlike in negotiation and mediation, the **arbitrator** can impose a solution on the adversarial parties. This third party (or a panel) is hired and paid by the parties to make a final decision on the matter. The arbitrator often has detailed skills in the area of law in question, and may have a wealth of knowledge in the subject area. Arbitration is usually private and confidential, and has little public attention, which can be beneficial to companies dealing with sensitive material. Arbitration hearings are often held in the same manner as a civil trial but typically in private. In arbitration, the emphasis is on the legal rights and duties of the parties. The goal is not to seek compromises or to ensure the mutual satisfaction of the parties. Arbitration is used frequently in the administrative law realm.

Arbitration allows the third party to make a final and binding decision (often called binding arbitration). Parties typically must agree beforehand that the arbitrator's decision will be final, or they can agree that it may be reviewed by a court, if necessary. Often the governing legislation of the parties will indicate whether binding arbitration is mandatory. The following box provides a sample arbitration clause.

WHAT DOES AN ARBITRATION CLAUSE LOOK LIKE?

A standard clause in many contracts may look like the following:

> *Any controversy or claim arising out of or relating to this contract, or the breach thereof, shall be settled by arbitration in accordance with the Commercial Arbitration Rules of ..., and judgment upon the award rendered by the arbitrator(s) may be entered in any court having jurisdiction thereof.*

24. Andrew J Pirie, *Alternative Dispute Resolution: Skills, Science, and the Law* (Toronto: Irwin Law, 2000) at 213.

Arbitration is often adversarial, and it is most like a traditional civil litigation scheme. The parties may enter evidence through a formal hearing, or may agree to make written submissions only. Both parties can retain lawyers, and each side will enter sworn evidence but it can still be more cost- and time-effective than litigation.

Advantages of Arbitration

Again, there is the obvious advantage of having more matters outside of the traditional court system. Cases are not decided with strict adherence to precedent, but the decision is made by a panel of experts who may be able to make a reasoned judgment based on their significant knowledge and with reference to social and economic factors. The arbitrator, or panel of arbitrators, has the power to gather information, hear witnesses, and examine evidence, and the remedy is tailored to the particular situation by those who have a great deal of knowledge in the subject. This can be a binding decision, so it can end the numerous appeals possible in the traditional system. A solution can be achieved without the pure adversarial positions in the civil litigation system.

Disadvantages of Arbitration

There are, however, disadvantages with arbitration. Notably, the parties are responsible for all of the actors involved, including the cost of the arbitrator, the reporter who makes a transcript, the cost of renting the space, and so forth. Usually, there is little right to appeal unless there was something procedurally wrong, and the courts give the utmost deference to arbitrators. Again, an appeal to the courts takes away from the benefits of arbitration. Despite the best intentions of the system, arbitration is not always a quick resolution. Like the civil litigation system, there is not always a win–win situation—it is likely that one party will lose. Again, the power differential of the parties is not always equal. Some say that the tribunal members are not always knowledgeable and that arbitration is just a poor copy of the civil litigation system.

Adjudication

As discussed in Chapter 3, adjudication is a public and formal method of resolving conflicts, and it is often found in the traditional court system. Courts can intervene in a dispute or impose a decision on both parties, and courts have the authority to enforce the decision. Courts require that disputes be narrowed down to the legally relevant facts and issues, and require that the parties come to a resolution of the issues. However, a court's decision may also leave a clear-cut winner and loser, or both parties may be unsatisfied.

Advantages of Adjudication

As discussed in Chapter 3, there are many benefits of our court system, including the system of precedent, deterrence and uniformity, and the ability of the parties to seek a full and final resolution of their issues. In addition, the system attempts to be independent from either of the parties.

Disadvantages of Adjudication

However, the court system can be extremely expensive, and it almost always requires lawyers to represent the parties, which takes the control from the individual parties. The decisions made by the court are not always understandable and justifiable, and the judge making the decision may have no expertise in the area. Judges are limited with the remedies they have at their disposal, and the average case can take years to resolve. This system is adversarial and necessarily makes the parties see each other as the enemy. There may be no compromise at the end of the day, and the parties may be left extremely unsatisfied.

CONCLUSION

Sentencing is, like many elements of the criminal justice system, more of an art than a science. It is a delicate balance between society, victim, and offender. The courts must come to the least restrictive medium that will protect society and also serve the offender. Even after the reforms in 1996, much work still needs to be done in Canadian sentencing to ensure a just sentence without resorting to warehousing those who may just need an alternative solution. Alternative dispute resolution techniques are relevant in both the criminal and civil law systems, and the entire system will be more effective by using these techniques rather than overburdening an already overwhelmed system.

LEARNING OUTCOMES SUMMARIZED

1. Analyze the purposes of sentencing.

Reforms were made to sentencing in 1996. The result was legislation that set out the purposes of sentencing. The purposes of sentencing are identified in s 718 of the *Criminal Code.* These factors must be used to promote respect for the law and a safe and peaceful society, and the following elements are important sentencing aims: denouncing offenders, deterring offenders, separating offenders, rehabilitating offenders, providing reparations to victims, promoting responsibility for offences, and acknowledging harm to the victims and society.

2. Evaluate the similarities between denunciation and general deterrence.

Denunciation emphasizes society's condemnation of the offensive behaviour. Denunciation has a symbolic value and performs two functions: (1) to educate and (2) to support societal values. Judges may talk directly to offenders to make them realize the harm that they have done. This punishment is often seen as a second chance for offenders with a relatively light sentence. General deterrence refers to harsh sentences designed to deter potential offenders from committing similar crimes, but some question if it is morally right to make an example of one offender to send a message to other potential law breakers.

3. Assess the appropriateness of restitution in the criminal law system.

Restitution comes from a time when offences were seen as private wrongs. The goal of sentencing at this time was to compensate the victim for the harm that was done, and restitution was a sentence in which the offender had to repay the *victim* for losses or to pay some equivalent amount. Today, this payment is usually made in monetary payments, though some (young offenders, for example) may be asked to provide services "in kind," mostly for damaged or stolen property or income lost because of a personal injury. Restitution is often used in addition to other sanctions, but the court must take into consideration the offender's financial resources. This type of order provides reparations to victims and promotes a sense of responsibility in the offender. Some criticize this aim and say that financial compensation should only have a place in the civil law. Others say that this is an appropriate measure because the victim might never be compensated for the monetary losses incurred.

4. List aggravating and mitigating factors in sentencing.

Aggravating factors:

- Evidence of hate against an identifiable group.
- Evidence of terrorism.
- Abuse of the offender's spouse or common-law partner or child.
- The offender was in a position of trust or authority in relation to the victim.
- The offender was a part of a criminal organization.

Mitigating factors:

- First offence?
- Out of character?
- Prior good character?
- Drugs or alcohol involved?
- Guilty plea?
- Remorse?
- Personal problems?
- Employment or school?
- Consequences to the offender?
- In a rehabilitation program?
- Unrelated meritorious conduct?
- Compensation to the victim?
- Provocation, duress, delay in the hearing?
- Gap in their criminal record?
- Lack of recidivism?
- Test case?
- Disadvantaged background or childhood?

5. Discuss the benefits of alternative dispute resolution.

Alternative measures can address issues within the criminal justice system in a way that traditional punishments cannot. Victims can have their voice heard, and offenders can be a contributing part of their own punishment and can be part of the process (making them much more likely to accomplish the goals of sentencing). In addition, the community can have closure to a crime that may have affected many people. These measures reduce recidivism and can provide help for those who would otherwise be lost within the system.

SELF-EVALUATION QUESTIONS

1. Provide an example of arbitration, mediation, and negotiation.
2. Why would a judge order restitution rather than a sentence emphasizing deterrence?
3. What does the Latin phrase *lex talonis* mean? What element of sentencing does it represent?
4. Describe the circumstances under which an individual may be punished by incarceration to a federal penitentiary.

CHAPTER

13

A Delicate Balance

I would urge any readers of this book who might be pressed by such reasons [such as pressure from family or friends, or seeing a law degree as a badge of honour] to resist them. If you find the examples of legal reasoning given in this book dull, or if they seem unrelated to anything of real value and importance, or if you think that the detailed discussion and the drawing of subtle distinctions between cases is a waste of time, you may well be a wiser person than the writer of this book. But the study of law is not likely to suit you.[1]

Learning Outcomes

After completing this chapter, you should be able to:

1. Identify what issues might warrant an investigation by the Canadian Judicial Council.
2. Identify some of the problems with forensic evidence.
3. Define a "chimera," and explain its implications for the criminal law (and law in general).

INTRODUCTION

As noted by Waddams in the opening quotation, the study of law is not for everyone. It is a very particular discipline, and some people find the topics dull and inapplicable to their lives. However, for those of us who are absolutely fascinated by these topics, the study of law can be extremely rewarding. But like any profession, there are those who pervert the practice, try to circumvent the rules, and to bring the administration of justice into disrepute. This chapter looks at when lawyers, judges, and experts may not uphold the goals of our system.

1. SM Waddams. *Introduction to the Study of Law*, 7th ed (Toronto: Carswell 2010) at 34. Reprinted by permission of Carswell, a division of Thomson Reuters Canada Ltd.

THE DELICATE BALANCE ... AND LAWYERS

> Lawyers suffer from depression, anxiety, hostility, paranoia, social alienation and isolation, obsessive-compulsiveness, and interpersonal sensitivity at alarming rates.[2]

Although we examined the discipline of lawyers in Chapter 2, there are many examples of lawyers being disbarred and disciplined for various matters. Consider these examples:

1. It does not matter how high profile a lawyer may be, if he or she does not live up to the responsibilities of lawyers, that person will be disbarred. In Guelph, Ontario, T. Sher Singh was disbarred after 22 years at the bar. Mr. Singh had the Order of Canada (his appointment was terminated in 2008), he was a member of the Ontario Police Commission, and he belonged to a provincial task force on race relations and policing. The prominent lawyer was found to have failed to serve clients, mishandled trust monies, and misappropriated money from clients. Singh said that he was burnt out from his 20 years in practice, his involvement in the community, and his role as a single parent. Mr. Singh did not attend his hearing, and said that he could not deal with the matter, and he was disbarred after a 15-minute hearing.[3]
2. Lawyers are only human and are subject to the same temptations and criminal offences that everyone else is, but they are held to a very high standard when it comes to their clients and a breach of trust. Alberta lawyer Paul Adams was disbarred for sexual misconduct with his client who was a 16-year-old prostitute. Police burst into his hotel room where the client was wearing a recording device. Mr. Adams pleaded guilty to a charge under s 153(1)(b) of the *Criminal Code,* which deals with those in a position of trust who invite a young person to sexually touch them, and served a 15-month sentence at home. At his disbarment hearing, the panel of the Alberta Law Society hearing committee said that a "professional must be above taking advantage of the client's feelings and vulnerability and must suppress his own desires ... It breaches the trust that underlays a solicitor–client relationship and cannot be tolerated if the profession is to continue to enjoy the respect of the public."[4]

Litigation Lawyers

> The hallmark of an outstanding trial lawyer is painstaking and meticulous preparation. There is no substitute for preparation. It has been said that "the lawyer who goes to trial without thorough preparation on both law and facts is bound to lose unless his opponent has been guilty of equal or greater negligence."[5]

Even when a lawyer has the best of intentions, sometimes litigation does not go well despite the best preparation. Richard Lederer has compiled a humorous list of actual questions asked in court from collections of Mary Louise Gilman, the editor of the *National Shorthand Reporter*, in a book called *More Humor in the Court.* One can be astonished what questions come out of your mouth when under pressure in court or in the discovery process, and these blunders are unfortunately recorded in the transcripts. The key rule of a litigation lawyer? Never ask a question unless you know what the answer will be:

Q. Doctor, how many autopsies have you performed on dead people?

A. All my autopsies have been performed on dead people.

Q. Mrs. Jones, is your appearance this morning pursuant to a [discovery] notice which I sent to your attorney?

A. No. This is how I dress when I go to work.

---

2. Patrick Schiltz, "Those Unhappy, Unhealthy Lawyers," Notre Dame Magazine (Autumn 1999) at 7.
3. Tracey Tyler, "Prominent Guelph Lawyer Disbarred for Misconduct" (12 September 2007), *Toronto Star*, online: <http://www.thestar.com/News/Ontario/article/255631>.
4. *Law Society of Alberta v Adams,* [1997] LSDD No. 157 as cited in Philip Slayton, *Lawyers Gone Bad: Money, Sex and Madness in Canada's Legal Profession* (Toronto: Penguin, 2007) at 136.
5. John A Olah, *The Art and Science of Advocacy.* (Toronto: Carswell, 1990) citing EM Morgan, *Some Problems of Proof in the Anglo-American System of Litigation* (New York: Columbia University Press, 1956) at 29.

Q. When he went, had you gone and had she, if she wanted to and were able, for the time being excluding all the restraints on her not to go, gone also, would he have brought you, meaning you and she, with him to the station?

Mr. Brooks: Objection. That question should be taken out and shot.

Q. You say you're innocent, yet five people swore they saw you steal a watch.

A. Your Honor, I can produce 500 people who didn't see me steal it.

Q. Now, I'm going to show you what has been marked as State's Exhibit No. 2 and ask if you recognize the picture?

A. John Fletcher.

Q. That's you?

A. Yes, sir.

Q. And you were present when the picture was taken, right?

Q. How long have you been a French Canadian.

Q. Do you recall approximately the time that you examined the body of Mr. Edington at the Rose Chapel?

A. It was in the evening, the autopsy started about 8:30 pm.

Q. And Mr. Edington was dead at the time, is that correct?

A. No, you stupid [jerk], he was sitting on the table wondering why I was doing an autopsy.

Q. What can you tell us about the truthfulness and veracity of this defendant?

A. Oh, she will tell the truth. She said she'd kill that sonofabitch—and she did!

Q. What is the meaning of sperm being present?

A. It indicates intercourse.

Q. Male sperm?

A. That is the only kind I know.

Q. And lastly, Gary, all your responses must be oral. O.K.? What school do you go to?

A. Oral.

Q. How old are you?

A. Oral.[6]

Passionate Lawyers

The devil makes his Christmas pies of Lawyers' tongues and clerks' fingers.[7]

It also is important for a lawyer not to go too far in overstating the case or (as we learned in Chapter 3) making a case too personal. Again, lawyers are human and sometimes go over the line—as in these cases:

1. A district attorney in Missouri got carried away saying what should happen to the accused he was prosecuting and said that he "ought to be shot through the mouth of a red hot cannon, through a barb wire fence into the jaws of hell ... [and] he ought to be kicked in the seat of the pants by a Missouri mule and thrown into a manure pile to rot."[8]

6. Reproduced by permission of Richard Lederer.

7. Thomas Adams, *The Works of Thomas Adams* (Edinburgh: James Nichol, 1861).

8. Lance S Davidson, *Ludicrous Laws and Mindless Misdemeanors: The Silliest Lawsuits and Unruliest Rulings of All Times* (Edison, New Jersey: Castle Books, 2004) at 161.

The Canadian Press/Jacques Boissinot

Jean Bienvenue

2. A trial lawyer in Illinois attempted to outwit the court throughout his ten years at the bar. He filed a complaint with the Pollution Control Board alleging contamination of the air with "character assassination" and pollution of the mind. He also said that the legal documents made out of paper were unconstitutional on "behalf of all the trees of the United States."[9] He was eventually disbarred.

THE DELICATE BALANCE ... AND JUDGES

Victims in the Criminal Justice System

Although, as we saw earlier, the law can be examined with a humorous lens, there are also some very serious repercussions of statements made by those in the justice system. Despite the years of work of women's and legal rights advocates, there is still a prejudice by some in the system that women somehow "deserve" the criminal actions of others. This prejudice is well documented in the comments of judges, particularly in sexual assault cases. The following comments have been made in the last three decades in Canadian courts:

1. Justice Jean Bienvenue of the Quebec Superior Court told a jury in 1995 that they were "simpletons" for convicting a woman of second-degree murder and not first-degree murder for slitting her husband's throat with a razor. He went on to say that "when women ascend the scale of virtues, they reach higher than men, and I have always believed this. But it is also said, and this, too, I believe, that when they decide to degrade themselves, they sink to depths to which even the vilest man could not sink." He went on to identify women who were a "sad part of our history," who have "debased the profile of women." Justice Bienvenue concluded that the accused woman before him was the "clearest living example" of this type of deficient woman, and that, unlike the accused, even the Nazis who killed millions of Jews did not do so "in a painful or bloody manner" but in "gas chambers, without suffering."[10]
2. In 1989, Quebec judge Justice Denys Dionne said that "rules are like a woman—they are made to be violated."[11]

Larry Wong/Edmonton Journal/ The Canadian Press

John McClung

3. In November 1988, Justice Peter van der Hoop sentenced an accused to just two years' probation because the three-year-old victim was "sexually aggressive."[12]
4. In 1998, Justice John McClung of the Alberta Court of Appeal acquitted a man (Mr. Ewanchuk) charged with sexually assaulting a 17-year-old girl because the female victim wore a t-shirt and shorts. The judge pointed out that the girl "did not present herself to [the accused] in a bonnet and crinolines." Justice Claire L'Heureux-Dubé of the Supreme Court addressed the comments made by Justice McClung in a separate opinion, criticizing McClung for what she called "archaic myths and stereotypes." The *National Post* wrote an article identifying all of the points made by Justice McClung, and the response by Justice L'Heureux-Dubé. A portion of the article is reprinted in the following box.

9. Lance S Davidson, *Ludicrous Laws and Mindless Misdemeanors: The Silliest Lawsuits and unruliest Rulings of All Times.* (Edison, New Jersey: Castle Books, 2004) at 161.
10. Sandra Martin, "Stupid Judge Tricks: Why Do Our Upholders of Justice Go off the Rails?" (13 March 1999) *Globe and Mail*, online: <http://www.fact.on.ca/newpaper/gm99031d.htm>. See the full inquiry, "Report to the Canadian Judicial Council by the Inquiry Committee Appointed under Subsection 63(1) of the *Judges Act* to Conduct a Public Inquiry into the Conduct of Mr. Justice Jean Bienvenue of the Superior Court of Quebec in *R v T Théberge*" (June 1996), online: <http://www.cjc-ccm.gc.ca/cmslib/general/conduct_inq_bienvenue_ReportIC_199606_en.pdf>.
11. Sandra Martin, "Stupid Judge Tricks: W hy Do Our Upholders of Justice Go off the Rails? (13 March 1999), *Globe and Mail*, online: <http://www.fact.on.ca/newpaper/gm99031d.htm>.
12. Associated Press, "Women's Group Wants Judge Ousted (27 November 1988), online: <http://news.google.com/newspapers?nid=2026&dat=19891127&id=o7EtAAAAIBAJ&sjid=odAFAAAAIBAJ&pg=6173,3944094>.

JUSTICE MCCLUNG AND JUSTICE L'HEUREUX-DUBÉ

Judge McClung said: "It must be pointed out the complainant did not present herself [to the accused] in a bonnet and crinolines."

Jonathan Hayward/The Canadian Press

Claire L'Heureux-Dubé

Judge L'Heureux-Dubé countered: "These comments made by an appellate judge help reinforce the myth that under such circumstances, either the complainant is less worthy of belief, she invited the assault, or her sexual experience signals probable consent to further sexual activity."

Judge McClung said: "She told Ewanchuk that she was the mother of a six-month-old baby and that, along with her boyfriend, she shared an apartment with another couple."

Judge L'Heureux-Dubé said: "One must wonder why he felt necessary to point out these aspects of the trial record. Could it be to express that the complainant is not a virgin?"

Judge McClung said: "There was no room to suggest that Ewanchuk knew, yet disregarded, her underlying state of mind as he furthered his romantic intentions."

Judge L'Heureux-Dubé said: "These were two strangers, a young 17-year-old woman attracted by a job offer trapped in a trailer with a man approximately twice her age and size. This is hardly a scenario that one would characterize as reflective of romantic 'intentions.' It was nothing more than an effort by Ewanchuk to engage the complainant sexually, not romantically."

Judge McClung said: "During each of three clumsy passes by Ewanchuk, when she said no, he promptly backed off."

Judge L'Heureux-Dubé said: "The expressions used by McClung to describe the accused's sexual assault, such as 'clumsy passes,' are plainly inappropriate in that context as they minimize the importance of the accused's conduct and the reality of sexual aggression against women."

Judge McClung said: "The sum of the evidence indicates that Ewanchuk's advances to the complainant were far less criminal than hormonal."

Judge L'Heureux-Dubé said: "According to this analysis, a man would be free from criminal responsibility for having non-consensual sexual activity whenever he cannot control his hormonal urges."

Judge McClung said: "In a less litigious age, going too far in the boyfriend's car was better dealt with on site, a well-chosen expletive, a slap in the face, or, if necessary, a well-directed knee."

Judge L'Heureux-Dubé said: "According to this stereotype, women should use physical force, not resort to the courts to 'deal with' sexual assaults and it is not the perpetrator's responsibility to ascertain consent ... but the woman's not only to express an unequivocal 'no' but also to fight her way out of such a situation."

In response to the article written by Justice L'Heureux-Dubé, Justice McClung wrote to the *National Post,* saying that "Madam Justice Claire L'Heureux-Dubé's graceless slide into personal invective in Thursday's judgment in the *Ewanchuk* case allows some response.... The personal convictions of the judge, delivered again from her judicial chair, could provide a plausible explanation for the disparate (and growing) number of male suicides being reported in the Province of Quebec."[13] Justice McClung apologized for this last part of his statement, as Justice L'Heureux-Dubé was from Quebec, and her husband had, in fact, committed suicide. Justice McClung denied knowing that her husband had died in this way.[14]

What do you think? Were Justice McClung's comments inappropriate?

Was it wrong for a Supreme Court judge to respond to the comments of a lower court judge?

Was it wrong for a lower court judge to make these comments aimed at a Supreme Court judge?

Some believe that these types of comments by judges are a thing of the past, but this is not necessarily true.

13. From Janice Tibbetts, "No means no in sex assaults, top court rules: 'Implied consent' doesn't exist, judges say," The Ottawa Citizen, 26 February 1999. Material reprinted with the express permission of: **Ottawa Citizen**, a division of Postmedia Network Inc.

14. CBC News, "Alberta Judge Apologizes for Part of his Letter" (November 10, 2000), online: <http://www.cbc.ca/news/canada/story/1999/02/27/judge990227.html>.

The Canadian Press/Winnipeg Free Press-Ken Gigliotti

Justice Robert Dewar

Justice Robert Dewar

In March 2011, the Canadian Judicial Council (CJC) launched an investigation into a decision of Justice Robert Dewar. Justice Dewar was not allowed to hear any cases that involved crimes of a sexual nature because of his comments made when sentencing a man for sexual assault.[15] The case that was the subject of the investigation was the criminal case of *R v Rhodes*, [2011] MJ No 67 (Man Ct QB).

The victim was sexually assaulted in the middle of the night at the side of a highway by Mr. Rhodes, who was convicted of sexual assault. It was the evidence of the victim that she fled without her pants through the woods nearby in an attempt to flag down assistance. The victim was intoxicated and sexually assaulted by someone who was larger and considerably older, and who had only known the victim for 20 minutes. The victim said that she had long-lasting emotional impact after the sexual assault as she now felt like a prisoner in her own house, and she had stress in her life and relationships.

At trial, Justice Dewar said that the parties met

> in what can only be described as "inviting" circumstances. At 2:30 on a summer morning two young women, one of which was dressed in a tube top without a bra and jeans and both of whom were made up and wore high heels in a parking lot outside a bar, made their intentions publically known that they wanted to party. Then the women, in particular S.M., made the suggestion that the group should go swimming, notwithstanding that not one of them had any bathing suit ... I conclude that although the accused was led by the circumstances to conclude that sex was in the air, he was insensitive to the fact the complainant was not a willing participant.

While giving a two-year conditional sentence for an incident of forced sexual intercourse (the Crown was seeking a three-year prison sentence), the judge said that this was a case of "misread signals and inconsiderate behaviour" and that the convicted man was a "clumsy Don Juan." The judge went on to say that he did not condone the behaviour, but that it "simply does not fit the archetypical cases cited" and that the sentence should be lower than the cases provided as precedent.

Critics of this decision organized a protest outside of the court house in Manitoba where the sentencing took place. Alanna Makinson of the Canadian Federation of Students, who organized the protest, said that she thought the decision was an "incredibly irresponsible ruling," and she felt that the judge "was wrong to question what the woman was wearing the night that she was raped ... under no circumstances does a flirt or a short skirt or a kiss ever imply consent to intercourse."[16] A reporter for the *National Post* commented on the case and said:

> So, there you have it: rape isn't rape, even when it is. No doesn't really mean no. And tight tops, by gum, they mean she wants IT. Bad. That she is dying for IT. That she is sending a signal to you, guys. And that forcing her to have sex with you is "inconsiderate behaviour," nothing more. Justice Dewar said his aim wasn't to blame the victim. What was it then? To send a message to men that raping a woman in a tube top because she gives you a suggestive wink is all part of the courtship process? My head aches from all the shaking.[17]

The CJC found that because there was an apology to the victim and all those offended, since Justice Dewar took steps to improve his knowledge of gender equality issues, and the fact that this was an isolated event dictated that no further action was taken by the CJC.

Justice Lori Douglas—Is It Important What a Judge Does in Her Spare Time?

Although the disciplinary process for judges was examined in Chapter 2, there are several other examples of when judges have been investigated for allegedly working contrary to the

15. *The Lawyers Weekly*, "Embattled Judge off Sex Crime Trials" (11 March 2011), online: <http://www.lawyersweekly-digital.com/lawyersweekly/3041?pg=3#pg3>.

16. Mia Rabson, "Outcry Grows Against Manitoba Judge who Did not Jail Rapist." (25 February 2011), *National Post*, online: <http://news.nationalpost.com/2011/02/25/outcry-grows-against-manitoba-judge-who-did-not-jail-rapist/>.

17. From Joe O'Connor, "Do a Tube Top and High Heels say, 'Go Ahead, Rape Me?,'' National Post, 24 February 2011. Material reprinted with the express permission of: **National Post**, a division of Postmedia Network Inc.

Justice Lori Douglas

Alex Chapman

justice system in the course of their duties as judge. However, what happens if a judge is caught in questionable circumstances when it comes to his or her personal life?

As of August 2012, Justice Lori Douglas is being investigated by the CJC. Justice Douglas was the associate chief justice of the Manitoba Court of Queen's Bench (family division) and is married to a lawyer named Jack King, who practised family law at the same firm where Justice Douglas once worked. Justice Douglas became a judge in Manitoba in 2005, and she is also a member who sits on the CJC, which is now investigating her. Mr. King posted naked photos of Justice Douglas using sex toys, performing oral sex, and engaging in bondage on a website. The CJC is investigating Justice Douglas, and Manitoba's Law Society is investigating Mr. King.

The complaint comes from a client of Mr. King's named Alexander Chapman. Mr. Chapman retained Mr. King to finalize his 2002 divorce. Mr. Chapman alleges he saw over 30 photographs of Justice Douglas that were posted on a porn website after Mr. King took Mr. Chapman out for a drink and mentioned a porn website devoted to interracial sex. Mr. King gave him the password for the site, where he saw numerous nude photos of Justice Douglas. These photos have since been removed. Mr. Chapman says that he did not have the money to switch lawyers, so he remained a client of Mr. King's until the finalization of his divorce.

The couple invited Mr. Chapman to their home, but Mr. Chapman says that he never attended and did not have sex with Justice Douglas. Mr. Chapman complained to the partners at the law firm after Mr. King left, but Mr. Chapman is alleged to have been given a $25 000 cash payment in return for not taking legal action. With the acceptance of the money, Mr. Chapman was asked to destroy all pictures and documents from Mr. King, but Mr. Chapman did not do so. Mr. Chapman decided to come forward seven years later to the CJC, and he also intends to sue both Justice Douglas and Mr. King civilly for sexual harassment and discrimination.

Mr. King says that he was suffering from depression at the time of the alleged incidents, and that he was coping with the death of his brother and his best friend. It is alleged that Justice Douglas did not know that her husband was posting nude pictures of her online. Mr. King left the firm and was put on sick leave after his interactions with Mr. Chapman. Mr. King says that he did not know that Mr. Chapman was uncomfortable with the conversations, but apologized for any effect these conversations may have had.

Experts are torn on the impact that these pictures should have. Alice Woolley, a professor at the University of Calgary, has said that "what you do in your bedroom is your business, regardless of whether or not you're a judge."[18] Others, however, disagree. Wayne MacKay, a professor at Dalhousie University, says that "in spite of the fact that it's obviously private—and judges still do have the right to a private life—that kind of picture when it's public ... I think it would clearly bring the judicial system or the administration of justice in question, or at least in some people's mind diminish the court's image."[19] Others say that a judge is a representative of our justice system, and that she would not have been appointed as a judge if she had disclosed that there were nude pictures of herself online. A line in the application asks, "is there anything in your past or present which could reflect negatively on yourself or the judiciary and which should be disclosed?"[20] If this was disclosed at the time of the application, Justice Douglas may not have been appointed.

The CJC decided in July 2011 that it will conduct a public inquiry into the conduct of Justice Douglas. The CJC announced that "after conducting a detailed review of a number of allegations ... a Review Panel of five judges has concluded that the matter may be serious enough to warrant the judge's removal from office."[21] The inquiry began in July 2012, and it is expected to continue in the fall of 2012.

18. CBC News, "Nude Photos of Judge Contained in Complaint" (31 August, 2010), online: <http://www.cbc.ca/news/canada/manitoba/story/2010/08/31/judge-manitoba-douglas.html>.

19. *Ibid.*

20. *Ibid.*

21. The Lawyers Weekly, "CJC launches Public Inquiry into Judge" (15 July, 2011), online: <http://www.lawyersweekly-digital.com/lawyersweekly/3111?pg=3#pg3>.

Canadian Judicial Council
http://www.cjc-ccm.gc.ca/english/news_en.asp?selMenu=news_2011_1206_en.asp

Do you think it matters what judges (or their spouses) decide to do in their personal time? Who do you agree with? Can a judge have a personal life, or does an incident like this reflect on the Canadian justice system? Should the CJC investigate Justice Douglas? What do you think the outcome will be? Is it because the complainant was a client that this case becomes more blameworthy?

Judges are not the only group who can make comments about those who are the victims of sexual assault. In a recent case at York University in Toronto, during a safety information session held at the law school, a police officer suggested that a safety tip for women was not to dress like "sluts."[22] The police officer later made a written apology for his comments.

There are other areas where the police are responsible for questionable conduct, but relevant to our discussion of the law is in the area of wrongful convictions and false confessions.

THE DELICATE BALANCE ... AND POLICE

Wrongful Convictions

Although a complete discussion of wrongful convictions in Canada and the role of the police and other actors is beyond the scope of this textbook, it is important to note that wrongful convictions are occurring in Canada today. Many researchers in the United States are also discussing this topic, particularly because many states still have the death penalty. Many of the areas currently being researched include police and Crown conduct, incompetent defence counsel, eyewitness error, **tunnel vision** by the police and prosecution, discrimination, and errors in science related to the law.[23]

The numbers of Canadians who have been wrongfully convicted of a crime are difficult to count, but the long list of names of those who have been wrongfully convicted include: James Driskell, Anthony Hanemaayer, Donald Marshall Jr., Simon Marshall, David Milgaard, Guy Paul Morin, William Mullins-Johnson, Romeo Phillion, Thomas Sophonow, Steven Truscott, Kyle Unger, and Erin Walsh, among others.[24] The problem became so troubling that in 2002 provisions have been added to the *Criminal Code* (s 696.1) allowing an accused to make an "application for ministerial review on the grounds of miscarriage of justice may be made to the Minister of Justice by or on behalf of a person who has been convicted of an offence under an Act of Parliament ... and whose rights of judicial review or appeal with respect to the conviction or finding have been exhausted." One particular area where the police have been involved in wrongful convictions is through false confessions.

False Confessions

> Common sense tells us that regular eyewitness[es] can make mistakes but that innocent people do not confess to crimes they did not commit.[25]

Ask yourself one question: Could you confess to a crime that you did not commit? A confession is defined by *Black's Law Dictionary* as a "criminal suspect's acknowledgement of guilt, usually in writing and often including details about the crime," and a "coerced confession" is defined as a "confession that is obtained by threats or force."[26] Police are trained to elicit confessions, and this function is considered an integral part of police enforcement, as a confession has long been held as the key any case. Indeed, some say that the "introduction of a confession makes the other aspects of a trial in court superfluous."[27]

22. Raymond Kwan, "Don't Dress Like a Slut: Toronto Cop" (17 February 2011) *Excalibur, York University's Community Newspaper*, online: <http://www.excal.on.ca/news/dont-dress-like-a-slut-toronto-cop/>.
23. Kathryn Campbell and Myriam Denov, "The Burden of innocence: Coping with a Wrongful Imprisonment" (2004) *Canadian Journal of Criminology and Criminal Justice* 139 at 140.
24. CBC News, "Canada's Wrongful Convictions," online: <http://www.cbc.ca.proxy.lib.uwaterloo.ca/news/canada/story/2009/08/06/f-wrongfully-convicted.html>.
25. SM Kassin, "Internalized false confessions," in M Toglia, R Lindsay, D Ross, and J Read, eds, *Handbook of Eyewitness Psychology: Volume 1, Memory for Events* (Mahwah, NJ: Erlbaum, 2007) 169 at 171.
26. Henry Campbell Black, ed, *Black's Law Dictionary*, 7th ed (St. Paul, MN: West Pub. Co., 1999).
27. SM Kassin, "The Psychology of Confession Evidence," *American Psychologist*, (1997) 52, 221 at 221.

It is a principle of law that a confession is not admissible unless the Crown shows that the statement was voluntary and was not obtained because the individual believed they would get an advantage, or because of fear of repercussions. This healthy skepticism of confessions obtained by threats or hope of advantage comes from the notion that confessions made in the face of threats may be untrue or untrustworthy. The use of fictitious evidence has been implicated in a vast majority of documented police coerced confessions, as has the use of deception and trickery by officers.[28]

Some researchers have also identified "investigator bias," whereby officers focus on one suspect because they are convinced he or she is guilty, as playing a significant role in false confessions.[29] The difficulty associated with reading body language and non-verbal cues also have the potential to lead to false confessions. Many scholars argue that a confession is highly persuasive, and is often a prosecutor's most powerful weapon of guilt. Theorists state that confessions have a compelling influence on jurors and that jurors are more likely to convict a suspect based on his or her confession than any other factor, even if the jurors are aware that the confession was coerced.[30]

False Confessions Generally

The Innocence Project in the United States estimates that in about "25 percent of DNA exoneration cases, innocent defendants made incriminating statements, delivered outright confessions or pl[eaded] guilty."[31] Richard Leo states that as of 2006 in the United States, there are "over 170 DNA exonerations of convictions, approximately 20 to 25 percent of which resulted in whole or in part from police-induced false confessions."[32] Most shockingly, of the inmates who claimed "to have made a false confession in the past during police interviewing ... (78 percent) were convicted of the offense to which they had allegedly made a false confession."[33]

The long history of false confessions in Canadian law was noted in the 2000 Supreme Court of Canada case of *R v Oickle,* [2000] 2 SCR 3 (SCC). The Supreme Court acknowledged that there is documentation on "hundreds of cases where confessions have been proven false by DNA evidence, subsequent confessions by the true perpetrator, and other such independent sources of evidence." Others maintain that false confessions are the product of individuals who are mentally deficient, but this is not supported in evidence. It is an easy answer to say that someone who might falsely confess is mentally disordered, but the following cases examine individuals who are not suffering from a recognized psychological illness.

The Typology of Coerced-Internalized Confessions

A typology of confessions was established by Saul Kassin and Lawrence Wrightsman in 1985 in order to distinguish among different types of confessions. They isolated three distinct types, including voluntary confessions, coerced-complaint confessions, and coerced-internalized confessions.[34] Although theorists have speculated that individuals voluntarily falsely confess because of reasons ranging for a desire for fame, a psychological condition making it difficult to tell reality from fantasy, or a desire to aid the

28. SM Kassin et al, "Police-Induced Confessions: Risk Factors and Recommendations," (2010) *Law and Human Behavior 34*, 3 at 12.

29. AD Redlich, and C Meissner, "Techniques and Controversies in the Interrogation of Suspects: The Artful Practice versus the Scientific Study," in JL Skeem, K Douglas, and S Lilienfeld, eds, *Psychological Science in the Courtroom: Controversies and Consensus* (New York, NY: Guilford, 2009) 2 at 5.

30. H Wakefield and R Underwager, "Coerced or Nonvoluntary Confessions," *Behavioral Sciences and the Law* (1998) 423 at 423.

31. Barry Scheck et al, "False Confessions" Innocence Project, online: <http://www.innocenceproject.org/understand/False-Confessions.php>

32. Richard A Leo et al, "Bringing Reliability Back in: False Confessions and Legal Safeguards in the Twenty-First Century" (2006) *Wis L Rev* 484 at 484.

33. H Wakefield and R Underwager, "Coerced or Nonvoluntary Confessions," *Behavioral Sciences and the Law* (1998) 423 at 425.

34. Saul M Kassin and Lawrence S Wrightsman, "Confession Evidence" in Saul M Kassin and Lawrence S Wrightsman, eds, *The Psychology of Evidence and Trial Procedure* (Beverly Hills, CA: Sage, 1985) at 76.

actual perpetrator, coerced-internalized confessions are those in which the individual actually *believes* he or she committed the crime, and is one of the most difficult types to comprehend. Legal theorist Dr. Kassin describes coerced-internalized false confessions as psychologically distinct because

> an innocent person—anxious, tired, confused, and subjected to highly suggestive methods of interrogation—actually comes to believe that he or she committed the crime. This type of false confession is particularly frightening because the suspect's memory of his or her own actions may be altered, rendering the original contents potentially irretrievable.[35]

These confessions are produced by a more gentle but persuasive interviewing. Coerced-internalized confessions must be distinguished from coerced-compliant confessions, where the individual does not believe the suggestions of interrogators, but only confesses to escape a situation that involves physical violence and aggressive interviewing techniques. Alternatively, coerced-internalized confessions are voluntary and not *actively* or necessarily *cognitively* coerced by police.

In the coerced-internalized typology, the suspect comes to believe that he or she has committed the crime, even if the individual has no actual memory. These individuals do not have a clear memory of *not* committing the crime they were accused of, and may have no recollection of the time when the offence was committed so believe that they must have committed the crime.[36] Because of the (sometimes subtle) manipulation of the interrogator, these individuals distrust their memory and adopt the suggestions of their examiner. In coerced-internalized confessions, the pressure is coerced by police and internalized to the extent that suspects change their beliefs about their innocence and they actively accept the interrogator's account of events.

These techniques have been supported by research. Researchers Saul Kassin and Katherine Kiechel ran a laboratory study in 1996 to see if those who are presented with false incriminating evidence in a high-stress situation are more likely to sign a confession, internalize guilt for the event, and create the details in memory consistent with that confession.[37] Seventy-nine undergraduates were asked to do an experiment on spatial awareness at a computer. Each of the participants was told not to hit the "ALT" key on the keyboard or the program would cease and the data would be lost. Each of the subjects experienced a crash of the computer and a distressed experimenter accused each student of pressing the key, and persuaded each participant to sign a confession saying they had pressed the key when none of the subjects had actually done so.

The students were met outside by another confederate who "overheard" the conversation and asked what happened. The students' internalized guilt was examined for study, and then they were asked to go back to the lab to show how they had hit the key to see how many would "confabulate" or create memories of past events and hit the prohibited key. Sixty-nine percent of the students signed the confession, 28 percent had evidence of internalization, and 9 percent confabulated details to support these false beliefs. The researchers concluded that when this research is examined in the realm of criminal confessions, the presentation of false incriminating evidence can lead some to confess, internalize blame, and confabulate details not only for remote past events, but for events that have just happened. The authors concluded that these effects were shown by intelligent college students who were "self-assured, and under minimal stress compared with crime suspects held in custody, often in isolation."[38]

---

35. SM Kassin, "The Psychology of Confession Evidence," *American Psychologist,* (1997) 52, 221 at 226.
36. GH Gudjonsson, and JAC MacKeith, "False Confessions: Psychological Effects of Interrogation. A discussion paper. In A Trankel, ed, *Reconstructing the Past: The Role of Psychologists in Criminal Trials.* Deventer: Kluwer (1982).
37. Saul M Kassin, and Katherine L Kiechel, "The Social Psychology of False Confessions: Compliance, Internalization, and Confabulation" 7 *American Psychological Society* (1996) 125 at 125.
38. Saul M Kassin, and Katherine L Kiechel, "The Social Psychology of false Confessions: Compliance, Internalization, and Confabulation," 7 *American Psychological Society* (1996) 125 at 127. Note that some researchers disagree with the way this research was completed.

Romeo Phillion

The Canadian Press/Chris Young

Case Examples

An example of the revelation of a false confession is the case of Romeo Phillion, who was arrested in Ottawa 1967 on another charge and instead confessed to the murder of Ottawa firefighter named Leopold Roy. In *R v Phillion,* [2009] OJ No 849, 2009 ONCA 202, the Court of Appeal quashed the conviction and ordered a new trial for Mr. Phillion in March 2009 after finding that his confession was unreliable. The court also mentioned that interrogation techniques used on Phillion were akin to brainwashing during the interrogation and polygraph test.[39]

In the United States, the 1988 case of Paul Ingram is often cited as one of the most shocking cases of coerced-internalized confessions. Mr. Ingram, a deeply religious deputy sheriff, county Republican Committee chair, and father of six children, was accused by his daughters of participating in satanic rituals, including the rape of his daughters and the murder of approximately 25 babies. Mr. Ingram had no history of mental illness. Dr. Kassin notes that "[a]fter 23 interrogations, which extended for five months, Ingram was detained, hypnotized, provided with graphic crime details, told by a police psychologist that sex offenders typically repress their offenses, and urged by the minister of his church to confess."[40]

Although Mr. Ingram first said that he had no memory of any of these accused crimes, he came to visualize (using a type of relaxation technique) scenes of group sexual assaults and cult activities, and then believed that he had committed these crimes and many additional charges. Mr. Ingram was very influenced by his fundamentalist Christian church who believed that Satan was a presence on earth. Mr. Ingram's two daughters, Ericka 22, and Julie, 17, made accusations against him after a church retreat. The allegations made by the girls kept evolving until they had accused their father of sexually assaulting them nearly every night, accused their brothers of sexual assault, and then reported that they were sexually assaulted by all of the men who attended the Saturday night poker parties at their home. Suspicions arose as the daughters were unable to describe the details of the 450 cult meetings they had attended, but they could describe the sexual assault and torture they had endured in graphic detail. No physical evidence was ever found to corroborate their accusations.

Mr. Ingram was subjected to at least 23 interrogations over five months. Mr. Ingram finally agreed that his daughters would not lie, and thus he must have raped them, been part of a cult, and committed various crimes, but had no memory. He said that he must have done the crimes.

Mr. Ingram received 20 years in prison for crimes for which there was absolutely no physical evidence. Mr. Ingram was given the option to plead guilty to six counts of third-degree rape or be charged with a host of other charges. Mr. Ingram's alleged 25–250 murders apparently no longer mattered. Mr. Ingram served the bulk of his sentence before he was released in 2003. Police need to be on guard for these types of suspects who might be persuaded to give a false confession, and should avoid the techniques that permit the conviction of the innocent.

THE DELICATE BALANCE ... AND EXPERTS

An expert witness is meant to assist the court with an unbiased perspective about the matters relating to the case before the court. Because of the Dr. Charles Smith case (discussed shortly), the rules of civil procedure have been changed in Ontario to provide that for an unbiased opinion in that:

> **4.1.01(1)** It is the duty of every expert engaged by or on behalf of a party to provide evidence in relation to a proceeding under these rules,
> (a) to provide opinion evidence that is fair, objective and non-partisan;

39. Christopher Sherrin, "False Confessions and Admissions in Canadian Law," *Queen's Law Journal,* (2004) 30, 615 at 621 622.
40. SM Kassin, "The Psychology of Confession Evidence," *American Psychologist,* (1997) 52, 221 at 226 227. See also Frances E Chapman, "Coerced Internalized False Confessions and Police Interrogations: The Power of Coercion" (2013) 37 *Law & Psychology Review* 1 (2013) (upcoming publication)

J.P. Moczulski/The Canadian Press

Dr. Charles Randal Smith

(b) to provide opinion evidence that is related only to matters that are within the expert's area of expertise.

An expert report that is given to the court must also be accompanied by a signed form by the expert confirming that he or she has a duty to be impartial. In the case of Dr. Charles Smith, it was the duty of the Crown, the defence lawyer, and judges to assure that the trusted expert giving testimony was actually an expert on that particular matter.

Dr. Charles Randal Smith

> Dr. Charles Randal Smith wreaked havoc in Ontario's criminal justice system: He destroyed many lives; he turned innocent parents and caregivers into killers; he had a propensity for finding murder where it did not exist. He believed his role as pathologist was to support the Crown Attorney, make the case look good and refute the defence counsel. And he single-handedly was probably responsible for more miscarriages of justice in the province than any other individual ... Charles Smith was able to do so much harm because the very people who were supposed to protect the public from fraudulent experts such as Smith—the province's prosecutors, defence lawyers and judges—were skillfully manipulated by him into believing that he was a brilliant, experienced, impartial and infallible forensic pathologist (when he was nothing of the sort) and dropped their guard.[41]

Dr. Charles Smith was one of the leading child pathologists in Canada, and frequently served as an expert in trials, including many child murder trials. Over 24 years, Dr. Smith performed more than 1000 child autopsies. An inquiry was called in Ontario in order to question his findings on 45 of his child autopsies. Twenty autopsies where Dr. Smith had found the cause of death to be homicide were called into question. Thirteen of those twenty cases (65 percent) resulted in a conviction of the accused in a criminal court.[42]

Justice Stephen Goudge was given the task of heading an inquiry to examine why Dr. Smith was permitted to appear as an expert witness in child homicide cases and why he was able to contribute to sending many individuals to jail for crimes they did not commit (and often for crimes against their own children). In October 2008, the Goudge Report came to several conclusions, including that Dr. Smith had misled those overseeing him in his medical duties, that he made false and misleading statements in court, and that he exaggerated his expertise in trials. In fact, the report found that Dr. Smith did not have basic knowledge about forensic pathology. Dr. Smith responded that his oversights were not intentional. Dr. Smith's licence to practise pathology was taken away, and he may no longer appear as an expert.[43] For the results of Dr. Smith's actions, see the Food for Thought box on page 354.

THE DELICATE BALANCE AND ... TECHNOLOGY

Is Forensic Evidence Infallible?

Forensic evidence can include material from a crime scene—a fingerprint, gun residue left when a firearm has been discharged, or trace materials, such as hair, fibres, soil, or paint that are left behind. However, evidence is not perfectly preserved at a crime scene. Experts may only recover a part of a sample or a smudged fingerprint. Although computers can help search for matches of the prints, the important thing to remember with all forensic evidence is that humans make mistakes, and humans are part of the process at so many of the key stages.

41. Harold Levy, "Foolish Pride or Malevolent Evil?" (June 2011) *Briefly Speaking*, p. 14-17. Reproduced by permission of the Ontario Bar Association.

42. CBC News, "Dr. Charles Smith: The Man Behind the Public Inquiry" (10 August 2010) CBC, online: <http://www.cbc.ca/news/canada/story/2009/12/07/f-charles-smith-goudge-inquiry.html>.

43. *Ibid*

FOOD FOR THOUGHT...

WHAT WERE THE RESULTS OF DR. SMITH'S ACTIONS?

The following are just a few of the examples of the harm done by Dr. Charles Smith:

1. William Mullins-Johnson was convicted of the murder of his four-year-old niece and served 12 years in prison. There was evidence that Dr. Smith had lost tissue samples in the case that could have proven that the child died of natural causes.
2. Marco Trotta was found guilty of abusing and murdering his eight-month-old son. Mr. Trotta spent nine years in jail. His wife Anisa was convicted of criminal negligence causing death and served five years in prison. A new trial has been ordered to re-examine the evidence.
3. Lianne Gagnon was accused of murder of her 11-month-old child. After other experts examined the evidence two years later, there was no evidence indicating that a murder had taken place.
4. Sherry Sherrett was convicted of the first-degree murder of her four-month-old son, and served one year in jail. Other pathologists eventually looked at the evidence and concluded that the child accidentally choked to death. During the course of the investigation and trial, Sherrett's older son was taken away and adopted by another family.
5. Louise Reynolds spent two years in prison for the death of her seven-year-old daughter who Dr. Smith said she stabbed to death with scissors. New evidence showed that the child was, in fact, attacked by a pit bull.
6. Brenda Waudby was charged with the second degree murder of her 21-month-old child. A key piece of evidence in the case was a pubic hair. Dr. Smith denied he knew about this hair, but in 2001 the hair was found in Dr. Smith's desk drawer.
7. Maureen Laidely was charged with the death of her boyfriend's three-year-old child, based on the report of Dr. Smith. When other pathologists reviewed the evidence, they concluded that the child accidentally fell off of a coffee table.
8. Tammy Marquardt served 14 years in prison for the murder of her two-year-old son. When the evidence was eventually called into question, the court said that it was tragic that it took so long to re-examine the evidence of Dr. Smith. The Crown dismissed the matter rather than re-trying the case.[44]

What do you think should happen to an expert who actively misleads the court?

Do you think that the responsibility lies with the lawyers and judges, who should make sure that experts know what they are testifying about?

Victims who were directly affected by Dr. Smith may now be eligible to receive up to $250 000 in compensation. Is this enough? Too much?

However, jurors often think that forensic and DNA evidence is perfect and conclusive evidence. However, DNA evidence breaks down over time, and may be contaminated, mixed with other samples, or mislabelled.[45] There have been many times when the DNA evidence has been wrong. There have been several cases which highlight these vulnerabilities:

1. British resident Peter Hamkin was charged with the murder of Annalisa Vincenti in Italy in 2003. Mr. Hamkin swore he had never been to Italy, and had witnesses who saw him in England at the time of the murder. However, there was a DNA match between Mr. Hamkin (from a DNA sample he had provided after an impaired driving conviction) and evidence collected at the crime scene. Twenty-three-year-old Hamkin spent

44. City News, "The Questionable Cases of Dr. Charles Smith: A Review" (12 November 2007), online: <http://www.citytv.com/toronto/citynews/news/local/article/18225--the-questionable-cases-of-dr-charles-smith-a-review>.

45. Pearl Tesler, "Shadows of Doubt: CSI Science Isn't as Solid as the TV Shows Lead us to Believe" (2010) *Current Science* 95.

20 days believing he was going to be deported to Italy. Before the extradition hearing, Mr. Hamkin got another opinion on the DNA evidence, which turned out not to be a match.[46]

2. Science has recently uncovered what are called "chimeras"—people with different strands of DNA in different parts of their body, or even different types of DNA found in their blood. Catherine Arcabascio, an American law professor, has looked at the implications to the law regarding individuals who may have no external differentiating features, but who can be hiding DNA characteristics that we did not even know existed a few years ago. Evidence found at a crime scene may not match the individual, even though he or she was the one that committed the crime.

   An example of how chimeras may be important to the law is the American example of Karen Keegan in 1998. Ms. Keegan was 52 years old and needed a kidney transplant. She was taken to a hospital to do testing to find a match, and her children were tested to see if they might be candidates. The tests revealed that Ms. Keegan was not the biological mother of two of her three sons. Upon further testing, doctors found that there were two different DNA types in her mouth swab, hair follicles, skin, and thyroid and bladder tissues. Doctors concluded that Ms. Keegan was the product of two female embryos that were fused at her conception; one embryo had one type of genetic material, and the other embryo had another type. Thus, if Ms. Keegan's DNA was used in a crime investigation, the results could be confusing and Ms. Keegan could easily be said to be lying to police. Further testing of Ms. Keegan's brothers and husband finally did prove that she was related to her sons, when material from her thyroid gland finally was a match.[47]

   Similarly in 2003, Lydia Fairchild had three children and was applying for public assistance in Washington state. She had to submit DNA samples to establish the paternity of her partner, but the tests came back and said that she was not the biological mother of any of her children. Ms. Fairchild was accused of defrauding the government, and prosecutors attempted to get her children taken and placed in foster care. Fortunately, Ms. Fairchild was pregnant, and the court ordered that a witness attend the birth of the child to ensure that she was the biological mother. DNA tests revealed that this fourth child, whose birth was witnessed by an officer of the court, was also not related to Ms. Fairchild. Further DNA testing was done and it was found that the children's DNA was consistent with their maternal grandmother, even though it did not match their mother. Finally, doctors found that samples from Ms. Fairchild's cervix did match the children, and it was concluded that she was a chimera and all four children were biologically hers.

   Dr. Arcabascio theorizes that a suspect could leave a sample of "hair, semen, saliva, perspiration, urine, earwax, mucus, bone, fingernail scrapings, blood, or skin ... If he is a chimera, however, the DNA from his saliva could, in theory, differ from the DNA in his semen, skin, blood, or some other sample left at the scene."[48] If there were no witnesses, the police would look for multiple perpetrators, or if there is a witness that saw only one person, this could lead to confusing results. Similarly, if a suspect was witnessed at the scene, the samples of a person who is a chimera may not match those left at the scene.

   Experts have theorized that for every eight babies born, one began as a twin, and the genetic material from that twin could have merged with the surviving baby. This means that approximately 10 percent of the population could be chimeras. Some have suggested that this number could be as high as 50–70 percent of the entire population.

---

46. James Careless, "An Imprecise Science" (March 2011) Canadian Bar Association, online: <http://cbanational.rogers.dgtlpub.com/2011/2011-03-31/pdf/An_imprecise_science.pdf>.

47. Catherine Arcabascio, "Chimeras" Double the DNA-Double the Fun for Crime Scene investigators, Prosecutors, and Defense Attorneys?" 40 *Akron Law Review* 435; Vivienne Lam "The Truth about Chimeras," (2011) 11 *Science Creative Quarterly*.

48. Catherine Arcabascio, "Chimeras: Double the DNA-Double the Fun for Crime Scene Investigators, Prosecutors and Defence Attorneys?" (2007) 40 *Akron Law Review* 435 at 443.

Dr. Arcabascio believes that in vitro fertilization and other reproductive assistance may create more chimeras, as many techniques involve implanting more than one embryo, resulting in a greater chance that the material may merge into a chimera. These scientific facts might be applicable to a variety of legal cases.[49]

3. DNA evidence can also be planted on the scene of a crime. However, those wishing to do this just got a whole new method. A company called Nucleix Ltd. has recently announced that it can synthesize DNA.[50]
4. German investigators pursued what they called the "Phantom of Heilbronn" across Western Europe. This female murderer left DNA at over 40 crime scenes, including 14 murders, and was thought to be a serial killer. DNA from this criminal was left on "a teacup at a murder scene in Germany, on a toy pistol after a robbery in France, at the scene of a burglary at an optometrist's store in Upper Austria, and on a car used to transport the bodies of three slain Georgians."[51] Eventually, a cotton swab manufacturer was embarrassed to reveal that the cotton swabs used at each of the crime scenes was contaminated by a single factory worker. The woman thought to be a serial killer was actually a woman working in a factory who touched the wrong material on the swabs.[52] Because of botched science, countless hours of police resources had been used chasing a killer who did not exist.

The "*CSI* Effect"

> These types of shows [like *CSI*] suggest that DNA samples are relatively easy to find, not easily contaminated, have a low error rate when they are profiled and can be examined in a matter of hours rather than days or weeks. In short, forensic sciences have been depicted as objective, reliable and infallible. The problem with this is that jurors are expecting to see the "technical wizardry" that appears in *CSI* in the courtroom, and when the prosecution fail to produce such reliable and objective results, "many Americans find themselves disappointed when they encounter the real world of law and order."[53]

CSI is a top-rated television show with millions of viewers across North America, and it has remained very popular for more than a decade. In 2002, in the first story on what has been termed the "*CSI* effect," journalist Robin Franzen pointed out that prosecutors were finding a change in the jury pool—potential jurors expected more criminal science in the courtroom. The *CSI* effect has snowballed since then, even though there is still more anecdotal evidence than actual research. There are believed to be three general effects of the phenomena:

1. Shows like *CSI* are making it more difficult for prosecutors to get convictions.
2. *CSI* raises scientific evidence to the rate of infallibility, making scientific evidence impenetrable.
3. *CSI* is allowing the average person understand scientific evidence.

1. Difficulty for Prosecutors to Get a Conviction

Some researchers have argued that people are increasingly romanticizing scientific evidence, thus leading to unreasonable expectations in jurors. Prosecutors report that jurors expect forensic science in every case, and particularly before they will consider convicting the accused. Some report that jurors feel that they are justified in an acquittal if there is no

49. Catherine Arcabascio, "Chimeras: Double the DNA-Double the Fun for Crime Scene Investigators, Prosecutors and Defence Attorneys?" (2007) 40 *Akron Law Review* 435 at 443.
50. Nucleix Ltd., online: <http://www.nucleix.com/pdf/Press_Release_Technology.pdf>.
51. Beverley Spencer, "Lessons from the Phantom of Heilbronn: Why DNA Evidence is Losing Its Lustre" (March 2001) Canadian Bar Association.
52. Kirk Makin, "The Dark Side of DNA" (13 March 2010), *The Globe and Mail*, online: <http://www.theglobeandmail.com/news/technology/science/the-dark-side-of-dna/article1499631/page3/>.
53. Jenny Wise, "Providing the CSI Treatment: Criminal Justice Practitioners and the CSI Effect." (2010) 21 *Current Issues in Criminal Justice* 383 at 384. Reproduced by permission of the Sydney Institute of Criminology.

forensic evidence. However, as we have discussed, the evidence presented on TV is perfectly left and recovered, but this rarely happens in real life. Thus, prosecutors are saying it is more difficult to get a conviction in cases without forensic evidence. Some say it is essential that law enforcement devote additional time and money to forensics, where it would previously not have been warranted.

2. Is Scientific Evidence Infallible?

As discussed, many blindly believe in scientific evidence, and there is a lure that makes this type of evidence insurmountable in the minds of some. The stories of those who have been wrongfully convicted because of forensic evidence are not as high-profile as those that imply that forensic evidence is always accurate and conclusive. But, different evidence can be interpreted differently by different technicians. DNA samples have been switched with evidence from other files, making it look like the victim in a robbery was actually the perpetrator of another crime; experts can lie under oath and/or present faked credentials; evidence can be planted; and it can be fabricated.

3. Does the Public Have More Information on Forensics?

Although there has been a huge increase in interest in the study of forensic sciences, police have noted they need to spend much more time explaining the forensics in a case and why it is not what is seen on TV. In an article, Toronto Police Forensic Identification Services Detective Constable Wade Knapp said that he spent several hours explaining why there was *not* forensic evidence at the scene of a home invasion.[54]

Inversely, many of those accused feel that they are in the clear if there is no forensic evidence. Both of these issues may mislead the jury, but it is difficult to tell the impact this evidence has on the jury because Canadian juries cannot talk about their deliberations. However, in the high-profile U.S. case of actor Robert Blake's trial, the jury members said that they acquitted him of murdering his wife because there was no gunshot residue on his hands or clothes. While this decision could be the result of the celebrity status of the accused, District Attorney Steve Cooley said the likely reason was that the jury was "incredibly stupid."[55]

Despite all of this material, largely collected from anecdotal sources and driven by the media, studies have been somewhat inconclusive. In a 2006 study by Kimberlianne Podlas, she found little correlation between watching *CSI* and what verdict would be given to a hypothetical court case. However, this knowledge (or supposed knowledge) of forensics might nonetheless result in longer jury deliberations and more juror questions, and it may have an impact on the process nonetheless. More research is being done, but this may be another myth driven by the media. Some have said that the *CSI* effect is simply a myth perpetrated by the program's network (CBS) to get controversy and publicity for the show. Yet others have theorized that the effect is a myth perpetrated by prosecutors (or perhaps defence counsel) to justify why they are not getting the convictions that they want.[56]

THE DELICATE BALANCE ... AND THE *CHARTER*

Some research has found that in the course of the rights revolution started by the inception of the *Charter of Rights and Freedoms* in 1982, the system has become plagued by questionable cases where individuals claim that their rights have been infringed by the government.

54. Deena Waisberg, "Battling the CSI Effect" (April 2001) *Canadian Lawyer*, online: <http://www.waisberg.ca/article_life_csi.html>.

55. Simon A Cole and Rachel Dioso-Villa, "Investigating the 'CSI Effect' Effect: Media and Litigation Crisis in Criminal Law" (2009) 61 *Stanford Law Review* 1335 at 1350 fn 73.

56. Kimberlianne Podlas, "'The CSI Effect': Exposing the Media Myth" (2006) 15 Fordham *Intellectual Property Media & Entertainment Law Journal* 429. Anyone addicted to the crime shows on TV should read Katherine Ramsland, *The C.S.I. Effect* (New York, Penguin: 2006). The author goes through the plots of these shows and discusses the real cases that deal with these issues.

Kevin Wiener

QMI Agency

Kevin Wiener and Zero Blood Alcohol

Ontario has recently changed driving rules to provide a greater incentive to new and young drivers to drive responsibly under a graduated licensing system (GLS), and to prevent first-time impaired driving offenders from becoming repeat offenders. As of August 1, 2010, all drivers under 21 must maintain a zero blood alcohol concentration level while driving. If novice drivers are found with blood alcohol under the GLS, they will have escalating sanctions for violations.[57] Those convicted under the new law will face a 30-day licence suspensions and a $500 fine, and those convicted of a second offence will have a 90-day suspension. A third offence could lead to a loss of all driving privileges. The new law came around as a result of the campaign by Tim Mulcahy, whose 20-year-old son was killed in a car accident after he and his friends were intoxicated.[58]

Four days after this change became effective, 20-year-old Kevin Wiener brought a *Charter* challenge against the new provision in the Ontario Superior Court of Justice. Mr. Wiener says that the law is unconstitutional because it restricts behaviour on the basis of age rather than experience. He argues that if young people are able to serve in the military and vote, they should be able to drink responsibly. Mr. Wiener says that "as a young person, I don't feel it's fair for the government [to do this]. I've been driving for four years, I have a clean driving record, I have no demerit points ever and the government's saying that because I'm 20, I can't be trusted to have a glass of wine with dinner."[59]

Osgoode Hall Law School Professor Allan Hutchinson doubts Wiener's challenge will get far, saying, "I can understand why he might feel irked by the legislation, but I have difficulty looking down the road and seeing success."[60] Many argue that young people are still permitted to drive—they are just unable to mix driving with alcohol. According to MADD Canada, drivers aged 16 to 24 make up 13 percent of the population but are involved in 33 percent of deaths caused by drunk driving. Transportation Minister Kathleen Wynne says that since ages 19–21 are dangerous years for young drivers, "as a society we've made a lot of decisions based on age.... Young people can't get their licence till they're 16, they can't vote till they're 18, they can't drink till they're 19."[61] It has yet to be seen if Mr. Wiener will be successful in his challenge.

Do you think that this law is discriminatory, or is it an allowable limit under the *Charter*?

THE DELICATE BALANCE ... AND LEGAL ODDITIES

Strange Laws Still on the Books

Different cities and towns still have some antiquated and interesting laws that are still on the books. Here are a few:

- Just in case you were planning on committing an indictable offence on a space station, s 7(2.3) of the *Criminal Code* provides that any crew member who commits an indictable offence during the space flight is deemed to have committed that act or omission in Canada.
- It is against the law to water your lawn during a rainstorm in Guelph, Ontario.[62]
- In Newfoundland, a school bus must stop the vehicle not less than five metres from the nearest railway track and, remaining stopped, shall listen and look in both directions

57. Ministry of Transportation, online: <http://www.mto.gov.on.ca/english/about/bill126.shtml>.
58. Robert Benzie, "Alcohol Ban for Young Drivers Faces Charter Challenge" (3 August 2010), *The Toronto Star*, online: <http://www.thestar.com/article/843521>.
59. *Ibid.*
60. Charlene Close, "20-year-old Challenges Ontario's Zero-Alcohol Law for Young Drivers" (4 August 2010), 680 News, online: <http://www.680news.com/news/local/article/85164--20-year-old-challenges-ontario-s-zero-alcohol-law-for-young-drivers>.
61. Robert Benzie, "Alcohol Ban for Young Drivers Faces Charter Challenge." (3 August 2010) *The Toronto Star*, online: <http://www.thestar.com/article/843521>
62. See s 8(1) of By-law Number (2003)-17106 [as amended]. A By-law to prescribe outside water use restrictions within the City of Guelph and to repeal By-law Number (2002)—16889, and to adopt Municipal Code Amendment #295, which amends Chapter 291-38 of The Corporation of the City of Guelph's Municipal Code.

along the track for an approaching train and for signals indicating the approach of a train and shall not proceed until it is safe to do so and should not change gears while crossing.[63] The odd part about this law is that the railway was abandoned in Newfoundland in 1988, and by 1990 most of the tracks were removed.[64]

- The term "vessel" is defined widely in the Canadian *Criminal Code.* Section 214 defines vessel as "a machine designed to derive support in the atmosphere primarily from reactions against the earth's surface of air expelled from the machine." Thus, the term "vessel" is not restricted to motorized vehicles; it simply includes them. Section 253 of the *Criminal Code* says that it is an offence to be impaired by alcohol or drugs while operating a vessel. Some have said that this is a broad definition and could include canoes and perhaps something as small as an inflatable boat.

  Police have long used this section to charge those who are boating drunk. Staff Sgt. Brad Schlorff of the Ontario Provincial Police Specialized Patrols unit has noted that the definition does not differentiate between types of boats and "basically, it's anything intended and used for navigation ... It's not your inflatable air mattress, but if you go out in a little rubber boat with a couple of paddles, it's a vessel."[65] Although drunk canoeing is not a common offence, 35 percent of boat fatalities are due to non-motorized boats, including canoes and kayaks. Be warned—do not drink and paddle your dinghy.
- In Oklahoma, statutes s 21 subsection 1772 provides that it is an offence to injure fruit, melons, or flowers at night. It provides that

> every person who shall maliciously or mischievously enter the enclosure, or go upon the premises of another in the night time, and knock off, pick, destroy, or carry away, any apples, peaches, pears, plums, grapes, or other fruit, melons, or flowers of any tree, shrub, bush, or vine, or having entered the enclosure or gone upon the premises of another, in the night time, with the intent to knock off, pick, destroy, or carry away any fruit or flowers, as aforesaid, be actually found thereon, shall, on conviction thereof, be punished by fine not exceeding One Hundred Dollars ($100.00) and not less than Ten Dollars ($10.00), or by imprisonment in the county jail not exceeding thirty (30) days.

Just Weird Cases!

Even with the best of intentions, weird cases that were never anticipated by the justice system arise. Our system has to determine how they will deal with those matters. Following are some cases that defy all classification.

Should Creative Law-Breaking Be Treated Less Severely?

1. *What do you do with the these criminals?* Border agents discovered through video evidence near Naco, Arizona, that a group of drug dealers were taking large amounts of marijuana and catapulting the drugs over the border from Mexico to the United States. The agents were able to seize 45 pounds of cannabis.[66]
2. *Does your boss make you sick?* New York housing authority superintendent Anthony Dingle has brought a lawsuit alleging that his boss's voice made him vomit. He says that her abuse at work got to the point that her voice made him sick and that he had to seek psychological assistance.[67] Mr. Dingle said that "I was constantly being attacked by her. I felt like attacks could come at any time. Every time I heard her voice, it triggered a sickening feeling in me."[68] Mr. Dingle had to seek prescription medication to calm

---

63. See s 134(1) and (2) of the Newfoundland *Highway Traffic Act*, RSNL 1990 Chapter H-3.

64. See the Railway Coastal Museum website, online: <http://www.railwaycoastalmuseum.ca/end.htm>.

65. Colin Campbell, "Don't Paddle Drunk" (24 July 2006) *Maclean's*, online: <http://www.macleans.ca/canada/national/article.jsp?content=20060724_130717_130717>.

66. Natalie Fraser, "The Case of the Cannabis Catapult" (13 May 2011) *The Lawyers Weekly*, online: <http://www.lawyersweekly-digital.com/lawyersweekly/3102?pg=17#pg17>.

67. Natalie Fraser, "Man Claims Boss's Voice Made him Vomit" (4 March 2011), *The Lawyers Weekly*, online: <http://www.lawyersweekly-digital.com/lawyersweekly/3040?pg=13#pg13>.

68. Jamie Schram, "Suit: My Boss' Voice Made Me Vomit" (15 February 2011) *New York Post*, online: <http://www.nypost.com/f/print/news/local/manhattan/suit_says_boss_pure_heave_il_kn63ZJzLT86dgGMMu85dqO>.

One little comma, one big difference.

© Frymire Archive/Alamy

his stomach and help his intestinal system, and he eventually suffered from a bleeding prostate that was treated by a urologist. Is this a legitimate lawsuit because of the quantifiable medical damage to Mr. Dingle?

3. *You know you have a problem with Facebook when ...* A burglar in Rome broke into a home and stole cash and jewellery. The case would have been much more difficult to solve if he had not logged into Facebook in the home where he was stealing property and forgot to log out. Similarly, in West Virginia a woman had two missing diamond rings, and noticed that her computer was logged onto a Facebook account she did not recognize. The Facebook page led directly to 19-year-old Jonathan Parker, who had broken into her home.[69]
4. *What difference does a comma make?* Many students of law think that the profession is far too rigid in its requirements for clarity. However, the importance of one comma was investigated by the Canadian Radio-television and Telecommunications Commission investigated a dispute between Rogers Communication and Aliant.

   A 14-page contract said that Rogers could use Aliant's poles for its communications purposes for a charge of $9.60 per pole starting in 2002. Page seven of the contract said that the agreement shall "continue in force for a period of five years from the date it is made, and thereafter for successive five year terms**,** unless and until terminated by one year prior notice in writing by either party." If the second comma was not there, the right to cancel would not have been available for five years. Rogers read the contract to say that it would have this price for five years from 2002, but Aliant read the contract to say that it could cancel the contract with one year's notice. Aliant raised the price of the poles to $28 per pole by 2006, and insisted that Rogers pay the new price. The difference in the arguments? A comma. The tribunal found that Aliant's reading of the contract was correct, costing approximately $2.1 million in pole costs for Rogers (not to mention the legal fees)—all because of one comma.[70]

CONCLUSION

> Law is an imperfect profession in which success can rarely be achieved without some sacrifice of principle. Thus all practicing lawyers—and most others in the profession—will necessarily be imperfect, especially in the eyes of young idealists. There is no perfect justice, just as there is no absolute in ethics. But there is perfect injustice, and we know it when we see it.[71]

The purpose of this final chapter of this textbook is simply to show (sometimes in a lighthearted way) that the law is not perfect, and we have a very delicate balance between the rights of all those involved. I have devoted much of my adult life to the study of the law, and I am the biggest supporter of the Canadian legal system. However, it does nothing to improve the system if we are blind to its problems. It is only with scrutiny of the law and the constant questioning of legislation, case law, and the actors involved, that we will have the best system possible.

It is up to those reading this textbook to take this knowledge with them to their careers as lawyers, judges, police officers, and corrections officers—and those who simply will face the law in their lives—to make sure that this system delivers on what it promises. There have been times where the law has failed us as a society, and it will again. The important part is how we respond to those failures and make sure that it never happens in that same way again. As the above quotation from Alan Dershowitz so perfectly illustrates, the law and the humans who tend to it are inherently imperfect; it is our job to make the delicate balance as perfect as we can imagine.

69. *Time*, "Jonathan Parker Is ... Allegedly Breaking into a House" (30 November 2009), online: <http://www.time.com/time/specials/packages/article/0,28804,1943680_1943678_1943557,00.html>.

70. Bob Tarantino, "Under Arrest: Canadian Laws You Won't Believe" (Toronto: Dundurn, 2007) at 150; and Grant Robertson, "Comma Quirk Irks Rogers" *Globe and Mail* (8 June 2006).

71. Alan Dershowitz, *Letters to a Young Lawyer* (New York: Basic Books, 2001) at 9.

LEARNING OUTCOMES SUMMARIZED

1. Identify what issues might warrant an investigation by the Canadian Judicial Council.

A variety of issues may warrant an investigation of a judge by the CJC. Not only issues that come up in the course of the justice system can be investigated; issues that arise in a judge's personal life may also be investigated, as it may bring the administration of justice into disrepute.

2. Identify some of the problems with forensic evidence.

Forensic evidence can include anything from a fingerprint at a crime scene, to gun residue left when a firearm has been discharged, or other trace materials like hair, fibres, soil, or paint that are left behind. However, fingerprints are not perfectly left at a crime scene, and investigators may only recover partial fingerprints. Although there may be a match on the prints, the important thing to remember with all forensic evidence is that humans make mistakes.

3. Define a "chimera," and explain its implications for the criminal law (and law in general).

Science has recently uncovered what are called "chimeras" or people with different strands of DNA in different parts of their body, or even different types of DNA in their blood. Evidence found at a crime scene may not match the individual even though they were the one who committed the crime. Experts theorize that a suspect could leave a sample of "hair, semen, saliva, perspiration, urine, earwax, mucus, bone, fingernail scrapings, blood, or skin ... If he is a chimera, however, the DNA from his saliva could, in theory, differ from the DNA in his semen, skin, blood, or some other sample left at the scene." This result could substantially confuse the investigation, witnesses, and suspects. Experts believe that in vitro fertilization and other reproductive assistance may create more chimeras.

SELF-EVALUATION QUESTIONS

1. How has technology been used in the legal system?
2. What is a chimera, and how could this discovery potentially affect evidence at a trial?
3. What is the "*CSI* effect"?
4. On what basis is Kevin Wiener challenging the zero blood alcohol and drinking provisions in Ontario?
5. What types of matters can a judge be investigated for?

Appendix: Becoming a Lawyer

BECOMING A LAWYER

Undergraduate University Degree

Before applying to law school, individuals must first complete at least two to three years of an undergraduate degree. However, most applicants will have at least a bachelor's degree before applying to law school. Very few applicants are accepted without first having an undergraduate degree for good reason—the level of critical thinking required in law school simply cannot be obtained with a few years of undergraduate work. Students should be advised to complete their undergraduate course of study so that they have this degree in hand whether or not they complete law school.

Grades are one of the key elements for an application to law school. On average, most successful law school applicants maintain an 80 percent cumulatively throughout their undergraduate years. However, some law schools place an emphasis on the last two years of undergrad (or top two years), so it is especially important to do well in those years. Each law school has particular ways in which it calculates your average and what is needed for admission. There may also be special categories for mature students and students who belong to particular minority groups (e.g., those with Aboriginal status.)

The LSAT

The Law School Admission Test (LSAT) is a half-day standardized test usually administered in February, June, September/October, and December, at testing centres around the world. Canadian law schools, and many other law schools worldwide, require a score from the LSAT as part of an application. The LSAT is designed to be a standard measure of reading comprehension, analytical reasoning, and logical reasoning that law schools use as a factor in selecting students applying to their school. Unfortunately, everything you have heard about the LSAT being a gruelling and demanding test is true. It is purposely designed to be difficult and is taken under very restricted time limits. Students are allowed to write three times in two years (and additional times with special permission), but law schools may average the scores or take only the highest score.

The LSAT score is based on how many questions are answered correctly, and there is no deduction for incorrect answers, nor are individual questions weighted differently. These scores are converted to an LSAT scale ranging from 120 (the lowest score possible) to 180 (the highest score possible), using a statistical procedure known as "equating," which adjusts for minor differences in difficulty between tests. A **percentile** rank is also reported for each LSAT score, which states the percentage of candidates scoring below (and above) your score. The percentile is based on the distribution of scores for the three-year period prior to the year in which the score is reported including those above and below. At the time of publication, a minimum score of 160 is required for many Canadian law schools, but this is by no means a cut-off. Check with the individual law schools for their requirements. The Law Society Admission Council (LSAC) is the body that administers the LSAT.

The Law Society Admission Council
http://www.lsac.org

Many criticize the LSAT test for inadequately measuring the skills required to be successful at law school and in practice. Some think that a U.S.-based test should not have such effect on whether a student is admitted to a Canadian institution. The criticisms that are levelled at other standardized tests are also relevant to the LSAT. Some say that the test is biased toward a particular middle-class culture, and that there may be a disadvantage to some groups.

Many think that interviews and more information on relevant work experience should instead be used. However, the interview process would take much more time and resources, and it can be subjective and biased in its own way. (For example, the interviewer can intangibly "like" one person over another). However, many countries have eliminated the test as a part of the law school admission process, including schools in the United Kingdom, Australia, and New Zealand.

Personal Statement

Applicants are expected to submit a personal statement for each law school they apply to. This is often the student's only ability to speak to the law school and convince the school why it should select him or her for admission over the thousands of other applicants. Each law school imposes different requirements for the statement, including character counts, word counts, and other length requirements. Students should reserve several weeks to edit and proofread these statements.

Law School

Historically, no formal university legal education existed for lawyers in Canada. Potential lawyers simply apprenticed with a practising lawyer and wrote several exams to be admitted to the bar. Starting in the 1950s and 1960s, university-based legal education began and law schools were formed that were approved by provincial law societies. Legal education has greatly expanded and now teaches many non-traditional areas of law. Today, to be admitted to the bar in the provinces and territories in Canada, the candidate must possess a law degree from an accredited law school. Table A.1 lists the approved law schools in Ontario, and Table A.2 lists the remainder of law schools in Canada.

For Ontario Law Schools, most recent information, see Ontario Law School Application Service (OLSAS) at **http://www.ouac.on.ca/docs/olsas/rc_olsas_e.pdf.**

In many schools in Canada, the law degree is an undergraduate degree called the LL.B. (a Bachelors degree in Law) but typically requires completion of a first degree for admission. However, many schools in Canada are transitioning to the degree offered in American law schools, which is called a J.D. (*juris doctor*). The University of Toronto was one of the first law schools to switch to the J.D. designation, and it has been followed by York University, the University of Western Ontario, Queen's University, the University of Windsor, the University of Ottawa, the University of British Columbia, and the University of Calgary. Many of the other Canadian schools are considering the change, and may have done so after publication. Note that a Canadian J.D. degree does not qualify an individual to practise in the United States where an American Bar Association approved J.D. is required.

Articling

After completing three years of law school in Canada, an applicant must work with a law firm under an apprenticeship, known as **articling**. Articling is a process where students learn from more experienced lawyers in order to find out what it is like to work under the pressure of deadlines. Articling length varies from province to province but typically lasts no more than a year (ten months in Ontario).[1] Law students typically apply for their articling job after their second year of law school. This is a required part of the licence to practise law. The firm, organization or sole practitioner that hires the articling student must provide a mentor or principal lawyer that evaluates the student's work and certifies that they are ready to practise law as a qualified lawyer. The principals must take an education course to teach them what is important to pass on to their students. At the end of the term,

1. The period is nine months in British Columbia, one year in Manitoba, 48 weeks in New Brunswick, one year in Nova Scotia, one year in Prince Edward Island, and one year in Saskatchewan.

Table A.1 Approved Law Schools in Ontario–Statistics from 2010–2012

School	Number of Applicants/First Year-Class	GPA	Median LSAT	References
Lakehead University http://www.law .lakeheadu.ca/	First year class of 55	B+ with at least an A- in the final two years.	No minimum, highest score used. Can write until February, but suggest take by December.	Two letters (at least one academic, but preferred two academic).
Queen's University http://www.law .queensu.ca Email: llb@post. queensu.ca	2797/168	Average of A- in last two years	Highest score used for admission. Average LSAT used for initial sorting. Write by December to be admitted in the first round.	Two required (at least one academic, but two preferred).
University of Ottawa http://www .commonlaw.uottawa. ca Email: comlaw@ uottawa.ca	3600/300	83% GPA is the most important factor.	Highest score is used. No minimum LSAT. Will look at the other elements of the file.	Two (at least one academic).
University of Toronto http://www.law .utoronto.ca Email: law. admissions@utoronto. ca	2111/199	86.5% Based on best three full-time years. See detailed info on website.	168 Highest score used. Will accept December and February LSAT after application prior November.	None
University of Western Ontario http://www.law .uwo.ca Email: lawapp@uwo.ca	2750/175	80–84% average GPA 3.7 Cumulative GPA of A–Focus on last two years.	General 80th percentile, discretionary more than 65th percentile. Highest score used. February LSAT accepted, but strongly recommend writing by December.	Two (one academic).
York University–Osgoode http://www.osgoode .yorku.ca Email: admissions@ osgoode.yorku.ca	3107/291	Cumulative GPA of A–. Based on best two years of undergrad.	LSAT 80th percentile or higher (163). Highest score is used.	Two required (academic and/or non-academic).
University of Windsor http://www.uwindsor. ca/law Email: uwlaw@ uwindsor.ca	1889/157 (J.D.) 635/60 (J.D./J.D.).	Based on seven criteria—see website.	Highest	One academic and one non-academic.

Table A.2 Canadian Law Schools Outside of Ontario—Statistics from 2010-2012

School	Number of Applicants/ First-Year Class	GPA	LSAT	Deadline	References
Dalhousie University www.dal.ca/law Email: law.admissions@dal.ca	1700/163	3.7	159 Highest score used.	Feb. 28 (but applications submitted by Nov. 30 will be considered for early admission)	Two; academic is preferable; there may be an interview.
McGill University* www.mcgill.ca/law1/ Email: undergradadmissions.law@mcgill.ca	1479/ 179	84%	162 Multiple scores averaged.	Nov. 1	Two letters of reference; must demonstrate ability in English *and* French.
Thompson Rivers University (first year 2012) http://www.tru.ca/law Email: lawadmissions@tru.ca	75	No stats.	December last date used.	Feb. 1	Three reference letters, two academic.
University of Alberta http://www.law.ualberta.ca Email: admission@law.ualberta.ca	1500/ 175	3.7	Scores averaged 161, 90th percentile or higher. Last accepted date is the December exam.	Nov. 1: Admission application deadline (online). Feb. 1 for supporting documents and supplemental form (online).	None (but two official transcripts are required).
University of British Columbia http://www.law.ubc.ca Email: admissions@law.ubc.ca	2261/ 185	83%	166 Highest score used.	Feb. 1	None (but some in discretionary categories).
University of Calgary Faculty of Law http://www.law.ucalgary.ca Email: law@ucalgary.ca	1360/ 110	3.57 (case by case; see website)	158 LSAT must be completed before application. Highest score. Must be written by December.	Nov. 1 for application form (found online), statement of interest, and fees. Feb. 1 for supporting documents. *Must be mailed in, not an online application.	Two letters, (both should be academic).

(*Continued*)

Table A.2 Canadian Law Schools Outside of Ontario—Statistics from 2010-2012 *(continued)*

School	Number of Applicants/ First-Year Class	GPA	LSAT	Deadline	References
University of Manitoba http://law.robsonhall.ca/ Email: um-law@ cc.umanitoba.ca	1211/ 110	3.9 Worst grades may be eliminated; see website.	162 Highest LSAT. Early offer must write by September. December and February only considered after first offers.	Nov. 1	None (only GPA and LSAT considered) but depends on the category.
University of New Brunswick http://www.law.unb.ca Email: lawadmit@unb.ca	989/92	3.8 Some marks may be eliminated; see website	159 Highest score used, under 150 unlikely to be admitted.	March 1. Earlier applications are strongly recommended.	Two letters are required in the Discretionary, Aboriginal, and Scholarship categories.
University of Saskatchewan http://www.usask.ca/law Email: doreen.petrow@usask. ca	1080/ 126	3.34	159 Highest score used. Suggested to write earlier than February.	Feb. 1: Grad work done is not added to GPA, but is considered. More weight to full-load basis.	None; will not be reviewed if provided.
University of Victoria http://www.law.uvic.ca Email: lawadmss@uvic.ca	1383/ 110	3.9	163, 88th percentile. Highest score used.	Dec. 1, but early applications encouraged (rolling admission starting in October). GPA: 70% LSAT: 30% of the decision	None

*Applicants should be aware that there is a language requirement for McGill Law, as you will be expected to read and understand complex French cases and materials. To assist applicants in determining if their French understanding is sufficient for McGill's curriculum, they have created a self-assessment questionnaire, and posted a French excerpt from a case. Both of these documents can be found at http://www.mcgill.ca/law-admissions/undergraduates/admissions/requirements/.

the articling student and the principal must meet to fill out law society documentation. If the principal does not feel that the student should be called to the bar, he or she can inform the law society that the student is not ready. If the student makes any errors during this period of time, the principal may face liability, and may withdraw as a mentor.

Bar Exams

Candidates must pass their bar admission exams administered by the provincial bar association before they are admitted to the bar. Students must graduate from a common or civil law program (civil law program is offered only at Ottawa and McGill), which is approved by the law society for the province. Students who attended law school in another country must have a Certificate of Qualification issued by the National Committee on Accreditation appointed by the Federation of Law Societies of Canada and the Committee of Canadian Law Deans. Students must also be up to date on all payment of fees to the law society.

The firm at which you are articling is required to provide five days of uninterrupted study time in order to take the bar exam, in addition to the one day to write a licensing examination for the first attempt. Each province is individual and slightly different exams are required. In Ontario, the Law Society of Upper Canada provides that there are two exams that must be completed. There were previously bar examination classes (but the attendance was low) so now the exams are exclusively self-study courses that are completed during the articling period.

In Ontario, the Barrister Examination will assess an individual's knowledge in ethical and professional responsibility, knowledge of the law (public law, criminal procedure, family law, and civil litigation), and establishing and maintaining the barrister client relationship. The Solicitor Examination assesses knowledge in ethical and professional responsibility, knowledge of the law (real estate, business law, wills, trusts, and estate administration and planning), and establishing and maintaining the solicitor client relationship. Each examination is approximately seven hours in length. The Law Society will provide the necessary materials to study from for the licensing examination, and this material is given to students one month before the exam.

Good Character

In order to be licensed in Canada, one must be deemed of "good character" under the governing legislation.[2] For example, under the Ontario *Law Society Act,* "it is a requirement for the issuance of every licence under this Act that the applicant be of good character." The rationale is that only individuals with integrity are admitted to the profession.

A lawyer being of "good character" dates back to Roman times and Anglo-Saxon England where lawyers were required to take an oath to fulfill their professional responsibilities in a good and virtuous manner. Before being admitted to the legal profession, applicants must be certified as being of good character, and one can be refused admission if deemed to be of low character. However, there is little consensus on what the requirement of moral character entails or demands. It is generally thought to include traits such as honesty, integrity, and reliability. Any prospective lawyer must report any criminal matters on their record, including speeding tickets (not parking tickets), substance abuse problems, and bankruptcy orders. Candidates are also required to have references completed by third parties vouching for their character.

Provincial bar associations seldom use this provision to deny applicants admission to the bar, but even in cases in which they do, the standards are not clear or consistent. In general, applicants are presumed to be of good character and suitable for legal practice unless there is evidence to the contrary. Law schools and bar associations do not do in-depth background checks. They make only a brief inquiry into an applicant's moral character (and this is largely confined to questions asked on application forms) and rely on the applicant being truthful. Some argue that the danger in a vague term such as "good character" is that it could be used to discriminate against groups who are arbitrarily deemed of low character. However, if there is an indication on the application form that there is an issue, the law society will investigate and this can have very serious consequences, as in the case of *The Law Society of Upper Canada v Burgess* (see the following case box).

THE LAW SOCIETY OF UPPER CANADA v BURGESS, 2006 ONLSHP 0066 (LAW SOCIETY HEARING PANEL)

Ms. Burgess was a 27-year-old student who completed her B.A. at the University of Toronto, law school at Queen's University, and had completed the bar admission course and articling. Ms. Burgess indicated on her application to the bar that there was a misunderstanding with a mark in her undergraduate degree. She went before the Law Society Hearing Panel to determine if she met s 27(2) of the *Law Society Act,* which requires that an "applicant for admission

2. Legal Profession Act, SA 1990, c L-9.1; Legal Profession Act, SBC 1998, c 9; Law Society Act, RSM 1987, c L100; Law Society Act, SNB 1996, c 89; Law Society Act, 1999, SNL 1999, c L-9.1; Legal Profession Act, RSNS 2004, c 28; Law Society Act, RSO 1990, c L-8; Legal Professions Act, SPEI 1992, c 39; Professional Code, RSQ, c C-26; Legal Profession Act, RSS 1990, c L-10.1; Legal Profession Act, R.S.Y. 2002, c 134 as amended by An Act to Amend the Legal Profession Act, SY 2004, c14; Legal Profession Act, SNWT 1988, c L-2; Legal Profession Act, RSNWT (Nu) 1988, c L-2.

to the Society shall be of good character" and (4) that "an application for admission to the Society may be refused only by the Hearing Panel after holding a hearing."

While in her fourth year at the University of Toronto, Ms. Burgess was alleged to have plagiarized a paper written by another person and attempted to pass off the work as her own. On her application for admission to the bar, she answered "yes" to the question: "while attending a post-secondary institution, have allegations of misconduct ever been made against you?" Although Ms. Burgess said there was an issue, Ms. Burgess was said to have misled the Law Society and said that she had simply handed in a paper that was too similar in content to a paper she handed in for another course, and the matter was simply a misunderstanding. She claimed that she did not proceed to fight this charge because she was graduating from the University of Toronto. Ms. Burgess gave this "false account" of the incident throughout the law society investigation, and told four of her six references this "false account."

The law society panel found that "the plagiarism, the lies told to the Law Society, and the lies told to her character references, go to the very heart of who lawyers are, and what lawyers do. Integrity is fundamental to the competence of a lawyer, competence necessarily includes integrity." The panel said that "good character" has been defined but continues to evolve as a "combination of qualities or features distinguishing one person from another. Good character connotes moral or ethical strength, distinguishable as an amalgam of virtuous attributes or traits which would include, among others, integrity, candour, empathy and honesty."

The onus was on the accused to show that she was of good character. The panel looked at the persistent lies told by Ms. Burgess to the law society and her character references. The panel found that there was not enough time passed between these lies and her application, and they could not find that she was a person of good character who could be admitted to the Law Society. They did suggest that at some time in the future Ms. Burgess could show that she was of good character, but this was not that time.

Should an otherwise qualified candidate be prevented from practising law based on what that person did as an undergraduate? Does it matter that it was a credibility issue?

Compare the case of *The Law Society of Upper Canada v Burgess* to the case of Sebastien Brousseau in the Food for Thought box.

FOOD FOR THOUGHT...

Sebastien Brousseau stabbed his mother 40 times, including a slash to her throat, during a heated argument when he was 21 years old. Mr. Brousseau was sentenced to four years and ten months in prison, and was released on parole in 1992. He completed law school and graduated in 1996. However, the Quebec Bar refused to admit Mr. Brousseau five times, saying that he had committed "one of the most revolting" acts, which would not lead to confidence in the administration of justice if he was permitted to be a lawyer.

Mr. Brousseau was described as having a stellar academic record, and articled in Quebec with a Montreal lawyer but was forced to fight for ten years to be sworn as a member of the Quebec Bar. Mr. Brousseau appealed to the "Tribunal des Professions," which is the judicial body that hears appeals in professional cases. Mr. Brousseau had several affidavits of support signed by lawyers and other supporters.

In a 2006 ruling, the tribunal overturned the Quebec Bar's refusal to admit Mr. Brousseau. The three-person tribunal said that he had the "morals, the conduct, the competence, the knowledge and the qualities to practise the profession of lawyer." They also noted that the applicant was "not the same person he was in 1990." Mr. Brousseau was sworn in as a lawyer in a private ceremony in 2006.[3]

Should a person who has been convicted of a serious crime be able to practise law?

Is it different when a person commits murder?

3. *Montreal Gazette*, "Murderer of Mother Becomes Lawyer" (15 May 2007) Canada.com, online: <http://www.canada.com/story_print.html?id=f11fb441-1130-4371-8840-b714817cf88e&sponsor=>.

The Call-to-the-Bar Ceremony

In Ontario, candidates who wish to be called to the bar must attend a ceremony to be presented with the Degree of "Barrister-at-Law" by the Law Society and a Court Certificate of Qualification. During the bar admission ceremony, graduates take an oath to uphold the highest standards of moral integrity. For example, in Alberta, lawyers must affirm or swear an oath saying that:

> That I will as a Barrister and Solicitor conduct all causes and matters faithfully and to the best of my ability. I will not seek to destroy anyone's property. I will not promote suits upon frivolous pretences. I will not pervert the law to favour or prejudice anyone, but in all things will conduct myself truly and with integrity. I will uphold and maintain the Sovereign's interest and that of my fellow citizens according to the law in force in Alberta.[4]

There is also an optional part of the oath in Ontario that provides that "I swear or affirm that I will be faithful and bear true allegiance to Her Majesty Queen Elizabeth the Second [or the reigning sovereign for the time being], Her heirs and successors according to law." In Ontario, a call-to-the-bar ceremony is normally held in January, June, and September of each year in various cities but this may change by province.

4. An Ethics Primer for Criminal Lawyers, Prepared For: Legal Education Society of Alberta, Criminal Law Boot, http://www.lesaonline.org/samples/24_21_04_p1.pdf

References

630393 Saskatchewan Ltd. v Antonishen 2003 SKPC 94 (Sask Prov Ct).

AA v BB, [2007] OJ No. 2 (Ont CA).

Access to Justice Act, SO 2006, c 21.

Adams v Law Society of Alberta, [2000] AJ No 1031 (Law Society of Alberta Hearing).

Adams, Thomas. *The Works of Thomas Adams* (Edinburgh: James Nichol, 1861).

Adjudicative Tribunals Accountability, Governance and Appointments Act, 2009 SO 2009, c 33, sch 5.

Administrative Justice Act RSQ, c J-3.

Administrative Procedures Act, RSA 2000, c A-3.

Age of Majority Act, RSNB 1973, c A-4.

Alberta Human Labour Relations Board, online: <http://www.alrb.gov.ab.ca/>.

Alberta Rules of Court

Alberta Rules of Court, Alta Reg 390/1968, *British Columbia and Yukon, Rules of Court*, BC Reg 221/90

Alberta, Law Society of Alberta Code of Professional Conduct http://www.lawsociety.ab.ca/lawyers/regulations/code.aspx>

Almrei v Canada (Minister of Citizenship and Immigration), [2011] FCJ No 781 (Fed Ct).

An Act Respecting the Class Action, RSQ c R-21; *The Class Actions Act*, SS, 2007, c 21.

An Act to Provide for a Change of Name Act, 1990, RSN, Chapter C-8.1

An Ethics Primer for Criminal Lawyers, prepared for Legal Education Society of Alberta, Criminal Law Boot, online: <http://www.lesaonline.org/samples/24_21_04_p1.pdf >.

Andrews v Grand and Toy Alberta Ltd., [1978] SCJ No 6.

Andrews, Michelle. "Prenuptial Agreements to Lose Weight, Have Sex." (28 August 2008) *U.S. News & World Report*, online: <http://health.usnews.com/health-news/blogs/on-health-and-money/2008/08/28/prenuptial-agreements-to-lose-weight-have-sex_print.html>.

Annual Report on the Operation of the Canadian Multiculturalism Act 2006–2007, online: <http://www.cic.gc.ca/english/pdf/pub/multi-report2007.pdf>.

Antle v NCC Financial Corp., [2009] BCJ No. 718 (BCSC).

Aquinas, Thomas. *Summa Theological*, translated by Fathers of the English Dominican Province, 1952.

Arcabascio, Catherine. "Chimeras: Double the DNA-Double the Fun for Crime Scene Investigators, Prosecutors and Defence Attorneys?" (2007) 40 *Akron Law Review* 435.

Arnold v Teno, [1978] SCJ No 8 (SCC).

Asimow, Michael. "Bad Lawyers In the Movies" (2000) 24 *Nova L Rev* 533.

Associated Press. "NYC to Fight Unicyclist Kyle Peterson's Lawsuit" (18 March 2011) CBS, online: <http://newyork.cbslocal.com/2011/03/18/nyc-to-fight-unicyclists-lawsuit/>.

Associated Press. "Women's Group Wants Judge Ousted" (27 November 1988), online: <http://news.google.com/newspapers?nid=2026&dat=19891127&id=o7EtAAAAIBAJ&sjid=odAFAAAAIBAJ&pg=6173,3944094>.

Atkinson, Paul. *The Canadian Justice System: An Overview*, 2nd ed (Markham, ON: LexisNexis, 2010).

Baker v Canada (Minister of Citizenship & Immigration), [1999] 2 SCR 817 (SCC).

Bala, Nicholas et al. *An International Review of Polygamy: Legal and Policy Implications for Canada* (Ottawa, ON: Status of Women Canada, 2005).

Bank of Nova Scotia v MacLellan (1977), 78 DLR (3d) 1 (NSSC App Div).

Barrick Gold Corp. v Lopehandia (2004), 71 OR (3d) 416 (CA).

Battered Men: The Hidden Side of Domestic Violence, online: <http://www.batteredmen.com/bathelpnatl.htm>.

Beacock v Wetter, [2006] BCJ No. 1416 (BCSC).

Beatty, David. *Constitutional Law in Theory and Practice* (Toronto: University of Toronto Press, 1995).

Bellomo, J Jerald. "Upper Canadian Attitudes Towards Crime and Punishment (1832 1851). (1972) *Ontario Historical Society* at 11.

Benetton, Luigi. "E-trials seen as 'Essential' for Justice in the Future." *Lawyers Weekly*, online: <http://www.lawyersweekly.ca/index.php?section=article&articleid=1396>.

Benzie, Robert. "Alcohol Ban for Young Drivers Faces Charter Challenge" (3 August 2010) *The Toronto Star*, online: <http://www.thestar.com/article/843521>.

Big Love: The Complete First to Fifth Seasons, DVD (US HBO Video, 2006 2011).

Black, Henry Campbell, ed. *Black's Law Dictionary*, 7th ed (St. Paul, MN: West Pub. Co., 1999).

Blackstone, William. *Commentaries on the Laws of England* (originally 1765 and 1769) (Boston, MA: Beacon Press, 1962).

Blake, Sara. *Administrative Law in Canada* (Toronto: Butterworths, 1992).

Bogart, WA. "'Guardian of Civil Rights ... Medieval Relic': The Civil Jury in Canada" 62 *Law and Contemporary Problems* 305.

Boucher v The Queen, [1955] SCR 16 (SCC).

Boyd, John-Paul. "Tsunami in a Teapot: *Leskun v Leskun*" (2007) 40 *UBC L Rev* 293.

Boyd, Neil. *Canadian Law: An Introduction,* 4th ed (Toronto: Nelson, 2007).

Boyd, Neil. *Canadian Law: An Introduction,* 5th ed (Toronto: Nelson, 2011).

Boyd, Susan B. "Spaces and Challenges: Feminism in Legal Academia" (2011) 44 *UBC. Law Review* 205.

Boyle, Christine, and David R Percy. *Contracts: Cases and Commentaries,* 6th ed (Toronto: Carswell, 1999).

British Columbia (Director of Civil Forfeiture) v Rai, [2011] BCJ No 241.

British Columbia Securities Commission, online: <http://www.bcsc.bc.ca/>.

British Columbia, *Evidence Act, s* 7

British Columbia, *Professional Conduct Handbook*, Law Society of British Columbia, online: <http://www.lawsociety.bc.ca/page.cfm?cid=383&t=Professional-Conduct-Manual>

Brogden v Metropolitan Railway Co. (1877), 2 AC 666.

Brown Commission, (second report), *Journal of the Legislative Assembly for Upper Canada*, 1849.

Browne, Angela, *When Battered Women Kill* (New York: The Free Press, 1987).

Brucker v Marcovitz, [2007] SCJ No. 54 (SCC).

Brudner, Alan. "A Theory of Necessity" (1987) 7 *Oxford J Legal Stud* 339.

Bruni v Bruni, 2010 ONSC 6568 (Ont. SCJ).

Brusegard, David. "The Implications of Demographic Change in the Legal Profession" (3 February 2004) Canadian Bar Association, online: <http://www.cba.org/CBA/about/main/>.

By-law Number (2003)-17106 [as amended] City of Guelph, Ontario.

Cairns-Way, R, and RM Mohr. *Dimensions of Criminal Law,* 2nd ed (Toronto: Emond Montgomery, 1996).

Cairns, David, JA. *Advocacy and the Making of the Adversarial Criminal Trial 1800 –1865,* (Oxford: The Hambledon Press, 1998).

Cameron, Deborah, and Elizabeth Frazer. *The Lust to Kill: A Feminist Investigation of Sexual Murder* (Cambridge: Polity in Association with Basil Blackwell, 1987).

Campbell, Angela, et al. *Polygamy in Canada: Legal and Social Implications for Women and Children* (Ottawa, ON: Status of Women Canada, 2005).

Campbell, Colin. "Don't Paddle Drunk" (24 July 2006) *Maclean's*, online: <http://www.macleans.ca/canada/national/article.jsp?content=20060724_130717_130717>.

Campbell, Kathryn, and Myriam Denov. "The Burden of innocence: Coping with a Wrongful Imprisonment" (2004) *Canadian Journal of Criminology and Criminal Justice* 139.

Canada (Attorney General) v JTI-Macdonald Corp., [2007] SJC No 30 (SCC).

Canada (Director of Investigation & Research, Combines Investigation Branch) v Southam, [1984] 2 SCR 145.

Canada Evidence Act, RSC 1985, c C-5.

Canadian Bar Association, "Addiction and Psychiatric Impairment of Lawyers and Judges: A Search for Meaningful Data" (Legal Profession Assistance Conference).

Canadian Bill of Rights, RSC 1970, App. III.

Canadian Centre for Justice Statistics through StatsCan, Legal Aid in Canada: Description of Operations, online: <http://publications.gc.ca/Collection-R/Statcan/85-217-XIB/0000185-217-XIB.pdf>.

Canadian Centre for Justice Statistics, *Family Violence in Canada: A Statistical Profile 2008* (Ottawa: Public Health Agency of Canada, 2008).

Canadian Human Rights Commission, online: <http://www.chrc-ccdp.ca/default-eng.aspx>.

Canadian Press, "Prisoners on Remand Far Outnumber those Serving Sentences, StatsCan Says" (17 May 2011), online: <http://www.citytv.com/toronto/citynews/news/national/article/131522--prisoners-on-remand-far-outnumber-those-serving-sentences-statscan-says>.

Canadian Press. "Cloverdale Students Caught in Facebook Sex Contest" (21 May 2010) CTV News, online: <http://www.ctvbc.ctv.ca/servlet/an/local/CTVNews/20100521/bc_sex_contest_100521/20100521?hub=BritishColumbiaHome>.

CanLII, online: <http://www.canlii.org/en/index.php>.

Cardinal and Oswald v Director of Kent Institution, [1985] 2 SCR 643 (SCC).

Careless, James. "An Imprecise Science" (March 2011) Canadian Bar Association, online: <http://cbanational.rogers.dgtlpub.com/2011/2011-03-31/pdf/An_imprecise_science.pdf>.

Carlill v Carbolic Smoke Ball Company, [1893] 1 QB 256 (CA).

CBC News. "A Timeline of Residential Schools, the Truth and Reconciliation Commission," online: <http://www.cbc.ca/news/canada/story/2008/05/16/f-timeline-residential-schools.html>.

CBC News. "Alberta Judge Apologizes for Part of his Letter" (November 10, 2000), online: <http://www.cbc.ca/news/canada/story/1999/02/27/judge990227.html>.

CBC News. "Dr. Charles Smith: The Man Behind the Public Inquiry" (10 August 2010), online: <http://www.cbc.ca/news/canada/story/2009/12/07/f-charles-smith-goudge-inquiry.html>.

CBC News. "Nude Photos of Judge Contained in Complaint" (31 August, 2010), online: <http://www.cbc.ca/news/canada/manitoba/story/2010/08/31/judge-manitoba-douglas.html>.

CBC News. "Talula Does the Hula from Hawaii, 9, Gets Court-Ordered Name Change." online: <http://www.cbc.ca/news/world/story/2008/07/24/talula-nz-name.html>.

Change of Name Act, RSNB, Chapter C-2.001

Change of Name Act, RSNS 1989, c 66

Change of Name Act, RSNWT (Nu) 1988, c C-3.

Change of Name Act, RSO 1990, Chapter C.7

Change of Name Act, RSPEI, Chapter C-3.1

Change of Name Act, RSY 2000, c 28

The Change of Name Act, 1995, Chapter RSS, Chapter C-6.1

The Change of Name Act, CCSM c C50

The Class Proceedings Act, CCSM c C130

The Court, online: <http://www.thecourt.ca/>.

Chapman, Frances E, "Intangible Captivity: The Potential for a New Canadian Criminal Defense for Brainwashing and Its Implications for the Battered Woman" (2012) 28 *Berkeley Journal of Gender, Law & Justice* (upcoming publication).

Charter of Human Rights and Freedoms, RSQ c C-12.

City News. "The Questionable Cases of Dr. Charles Smith: A Review" (12 November 2007), online: <http://www.citytv.com/toronto/citynews/news/local/article/18225--the-questionable-cases-of-dr-charles-smith-a-review>.

Civil Code of Quebec, LRQ 1977, c C-25.

Civil Code of Quebec, LRQ, c C-1991, s 1471

Civil Code of Québec, SQ, 1991, c 64.

Civil Forfeiture Act, SBC 2005, Chapter 29

Civil Marriage Act, SC 2005, c 33

Civil Procedure Rules, R 20.03, 20.04 and 20.05

Claridge, Thomas. "Complaints Against Ontario Lawyers Jump Nine Per Cent" (4 March 2011) *The Lawyers Weekly.*

Claridge, Thomas. "Justice Cosgrove Pleads for his Job: Judge Delivered a Second Apology to the Full Council of Chief Justices in Toronto" (20 March 2009) *The Lawyers Weekly.*

Class Proceedings Act, 1992, SO 1992, c 6

Class Proceedings Act, RSBC 1996, c 50

Class Proceedings Act, SA 2003, c C-16.5

Class Proceedings Act, SNB 2006, c C-5.15

Class Actions Act, SNL 2001, c C-18.1

Class Proceedings Act, SNS 2007, c 28

Close, Charlene. "20-year-old Challenges Ontario's Zero-Alcohol Law for Young Drivers" (4 August 2010) 680 News, online: <http://www.680news.com/news/local/article/85164--20-year-old-challenges-ontario-s-zero-alcohol-law-for-young-drivers>.

Code of Professional Conduct, CBA, online: <http://www.cba.org/CBA/activities/pdf/codeofconduct.pdf>

Cojocaru (Guardian Ad Litem) v British Columbia Women's Hospital and Health Centre, [2011] BCJ No 680 (BC CA).

Cole, Simon A, and Rachel Dioso-Villa. "Investigating the 'CSI Effect' Effect: Media and Litigation Crisis in Criminal Law" (2009) 61 *Stanford Law Review* 1335.

Commission for Public Complaints Against the RCMP, online: <http://www.cpc-cpp.gc.ca/>.

Committee for Justice & Liberty v Canada (National Energy Board), [1978] 1 SCR 369 (SCC).

Commrs. of Customs and Excise v Harz, [1967] 1 AC 760.

Community Justice Initiatives of Waterloo Region, Kitchener, Ontario, online: <http://www.cjiwr.com/>.

Constitution Act, 1982, Schedule B to the *Canada Act 1982* (U.K.), 1982, c 11.

Contributory Negligence Act, RSA 2000, c C-27

Contributory Negligence Act, RSNB 1973, c C-19

Contributory Negligence Act, RSNL 1990, c C-33

Contributory Negligence Act, RSNS 1989, c 95

Contributory Negligence Act, RSNWT 1988, c C-18

Contributory Negligence Act, RSPEI 1988, c C-21

Contributory Negligence Act, RSS 1978, c C-31

Contributory Negligence Act, RSY 2002, c 42

Contributory Negligence Act, RSNWT (Nu.) 1988, c C-18

Controlled Drugs and Substances Act, SC 1996, c 19.

Cooligan, Katherine. "You've Got Mail: Snooping Emails, Privacy Law, and Admissibility of Evidence" (2011) *Ontario Bar Association* 26.

Corbett v Corbett, [1970] 2 All ER 33 (PDA).

Correctional Services Canada. "So You Want to Know the Recidivism Rate," http://www.csc-scc.gc.ca/text/pblct/forum/e053/e053h-eng.shtml.

Corrections Canada, "Corrections and Conditional Release Statistical Overview 2011," http://www.securitepublique.gc.ca/res/cor/rep/2011-ccrso-eng.aspx.

Courts of Justice Act, RS 1992, c s 106, class 2, s 160, s 181

Courts of Justice Act, RSO 1990, Chapter C.43.

Courts of Justice Act, RSQ, c T-16

Craik, Neil et al. *Public Law: Cases, Materials, and Commentary* (Toronto: Emond Montgomery, 2006).

Criminal Code, RSC 1985, c C-46, s 17; RSC 1985, c 27 (1st Supp.).

Crown Attorneys Act, RSO 1990, c C.49.

Cruz, Michael J. "Why Doesn't He Just Leave?" Gay Male Domestic Violence and the Reasons Victims Stay" (2003) The Journal of Men's Studies 1.

Cumming v Ince (1847), 116 ER 418 (QB).

Currency Act, RSC, 1985, c C-52.

Currie v Misa (1875), LR, 10 Exch. 153 at 162.

Darrow, Clarence. *Crime: Its Cause and Its Treatment* (New York: Kaplan, 2009).

Davidson, Lance S. *Ludicrous Laws and Mindless Misdemeanors: The Silliest Lawsuits and unruliest Rulings of All Times.* (Edison, New Jersey: Castle Books, 2004).

Declarations of Death Act, SO 2002, Chapter 14.

Defamation Act, CCSM c D20

Defamation Act, RSA 2000, c D-7

Defamation Act, RSNB 1973, c D-5

Defamation Act, RSNL 1990, c D-3

Defamation Act, RSNS 1989, c 122

Defamation Act, RSNWT 1988, c D-1

Defamation Act, RSNWT (Nu.) 1988, c D-1.

Defamation Act, RSPEI 1988, c D-5

Defamation Act, RSY 2002, c 52

Delgado, Richard. "Ascription of Criminal States of Mind: Toward a Defense Theory for the Coercively Persuaded ("Brainwashed") Defendant" in Michael Louis Corrado, ed, *Justification and Excuse in the Criminal Law, A Collection of Essays* (New York: Garland, 1994).

Department of Justice. "Fair and Effective Sentencing—A Canadian Approach to Sentencing Policy" (9 April 2009), online: <http://www.justice.gc.ca/eng/news-nouv/nr-cp/2005/doc_31690.html>.

Department of Justice. "Mandatory Sentences of Imprisonment in Common Law Jurisdictions: Some Representative Models" (8 January 2010), online: <http://www.justice.gc.ca/eng/pi/rs/rep-rap/2005/rr05_10/p2.html>.

Department of Justice. "Restorative Justice" (31 October 2010), online: <http://www.justice.gc.ca/eng/pi/pcvi-cpcv/res-rep.html>.

Department of Justice. "Unified Family Court, Summative Evaluation" (March 2009), online: < http://www.justice.gc.ca/eng/pi/eval/rep-rap/09/ufc-tuf/ufc.pdf>.

Department of Justice. "Victim Participation in the Plea Negotiation Process in Canada" (15 May 2011), online: <http://www.justice.gc.ca/eng/pi/rs/rep-rap/2002/rr02_5/d.html>.

Dershowitz, Alan. *Letters to a Young Lawyer* (New York: Basic Books, 2001).

Deserted Wives' and Children's Maintenance Act, RSO, 1937, c 211.

Deslisle, Ronald Joseph, and Don Stuart. *Learning Canadian Criminal Procedure*, 6th ed (Scarborough: ON: Carswell, 2000).

DFS Ventures Inc. v Manitoba (Liquor Control Commission), 2003 MBCA 33 (CA).

Divorce Act, RSC, 1985, c 3 (2nd Supp) D-3.4.

Dobson (Litigation Guardian of) v Dobson, [1999] SCJ No 41 (SCC).

Dodek, Adam M. "Canadian Legal Ethics: Ready for the Twenty-First Century at Last" (2008) 46 *Osgoode Hall Law Journal* 1.

Domestic Relations Act, RSA 2000, c D-14

Donoghue v Stevenson, [1932] AC 562 (HL).

DPP v Camplin, [1978] AC 705.

Dube v Labar, [1986] SCJ No 29 (SCC).

Dukelow, DA. *Dictionary of Canadian Law*, 3rd ed (Toronto: Thomson Carswell, 2004).

Dunlop v Major, [1998] OJ No. 2553 (Ont CA).

Eastwood v Kenyon (1840), 11 Ad & E 438, 113 ER 482 (QB).

Edwards v Canada (Attorney General), [1930] AC 124.

Eizenshtein v Eizenshtein (2008), 62 RFL (6th) 182 (Ont Sup Ct).

Ekstedt, John W, and Curt T Griffiths, *Corrections in Canada: Policy and Practice*, 2nd ed (Toronto: Butterworths, 1988).

Electronic Commerce Act, 2000 SO 2000, c 17

Electronic Commerce Act, RSPEI 1988, c E-4.1

Electronic Commerce Act, RSY 2002, c 66.

Electronic Commerce Act, S Nu 2004, c 7

Electronic Commerce Act, SNL 2001, c E-5.2

Electronic Commerce Act, SNS 2000, c 26

The Electronic Commerce and Information Act, CCSM c E55

Electronic Information and Documents Act, 2000, SS 2000, c E-7.22

Electronic Transactions Act, SA 2001, c E-5.5

Electronic Transactions Act, SBC 2001, c 10

Electronic Transactions Act, SNB 2001, c E-5.5

Embry, Jessie. *Mormon Polygamous Families* (Salt Lake City, UT: University of Utah Press, 1987).

Emergency Medical Aid Act, RSA 2000, c E-7

Emergency Medical Aid Act, RSNL 1990, c E-9

Emergency Medical Aid Act, RSNWT (Nu) 1988, c E-4

Emergency Medical Aid Act, RSNWT 1988, c E-4

Emergency Medical Aid Act, RSS 1978, c E-8

Emergency Medical Aid Act, RSY 2002, c 70.

Environmental Protection Act, RSO 1990, c E.19.

Errington v Errington and Woods, [1952] 1 KB 290 (CA).

Evidence Act, Alberta Evidence Act, 4(3)

Family Law Act (Nunavut) SNW 1997, c 18, *Family Law Act*, SPEI 1995, c 12

Family Law Act, RSNL 1990, c F-2

Family Law Act, RSO 1990, c F.3

Family Law Act, SA 2003, c F-4.5

Family Relations Act, RSBC 1996, Chapter 128.

Family Law Act, SNWT (Nu) 1997, c 18

Family Law Act, SNWT 1997, c 18

The Family Law Act, RSPEI 1988, c F-2.1

Family Maintenance Act, 1997, SS 1997, c F-6.2

Family Maintenance Act, CCSM c F20,

Family Services Act, SNB 1980, c F-2.2

Family Maintenance Act, RSNS 1989, c 465

Family Orders and Agreements Enforcement Assistance Act, RSC, 1985, c 4 (2nd Supp).

Family Property & Support Act, RSY 2002, c 83.

Family Property and Support Act, RSY 1986, c 63.

Family Relations Act, RSBC 1996, Chapter 128.

Family Relations Act, RSBC, 1996, c 128

Fasken Martineau. "2008 Litigation Trends in Canada," online: <http://www.fasken.com/files/FileControl/04da904b-f84e-4d9f-b2f4-0a8efcbb47e3/7483b893-e478-

44a4-8fed-f49aa917d8cf/Presentation/File/LTS_English_WEB.pdf>.

Federal Court Act, RSC, 1985, c F-7.

Federation of Law Societies of Canada (FLSC), online: <http://www.flsc.ca/en/about/about.asp>.

Feng v Sung Estate, [2004] OJ No. 4496 (Ont CA).

Firearms Act, SC 1995, c 39.

Fiske, Kenneth WF. "Sentencing Powers and Principles" in Joel E Pink and David C Perrier, eds, *From Crime to Punishment* (Toronto: Thomson Carswell, 2007).

Fitzgerald, Patrick, Barry Wright, and Vincent Kazmierski. *Looking at Law: Canada's Legal System,* 6th ed (Markham: ON: LexisNexis, 2010).

Foakes v Beer (1884), 9 App Cas 605 (HL).

Food and Drugs Act, RSC 1985, C.F-27.

Forest Practices Code of British Columbia Act, RSBC 1996, c 159.

Foucault, Michel. *Discipline and Punishment: The Birth of the Prison* (London: Penguin, 1977).

Fraser v Canada (Treasury Board), [1985] 1 SCR 441.

Fraser, Laura. "Sterilization: Choice, Right, or Requirement? A Comment on the Best Interests Test in *Re Eve*" (1998) 7 *Dalhousie Journal of Legal Studies* 163.

Fraser, Natalie. "The Case of the Cannabis Catapult." (13 May 2011) *The Lawyers Weekly*, online: <http://www.lawyersweekly-digital.com/lawyersweekly/3102?pg=17#pg17>.

Fraser, Natalie. "Unicyclist Fights Two-Wheel Rule" (10 June 2011) *The Lawyers Weekly*, online: <http://www.lawyersweekly-digital.com/lawyersweekly/3106#pg15>.

Frustrated Contract Act, RSBC 1996, c 166, s 7.

Frustrated Contracts Act, RSA 2000, c F-27, s 4

Frustrated Contracts Act, RSNB 1973, c F-24, s 3

Frustrated Contracts Act, RSNL 1990, c F-26, s 4

Frustrated Contracts Act, RSNWT (Nu) 1988, c F-12, s 4

Frustrated Contracts Act, RSNWT 1988, c F-12, s 4

Frustrated Contracts Act, RSO 1990, c F.3, s 3

Frustrated Contracts Act, RSPEI 1988, c F-16, s 3

Frustrated Contracts Act, RSY 2002, c 9, s 5

Frustrated Contracts Act, SS 1994, c F-22.2, s 6

Funston, Bernard W, and Eugene Meehan. *Canada's Constitutional Law in a Nutshell*, 2nd ed (Toronto: Carswell, 1998).

Gajamugan v Gajamugan (1979), 10 RFL (2d) 280 (Ont HC).

Gibb, Frances. "Actually, the Public Do Trust Lawyers ..." (31 March 2009) *Times Online*, online: <http://business.timesonline.co.uk/tol/business/law/article6010141.ece>.

Gibson, Dwight L, et al. *All About Law,* 5th ed (Toronto: Thomson Nelson, 2003).

Gill v Grant, [1998] BCJ No. 1705 (BCSC).

Glick, Leonard, and J Mitchell Miller. *Criminology,* 2nd ed (Boston: Pearson, 2008).

Glover v Canada Pension Plan, 2010 HRTO 1364 (Human Rights Tribunal of Ontario).

Gold, Alan D. *The Practitioner's Criminal Code* (Toronto: LexisNexis, 2008).

Goldthorpe v Logan, [1943] OWN 215, [1943] 2 DLR 519 (CA).

Good Samaritan Act, 2001, SO 2001, c 2

Good Samaritan Act, RSBC 1996, c 172

The Good Samaritan Protection Act, CCSM c G65

Green v US (1957), 355 US 184.

Greene, Ian. *The Courts* (Vancouver: UBC Press, 2006).

Grosman, Brian A. *The Prosecutor: An Inquiry into the Exercise of Discretion* (Toronto: University of Toronto Press, 1969).

Gudjonsson, GH, and JAC MacKeith. "False Confessions: Psychological Effects of Interrogation." A discussion paper. In A Trankel, ed, *Reconstructing the Past: The Role of Psychologists in Criminal Trials* (Deventer: Kluwer, 1982).

Hainsworth, Jeremy. "Donor Offspring Rights and Estate Law" (24 June 2011) *The Lawyers Weekly*, online: <http://www.lawyersweekly.ca/index.php?section=article&articleid=1446>.

Hainsworth, Jeremy. "Polygamous Society 'Consumes its Young,' says Crown." (15 April 2011) *The Lawyers Weekly*, online: <http://www.lawyersweekly-digital.com/lawyersweekly/3046?pg=14#pg14>.

Hall v Hebert, [1993] SCJ No. 51 (SCC).

Hamer v Sidway (1891), 124 NY 538, 27 NE 256 (CA NY).

Harper, Stephen, "*Citizen's Arrest and Self-Defence Act*" (17 February 2011) Prime Minister of Canada, online: <http://pm.gc.ca/eng/media.asp?id=3966>.

Hart, HLA, "Positivism and the Separation of Law and Morals" (1958) 71 *Harvard Law Review* 593.

Hausegger, Lori, Matthew Hennigar, and Troy Riddell, *Canadian Courts: Law, Politics and Process* (Don Mills, ON: Oxford, 2009).

Hawkin, William. *William Hawkin's Pleas of the Crown*, Vol 1 (London: Professional Books, 1716).

Henderson v Pearlman et al, [2009] OJ No 3444 (Ont SCJ).

Highway Act, RSNB 1973, c H-5

Highway Safety Code, RSQ, c C-24.2

Highway Traffic Act, CCSM c H60

Highway Traffic Act, RSNL 1990 Chapter H-3.

Highway Traffic Act, RSO 1990, c H.8

Highway Traffic Act, RSPEI 1988, c H-5

Hogan, Shanna. "Conditional Love: Despite Critics, Prenuptial Agreements More Popular and Outrageous than Ever" (March 2008) *Times Publications*, online: <http://www.shannahogan.com/?page_id=123>.

Horner, Jessie J. *Canadian Law and the Canadian Legal System* (Toronto: Pearson, 2007).

Hovius, Berend. *Family Law: Cases, Notes and Materials,* 6th student ed (Toronto: Thomson Carswell, 2005).

Human Rights Code RSBC 1996, c 210.

Iliescu v Voicegenie Technologies Inc., [2009] OJ No 85 (Ont SCJ) affirmed by *Iliescu v Voicegenie Technologies Inc.,* [2010] OJ No 480 (Ont CA).

Immigration and Refugee Board of Canada, online: <http://www.irb.gc.ca/eng/pages/index.aspx>.

Immigration and Refugee Protection Act, SC 2001, c 27.

Immigration and Refugee Protection Regulations, SOR /2002-227.

Institute of Marriage and Family Canada. "Canadian Divorce Statistics" (2 June 2010), online: <http://imfcanada.org/default.aspx?go=article&aid=1182&tid=8>.

Interpretation Act, RSC 1985, c I-21.

Interpretation Act, RSO 1990, c I11.

Jacobsen, Carol, Kammy Mizga, and Lynn D'Orio. "Battered Women, Homicide Convictions, and Sentencing: The Case for Clemency" (2007) 18 *Hastings Women's Law Journal* 31.

Johnson, Michael P. "Conflict and Control: Gender Symmetry and Asymmetry in Domestic Violence" (2006) 12 *Violence Against Women* 1003.

Johnson, Samuel. *Tour to the Hebrides* (15 August 1773).

Judicial Review Act, RSPEI 1988, c J-3

Judicial Review Procedure Act, RSBC 1996 c 241

Judicial Review Procedure Act, RSO 1990, c J.1

Juries Act RSO 1990, c C.43.

Jury Act, RSBC 2006, c 242.

Justice of Peace Act, RSNS 2000, c s 7

Justice of Peace Act, RSO 2009, c s 13, s 15, s 17

Justice of Peace Act, SS 1988, c J- 5.1. s 13, s 15

The Justice of Peace Act, RSA 1998, c s 6

Justice of Peace Regulation, CCSM 2006, c C275, s 5, s 11

Justice of the Peace Act, RSNWT 1988, c J-3, s 4

Justice of the Peace Act, SNWT 1998, c 34, s 2, s 7

Justices Act, RSNL 1990, c s 7

Kanitz v Rogers Cable Inc., [2002] OJ No 665 (Ont SCJ).

Kassin, Saul M, and Katherine L Kiechel. "The Social Psychology of false Confessions: Compliance, Internalization, and Confabulation" (1996) 7 *American Psychological Society* 125.

Kassin, Saul M. "False Confessions: Causes, Consequences, and Implications for Reform" (2008) 17 *Current Directions in Psychological Science* 249.

Kassin, SM, et al. "Police-Induced Confessions: Risk Factors and Recommendations" (2010) 34 *Law and Human Behavior* 3.

Kassin, SM. "Internalized False Confessions" in M Toglia, R Lindsay, D Ross, and J Read, eds, *Handbook of Eyewitness Psychology: Volume 1, Memory for Events* (Mahwah, NJ: Erlbaum, 2007).

Kassin, SM. "The Psychology of Confession Evidence" (1997) 52 *American Psychologist* 221.

Kauffman v T.T.C., [1959] OJ No 657 (Ont CA).

Kelly, Owen. "Lawyers and Depression: Three Case Studies" Canadian Bar Association, online: <http://www.cba.org/cba/practicelink/bwl/depression.aspx>.

Kenny v Schuster Real Estate Co., [1990] BCJ No. 1420 (BCSC).

Kerr, Margaret, et al. *Canadian Tort Law in a Nutshell,* 2nd ed (Toronto: Thomson Carswell, 2005).

Khan v The University of Ottawa, (1997), 2 Admin LR (3d) 298 (Ont CA).

King's College of Law, London, International Centre for Prison Studies. "Prison Brief—Highest to Lowest Rates" (18 March 2010), online: <http://www.kcl.ac.uk/depsta/law/research/icps/worldbrief/wpb_stats.php?area=all&category=wb_poprate>.

Knight v Indian Head School Division No. 19, [1990] 1 SCR 653 (SCC).

Knoll v Knoll, 1 RFL 141 (Ont Ca).

Koppel, Nathan. "Objection! Funny Legal Ads Draw Censure," *Wall Street Journal,* online: <http://online.wsj.com/article/SB120234229733949051.html>.

Kwan, Raymond. "Don't Dress Like a Slut: Toronto Cop. Excalibur, York University's Community Newspaper, online: <http://www.excal.on.ca/news/dont-dress-like-a-slut-toronto-cop/>.

Lavin McEleney, Barbara. *Correctional Reform in New York: The Rockefeller Years and Beyond* (New York: University Press of America, 1985).

Law School Admission Council, online: <http://www.lsac.org>.

Law Society Act, 1999, SNL 1999, c L-9.1

Law Society Act, RSM 1987, c L100

Law Society Act, RSO 1990, c L-8

Law Society Act, SNB 1996, c 89

Law Society of Alberta v Adams, [1997] LSDD No 157.

Law Society of British Columbia v Mangat [2001], 3 SCR 113 (SCC).

Law Society of Upper Canada v Boldt, [2006] OJ No 1142 (Ont SCJ).

Law Society of Upper Canada v Burgess, 2006 ONLSHP 0066 (Law Society Hearing Panel).

Law Society of Upper Canada: Bar Admissions Course. *Family Law* (Toronto: Law Society of Upper Canada, 2003).

Law Society of Upper Canada: Bar Admissions Course. *Public Law: Introduction and Overview,* Chapter 2 (Toronto: Law Society of Upper Canada, 2002).

Law Society of Upper Canada. "Diversity and Change: The Contemporary Legal Profession in Ontario," online: <http://rc.lsuc.on.ca/pdf/equity/diversityChange.pdf>.

Law Society of Upper Canada. "Final Report—Retention of Women in Private Practice Working Group," May 22, 2008.

Leduc v Roman, [2009] OJ No 681 (Ont SCJ).

Legal Profession Act, RSNS 2004, c 28

Legal Profession Act, RSNWT (Nu) 1988, c L-2.

Legal Profession Act, RSS 1990, c L-10.1

Legal Profession Act, RSY 2002, c 134 as amended by *An Act to Amend the Legal Profession Act*, SY 2004, c14

Legal Profession Act, SA 1990, c L-9.1

Legal Profession Act, SBC 1998 Chapter 9.

Legal Profession Act, SNWT 1988, c L-2

Legal Professions Act, SPEI 1992, c 39

Leo, Richard A, et al. "Bringing Reliability Back in: False Confessions and Legal Safeguards in the Twenty-First Century" (2006) *Wis L Rev* 484.

Leskun v Leskun, [2006] SCJ No 25 (SCC).

Lévis (Ville) c Tétreault (2006), 36 CR (6th) 215 (SCC).

Levy, Harold. "Foolish Pride or Malevolent Evil?" (June 2011) *Briefly Speaking.*

Licence Appeal Tribunal Act, SO 1999, c 12. Schedule G.

Lieb, Glynnis, et al, "The Alberta Legal Services Mapping Project: Final Report for the Calgary Judicial District" (Edmonton: Canadian Forum on Civil Justice, 2009), online: <http://cfcj-fcjc.org/docs/2011/mapping-final-en.pdf>.

Linden, Rick. *Criminology: A Canadian Perspective*, 6th ed (Toronto: Nelson, 2009).

Linden, Rick. *Criminology: A Canadian Perspective*, 7th ed (Toronto: Nelson, 2012).

Llewellyn, Karl. *The Bramble Bush* (New York: Oceana, 1960).

Lombroso, Cesare, and William Ferrero. *The Female Offender* (New York: Appleton, 1895).

Lombroso, Cesare. *Criminal Man*, translation and introduction by Mary Gibson, Nicole Hahn Rafter (North Carolina: Duke University Press, 2006).

M v H (1999), 46 RFL (4th) 32 (SCC).

M'Naghten's Case (1843), 10 Cl & Fin 200.

MacGuigan, Mark. *Report to Parliament, by the Sub-Committee on the Penitentiary System in Canada* (Ottawa: Government of Canada, 1977).

Maclennan v Maclennan, [1958] Sess Cas 105 (Scotland Ct Sess).

Mahmoodi v University of British Columbia (1999), 2001 BCSC 1256 (BCHRT).

Makin, Kirk. "The Dark Side of DNA" (13 March 2010) *The Globe and Mail*, online: <http://www.theglobeandmail.com/news/technology/science/the-dark-side-of-dna/article1499631/page3/>.

Malkin, Bonnie. "'Talula Does the Hula from Hawaii' Not a Girl's Name, New Zealand Court Rules," Telegraph.co.uk, online: <http://www.telegraph.co.uk/news/newstopics/howaboutthat/2452593/Talula-Does-The-Hula-From-Hawaii-not-a-girls-name-New-Zealand-court-rules.html>.

Malong v The Minister of Citizenship and Immigration, (2009) IAD File No: VA7-02330.

Manitoba Evidence Act, s 4.

Manitoba Pensions Commission, online: <http://www.gov.mb.ca/labour/pension/>.

Manitoba, Code of Professional Conduct, Law Society of Manitoba, online: <http://www.lawsociety.mb.ca/lawyer-regulation/code-of-professional-conduct/english-version>

Manitoba, Court of Queen's Bench Rules, Man Reg 553/88

Manning, Morris, and Peter Sankoff, *Manning, Mewett & Sankoff: Criminal Law*, 4th ed (Markham ON: Lexis Nexis, 2009).

Manson, Allan, Patrick Healy, and Gary Trotter. *Sentencing and Penal Policy in Canada: Cases, Materials, and Commentary* (Toronto: Emond Montgomery, 2000).

Marcon v Cicchelli (1993), 47 RFL (3d) 403 (Ont Gen Div).

Marital Property Act, CCSM c M45

Marital Property Act, SNB 1980, c M-1.1

Marriage (Prohibited Degrees) Act, SC 1990, c 46.

Marriage Act CCSM c M50, s 18

Marriage Act, RSA 2000, c M-5 s 17

Marriage Act, RSBC 1996, c 282, s 28

Marriage Act, RSNB c M-3, s 19

Marriage Act, RSNWT (Nu) 1988, c M-4, s 21

Marriage Act, RSNWT, 1988, c M-4, s 21

Marriage Act, RSO 1990, c M-3.

Marriage Act, RSO 1990, c M.3, s 5

Marriage Act, RSPEI 1988, Cap. M-3, s 17

Marriage Act, RSS, 1995 c M-4.1, s 25

Marriage Act, RSY 2002, c 146.

Martin, Sandra. "Stupid Judge Tricks: Why Do Our Upholders of Justice Go off the Rails?" (13 March 1999) *Globe and Mail*, online: <http://www.fact.on.ca/newpaper/gm99031d.htm>.

Matrimonial Property Act, 1997, c M-6.11

Matrimonial Property Act, RSA 2000, c M-8

Matrimonial Property Act, RSNS 1989, c 275

Maxwell v Stable, [1974] QB 523.

McArthur v Zaduk, 2001 CanLII 28143 (Ont SCJ).

McCormick, CT. *Handbook of the Law of Evidence*, 2nd ed (St. Paul, MN: West, 1972) at 316 cited in Saul M Kassin, "The Psychology of Confession Evidence" (1997) 52 *American Psychologist* 221.

McGillivray, Anne. "'A Moral Vacuity in her Which is Difficult if Not Impossible to Explain': Law, Psychiatry and the Remaking of Karla Homolka" (1998) 5 *International Journal of the Legal Profession* 255.

McIntosh v Metro Aluminum Products Ltd. and Zbigniew Augustynowicz 2011 BCHRT 34 (BC Human Rights Tribunal).

McNulty, Tim. "Boomer the Dog to Remain Gary Guy Mathews: Judge Denies Green Tree Man's Petition to Change his Name," post-gazette.com, online: <http://www.post-gazette.com/pg/10224/1079431-455.stm>.

McPhail v McPhail, 2001 BCCA 250 (BCCA).

Mercantile Law Amendment Act RSO 1990, c M.10.

Miller v Carley, 2009 CanLII 39065 (Ont SCJ).

Miller v F Mendel Holdings Ltd. (1984), 30 Sask R 298 (QB).

Miller, JR. "Troubled Legacy: A History of Native Residential Schools" (2003) *Saskatchewan Law Review* 357.

Minaker, Joanne, and Laureen Snider. "Husband Abuse: Equality with a Vengeance?" (2006) *Canadian Journal of Criminology and Criminal Justice* 754.

Minister of the Attorney General for Ontario, "Supporting Vulnerable Victims and their Families" (10 April 2011), online: <http://www.attorneygeneral.jus.gov.on.ca/english/news/2011/20110410-victims-nr.asp>.

Ministry of Transportation, online: <http://www.mto.gov.on.ca/english/about/bill126.shtml>.

MO v EN, [2004] BCJ No 2350 (BCPC).

Modernization of Obligations and Benefits Act, SC 2000, c 12.

Moge v Moge, [1992] 3 SCR 813 (SCC).

Monahan, Patrick J. *Constitutional Law,* 3rd ed (Toronto: Irwin Law, 2006).

Montreal Gazette. "Murderer of Mother Becomes Lawyer" (15 May 2007), Canada.com, online: <http://www.canada.com/story_print.html?id=f11fb441-1130-4371-8840-b714817cf88e&sponsor=>.

Moore v Bertuzzi, [2007] OJ No 5113 (Ont SCJ).

Morgan, EM. *Some Problems of Proof in the Anglo-American System of Litigation* (New York: Columbia University Press, 1956).

Morgan, Steven M. *Conjugal Terrorism—A Psychological and Community Treatment Model of Wife Abuse* (Palo Alto, CA: R and E Research, 1983) citing T Davidson, "Wifebeating: A Recurring Phenomenon Throughout History" in M Roy, ed, *Battered Women: A Psychological Study in Domestic Violence* (New York: Van Norstand Reinhold, 1977) 233.

Mosher v Benson, [2008] NSJ No 464 (NS Small Claims).

Moston, Stephen. "From Denial to Admission in Police Questioning of Suspects" in G Davies et al, eds, *Psychology, Law and Criminal Justice: International Developments in Research and Practice* (New York: de Gruyter, 1996).

Motherwell v Motherwell, [1976] AJ No 555 (Alta CA).

Motor Vehicle Act, RSBC 1996, c 318

Motor Vehicle Act, RSNS *1989 c 293*

Motor Vehicle Act, RSNWT (Nu) 1988, c M-16

Motor Vehicles Act, RSNWT 1988, c M-16

Motor Vehicles Act, RSY 2002, c 153.

Mullan, David J. *Administrative Law* (Toronto: Irwin Law, 2001).

Murdoch v Murdoch, [1975] 1 SCR 423 (SCC).

Murphy, Jeffrie G, and Jules L Coleman. *Philosophy of Law: An Introduction to Jurisprudence* (Boulder, CO: Westview, 1990).

MyWedding.com, "Ten Craziest Prenuptial Agreements," online: <http://www.mywedding.com/blog/planning/life-style/just-for-fun/ten-craziest-prenuptial-agreements/>.

Name Act, RSBC, 1996, c 328

Narcotics Control Act, RSC 1970, c N-1.

National Bank of Canada v Chace [1996] OJ No. 3251 (Ont SCJ).

National Post, "Justice Comes at Too High a Price: McLachlin," nation-alpost.com, online: <http://www.canada.com/nationalpost/news/story.html?id=54c6a41b-4d85-460f-a21f-524087fbcf2e&k=18398>.

Negligence Act, RSBC 1996, c 333

Negligence Act, RSO 1990, c N.1

New Brunswick Code of Professional Conduct, Law Society of New Brunswick, online: <http://www.lawsociety-barreau.nb.ca/assets/documents/CODEOFPROFESSIONALCONDUCT_February_2009.pdf>

New Brunswick, *Evidence Act,* ss 5 and 9

New Brunswick, Rules of Court, NB Reg 82-73

Newfoundland and Labrador, Rules of the Supreme Court, SNL 1986, c 42, Sch DR

Newfoundland Code of Professional Conduct, Adopted by Benchers, December 7, 1998. In Force, June 4, 1999.

Newfoundland, Code of Professional Conduct, online: <http://www.lawsociety.nf.ca/code/code.asp>

Newfoundland, *The Evidence Act,* ss 2 and 4(a)

Nichol v London (City) Police Services, [2003] OJ No 1857 (Ont SCJ).

Nind, Naomi. "Solving an "Appalling" Problem: Social Reformers and the Campaign for the Alberta *Sexual Sterilization Act,* 1928" (2000) 38 *Alberta Law Review* 536.

Nishnawbe Aski Nation v Eden, [2011] OJ No 988 (Ont CA).

Nix v Whiteside, 475 US 157 (1986) (United States Supreme Court).

Norberg v Wynrib, [1992] SCJ No 60 (SCC).

Northwest Territories and Nunavut, Rules of the Supreme Court, NWT Reg 010-96

Northwest Territories uses the CBA's code of professional conduct but also has *Legal Profession Act*, online: <http://www.justice.gov.nt.ca/Legislation/..%5CPDF%5CACTS%5CLegal%20Profession.pdf>

Northwest Territories, *Evidence Act,* s 4(2)

Nova Scotia Alcohol and Gaming Commission, online: <http://www.gov.ns.ca/lae/agd/liquor.asp>.

Nova Scotia, *Evidence Act,* ss 45 and 48

Nova Scotia, Judicature Act, RSNS 1989, c 240

Nova Scotia, *Legal Ethics Handbook*, Nova Scotia Barristers' Society, online: <http://www.nsbs.org/legalethics/toc.htm>

Nucleix Ltd., online: <http://www.nucleix.com/pdf/Press_Release_Technology.pdf>.

Nunavut, Rules of the Law Society of Nunavut, online: <http://lawsociety.nu.ca/act_and_rules/2009%2005%2002%20_%20Con_Rules.pdf>

The Nunavut Judicial System Implementation Act, SNWT 1998, c 34

O'Connor, Joe, "Do a Tube Top and High Heels say, 'Go Ahead, Rape Me?'"

(24 February 2011) *National Post*, online: <http://fullcomment.nationalpost.com/2011/02/24/joe-oconnor-do-a-tube-top-and-high-heels-say-go-ahead-rape-me/>.

O'Sullivan, Mary Catherine. *The Sacrifice of the Guilty: The Importance of Narrative Resonance in Understanding Criminal Justice and Media Responses to Aberrant Offenders* (North York ON: Osgoode, 1996) [unpublished].

Oakes, Gary "BC Landlord's Home Seized for Housing Marijuana Grow-Op," *Lawyers Weekly*, http://www.lawyersweekly-digital.com/lawyersweekly/3040?pg=9#pg9.

Oakes, Gary, "Trial Decision Overturned for Plagiarism" (29 April 2011) *The Lawyers Weekly*, 2.

Occupiers' Liability Act, RSA 2000, c O-4

Occupiers' Liability Act, RSBC 1996,c 337

Occupiers' Liability Act, RSO 1990, c O.2

Occupiers' Liability Act, RSPEI 1988, c O-2

Occupiers' Liability Act, SNS 1996, c 27

The Occupiers' Liability Act, CCSM c O.8

Olah, John A. *The Art and Science of Advocacy* (Toronto: Carswell, 1990).

Olivio, Laurence. *Introduction to Law In Canada* (Concord ON: Captus Press, 1995).

Olivo, Laurence M. *Introduction to Law in Canada.* (Concord ON: Captus Press, 2006).

Ontario Civil Legal Needs Project, *Listening to Ontarians* (Toronto: Ontario Civil Legal Needs Project Steering Committee, 2010), online: <http://www.lsuc.on.ca/media/may3110_oclnreport_final.pdf>.

Ontario Lawyers Assistance Plan. "Annual Report: 2010," online: <http://www.olap.ca/ANNUAL%20REPORT%202010_V2.pdf>.

Ontario Minister of Finance, online: <http://www.fin.gov.on.ca/en/publications/salarydisclosure/2010/judiciary10.html>.

Ontario Ministry of the Attorney General, *Ontario Law Reform Commission, Report on Amendment of the Law of Contract* (Toronto: ON, Ministry of the Attorney General, 1987).

Ontario, *Evidence Act*, s 8, and *The Provincial Offences Act*, ss 46(5)

Ontario, Law Society of Upper Canada, online: <http://www.lsuc.on.ca/WorkArea/DownloadAsset.aspx?id=10272>

Osborne, Coulter A, *Civil Justice Reform Project* (Toronto: Ministry of the Attorney General, 2007), online: <http://www.attorneygeneral.jus.gov.on.ca/english/about/pubs/cjrp/090_civil.asp>.

Osborne, Philip H. *The Law of Torts* (Toronto: Irwin Law, 2000).

Oxaal, Zoe. "'Removing That Which Was Indian from the Plaintiff': Tort Recovery for Loss of Culture and Language in Residential Schools Litigation," (2005) 68 *Saskatchewan Law Review* 367.

P.E.I., Code of Professional Conduct, Law Society of P.E.I., online: <http://www.lspei.pe.ca/ethics_and_code.php>

Paciocco, David, and Lee Stuesser, *The Law of Evidence*, 2nd ed (Toronto: Irwin, 1999).

Packer v Packer, [1953] 2 All ER 127 (CA).

Palsgraf v Long Island Ry. Co. (1928), 248 NY 339 (NYCA).

Pao On v Lau Yiu Long, [1980] AC 614 (PC).

Parental Responsibility Act, SBC 2001, c 45; *Parental Responsibility Act*, 2000, SO 2000, c 4; *The Parental Responsibility Act*, 1996, CCSM c P8.

Parker, Shane G. "Solicitor/Client Privilege" in Joel E Pink and David C Perrier, *From Crime to Punishment*, 6th ed (Toronto: Thomson Carswell, 2007).

Parole Board of Canada, online: <http://www.pbc-clcc.gc.ca/index-eng.shtml>.

Paul v British Columbia (Forest Appeals Commission), [2003] SCJ No 34 (SCC).

Paxton et al *v Ramji* (2008), 92 OR (3d) 401 (Ont CA).

Payne, Julien D, and Marilyn A Payne. *Canadian Family Law*, 3rd ed (Toronto: Irwin Law, 2008).

Pearce v Brooks [1861–1873] All ER Rep 102 (C Ex).

Pearson, Patricia. *When She Was Bad: Violent Women and the Myth of Innocence* (Toronto: Random House, 1997).

Personal Information Protection and Electronic Documents Act (PIPEDA), SC 2000, c 5.

Pink, Joel E, and David C Perrier. *From Crime to Punishment*, 6th ed (Toronto: Thomson Carswell, 2007).

Pirie, Andrew J. *Alternative Dispute Resolution: Skills, Science, and the Law* (Toronto: Irwin Law, 2000).

Podlas, Kimberlianne. "'The CSI Effect': Exposing the Media Myth" (2006) 15 *Fordham Intellectual Property Media & Entertainment Law Journal* 429.

Pratten v British Columbia, (Attorney General), [2011] BCJ No. 931 (BCSC).

Prince Edward Island, Supreme Court Act, RSPEI 1988, c S-10, Rules of Civil Procedure

Professional Code, RSQ, c C-26

Proulx, Michel, and David Layton. *Ethics and Canadian Criminal Law* (Toronto: Irwin Law, 2001).

Provincial Court Act, 1991 SNL 1991, c 15

Provincial Court Act, CCSM c C275

Provincial Court Act, RSA 2000, c P-31

Provincial Court Act, RSBC 1996, c 379

Provincial Court Act, RSBC 1996, c s 30, s 31

Provincial Court Act, RSNB 1973, c P-21

Provincial Court Act, RSNB 1973, c s 4, s 8, s 13

Provincial Court Act, RSNS 1989, c 238

Provincial Court Act, RSPEI 1988, c P-25

Provincial Court Act, RSPEI 1988, c s 14

The Provincial Court Act, SS 1998, c P-30.11

Quebec Charter of Human Rights and Freedoms, RSQ c C-12.

Quebec, Barreau du Québec, online: <http://www.barreau.qc.ca/?Langue=en>

R v AM, [2008] SCJ No 19 (SCC).

R v Ancio, [1984] 1 SCR 225 (SCC).

R v Askov, [1990] 2 SCR 1199 (SCC).

R v Aussem, [1997] OJ No 5582 (Ont CJ).

R v Barron, [1985] OJ No. 231 (Ont CA).

R v Bleta, [1964] SCR 561 (SCC).

R v Brown, [2006] PEIJ No 44 (PEI Sup Ct App).

R v Buzzanga and Durocher, [1979] OJ No 4345 (Ont CA).

R v Castro, 2010 ONCA 718 (Ont CA).

R v Chamandy (1934), 61 CCC 224 (Ont CA).

R v Chan (2003), 178 CCC (3d) 269 (Ont CA).

R v Chaulk, [1990] 3 SCR 1303 (SCC).

R v Chen, [2010] OJ No 5741 (Ont CJ).

R v Cline (1956), 118 CCC 18 (Ont CA).

R v Collins, [2011] OJ No 978 (Ont CA).

R v Cornell, [2010] SCJ No 31 (SCC).

R *v Daviault*, [1994] 3 SCR 63 (SCC).

R v Delisle (1999), 133 CCC (3d) 541 (Que CA).

R v Deutsch, [1986] SCJ No 44 (SCC).

R v Drummond, [1996] OJ No 4597 (Ont CJ).

R v Dudley & Stephens (1884), 14 QBD 273 (CCR).

R v Ekman, [2006] SCCA No. 339 (SCC).

R v Fagan, [1968] 2 All ER 442 (QB Div).

R v Feeney (1997), 146 DLR (4th) 609 (SCC).

R v Field, [2011] AJ No 122 (ABCA).

R v Fontaine, [2002] MJ No 363 (Man CA).

R v Fraser, [2002] NSJ No 401(NS PC).

R v Goltz, [1991] 3 SCR 485 (SCC).

R v Greyeyes, [1997] SCJ No 72 (SCC).

R v Hamilton, [2005] SCJ No 48 (SCC).

R v Harding,[2001] OJ No 4953 (Ont CA).

R v Harrison, [2008] OJ No 427 (SCC).

R v Hawkins, [1996] 111 CCC (3d) 129 (SCC).

R v Hibbert, [1995] 2 SCR 973 (SCC).

R v Howe & Burke, [1987] AC 417 (HL).

R v Hundal, [1993] 1 SCR 867 (SCC).

R v Kagan (2009), 276 NSR (2d) 381 (NS CA).

R v Kulbacki, [1965] MJ No 9 (Man CA).

R v Lachance, [1963] 2 CCC 14 (Ont CA).

R v Ladue, [1965] 4 CCC 264 (YT CA).

R v Laliberté, [2000] SJ No 138 (Sask CA).

R v Lamb, [1967] 2 QB 981 (CA).

R v Latimer, [2001] 1 SCR 3 (SCC).

R v Laurencelle (1999), 28 CR (5th) 157 (BC CA).

R v Lavallee, [1990] SCJ No 36 (SCC).

R v Li, [1993] BCJ No 2312 (BC CA).

R v Lotufo, [2008] OJ No 2894 (Ont SCJ).

R v Luedecke [2008] OJ No 4049 (Ont CA).

R v Mack, [1988] SCJ No 91 (SCC).

R v Malfara (2006), 211 OAC 200 (Ont CA).

R v Malone (1984), 11 CCC (3d) 34.

R v Malot, [1996] OJ No 3511 (Ont CA).

R v Manley, 2001 ONCA 128 (Ont CA).

R v McCraw, [1991] 3 SCR 72 (SCC).

R v McRae, [2005] OJ No 3200 (Ont CA).

R v MLC, [2010] OJ No 5310 (Ont CA).

R v Morris, [1981] AJ No 561, 61 CCC (2d) 163 (Alta QB).

R v MPD, [2003] BCJ No 771 (BC Prov Ct).

R v Murray (2000), 144 CCC (3d) 289 (Ont SCJ).

R v Nahar (2004), 181 CCC (3d) 449 (BCCA).

R v Nelson, [1953] BCJ No 98 (BCCA).

R v Nevin, [2006] NSJ No 235 (NS CA).

R v Oakes, [1986] 1 SCR 103 (SCC).

R v Oickle, [2000] 2 SCR 3 (SCC).

R v Oluwa (1996), 107 CCC (3d) 236 (BC CA).

R v Oommen, [1994] SCJ No 60 (SCC).

R v Pake, [1995] AJ No 1152 (Alta CA).

R v Parks, [1992] 2 SCR 871 (SCC).

R v Perka, [1984] SCJ No 40 (SCC).

R v Perrigo (1972), 10 CCC (2d) 336 (Ont Dist Ct).

R v Phillion, [2009] OJ No 849, 2009 ONCA 202 (Ont CA).

R v Ramage, [2010] OJ No 2970 (Ont CA).

R v Rhodes, [2011] MJ No 67 (Man Ct QB).

R v Romas, [2002] BCJ No 3256 (B.C. Prov. Ct.).

R v Ruzic, [2001] SCJ No 25 (SCC).

R v Ryan (1967), 40 ALJR 488 (Aus HC).

R v Salvador (1981), 21 CR (3d) (NSCA).

R v Sansregret, [1985] 1 SCR 570 (SCC).

R v Sault Ste. Marie (1978), 85 DLR (3d) 161 (SCC).

R v Scott, [1964] 2 CCC 257 (Alta CA).

R v Sellars,[1980] 1 SCR 527 (SCC).

R v Shanks, [1996] OJ No. 4386 (Ont CA).

R v Smith, [2000] 4 All ER 289.

R v Sorrell & Bondett (1978), 41 CCC (2d) 9 (Ont CA).

R v Stone, [1999] SCJ No 27 (SCC).

R v Sussex Justices, Ex Parte McCarthy, [1924] 1 KB 256.

R v Thibert, [1996] 1 SCR 37 (SCC).

R v Tolson (1889), 23 QBD 168.

R v Tran, [2010] SCJ No 58 (SCC).

R v Tse, [2012] SCJ No 16 (SCC)

R v Whittle (1994), 32 CR (4th) 1 (SCC).

R v Wholesale Travel Group Inc., [1991] 3 SCR 154 (SCC).

Rabson, Mia. "Outcry Grows Against Manitoba Judge who Did not Jail Rapist" (25 February 2011) *National Post*, online: <http://news.nationalpost.com/2011/02/25/outcry-grows-against-manitoba-judge-who-did-not-jail-rapist/>.

Railway Coastal Museum, online: <http://www.railwaycoastalmuseum.ca/end.htm>.

Rakus v Piccolo, [1989] OJ No 2435 (Ont Gen Div).

Ralston v Fomich, [1992] BCJ No 463 (BC Sup Ct).

Ramsland, Katherine. *The C.S.I. Effect* (New York, Penguin: 2006).

Rappaport, Michael. "Nobody Likes a Lawyer Until they Need One" (2008) *Lawyers Weekly*.

Ratych v Bloomer (1990), 30 CCEL 161(SCC).

Re Reitzel and Rej-Cap Manufacuring Ltd (1985), 53 OR (2d) 116 (HC).

Redlich, AD, and C Meissner. "Techniques and Controversies in the Interrogation of Suspects: The Artful Practice versus the Scientific Study," in JL Skeem, K Douglas, and S Lilienfeld, eds, *Psychological Science in the Courtroom: Controversies and Consensus* (New York, NY: Guilford, 2009).

Reference Re Firearms Act (Canada), [2000] 1 SCR 783 (SCC).

Reference Re Section 94(2) of the Motor Vehicle Act, [1985] 2 SCR 486 (SCC).

Reference Re Validity of x. 5(a) of Dairy Industry Act (Canada), [1949] SCR 1.

Reference re: Criminal Code of Canada (B.C.), [2011] BCJ No 2211 (BCSC).

Rex v Arnold 16 Howell's State Trials 695 (10 George I. A.D. 1724).

Robertson, Grant. "Comma Quirk Irks Rogers" *Globe and Mail* (8 June 2006).

Rogler v Rogler (1977), 1 RFL (2d) 398 (Ont HC).

Roncarelli v Duplessis, [1959] SCR 121 (SCC).

Rothman, DJ. *The Discovery of the Asylum: Social Order and Disorder in the New Republic* (Hawthorne, NY: Little Brown, 1971).

Ruby, Clayton. "The Shame of Legal Aid Ontario," *Lawyers Weekly*, online: <http://www.lawyersweekly.ca/index.php?section=article&articleid=1355>.

Rudder v Microsoft Corp. [1999] OJ No 3778 (SCJ).

Rules of Civil Procedure RRO 1990, Regulation 194

Rushton v Rushton (1969), 1 RFL 215 (BCSC).

Sale of Goods Act, CCSM c S10

Sale of Goods Act, RSA 2000, c S-2

Sale of Goods Act, RSNB 1973, c S-1

Sale of Goods Act, RSNL 1990, c S-6

Sale of Goods Act, RSNS 1989, c 408

Sale of Goods Act, RSNWT 1988, c S-2

Sale of Goods Act, RSNWT (Nu) 1988, c S-2

Sale of Goods Act, RSO 1990, c S.1

Sale of Goods Act, RSPEI 1988, c S-1

Sale of Goods Act, RSS 1978, c S-1

Sale of Goods Act, RSY 2002, c 198.

Saskatchewan Evidence Act, 35(1) and (2) and Yukon Territory, *Evidence Act*, s 8, Prince Edward Island, *Evidence Act*, s 4

Saskatchewan Queen's Bench Rules.

Saskatchewan, Law Society of Saskatchewan Code of Professional Conduct, online: <http://www.lawsociety.sk.ca/newlook/Publications/Code2003/CodeCompleteNov03.pdf>

Saskatchewan, Queen's Bench Act, RSS 1978, c Q-1, *Queen's Bench Rules, R 214 and Quebec, Code of Civil Procedure*, RSQ c C-25.

Savirimuthu, Joseph. "Online Contract Formation: Taking Technological Infrastructure Seriously" (2005) 2:1 *UOLTJ* 105.

Scheck, Barry et al. "False Confessions" Innocence Project, online: <http://www.innocenceproject.org/understand/False-Confessions.php>.

Scheflin, Alan W, and Edward M Opton. *The Mind Manipulators: A Non-Fiction Account* (New York: Paddington, 1978).

Schiltz, Patrick. "Those Unhappy, Unhealthy Lawyers" (Autumn 1999) *Notre Dame Magazine 7.*

Schneider, Elizabeth M. "Feminism and the False Dichotomy of Victimization and Agency" (1993) 38 *NYL Sch L Rev* 387.

Schram, Jamie. "Suit: My Boss' Voice Made Me Vomit" (15 February 2011) *New York Post*, online: <http://www.nypost.com/f/print/news/local/manhattan/suit_says_boss_pure_heave_il_kn63ZJzLT86dgGMMu85dqO>.

Schuller, Regina A, and Gwen Jenkins. "Expert Evidence Pertaining to Battered Women: Limitations and Reconceptualizations" in Mark Costanzo, Daniel Krauss and Kathy Pezdek, eds, *Expert Psychological Testimony for the Courts* (Mahwah: NJ, Lawrence Erlbaum, 2007) 203.

Schuller, Regina, and Sara Rzepa. "The Scientific Status of Research on Domestic Violence Against Women" in David L Faigman et al, eds, *Modern Scientific Evidence: The Law and Science of Expert Testimony* (St. Paul MN: West, 2002).

Serra v Serra, [2009] OJ No 432 (Ont CA).

Sexual Sterilization Act, SA 1928, c 37.

Shakespeare, William. *King Henry VI*, Act IV, Scene II.

Sherrin, Christopher. "False Confessions and Admissions in Canadian Law." (2004) 30 *Queen's Law Journal* 615.

Simpson, AWB. *Cannibalism and the Common Law: The Story of the Tragic Last Voyage of the Mignonette and the Strange Legal Proceedings to Which It Gave Rise* (Chicago: University of Chicago Press, 1984).

Skoke-Graham v R, [1988] 1 SCR 513 (SCC).

Slayton, Philip. *Lawyers Gone Bad: Money, Sex and Madness in Canada's Legal Profession* (London: Penguin, 2007).

Smith v Jones, [1999] SCJ NO. 15 (SCC).

Smith v Leech Brain & Co., [1962] 2 QB 405.

Smith, Joanna. "Statistics Canada to Stop Tracking Divorce Rates" (20 July 2011) *Toronto Star*, online: <http://www.thestar.com/news/canada/politics/article/1027273--statistics-canada-to-stop-tracking-divorce-rates>.

Smyth, JE, DA Soberman, and AJ Easson. *The Law and Business Administration in Canada* (Toronto: Pearson Prentice Hall, 2007).

Solemnization of Marriage Act, RSNL 1990, c S-19, s 12

Solemnization of Marriage Act. RSNS, c 436, s 1

Solomon, Robert M, et al. *Cases and Materials on the Law of Torts* (Toronto: Carswell, 1996).

Sorrells v United States, 287 US 435 (1932).

Southwark London Borough Council v Williams, [1971] 1 Ch 734.

Spencer v Rozon et al. 2000 BCSC 674 (BCSC).

Spencer, Beverley. "Lessons from the Phantom of Heilbronn: Why DNA Evidence is Losing its Lustre" (March 2001) Canadian Bar Association.

Spousal Relationships Statute Law Amendment Act, SO 2005, c 5; *Support and Custody Orders Enforcement Act*, SO 1996, Chapter 31; *Family Maintenance Enforcement Act*, RSBC 1996, Chapter 127; *Maintenance Enforcement Act*, RSA 2000, c M-1; *Maintenance Enforcement Act*, SNS 1994-95, c 6.

Statistics Canada. "2006 Census: Family Portrait: Continuity and Change in Canadian Families and Households in 2006" (20 November 2009), online: <http://www12.statcan.ca/census-recensement/2006/ref/dict/fam007-eng.cfm>.

Statistics Canada. "Population Projections by Aboriginal Identity in Canada, 2011," online: <http://www.statcan.gc.ca/daily-quotidien/111207/dq111207a-eng.htm>.

Statistics Canada. *Legal Aid in Canada*, online: <http://dsp-psd.tpsgc.gc.ca/Collection-R/Statcan/85-217-XIB/0000185-217-XIB.pdf>.

Statute of Frauds, 1677 Chapter 3 29 Chapter 2, from 1677.

Statutory Powers Procedure Act, RSO 1990, c S.22.

Stenning, Phillip C. *Appearing for the Crown* (Toronto: Brown Legal Publications, 1986).

Stergios v Kim, [2010] OJ No 3299 (Ont SCJ).

Stewart v Pettie, [1995] SCJ No 3 (SCC).

Stone, Richard. *The Modern Law of Contract*, 8th ed (London: Routledge Cavendish, 2009).

Stuart, Don, RJ Delisle, and Steve Coughlan. *Learning Canadian Criminal Law*, 10th ed (Scarborough, ON: Toronto, 2006).

Supreme Court Act, RSC 1985, c S-26.

Sutherland, Kate. *Tort Law: Cases and Materials* (Toronto: Osgoode Hall, 2007).

Swan, Angela. *Canadian Contract Law*, 2nd ed (Markham, ON: LexisNexis, 2009).

Szarfer v Chodos, [1986] OJ No 256 (Ont HCJ).

Szasz, Thomas. "Psychiatry, Ethics and the Criminal Law" (1958) 58 *Columbia Law Review* 183.

Tarantino, Bob. *Under Arrest: Canadian Laws You Won't Believe* (Toronto: Dundurn, 2007).

Tercon Contractors Ltd. v British Columbia, 2010 SCC 4 (SCC).

Territorial Court Act, RSNWT, 1988, c T-2

Territorial Court Act, RSY 2002, c 217.

Territorial Court Act, RSY 2002, c s 79.

Terry v Mullowney, [2009] NJ No 86 (Nfld & LSC).

Tesler, Pearl. "Shadows of Doubt: CSI Science Isn't as Solid as the TV Shows Lead Us to Believe" (2010) *Current Science* 95.

Thomas v Thomas (1842), 2 QB 851, 114 ER 330.

Thornton (Next Friend of) v Prince George School District No 57 [1978] SCR No 7 (SCC).

Tibbetts, Janice, and Shawn Ohler. "Judges Clash Over Landmark Sex-Assault Ruling: No Definitely Means No: Supreme Court Judge Castigated for 'Graceless Slide into Personal Invective'" *National Post*, online: <http://www.fact.on.ca/newpaper/np990226.htm>.

Time. "Jonathan Parker Is ... Allegedly Breaking into a House" (30 November 2009), online: <http://www.time.com/time/specials/packages/article/0,28804,1943680_1943678_1943557,00.html>.

Time. "Saved by a Status Update" (30 November 2009), online: http://www.time.com/time/specials/packages/article/0,28804,1943680_1943678_1943652,00.html>.

Tjaden, Ted. *Legal Research & Writing*, 2nd ed (Toronto: Irwin Law, 2004).

Topping, Alexandra. "Fugitive Caught after Updating His Status on Facebook" (14 October 2009), Guardian.co.uk, online: <http://www.guardian.co.uk/technology/2009/oct/14/mexico-fugitive-facebook-arrest/print>.

Traffic Safety Act, RSA 2000, c T-6

Tortfeasors and Contributory Negligence Act, CCSM c T90.

Traffic Safety Act, SS 2004, c T-18.1

Tuckiar v R (1934), 52 CLR 335 (HC Australia).

Tyler, Tracey, "Prominent Guelph Lawyer Disbarred for Misconduct" (12 September 2007) *Toronto Star*, online: <http://www.thestar.com/News/Ontario/article/255631>.

Tyler, Tracey. "Cosgrove Resigns Ahead of Ouster" (3 April 2009), *Toronto Star*, online: <http://www.thestar.com/article/612960>.

Tyler, Tracey. "Judge's Peers Want him Off the Bench" (1 April 2009), *Toronto Star*, online: <http://www.thestar.com/article/611546>.

Uniform Electronic Commerce Act (UECA).

United States v Holmes, 26 F Cas 360 (1842).

United States v Russell (1973), 411 US 428.

Universe Tankships of Monrovia v International Transport Workers' Federation, [1983] 1 AC 366, 400 (HL).

Van Ness, D. "Pursuing a Restorative Vision of Justice" at in, *Justice: The Restorative Vision, New Perspectives on Crime and Justice*, Occasional papers of MCC Canada/U.S. February 1989.

Veninot v Kerr-Addison Mines Ltd., [1975] 2 SCR 311 (SCC).

Verdun-Jones, SN. *Criminal Law in Canada: Cases, Questions & the Code*, 5th ed (Toronto: Nelson, 2011).

Victims of Violence. "Research—Plea Bargaining" (28 February 2011), online:

<http://www.victimsofviolence.on.ca/rev2/index.php?option=com_content&task=view&id=378&Itemid=197>.

Volokh, Eugene. "Talula Does the Hula from Hawaii And Other Names So Weird that Judges Forbade Them" *Slate*, online: <http://www.slate.com/id/2196204/pagenum/all/#p2>.

Volunteer Services Act, RSNS 1989, c 497

Waddams, SM. *Introduction to the Study of Law*, 5th ed (Toronto: Thompson 1997).

Waddams, SM. *The Law of Contracts*, 4th ed (Toronto: Canada Law Book, 1999).

Waisberg, Deena. "Battling the CSI Effect" (April 2001) *Canadian Lawyer*, online: <http://www.waisberg.ca/article_life_csi.html>.

Wakefield, H, and R Underwager. "Coerced or Nonvoluntary Confessions" (1998) *Behavioral Sciences and the Law* 423.

Wakefield, Hollida, and Ralph Underwager, "Coerced or Nonvoluntary Confessions" (1998) 16 *Behavioral Sciences and the Law* 423.

Walford v Jacuzzi Canada Ltd, 2007 ONCA 729 (Ont CA).

Walker, Lenore E. *The Battered Woman*, (New York: Harper & Row, 1979).

Walker, Lenore. *The Battered Woman Syndrome* (New York: Springer, 1984).

Wang v HMTQ (2006) BCSC 2001 (SCBC).

Ward v Byham, [1956] 1 WLR 496.

Ware's Taxi Ltd. v Gilliham, [1949] SCR 637 (SCC).

Watkins v Watkins (1980), 14 RFL (2d) 97 (Nfld TD).

Watmough v Cap's Construction Ltd, 1976 CanLII 268 (AB QB).

Watson, Garry D, et al. *The Civil Litigation Process: Cases and Materials*, 5th ed (Toronto: Emond Montgomery, 1999).

White, Rob, Fiona Haines, and Lauren Eisler. *Crime and Criminology, An Introduction*. Canadian ed (Don Mills ON: Oxford, 2004).

Whiten v Pilot Insurance Co., [2002] 1 SCR 595 (SCC).

Wickberg v Patterson (1997), 145 DLR (4th) 263 (Alta CA).

Wilkinson v Downton, [1897] 2 QB 57.

Williams v Carwardine (1833), 4B & Ad. 621, 110 ER 590 (KB).

Williams, Glanville. *Learning the Law*. 11th ed (London: Stevens, 1982).

Wilson, Colin. *A Criminal History of Mankind* (London: Mercury, 2005).

Wise, Jenny, "Providing the CSI Treatment: Criminal Justice Practitioners and the CSI Effect." (2010) 21 *Current Issues in Criminal Justice* 383

Wojna, Lisa. *Weird Canadian Laws: Strange, Bizarre, Wacky & Absurd.* (Toronto, Blue Bike Books, 2006).

Wolfgang, Marvin E. "Cesare Lombroso," in Hermann Mannheim, ed, *Pioneers in Criminology* (Montclair, NJ: Patterson Smith, 1972).

Woolley, Alice, Richard Devlin, Brent Cotter, and John M Law. *Lawyers' Ethics and Professional Regulation* (Markham, ON: LexisNexis, 2008).

Worker's Compensation Act, RSA 2000 c W-15.

Yates, Richard A, Ruth Whidden Yates, and Penny Bain. *Introduction to Law in Canada*, 2nd ed (Scarborough, ON: Prentice Hall, 2000).

Yukon Forest Commission, online: <http://www.emr.gov.yk.ca/forestry/>.

Yukon, Code of Professional Conduct, Law Society of Yukon, online: <http://www.lawsocietyyukon.com/pdf/codeofconduct10.pdf>.

Zerr, H. *Changing Lenses: A New Focus for Crime and Justice* (Scottsdale, PA: Herald Press, 1990).

Glossary

Abandonment: the giving up of an action by the parties with no intention of claiming anything in the future. This may occur because the plaintiff no longer has money or because of the emotional toll of this onerous litigation process. (72)

Abettor: a person who encourages another to commit a crime. (242)

Absolute liability offences: violations of law where proof of a guilty mind is not necessary; only the act is important. (249)

Access: the ability to go and visit one's child in the care of someone else, although custody of a child has been given to another person. (179)

Acrimonious: bitter or contentious. (170)

Actionable: capable of sustaining a proceeding in court. (25)

***Actus reus*:** the voluntary act, whether by act or omission, that is the basis of a criminal offence. (230)

Administrative tribunal: a body where a legal matter is heard, but is outside of the traditional court system. (185)

Admissible: relevant and allowed by the court. The decision of the judge whether relevant evidence may be received by the court to help the fact-finder resolve the inquiry. (227)

Adultery: voluntary sexual intercourse with a person other than a spouse while married. (168)

Adversarial system: a system where disputes between parties are decided by an impartial individual after hearing the evidence presented to the court. (222)

Adverse inference: a negative conclusion reached through logic; the principle dictating that a judge or lawyer may not infer something negative from the actions of one of the parties. For example, a trial judge cannot assume that an accused is not testifying because it would hurt his or her case. Every individual has the right to testify (or not to testify) in his or her trial. (272)

Advisement: deliberation allowing the lawyer to gather more information. (78)

Affidavit: a written statement that is supported by a promise and sworn by a person who is authorized to administer an oath. (74)

Affidavit of documents: a listing of documents that the party possesses, controls, or has in its power. (78)

Affidavit of service: a document certifying that a document has been delivered to another party in the proceeding. (74)

Affirmation: a solemn declaration to tell the truth. (78)

Affirmative defence: a type of defence in which all the elements of the offence are present and acknowledged, but the defendant wishes to provide other grounds why he or she should not be culpable. (296)

Aggravated damages: money awarded to punish for particularly malicious and high-handed actions of the defendant. (82)

Aider: a person who enables (or omits doing something) that allows someone else to commit a crime. (242)

Air of reality: a test to determine if a defence should be left with a trier of fact. The test is whether a properly instructed and functioning jury would reasonably acquit the accused. This prevents using defences that are completely unbelievable. (279)

Alimony: a historic term for court-ordered amount of money one spouse pays to the other for financial support while they are separated, in a family law dispute, or after they are divorced. (172)

Amending formula: the statutory method used to change the Canadian Constitution. (205)

Annulment: finding a marriage void. Unlike a divorce, annulment is a declaration that the marriage never existed in law. (170)

Anticipatory breach: repudiation of a contract before the obligations are supposed to be performed. (108)

Appeal: a review of a decision of one level of court by one or more judges at a higher level of court. (194)

Apportionment: a division into parts according to the rights or responsibilities of the parties. (140)

Arbitrator: a person who decides disputes on the consent of the parties or under an agreement. (338)

Articling: the process whereby a student of law works for a lawyer in exchange for learning the profession; a type of apprenticeship. (363)

Atavistic: having physical features of a human at an earlier stage of development that could identify an individual as a born criminal. (16)

Authority: a statute or case cited to prove a legal argument. (68)

***Autrefois acquit*:** a defence that may be entered to show that the accused was already acquitted or convicted. It can be entered when two charges are the same in subject matter, the new count is the same as the first trial, or that the charge is implicitly included in the first trial in law or evidence if it was possible to make amendments to include this in the first trial. (309)

Bad faith: an act to mislead or disregard the rights of another. It has been found to include discrimination, abuse of power, fraud, bias, unfairness, unreasonable conduct, dishonesty, and conflict of interest. (191)

Balance of probabilities: a tool used by the court to examine if there is a greater likelihood of one thing occurring more than another. Standard used in a civil trial to determine which party has the stronger evidence, regardless of how small the margin. This is a lesser standard than the criminal burden of "beyond a reasonable doubt."(79)

Banishment: expulsion from a country; loss of nation. (312)

Barrister: a lawyer who is an advocate in court, or one who is a lawyer in front of the "bar" (the barrier that separates the judge's bench and lawyers from the rest of the court). Barristers may work in areas of the law such as civil litigation (especially areas like commercial law or personal injury law), family law, or criminal law, where they get extensive exposure to courtroom work. (23)

Barrister and solicitor: the title given to a lawyer who is a member of a provincial law society in the common law provinces and territories in Canada. (25)

Bencher: a lawyer that is elected by other lawyers to the "convocation," or the governing body of the law society. There are also benchers who are not lawyers but are appointed by the government to represent the general public interest. (24)

Best interest of the child: the welfare of the child including the general, psychological, spiritual and emotional needs. (179)

Beyond a reasonable doubt: the standard of proof required in criminal law cases to a level of certainty which excludes the possibility of innocence. The Crown must prove all elements of a crime to this standard. (222)

Bias: a state of mind that is predisposed to a certain result or that is closed to evidence or issues. (192)

Bigamy: being married in Canada and going through another marriage ceremony with another person, or knowing that the other person is married and marrying him or her anyway. May also include marrying more than one person on the same day. (151)

Bilateral contract: an agreement where each of the two parties is bound to complete the obligations promised to the other. (90)

Bind (binding) authority: a decision of a higher court which a lower court *must* follow. (42)

Black-letter law: legal principles that are fixed and settled and should be applied strictly; the term comes from the Gothic font used in books, which is in a black, bold font. (7)

Board: a body of persons with delegated powers who are elected for certain purposes; for example, the Workers' Compensation Board of Manitoba. (7)

Brainwashing: the forcible indoctrination of implanted beliefs that are alien to the brainwashee. (304)

Branding: punishment of an offender through permanently marking the body with a hot iron. (313)

Breach: the failure to complete the contract per the terms agreed to. (108)

Burden: the act of convincing the court of the existence or non-existence of a fact. (79)

But-for test: test in which causation in negligence is proven where the plaintiff shows, on a balance of probabilities, that the defendant contributed to the injuries, and the injury would not have occurred without the negligence of the defendant. (232)

Canon law: law that is developed within a religious tradition; also called "church law" or "canonical law."(15)

Capacity: the ability to understand the nature of an agreement. (17)

Capital punishment: the death penalty. (312)

Case at hand: also called the case at bar, instant case, present case; the case immediately before the consideration of the court. Refers to the matter that is currently under consideration. (67)

Case law: the decisions of judges as opposed to statute law. These judgments form the source of law and legal precedent. (67)

Cause of action: a fact situation that allows one individual to obtain a remedy from another; a legal right to start a law suit. (73)

***Caveat emptor*:** buyer beware. (104)

***Certiorari*:** a tool to quash a decision based on an error of law on the record. (197)

Challenge for cause: a reason to object to a particular juror for certain enumerated reasons. (228)

Chambers: a judge's office where meetings with parties may occur.(78)

Charge to the jury: instructions given to the jury after the trial but before the decision is made. (310)

Chattel: personal property that is movable or transferrable. (145)

Citation: a precise reference for cataloguing at the beginning of a case. (69)

Civil law: a type of private law that is used within Quebec and is based on the *Civil Code of Lower Canada* and the *Civil Code of Quebec*, LRQ 1977, c C-25; the legal system of Quebec based on a Civil Code, which was formed from Roman law; also the types of law that deal with non-criminal matters, such as contracts law, torts law, property law, administrative law, and so forth. (4)

Clean hands doctrine: principle that the court will not assist someone who has committed fraud, misrepresentation, illegality, or impropriety. If the person seeking help from the court of equity has not behaved in a way that is fair and honourable, the court will not help. (89)

Closing argument: a statement made at the conclusion of the trial before a judge and/or jury. (47)

Cohabitation: living together as spouses; can refer to either opposite-sex or same-sex couples. (158)

Cohabitation agreement: a contract between two persons who are cohabiting or intend to cohabit and are not married. Can include statements on rights and obligations during cohabitation, on the breakdown of the relationship, or death, including property, support, education of children, and other matters. (158)

Commission: a body given the authority to administer a statute or perform a public function; for example, the Disabled Persons Commission of Nova Scotia. (184)

Common law: the law that comes from the decisions of the court. Also called "judge-made" law, it often has a written component where the judge explains his or her decision in a particular case. (220)

Common law defence: a defence that only exists in the common law, and not in legislation. (220)

Complete defence: a defence that results in a full absence of liability without any terms. (138)

Compurgation: a historic type of trial where the accused would gather supporters to testify that the defendant was telling the truth; also called trial by oath or "wager of law." If the accused cannot get the people to swear an oath in the proper form, the oath "bursts" and the accused loses the trial. (15)

Concurring decision: a separate written decision by a judge in favour of the majority decision reasoned on grounds different from the majority. (60)

Condition precedent: an act or event that must exist before a duty to perform something promised arises. (107)

Condition subsequent: a condition that will bring an agreement to an end and that discharges the duties. (107)

Condonation: acquiescence or forgiveness for a marital wrong by one spouse who knows and forgives the incident, so that there is no further matrimonial offence. (169)

Conduct unbecoming: actions that are contrary to the best interest of the public or the profession, and may harm the standing of the legal profession. (50)

Conjugal: relating to a married or marriage-like state, often with sexual relations. (144)

Connivance: an agreement to do wrong by the plaintiff; a bad intent by the plaintiff about the matter complained of. (169)

Consanguinity: blood relationship by descent from a common ancestor or from the same line (e.g., daughter and father). (149)

Consensus *ad idem*: a "meeting of the minds;" an agreement of the parties to the same terms. (93)

Consent: free agreement. (138)

Consideration: an interest or right that accrues to one party with some loss suffered by the other party. Something of value received by the promisor from the promisee to make an agreement enforceable. (96)

Consummation: sexual intercourse after marriage, which finalizes the union. (149)

Contempt of court: a tool used to ensure compliance with orders and the process. Contempt of court has existed in the civil and criminal law for centuries. It punishes public acts that bring the administration of justice into disrepute. May include fine and/or jail. (25)

Contingency fee: an arrangement with a lawyer that no money will be payable until there is a successful judgment at the completion of the matter. (136)

Contract: an agreement between two or more persons creating legally recognized rights and obligations that are enforceable at law. (104)

Contracting out: the unlawful creation of a contract to escape provisions that would apply under the law. (106)

Contributory negligence: a situation where the plaintiff's negligence was a factor in causing his or her own injury, and the plaintiff should be responsible for that portion of the damages. (125)

Convention: an informal agreement or rules that limit political power and are recognized (even if they may not be enforced) by the courts. (202)

Coroner's inquest: a hearing held regarding a death of an individual under suspicious circumstances. (228)

Corporal punishment: punishment physically inflicted on the body (such as whipping). Corporal punishment was abolished for prisoners in Canada in 1972. (312)

Counsellor: an individual who, through acts or words, induces a person to commit the offences he or she desires. (242)

Counterclaim: an action raised by the defendant, which can be heard at the same time as the plaintiff's statement of claim. (76)

Counteroffer: an offer made by an offeree by rejecting the initial offer and creating a new offer. (94)

Course of employment: work or job related. (134)

Court of equity: a court system used until the late nineteenth century that provided remedies not available at common law. (84)

Courts of first instance: the first judicial proceeding that addresses a case. (59)

Craniometry: the science of measuring skulls. (17)

Credibility: believability, worthiness of belief. (271)

Criminal law: law that concerns conduct that interferes with the security of a society. (18)

Crossclaim: a claim of one defendant against a co-defendant. (76)

Cross-examination: questioning of a witness by the party who did not call the individual for an examination in chief. The goal is to get evidence from the witness favourable to the party who is cross-examining him or her. (79)

Crown: head of state or the monarchy. The Queen of England is the formal head of state, and the government (federal and provincial) is also referred to as the Crown. (205)

Cruel and unusual punishment: punishment so disproportionate to the offence that it is inappropriate. (315)

Custodial sentence: a prison sentence. (317)

Custody: care and control of a child, and a right of guardianship. (179)

Damages: a monetary payment for a violation of a right in law. Money is the most common form of damages, as it is the easiest to value and award. (72)

Declaratory order: a binding proclamation by the court on the rights of the parties, regardless of whether or not any other remedy is appropriate. (85)

Decree of nullity: a document declaring a marriage to be void. No divorce is required to end the marriage because it is as if the marriage never existed. (171)

Defamation: the publication of material that injures the reputation of an individual in the community by exposing him or her to ridicule or hatred. (131)

Default judgment: final judgment given to the plaintiff when the defendant fails to file a statement of defence. (72)

Defence: a denial of guilt that would negate the crime and, if accepted, would result in an acquittal or reduction of charges. (279)

Defendant: a person against whom an action is started. (116)

Deference: respect shown to other judges; the degree to which an appeal court will refuse to interfere with the decision of a lower court; or respect to the administrative tribunal by the courts. (194)

Delegates: to give someone's powers to someone else. One may only delegate the powers that one possesses. (185)

Deliberate: to consider on the basis of all available and admissible evidence. (52)

Denunciation: communication of society's condemnation of an action. (315)

Deportation: the removal of an individual from Canada to the place where he or she has citizenship. (193)

Disbarment: a termination of a membership in the law society. A lawyer's name is taken from the list of barristers and solicitors in the province. (50)

Discretion: the ability of public officials to use their power in certain circumstances according to their judgment. (191)

Disposition: the final decision of the case. Courts are said to release cases as they finally determine the rights of the parties or terminate the proceedings. (270)

Dissent: a decision of a judge who does not agree with the majority of the judges on the case. (62)

Distinguishing the case: showing that a particular case (or series of cases) has a factual, procedural, or legal difference in order to minimize its precedential value or to show that it is wholly or partially inapplicable. (67)

Diversion: a program that shifts the dispute from the justice system to an alternate form of resolution. (72)

Division of powers: the exhaustive provisions of the *Constitution Act* that dictate which levels of government have jurisdictions over particular matters. For example, the criminal law is largely under the jurisdiction of the federal government according to the *Constitution*. (219)

Divisional Court: a division of the Ontario Superior Court of Justice, which sits in panels of three adjudicators and is often the first arena of judicial review of appeals from administrative decisions. (194)

Double recovery: a judgment that awards damages twice for the same loss, or beyond the maximum loss sustained. (141)

Due diligence defence: a defence that the accused held a reasonable belief in mistaken facts or that the accused took all reasonable steps to avoid offending. (250)

Due process: the right to a fair hearing before a tribunal with the power to decide a case according to the legal processes established by Parliament and Canadian courts; the law of the land. (189)

Duress: threats to induce a person to enter into an agreement or crime. (105)

Duty of care: to be successful in a negligence action, the plaintiff must show that the defendant had a legal responsibility to be careful and to not cause harm. (119)

Duty to act fairly: duty to adhere to natural justice for administrative law purposes. (188)

Election: choosing what type of offence (summary or indictable) that the Crown wishes to pursue. (222)

Eugenics: the belief that humans should protect the best gene pool by encouraging those with "good genes" to breed, and those with "bad genes" to abstain from procreation. (17)

Evidentiary burden: a responsibility to produce information to the court. A requirement that a party must put an issue before the court and show that certain facts exist. (273)

Examination for discovery: disclosure of information and documents of the parties before trial through a question-and-answer process. (78)

Examination in chief: questioning of a person under oath by the party that called that person as a witness. (276)

Excuse: an explanation that makes a person not responsible. In criminal law, a declaration by the accused that he or she did the wrongful action, but should not be held responsible for these actions. The person may have committed criminal actions, but the law should not punish him or her. (279)

Exemplary damages: monetary award that is given to acknowledge the defendant's bad conduct, which warrants punishment for malice, fraud, or other abusive behaviour. (140)

Fair comment: a comment made in good faith and without malice on an issue of public interest. (132)

Fair market value: the highest price that a seller could obtain in a free market. (110)

Fiduciary relationship: a duty where the law tries to protect vulnerable individuals with their dealings with others. A client must be able to be in a trust relationship with his or her lawyer or a person whom a party owes good faith, trust, and confidence, by means of their relationship. (38)

Firm: persons who are associated by partnership in a business to carry on the organization under a registered business name. Many lawyers in Canada are employed within the structure of a law firm. (35)

Forensic evidence: scientific testimony or reports used in court. Can include ballistic or medical information. (353)

Foreseeable plaintiff test: test to determine who is reasonably a plaintiff in a particular tort matter. (120)

Forfeiture order: a surrender of goods or property to punish someone for a crime. (269)

Frustration: the prevention of performance of a contract. (107)

Fundamental breach: an event caused by the failure of one party to perform an obligation; it denies the other party the benefit that he or she should have received from the contract. (106)

Gaol: a prison where lesser offences are punished. (312)

Garnish: to attach a debt. (84)

Gazette: a publication issued by the government (often weekly) containing notices and announcements; it is the location where regulations are first published. A regulation takes effect at the time of publication in the gazette. (62)

General damages: damages for things much less tangible than special damages, including pain and suffering. (81)

General deterrence: a sentence to discourage others from committing a particular crime. (316)

Gift in contemplation of marriage: the transfer of property when the parties commit themselves to marriage. (148)

Gratuitous promise: a promise in exchange for nothing, which is not supported by consideration, and is usually unenforceable. (97)

Grievance: a complaint made by an individual. Term is often used in the context of dismissal, working conditions, or employment. (187)

***Habeas corpus*:** a check on the court or tribunal to confirm the rightful detention of a person. *Habeas corpus* may be used to secure the release of a person wrongfully held in custody. (198)

Hansard: the official transcripts of parliamentary debates. (64)

Headnote: a summary of what the editor of the journal considers important in a particular case. A student should always read the entirety of the case to ensure that the summary is accurate. (69)

Hearsay: telling the court what others have said rather than giving personal knowledge. Evidence of a person who is not testifying is inadmissible as to the truth of the statements. (275)

Home Office: The Department of State in England responsible for overseeing the internal affairs of the country. (219)

Hung jury: a jury that cannot make a unanimous decision in a criminal case. (319)

Hybrid offence: a crime that is tried either summarily or by indictment at the option of the prosecution. (222)

Impartiality: a state of mind of the judge that he or she disinterested in the outcome and that is open to the evidence and submissions of the lawyers. (52)

In kind: goods or services rather than money. A return in an equivalent way to what has been taken. (326)

Inadmissible: relating to evidence that is not found worthy of being considered by the court. Such information excluded under a rule of evidence. (227)

Inchoate offence: an offence in which there is some preparation, such as an attempt, which has the agreement of the parties but does not require those acts to be fully carried out. Pronounced in-KOH-it. (245)

Independent legal advice: impartial legal opinion from another lawyer to ensure that the rights of the client are maintained. (39)

Indictable offence: a crime that is tried by way of "indictment" and is considered more serious than a summary offence. (222)

Indictment: the formal legal document containing the alleged indictable offences, including the relevant information. (276)

Inferior courts: courts where a Justice of the Peace or magistrate decides minor criminal offences. (229)

Information: a document that alleges that an accused person committed an offence. One begins a criminal proceeding with an indictment by laying an information. (276)

In-house counsel: one or more lawyers employed by a business to attend to only the corporate affairs of that one company. (26)

Injunction: an order that a party either act in a certain way or refrain from acting in a certain way.

Intention: the willingness to bring about something planned. (89)

Intentional tort: a wrong in which the person wishes to harm another, or believes that this harm may follow from his or her actions, and injury results to the plaintiff. Examples are battery, false imprisonment, and trespass to land. (116)

***Intra vires*:** within the power or authority of a body. (211)

Invitations to treat: a wish of a party to contract with another if the parties can agree on an arrangement; but this is not yet a contract. (93)

Issuing: the process by which the registrar at the court house dates, signs, and seals the document with the official stamp of the court, and a court file number is assigned to the case. (74)

Joint and several tortfeasors: liability that may be apportioned to two or more parties who are responsible individually or who are together liable. (141)

Joint custody: custody arrangement where both parents have responsibility for the child. (179)

Joint tortfeasors: multiple defendants acting in concert to a common end who are all liable for the plaintiff's damage. (141)

Judicial realism: theory that the background and social/economic status of the judge impacts how he or she deals with the law. (8)

Judicial review: the subjection of a tribunal decision to the scrutiny of the courts, or the actual setting aside of the decision. (195)

Jurisdiction: the power of the tribunal (or court) to hear a particular matter. The authority to hear a particular matter is found in the tribunal's authorizing legislation. (185)

Justification: a declaration that challenges the wrongfulness of the action that constitutes a crime. The accused would admit committing the crime, but claim to be right to have acted as he or she did. (279)

Law Reform Commission of Canada: a body established by the federal government of Canada to review the laws of Canada. (268)

Leave of the court: permission of the court. (229)

Leave to appeal: permission sought from the appeal court by the party who wishes to appeal. The appealing party must convince the appeal court that the party should be heard and that this is an efficient use of the court's time. (276)

Legal aid: legal advice and services provided for those who are financially unable to hire a lawyer. (30)

Legal positivism: the theory that law can be scientifically determined through precedent rather than the application of morality. (6)

Legislation: a collection of written laws created by passing bills into law. (220)

Lesser but included offence: an offence where the elements constitute a part of a greater offence (but there might not be evidence to constitute the greater offence). For example, manslaughter is a lesser offence in relation to murder. The Crown may not have proof of murder, but may have enough evidence to constitute manslaughter. (269)

***Lex iniusta non est lex*:** an unjust law is not a law. (6)

***Lex talionis*:** an eye for an eye, or the law of retribution in kind; the principle of retribution to seek punishment for offenders just as the victim has been hurt. (314)

Liable: accountable or responsible. (79)

Life in prison: a sentence given by Canadian courts that imprisons the convicted person for a defined period of time. Section 745 of the *Criminal Code* provides that a person who is sentenced to life in prison shall serve 25 years of the sentence without eligibility for parole for a period of 10–25 years depending on the crime. (222)

Litigation: the lawsuit and the related matters. Refers to any proceeding before a court or tribunal. (73)

Living tree approach: originally a term of constitutional interpretation, which says that the law must grow like a tree to expand to current needs. (10)

Magistrate: a provincial or territorial judge authorized to accept documents, commence criminal proceedings, and hear regulatory offences and lesser criminal offences. Also known as Justice of the Peace. (229)

Majority decision: a court's written statement explaining its finding in a case expressed by more than half of the judges hearing a case. (68)

***Mala in se*:** crimes that are considered inherently immoral, such as murder, arson, or sexual assault. (231)

***Mala prohibita*:** an action that is illegal simply because the law says it is wrong, such as unlawful assembly or regulatory offences like driving offences. (231)

***Mandamus*:** an order to make a public official act. If legislation provides that the official should make a decision, he or she must make that decision. (197)

Mandatory mediation: a required part of the process which makes parties sit with a neutral third party to attempt to settle their dispute. (73)

Marriage contract: an agreement between two people entered into before marriage, or during marriage (or drafted when cohabiting), which will deal with marital rights or obligations during the marriage, at separation, on divorce, or at death. (158)

Material fact: an element that is essential to the matter at hand. (105)

Matrimonial home: the property (including a house, mobile home, condo, or any dwelling) that is owned or leased by one or both spouses and occupied as their family home. (158)

Mediation: sitting down with a neutral third party to try to resolve a dispute. (78)

***Mens rea*:** the mental state of the accused. *Actus reus* and *mens rea* are the basis for liability in criminal law. (230)

Minor child: a person who has not reached full legal age. (102)

Minority decision: an opinion by one or more judges who disagree with the decision reached by the majority; also called dissenting opinion. (258)

Misrepresentation: a false or misleading statement, often with the intent to deceive. (98)

Mistake of fact: a defence where the accused does not have the *mens rea* required for the offence because he or she misunderstood the circumstances. (280)

Mistake of law: an error that does not go to the facts of the case, but relates to the legal implications or significance. This could include things such as not asking the right legal questions, applying the wrong principles, or failing to apply a principle of law. (280)

Mitigate: to reduce the damages suffered. (109)

Modified objective test: an objective test that takes some subjective factors into account. (235)

Moral panic: term first used by sociologist Stanley Cohen in 1972 to discuss the overt reaction (or overreaction) to crime or deviance and its threat to society. Moral panics are used to create fear and allow those in power to change laws or practices. (15)

Morality: conformity with rules of conduct dictating what is right and what is wrong. A standard by which an action is determined to be either virtuous or immoral. (61)

Motion: an oral or written request to the court, which may be opposed by the other party. (73)

Natural justice: the right to be heard and the right to be free from an unbiased tribunal. (187)

Natural law: a philosophical system of law that derives from a universal concept of natural justice based on morality. (6)

Necessity: a defence in criminal law that is applicable in limited circumstances, which excuses behaviour that was the result of some imminent disaster, often from the natural elements. One would say that the evil that the accused seeks to avoid is greater than breaking the law, and thus the accused should be absolved from liability. (218)

No force or effect: no effectiveness. According to the *Constitution Act, 1982,* anything that is inconsistent with the Constitution is no longer good law and is referred to as being "struck down" and is no longer applicable. (255)

Nominal damages: a recognition by the court of the violation of rights, even though the party had no (or minimal) monetary loss. (82)

Notary: legal practitioner in Quebec who drafts deeds and contracts and ensures the accurate date and legality of those documents. In other provinces, notaries also ensure that authentic copies of deeds are created. (82)

Notice of action: a document that contains a short summary of what the case is going to be about. (73)

***Nulla poena sine lege*:** no punishment without a law authorizing that action. (7)

Oath: a solemn declaration to God or a revered person or thing that a statement is true or that one will be bound to a promise. (78)

***Obiter dicta*:** comments made by a judge in the course of making a decision in a case. While it may not be a precedent in future cases, it may be persuasive. (68)

Offence: a technical term for a law or regulation that is broken and liable to fine, imprisonment, or other punishment. (219)

Offeree: a person to whom a proposal is made in contract. (90)

Offeror: a person who makes the proposal in contract. (90)

Opening statement: a lawyer's outline of the case and what will be proved through witnesses and evidence. (79)

Originating process: the first document that starts a case. (73)

Out of court settlement: an agreement to end to a civil suit (or potential suit) without going through the court system. (72)

Overinclusive: too broad in application. Legislation that extends beyond the persons intended to be regulated; it may involve more persons than is necessary to solve a problem. (266)

Paralegal: a non-lawyer who performs legal services. (51)

Parallel parenting: custody arrangement where each of the parents has jurisdiction over particular decisions. (179)

Parliamentary supremacy: the doctrine that Parliament is the only lawmaker and this ability cannot be overridden or set aside by the courts or anyone else. (204)

Partial defence: a defence that goes to some of the issues of the crime, but does not result in a finding of no liability. (138)

Peace bond: a written promise made to the court to behave as a good citizen for a period of time. Often the person will be ordered to stay away from certain persons, not to possess weapons, and so forth. (269)

Peace officer: a person employed to preserve and maintain the public peace. (260)

Penitentiary: a federal facility operated by the correctional service for detaining prisoners. (313)

Percentile: in the LSAT, a statistical value placed on the raw score that indicates how many scores were above or below your score. (362)

Perjury: a false statement made under oath. A *Criminal Code* offence in which an individual, before a court, with intent to mislead, makes a false statement under oath or in a solemn affirmation orally or in writing. (46)

Personal service: delivering the legal documents by bringing the material into the hands of another, or by bringing it personally to their awareness.

Persuasive: description of a case that should be given respect and may be followed, but it is not binding. (60)

Petition for Divorce: the document that starts a divorce action. (170)

Petitioner: a person who applies to court for a divorce. (170)

Phrenology: the study of the shape of the head and its relation to human behaviour. (16)

Physiognomy: science of human faces in relation to behaviour. (16)

Pillory: a wooden framework that an offender must stand behind with the heads and hands in holes. It was usually used in a public location for public shaming. (313)

Pith and substance: the dominant purpose, or most important characteristic. (213)

Plaintiff: a person who commences an action. (116)

Pleadings: the process in which the parties set out a written account of their allegations, and respond to any previous statements. This paperwork is exchanged prior to trial. (73)

Polygamy: the state of having multiple wives or husbands. (151)

Post box rule: the rule that acceptance occurs at the precise moment when an envelope goes into a mailbox if traditional mail is an accepted mode of acceptance. (95)

Preamble: phrases at the beginning of the legislation after the title. The preamble sets out why the legislature thought it necessary to create this legislation. (65)

Precedent: a decided case that provides the basis for decisions for later cases based on the same, or similar, facts. (67)

Prejudicial effect: tending to cause harm to the case or the administration of justice. (170)

Preliminary hearing: a hearing under part XVIII of the *Criminal Code* in which a judge determines if there is sufficient evidence for an accused to go to trial. (272)

Premises: the grounds immediately around a house; may include buildings and structures. (256)

Prerogative powers: privileges that the law gives to the Crown. (205)

Pre-sentence report: a report that describes the offender's situation and whether he or she would be a suitable candidate for particular sentences or release. Under s 721 of the *Criminal Code* a probation officer "shall, if required to do so by a court, prepare and file with the court a report in writing relating to the accused for the purpose of assisting the court in imposing a sentence or in determining whether the accused should be discharged."(315)

Presumption of innocence: the right not to be convicted until proven so according to the law in a fair, public hearing by an independent tribunal. (265)

Pre-trial conference: a meeting with a judge to discuss the case and to consider the possibility of settlement, simplifying the issues, or agreeing on other matters that would shorten a trial. (78)

Principal: someone who actually committed the offence and has the *mens rea* and *actus reus* required for the particular crime. There may be more than one principal. (242)

Private law: the law governing conflict between persons. (5)

Privative clause: a declaration that the decisions of a tribunal are final with no appeal and that excludes all judicial review. (196)

Privity: rule that a contract cannot confer rights or demand obligations on anyone but the parties to the agreement. (106)

***Pro bono*:** legal services donated to groups or individuals to provide access to law for disadvantaged individuals, organizations, or for the improvement of laws or the legal system. From the Latin term, *pro bono publico*, meaning "for the public good."(31)

Probative value: information tending to prove facts or evidence. To have legal value, evidence must give some credence to the case other than the accused is a bad person. (170)

Prohibition: an order of the court preventing a tribunal from acting outside of its jurisdiction or outside of the rules of natural justice; an order of the court that stops an individual from acting in a particular way, such as not possessing a firearm or driving a motor vehicle. (197)

Promise: an intention to act or refrain from acting in a certain way to benefit another person. (90)

Promulgation: the act of publishing. (62)

Public law: the law between individuals and the state. (5)

Publishing or broadcasting: transmitting or making public through written material, pictures, or sounds. (132)

Punitive damages: money awarded to punish the defendant and make an example of him or her to deter others from committing this same wrong. (82)

***Quantum meruit*:** the reasonable value of services. (109)

Quash: the act of setting aside a decision of a tribunal on judicial review. (192)

Quasi-criminal offence: an offence created by provincial law, which carries a penalty similar to a crime. (248)

Question of fact: a grounds for appeal on a disputed *fact*; a much more limited grounds for appeal than a question of law. (276)

Question of law: a mistake by the court in its use of the applicable law. A question of law is the reason used as grounds for appeal for things like the misinterpretation of legislation, a trial judge's mistaken instructions to the jury, and the determination of whether rights were violated under the *Charter*. (276)

***Ratio decidendi*:** the principle upon which the case is decided. (67)

Read in: a litigation tool used so that the written record of another hearing may be read out loud at trial and may be recorded as the evidence of the witness. (275)

Reading in: adding a group or circumstance to a statute that had been inconsistent or wrongly excluded. (255)

Reading down: technique used to interpret a statute as narrowly as possible to keep it within the scope of power of the province or territory. (255)

Reasonable person: is a hypothetical prudent and careful individual who is entering into a contract. The court uses this standard to determine what this person would understand the contract to be. Also used in other areas of law to determine the actions of a prudent and careful person. (93)

Recidivist: someone who is repeatedly caught committing crimes. (317)

Reference: a question that the government brings to the court to give an opinion about the constitutionality or legality of a provision, even though it is not currently in dispute in an actual case. (210)

Regulation: a rule of conduct by a law-making authority that has the force of the law. (62)

Remedy: legal relief for the wrong that has been committed against you. (85)

Reopening clause: a part of an agreement that says that negotiations can be restarted during the term of the agreement if circumstances change. (164)

Replevin: getting back a particular possession that the victim has lost. (140)

Representation: words or conduct meant to induce someone to act in contract. (98)

Repudiate: refuse to perform obligations under a contract to make the contract come to an end. (104)

***Res judicata*:** "a thing adjudicated." The final judicial decision or a defence to a subsequent action. (68)

Rescission: to end a contract for a legally valid reason. (105)

Respondent: in family law, the person against whom a petition is brought. This is usually the spouse not initially seeking the divorce. (170)

Retainer: the act of hiring a lawyer, the document which is signed to secure this relationship, or the initial amount of money given to have the lawyer work on that matter. A private retainer is one without legal aid, and the lawyer can decide how much to charge. (31)

Retribution: punishment based on the idea that every crime needs payment in the form of punishment. A sanction representing the moral blameworthiness of the offender. (314)

Reverse onus: a burden or obligation that shifts to the defence from the Crown. The legal principle which states that instead of the usual presumption that the Crown has to prove all elements of the crime beyond a reasonable doubt, in a reverse onus situation, the requirement is instead that the *accused* proves the defence (or issue) on the balance of probabilities. (265)

Revocation: destroying or voiding a contract; undoing something that has been granted. (94)

Royal Prerogative of Mercy: powers and privileges that are given by the common law to the Crown to set aside a decision of the court. These are powers left over from when the royalty had an absolute monarchy. (218)

Rule of law: principle that no one is above the law, not even the state. The rule of law protects citizens and provides a predictable and ordered society free from the arbitrary exercise of individual or state power. (58)

Runs with the land: rule that the advantages and liabilities assigned to land pass to the person who takes over than land by purchase or lease. (106)

Seal: an impression made on documents with a stamp that makes the paperwork official. (74)

Search and seizure: a police practice where they can view property and take evidence that may be needed in the investigation and prosecution of crime. (255)

Segregation: the act of placing a person or body away from the general group of persons. (188)

Sentencing circle: common in Aboriginal communities, a sentencing circle brings together the offender and his or her supporters, the victim and his or her supporters, community leaders, judges, lawyers, police, and other interested parties to decide how best to hold the offender responsible for his or her actions. (335)

Separate and apart: a term representing the end of a matrimonial obligation and the intent to end a marriage, as well as possible physical separation. (167)

Separation: the decision of a conjugal couple to live apart. (163)

Service: delivery of a copy of the legal paperwork to the other parties so that they know of the court case. (74)

Set down the matter for trial: a step in a civil matter where one of the parties states that they are ready for trial. (78)

Settlement: an agreement by the parties in the dispute about how they will resolve the matter. (72)

Several tortfeasors: multiple defendants who act in the same event, but who have not acted in common with each other. They are responsible for the same damage, but not necessarily the same tort. (141)

Sexual sadist: an offender who is characterized by the most severe forms of sexual and other violence. (305)

Shared parenting or co-parenting: custody arrangement where the child lives with each of the parents for a significant time. (179)

Sharp practice: unethical actions or trickery by a lawyer. (36)

Sole practitioner: a lawyer who practises law without partners or associate lawyers. (26)

Solicitor: a lawyer who does not appear in court regularly, but does other work of lawyers. Solicitors were formerly called "attorneys," which is still a term used in the United States. Solicitors may work in areas of the law such as real estate law, corporate law, or wills and estates law, which are more paperwork-intensive and involve very little (if any) courtroom experience. (23)

Solicitor-client privilege: the principle that communications between a lawyer and his or her client are confidential. (38)

Special damages: compensation for out-of-pocket expenses. They include things like specific lost wages between an accident and trial, hospitalization, and so forth. (81)

Special verdict: a decision made by the jury to give a written finding for each issue, but leaves the application of the law to the judge. (218)

Specific deterrence: a sentence to discourage that particular offender from committing that crime an additional time. (316)

Specific performance: a remedy ordered by the court to fulfill a legal obligation when money is inappropriate or inadequate; an order to compel someone to complete what was promised pursuant to the contract. (85)

Split custody: custody arrangement where one or more children are in the custody of each parent. (179)

Spousal or child support: financial assistance to allow a dependant (child or spouse) to maintain a standard of living, including the necessities of life. (172)

Standard form contracts: a preprinted contract used in a certain industries. (92)

Standing: status to engage in the legal system; to gain standing, a person must show that they have a direct interest in the lawsuit. (73)

***Stare decisis*:** means to stand by what has been decided. The doctrine of precedent that the court must follow earlier decisions when the same principle of law arises. (67)

Statement of claim: a document that states only the facts on which the plaintiff is relying on to sue the defendant, and sets out the amounts that are being sought. (74)

Statement of defence: a document created by the defendants to respond to the allegations in the statement of claim. (74)

Statement of facts: a statement that outlines the facts of the case that both parties agree and on which the case will be decided. (271)

Stay of proceedings: an action by the court to suspend proceedings. It is a remedy that redresses a past wrong and prevents it from happening again, which may mean the total discontinuance of the action; the decision to stop one type of action until something happens (e.g., the completion of a criminal trial). (171)

Strict liability: criminal liability based on simple negligence with only one possible defence of due diligence. (134)

***Subpoena*:** a document issued by the court compelling a person to attend legal proceedings as a witness to give testimony. This request is made under threat of penalty. (274)

Subrogation: a tool that lets the insurer pursue claims against a third party for losses that the insurance company has had to pay out. (136)

Subsidiary promise: implied promise that the person making the offer cannot revoke once the individual begins performing, in good faith, and continues to perform. (91)

Substantive criminal law: law that determines the party's conduct and relations to others. (220)

Summary offence: a crime that is tried "summarily" and is considered less serious. (222)

Summons: a document that tells a person that he or she must appear in court on a particular day and time. (227)

Suspended sentence: a sentence that includes the release of the offender on certain conditions in a probation order. (315)

Term: the part of a contract that explains the obligation of one or more parties. (90)

Test case: a lawsuit brought to establish a widespread and important principle of law or right. Sometimes many cases all agree to be bound by the decision in the test case. For example, in the case of *Tremblay v Daigle,* [1989] 2 SCR 530 (SCC), which dealt with the ability of a woman to have an abortion regardless of the objection of her partner, Ms. Daigle had an abortion during the course of the appeal but the parties involved thought this was so important that the matter continued to the Supreme Court. (2)

Third-party claim: claim in which a defendant can add a person who is not named in the statement of claim, who might be liable to the defendant for the plaintiff's claim, or may be liable to the defendant for another or related claim. (76)

Tort: a civil wrong that results in injuries to the plaintiff for which damages can be sought; a means by which a citizen can sue another in court, usually for money, to compensate the individual for the injuries suffered as a result of the wrongdoer's conduct. (12)

Tortfeasor: a wrongdoer. (118)

Trafficking: buying, selling, or dealing in drugs. (220)

Transferred intent: situation in which if person A intends to injure person B, but instead unintentionally harms C, the tortious intent of A toward B still applies against C as well. (128)

Trial record: a copy of all pleadings and orders of the court regarding that matter. (78)

Tribunal: a court or an adjudicative body. All courts are tribunals, but not all tribunals are courts. Examples of tribunals include the Federal Canadian Human Rights Commission, or the Labour Standards Tribunal of Nova Scotia. (184)

Trier of fact: someone (like a judge alone) or a group of persons (jury) who hear testimony and review evidence to decide a factual issue. (227)

Tunnel vision: a situation arising when police put all of their resources into convicting the one person they believe to be guilty, ignoring all other evidence and suspects. (349)

***Ultra vires*:** acting outside of the power given to the legislative body by a particular statute. If a legislative body (e.g., a tribunal) acts beyond its authority, the decision is invalid. (62)

Unconscionable: contrary to beliefs of fairness; relating to unscrupulous behaviour that shows no regard for justice or reasonableness. (89)

Uncontested divorce: a divorce proceeding in which the respondent does not file documentation to fight the divorce. (170)

Undertaking: an assurance given to the other lawyer in his or her role as a lawyer. (78)

Undue influence: unscrupulous use of power to induce another person to act in a certain way. (105)

Unified family courts: courts established to civil and criminal matters involving families, even though some aspects might usually be heard in other courts. (147)

Unilateral contract: an agreement where one party makes a promise in return for performance. (90)

Unintentional tort: a wrong that fails to observe the standard of care required, and damages are caused. An example is negligence. (116)

Vagabond: a historic term for a homeless wanderer (vagrant) who cannot make an honest wage. (13)

Verdict: the decision of a judge or jury. (79)

Victim impact statement: a written statement from the victim describing the harm done, and any losses suffered by the victim because of the offence. (315)

Victim surcharge: a fee that is paid by an individual convicted under the *Criminal Code* that goes to a fund instead of to the person injured by the criminal action. (326)

Victim/Witness Assistance Programs: various programs that provide victims and witnesses of crime help through the court process to understand the stages of the justice system. This assistance is particularly for those who have experienced violent crime, domestic violence, child abuse, sexual assault, homicide, and hate crimes. (326)

Victimless crime: a crime that is said to have no direct victim such as possession of drugs or participation in prostitution. (249)

Victims' Justice Fund: provincial fund used to assist victims through grants to community agencies, and other services for victims. (326)

Void: without legal force and of no legal effect. (103)

Voidable: valid until affirmed or rejected at the option of one of the parties. (103)

Warrant: an order from a judicial authority that an officer may arrest, seize, search, or carry out a judicial sentence. (227)

Warranty: a lesser obligation than a term of a contract, which does not go to the root of the agreement. (104)

Witness stand: place in a courtroom that is often set aside in a boxed area where witnesses sit or stand while testifying. Often shortened to the "stand."(79)

Writs: the formal order of a court that makes a person do, or not do, some action. (196)

Writ of seizure and sale: a document from the court that is evidence of an unpaid debt given to the sheriff to enforce when a party attempts to sell his or her property. (84)

Index